International Rare
Book Prices

EARLY PRINTED
BOOKS

1988

International Rare
Book Prices

EARLY PRINTED
BOOKS

Series Editor: Michael Cole

1988

Picaflow Ltd., York

© **Picaflow Limited 1988**

7 Pulleyn Drive, York YO2 2DY, England

ISBN 1 870773 02 0

North America

Spoon River Press, P.O. Box 3635
Peoria, Illinois 61614, U.S.A.

Cover illustration by courtesy of Ken Spelman, York, England
Typesetting by Maxiprint, York, England
.Printed and bound by Unwin Brothers Ltd., Woking, England

Contents

Introduction and Notes

Early Printed Books (being books published prior to 1800) is the second title in the annual series *International Rare Book Prices*. The other titles are *The Arts & Architecture, Modern First Editions, Science & Medicine, Voyages, Travel & Exploration.*

IRBP was established in 1987 so as to provide annual records of the pricing levels of out-of-print, rare or antiquarian books within a number of specialty subject areas and to give likely sources and suppliers for such books in Britain and the United States of America.

Sources of information:

The books recorded each year in the various subject volume of *IRBP* have been selected from catalogues of books for sale issued during the previous year by numerous bookselling firms in Britain and the United States. These firms, listed at the end of this volume, range in nature from the highly specialized, handling books solely with closely defined subject areas, through to large concerns with expertise across a broad spectrum of interests.

Extent of coverage:

IRBP concentrates exclusively on books published in the English language and, throughout the series as a whole, encompasses books published between the 16th century and the 1970s.

The specific titles recorded in the annual volumes of *IRBP* vary greatly from year to year although naturally there is a degree of overlap, particularly of the more frequently found titles. Consecutive annual volumes do not, therefore, merely update pricings from earlier years; they give substantially different listings of books on each occasion. The value of the *IRBP* volumes lies in providing records of an ever-increasing range of individual titles which have appeared for sale on the antiquarian or rare book market.

Emphasis is placed on books falling within the lower to middle range of the pricing scale rather than restricting selection to the unusually fine or expensive. In so doing, *IRBP* provides a realistic overview of the norm, rather than the exception, within the booktrade.

Further details of the scope of the individual titles in the series are given on the final page of this volume.

Authorship and cross-references:

Authors are listed alphabetically by surname.

Whenever possible, the works of each author are grouped together under a single form of name irrespective of the various combinations of initials, forenames and surnames by which the author is known.

Works published anonymously, or where the name of the author is not recorded on the title-page, are suitably cross-referenced by providing the main entry under the name of the author (when mentioned by the bookseller) with a corresponding entry under the first appropriate word of the title. In cases of unknown, or unmentioned, authorship, entry is made solely under the title.

Full-titles:

Editorial policy is to eschew, whenever possible, short-title records in favour of full-, or at least more complete and explanatory, titles. Short-title listings do little to convey the flavour, or even the content, of many books - particularly those published prior to the nineteenth century.

Descriptions:

Books are listed alphabetically under each author's name, using the first word of the title ignoring, for alphabetical purposes, the definite and indefinite articles *the*, *a* and *an*. Within this alphabetical grouping of titles, variant editions are not necessarily arranged in chronological order, i.e., a 2nd, 3rd or 4th edition might well be listed prior to an earlier edition.

Subject to restrictions of space and to the provisos set out below, the substance of each catalogue entry giving details of the particular copy offered for sale has been recorded in full.

The listings have been made so as to conform to a uniform order of presentation, viz: Title; place of publication; publisher or printer; date; edition; size; collation; elements of content worthy of note; description of contents including faults, if any; description and condition of binding; bookseller; price; approximate price conversion from dollars to sterling or vice versa.

Abbreviations of description customary within the booktrade have generally been used. A list of these abbreviations will be found on page *x*.

Collations:

Collations, when provided by the bookseller, are repeated in toto although it should be borne in mind that booksellers employ differing practices in this respect; some by providing complete collations and others by indicating merely the number of pages in the main body of the work concerned. The same edition of the same title catalogued by two booksellers could therefore have two apparently different collations and care should be taken not to regard any collation recorded in *IRBP* as being a definitive or absolute record of total content.

Currency conversion:

IRBP lists books offered for sale priced in either pounds sterling (£) or United States dollars ($). For the benefit of readers unaccustomed to one or other of these currencies, an approximate conversion figure in the alternative currency has been provided in parentheses after each entry, as, for example, "**£100 [= $180]**", or, "**$60 [= £33]**". The conversion is based upon an exchange rate of £1 sterling ≃ US $1.80 (US $1 ≃ £0.556 sterling), the rate applicable at the date of going to press.

It must be stressed that the conversion figures in parentheses are provided merely as an indication of the approximate pricing level in the currency with which the reader may be most familiar and that fluctuations in exchange rates will make these approximations inaccurate to a greater or lesser degree.

Acknowledgements:

I am indebted to those booksellers who have provided their catalogues during 1987 for the purposes of *IRBP*. A list of the contributing booksellers forms an appendix at the rear of this volume.

This appendix forms a handy reference of contacts in Britain and the United States with proven experience of handling books within the individual specialist fields encompassed by the series. The booksellers listed therein are able, between them, to offer advice on any aspect of the rare and antiquarian booktrade.

Many of the listed books will still, at the time of publication, be available for purchase. Readers with a possible interest in acquiring any of the items may well find it worth their while communicating with the booksellers concerned to obtain further and complete details.

Caveat:

Whilst the greatest care has been taken in transcribing entries from catalogues, it should be understood that it is inevitable that an occasional error will have passed unnoticed. Obvious mistakes, usually typographical in nature, observed in catalogues have been corrected. I have not questioned the accuracy in bibliographical matters of the cataloguers concerned.

Michael Cole
Series Editor IRBP

Abbreviations

advt(s)	advertisement(s)	jnt(s)	joint(s)
addtn(s)	addition(s)	lge	large
a.e.g.	all edges gilt	lea	leather
a.l.s.	autograph letter signed	lib	library
altrtns	alterations	ltd	limited
Amer	American	litho(s)	lithograph(s)
bibliog(s)	bibliography(ies)	marg(s)	margin(s)
b/w	black & white	ms(s)	manuscript(s)
bndg	binding	mrbld	marbled
bd(s)	board(s)	mod	modern
b'plate	bookplate	mor	morocco
ctlg(s)	catalogue(s)	mtd	mounted
chromolitho(s)	chromo-lithograph(s)	n.d.	no date
ca	circa	n.p.	no place
cold	coloured	nu⸏	numerous
coll	collected	obl	oblong
contemp	contemporary	occas	occasional(ly)
crnr(s)	corner(s)	orig	original
crrctd	corrected	p (pp)	page(s)
cvr(s)	cover(s)	perf	perforated
dec	decorated	pict	pictorial
detchd	detached	port(s)	portrait(s)
diag(s)	diagram(s)	pres	presentation
dw(s)	dust wrapper(s)	ptd	printed
edn(s)	edition(s)	qtr	quarter
elab	elaborate	rebnd	rebind/rebound
engv(s)	engraving(s)	rec	recent
engvd	engraved	repr(d)	repair(ed)
enlgd	enlarged	rvsd	revised
ex lib	ex library	roy	royal
f (ff)	leaf(ves)	sep	separate
facs	facsimile	sev	several
fig(s)	figure(s)	sgnd	signed
fldg	folding	sgntr	signature
ft	foot	sl	slight/slightly
frontis	frontispiece	sm	small
hand-cold	hand-coloured	t.e.g.	top edge gilt
hd	head	t.l.s.	typed letter signed
ill(s)	illustration(s)	unif	uniform
illust	illustrated	v	very
imp	impression	vell	vellum
imprvd	improved	vol(s)	volume(s)
inscrbd	inscribed	w'engvd	wood-engraved
inscrptn	inscription	w'cut(s)	woodcut(s)
iss	issue	wrap(s)	wrapper(s)

Books published prior to 1800
1987 Catalogue Prices

'a Wood, Anthony
- The history and antiquities of the University of Oxford ... now first published in English. Oxford: for the editor, 1792-96. 2 vols in 3. 4to. [lxxx],667; [viii],500; [vi],501-997, [lxxix] pp. 3 plates, vignette port. Contemp calf, rubbed, jnts cracked.   *(Clark)* £85 [≈ $153]

Abelard, Peter & Heloise
- Letters of Abelard and Eloisa ... their lives, amours and misfortunes ... to which are added several poems by Mr. Pope and other authors. London: for W. Lowndes ..., 1788. 8vo. 6 plates. Contemp str-grained mor, gilt spine & edges.   *(Waterfield's)* £65 [≈ $117]

Abstract ...
- An abstract of the remarkable passages in the life of a private gentleman. London: Joseph Downing, 1715. 1st edn. 12mo. 192 pp. Contemp calf, rebacked.
    (Bennett) £150 [≈ $270]

Account ...
- An account of Denmark ... See Molesworth, Robert
- An account of several new inventions ... See Hale, Thomas
- An account of some new microscopical discoveries ... See Needham, John Turbeville
- An account of the European settlements in America. London: for R. & J. Dodsley, 1757., 1st edn. 2 vols. 8vo. 2 fldg map frontis. Some browning & foxing, 1 map reinforced, reprs to title verso. Rec mor spine over mrbld bds.
    (Pirages) $325 [≈ £180]
- An account of the expedition to Carthagena ... See Knowles, Sir Charles
- An account of the origin ... and intentions of the Society for the Promotion of Industry in ... parts of Lindsey, in the County of Lincoln

... Louth: R. Sheardown, [1790]. 3rd edn. 8vo. [iv],ix, [iii]-xiv, 152 (i.e.168) pp. Fldg table. Contemp half calf.
    (Burmester) £200 [≈ $360]
- An account of the proceedings of the House of Peers, upon the observations of the commissioners for taking ... the publick accounts of the kingdom. London: Charles Bill, 1702. Folio. 86 pp. Disbound.
    (C.R. Johnson) £25 [≈ $45]
- An account of the proceedings ... in parliament assembled in relation to the Bill instituted an Act for preventing occasional conformity. London: Charles Bill, 1702. Folio. 28 pp. Disbound.
    (C.R. Johnson) £15 [≈ $27]
- An account of the transactions of the late King James in Ireland, wherein is contain'd the Act of Attainder ... with other Proclamations and Acts ... London: for Robert Clavell, 1690. Sm 4to. [2],63 pp. Advts. Calf, rebacked.
    (Emerald Isle) £150 [≈ $270]
- An account of two voyages. First of Feodor Iskowitz Backhoff ... into China ... Translated from the High Dutch ... N.d. [ca 1764]. Sm folio. 10 pp. Mod cloth.
    (Old Cinema) £20 [≈ $36]
- A brief account of the General Meeting of Catholic Delegates held in Dublin, December, 1792. By a Delegate. Dublin: H. Fitzpatrick, 1793. 33 pp. Disbound.
    (C.R. Johnson) £28 [≈ $50]
- A faithful and authentic account of the siege and surrender of St. Philip's Fort in the Island of Minorca ... from the minutes of each day, taken by an officer ... London: for S. Crowder ..., 1757. 1st edn. 8vo. [iv],ii, 49 pp. Half-title. Stitched as issued.
    (Burmester) £90 [≈ $162]
- A genuine account of the lives, behaviour, confession, and dying words of the five rebels

... executed at Kennington-Common, for High-Treason. London: J. Nicholson, [1746]. 4to. Cased in new bds.
(Marlborough) £65 [≈ $117]

- An historical account of the expedition against the Ohio Indians ... See Smith, William

- A particular account of the late action in the Mediterranean ... See Mathews, Thomas

- A short account of such parts of his Majesty's hereditary revenue on the Kingdom of Ireland as are unappropriated; and of his private estate therein. Dublin: 1754. 2nd edn. 24 pp. Half-title. Disbound.
(C.R. Johnson) £50 [≈ $90]

- A short account of the Spanish Juros. In a letter to a citizen of London. Awake thou, that sleepest. London: for S. Popping, 1713. Sm 4to. Title, 11 pp. Unbound.
(Traylen) £20 [≈ $36]

- A true account and declaration of the horrid conspiracy against the late King ... See Sprat, Thomas

- A true and impartial account of the murder of his Grace the Duke of Hamilton and Brandon, by Mr. Mackartney. Edinburgh: reprinted by Mr. Robert Freebairn, [1712]. 8vo. 14 pp. Stitching loose. Disbound.
(Clark) £30 [≈ $54]

Adam, Alexander
- Roman antiquities: or, an account of the manners and customs of the Romans ... Edinburgh: for A. Strahan, 1792. 2nd edn. Thick 8vo. Uncut in orig bds, sl chipped.
(Hughes) £30 [≈ $54]

Adam, Robert
- Ruins of the Palace of the Emperor Diocletian at Spalatro in Dalmatia. London: for the author, 1764. 1st edn. Folio. iv,[vii],33 pp. Addtnl engvd frontis, 61 engvd plates (11 fldg, 1 fractionally trimmed). Contemp diced russia, rebacked, crnrs bumped.
(Frew Mackenzie) £2,300 [≈ $4,140]

Adams, George, Jr.
- Essays on the microscope; containing a practical description of the most improved microscopes ... London: for the author, 1787. 1st edn. 2 vols. 4to & obl folio. Frontis, 4 pp ctlg of instruments, atlas of 32 engvd plates. Contemp tree-calf, gilt spines.
(Traylen) £1,200 [≈ $2,160]
- Essays on the microscope; containing a practical description of the most improved microscopes ... London: for the author, 1787. 1st edn. 2 vols. 4to & obl folio atlas. Frontis,

32 engvd plates. Bds.
(Halewood) £240 [≈ $432]

Adams, George, Sr.
- Micrographia illustrata: or the microscope explained. London: for the author, 1771. 'Fourth' (i.e. 3rd) edn. 8vo. [12],lxi,[1],325 pp. 72 engvd plates, many fldg. Some spotty foxing. Contemp diced calf, rebacked.
(Antiq Sc) £650 [≈ £361]
- Micrographia illustrata: or the microscope explained. London: 1771. 4th edn. lix,325 pp. 72 copper plates. Frontis reprd. Mod qtr lea, mrbld bds.
(Scientia) $575 [≈ £319]

Adams, Joseph
- Observations on morbid poisons, phagadaena, and cancer ... on the laws of the venereal virus ... London: for J. Johnson, 1795. 1st edn. 8vo. [4],iv,328,[2] pp. Contemp half mor. Wellcome Lib withdrawal stamp.
(Rootenberg) $500 [≈ £277]

Adams, William
- Pastoral advice to young persons before confirmation. Shrewsbury: J. Eddowes, 1772. 2nd edn. 30,1 advts pp. Orig wraps.
(C.R. Johnson) £15 [≈ $27]

Addison, Joseph
- The evidences of the Christian religion ... with a preface, containing the sentiments of Mr. Boyle, Mr. Lock, and Sir Isaac Newton. London: Tonson, 1730. 1st edn. Sm 8vo. Marg wormhole. Contemp calf, jnts worn.
(Marlborough) £40 [≈ $72]
- The free-holder, or political essays. London: for D. Midwinter ..., 1716. 1st coll edn. 8vo. Some dust & other marks, tiny wormholes through some margs. Rec half calf, mrbld bds.
(Bow Windows) £46 [≈ $82]
- The free-holder, or political essays. London: for D. Midwinter ..., 1716. 1st coll edn. Lge 12mo. [xii],312 pp. Half-title. Contemp panelled calf.
(Lloyd-Roberts) £60 [≈ $108]
- The miscellaneous works in verse and prose ... London: for J. & R. Tonson, 1765. 4 vols. Lge paper (?). Contemp speckled calf, gilt, v sl & minor imperfections.
(Pirages) $275 [≈ £152]
- Remarks on several parts of Italy. London: Jacob Tonson, 1705. 1st edn. 8vo. [xii],534,[x] pp. Half-title, engvd ills. A few leaves with sl dampstain. Contemp Cambridge calf.
(Pirages) $175 [≈ £97]
- Remarks on several parts of Italy, &c. in the years 1701, 1702, 1703. London: for Jacob Tonson, 1705. 1st edn. 8vo. 4ff, 534 pp.

Index at end. Contemp panelled calf.
(Argosy) **$200 [≈£111]**
- Remarks on several parts of Italy, etc. London: Tonson, 1705. 1st edn. 8vo. Sl browning. Contemp mrbld bds, later calf spine. *(Stewart)* **£140 [≈$252]**
- Remarks on several parts of Italy, etc. London: Tonson, 1736. 5th edn. Lge 12mo. 304,[8] pp. Contemp calf, gilt, little worn but sound. *(Fenning)* **£24.50 [≈$43]**
- The works. London: for Jacob Tonson, 1721. 1st coll edn. 4 vols. Lge 4to. Contemp panelled calf. *(Lloyd-Roberts)* **£180 [≈$324]**
- The works. London: for Jacob Tonson, 1721. 1st coll edn. 4 vols. 4to. Port. Contemp panelled calf, rebacked.
(Traylen) **£120 [≈$216]**
- The works. London: for Jacob Tonson, 1730. 2nd edn. 4 vols. 4to. Engvd frontis, 6 plates. Contemp calf, gilt, later rebacking.
(Gough) **£225 [≈$405]**
- The works. Birmingham: J. Baskerville for J. & R. Tonson, 1761. 4 vols. Thick lge 4to. Contemp calf, newer backstrips elab gilt.
(Argosy) **$900 [≈£500]**
- The works. Birmingham: J. Baskerville for J. & R. Tonson, 1761. 4 vols. 4to. Engvd port, 3 engvd plates, 6 pp of medals. Contemp strgrain red mor, elab gilt, a.e.g. Ex lib 5th Duke of Leeds with his b'plates.
(Gough) **£1,750 [≈$3,150]**

Address ...
- An address to the ... Lords Commissioners of the Admiralty; upon the degenerated, dissatisfied state of the British Navy ... By a sailor. Second edition. London: J. Stockdale, 1784. 98,8 advts pp. Orig sewn pamphlet, uncut. *(C.R. Johnson)* **£85 [≈$153]**
- An address to the people of Ireland ... See O'Connor, Roger
- The humble address of the lords spiritual and temporal in parliament assembled presented to his majesty. On Tuesday 6th of January, 1701. London: Charles Bill, 1701. Folio. 4 pp. *(C.R. Johnson)* **£20 [≈$36]**

Administration ...
- The administration of the Colonies ... See Pownall, Thomas

Adriano ...
- Adriano; or the first of June ... See Hurdis, James

Advantages ...
- The advantages and disadvantages of the

marriage state ... See Johnson, John

Adventures ...
- The adventures of Sigr. Gaudentio di Lucca ... See Berington, Simon
- The adventures of Sir Launcelot Greaves ... See Smollett, Tobias

Advice ...
- Advice from a lady of quality to her children in the last stage of a lingering illness. Translated ... by S. Glasse. Glocester: R. Raikes, 1786. 4th edn. 8vo. xvi,245 pp. Calf, gilt, crnrs sl bumped. *(Titles)* **£80 [≈$144]**

Aeschylus
- The tragedies. Translated by R. Potter. Norwich: J. Crouse, 1777. Lge paper. Thick 4to. Old mrbld wraps, uncut, lacking spine.
(Argosy) **$135 [≈£75]**

Aesop
- Aesop fables, in English and Latin, interlineary, for the benefit of those who ... would learn either of these tongues. London: A. & J. Churchill, 1703. 8vo. [14],337 pp. 74 ills on 5 engvd plates. Contemp mottled calf, rebacked. *(Spelman)* **£120 [≈$216]**
- Fables of Aesop and others. Translated into English with instructive applications ... London: for W. Strahan ..., 1775. 10th edn of this trans. 18ff,329,[7] pp. Engvd frontis, 196 w'cuts in text. Sl uniform yellowing. Contemp sprinkled calf, jnts reprd.
(Pirages) **£125 [≈$69]**
- The fables of Aesop, with a life of the author ... London: for John Stockdale, 1793. 2 vols. Lge 8vo. [lxvi],189; [xii],248 pp. Engvd titles, 110 engvd plates (some offsetting). Some sl foxing & other marks. Half calf, gilt panelled spines. *(Bow Windows)* **£235 [≈$423]**
- Fables of Aesop. With a life of the author. London: John Stockdale, 1793. 1st iss of 1st Stockdale edn. 2 vols. 2 engvd titles, 110 engvd plates. Scattered light foxing. Contemp polished tree-calf, spines gilt, outer hinges cracked. Lge & thick paper copy.
(Argonaut) **$375 [≈£208]**
- Select fables of Esop and other fabulists. [Birmingham:] Baskerville for R. & J. Dodsley, 1761. lxxviii,204,[28] pp. Vignette title, engvd frontis, 15 plates, 6 engvd vignettes. Some browning by plates. Contemp sprinkled calf, rebacked, 2 crnrs reprd. *(Pirages)* **$185 [≈£102]**

Affairs of Scotland ...
- An account of the affairs of Scotland ... See

Lindsay, Colin, Earl of Balcarres

Agricola, G.A.
- The experimental husbandman and gardener ... to which is now added an appendix, containing a variety of experiments ... by R. Bradley. London: 1726. 2nd edn. 4to. [xxiv],314,[4] pp. 22 plates (13 double-page). Contemp calf, trifle worn.
        (Wheldon & Wesley) **£150 [≈ $3,106]**

Agriculture & Rural Affairs ...
- Essays relating to agriculture and rural affairs ... See Anderson, James

Aiken, John
- Essays on song-writing; with a collection of such English songs as are most eminent for poetical merit. Warrington: 1774. 2nd edn. Contemp green mor, gilt, a little rubbed.
        (Robertshaw) **£45 [≈ $81]**

Aikin, Arthur
- Journal of a tour through North Wales and part of Shropshire, with observations in mineralogy ... London: for J. Johnson, 1797. 1st edn. 8vo. xvi,232,[viii index] pp. Fldg chart. Uncut in rec calf, gilt spine, mrbld bds.
        (Lloyd-Roberts) **£100 [≈ $180]**

Aikin, J.
- A description of the country thirty to forty miles round Manchester ... London: 1795. 4to. Allegorical frontis, engvd & ptd titles, lge fldg plan, cold map, 71 engvd plates. Qtr calf.
        (Halewood) **£295 [≈ $531]**
- England delineated: or a geographical description of every County in England and Wales. 1795. 3rd edn. Engvd fldg map, 42 outline county maps. Contemp half calf, worn.   *(Tooley)* **£150 [≈ $270]**

Aikin, J.
- A manual of materia medica ... account of all the simples directed in the London and Edinburgh Dispensatories ... Yarmouth printed: Downes & March, 1785. 1st edn. 8vo. ix,194,viii index,[i advt] pp. Title laid down, spotted, ink-mark at ft. 19th c cloth.
        (Gough) **£80 [≈ $144]**

Aikin, John
- Biographical memoirs of medicine in Great Britain from the revival of literature to the time of Harvey. London: 1780. 8vo. 12,338 pp, 6ff index, advt leaf. Cloth.
        (Halewood) **£150 [≈ $270]**
- Letters from a father to his son, on various

topics, relative to literature and the conduct of life. Phila: Samuel Harrison Smith, 1794. 1st edn. 8vo. 328 pp. Contemp mottled calf, extremities rubbed, front hinge cracked at top.   *(Karmiole)* **$60 [≈ £33]**

Aikin, John
- Essays on song-writing: with a collection of such English songs as are most suitable for poetical merit. London: for J. Johnson, 1774. 2nd edn. xix,286 pp. Title a little browned & soiled. Contemp calf, rubbed, rebacked, crnrs reprd.   *(Claude Cox)* **£45 [≈ $81]**

Ainsworth, Henry
- The communion of Saintes. Amsterdam: 1640. Sm 8vo. Title backed. Old half calf, worn. NSTC 232.
        (Marlborough) **£60 [≈ $108]**

Air, Weather ...
- A general chronological history of the air, weather, seasons ... See Short, Thomas

A Kempis, Thomas
- The Christian's pattern: or, a treatise of the imitation of Jesus Christ. Now render'd into English. London: D. Brown, 1708. Sm 8vo. 2,[ii],271,[ii], 38 pp. Frontis. Contemp panelled calf. crnrs worn.
        (Spelman) **£20 [≈ $36]**

Akenside, Mark
- The pleasures of imagination. A poem in three books. London: for R. Dodsley, 1744. 3rd edn. 8vo. 142 pp. Half-title, engvd title vignette. Occas browning. Contemp qtr calf, rebacked.   *(Young's)* **£22 [≈ $39]**
- The pleasures of imagination. To which is prefixed a critical essay on the poem by Mrs. Barbauld. London: 1795. 12mo. Half-title, title, xxxvi,[2] pp. Frontis, 3 plates (offset to text & foxed). Contemp calf, gilt, sl rubbed, upper jnt a little cracked.
        (Bow Windows) **£25 [≈ $45]**
- The poems. London: Bowyer & Nichols, 1772. 1st edn. 4to. On fine paper. xii,380 pp. Mezzotint port frontis. Without half-title, title lightly soiled. 19th c half calf, mrbld sides, extremities rubbed.
        (Claude Cox) **£85 [≈ $153]**
- The poems. London: Bowyer & Nichols, 1772. 8vo. Contemp calf, rebacked.
        (Waterfield's) **£100 [≈ $180]**

Alanson, Edward
- Practical observations on amputation and the after-treatment ... an account of amputation

above the ankle ... London: 1782. 2nd edn, greatly enlgd. 8vo. 31,296 pp. Half calf.
(Halewood) **£90 [≈ $162]**

Albinus, Bernhard Siegfried
- Tables of the skeleton and muscles of the human body. Translated ... London: for John & Paul Knapton, 1749. 1st edn in English, Lge folio. 48 ff. 40 engvd plates, 12 in outline. Some browning, mainly marginal, title soiled. Mod half mor.
(Pickering) **$4,250 [≈ £2,361]**
- Tables of the skeleton and muscles of the human body. Edinburgh: for Andrew Bell, 1777-78. 2nd English edn. 2 parts in 1 vol. Folio. Engvd title vignettes, 28 engvd, 13 outline plates. Some offsetting & spotting. Contemp mrbld bds, rebacked in mor.
(Quaritch) **$550 [≈ £305]**

Aleman, Mateo
- The Rogue or the life of Guzman de Alfarache. London: for Edward Blount, 1623. 1st edn in English, 2nd iss. 2 pts in 1 vol. Title re-margined & rebacked, sl dampstained throughout, some old pencil notes, final sgntr from a smaller copy. Mod 3/4 mor. STC 289.
(Pirages) **$250 [≈ £138]**
- The Rogue or the life of Guzman de Alfarache. Oxford: W. Turner for R. Allot, 1630. 2 pts in 1 vol. Thick folio. Old stain to a few leaves. Contemp calf. STC 290.
(Stewart) **£300 [≈ $540]**

Alexander, William
- The history of women, from the earliest antiquity to the present time ... London: for W. Strahan, 1779. 1st edn. 2 vols. 4to. Rebound qtr calf. *(Hughes)* **£165 [≈ $297]**

Algarotti, Count Francesco
- Letters military and political. From the Italian. London: T. Egerton, 1783. 2nd edn. [ii],vii, xxviii,319 pp. Contemp calf, spine gilt, minor wear at extremities.
(Clark) **£20 [≈ $36]**

Allen, Charles
- A new and improved history of England ... London: for J. Johnson, 1798. 2nd edn. 552 pp, fldg chart, 4 plates engvd by William Blake. Contemp sheep, somewhat worn.
(C.R. Johnson) **£325 [≈ $585]**
- The polite lady, or a course of female education in a series of letters, from a mother to her daughter. London: Newberry & Carnan, 1769. 2nd edn. Engvd frontis. Rebound in roan.
(C.R. Johnson) **£260 [≈ $468]**

Allestree, Richard
- The causes of the decay of Christian piety. Or an impartial survey of the ruines of Christian religion. London: for Robert Pawlett, 1679. 8vo. Vignette title, 2 pp bookseller's ctlg. 1 crnr torn. Lib stamp on title. Contemp calf. Wing 1105. *(Stewart)* **£40 [≈ $72]**
- A discourse concerning the period of humane life: whether mutable or immutable. London: J.R. for Enoch Wyer, 1677. 2nd edn crrctd. Sm 8vo. [x],134 pp. Contemp sheep, backstrip defective. New Wing A1111.
(Blackwell's) **£65 [≈ $117]**
- The gentleman's calling. London: for T. Garthwait, 1660. 8vo. xxx,176 pp. Engvd title, 2 engvd plates. Names on endpapers. Contemp calf. Wing A1115.
(Lloyd-Roberts) **£75 [≈ $135]**
- The gentleman's calling. London: R. Norton, 1674. Cr 8vo. Engvd frontis, 2 pp pub ctlg. 19th c half mor, mrbld bds. Wing 1124.
(Stewart) **£35 [≈ $63]**
- The ladies calling. In two parts. Oxford: at the Theater, 1673. 1st edn. 8vo. Frontis. Later calf, a.e.g. Wing A1141.
(Argosy) **$200 [≈ £111]**
- The ladies calling. In two parts. Oxford: at the Theater, 1673. 1st edn. 8vo. Lacking front endpaper. Contemp polished calf. Wing A1141. *(Charles Cox)* **£40 [≈ $72]**
- The lively oracles given to us. Or the Christian's birth-right and duty ... Oxford: at the Theater, 1678. Cr 8vo. Vignette title. Old stain in crnr of early leaves, minimal marg worming to a few leaves. Contemp calf.
(Stewart) **£45 [≈ $81]**

Alleyne, James
- A new English dispensatory, in four parts. London: Tho. Astley, 1733. 1st edn. 8vo. xiv,646,[56] pp. Prelim & final advt leaf. Contemp calf. *(Spelman)* **£160 [≈ $288]**

Allix, Peter
- An examination of the scruples of those who refuse to take the oath of allegiance. London: Richard Chiswell, 1689. 4to. 34,2 advts pp. Wing A1222. *(C.R. Johnson)* **£25 [≈ $45]**

Almoran ...
- Almoran and Hamet: an oriental tale ... See Hawkesworth, John

Alonzo ...
- Alonzo. A tragedy ... See Home, John

Amboyna ...
- A true relation of the unjust, cruell, and

barbarous proceedings against the English at Amboyna in the East Indies, by the Neatherlandish Governour ... London: for N. Newberry, 1624. viii,38; ii,20; ii,34 pp. Vellum.   *(Farahar)* **£750 [≈ $1,350]**

Amelott, A.N. de la Houssaie

- The history of the government of Venice ... the use of the balloting box exactly described. London: for John Starkey, 1677. 8vo. 7 advt leaves. Later half mor, jnts rubbed, spine gilt. Wing A2974.   *(Stewart)* **£95 [≈ $171]**

Amendments ...

- Amendments of Mr. Collier's false and imperfect citations ... See Congreve, William

Amos, William

- The theory and practice of drill husbandry; founded upon philosophical principles and confirmed by experience ... London: for G.G. & J. Robinson, 1794. 1st edn. 4to. Advt leaf, 9 fldg engvd plates. Orig blue-grey bds, lacking spine, uncut edges.
                         (Traylen) **£295 [≈ $531]**

Amours of Lais ...

- The amours of Lais: or, the misfortunes of love. London: M. Folingsby, 1766. Contemp sheep.   *(C.R. Johnson)* **£300 [≈ $540]**

Les Amusemens de Spa ...

- Les amusemens de spa, or the gallantries of the spaw in Germany ... Dublin: James Kelburn, 1740. 2nd edn. 8vo. Contemp calf.
                      (Emerald Isle) **£165 [≈ $297]**

Amyntor and Theodora ...

- Amyntor and Theodora ... See Mallett, David

Anacreon and Sappho ...

- The works of Anacreon and Sappho ... See Greene, Edward Burnaby

Anatomy & Physiology ...

- A system of anatomy and physiology with the comparative anatomy of animals compiled from the latest and best authors .... Edinburgh: Creech, 1795. New edn. 3 vols. 8vo. Frontis, 20 copperplates. Contemp calf, worn, jnts weak.   *(Goodrich)* **$175 [≈ £97]**

Anatomy ...

- The anatomy of humane bodies epitomized ... See Gibson, Thomas

Anburey, Thomas

- Travels through the interior parts of America.

London: for William Lane, 1789. 1st edn. 2 vols. 8vo. 8 plates (5 fldg), fldg map. Without the subscribers' list, minor browning & offsetting, some short tears in marg. Contemp speckled calf, jnts cracked.
                       (Pirages) **$750 [≈ £416]**

Anderson, Aeneas

- A narrative of the British Embassy to China, in the years 1792, 1793, and 1794 ... London: J. Debrett, 1795. 1st edn. 4to. xxiv,278, [25 appendix & glossary], [1 advts] pp. Lacking half-title. Contemp half calf, spine gilt, mrbld bds, jnts weak, crnrs worn.
                        (Morrell) **£160 [≈ $288]**
- A narrative of the British Embassy to China, in the years 1792, 1793, and 1794 ... London: J. Debrett, 1795. 2nd, 1st 8vo, edn. Rec half calf, mrbld bds, uncut & partly unopened.
                          (Clark) **£90 [≈ $162]**

Anderson, James

- Essays relating to agriculture and rural affairs ... by a farmer. Edinburgh: for T. Cadell, London, 1775. 1st edn. 2 pts in 1. 8vo. xxxiii,[i],196; [v],200-472 pp. 24 ills on 3 fldg engvd plates. Contemp calf, minor split on top of spine.   *(Burmester)* **£240 [≈ $432]**

Anderson, Robert

- The life of Samuel Johnson ... with critical observations on his works. London: for J. & A. Arch ..., 1795. 1st edn. 8vo. [iv],307 pp. Half-title, traces of old lib stamp on title. Early 19th c half calf, rubbing, lacking label, white lib mark on spine.
                      (Burmester) **£125 [≈ $225]**

Andrews, James Petit

- Anecdotes, &c. ancient and modern. With observations. London: 1790. 8vo. 470; 106 pp. Engvd frontis. Half red mor, g.e.
                         (Argosy) **$150 [≈ £83]**

Andrews, Lancelot

- Apostolica Sacra: or a collection of posthumous and orphan lectures ... Never before extant. London: R. Hodgkinsonne, 1657. Sm folio. Some sl marg worming, margs of endleaves strengthened. Later half calf, mrbld bds. Wing 3125.
                        (Stewart) **£100 [≈ $180]**
- The pattern of catechistical doctrine at large. London: Roger Norton, 1650. Folio. Port frontis. Contemp calf, rebacked in cloth, upper jnt cracked. Wing 3147.
                        (Stewart) **£85 [≈ $153]**

Andrews, Miles Peter
- The Baron Kinkvervankotsdorsprakin-gatchdern. A new musical comedy ... London: T. Cadell, 1781. Sole edn. xi,[v],71 pp.
(Clark) £24 [≈ $43]

Queen Anne ...
- Good Queen Anne vindicated ... See Swift, Jonathan
- The life of Queen Anne. In which is contained the most considerable transactions of her reign ... particular relation to her sickness and death ... London: for A. Bell, 1714. Cr 8vo. Fldg frontis. Contemp calf, rubbed. *(Stewart)* £25 [≈ $45]

Anson, George
- A voyage round the world ... London: for the author, 1748. 1st edn. 1st iss. 4to. [xxxiv],[420] pp. 42 fldg plates, maps & charts. Some sl wear to plates, 1 hole reprd with sl loss, some offsetting, some anntns. Mod half mor by Sangorski.
(Ash) £800 [≈ $1,440]
- A voyage round the world. In the years MDCCXL, I, II, III, IV. London: for the author, 1748. 1st edn. 4to. [xxxiii],[i blank],417,[1 blank],[2 directions] pp. 14 maps & charts inc addtnl track chart from 2nd edn, 29 fldg plates. Contemp panelled calf, rebacked. *(Morrell)* £580 [≈ $1,044]
- A voyage round the world ... London: for John & Paul Knapton, 1748. 2nd edn. Thick 8vo. 3 fldg engvd charts. repr to 1 chart, marg reprs to 2 leaves (1 with loss of a few letters), some spotting. Rebound qtr red mor.
(Hughes) £75 [≈ $135]
- A voyage round the world. In the years MDCCXL, I, II, III, IV. Compiled from his papers and materials ... London: for T. Osborne ..., 1767. 12th edn. 4to. [20],417 pp, 1f directions to binder. 41 engvd maps, charts, plates. 3/4 calf, mrbld bds.
(Argonaut) £650 [≈ £361]
- A voyage round the world. In the years 1740 [to] 1744 ... compiled from his papers and materials, by Richard Walter ... For Bowyer & Nichols, 1776. 15th edn. 4to. xx,417 pp. 43 fldg maps, charts. Contemp calf, spine gilt, extremities chipped, jnt tender.
(Frew Mackenzie) £320 [≈ $576]

Answer ...
- An answer to a book intituled The state of the Protestants of Ireland ... See Leslie, Charles
- An answer to a late pamphlet, intituled a free and candid inquiry, addressed to the representative etc. of this Kingdom. Dublin:

1753. 46 pp. Disbound.
(C.R. Johnson) £38 [≈ $68]
- An answer to Mr. Mist's journal ... See Curll, Edmund
- Answer to the considerations of the establishment of a Regency. London: for J. Debrett, 1788. 1st edn. 8vo. [iv],23 pp. Half-title. Orig plain blue wraps.
(Burmester) £20 [≈ $36]
- An answer to the dissenters pleas ... See Bennet, Thomas
- A final answer to the remarks on the Craftsman's vindication ... See Bolingbroke, Henry St. John, Viscount

Antonius, Marcus Aurelius
- The meditations of the Emperor. Newly translated from the Greek. Glasgow: 1742. 1st edn thus. 12mo. Title, 308,[i advt] pp. Wormhole through ft of lower marg. Contemp sheep, gilt panelled spine, light wear. *(Barbary)* £55 [≈ $99]

Apology ...
- An apology for the failures charg'd on the Reverend Mr. George Walker's account of the Siege of Derry. In a letter to the undertaker of a more accurate narrative. 1689. 4to. 27 pp. Disbound. With the licence leaf. Wing A3549. *(C.R. Johnson)* £110 [≈ $198]

Appeal ...
- An appeal from the new to the old Whigs ... See Burke, Edmund
- A free appeal to the people of Great Britain, on the conduct of the present administration, since the thirteenth of July, 1766. London: J. Almon, 1767. 2nd edn. 45,3 advts pp. Disbound. *(C.R. Johnson)* £38 [≈ $68]

Appleton, Nathaniel
- God, and not ministers, to have the glory of all success given to the preached gospel ... Boston: Rogers & Fowle, 1741. 1st edn. 44 pp. *(Jenkins)* £45 [≈ £25]

Aram, Eugene
- The genuine account of the trial of Eugene Aram, for the murder of Daniel Clark, late of Knaresborough ... York: for C. Etherington, 1759. 2nd edn. 8vo. [ii],42 pp. Title dusty. Disbound. *(Burmester)* £85 [≈ $153]
- The genuine account of the trial of Eugene Aram, for the murder of Daniel Clark, late of Knaresborough ... York: E. Hargrove, 1792. 8th edn. 19th c qtr calf.
(C.R. Johnson) £45 [≈ $81]

Arbuthnot, John

- An essay concerning the effects of air on human bodies. London: for J. Tonson, 1733. 1st edn. 8vo. Half-title. Contemp calf, rebacked, crnrs worn.
  (Chaucer Head) £340 [≈ $612]
- Tables of the Grecian, Roman and Jewish measures. London: Smith, n.d. [?1705]. 1st edn. Obl 4to. Title, 13ff. Engvd throughout. Contemp red mor gilt, refurbished.
  (Marlborough) £350 [≈ $630]

Argens, Jean Baptiste de Boyer

- Chinese letters. being a ... correspondence between a Chinese traveller at Paris and his countrymen in China ... London: D, Browne ..., 1741. 1st edn in English. 12mo. xx,314,[22] pp. Edges of title & half-title browned, some foxing. Contemp calf, rebacked.
  (Dailey) $225 [≈ £125]

Argenson, Marquis d'

- Essays, civil, moral, literary and political. Worcester, Mass: Thomas ..., 1797. 1st Amer edn. Cr 8vo. Contemp calf, sl rubbed.
  (Stewart) £145 [≈ $261]

Argument ...

- An argument ... that a standing army is inconsistent with a free government ... See Trenchard, John

Arguments ...

- Arguments for and against a union between Great Britain and Ireland ... See Cooke, Edward

Argumentum ...

- Argumentum anti-Normanicum: or an argument proving ... that William, Duke of Normandy, made no absolute conquest of England. London: John Darby, 1682. 1st edn (?). 8vo. Frontis. Later calf, rebacked. Wing C4907A.
  (Charles Cox) £175 [≈ $315]

Ariosto, Ludovico

- The Orlando of Ariosto. Reduced to xxiv books ... by John Hoole. London: 1791. 2 vols. 8vo. 6 plates. Contemp calf, gilt spine, jnt mended.
  (Argosy) $150 [≈ £83]

Armstrong, John

- The history of the Island of Minorca. London: for C. Davis, 1752. 1st edn. 8vo. Lge fldg map, 2 plates, half-title. Contemp calf, old rebacking. *(Chaucer Head)* £280 [≈ $504]
- The oeconomy of love. A poetical essay. London: T. Cooper, 1739. 3rd edn. 43 pp. Half-title. Disbound.
  (C.R. Johnson) £65 [≈ $117]

Armstrong, John (1709-1779)

- The art of preserving health: a poem. London: 1774. Sgntr on title erased. Orig calf, top bd & endpapers detchd.
  (Rittenhouse) $75 [≈ £41]

Army List

- Army List. 1766. Calf, sl worn, sm owner's stamp on endpaper. *(Edwards)* £130 [≈ $234]
- Army List. 1794. Tree-calf, hd & tail of spine sl worn, crnrs bumped.
  (Edwards) £120 [≈ $234]
- Army List. 1795. Tree-calf, lower bd sl worn, crnrs bumped. *(Edwards)* £120 [≈ $234]

Arnaud de Ronsil, G.

- A dissertation on hernias or ruptures ... London: 1748. vii pp, 4ff, 412 pp. Pp 413-439 (vocabulary of terms) omitted by binder. Endpapers sl stained. Orig lea, worn, rebacked. *(Whitehart)* £65 [≈ $117]

Arnot, Hugo

- The history of Edinburgh. From the earliest accounts to the present time. Edinburgh: 1788. 4to. Plan, 20 engvs. Contemp calf.
  (Halewood) £220 [≈ $396]

Art of Cookery ...

- The art of cookery, in imitation of Horace's art of poetry ... See King, William

Art of Drawing ...

- The art of drawing and painting in water-colours. Wherein the principles of drawing are laid down ... London: G. Keith, 1779. 5th edn. Sm 8vo. 96 pp. 2 fldg plates. Margs a little dusty. Soiled orig wraps.
  (Spelman) £120 [≈ $216]

Art of Painting ...

- The art of painting in miniature ... See Boutet, Claude

Ascham, Roger

- The English works ... I. A report of the affairs of Germany. II. Toxophilus ... III. The schoolmaster ... IV. Letters to Queen Elizabeth ... London: for R. & J. Dodsley ..., 1761. 4to. New half calf.
  (Traylen) £220 [≈ $396]
- The scholemaster: shewing a plain and perfect way of teaching the learned languages. London: Innys & Burt, 1743. 8vo. xxii,274 pp. Plate. Sl waterstaining to lower half. Calf,

later rebacking. *(P & P)* **£95** [≈ **$171**]
- Toxophilus, the schole, or partitions, of shooting. Contayned in 11 bookes ... Wrexham: R. Marsh, 1788. New edn. 23,230,2 pp. Orig tree-calf, gilt extra.
(Jenkins) **$175** [≈ **£97**]

Ashmole, Elias
- The history and antiquities of Berkshire ... and a particular account of the castle, college, and town of Windsor. Reading: Carnan, 1736. Folio. xvii,340,[ii] pp. Red & black title, fldg map. Later russia, gilt, a.e.g., jnts sl rubbed. *(Frew Mackenzie)* **£250** [≈ **$450**]
- The institution, laws and ceremonies of the most noble Order of the Garter. London: for N. Brooke, 1672. Folio. 6ff, 720 pp, 52 ff. Engvd port, 36 engvd plates, 18 text ills. Early 19th c mor, gilt, a.e.g., edges a little rubbed. Wing A3983.
(Marlborough) **£850** [≈ **$1,530**]

Ashworth, Caleb
- Reflections on the fall of a great man. A sermon preached to ... dissenters at Daventry ... on the death of ... Isaac Watts. London: J. Waugh, 1749. 42,2 advts pp. Disbound.
(C.R. Johnson) **£25** [≈ **$45**]

Asiatic Researches ...
- Asiatic researches: or, Transactions of the Society [Asiatic Soc of Bengal] ... for inquiring into the history ... the arts, science, and literature of Asia ... London: 1799. 2nd series, 5 vols. 4to. Little foxing & browning. Contemp calf, rubbed, jnts weak.
(Morrell) **£230** [≈ **$414**]

Astle, Thomas
- The origin and progress of writing. As well hieroglyphic as elementary. London: the author, 1784. vii,xxv,235 pp. 31 plates (25 with blank verso, 3 ptd both sides; 10 fldg, 6 cold; minor offsetting). Contemp tree-calf, rebacked, crnrs renewed, sides sl marked.
(Pirages) **$450** [≈ **£250**]
- The origin and progress of writing. As well hieroglyphic as elementary ... some account of the origin and progress of printing. London: the author, 1784. 1st edn. 31 plates (9 fldg, some part cold). Contemp half calf, rebacked, orig spine laid down. *(Traylen)* **£120** [≈ **$216**]

Astronomical Catechism ...
- An astronomical catechism, for the instruction of young gentlemen and ladies. By a minister in the country for the use of his own children. London: T. Wilkins, 1792. 53pp plus table. Stabbed pamphlet as issued,

enclosed in early wraps.
(C.R. Johnson) **£50** [≈ **$90**]

Athenian Letters ...
- Athenian letters, or the epistolatory correspondence of an agent of the King of Persia during the Peloponesian War etc. Dublin: Archer, 1792. 2 vols. 8vo. Frontis. Mod half calf, mrbld bds.
(Emerald Isle) **£50** [≈ **$90**]

Athenian Sport ...
- Athenian sport ... See Dunton, John

Atkinson, James & Wilson, H.
- A compleat system of navigation ... or the whole art performed ... by a new method, not yet published. Dublin: 1767. 412,150 tables pp. 16 fldg plates. Sl cropping at top edge. Mod gilt dec crushed mor.
(Gough) **£325** [≈ **$585**]

St. Augustine
- Confessions ... divers antiquities are explained; and the marginal notes of a former Popish translation, answered. London: for Abel Roper, 1650. 12mo. [x],513,[iii] pp. Marg fraying of 1st 2 leaves, 1st & last few pp dusty. Contemp calf, rebacked. Wing A4206.
(Clark) **£50** [≈ **$90**]
- Of the citie of God: with the learned comments of I.L. Vives. London: Eld & Flesher, 1620. 2nd edn. Folio. Engvd title, [xiv],921 pp. Engvd title & 1st leaf of text cut & laid down. Contemp calf, gilt, rebacked, crnrs bumped. STC 917.
(P & P) **£145** [≈ **$261**]

Auteroche, L'Abbe Chappe d'
- A journey into Siberia ... containing an account of the manners and customs of the Russians ... London: T. Jefferys, 1770. 1st English edn. 4to. xiii,[vi contents],[i advts], 395,[1 errata] pp. Fldg engvd map, 9 engvd plates. Contemp calf, jnts cracked.
(Morrell) **£420** [≈ **$756**]

Avila, Juan de
- The audi filia or rich cabinet full of spirituall jewells. [St. Omer: English College Press], 1620. 4to. Title spotted. Half brown mor by Winstanley. NSTC 983.
(Marlborough) **£120** [≈ **$216**]

Awsiter, John
- An essay on the effects of opium considered as a poison. London: G. Kearsly, 1763. 1st edn. 8vo. vii,70 pp. Uncut & sewn as issued.

Preserved in a cloth box.
(Rootenberg) **$650 [≈ £361]**

Ayloffe, Sir Joseph
- An historical description of an ancient picture in Windsor Castle. 1773. Demy 4to. 41 pp. Rec cloth.   *(Deighton Bell)* **£20 [≈ $36]**
- An historical description of an ancient picture in Windsor Castle. London: 1773. Sm 4to. 2ff, 45 pp, 1 leaf advts. New qtr calf.
(Marlborough) **£65 [≈ $117]**

Ayres, John
- Arithmetick made easie for the use and benefit of trades-men ... London: for Tho. Norris ..., 1716. 13th edn. 12mo. A little browned, sm repr to crnr of last leaf, frontis marg reinforced. Contemp sheep, rebacked.
(Charles Cox) **£50 [≈ $90]**

Ayres, Philip
- Emblems of love in four languages. [L:] for John Wren, n.d. [ca 1690]. Sm 8vo. Title, 1 f, 44ff emblematic plates, 44ff text, engvd throughout. Sev plates cut loose. 18th c calf, upper jnts cracked.
(Marlborough) **£500 [≈ $900]**
- Lyric poems. Made in imitation of the Italians. London: for Jos. Knight ..., 1687. 1st edn. Lacking engvd frontis, sl browned. Mod blindstamped half calf. Wing A4312.
(Charles Cox) **£90 [≈ $162]**

Ayscough, James
- A short account of the eye and nature of vision. The sixth edition. Printed for John Gilbert, n.d. [1760?]. 8vo. Fldg engvd frontis. Mod mrbld bds, calf spine, red mor label.
(Bickersteth) **£225 [≈ $405]**

Bacon, Sir Francis
- Baconiana. Or certain genuine remains ... in arguments civil and moral, natural, medical ... for the first time faithfully published. London: Richard Chiswell, 1679. 1st edn. Cr 8vo. Lacks port & 2nd divisional title. Contemp calf, worn, jnt cracked.
(Stewart) **£100 [≈ $180]**
- Baconiana. Or certain genuine remains ... now for the first time faithfully published. London: for Richard Chiswell, 1679. 1st edn. 8vo. Old calf, rebacked, new endpapers.
(Charles Cox) **£50 [≈ $90]**
- The elements of the common lawes of England, branched into a double tract. London: assignes of Iohn More, 1639. 3rd edn. 4to. Title & fly-title chipped. Old calf, rebacked & refurbished. STC 1136.

(Charles Cox) **£225 [≈ $405]**
- The essayes or counsels, civill and morall ... Newly enlarged. John Haviland, 1632. Sm 4to. [viii],340,[xlii] pp. A1 blank. 2X2 & [a2] transposed. Contemp calf, extremities lightly rubbed, front jnt beginning to split at hd. STC 1150.   *(Frew Mackenzie)* **£225 [≈ $405]**
- The essayes or counsels, civill and morall. London: Iohn Beale, 1639. 4to. Lacking prelim blank, a few sl stains & watermarks. Old calf, rebacked. STC 1151.
(Charles Cox) **£75 [≈ $135]**
- The essayes or counsels, civill and morall ... discourse of the wisdom of the ancients ... added the character of Queen Elizabeth ... London: A. Swalle ..., 1696. Browned & spotted. Sgntrs X & Y misbound after table & advts. 18th c calf, rebacked. Wing B295B.
(Charles Cox) **£55 [≈ $99]**
- The essays or councils, civil and moral ... London: George Sawbridge, 1696. 8vo. [8],167, [8],21,[1], [9],16-98,[1], [4 advts], 99-123 pp. Ms contents list at end, sm tear in 1 marg without loss. Contemp calf.
(Spelman) **£300 [≈ $540]**
- The historie of life and death with observations natural and experimental for the prolonging of life. London: 1638. 12mo. 323 pp. Title reprd. Old calf, rebacked.
(Goodrich) **£225 [≈ £125]**
- The historie of the reigne of King Henry the Seventh ... London: 1641. 3rd edn. Folio. [14],248 pp. Lacking engvd frontis, sl cropped throughout with loss of fore-edge rule, unobtrusive worm slit in marg of 25 leaves. Early 19th c calf. New Wing B299.
(Claude Cox) **£48 [≈ $86]**
- The historie of the reigne of King Henry the Seventh ... London: 1641. Sm folio. Contemp calf, 19th c recasing. Wing B299.
(Stewart) **£85 [≈ $153]**
- The history of Henry VII of England ... Now first new written 1786. London: for the editor, at the Logographic Press, 1786. 1st edn thus. 8vo. iv,288,4 pp. 19th c half cloth.
(Young's) **£30 [≈ $54]**
- Law tracts, containing 1. A proposition ... 8. Reading on the Statute of Uses. London: for R. Gosling, 1737. 2nd edn. A few light marg stains. edges cut a little close. Old calf, rebacked.   *(Charles Cox)* **£65 [≈ $117]**
- Of the advancement and proficience of learning, or the partitions of sciences ... interpreted by Gilbert Wats. Oxford: for Rob. Young ..., 1640. 1st edn of this trans. Folio. 19ff, 477 pp, 10ff. Sl waterstained. Contemp calf, jnt mended. STC 1167.
(Argosy) **$750 [≈ £416]**

- Of the advancement and proficience of learning ... interpreted by Gilbert Wats. Oxford: for Rob. Young ..., 1640. 1st edn in English. Folio. Port (laid down), engvd title. Later panelled calf, rebacked, new endpapers. STC 1167. *(Charles Cox)* **£275 [≈ $495]**
- Of the advancement and proficience of learning, or the partitions of sciences ... interpreted by Gilbert Wats. London: Thomas Williams, 1674. Sm folio. Port frontis. Contemp calf, recased. Wing B312. *(Argosy)* **$300 [≈ £166]**
- The philosophical works ... methodized and made English ... with occasional notes ... London: for J.J. & P. Knapton ..., 1733. 1st coll edn. 3 vols. 4to. Contemp speckled calf, gilt, gilt dec spines. *(Traylen)* **£350 [≈ £630]**
- The philosophical works ... methodized and made English ... with occasional notes ... by Peter Shaw. London: for J.J. & P. Knapton ..., 1733. 3 vols. 4to. Contemp calf, rebacked. *(Waterfield's)* **£450 [≈ $810]**
- Sylva sylvarum: or, a natural historie. In ten centuries ... London: for William Lee, 1635. 4th edn. Folio. [xx],260, [xxxii],47,[i] pp. Engvd frontis, addtnl title. Lacking 1 leaf of "Magnalia naturae". Old calf, later rebacking, worn, loose in binding. *(Clark)* **£60 [≈ $108]**
- Sylva sylvarum: or, a natural historie. In ten centuries ... London: for William Lee, 1639. 5th edn. Folio. Port, engvd frontis, vignette title. Contemp calf, rebacked, orig spine laid down. STC 1173. *(Traylen)* **£85 [≈ $153]**
- Three speeches ... concerning the post-nati, naturalization of the Scotch in England, union of the laws of the kingdomes of England and Scotland. London: for Samuel Broun, 1641. 1st edn. 4to. Top crnrs of 1st few leaves reprd. Mod half mor. Wing B337. *(Charles Cox)* **£105 [≈ $189]**
- The two bookes of Francis Bacon. Of the proficience and advancement of learning, divine and humane. London: for Henrie Tomes, 1605. 1st edn. 4to. Early engvd port mtd to face title. Some light waterstains & early underlining. Early 19th c calf. STC 1164, *(Charles Cox)* **£650 [≈ $1,170]**
- The works ... London: R. Gosling ..., 1730. 4 vols. Folio. 4 engvd frontis. Contemp speckled calf, gilt, rebacked, mor labels, gilt. *(Traylen)* **£250 [≈ $450]**
- The works ... London: R. Gosling ..., 1730. 4 vols. Sm folio. 4 engvd frontis. Mottled calf, early rebacking, jnts worn. *(Book Block)* **$175 [≈ £97]**
- The works ... in four volumes. London: A. Millar, 1740. Folio. Lge paper. 4 engvd frontis, 4 vignette titles, 2 fldg tables.

Sporadic dampstaining, insignificant worming towards end of vol 2. Contemp calf, worn, calf pitted & defective in parts, jnts cracked. *(Clark)* **£130 [≈ $234]**
- The works ... London: A. Millar, 1765. 5 vols. 4to. Red & black titles with vignettes, 4 port frontis, 2 fldg tables. Contemp calf, gilt, light rubbing, jnts cracked but holding. B'plates. *(Frew Mackenzie)* **£240 [≈ $432]**

Bacon, Nathaniel
- A relation of the fearful estate of Francis Spira, after he turn'd apostate ... to popery. As also ... John Child, who desperately hang'd himself ... London: for B. Harris, 1715. 12mo. W'cut frontis. Sgntrs on title marg. Contemp sheep, spine chipped, cracked. *(Chaucer Head)* **£60 [≈ $108]**

Badcock, William
- A touch-stone for gold and silver wares; or, a manual for goldsmiths, and all other persons ... London: for Bellinger & Bassett, 1677. 1st edn. Sm 8vo. 26,115,[11] pp. Engvd frontis, engvd plate. Prev owner's sgntr. Contemp calf, spine reprd. Wing B382. *(Rootenberg)* **$850 [≈ £472]**

Badeslade, Thomas
- Chorographia Britanniae or a set of maps of all the Counties of England and Wales ... London: 1742. 8vo. Engvd fldg title & dedn, 46 double-page maps, 5 tables. Calf, rebacked. *(Tooley)* **£600 [≈ $1,080]**

Badger, John
- A collection of remarkable cures of the King's Evil, perfected by the Royal Touch, collected from the writings of many eminent physicians and surgeons, and learned men. London: Cooper, 1748. Half-title. 64 pp. Some foxing & underlining. New bds. *(Goodrich)* **$135 [≈ £75]**

Bailey, Nathaniel
- An universal etymological English dictionary ... the second edition. London: [n.d.]. 8vo. 8 prelims, 476 unpaginated leaves. Lower crnr of title torn away with loss of date. Some dampstains & smudges. Old half roan, worn, rec rebacked with calf. *(Bow Windows)* **£48 [≈ $86]**
- An universal etymological English dictionary ... the twentieth edition. London: for T. Osborne ..., 1763. Tick 8vo. Rebound in qtr calf, mrbld sides. *(Hughes)* **£68 [≈ $122]**
- An universal etymological English dictionary ... the four and twentieth edition. London: for J. Buckland ..., 1782. 8vo. Later half calf,

rubbed.   *(Waterfield's)* **£25 [≃ $45]**

Baillie, Matthew
- The morbid anatomy of some of the most important parts of the human body. Albany: Thomas Spencer, 1795. 1st Amer edn. 8vo. [2],viii, 248,[12] pp. Some waterstaining & browning. Contemp calf, lower front jnt broken.   *(Antiq Sc)* **$185 [≃ £102]**
- The morbid anatomy of some of the most important parts of the human body. London: 1797. 2nd edn. 8vo. xxxvi,460 pp. Lacking cloth spine, bds detchd or nearly so.
        (Rittenhouse) **$150 [≃ £83]**

Baillie, Robert
- Letters and journals ... Containing an impartial account of public transactions, civil, ecclesiastic, and military ... from 1637 to 1662 ... Edinburgh: W. Gray ..., 1775. 8vo. viii,456,[ii]; [ii],464.[ii] pp. Occas foxing. Old qtr mor, crnrs worn.   *(Clark)* **£40 [≃ $72]**

Baillie, Thomas
- A solemn appeal to the public ..., London: for Captain Baillie, 1779. Sole edn. Folio. [8],xliv, 190,[6] pp. Index, errata, dedn. Contemp red mor, elab gilt dec.
        (Rootenberg) **$550 [≃ £305]**

Baker, John Wynn
- Considerations upon the exportation of corn. Dublin: [The Dublin Society], 1771. 1st edn. 8vo. 48 pp. Disbound.
        (Burmester) **£75 [≃ $135]**

Baker, Richard
- Meditations and disquisitions upon the one and fiftiethe Psalme of David. London: Edward Griffin, 1638. 1st edn. Sm 4to. [6],75 pp. Some old waterstaining. 19th c mrbld paper wraps, cloth spine.
        (Spelman) **£30 [≃ $54]**

Balbani, Niccolo
- The Italian convert ... or the life of Galaecius Caracciolus. London: for Abel Roper, 1677. 8vo. 2ff advts at end. Frontis cut down & mtd, 2 margs cut short with loss of a few letters, sev marks & brief tears. Later sheep, rubbed, jnts weak. Wing B544A.
        (Charles Cox) **£40 [≃ $72]**

Balfour, Sir James
- Practicks: or, a system of the most ancient law of Scotland. Edinburgh: for Kincaid & Donaldson, 1755. 1st edn. Folio. Early law calf, rebacked, mod blanks.
        (Chaucer Head) **£170 [≃ $306]**

Balzac, John Luis Guez, Sieur de
- Aristippus, or Monsr. de Balsac's masterpiece. Being a discourse concerning the court ... Englished by R.W. London: for Nat. Eakins ..., 1659. 12mo. [xvi],159,[17] pp. Royal Institution blindstamp on title. Contemp sheep, rebacked. Wing B612.
        (Burmester) **£60 [≃ $108]**

Bancroft, Edward
- Essay on the natural history of Guiana, in South America ... together with an account of the religion, manners, and customs of several tribes of its Indian inhabitants. London: Becket & de Hondt, 1769. 1st edn. 8vo. Engvd frontis. New half calf, mor label.
        (Traylen) **£275 [≃ $495]**

Bancroft, Richard
- Dangerous positions and proceedings, published and practised within this island of Britaine, under pretence of Reformation ... London: R. Young & R. Badger, 1640. 2nd edn. Sm 4to. Qtr mor gilt, cloth bds. STC 1345.   *(Deighton Bell)* **£50 [≃ $90]**

Bancroft, Thomas
- The poetical correspondent; or sketches of Manchester in verse, written in letters by a person in town to his friend at Cambridge. Manchester: J. Harrop, 1777. 4to. 20 pp. Rebound in qtr calf, mrbld bds, spine gilt.
        (C.R. Johnson) **£750 [≃ $1,350]**

Banks, John
- History of John Duke of Marlborough ... commander-in-chief of the armies of Her Britannic Majesty ... London: for J. Hodges, 1755. 3rd edn, crrctd. 8vo. Engvd frontis. Calf, gilt, rubbed, ex lib with stamps & labels.
        (Hughes) **£35 [≃ $63]**

Banks, John (fl. 1696)
- Vertue betray'd; or, Anna Bullen. A tragedy at His Royal Highness the Duke's Theatre. London: R. Bentley ..., 1682. 1st edn. Sm 4to. Title backed, imprint cropped. Mod green mor. Wing B567.
        (Traylen) **£135 [≃ $243]**

Baptist de la Fontaine, John
- The French spy: or, the memoirs of ... late brigadier and surveyor of the French King's army, now a prisoner in the Bastile ... Translated ... 1700. A-Bb8. Calf, gilt, a.e.g., upper bd detchd.   *(Edwards)* **£100 [≃ $180]**

Baratariana ...
- Baratariana, a select collection of fugitive

political pieces etc. Dublin: 1772. 12mo. Engvd frontis. Mod half calf.
(Emerald Isle) **£50 [≈ $90]**
- Baratariana, a select collection of fugitive pieces ... Published during the administration of His Excellency Lord Viscount Townsend in Ireland. Dublin: 1772. Port frontis. Contemp calf. *(C.R. Johnson)* **£165 [≈ $297]**

Barbauld, Anna Laetitia
- Epistle to William Wilberforce, Esq. On the rejection of the Bill for abolishing the slave trade ... London: J. Johnson, 1791. 2nd edn. 4to. Half-title, 14 pp. Rebound in bds.
(C.R. Johnson) **£145 [≈ $261]**

Barclay, James
- A complete and universal English dictionary ... A new edition ... London: J.F. & C. Rivington ..., 1792. 8vo. A1-3S8, T4 (without pagination). Contemp tree-calf, spine gilt, vertical crack in backstrip.
(Clark) **£60 [≈ $108]**

Barclay, Robert
- An apology for the true Christian divinity ... the principles and doctrines of the people called Quakers. Phila: 1788. Old lea, lacking front cvr. *(Allen)* **$17.50 [≈ £9]**
- An apology for the true Christian divinity, as the same is held forth ... by ... Quakers. London: T. Sowle, 1703. 5th edn in English. 8vo. Endpaper torn. Contemp panelled calf, upper jnt cracked & sl worn.
(Stewart) **£35 [≈ $63]**

Barclay, William
- Callirhoe; commonly called the Well of Spa ... what diseases may be cured by drinking of the well ... Aberdeen: Burnett & Rettie, 1799. 12mo. 26,[2] pp. W'cut arms & ms notes on title verso. Uncut in old bds, cloth spine.
(Burmester) **£30 [≈ $54]**

Barcroft, John
- A brief narrative of the life, convincement, conversion and labours of John Barcroft ... Dublin: Sam Fuller, 1730. 12mo. Calf.
(Emerald Isle) **£85 [≈ $153]**

Bardwell, Thomas
- The practice of painting and perspective made easy ... the art of painting in oil ... London: for the author, 1756. 1st edn. 4to. v,[i blank],64 pp. 6 engvd plates. Privilege leaf before title, tipped-in errata. Minor foxing. Rec qtr calf, fresh endpapers.
(Spelman) **£200 [≈ $360]**

Baretti, Joseph
- A journey from London to Genoa. London: Davies, 1770. 4 vols. 8vo. Contemp mottled calf, gilt, worn, jnts cracking, lacking 2 labels.
(Marlborough) **£220 [≈ $396]**

Barlow, P.
- The general history of Europe; and entertaining traveller ... all the empires, kingdoms, &c. in Europe. London: Stratford, n.d. [ca 1790]. 1st edn. Thick folio. Engvd frontis, 70 plates inc 19 extndg maps, 40 views, 12 ports. Browning. Contemp calf, rebacked. *(Bow Windows)* **£510 [≈ $918]**

Barlow, Thomas
- A letter concerning invocation of Saints and Adoration of the Cross wrote ten years since to John Evelyn. London: for John Martyn 1679. 4to, Disbound. Wing B834.
(Waterfield's) **£25 [≈ $45]**

Barlow, Thomas, Bishop of Lincoln
- The gunpowder-treason: with a discourse of the manner of its discovery. London: Tho. Newcomb ..., 1679. 1st edn. Sm 8vo. Rec qtr calf over mrbld bds, mottled edges.
(Sotheran) **£98 [≈ $176]**

Barnard, Thomas
- An historical character of the holy and exemplary life of ... Lady Elisabeth Hastings. 1742. Calf, jnts broken. *(Allen)* **£30 [≈ £16]**

Barnes, Joshua
- Gerania: a new discovery of a little sort of people anciently discoursed of, called Pygmies ... London: W.G. for Obadiah Blagrove, 1675. 1st edn. Sm 8vo. [iv],110,[x pub ctlg] pp. Engvd frontis (sl stained), sl loss to H3. Later endpapers, mod calf. Wing B870. *(P & P)* **£380 [≈ $684]**
- Gerania: a new discovery of a little sort of people anciently discoursed of, called Pygmies ... London: W.G. for Obadiah Blagrove, 1675. 1st edn. Sm 8vo. [vi],110,[x pub ctlg] pp. Engvd frontis. Contemp gilt-panelled mor, spine elab gilt, rubbed. Wing B870. *(Bennett)* **£550 [≈ $990]**
- The history of that most victorious monarch Edward IIId. Cambridge: the author, 1688. 1st edn. Folio. Frontis, 2 ports. Frontis & title laid down, A2 marg reprd, 1 leaf torn without loss, sl fraying. Contemp black mor, gilt, spine worn at ft. Wing B871.
(Charles Cox) **£120 [≈ $216]**
- The history of that most victorious monarch Edward IIId. Cambridge: for the author,

1688. 1st edn. Folio. 8ff,911 pp. 3 engvd ports. Isolated minor stains or tears. Contemp mottled calf, crnrs & edges worn, jnts patched.   *(Pirages)* **$200 [≈ £111]**

Barrington, Daines
- Miscellanies. London: J. Nichols, 1781. 1st edn. 4to. iv,viii,557 pp. 2 ports, 2 maps (1 fldg), 4 tables. A little browned, early ink inscrptn on title. Armorial b'plate. Contemp half calf, reprd, crnrs worn.
            (Morrell) **£580 [≈ $1,044]**
- Observations on the most ancient statutes from Magna Charta to the twenty-first of James I. Cap XXVII. 1775. 4th edn. 4to. xii,578 pp. Orig paper bds, rebacked. Barrington's pres inscrptn on front pastedown.   *(Edwards)* **£170 [≈ $306]**
- Observations upon the statutes. Chiefly the most ancient, from Magna Charta to the twenty-first of James the First, Ch. xxvii. Dublin: Boulter Grierson ..., 1767. 2nd edn 8vo. xii,428 pp. Contemp calf, hinges cracked. (A piracy?).
            (Edwards) **£140 [≈ $252]**

Barron, Richard
- A faithful account of Mr. Archibald Bower's motives for leaving his office of secretary to the Court of Inquisition ... Dublin: for George Faulkener ..., 1750. 1st Dublin edn. 8vo. 15 pp. Rec bds. *(Burmester)* **£45 [≈ $81]**

Barron, William
- History of the colonization of the free states of antiquity applied to the present contest between Great Britain and her American Colonies. London: T. Cadell, 1777. 4to. 151 pp. Mrbld bds, rebacked.
            (C.R. Johnson) **£165 [≈ $297]**

Barrough, Philip
- The method of physick, containing the causes, signes, and cures of inward diseases in mans body from the head to the foote. London: 1610. 4th edn. Sm 4to. 8ff, 477,7 pp. Inconspicuous worming in last 30 leaves. Rec calf.   *(Hemlock)* **£650 [≈ $361]**

Barrow, Isaac
- A defence of the B. Trinity. Never before printed. London: for Aylmer, 1697. Sm 8vo. Marg tear in E3 just touching text. Contemp calf, upper jnt cracked. Wing 931.
            (Stewart) **£20 [≈ $36]**
- Euclide's elements; the whole fifteen books compendiously demonstrated. London: For E. Redmayne, 1705. Sm 8vo. [vi],366 pp. Advt leaf, num w'cut diags in text. Crnr torn

from 1 leaf, just touching page numeral. New qtr calf, mrbld bds.
            (Bickersteth) **£160 [≈ $288]**
- Euclide's elements; the whole fifteen books compendiously demonstrated ... and a brief treatise of regular solids. London: 1714. Contemp lea, rebacked.
            (Whitehart) **£80 [≈ $144]**
- Euclide's elements; the whole fifteen books compendiously demonstrated ... a brief treatise of regular solids. By Thomas Haselden. London: for Daniel Midwinter, 1732. 8vo. Port frontis, text figs. Lacking final endpaper. Contemp calf, sl rubbed, jnts cracked.   *(Stewart)* **£100 [≈ $180]**
- The usefullnesse of mathematical learning explained and demonstrated ... London: 1734. 1st edn. xxxii,440,[23] pp. Port frontis, fldg plate. Contemp calf, rebacked, spine gilt, crnrs worn.   *(Whitehart)* **£150 [≈ $270]**

Barruel, Augustin
- The history of the clergy during the French Revolution. London: ... sold by J. Debrett ..., 1794. 8vo. Later half calf, front jnt breaking.
            (Waterfield's) **£20 [≈ $36]**

Barry, Edward
- Observations historical, critical and medical on the wines of the ancients ... principles and qualities of water ... particular those of Bath. London: 1775. 4to. xii,479,[i] pp. Engvd frontis, engvs on title. Old calf, v worn, rebacked.   *(Weiner)* **£325 [≈ $585]**
- A treatise on three different digestions, and discharges of the human body ... London: A. Millar, 1759. 1st edn. 8vo. xvi,434 pp. 1 text ill. Marg repr to lower edge of title. Qtr calf.
            (Rootenberg) **$275 [≈ £152]**

Barthelemy, Jean Jacques
- Travels of Anarchis the Younger in Greece, during the middle of the fourth century before the Christian era. Translated from the French. London: Robinson, 1796. 5 vols. 8vo. 17 fldg maps, 10 fldg plans, 4 fldg plates. Contemp tree-calf, lightly rubbed.
            (Frew Mackenzie) **£130 [≈ $234]**

Bartram, William
- Travels through North and South Carolina, Georgia ... Florida ... and the Country of the Choctaws. Phila: James ..., 1791. xxxiv,522 pp. Port frontis, 7 plates (1 fldg). Fldg map (half supplied in facs). Foxing, pencil anntns. Contemp calf, rebacked.
            (Reese) **$2,750 [≈ £1,527]**

Bate, George

- Pharmacopoeia Bateana: or, Bate's dispensatory ... containing his choice and select recipes ... London: Innys, 1713. 4th edn. 8vo. [16],744,[16] pp. Double column. Lacking front endpaper. Contemp panelled calf, rear hinge split.
(Hemlock) **$200** [≈£111]

Bateman, Dr.

- A short treatise of ... Dr. Bateman's pectoral drops ... See Okell, Benjamin

Bates, Ely

- A Chinese fragment, containing an enquiry into the present state of religion in England. 1786. Rubber stamp on sev leaves, flyleaf reprd with tape, a few pages spotted.
(Allen) **$25** [≈£13]

Bath ...

- Bath and its environs, a descriptive poem ... See Hippesley, R.
- Bath: its beauties and amusements ... See Ellis, George (1758-1815)
- A description of Bath: a poem ... See Chandler, Mary

Batteley, John

- The antiquities of Richborough and Reculver. Abridged from the Latin ... J. Johnson, 1774. 8vo. 8vo. [i],ix,[i],152 pp. Map frontis, engvd plate. Contemp calf, sides ruled in gilt. Extremities rubbed, jnts tender.
(Frew Mackenzie) **£85** [≈$153]

Baviad ...

- The Baviad ... See Gifford, William

Baxter, Andrew

- An enquiry into the nature of the human soul; wherein the immateriality of the soul is evinced from the principles of reason and philosophy. London: [1733]. 1st edn. 4to. [6]ff,376 pp. Orig calf, worn.
(Elgen) **$125** [≈£69]
- Matho: or, the cosmotheoria puerilis; in ten dialogues ... phaenomena of the material world ... principles of natural religion ... London: for A. Millar, 1765. 3rd edn. 2 vols. 12mo. 2 fldg engvd tables. Contemp calf, spines gilt, 2 jnts sl cracking.
(Burmester) **£45** [≈$81]

Baxter, Richard

- The crucifying of the world. London: for Nevill Simmons, 1658. 1st edn. 4to. Contemp calf, jnts & crnrs worn, lacking front free

endpaper. New Wing B1233.
(Marlborough) **£80** [≈$144]
- The saints everlasting rest. Salop: J. Cotton ..., 1759. Cr 8vo. New calf.
(Stewart) **£15** [≈$27]

Bayle, Pierre

- The dictionary historical and critical ... to which is prefixed the life of the author ... London: J.J. & P. Knapton ..., 1734-38. 2nd edn. Lge paper. 5 vols. Folio. Engvd port, red & black titles. Contemp diced calf, orig spines laid down. (Traylen) **£375** [≈$675]
- The dictionary, historical and critical. London: J.J. & P. Knapton, 1734. 2nd English edn. 5 vols. Folio. Half-titles in each vol, red & black titles. Contemp tan calf, vol 1 jnts cracked, others beginning to split at hd & tail, some crnrs bumped.
(Frew Mackenzie) **£360** [≈$648]
- The dictionary, historical and critical. London: 1734-38. 2nd edn. 5 vols. Folio. Red & black titles, engvd port. Old calf, worn & shabby. (Hemlock) **£250** [≈£138]
- An historical and critical dictionary ... Translated into English ... London: C. Harper ..., 1710. 1st edn in English. 4 vols. Folio. 4 title vignettes. Some minor marg worming vols 1-3, occas light dampstaining. Contemp calf, old rebacking, worn.
(Clark) **£165** [≈$297]

Baylie, Thomas

- Certamen religiosum: or, a conference between ... [King] Charles and Henry, Earl of Worcester, concerning religion ... London: 1649. 1st edn. Sm 8vo. Errata leaf at end. Some dampmarks at beginning. Contemp calf, hd & ft of spine worn. Wing B1506.
(Robertshaw) **£38** [≈$68]
- Certamen religiosum: or, a conference between ... [King] Charles and Henry, Earl of Worcester, concerning religion ... London: H. Hils, 1649. 8vo. [xvi],232,[ii] pp. Title cropped at outer marg, sm paper flaw at G1. Contemp calf. Wing B1506.
(Clark) **£75** [≈$135]

Baynard, Edward

- Health, a poem shewing how to procure, preserve, and restore it. To which is annex'd The Doctor's Decade. London: J. Roberts, 1740. 48 pp. Half-title.
(C.R. Johnson) **£65** [≈$117]

Beale, Thomas

- A true discovery of a bloody plot ... against ... some of the chiefe of the Lords and Commons

in Parliament assembled by bloody minded
Papists. London: 1641. 4to. 6 pp. Disbound.
Wing B1559A.   *(Robertshaw)* **£38 [≈ $68]**

Bearcroft, Philip
- An historical account of Thomas Sutton Esq.,
and of his foundation in Charter-House.
London: 1737. 1st edn. 8vo. xvi,275,[1 errata]
pp. Double-page view, 2 plates. Some minor
dust & other marks, notes on blank prelims.
Old mottled calf, rebacked & reprd.
      (Bow Windows) **£75 [≈ $135]**

Beattie, James
- The minstrel ... with some other poems to
which are now added miscellanies ... London:
for C. Dilly, 1799. 2 vols. 8vo. 6 plates. Early
sgntrs on titles. Contemp tree-calf.
      (Waterfield's) **£35 [≈ $63]**
- The minstrel; in two books; with some other
poems. London: E. & C. Dilly, 1779.
Contemp calf. Ex lib Newby Hall.
      (C.R. Johnson) **£25 [≈ $45]**
- The minstrel; or the progress of genius. A
poem. In two books. Dublin: James Williams.
1775. 66 pp. Disbound.
      (C.R. Johnson) **£25 [≈ $45]**
- Poems on several occasions. Edinburgh: W.
Creech, 1796. 83 pp. Contemp tree-calf.
      (C.R. Johnson) **£120 [≈ $216]**

Beattie, James (1735-1803)
- An essay on the nature and immutability of
truth in opposition to sophistry and
scepticism. For E. & C. Dilly ..., 1774. 5th
edn, crrctd. 8vo. Lacking free endpapers,
sgntr on title, marg staining at beginning.
Contemp sheep, rubbed.
      (Waterfield's) **£65 [≈ $117]**
- Essays on poetry and music as they affect the
mind; on laughter and ludicrous composition
... For E. & C. Dilly, 1778. Re-iss of 1776 edn
with cancel-title. 8vo. Contemp calf, jnts
cracked.   *(Waterfield's)* **£90 [≈ $162]**
- Essays. On the nature and immutability of
truth ... Edinburgh: Creech, 1776. 4to. Occas
light foxing. Later polished calf, a.e.g., by
Cavenach of Dublin, a little rubbed.
      (Marlborough) **£300 [≈ $540]**

Beatty, Charles
- The journal of a two-months tour; with a view
of promoting religion among the frontier
inhabitants of Pennsylvania ... Edinburgh:
1798. 8vo. 50 pp. Wraps.
      (Farahar) **£85 [≈ $153]**

Beaufort, Daniel Augustus
- Memoir of a map of Ireland ... and containing
a short account of its present state. Dublin:
Slater, 1792. 4to. Uncut in later half calf.
      (Emerald Isle) **£120 [≈ $216]**
- Memoir of a map of Ireland illustrating the
topography of that Kingdom and containing a
short account of its present state. Dublin:
Slater, 1792. 4to. Full diced russia, by Mullan
of Dublin, ex lib Earl of Leitrim.
      (Emerald Isle) **£185 [≈ $333]**

Beaumont, Francis & Fletcher, John
- The dramatick works ... London: for T.
Evans & P. Elmsley ..., 1778. 10 vols. 8vo.
Engvd port frontis, 53 engvd plates. Contemp
speckled calf, vol I rebacked, spines a trifle
worn.   *(Sotheran)* **£98 [≈ $176]**
- Philaster or, love lies bleeding. The fifth
impression. London: for William Leake,
1652. 4to. 34ff, unnumbered. Uniformly
browned throughout, lower outer crnr of title
chipped affecting 4 letters, many headlines,
catchwords & sgntrs cropped. 19th c half mor.
      (Claude Cox) **£85 [≈ $153]**

Beauties ...
- Beauties of the Anti-Jacobin; or, Weekly
Examiner; containing every article of
permanent utility in that valuable and highly
esteemed paper ... 1799. Cr 8vo. Contemp
half calf, rubbed.   *(Halewood)* **£40 [≈ $72]**

Beauties of England ...
- A new display of the beauties of England ...
the most elegant ... public edifices, royal
palaces, noblemen's and gentlemen's seats ...
London: R. Goadsby, 1772. 1st ed thus. 2
vols. 8vo. 181 engvd plates (1 torn). Lightly
browned. 18th c diced russia.
      (Frew Mackenzie) **£450 [≈ $810]**

Beccaria, Cesare
- An essay on crimes and punishment,
translated from the Italian ... Edinburgh: Bell
& Murray ..., 1778. New edn. 12mo in 6's.
Some staining of last few leaves. Rebound in
qtr calf.   *(Hughes)* **£125 [≈ $225]**
- An essay on crimes and punishment. With a
commentary, by M. de Voltaire. A new
edition corrected. Glasgow: for Robert Urie,
1770. 12mo. 214 pp. Flyleaves torn out, sl
damage caused by adhesion of final advt leaf
to lower cvr. Contemp sheep, rubbed.
      (Burmester) **£90 [≈ $162]**
- An essay on crimes and punishment ... With
a commentary attributed to Mons. de
Voltaire. London: for J, Almon ..., 1767. 1st

edn in English. 8vo. xii,179, lxxiv pp. Contemp sprinkled calf, crnrs & edges a little scuffed.   *(Pickering)* **$1,000 [≈ £555]**

Beckford, Peter
- Thoughts upon hare and fox hunting ... London: 1796. 1st illust edn. 8vo. [xvi],340 pp. 20 engvd plates (minor offsetting). Upper crnr sev leaves creased, minor offsetting. Contemp calf, richly gilt. Ex lib Colquhoun of Luss.   *(Pirages)* **$650 [≈ £361]**

Beckford, William
- [Vathek.] An Arabian tale, from an unpublished manuscript: with notes critical and explanatory. London: J. Johnson, 1786. 1st edn. 8vo. vii,334 pp. Without the final blank. 19th c green str-grain mor, gilt, a.e.g., extremities v lightly rubbed.   *(Frew Mackenzie)* **£600 [≈ $1,080]**

Beddoes, Thomas
- Observations on the nature and cure of calculus, sea scurvy, catarrh, and fever: together with conjectures upon several other subjects of physiology and pathology. London: 1793. 8vo. xvi,278 pp. Half mor, 2 b'plates. *(Rittenhouse)* **$375 [≈ £208]**
- Observations on the nature and cure of calculus, sea scurvy, catarrh, and fever: together with conjectures upon several other subjects of physiology and pathology. Phila: 1797. Sgntr on title. 1st Amer edn. Orig lea, worn.   *(Rittenhouse)* **$350 [≈ £194]**

Bedingfield, Robert
- A sermon preached at Pauls Crosse the 24. of October, 1624. Oxford: John Lichfield ..., 1625. 8vo. New wraps. STC 1792.   *(Stewart)* **£35 [≈ $63]**

Behn, Aphra
- Lycidus: or the lover in fashion ... From the French ... together with a miscellany of new poems. London: for Joseph Knight, 1688. 1st edn. 8vo. [xiv],64, 176,[iv] pp. Red & black title. A little minor soiling. Contemp mottled calf, crnrs worn. Wing T129.   *(Bennett)* **£450 [≈ $810]**
- Plays written by the late ingenious Mrs. Behn ... London: for Mary Poulson ..., 1724. 3rd edn. 4 vols. 12mo. Port. Contemp polished calf, gilt panelled spines.   *(Traylen)* **£295 [≈ $531]**
- The Rover; or, the banish't cavaliers. London: 1697. 2nd edn. 4to. [iv],68 pp. Title mtd, A2 reprd, browned throughout. [with] The second part of the Rover ... Tonson, 1681. 4to. [viii],85,[iii] pp. Title stained. Mod

mor-backed wraps. Wing B1764 & B1765.   *(Clark)* **£100 [≈ $180]**

Belknap, Jeremy
- Sacred poetry, consisting of psalms and hymns, adapted to Christian devotion ... Boston: Nov. 1797. 2nd edn. 240; 262 pp. Later lea, gilt.   *(Xerxes)* **$150 [≈ £83]**

Bell, Benjamin
- A treatise on gonorrhea virulenta and lues venerea. Phila: 1795. 1st Amer edn. 2 vols in 1. 220; 250, index, contents pp. Lea.   *(Scientia)* **$275 [≈ £152]**

Bell, Henry
- An historical essay on the original of painting. London: Worrall, 1728. 12mo. 2ff, 138 pp, 3ff tables & advts. New qtr calf, spine gilt.   *(Marlborough)* **£210 [≈ $378]**
- The perfect painter: or, a compleat history of the original, progress and improvement of painting. London: 1730. Sm 8vo. [4],138 pp. Frontis & title mtd. Crude rebacking.   *(Spelman)* **£75 [≈ $135]**
- The perfect painter: or, a compleat history of the original, progress and improvement of painting. London: 1730. Lge 12mo. Engvd frontis, title, 1f, 138 pp, 2ff. Dusty, possibly lacking leaf of advts at end. Contemp calf, rebacked.   *(Marlborough)* **£195 [≈ $351]**

Bell, John
- Engravings explaining the anatomy of the bones, muscles, and joints. Edinburgh: 1794. 4to. [iv],xxii, 191,[i] pp. 2 extra leaves 37* & 109*. 32 plates (4 outline), 2 text engvs. A poor copy, 2 plates loose, frayed. Contemp calf, rubbed.   *(Pollak)* **£150 [≈ $270]**

Bellamy, George Anne
- Memoirs of George Anne Bellamy, including all her intrigues; with genuine anecdotes of all her public and private connections. By a gentleman of Covent-Garden Theatre. London: J. Walker, 1785. 204 pp. Contemp qtr calf, mrbld bds, hinges worn.   *(C.R. Johnson)* **£180 [≈ $324]**

Belleisle, Duke de
- Letters to Marechal de Contades, found among the papers of Mons. de Contades, after the battle of Minden. Translated ... London: for Thomas Payne, 1759. 8vo. Title dusty. Rebound in half cloth, mrbld bds.   *(Stewart)* **£20 [≈ $36]**

Bellendenus ...
- A free translation of the preface to Bellendenus ... See Parr, Samuel

Benezet, Anthony
- A caution to Great Britain and her colonies, in a short representation of the calamitous state of the enslaved negroes, in the British Dominions. Philadelphia printed, London reprinted. 1767. 46 pp. Disbound.
(C.R. Johnson) **£160 [≈ $288]**
- Some historical account of Guinea, its situation, produce, and the general disposition of its inhabitants ... the rise and progress of the slave-trade ... Phila: Joseph Crukshank, 1771. 1st edn. 12mo. [vi],iv,144; 53,[6] pp. A bit browned. Rec half calf.
(Burmester) **£275 [≈ $495]**

Benfield, Paul
- Catalogue of the superb, valuable and well-chosen selection of original performances ... [London:] Coxe, Burell ..., 1799. 4to. 10 pp. 66 lots. Orig mrbld wraps.
(Marlborough) **£225 [≈ $405]**

Bennet, Thomas
- An answer to the dissenters pleas for separation: or, an abridgement of the London cases ... London: for James Knapton, 1711. 5th edn. 8vo. Contemp panelled calf, a little rubbed at extremities.
(Waterfield's) **£40 [≈ $72]**

Bentham, Jeremy
- Defence of usury; shewing the impolicy of the present legal restraints on the terms of pecuniary bargains. Dublin: 1788. 1st edn. 12mo. 232 pp. Contemp half mor.
(Argosy) **$400 [≈ £222]**
- A fragment on government ... an examination of ... the introduction to Sir William Blackstone's Commentaries ... London: for T. Payne ..., 1776. 1st edn. 8vo. [iv],lvii, [i blank], [ii fly title], 208 pp. V minor staining on title. Resewn & rebound in buckram.
(Pickering) **$2,400 [≈ £1,333]**

Bentham, Joseph
- A disswasive from error much increased. A Perswasive to order much decayed. London: William Thompson, 1669. Sm 4to. 86 pp. Contemp ms crrctns. Stitched. Wing B1909.
(Argosy) **$175 [≈ £97]**

Bentivoglio, Guido
- The history of the warrs of Flanders, written in Italian ... Englished ... London: 1678.

Folio. [viii],387, [xviii],56 ['A continuation...'] pp. Port frontis, lge fldg map (minor tear), 23 half-page ports in text. Contemp calf, rebacked.
(Frew Mackenzie) **£85 [≈ $153]**

Bentley, R.
- Designs by Mr. R. Bentley, for six poems by Mr. T. Gray. London: R. Dodsley, 1753. 1st edn, 1st iss. Folio. 2,36 pp, 2ff. Half-title, 19 engvs (6 full-leaf), text ptd 1 side only. Sl foxing & browning. Contemp calf, mrbld sides, jnts & sides rubbed, worn.
(Pirages) **$250 [≈ £138]**
- Designs by Mr. R. Bentley, for six poems by Mr. T. Gray. London: for R. Dodsley, 1753. 1st edn. Folio. Title vignette, 6 full-page plates, 12 vignettes. Contemp calf, rebacked.
(Traylen) **£395 [≈ $711]**

Bentley, Richard
- The folly and unreasonableness of atheism [and 8 other sermons]. London: Mortlock, 1693. 1st coll edn. 4to. Contemp panelled calf, rebacked. New Wing B1930.
(Marlborough) **£450 [≈ $810]**
- The folly and unreasonableness of atheism. London: for H. Mortlock, 1699. 4th edn, crrctd. 4to. 280 pp. Contemp calf. Wing B1931.
(Argosy) **$150 [≈ £83]**
- Remarks upon a late discourse of freethinking ... The eighth edition. With further additions ... Cambridge: J. Bentham, 1743. 8vo. 4 pp advts at end. Blind lib stamp on title. Rebound in qtr calf.
(Hughes) **£65 [≈ $117]**

Berenger, Richard
- The history and art of horsemanship. 1771. 1st edn. 2 vols. 4to. [6],319,[5]; [2],246,[2] pp. 17 engvd plates. Without half-titles. Sl later half calf, jnts cracked. *(Kerr)* **£245 [≈ $441]**

Bergman, Torbern
- A dissertation on elective attractions. London: Murray, and C. Elliot, Edinburgh, 1785. 1st edn in English. 8vo. xiv,[2], 382,[1 errata] pp. 3 extra-lge fldg tables, 4 fldg engvd plates. Contemp speckled calf.
(Antiq Sc) **$475 [≈ £263]**

Berington, Joseph
- The history of the lives of Abeillard and Heloisa ... with their genuine letters from the collection of Amboise. Birmingham: M. Swinney, 1787. 1st edn. 4to. Half-title. Contemp half calf, gilt back.
(Argosy) **$150 [≈ £83]**

Berington, Simon
- The adventures of Sigr. Gaudentio di Lucca ... The second edition. Faithfully translated ... London: for W. Innys ..., 1748. 8vo. xii,24,291 pp. V light foxing in places. Contemp calf, rebacked.
(Fenning) **£145 [≈ $261]**
- The memoirs of Gregorio Panzani; giving an account of his agency in England in the years 1634-6, translated ... and now first published. Birmingham: Swinney & Walker, 1793. Lge 8vo. Later half mor, spine gilt, t.e.g., rubbed.
(Marlborough) **£90 [≈ $162]**

Berkeley, George
- An essay towards a new theory of vision. Dublin: 1709. 2nd edn. 8vo. xiv,198 pp. Contemp lea, back hinge broken.
(Argosy) **$100 [≈ £55]**
- Siris: a chain of philosophical reflexions and inquiries concerning the virtues of tar water ... Dublin printed, London re-printed: 1744. 2nd edn, imprvd & crrctd.
(Traylen) **£70 [≈ $126]**
- Siris: a chain of philosophical reflexions and inquiries concerning the virtues of tar water ... Dublin printed, London re-printed: 1744. [Bound with] Anti-Siris, or English wisdom ... For M. Cooper, 1744. Repr to top of 1st title. Contemp half calf.
(Waterfield's) **£185 [≈ $333]**
- Siris: a chain of philosophical reflexions ... Dublin printed, London re-printed: 1744. [Bound with] Prior, Thomas - An authentick narrative of the success of tar-water in curing ... distempers. 1746. Contemp mottled calf. Ex Signet Library.
(Waterfield's) **£135 [≈ $243]**

Berkeley, George Monck
- Heloise, or the Siege of Rhodes. A legendary tale ... The third edition, to which is added Harriet, or the Vicar's Tale. Dublin: P. Byrne, 1789. 2 vols in 1. 12mo. Contemp half calf.
(Emerald Isle) **£85 [≈ $153]**

Berkenhout, Dr. John
- A volume of letters [on mathematics, botany, geography, &c., &c.] ... to his son at the University. Cambridge: for T. Cadell, 1790. 8vo. [iv],iv,374, [ii] pp. Final errata leaf. Contemp speckled calf, rebacked, crnrs rubbed.
(Clark) **£100 [≈ $180]**

Bernard, Nicholas
- The life and death of the most reverend and learned father of our church Dr. James Usher ... primate of all Ireland. London: E. Tyler,

1656. Contemp calf, rubbed. Wing B2012.
(C.R. Johnson) **£75 [≈ $135]**

Bernard, Richard
- The faithfull shepheard amended and enlarged: with the shepheard's practise in preaching. London: for John Bill, 1609. S, 4to. With final blank. Title dust-soiled. Mod mor backed bds.
(Robertshaw) **£40 [≈ $72]**

Bernier, Francois
- The history of the late revolution of the Empire of the Great Mogol ... English'd ... London: Moses Pitt ..., 1671. 8vo. [xvi],258, [ii],176, 102,[ii] pp. Final advt leaf, fldg map. Some pages poorly inked. Contemp qtr calf, mrbld bds. Wing B2043.
(Clark) **£80 [≈ $144]**

Berriman, William
- Youth, the proper season of discipline ... a sermon for promoting English Protestant working schools in Ireland. London: Downing, 1742. Sm 4to. Wraps.
(Emerald Isle) **£25 [≈ $45]**

Berrow, Capel
- A lapse of human souls in a state of pre-existence ... London: for J. Dodsley ..., 1766. Vignette title. K1 sgnd K* (a cancel?). Contemp calf.
(Waterfield's) **£40 [≈ $72]**
- A short and easie method with the deists, wherein the certainty of the Christian religion is demonstrated ... London: for Geo. Strahan, 1711-15. 2 pts in 1 vol. 5th edn, crrctd. Cr 8vo. Contemp panelled calf, upper jnt cracked.
(Stewart) **£30 [≈ $54]**

Bertram (fl. ca 800)
- Concerning the body and blood of Christ ... first translated into English in 1549. London: Griffin, 1686. 12mo. Engvd port frontis. Contemp calf, hd of spine bumped. New Wing B2049B.
(Marlborough) **£50 [≈ $90]**

Besse, Joseph
- A collections of the sufferings of the people called Quakers ... London: Luke Hinde, 1753. 2 vols. Folio. Over 1400 pp. Old half calf, reprd. Jonathan Pim's set, with his sgntr on title.
(Emerald Isle) **£125 [≈ $225]**

Beveridge, William
- The works of Dr. William Beveridge, late Lord Bishop of St. Asaph. London: for A. Bettesworth ..., 1729. 2nd edn. 2 vols. Folio. Engvd port frontis. Contemp calf.
(Lloyd-Roberts) **£75 [≈ $135]**

Bewick, Thomas

- A general history of quadrupeds. Newcastle-upon-Tyne: 1791. 2nd edn. One of 300 on royal paper. 8vo. 212 w'cut figs. 19th c strgrained mor, gilt borders & inner dentelles, edges gilt, by Hammond.
(Traylen) **£225 [≈ $405]**
- A general history of quadrupeds. Newcastle-upon-Tyne: 1791. 2nd edn. 8vo. 212 w'cut figs. 1 leaf reprd. Contemp calf, rebacked, orig mor label, gilt. *(Traylen)* **£120 [≈ $216]**
- A general history of quadrupeds. Newcastle-upon-Tyne: 1792. 3rd edn. 8vo. x,483 pp. Tear in 1 leaf reprd, some foxing & stains. Rec dark green mor, mrbld sides.
(Bow Windows) **£160 [≈ $288]**
- History of British birds. Newcastle: 1797-1804. 1st edn. 2 vols. 8vo. Contemp half calf. *(Edwards)* **£245 [≈ $441]**
- History of British birds. Newcastle: 1797-1804. 2 vols. Demy 8vo. xxx,335,[i advt]; xx,400 pp. Half-title vol 1, 218 figs, 227 vignettes. V sl browning. Contemp half calf, mrbld sides, rebacked, spines gilt, lightly rubbed. *(Frew Mackenzie)* **£320 [≈ $576]**
- History of British birds. Newcastle: 1797-1804. 1st edn. 2 vols. Roy 8vo. 261 w'cuts of birds, 192 vignettes & tail-pieces. Contemp calf, rebacked. Vol 2 the imperial iss, trimmed to size of the vol 1 royal.
(Wheldon & Wesley) **£250 [≈ $450]**

Bible

- Old Testament: Psalms. A new version of the Psalms of David fitted to the tunes used in churches by N. Tate and N. Brady. London: for the Company of Stationers, 1698. 8vo. Contemp panelled mor, gilt, gilt backstrip & edges, mrbld endpapers. Wing B2606.
(Waterfield's) **£105 [≈ $189]**

Bignon, Jean-Paul

- The adventures of Abdalla ... sent by the Sultan of the Indies, to make a discovery of the Island of Borico. London: for T. Worrall, 1730. 2nd edn. [6],xvi, [2],169,[7 advt] pp. 8 plates. 1st & last few leaves waterstained & a few tears in margs. Mod calf.
(Claude Cox) **£75 [≈ $135]**

Bilguer, Johann Ulrich von

- A dissertation on the inutility of the amputation of the limbs ... Now first translated into English ... London: for R. Baldwin ..., 1764. 1st edn in English. 8vo. xvi,100 pp. Disbound.
(Burmester) **£120 [≈ $216]**

Bill ...

- The Bill entitled, An Act for Preventing Occasional Conformity ... London: Edward Jones, 1702. Folio. Licence leaf. 64 pp. Disbound.   *(C.R. Johnson)* **£20 [≈ $36]**

Bilson, Thomas

- The effect of certaine sermons. London: Burre, 1599. 1st edn. 4to. Title grubby, margs thumbed. Contemp calf, rebacked & refurbished. NSTC 3064.
(Marlborough) **£140 [≈ $252]**

Bingham, Joseph

- The works ... London: Robert Knaplock, 1726. 1st coll edn. 2 vols. Folio. [iv],xxxi, [i],831,[viii index]; [xvi],842,[ii advts] pp. Red & black titles, engvd map. Sl dampstaining & worming (in index mainly). Contemp panelled calf, reprd, rebacked.
(Frew Mackenzie) **£130 [≈ $234]**

Biographia Britannica ...

- Biographia Britannica: or the lives of the most eminent persons who have flourished in Great Britain and Ireland ... London: W. Innys ..., 1747-66. 1st edn. 6 vols in 7. Folio. Half-titles. Contemp russia, rebacked, 1 jnt cracked. Ex lib with stamps on bds.
(Clark) **£300 [≈ $540]**

Bion, M.

- The construction and principle uses of mathematical instruments ... London: 1723. 1st English edn. Folio. viii,264 pp. 26 fldg plates. A few pages at rear sl torn & reprd, light waterstain top outer crnr, a few pages grubby. Contemp panelled calf, rebacked.
(Whitehart) **£380 [≈ $684]**

Birch, Thomas

- The history of the Royal Society of London for improving of natural knowledge ... 1756-57. 1st edn. Vols 1-3. 4to. Fldg plates, text diags. A little foxing. Contemp bds, late 19th c mor backed. *(Halewood)* **£300 [≈ $540]**
- An inquiry into the share which King Charles I had in the transactions of the Earl of Glamorgan ... for bringing over a body of Irish rebels ... London: Millar, 1747. 1st edn. 8vo. Speckled calf.
(Emerald Isle) **£110 [≈ $198]**
- An inquiry into the share which King Charles I had in the transactions of the Earl of Glamorgan ... for bringing over a body of Irish rebels ... London: Millar, 1756. 2nd edn. 8vo. 376 pp. Half calf.
(Emerald Isle) **£85 [≈ $153]**

Birckbek, Simon
- The protestants evidence. London: Milbourne, 1635. 2nd iss. 4to. Contemp calf, spine gilt, worn, label gone, new endpapers. NSTC 3083. *(Marlborough)* **£130** [≈ $234]

Birth ...
- The birth of man-kinde ... See Roesslin, Eucharius

Bishop of Carlisle ...
- The Bishop of Carlisle's speech ... See Merke, Thomas

Bishop, Matthew
- The live and adventures ... containing an account of several actions by sea, battles and sieges ... from 1701 to 1711 ... London: for J. Brindley, 1744. 1st edn. 8vo. viii,[iv], 283,[i] pp. Marg tear reprd. Contemp gilt-ruled calf, rebacked. *(Bennett)* **£325** [≈ $585]

Bisse, Thomas
- The beauty of holiness in the Common-Prayer, as set forth in four sermons ... London: for W. Taylor ..., 1721. 8th edn. Contemp calf, spine rubbed.
(Lloyd-Roberts) **£12** [≈ $21]

Blackerby, Samuel
- Cases in law: wherein Justices of Peace have a jurisdiction ... being the second part of the Justice of the Peace's Companion. London: for J. Walthoe ..., 1717. 1st edn. Contemp calf. *(Charles Cox)* **£45** [≈ $81]

Blacklock, Thomas
- Poems ... to which is prefix'd, an account of the life, character, and writings, of the author ... London: R. & J. Dodsley, 1756. 8vo. Fore-edge of title & last leaf browned, lib stamp on contents leaf. Rebound half calf, mrbld sides.
(Hughes) **£85** [≈ $153]

Blacklock, Thomas, et al.
- A collection of original poems. By ... and other Scotch gentlemen. Edinburgh: for A. Donaldson, 1760. 1st edn. 12mo. Some stains & ink-marks, some wear. Contemp mottled calf, gilt. *(Charles Cox)* **£65** [≈ $117]

Blackmore, Sir Richard
- A short history of the last parliament. London: Jacob Tonson, 1699. 1st edn. 8vo. 64 pp. Mod bds. *(Pirages)* **$100** [≈ £55]
- A true and impartial history of the conspiracy against the person and government of King William III of glorious memory. In the year

1695. London: for James Knapton, 1723, 1st edn. 8vo. Title dust-soiled & marked. Sep title for 'Authentick Copies'. Qtr calf.
(Hughes) **£35** [≈ $63]

Blackstone, Sir William
- An analysis of the laws of England. Oxford: Clarendon Press, 1758. 3rd edn. 8vo. lxx,189,160 pp. Fldg table. [with] An introduction to the knowledge of the laws ... By a gentleman of the Middle Temple. London: 1763. Fldg table. Contemp calf. Armorial b'plate. *(Edwards)* **£300** [≈ $540]
- Commentaries on the laws of England. Oxford: Clarendon Press, 1766-69. 4 vols. 2nd, 2nd, 1st, 1st edns. 4to. Endpapers spotted, some spotting elsewhere, occas trivial marg dampstain vol 4. Contemp calf, rebacked & recrnrd, spines gilt.
(Frew Mackenzie) **£1,050** [≈ $1,890]
- Commentaries on the laws of England ... Oxford: Clarendon Press, 1766-69. 4 vols. 2nd, 2nd, 1st, 1st edns. 4to. 2 tables (1 fldg). Vol 4 title torn across & reprd, occas spotting. Contemp half calf, mrbld bds.
(Chaucer Head) **£950** [≈ $1,710]
- Commentaries on the laws of England. In four books. Oxford: Clarendon Press, 1768-70. 4 vols. 4th, 4th, 1st, 1st edns. 4to. Sgntr & stamps on titles, minor worming in appendix marg vol 2 & single wormhole in some margs vol 3. Contemp calf, scuffed. *(Edwards)* **£950** [≈ $1,710]
- Commentaries on the laws of England ... Oxford: at the Clarendon Press, 1770. 4th edn. 4 vols. 4to. 2 engvd plates (1 fldg). Contemp calf, rebacked, orig mor labels, gilt. *(Traylen)* **£850** [≈ $1,530]
- Commentaries on the laws of England. In four books. The sixth edition. London: Strahan & Cadell, 1774. 4 vols. 4to. Engvd port frontis, fldg table. Sl occas browning. Contemp calf, spines elab gilt, jnts beginning to split. *(Frew Mackenzie)* **£800** [≈ $1,440]
- The Great Charter and Charter of the Forest ... Oxford: 1759. 4to. lxxvi,86 pp. Imprim & dedn leaf. Contemp calf, rubbed, hinges splitting. *(Edwards)* **£550** [≈ $990]
- A treatise on the law of descents in fee-simple. Oxford: Clarendon Press, 1759. 1st edn. 8vo. 2 fldg tables, advt leaf. Mod half polished calf, mrbld bds.
(Chaucer Head) **£180** [≈ $324]

Blair, Hugh
- Lectures on rhetoric and belles lettres. London: for Strahan ..., 1783. 1st edn. 2 vols. 4to. Engvd frontis vol 1. Contemp calf,

rebacked.   *(Chaucer Head)* **£320 [≈ $576]**

Blome, Richard
- Britannia; or, a geographical description of the Kingdoms of England, Scotland and Ireland, with the Isles and territories thereto belonging etc. London: 1673. Folio. 50 fldg engvd maps, engvd plan, 24 pp engvd coats of arms. Disbound.
(Halewood) **£1,850 [≈ $3,330]**

Blondel, D.
- A treatise of the Sibyls, so highly celebrated as well by the ancient heathens, as the Holy Fathers of the Church ... 1661. 1st English edn. Sm 4to. 293,vii pp. Title sl frayed & lacking previous leaves, occas browning. Mod half calf, mrbld bds. *(Edwards)* **£200 [≈ $360]**

Blount, Charles
- King William and Queen Mary conquerors: or, a discourse endeavouring to prove that their Majesties have on their side ... London: for Richard Baldwin ..., 1693. Sole edn. 4to. [viii],59 pp. Uncut in green mor, gilt lettering. Wing B3309.
(Young's) **£170 [≈ $306]**

Blount, Thomas
- Boscobel: or, the compleat history of his sacred majesties most miraculous preservation after the Battle of Worcester 3 Sept. 1651 ... London: 1680. 3rd edn. 2 pts in 1. 8vo. Port, addtnl engvd title, 2 maps. Contemp panelled calf, jnts cracked.
(Robertshaw) **£75 [≈ $135]**
- Fragmenta antiquitatis. Antient tenures of land, and jocular customs of some mannors ... London: 1679. 1st edn. 8vo. A little marg worming at beginning. Later half calf, spine defective. Wing B3333.
(Robertshaw) **£38 [≈ $68]**

Blount, Sir Thomas Pope
- A natural history: containing many not common quotations: extracted out of the best modern writers. London: for R. Bentley ..., 1693. 1st edn. 12mo. [xvi],469,3 advts] pp. Some browning. Old panelled calf, crnrs worn, rec rebacking, new endpapers. Wing B3351.   *(Bow Windows)* **£275 [≈ $495]**

Blumenbach, Johann Friedrich
- Elements of physiology, translated ... to which is subjoined ... an appendix ... of the existing discoveries relative to ... animal electricity. Phila: Thomas Dobson, 1795. 1st edn in English. 2 vols in 1. 8vo. xvi,229 pp;

1f, 247 pp. Contemp calf.
(Offenbacher) **$500 [≈ £277]**

Boate, Gerard & Molineux, Thomas
- A natural history of Ireland in three parts ... description of its situation ... nature of its air and seasons ... advancement of navigation ... discourse concerning Danish forts etc. Dublin: Ewing, 1755. Sm 4to. Plates. Contemp calf. *(Emerald Isle)* **£285 [≈ $513]**

Bobbin, Tim (pseud.)
- See Collier, John

Bodley, Sir Thomas
- The life of Sir Thomas Bodley, the hon. founder of the publique library in the University of Oxford. Written by himself. Oxford: Henry Hall, 1647. 4to. 16 pp. Calf. Wing B3392. *(C.R. Johnson)* **£550 [≈ $990]**

Boerhaave, Herman
- Aphorisms: concerning knowledge and cure of diseases. London: 1735. 8vo. [14],444 pp. Index. Contemp lea.
(Rittenhouse) **$225 [≈ £125]**
- Aphorisms: concerning knowledge and cure of diseases. London: 1755. 3rd edn. 8vo. xvi,444 pp. Index. Names, dates & a b'plate on front endpaper. Orig binding, hinges weak.   *(Rittenhouse)* **$195 [≈ £108]**
- A new method of chemistry including the theory and practice of that art ... London: for J. Osborn & T. Longman, 1727. 1st edn. 4to. Contemp calf, jnts cracked.
(Waterfield's) **£450 [≈ $810]**
- A new method of chemistry including the theory and practice of that art ... London: for J. Osborn & T. Longman, 1727. 1st edn. 4to. 2 pts in 1 vol. 2 engvd plates. 18th c calf, rebacked.   *(Chaucer Head)* **£620 [≈ $1,116]**
- A new method of chemistry ... the history, theory and practice of the art ... London: Longman, 1741. 2nd edn. 2 vols. 4to. xxx,593,[i]; [i],410, [xxxviii index] pp. 41 fldg engvd plates on 25 sheets. Occas spotting. Contemp calf, jnts & extremities reprd.
(Frew Mackenzie) **£450 [≈ $810]**

Boethius
- The five books on the consolation of philosophy, translated ... by Robert Duncan. Edinburgh: Creech, 1789. 1st edn of this trans. 8vo. Paper flaw in 1 leaf. Later half calf.   *(Marlborough)* **£60 [≈ $108]**

Bohun, Edmund
- The history of the desertion ... all the publick

affairs in England, from the beginning of September 1688 to the twelfth of February following ... London: for Ric. Chiswell ..., 1689. 1st edn. 4to. [viii],168 pp. Rec calf. Wing B3456. *(Young's)* **£68 [≈ $122]**

Boileau, Nicholas
- The Lutrin: an heroi-comical poem. In six cantos ... Adorn'd with cuts. London: for E. Curll ..., 1714. 3rd edn, crrctd & revsd. 8vo. xxiv,83 pp. 6 engvd plates. Calf-backed bds. *(Young's)* **£40 [≈ $72]**

Bolingbroke, Henry St. John, Viscount
- A final answer to the remarks on the Craftsman's vindication; and to all the libels, which have come, or may come, from the same quarter ... London: R. Francklin, 1731. 32 pp. Rebound in bds. *(C.R. Johnson)* **£25 [≈ $45]**
- The freeholder's political catechism. London: for John Roberts, 1733. 1st edn. 8vo. 24 pp. Text browned, title ink-spattered. Later half calf, rebacked, new mor label, crnrs reprd. Ex Signet Library. *(Claude Cox)* **£35 [≈ $63]**
- A letter to Sir William Windham. II. Some reflections ... III. A letter to Mr. Pope. London: for A. Millar, 1753. 1st edn. 8vo. 531 pp. Port. Contemp calf, rebacked. *(Claude Cox)* **£35 [≈ $63]**
- Letters on the study and use of history. London: for A. Millar, 1752. 2 vols. 8vo. New half calf. *(Lloyd-Roberts)* **£60 [≈ $108]**
- Letters on the study and use of history. London: for A. Millar, 1752. 1st edn. 2 vols. 8vo. [4],315; [4],286,[4 contents] pp. Worm slit in marg on final 7ff vol 1. Contemp panelled calf, little worn at extremities. *(Claude Cox)* **£38 [≈ $68]**
- Letters, on the spirit of patriotism: on the idea of a patriot king ... London: for A. Millar, 1749. 1st edn. 8vo. xii,[9]-251 pp. Half-title, lge margins. Sm worm slit at ft of final leaf & endpapers. Contemp calf, rebacked, crnrs reprd. *(Claude Cox)* **£48 [≈ $86]**
- The occasional writer. Numb. I. With an answer paragraph by paragraph. London: for A. Moore, 1727. 8vo. 31,[1] pp. Disbound. *(Burmester)* **£30 [≈ $54]**

Bolton, Sir Richard
- A Justice of the Peace for Ireland ... with all the statutes ... also some precedents of committals, convictions, summonses, etc. Dublin: Leathley, 1750. Sm 4to. 586,292 pp. Cloth. *(Emerald Isle)* **£65 [≈ $117]**

Bolton, Robert
- A translation of the Charter and Statutes of Trinity College, Dublin ... with the library-statutes, and the rules of the University. Dublin: the translator, 1749. 1st edn of this trans. 3 pts in 1. Lge 12mo. 161,v pp. Contemp calf. Lacking blank flyleaf. *(Fenning)* **£85 [≈ $153]**

Bonnet, Charles
- The contemplation of nature. London: 1766. 1st edn in English. 2 vols. 256; 230 pp. Sm section cut from 1st blank in each vol. Lea. *(Scientia)* **$350 [≈ £194]**
- Interesting views of Christianity being a translation of part of ... Recherches Philosophiques sur les Preuves de Christianisme. Dublin: P. Byrne, 1798. A few leaves browned & fragile, faint pencil marks throughout. Contemp sheep, worn. *(Waterfield's)* **£45 [≈ $81]**

Bonneval, Claudius Alexander de
- Memoirs of the Bashaw Count Bonneval. London: E. Withers ..., 1750. 8vo. x,326. Engvd port frontis. Contemp calf, rubbed, upper jnt cracked. (Probably spurious). *(Clark)* **£85 [≈ $153]**

Bonneval, Count
- A complete history of the wars in Italy ... translated from the original French by J. Sparrow. London: for W. Mears, 1734. 8vo. [xvi],376 pp. Fldg map. Contemp calf, head of spine worn, lacking label. *(Lloyd-Roberts)* **£55 [≈ $99]**

Bonnycastle, John
- An introduction to algebra ... for the use of schools and places of public education. 1788. 2nd edn. x,[1],208 pp. Light marg waterstaining on a few pp. Contemp lea, sl worn, hinges cracked. *(Whitehart)* **£50 [≈ $90]**

Book of Drawing ...
- A book of drawing, limning, washing or colouring of maps and prints: and the art of painting, with the names and mixtures of colours ... London: for T. Jenner, 1652. Sm folio. Title, 40 pp inc 20 full-page engvd plates. Loose in contemp wraps, in fitted case. *(Marlborough)* **£1,250 [≈ $2,250]**

Book of Martyrs
- An account of holy men who died for the Christian Religion. Bath: sold by S. Hazard, [1795]. Sewn as issued, partly unopened. *(Waterfield's)* **£30 [≈ $54]**

Booth, Henry, Lord Delamere
- An impartial enquiry into the causes of the present fears and dangers of the Government ... for raising the militia. London: 1692. 1st edn. 4to. 20 pp, imprim leaf. Ptd in double column. Disbound. Wing D877.
(Young's) £40 [≈ $72]

Borlase, Edward
- The history of the Irish rebellion traced to 1641 ... Dublin: Oli Nelson, 1743. Sm folio. Calf.   *(Emerald Isle)* £240 [≈ $432]

Borlase, William
- Antiquities, historical and monumental of the County of Cornwall. London: 1769. Folio. xvi,464 pp. 37 plates inc fldg map, another map, 24 ills (1 fldg). Contemp calf, rebacked & reprd.   *(Bow Windows)* £375 [≈ $675]
- The natural history of Cornwall. The air, climate, waters, rivers ... tin and the manner of mining ... Oxford: for the author, 1758. 1st edn. Folio. xix,426,[1 errata, 1 directions] pp. 29 plates inc extndg map. Minor dust marks. Contemp calf, rebacked.
(Bow Windows) £350 [≈ $630]
- The natural history of Cornwall. Oxford: 1758. Folio. xix,326,[2] pp. Double-page map, 28 engvd plates. A little minor foxing, sm tears in map & 1 plate reprd, occas ms crrctns in text. Contemp calf, jnts cracked,
(Wheldon & Wesley) £250 [≈ $450]
- Observations on the ancient and present state of the Islands of Scilly ... Oxford: W. Jackson, 1756. 1st edn. 4to. [iv],140 pp. Half-title, 4 engvd plates (2 fldg), 1 text engv. Trivial dust soiling to some edges. Uncut & unopened in orig bds, rebacked.
(Frew Mackenzie) £300 [≈ $540]
- Observations on the ancient and present state of the Islands of Scilly ... Oxford: W. Jackson, 1756. 4to. 4 plates, plus 1 on a text leaf. Contemp mottled calf, jnts cracked.
(Waterfield's) £225 [≈ $405]

Boscobel ...
- Boscobel ... See Blount, Thomas

Bosman, William
- A new and accurate description of the Gulf of Guinea. Divided into the Gold, the Slave, and the Ivory Coasts. London: F. Knapton ..., 1705. 493,16 index,3 ctlg pp. Ills. lea, crnrs worn, backstrip with cracks.
(Ottenberg) $325 [≈ £180]
- A new and accurate description of the Coast of Guinea ... London: Knapton & Midwinter, 1705. 1st English edn. 8vo. [viii],493, [16 index],3 advts] pp. Fldg engvd map, 7 engvd plates. Index & last few leaves browned, a little worming. Contemp calf, sl rubbed.
(Morrell) £560 [≈ $1,008]
- A new and accurate description of the Coast of Guinea ... now faithfully done into English. London: 1721. 2nd edn. 8vo. Fldg map, 7 engv plates. A few minor blemishes. Half old style calf. *(Halewood)* £195 [≈ $351]

Bossuet, J.B.
- An exposition of the doctrine of the Catholic Church in matters of controversie. London: Henry Hills, 1686. Sm 4to. [8],55 pp. 1st 4ff stained along inner marg. Contemp qtr sheep.
(Spelman) £60 [≈ $108]

Boswell, James
- An account of Corsica, the journal of a tour to that island ... London: for Edward & Charles Dilly, 1768. 1st edn. 8vo. xxi,[iii],382 pp. Fldg engvd map (in 1st state). Wanting half-title, sl browning & some old underlining, lib stamp on title. New half calf.
(Burmester) £90 [≈ $162]
- An account of Corsica, the journal of a tour to that island ... London: 1768. 2nd edn. 8vo. 384 pp. Lge fldg map, engvd title vignette. Contemp calf, worn, spine split, re-inforced hinges.   *(Argosy)* $200 [≈ £111]
- An account of Corsica, the journal of a tour to that island ... The second edition. Edward & Charles Dilly, 1768. 8vo. xxii,384 pp. Half-title, fldg map (faint marg dampstains, browned). Tiny wormhole in gutter of 1st half. Contemp sprinkled calf, gilt.
(Frew Mackenzie) £300 [≈ $540]
- Dr. Johnson's table-talk. London: C. Dilly, 1798. 1st edn. 8vo. [4],446,[2] pp. 19th c half calf over mrbld bds, top of spine chipped.
(Karmiole) $125 [≈ £69]
- The life of Samuel Johnson. London: for Charles Dilly, 1793. 2nd edn. 3 vols. 8vo. Port frontis, 2 fldg plates. Isolated stains & foxing. Contemp tree-calf, 20th c rebacking, with minor wear.   *(Pirages)* $325 [≈ £180]
- The life of Samuel Johnson. London: 1793. 2nd edn. 3 vols. 8vo. Inserted leaf of 'Additional Corrections'. Contemp tree-calf, early rebacking, all edges stained yellow.
(Book Block) £650 [≈ £361]

Boswell, John
- A method of study: or, an useful library. In two parts ... study of several valuable parts of learning ... study of divinity ... London: for the author, 1738. 1st edn. 8vo. Rebound in qtr calf, mrbld sides. *(Hughes)* £95 [≈ $171]

Bouhours, Dominick
- The life of St. Ignatius, founder of the Society of Jesus. London: Henry Hills, 1686. 8vo. Contemp calf. Wing B3825.
(Stewart) £70 [≈ $126]

Bourne, John
- The history of Newcastle upon Tyne. Newcastle: John White, 1736. 1st edn. Folio. Fldg engvd map (mtd on linen, some defects & browning), some creasing & spotting on title & prelims. Early 20th c full red mor.
(Hughes) £65 [≈ $117]

Bourne, Vincent
- Miscellaneous poems, consisting of originals and translations. London: for W. Ginger ..., 1772. 4to. 352 pp. Tear on N2. 19th c dark blue calf, gilt. *(Burmester)* £35 [≈ $63]

Boutcher, William
- A treatise on forest-trees ... best methods of their culture ... new and useful discoveries ... Edinburgh: R. Fleming, 1775. 1st edn. 4to. Author's authentication, sgnd, on title verso. Contemp calf, rebacked with orig spine, gilt.
(Traylen) £120 [≈ $216]
- A treatise on forest-trees ... best methods of their culture ... new and useful discoveries ... Edinburgh: for the author, 1778. 2nd edn. 4to. xlviii,259,[5] pp. Contemp calf-backed mrbld bds, spine rubbed, hinges starting.
(Karmiole) $200 [≈ £111]

Boutet, Claude
- The art of painting in miniature ... now added, I ... II ... III The usefulnesse and benefit of prints. London: 1752. 6th edn. 12mo. [x],1-132, 135-150,[6 contents] pp without apparent loss. Frontis, page of diags. Tear in 1 lf reprd. Later calf, jnt rubbed.
(Bow Windows) £75 [≈ $135]
- The art of painting in miniature: teaching the speedy and perfect acquisition of that art ... London: Longman Hitch, 1752. 6th edn. 8vo. [10],1-132, 135-150,[6] pp without loss of text. Engvd frontis, engvd plate. Rec gilt calf.
(Spelman) £140 [≈ $252]
- The art of painting in miniature London: 1752. 6th edn. Sm 8vo. 150 pp. Engvd frontis, 1 other plate. Orig calf, spine sl rubbed at lower end. *(Camden)* £150 [≈ $270]

Bowdler, John
- Reform or ruin; take your choice. London: J. Hatchard, 1797. 42 pp. Rebound in bds.
(C.R. Johnson) £28 [≈ $50]
- Reform or ruin; take your choice. In which

the conduct of the King ... is considered. And that reform pointed out, which alone can save the country. Dublin: John Milliken, 1798. 3rd edn. 32 pp. Rebound in bds.
(C.R. Johnson) £38 [≈ $68]

Bowen, Captain Essex
- Statement of facts, in answer to Mrs Gunning's letter, addressed to His Grace the Duke of Argyll. London: for J. Debrett, 1791. 1st edn. xv,60 pp. Lacking half-title. New canvas-backed paper bds.
(Claude Cox) £25 [≈ $45]

Bower, Archibald
- A faithful account of Mr. Archibald Bower's motives ... See Barron, Richard

Bowles, John
- French aggression proved from Mr. Erskine's "View of the causes of war" ... London: J. Wright, 1797. 179 pp. Disbound.
(C.R. Johnson) £25 [≈ $45]

Bownas, Samuel
- An account of the life, travels, and Christian experiences in the work of the ministry of Samuel Bownas. London: Luke Hinde, 1756. 1st edn. 8vo. Final advt leaf. Contemp calf, rebacked, crnrs worn.
(Stewart) £115 [≈ $207]
- An account of the life, travels, and Christian experiences in the work of the ministry of Samuel Bownas. London: Luke Hinde, 1756. 1st edn. 8vo. viii,3-198, ii pp. Advt leaf at end. Contemp speckled calf, jnts & extremities worn, a bit soiled & marked.
(Pirages) $300 [≈ £166]
- A description of the qualifications necessary to a Gospel Minister. London: 1767. 2nd edn. 8vo. 112 pp. Some minor marg stains, early inscrptns on title & flyleaf. Contemp Cambridge calf, rubbed, jnts a little cracked.
(Bow Windows) £48 [≈ $86]

Boyce, William
- Solomon, a serenata, in score, taken from the canticles. Set to musick. London: for the author, 1743. 1st edn. Folio. [vi],101 pp. List of subscribers. Title sl soiled, last leaf with short tear reprd. 19th c mor-backed cloth.n
(Bennett) £250 [≈ $450]

Boydell, John
- The school of Raphael; or the student's guide to expression in historical painting. London: Boydell, 1759. Lge folio. Title, 24 pp. 56 engvd plates inc 45 in 2 states. Contemp calf,

worn, newly rebacked.
(Marlborough) **£550 [≈ $990]**

Boyle, John, Earl of Orrery

- Remarks on the life and writings of Dr.
  Jonathan Swift ... London: Millar, 1752. 1st
  edn. 8vo. Lge paper on thicker paper.
  339,[11] pp. Ink inscrptns on front free
  endpaper. Frontis. Old calf, spine rubbed.
  (Karmiole) **$200 [≈ £111]**
- Remarks on the life and writings of Dr.
  Jonathan Swift ... London: A. Millar, 1752.
  3rd edn. 8vo. [ii],214,[x] pp. Port frontis.
  Final advt leaf. Contemp calf, lightly rubbed,
  jnts split.   *(Clark)* **£40 [≈ $72]**
- Remarks on the life and writings of Dr.
  Jonathan Swift ... London: A. Millar, 1752.
  4th edn. 8vo. [ii],321,[xi] pp. Port frontis.
  Some spotting. Contemp calf, worn, jnts
  cracked, 1 hinge internally re-inforced with
  tape. Working copy.   *(Clark)* **£20 [≈ $36]**

Boyle, Robert

- Certain physiological essays and other tracts
  written at distant times ... a discourse upon
  the absolute rest in bodies. London: for H.
  Herringman, 1669. 2nd edn (1st of 2nd part).
  2 pts in 1. Contemp calf, rebacked, mor label,
  gilt. Wing B3930.   *(Traylen)* **£495 [≈ $891]**
- Certain physiological essays and other tracts
  ... London: for H. Herringman, 1669. 2nd
  enlgd edn. 4to. Collation as in Fulton, with
  the final blank. 18th c sgntr on title scored
  through, some browning. Contemp calf,
  rebacked, orig spine preserved. Wing B3930.
  (Pickering) **$850 [≈ £472]**
- Medicina hydrostatica: or, hydrostaticks
  applyed to the materia medica. London:
  Smith, 1690. 1st edn. 12mo. [20],217,[7], t.p.,
  14 [ctlg with title dated 1690] pp. Half-title,
  engvd frontis. A few crnrs strengthened.
  Contemp speckled calf, early rebacking.
  (Antiq Sc) **$2,100 [≈ £1,166]**
- Medicinal experiments, or a collection of
  choice remedies. London: Smith, 1692. 1st
  edn. 12mo. [10],88 pp. Imprim leaf & 17 pp
  pub ctlg. Crnr torn from p 5 with loss of a few
  letters, headlines closely shaved, some pages
  worn at crnrs. Old calf, rebacked.
  (Oasis) **$225 [≈ £125]**
- The origine of formes and qualities ...
  illustrated by considerations and experiments.
  Oxford: 1667. 2nd edn, 1st iss. 8vo. Contemp
  calf, rebacked. Wing B4015.
  (Argosy) **$500 [≈ £277]**
- The philosophical works; abridged,
  methodized and disposed under the general
  heads of physics ... and medicine. London:

Innys, 1725. 1st edn. 3 vols. 4to. [iv],xliii,
730; xx,726; [iv],xv,756 pp. 21 fldg engvd
plates. Contemp calf, some jnts splitting,
rubbed.   *(Frew Mackenzie)* **£780 [≈ $1,404]**
- Some considerations touching the usefulnesse
  of experimental natural philosophy ...
  Oxford: 1664-71. 2 vols in 1. 4to. 2nd edn vol
  1; 1st edn vol 2. Complex collation, complete,
  with all blanks, &c. Contemp blindstamped
  calf.   *(Hemlock)* **$900 [≈ £500]**
- Some considerations touching the usefulnesse
  of experimental natural philosophy ... A
  second edition ... Oxford: for Ric. Davis,
  1664-71. 2 vols in 1. 8vo. Lacking ddd4 (label
  title). Contemp panelled calf, rebacked. Wing
  B4029 & B4030.
  (Waterfield's) **£700 [≈ $1,260]**
- The works ... In five volumes. To which is
  prefixed the life of the author. London: A.
  Millar, 1744. 1st edn. 5 vols. Folio. Engvd
  port frontis, red & black titles, 24 engvd
  plates on 15 fldg sheets. Contemp calf, gilt,
  jnts & extremities restored.
  (Frew Mackenzie) **£1,300 [≈ $2,340]**
- The works ... In six volumes. To which is
  prefixed the life of the author. London: for F.
  & J. Rivington, 1772. New edn. 6 vols. 4to.
  Engvd port frontis, 24 plates on 16 leaves, 6
  engvd vignette titles. Contemp calf, worn,
  crnrs reprd, rebacked, mor labels.
  (Traylen) **£1,100 [≈ $1,980]**
- The works ... To which is prefixed the life of
  the author. London: A. Millar, 1744. 5 vols.
  Folio. Port frontis, 22 plates, subscribers' list.
  Contemp calf, 3 jnts cracking.
  (Waterfield's) **£650 [≈ $1,170]**

Boyles ...

- Memoirs of the ... family of the Boyles ... See
  Budgell, Eustace

Boyles, John

- Table calculated to shew the contents (in feet
  and twelfth parts of a foot) of any sled load or
  cart load of wood. Boston: John Boyles, 1771.
  16 mo. 7 pp. 3 leaves torn without loss,
  contemp ink notes in margs. Disbound.
  (Xerxes) **$200 [≈ £111]**

Bracken, Henry

- The traveller's pocket-farrier: or a treatise
  upon the distempers and common incidents
  happening to horses upon a journey ...
  London: B. Dod, 1743. 1st edn. 12mo.
  [6],151,[9] pp. Red & black title. Contemp
  calf, cvrs loose.   *(Rootenberg)* **$175 [≈ £97]**

Braddon, Lawrence
- Essex's innocency and honour vindicated: or, murther. subornation, perjury and oppression, justly charged on the murtherers of ... Earl of Essex. London: for the author, 1690. 1st edn. 4to. [viii],62 pp. Engvd frontis. Disbound. Wing B4101.
(Young's) £65 [≈ $117]

Bradford, E.
- Preaching the unsearchable riches of Christ. S. Hall in Salem, 1785. 8vo. 44 pp. Later half mor, spine worn. *(Spelman)* £35 [≈ $63]

Bradley, Richard
- A complete body of husbandry, collected from the practice and experience of the most considerable farmers in Britain. Woodman, 1727. 1st edn. 8vo. [i],xi,372 pp, 2ff pub advts. 4 fldg engvd plates. Light dust-soiling. Contemp calf, rebacked, recrnrd.
(Frew Mackenzie) £190 [≈ $342]
- New improvements of planting and gardening, both philosophical and practical London: 1739. 7th edn. 8vo. [xvi],608,[23] pp. Engvd frontis, 13 engvd plates. Mod half calf. *(Wheldon & Wesley)* £70 [≈ $126]

Brady, Nicholas
- The antiquity and usefulness of Episcopal Confirmation ... a sermon at Richmond ... London: John Chantrey, 1708. Sm 4to. 20 pp. Mod wraps, *(Emerald Isle)* £38 [≈ $68]

Brag, Robert
- The journey of Dr. Robert Bongout and his lady to Bath performed in the year 177-. London: for J. Dodsley, 1778. Frontis port. Orig blue wraps, uncut.
(C.R. Johnson) £220 [≈ $396]

Brand, John
- History and antiquities of the town and county of Newcastle-upon-Tyne ... the coal trade ... engraved views of the publick buildings ... 1789. 1st edn. 2 vols. Lge 4to. xvi,676; 724 pp. Calf, rubbed, worn, crnrs bumped, upper hinge vol 2 split.
(Edwards) £160 [≈ $288]

Brathwait, Richard
- The English gentleman; containing sundry excellent rules or exquisite observations, tending to direction of every gentleman ... London: J. Haviland, 1630. 1st edn. 4to. Engvd title, fldg "Draught of the frontispiece", errata leaf. Contemp limp vell. STC 3563. *(Traylen)* £525 [≈ $945]

- A survey of history: or, a nursery for gentry. London: 1638. 4to. Engvd title in facsimile. Contemp calf, rebacked.
(Robertshaw) £95 [≈ $171]
- Times treasury: or, academy for gentry ... inlarged with a ladies love-lecture ... London: Brooke, 1652. Folio. vi,454; 52,[viii] pp. 4 titles, fldg sheet. 1st & last few leaves sized, a few crnrs frayed & reprd, sl browned. Contemp calf, rebacked. Wing B4276.
(P & P) £370 [≈ $666]

Bremner, Robert
- The rudiments of music ... to which is added, a collection of the best Church-tunes ... Edinburgh: for the author, 1756. Sm 8vo. 58 engvd plates of music (2 fldg). Contemp red mor, gilt, rebacked.
(Marlborough) £220 [≈ $396]

Brerewood, Edw.
- Enquiries touching the diversity of languages, and religions, through the chiefe parts of the world. London: John Bill, 1722. Sm 4to. Title vignette. Title reprd, headlines cropped. 19th c vellum. STC 3619.
(Stewart) £95 [≈ $171]

Brevint, D.
- Saul and Samuel at Endur, or, the new waies of salvation and service, which usually tempt men to Rome ... Truly represented and refuted. Oxford: at the Theater, 1674. 8vo. 413 pp. Contemp calf.
(Halewood) £35 [≈ $63]

Bridge, Josiah
- A sermon preached before his Excellency John Hancock, Esq., Governour; his honour Benjamin Lincoln, Esq., Lieutenant-Governour ... Boston: Adams & Nourse, 1789. 8vo. 54 pp. half-title. 19th c half mor, upper bd detchd. *(Spelman)* £30 [≈ $54]

Brissot, Jacques Pierrot
- J.P. Brissot, deputy of Eure and Loire, to his constituents. On the situation of the National Convention ... Dublin: P. Byrne, 1794. 8vo. Title & last leaf sl soiled. New bds.
(Stewart) £120 [≈ $216]

Britannicus (pseud.)
- A review of a late treatise entitled An account of the conduct of the Dowager D----- of M------- ... in a letter to a person of distinction. London: J. Roberts, 1742. 74 pp. Rebound in bds. *(C.R. Johnson)* £25 [≈ $45]

Britton, John (d. 1275)
- Britton. [A treatise on the laws of England]. London: ... J. Moore, 1640. 2nd edn, crrctd. Cr 8vo. Black letter. Some marginal soiling of a few prelims. Contemp calf, jnts reprd, orig spine laid down. New STC 3804.
(Traylen) **£450 [≈ $810]**

Brokesby, Francis
- The life of Henry Dodwell; with an account of his works ... to which is added, a letter to Robert Nelson from Dr. Edmund Halley ... London: Geo. James, 1715. 1st edn. 8vo. [xxviii],638 pp. Engvd port. Early 19th c panelled calf. *(Bennett)* **£75 [≈ $135]**
- The life of Henry Dodwell; with an account of his works ... London: 1715. 1st edn. 2 vols. 8vo. Port. Some light browning. Contemp panelled calf, some wear, 1 jnt cracked.
(Robertshaw) **£25 [≈ $45]**

Brome, Alexander
- Songs and other poems. London: for Henry Brome, 1661. 1st edn. Sm 8vo. [xviii],202 pp. Engvd port. Ms crrctns. Rec calf. Wing B4852. *(Bennett)* **£325 [≈ $585]**

Bromley, Henry
- A catalogue of engraved British portraits ... effigies of persons in every walk of life ... T. Payne, 1793. 4to. xiv,[2], 479,[i], 56,[80 appendix] pp. Num contemp anntns by W. Bateman, Jnr, with his sgntr crossed out on title. Rebound in qtr calf.
(Spelman) **£120 [≈ $216]**
- A catalogue of engraved British portraits from Egbert the Great to the present time. London: Payne ..., 1793. 4to. xiv,479 pp, 40ff index, 56 appendix pp. Contemp calf, rebacked, rubbed & worn. *(Marlborough)* **£65 [≈ $117]**
- A catalogue of engraved British portraits from Egbert the Great to the present time. London: 1793. xiv,479,[56] pp. Half lea, mrbld bds, gilt, rebacked, hinges strengthened.
(Fine Art) **£35 [≈ $63]**

Bromley, William
- Remarks in the Grand Tour of France and Italy. perform'd by a person of quality, in the year 1691. London: John Nutt, 1705. 2nd edn. 8vo. [xi],250,[vi] pp. Lightly browned, marg tear in 1 leaf. Contemp panelled calf, old rebacking, recrnrd.
(Frew Mackenzie) **£180 [≈ $324]**

Brooke, Charlotte
- A dialogue between a lady and her pupils, describing a journey through England and Wales; in which a detail of different arts and manufactures of each city and town is accurately given ... London: Rickman, n.d. [ca 1790]. 1st edn. 12mo. 280 pp. Contemp calf. *(Argosy)* **$250 [≈ £138]**

Brooke, Mrs. Frances
- The history of Charles Mandeville, a sequel to Lady Julia ... Dublin: Chamberlaine, 1790. 12mo. Half-title. Sm tear in 1 leaf reprd. Contemp half calf.
(Emerald Isle) **£110 [≈ $198]**

Brooke, Henry
- The fool of quality; or, the history of Henry Earl of Moreland. London: Edward Johnston, 1782. New edn. 5 vols. 12mo. 300; 273; 275; 244; 280 pp. Sporadic browning. Contemp sheep, extremities a bit worn, some jnts tender. *(Clark)* **£50 [≈ $90]**

Brooke, R.
- A discoverie of certaine errours published in print in the much commended Britannia, 1594 ... Mr. Camden's answer to this book; and Mr. Brooke's reply. 1724. 1st edn. vi, approx 320 pp. Engvd port frontis, engvd plate. Calf, sl rubbed, backstrip chipped.
(Edwards) **£120 [≈ $216]**

Brookes, R.
- An introduction to physic and surgery. Containing I. Medical institutions ... II ... anatomy ... London: Newbury. 1754. 1st eden. 8vo. vii,556 pp. Later qtr calf.
(Goodrich) **$150 [≈ £83]**

Broome, Ralph
- Letters from Simkin the Second to his dear brother in Wales, for the year 1790 ... London: for John Stockdale, 1790. 1st edn. 8vo. [2],124,[8 advts] pp. 8vo. Sl later half calf by G. Bellew of Dublin.
(Fenning) **£45 [≈ $81]**

Broughton, R.
- Monastichon Britanicum: or, a historical narration of the ... antient monasteries, religious rules ... London: Herringman, 1655. 8vo. [vi],411 pp. Lacking both paste-downs. Sl soiled calf. *(P & P)* **£28 [≈ $50]**

Brown, Andrew
- History of Glasgow; and of Paisley, Greenock and Port-Glasgow. Glasgow: William Paton, 1795-97. 2 vols in 1. Contemp tree calf, red & green labels. Ex lib Colquhoun of Luss.
(C.R. Johnson) **£350 [≈ $630]**

- History of Glasgow; and of Paisley, Greenock and Port-Glasgow. Glasgow: 1795 [and, Vol 2] Edinburgh: for the author, 1797. 1st edns. 2 vols. 8vo. 28,195; 385,11 pp. 2 fldg tables. Orig bds, uncut, worn.
(Young's) **£95 [≈ $171]**

Brown, Christopher
- Itinerarium Novi Testamenti: or, the sacred history ... of the New Testament ... added, a supplement describing the universe, the calculation of time ... regulation of the seasons ... London: the author, 1753. 3rd edn. 8vo. Frontis, 9 plates. Contemp roan.
(Chaucer Head) **£35 [≈ $63]**

Brown, John
- An estimate of the manners and principles of the times. London: for L. Davis ..., 1757. 8vo. Red & black title. Advt leaf at end reprd. Contemp calf, reprd & rebacked, orig spine laid down. *(Hughes)* **£55 [≈ $99]**
- An estimate of the manners and principles of the times. London: for L. Davis ..., 1757. 3rd edn. 8vo. Red & black title. Contemp calf, tail of backstrip chipped, jnts cracked.
(Waterfield's) **£75 [≈ $135]**
- Thoughts on civil liberty, on licentiousness, and faction. London: for L. Davis ..., 1765. 2nd edn. 8vo. 168 pp. A little foxing, a few sm paper-flaw holes. Rec half calf, gilt.
(Burmester) **£120 [≈ $216]**

Brown, Levinius
- The protestant's tryal (in controverted points of faith) by the written word. Brussels: 1745. 1st edn. 8vo. Errata leaf. Title reprd in marg & crnr. Early sheep, old rebacking.
(Chaucer Head) **£110 [≈ $198]**

Brown, William Lawrence
- An essay on the natural equality of men ... Phila: 1793. 191 pp. Ink notations throughout, some marg paper loss on 2 leaves not affecting text. Calf. *(Reese)* **£200 [≈ £111]**

Browne, Edward
- An account of several travels through a great part of Germany: in four journeys ... London: B. Tooke, 1677. 1st edn. 4to. 6 plates. Old red mor, gilt tooled, jnts worn.
(Argosy) **$350 [≈ £194]**

Browne, Isaac Hawkins
- Poems upon various subjects, Latin and English, published by his son. London: J. Nourse ..., 1768. 1st coll edn. 8vo. Port frontis. A few leaves cropped along fore-edge. Unbound. *(Traylen)* **£24 [≈ $43]**

Browne, John
- Myographia nova: or, a graphical description of all the muscles in the humane body ... London: 1697. 3rd edn. 4to. [xl],109 pp. Engvd port frontis, 40 engvd plates (tear in 1 without loss). 17th c b'plate. Sl browning. Contemp calf, rebacked. Wing B5128.
(Pickering) **$850 [≈ £472]**

Browne, Moses
- Angling sports; in nine piscatory eclogues. 1773, 3rd edn. 8vo. 136 pp. Engvd frontis, Mor, raised bands. *(Edwards)* **£195 [≈ $351]**

Browne, Peter
- The procedure, extent, and limits of human understanding. London: for W. Innys ..., 1737. 3rd edn. 8vo. Mod half calf.
(Waterfield's) **£125 [≈ $225]**
- Things divine and supernatural conceived by analogy with things natural and human ... London: for William Innys ..., 1733. 1st edn. 8vo. B6 cancelled. Contemp calf, rather rubbed, jnts cracked.
(Waterfield's) **£150 [≈ $270]**

Browne, Sir Thomas
- Certain miscellany tracts ... London: Mearne ..., 1684. 1st edn, 2nd iss. x,215,6 pp. Engvd port. Contemp calf, rebacked.
(Goodrich) **$295 [≈ £163]**
- Certain miscellany tracts ... London: for Charles Mearne, 1684. 1st edn, 2nd iss. 8vo. Engvd port. Contemp mottled calf. Wing B5152. *(Traylen)* **£240 [≈ $432]**
- Hydriotaphia: Urn-buriall, or a discourse of the sepulchrall urnes lately found in Norfolk. London: for Hen. Brome ..., 1658. 1st edn. 4to. 4ff, 73 pp. 2 engvd plates. [Bound with, in mod cloth] Pseudodoxia Epidemica. London: 1658. 4th edn. 2nd work lacking title. *(Argosy)* **$750 [≈ £416]**
- Pseudodoxia epidemica: or, enquiries into very many received tenets ... London: for Edward Dod ..., 1650. 2nd edn. Folio. Blind-tooled brown mor, a.e.g., by Bayntun. Wing B5160. *(Traylen)* **£375 [≈ $675]**
- Pseudodoxia epidemica: or, enquiries into very many received tenets ... urn-burial ... Garden of Cyrus ... London: E. Dod, 1658. 4to. [xvi],468 (440), [xvi],[xii], 73,[iii] pp. 3 engvs, longitudinal title. Contemp calf, backstrip worn, jnt cracked.
(Clark) **£160 [≈ $288]**
- Religio medici ... with annotations never before published ... London: for Andrew Crook, 1656. 4th edn. Cr 8vo. Engvd frontis (crnr torn), 4 pp advts. B6 reprd, marg

wormhole, old names on title. Contemp calf, crnrs worn, rebacked. *(Stewart)* **£60 [≈ $108]**
- The works. London: Bassett ..., 1686. 1st collected edn. Folio. Engvd port. Contemp calf, rebacked. *(Goodrich)* **$295 [≈ £163]**

Browne, Thomas
- Christian morals ... the second edition. With a life of the author, by Samuel Johnson. London: for J. Payne, 1756. 1st edn edited by Johnson. 12mo. [iv],lxi, [iii],136 pp. Half-title, Dd8 blank. Trace of old stamp on title & last leaf. Contemp calf, rebacked. *(Burmester)* **£125 [≈ $225]**
- Christian morals ... With a life of the author, by Samuel Johnson. London: for J. Payne, 1756. 2nd edn. Cr 8vo. Half-title, blank d8. Contemp calf, rebacked, *(Traylen)* **£275 [≈ $495]**

Browne, W.G.
- Travels in Africa, Egypt and Syria, from the year 1792 to 1798. 1799. 1st edn. 4to. xxxviii,496 pp. Engvd frontis (waterstained), 2 fldg maps (some foxing, both with tears reprd), engvd plan. Tear on title reprd. Orig suede bds, amateurishly rebacked. *(Edwards)* **£100 [≈ $180]**

Bruce, James
- Travels to discover the source of the Nile in six volumes. Dublin: William Sleater, 1790. 6 vols. Plates & maps (2 plates supplied in facs). Contemp Irish calf. *(Emerald Isle)* **£350 [≈ $630]**

Brulart de Genlis, Stephanie
- Tales of the castle: or, stories of instruction and delight .. translated ... by Thomas Holcroft. London: for G. Robinson, 1785. 1st English edn. 5 vols. 12mo. Half-titles. Some marg worming vol 4. Contemp tree-calf, gilt spines. *(Traylen)* **£180 [≈ $324]**

Brune, Jean de la
- The life of that most illustrious prince Charles V late Duke of Lorraine and Bar ... London: for Francis Saunders, 1691. 1st English edn. 8vo. [iv],192, 241-362, [2 advts] pp. (Complete, despite pagination jump). Contemp mottled calf, hd & ft of spine reprd. *(Deighton Bell)* **£65 [≈ $117]**

Bryant, Jacob
- A new system, or, an analysis of ancient mythology. London: T. Payne ..., 1774-77. 1st edn. 3 vols. 4to. 27 plates, 3 maps (2 fldg), 3 vignettes, half-title in vol 3. Contemp calf,

gilt panelled spines, a little worn, jnts reprd. *(Traylen)* **£250 [≈ $450]**
- A new system, or, an analysis of ancient mythology. London: T. Payne ..., 1775-77. 2nd, 2nd, 1st edns. 3 vols. 4to. 25 plates, 3 maps (2 fldg), 3 vignettes, half-title & final blank in vol 3. Contemp speckled calf, gilt panelled spines, jnts sl worn. *(Traylen)* **£175 [≈ $315]**
- Observations and inquiries relating to various parts of ancient history. Cambridge: 1767. 1st edn. 8vo. 324 pp. 6 fldg maps. Orig mottled calf, spine gilt, edges rubbed. *(Edwards)* **£125 [≈ $225]**
- Observations upon the poems of Thomas Rowley: in which the authority of those poems is ascertained. London: for T. Payne ..., 1781. 8vo. 597 pp. Half green calf, gilt back, mrbld bds & edges. *(Dailey)* **$150 [≈ £83]**

Brydges, Samuel Egerton
- Sonnets and other poems. A new edition. London: B. & J. White, 1795. Disbound. *(C.R. Johnson)* **£38 [≈ $68]**

Brydone, Patrick
- A tour through Sicily and Malta. London: Strahan & Cadell, 1773. 1st edn. 2 vols. 8vo. 2 pp a little soiled. Contemp smooth calf, gilt ruled, yellow edges. Ex lib Colquhoun of Luss with 2 b'plates. *(Pirages)* **$650 [≈ £361]**

Buchan, William
- Domestic medicine; or, the family physician: being an attempt to render the medical art more generally useful ... Edinburgh: Balfour ..., 1769. 1st edn. 8vo. 624 pp. Some thumbing. Contemp calf, rebacked. *(Goodrich)* **$750 [≈ £416]**
- Domestic medicine; or, the family physician ... Edinburgh: Balfour ..., 1769. 1st edn. 8vo. xv,[i],624 pp. Occas foxing, 1 leaf lacking portion of lower marg, marg tear reprd, some tips creased. Contemp calf, rebacked, crnrs worn. *(Pollak)* **£250 [≈ $450]**
- Domestic medicine ... The ninth edition: to which is now added, an additional chapter on cold bathing ... London: for A. Strahan ..., 1786. 8vo. Contemp speckled calf, jnts cracked but sound. *(Sotheran)* **£78 [≈ $140]**
- Domestic medicine ... London: 1792. 13th edn. Light foxing. Contemp calf, rebacked with simulated lea spine. *(Goodrich)* **$115 [≈ £63]**

Buchius, Paulus
- The Divine Being and its attributes

philosophically demonstrated from the Holy Scriptures and original nature of things ... London: Randal Taylor, 1693. With a1 (blank). 18th c panelled calf. Wing B5299.
(Waterfield's) **£200 [≈ $360]**

Buchoz, Pierre Joseph
- The toilet of flora; or a collection of the most simple methods of preparing baths, essences ... perfumes ... cosmetics of every kind ... take off the appearance of old age and decay. London: Nicoll, 1772. 8vo. [16],272 pp. Contemp calf, hd of spine chipped.
(Spelman) **£300 [≈ $540]**
- The toilet of flora; or a collection of the most simple methods of preparing baths, essences ... perfumes ... cosmetics of every kind ... London: for J. Murray, 1779. New edn, imprvd. [xii],342 pp. Frontis. Orig sheep, crnr worn, upper hinge cracked.
(Claude Cox) **£120 [≈ $216]**

Budgell, Eustace
- Memoirs of the lives and characters of the most illustrious family of the Boyles ... Dublin: J. Esdall, 1754. 1st edn. 8vo. Contemp calf, spine worn, upper cvr detchd.
(Robertshaw) **£32 [≈ $57]**
- The moral characters of Theophrastus ... Translated ... London: for Jacob Tonson ..., 1714. 1st edn. [xxxiv],80,4 ctlg pp. Engvd frontis. Calf-backed bds.
(Young's) **£30 [≈ $54]**

Budworth, Joseph
- Windermere, a poem. London: T. Cadell ..., 1798. Half-title. Lgely uncut. Qtr blue mor.
(C.R. Johnson) **£650 [≈ $1,170]**

Bugg, Francis
- New Rome arraigned and out of her own mouth condemned ... the dangerous errours ... of the people called Quakers ... London: for the author, 1693. 1st edn. Sm 4to. 8ff,63 pp. Some mispagination, some pp cut close or shaved. Old half calf, worn. Wing B5376.
(Bow Windows) **£70 [≈ $126]**

Bull, Dr.
- The corruptions of the Church of Rome in relation to ecclesiastical government ... in answer to the Bishop of Meaux's queries. London: 1707. 12mo. Title a little soiled. Contemp calf. *(Robertshaw)* **£18 [≈ $32]**

Bulstrode, Sir Richard
- Memoirs and reflections upon the reign and government of King Charles the 1st and King Charles the IId ... London: N. Mist, 1721.

[vi],439,[xvii] pp. Title torn & reprd, crnr torn from 1st & last leaf without loss. Contemp calf, rebacked, crnrs reprd. Ex lib.
(Clark) **£48 [≈ $86]**

Bunyan, John
- Come and welcome to Jesus Christ. Or, a plain and profitable discourse. London: Benj. Harris, 1715. 11th edn. 12mo. [iv],164 pp. W'cut frontis. Some worming throughout affecting letters. Contemp sheep, worn.
(Bennett) **£35 [≈ $63]**
- The pilgrim's progress ... to which is prefixed the life of the author. 1796. 2 parts. 8vo. Engvd port frontis, 8 engvd plates (a trifle foxed). Contemp red str-grained mor, dulled.
(Sotheran) **£72 [≈ $129]**

Burbury, John
- A relation of a journey of the right honourable my lord Henry Howard from London to Vienna, and thence to Constantinople ... London: Collins & Ford, 1671. 12mo. Title dusty. Later calf, rebacked. New Wing B5611. *(Marlborough)* **£130 [≈ $234]**

Burchett, Josiah
- A complete history of the most remarkable transactions at sea from the earliest accounts of time to the conclusion of the last war with France. 1720. 1st edn. 4to. 800 pp. Red & black title, port frontis, 9 double-page maps. Contemp calf, worn, rebacked.
(Edwards) **£400 [≈ $720]**
- A complete history of the most remarkable transactions at sea from the earliest accounts of time to the conclusion of the last war with France. 1720. Folio. Port frontis, 9 double-page maps. Final leaves damp-wrinkled. Panelled calf, crnrs worn, rebacked.
(Allen) **$250 [≈ £138]**

Burgess, Anthony
- True doctrine of justification asserted and vindicated, from the errours of Papists, Arminians ... and more especially Antinomians. London: for Tho. Underhil, 1651. 2nd edn. 272,[7] pp. Contemp ms notes on end-pages. Lea, hinges cracked.
(Xerxes) **$250 [≈ £138]**

Burgh, James
- The dignity of human nature. London: for J. Johnson ..., 1767. 2nd edn. 2 vols. 8vo. xxxv,[i],322; 504 pp. Contemp speckled calf, jnts cracked, spines sl rubbed, labels renewed.
(Burmester) **£110 [≈ $198]**

Burgher, G.A.
- Leonora. Translated ... With designs by the right honourable lady Diana Beauclerc. London: for J. Edwards ..., 1796. 1st edn. Folio. [viii],35 pp. Symbolic title, 4 etched & engvd vignettes, 4 engvd plates. Some fingering. Old mrbld bds, mor spine, rebacked.   *(Bow Windows)* **£105 [≈ $189]**

Burgoyne, John
- The lord of the manor, a comic opera ... with a preface by the author. London: for T. Evans, 1781. 1st edn. 8vo. xxvi,96 pp. Possibly wanting half-title. Later wraps.
        (Burmester) **£45 [≈ $81]**
- The maid of the oaks. A new dramatic entertainment. As it is performed at the Theatre Royal, in Drury Lane. A new edition. London: for T. Beckett, 1775. 8vo. [xii],68 pp. Title silhouetted in ink, last leaf torn at inner marg. Disbound.
        (Burmester) **£15 [≈ $27]**

Burke, Edmund
- An appeal from the new to the old Whigs ... relative to the reflections on the French Revolution. London: J. Dodsley, 1791. 3rd edn. 143 pp. Disbound.
        (C.R. Johnson) **£28 [≈ $50]**
- A letter ... to a noble Lord, on the attacks made upon him and his pension in the House of Lords ... London: J. Owen, 17796. 80 pp. Disbound.   *(C.R. Johnson)* **£30 [≈ $54]**
- A letter ... to John Farr and John Harris, Sheriffs of that City [Bristol], on the affairs of America. London: for J. Dodsley, 1777. 3rd London edn. 8vo. 75 pp. Occas v minor foxing. Green cloth. *(Heritage)* **$75 [≈£41]**
- Mr. Burke's speech, on the motion made for papers relative to the directions for charging the Nabob of Arcot's private debts to Europeans on the revenues of the Carnatic ... London: J. Dodsley, 1785. 93 pp. Sewn pamphlet as issued, partly unopened.
        (C.R. Johnson) **£55 [≈ $99]**
- A philosophical enquiry into the origin of our ideas of the sublime and beautiful. London: R. & J. Dodsley, 1757. 1st edn. 8vo. Half-title. Occas contemp inked marginalia. Contemp calf, hinges reprd.
        (Argosy) **$750 [≈£416]**
- A philosophical enquiry into the origin of our ideas of the sublime and beautiful. London: R. & J. Dodsley, 1757. 1st edn. 8vo. viii,[viii],184 pp. Half-title. Lacking front free endpaper, edges sl dustsoiled. Uncut in contemp sheep-backed mrbld bds.
        (Frew Mackenzie) **£380 [≈ $684]**

- A philosophical enquiry into the origin of our ideas of the sublime and beautiful. London: R. & J. Dodsley, 1752. 1st edn. Sm 8vo. [xvi],184 pp. Half-title. Hole in B8 with trivial loss. Contemp speckled calf, rebacked & recrnrd, front cvr reprd.
        (Blackwell's) **£240 [≈ $432]**
- A philosophical enquiry into the origin of our ideas of the sublime and beautiful. London: R. & J. Dodsley, 1764. 4th edn. 8vo. ix,[7],342 pp. Contemp calf, rebacked, crnrs worn, new label.   *(Spelman)* **£45 [≈ $81]**
- A philosophical enquiry into the origin of our ideas of the sublime and beautiful. London: J. Dodsley, 1776. 8th edn. 8vo. ix,[7],342 pp. Contemp calf, hd of spine reprd.
        (Spelman) **£50 [≈ $90]**
- Reflections on the Revolution in France ... London: for J. Dodsley, 1790. 1st edn, 1st iss. 8vo. Half red mor gilt, t.e.g., other edges uncut.   *(Traylen)* **£375 [≈ $675]**
- Reflections on the Revolution in France ... London: for J. Dodsley, 1790. 1st edn, 1st iss. 8vo. New half antique calf, mor label.
        (Traylen) **£330 [≈ $594]**
- Reflections on the Revolution in France ... London: 1790. 7th edn. 8vo. 364 pp. Contemp half calf.   *(Argosy)* **$100 [≈£55]**
- A representation to his Majesty, moved in the House of Commons ... Monday, June 14th, 1784, and negatived. With a preface and notes. A new edition. London: J. Debrett, 1785. 81,3 advts pp. Half-title. Rebound in qtr calf.   *(C.R. Johnson)* **£35 [≈ $63]**
- A speech ... at the Guildhall, in Bristol, previous to the late election in that city, upon certain points relative to his parliamentary conduct. London: J. Dodsley, 1780. 3rd edn. 68 pp. Disbound. *(C.R. Johnson)* **£25 [≈ $45]**
- A speech ... at the Guildhall, in Bristol, previous to the late election in that city, upon certain points relative to his parliamentary conduct. London: J. Dodsley, 1782. 5th edn. 68 pp. Disbound. *(C.R. Johnson)* **£25 [≈ $45]**
- Speech ... on American taxation April 19, 1774. London: for J. Dodsley, 1775. 3rd edn. 8vo. Mod mrbld bds, sm hole on title affecting 2 letters of the price. Todd 24c but no press figure on p 22.
        (Waterfield's) **£40 [≈ $72]**
- Speech ... on American taxation April 19, 1774. London: J. Dodsley, 1783. 4th edn. 97 pp. Disbound.   *(C.R. Johnson)* **£45 [≈ $81]**
- Speech ... on American taxation April 19, 1775. London: for J. Dodsley, 1775. 4th edn. 8vo. Disbound. Todd 24e.
        (Waterfield's) **£40 [≈ $72]**
- Speech ... on moving his resolutions for

conciliation with the colonies. March 22, 1775. London: for J. Dodsley, 1775. 8vo. 19th c anntns in text. Disbound. Todd 25b.
(Waterfield's) £50 [≈ $90]
- Speech ... on moving his resolutions for conciliation with the colonies. March 22, 1775. London: J. Dodsley, 1775. 3rd edn. 107 pp. Disbound. Todd 25e.
(C.R. Johnson) £38 [≈ $68]
- Speech ... on presenting to the House of Commons a plan for the better security of the independence of parliament ... London: J. Dodsley, 1780. 95 pp. Disbound.
(C.R. Johnson) £25 [≈ $45]
- Three memorials on French affairs. London: for F. & C. Rivington, 1797. 1st edn, 2nd imp. 8vo. [ii],xxxi, 4,199,[11 blank & appendix] pp. Wanting half-title, occas early pencilled notes. New bds.
(Pickering) $150 [≈ £83]
- Two letters addressed to a member of the present parliament on the proposals for peace with the Regicide Directory of France. London: for F. & C. Rivington, 1796. 8vo. 1st authorised edn, 1st iss. Lacking half-title. Todd 66b. *(Waterfield's)* £45 [≈ $81]
- A vindication of natural society: or, a view of the miseries and evils arising to mankind from every species of artificial society. London: J. Dodsley, 1780. 3rd edn. 106 pp. Disbound.
(C.R. Johnson) £38 [≈ $68]

Burlamaqui, J.J.
- The principles of natural law. Dublin: for J. Sheppard, 1769. 3rd edn, revsd & crrctd. 2 pts in 1. Translated. Contemp ms notes on endpaper. Contemp calf. Armorial b'plate.
(Edwards) £100 [≈ $180]

Burn, John
- A new law dictionary for general use as well as for gentlemen of the profession. Dublin: Brett Smith, 1792. 8vo. 739 pp. Irish calf.
(Emerald Isle) £65 [≈ $117]

Burnby, John
- An historical description of the Cathedral and Metropolitical Church of Christ, Canterbury ... Canterbury: 1772. 1st edn. 8vo. vi,3-105 pp. Engvd frontis, half-title. 19th c half roan, trifle rubbed. *(Burmester)* £60 [≈ $108]

Burnet, Elizabeth
- A method of devotion: or, rules for a holy and devout life ... added, some account of her life ... London: for Joseph Downing, 1709. 8vo. Port frontis (stuck to pastedown), 3 pp bookseller's ctlg. Lacking endpapers.

Contemp panelled calf, crnrs worn.
(Stewart) £40 [≈ $72]

Burnet, Gilbert
- The abridgement of the history of the Reformation of the Church of England. London: for R. Chiswell, 1683. 2nd edn. 8vo. xxx,320, 384 pp. Engvd frontis, 4 pp engvd ports. Contemp calf, spine rubbed. Wing B5756. *(Lloyd-Roberts)* £55 [≈ $99]
- Bishop Burnet's history of his own time from the Restoration of King Charles II ... London: for Thomas Ward, 1724; Joseph Downing, 1734. 1st edn. 2 vols. Folio. Contemp calf, gilt, hinges worn & tender.
(Lloyd-Roberts) £130 [≈ $270]
- A collection of eighteen papers, relating to the affairs of Church and state ... Reprinted at London: for John Starkey ..., 1689. 4to. Half-title soiled. Disbound. *(Stewart)* £30 [≈ $54]
- A discourse of the pastoral care. London: for Ric. Chiswell ..., 1692. 2nd edn. [xxxiv],252 pp. Old calf. Wing B5777.
(Young's) £40 [≈ $72]
- Dr. Burnet's travels, or letters containing an account of what seemed most remarkable in Switzerland, Italy, France, and Germany ... Amsterdam: for Peter Savouret ..., 1687. 12mo. Old polished sheep, rebacked & refurbished. *(Charles Cox)* £35 [≈ $63]
- An exposition of the thirty-nine articles of the Church of England. London: for Ri. Chiswell, 1705. 3rd edn, crrctd. Folio. [vi],396 pp. Contemp panelled calf, spine worn. *(Lloyd-Roberts)* £50 [≈ $90]
- Four letters which passed between the ... Lord Bishop of Sarum and Mr. Henry Dodswell. London: for Richard Smieh [sic], 1713. 1st edn. 39 pp. Half-title. Disbound.
(Young's) £40 [≈ $72]
- History of his own time ... To which is added, the author's life, by the editor. London: for Thomas Ward, 1724-34. 1st edn. 2 vols. Folio. [xvi],836; xxii,765,[xii] pp. Contemp calf, jnts splitting at hd & tail, rubbed, extremities bumped.
(Frew Mackenzie) £85 [≈ $153]
- The history of the Reformation of the Church of England. Part one ... Part two ... Part three. Being a supplement ... London: R. Chiswell (pt 3 J. Churchill), 1679-81, 1715. 1st edn. 3 vols. Folio. 16 engvd ports, engvd titles vols 1 & 2. 19th c half mor.
(Stewart) £150 [≈ $270]
- The history of the Reformation of the Church of England in two parts. London: for R. Chiswell, 1681-83. 2nd edn. Wing B7598 & B7599. [with] ... Third part. For J. Churchill,

1715. 1st edn. Together, 3 vols, folio. Contemp calf, vols 1 & 2 rubbed & sl worn.
(Lloyd-Roberts) **£150 [≈ $288]**
- The life and death of Sir Matthew Hale, Kt. London: for William Shrowsbery, 1682. Port. 1st 2 leaves sl tattered, A3 marg cut down, some sl worming. Old calf, rebacked. Wing 5823.
(Charles Cox) **£45 [≈ $81]**
- The life and death of Sir Matthew Hale, Kt. London: for D. Brown ..., 1721. 12mo. [8],95 pp. Some light browning & soiling. Contemp calf.
(Claude Cox) **£28 [≈ $50]**
- Reflections on a late pamphlet entitled Parliamentum Pacificum .... Amsterdam: for P. Savouret, 1688. 4to. 8 pp. Some page numerals cropped. Disbound. Wing B5849.
(Burmester) **£30 [≈ $54]**
- A sermon preached at the funeral of the Honourable Robert Boyle ... January 7. 1691/2. London: for Richard Chiswell ..., 1692. 1st edn. Sm 4to. [3]-40 pp, without the half-title. 2 catchwords touched by binder's knife. New bds. Wing B5899.
(Pickering) **$400 [≈ £222]**
- Six papers ... to which is added I. An apology for the Church of England ... II. An enquiry into the measures of submission ... London: printed in the year 1689. 4to. Disbound. Wing B5913.
(Waterfield's) **£40 [≈ $72]**
- Some letters. Containing an account of what seemed most remarkable in Switzerland, Italy, &c. Rotterdam: 1686. 12mo. 310 (i.e. 300) pp. Cropped at hd affecting 1st word of title & some page numerals, marg tear in E10. Mod half calf. Wing B5916.
(Clark) **£68 [≈ $122]**
- Some letters. Containing an acccount [sic] of what seemed most remarkable in ... Switzerland, Italy ... Rotterdam: 1687. [With] Three letters ... a supplement ... 1688. 8vo. [xxii],336; [xvi],191,[i errata] pp. Contemp calf, rebacked. Wing B5918 & B5932.
(Frew Mackenzie) **£175 [≈ $315]**
- Some passages of the life and death of the ... Earl of Rochester ... London: for Richard Chiswel, 1680. 8vo. Port frontis, 8 pp bookseller's ctlg. Contemp calf, later spine & recased. Wing B5922. *(Stewart)* **£60 [≈ $108]**
- Some passages of the life and death of the ... Earl of Rochester ... London: for Richard Chiswel, 1680. 1st edn. 8vo. Port frontis, addtnl port after preface, 8 pp pub ctlg at end. 19th c calf, worn, jnts cracking.
(Charles Cox) **£45 [≈ $81]**

Burnet, T.
- The theory of the earth ... A review of the theory of the earth. London: Norton,

1684-90. 1st edns. 2 vols. Folio. 2 engvd frontis, 12 engvs, 3 plates (2 fldg), advt leaf. Minor repr to vol 2 title, a few sm lib stamps. Contemp calf, spines gilt. Wing B5950/1.
(P & P) **£195 [≈ $351]**

Burney, Charles
- An account of the musical performances in Westminster-Abbey, and the Pantheon, May 26th ... 1764. in commemoration of Handel. Dublin: Moncrieffe ..., 1785. Contemp calf, spine gilt. Leading hinge weakening.
(C.R. Johnson) **£385 [≈ $693]**
- A general history of music ... to the present period ... London: for the author, 1782-89. 4 vols. 4to. 2nd edn vol 1; 1st edns o/w. Port, 9 plates (2 fldg), lge fldg w'cut, errata leaves vols 2 & 4. marg worming vol 4. Contemp calf, 2 vols rebacked. *(Traylen)* **£400 [≈ $720]**
- The present state of music in France and Italy: or, a journal of a tour through those Countries ... London: T. Becket, 1771. 8vo. Browning to edge of margs of 1st few leaves. Contemp calf, red label. Ex lib Colquhoun of Luss. *(C.R. Johnson)* **£650 [≈ $1,170]**
- The present state of music in France and Italy: or, a journal of a tour through those Countries ... T. Becket, 1771. 1st edn. 8vo. vii,396, [xiii index, advt leaf, errata leaf] pp. Prelim & final leaves browned. Rec qtr mor, gilt, cloth sides. *(Blackwell's)* **£150 [≈ $270]**

Burney, Frances, Madame d'Arblay
- Camilla. London: Payne, 1796. 1st edn. 5 vols. 8vo. Binder's blanks in 1st vol reprd. Contemp calf, rebacked, spines gilt, mor labels. *(Ash)* **£200 [≈ $360]**
- Camilla. Dublin: William Porter, 1796. Pirated edn. 3 vols. Cr 8vo. A few sections browned. Contemp calf, 1 spine worn.
(Stewart) **£40 [≈ $72]**

Burns, Robert
- Poems chiefly in the Scottish dialect. Edinburgh: for the author, 1787. 1st Edinburgh edn (iss with "skinking'). Lacking half-title. 19th c qtr calf.
(C.R. Johnson) **£225 [≈ $405]**
- Poems chiefly in the Scottish dialect. The third edition. London: for A. Strahan ... and W. Creech, Edinburgh, 1787. 1st London edn. 8vo. xlviii,13-372 pp. Engvd port, half-title. Uncut in orig grey bds.
(Burmester) **£225 [≈ $405]**
- Poems chiefly in the Scottish dialect. Edinburgh: for the author, 1787. Half-title, port frontis, subscribers' list. Full red mor, gilt, by Riviere. Ownership inscrptn of

Charles Kirkpatrick Sharpe.
(C.R. Johnson) **£650 [≃ $1,170]**
- Poems chiefly in the Scottish dialect. Edinburgh: for the author, 1787. 1st Edinburgh edn. 368 pp. Frontis. Orig calf, gilt, red mor label. *(Jenkins)* **$350 [≃ £194]**
- Poems chiefly in the Scottish dialect. Edinburgh: for the author, 1787. 1st Edinburgh edn, 1st iss (with "skinking" & "Boxburgh" misprints). Half-title & port frontis. Isolated minor spotting, a few leaves browned. Old half calf, mrbld paper sides, worn. *(Pirages)* **$275 [≃ £152]**
- Poems chiefly in the Scottish dialect. Dublin: William Gilbert, 1789. Port frontis. Rebound in calf. *(C.R. Johnson)* **£285 [≃ $513]**
- Poems, chiefly in the Scottish dialect ... The second edition considerably enlarged ... Edinburgh: for T. Cadell, London ..., 1793. 12mo. xi,237; [iv],283 pp. Port frontis vol 1, 2 half-titles. Minor staining. Contemp calf, scuffed, 3 jnts cracked. *(Clark)* **£100 [≃ $180]**

Burrish, Onslow
- Batavia illustrata ... the policy and commerce of the United Provinces ... In three parts ... London: W. Innys ..., 1731. 1st edn, 2nd iss, with cancel title. [ii],vi,[ii contents], 580 pp. Occas browning & soiling. Contemp polished calf, rebacked, sl rubbed.
(Pickering) **$400 [≃ £222]**

Burrough, Edward
- A declaration of the present sufferings of above 140 persons ... (who are now in prison) called Quakers. London: for Tho. Simmons, 1659. 4to. [ii],44 pp. Title soiled & with sm hole affecting imprint. Later mrbld wraps. Wing B5993. *(Clark)* **£85 [≃ $153]**

Burtenshaw, Henry
- Specimens of justice, humility, and uniformity, in another letter to the ... Earl of Mansfield. London: for the author ..., 1782. 4to. iv,157 pp. Piece torn without loss from blank crnr of 1st text leaf. Mod qtr calf.
(Kerr) **£150 [≃ $270]**

Burton, Robert
- The anatomy of melancholy. Oxford: for Henry Cripps, 1624. 1st folio edn. Sm folio. [iv],64,[iv], 189-332, [ii],333-557, [vii] pp. Paper fault on 1 leaf, pen markings on prelims & some margs. Later calf, mrbld sides, rebacked. STC 4160.
(Frew Mackenzie) **£600 [≃ $1,080]**
- The anatomy of melancholy. What it is, with all the kinds, causes ... and several cures of it.

Oxford printed: for Henry Cripps. 1632. 4th edn. Sm folio. Prelim leaf mtd, engvd title frayed, lacking final index leaf. Calf, rebacked. *(Goodrich)* **$195 [≃ £108]**
- The anatomy of melancholy ... London: Henry Cripps. 1662. 7th edn. Sm folio. Argument leaf & engvd allegorical title. Foxing. Contemp calf, rubbed.
(Goodrich) **$450 [≃ £250]**

Butler, John
- The political fugitive: being a brief disquisition into the modern system of British politics ... Written during a voyage from London to New York. Thomas Greenleaf, for the author, 1794. 8vo. 115 pp. Wraps.
(Farahar) **£90 [≃ $162]**

Butler, Samuel
- The genuine remains in verse and prose ... with notes by R. Thyer. London: for J. & R. Tonson, 1759. 1st edn. 2 vols. Contemp calf, rebacked. *(Charles Cox)* **£35 [≃ $63]**
- The genuine remains in verse and prose ... with notes by R. Thyer. London: for J. & R. Tonson, 1759. 1st edn. 2 vols. Rec qtr calf, uncut. *(Lloyd-Roberts)* **£75 [≃ $135]**
- Hudibras. The first and second parts. London: for John Martyn ..., 1674. Sl browned, a few trifling tears. Old calf, rebacked. Wing B6311.
(Charles Cox) **£50 [≃ $90]**
- Hudibras ... Corrected and amended. London: 1684. 3 pts in 1 vol. Thick 8vo. 1st title reprd with loss of a few letters. Old bds, later mor reback. *(Argosy)* **$50 [≃ £27]**
- Hudibras. In three parts ... London: for D. Browne ..., 1726. Cr 8vo. Engvd frontis, 16 plates (2 reprd) by William Hogarth. New bds. *(Stewart)* **£65 [≃ $117]**
- Hudibras. In three parts ... Cambridge: J. Bentham, 1744. 2 vols. 8vo. Port frontis, 16 plates (5 fldg) after Hogarth, subscribers' list. Brief ink notes on 1 page. Later mor, gilt, spines a bit darkened, jnts sl rubbed.
(Pirages) **$150 [≃ £83]**
- Hudibras. Glasgow: Foulis, 1774. 2 vols. xvi,476. Contemp red mor, spines heavily gilt, mrbld endpapers, jnts & extremities sl rubbed. B'plate of Edward, Lord Suffield in each vol. *(Pirages)* **$125 [≃ £69]**
- The posthumous works ... compleat in one volume ... London: for R. Reily, 1730. 3rd edn, crrctd. Tall 12mo. viii,312 pp. Contemp panelled calf, pine rubbed.
(Lloyd-Roberts) **£50 [≃ $90]**

Butt, George
- A sermon preached at the Octagon Chapel in the City of Bath on the day the Lord Bishop of Winchester was buried. Oxford: J. & J. Fletcher, 1775. 4to. 22 pp. Half-title. Disbound.   *(C.R. Johnson)* **£22 [≈$39]**

BW
- See Badcock, William

Byng, John, Admiral
- A candid examination of the resolutions and sentence of the court-martial on the trial of Admiral Byng. London: for J. Cooke, 1757. 1st edn. 8vo. [ii],38 pp. 19th c red half mor.
      (Burmester) **£75 [≈$135]**
- An exact copy of a remarkable letter from Admiral Byng to the Right Honourable W--- P---, Esq. dated March 12, 1757. Two days before his execution. London: J. Reason, 1757. 22 pp. Disbound.
      (C.R. Johnson) **£48 [≈$86]**
- A letter to a member of parliament in the country, from his friend in London, relative to the case of Admiral Byng. London: 1756. 1st edn. Half-title, 31 pp. Some spotting. Disbound.   *(Robertshaw)* **£25 [≈$45]**
- The trial of ... at a Court Martial ... London: for R. Manby ..., 1757. 1st edn. Folio. 1-36, 37*, 38*, 37-76, 73*-76*, 77-130, 19 appendix pp. Sl browning, spotting & staining. Old cloth, spine ends, jnts, crnrs & edges worn.   *(Bow Windows)* **£135 [≈$243]**

Byrom, John
- The universal English short-hand; or, the way of writing English ... Manchester: Joseph Harrop, 1767. [vi],ix,[i], [3]-92 pp. 13 engvd plates. Lacking rear endpaper. Contemp calf, rebacked.   *(Clark)* **£200 [≈$360]**
- The universal English short-hand; or, the way of writing English ... Manchester: Joseph Harrop, 1767. 1st edn. 8vo. [2],x,92 pp. Engvd table, 12 plates. Title mtd, occas light soiling. Old calf, mod rebacking.
      (Claude Cox) **£75 [≈$135]**

Byron, John
- Narrative ... an account of the great distresses ... on the coast of Patagonia ... with a description of St. Jago de Chili ... London: Baker ..., 1768. 2nd edn. 8vo. [ii],viii,257 pp. Engvd frontis. Title reprd in marg. Contemp half calf, crnrs restored.
      (Morrell) **£125 [≈$225]**

Cabala ...
- Cabala, mysteries of State in letters to the

great Ministers of King James and King Charles. Wherein much of the publique manage of affaires is related. London: 1654. 1st edn. m 4to. Contemp unlettered calf, upper jnt reprd. Wing C183.
      (Robertshaw) **£80 [≈$144]**

Cadogan, William
- A dissertation on the gout, and all chronic diseases ... addressed to all invalids. London: Dodsley, 1771. 7th edn. 8vo. 100 pp. Half-title. Contemp calf-backed mrbld bds, some worming to hd of spine, extndg to last gathering, extremities rubbed.
      (Frew Mackenzie) **£130 [≈$234]**

Calamy, Benjamin
- Sermons preached upon several occasions. London: John Darby, 1700. Cr 8vo. Port frontis. Contemp calf, sl rubbed. Wing 223.
      (Stewart) **£40 [≈$72]**

Calamy, Edmund
- The Saints' transfiguration ... a sermon preached at the funerall of ... Dr. Samuel Bolton ... London: for Joseph Crauford, 1655. Disbound. Wing C265.
      (Waterfield's) **£25 [≈$45]**

Calcott, Wellins
- A candid disquisition of the principles and practices of the most free and accepted masons ... For the author, 1769. 1st edn, 2nd iss. 8vo. [ii],xxxii subscribers, 243 pp. Lge & untrimmed in orig qtr calf, mrbld bds, cvrs rubbed, front jnt cracking.
      (Blackwell's) **£225 [≈$405]**

Calculations ...
- Calculations deduced from first principles ... See Dale, W.

Callimachus
- The hymns of Callimachus. Translated from the Greek ... by William Dodd. London: 1755. 1st edn. 4to. 212 pp. Engvd port on title, 6 other engvs. Contemp half mor.
      (Argosy) **$200 [≈£111]**
- The works ... Translated into English verse ... and notes ... and additional observations by H.W. Tytler. London: for Charles Dilly, 1793. 1st edn of this trans. 4to. iii,268,[6 subscribers] pp. Rec half calf over gray bds, uncut.   *(Karmiole)* **$200 [≈£111]**

Callis, Robert
- The reading of that most famous and learned gentleman upon the Statute of 23, H. 8. Cap. 5 of sewers. London: for William Leake,

1647. 1st edn. 4to. 235 pp. Mod half calf. Wing C304.   *(Edwards)* **£170 [≈ $306]**

Calonne, Charles Alexandre de
- Museum Calonnianum. Specification of the various articles of natural history collected by M. de Calonne. London: George Humphrey, 1797. 8vo. 84 pp. 1,439 lots. Added engvd port. Old wraps, dusty.
          (Marlborough) **£250 [≈ $450]**

Calvin, John
- A harmonie upon the three Evangelistes Matthewe, Marke, and Luke ... a commentarie upon ... S. Iohn ... London: Thos. Adams, 1610. 4to. Reprs to crnrs of 1st 6 & last 3 leaves, minor worming to some margs, few tears & stains. Early sheep, rebacked. STC 2963.
          (Charles Cox) **£85 [≈ $153]**
- The institution of the Christian religion: in four books ... Glasgow: for Alexander Irvine ..., 1762. 4to. Engvd ptd frontis (sl creased & dusty & reprd to inner marg). 1 leaf reprd, some browning. Rebound in mod lib cloth, brown mor spine. Ex lib.
          (Hughes) **£45 [≈ $81]**
- Sermons of Master John Calvin upon the Booke of Job. Translated ... Lucas Harison & George Byshop, [1574]. 1st ed. Folio. [lxiv],[819] pp. Pagination erratic. Occas marg staining, 2ff torn, 1 with loss of 8 letters. 17th c calf, gilt, rebacked. STC 4445.
          (Frew Mackenzie) **£385 [≈ $693]**

Cambridge, Richard Owen
- The Scribleriad: an heroic poem. In six books. London: for R. Dodsley ..., 1751. 1st edn. 6 pts in 1 vol. 4to. Sep paginated. Engvd frontis, 6 other plates as frontis to each pt, sep titles to each book. Contemp calf, later label.
          (Burmester) **£65 [≈ $117]**
- The Scribleriad: an heroic poem. In six books. London: for R. Dodsley ..., 1751. Explntn of the frontis, 12 pp preface, 7 pp index, errata pp. 7 engvd plates. Old half calf, tiny wormhole through lower jnts, tips of crnrs & base of spine rubbed.
          (Bow Windows) **£210 [≈ $378]**

Camden, William
- Annals, or, the historie of ... Princesse Elizabeth, late queen of England ... Trans. by R.N. London: for Benjamin Fisher, 1635. 3rd edn. Folio. Sm hole in d3 with sl loss of text, marg reprs to some leaves. New panelled calf. STC 4501.   *(Stewart)* **£150 [≈ $270]**
- Britannia ... revised by Edmund Gibson. London: for R. Ware ..., 1753. 2 vols. Folio.

Engvd port, 51 double-page or fldg maps, red & black titles, 9 plates. Text sl browned. Contemp sprinkled calf, crnrs worn, hinges cracked.   *(Claude Cox)* **£1,250 [≈ $2,250]**
- Remains concerning Britaine. The fift impression, with many rare antiquities never before imprinted. London: for John Waterson, 1637. 5th edn, 2nd iss. 4to. Port & title both laid down, A3 reprd at ft. Early 19th c diced calf, gilt. STC 4526.   *(Charles Cox)* **£80 [≈ $144]**

Cameron, William
- Poems on various subjects. Edinburgh: Gordon & Murray, 1780. Qtr roan, cloth bds, hinges weakening.
          (C.R. Johnson) **£165 [≈ $297]**

Camoens, Luis de
- The Lusiad; or, the discovery of India, an epic poem. Oxford: for J. Bew ..., 1778. 4to. 2ff, ccxxxvi,496 pp. A little foxing, spotting & creasing. Old blue paper bds, somewhat soiled & wrinkled, with short tears.
          (Pirages) **$195 [≈ £108]**

Campbell, Archibald
- The doctrines of a middle state between death and the resurrection. London: for the author, 1721. Folio. Mod half calf.
          (Waterfield's) **£65 [≈ $117]**

Campbell, Donald
- A journey overland to India, partly by a route never gone by before by any European ... 1795. 1st edn. 4to. Orig tree-calf, jnts a little tender.   *(Farahar)* **£220 [≈ $396]**

Campbell, Duncan
- Secret memoirs of the late ... the famous deaf and dumb gentleman written by himself. London: for Milland & Crichley, 1732. 8vo. Port frontis. Mod qtr calf.
          (Waterfield's) **£150 [≈ $270]**

Campbell, John
- A political survey of Britain: being a series of reflections on the situation, lands, inhabitants ... London: for the author, 1774. 1st edn. 2 vols. 4to. Half-titles & indexes to each vol. Contemp calf, rebacked, orig spines laid down.   *(Traylen)* **£140 [≈ $252]**
- A political survey of Britain: being a series of reflections on the situation, lands, inhabitants ... of this island. London: for the author, 1774. 1st edn. 2 vols. 4to. Half-titles & indexes to each vol. Sm lib stamp on title & elsewhere. Rec half calf.
          (Bow Windows) **£245 [≈ $441]**

- A political survey of Britain: being a series of reflections on the situation, lands, inhabitants ... London: for the author, 1774. 2 vols. 4to. Rec half calf, mrbld sides.
(Lloyd-Roberts) **£180 [≈ $324]**

Campbell, John
- Lives of the admirals and other eminent British seamen ... curious passages relating to our discoveries and commerce ... 1750. 2nd edn. 4 vols. 8vo. Sl marg dampstaining in 2 vols. Contemp calf, gilt ruled, worn.
(Edwards) **£120 [≈ $216]**

Campbell, Thomas
- A philosophical survey of the South of Ireland, in a series of letters to John Watkinson, M.D. Dublin: for W. Whitestone, 1778. 1st Irish edn. 8vo. xvi,478,[2 blank] pp. 6 engvd plates (2 fldg). Rec calf-backed mrbld bds.
(Fenning) **£125 [≈ $225]**

Camper, Petrus
- The works ... connexion between ... anatomy and the arts of drawing, painting ... London: Dilly, 1794. 1st English edn. 4to. xxiii,[i errata], 175,[i] pp. Port frontis, 17 fldg plates (foxed), 7 outline plates. Dampstained. Later half calf, spine worn at ends.
(Pollak) **£400 [≈ $720]**

Canterbury ...
- An historical description of the Cathedral and Metropolitical Church of Christ, Canterbury ... See Burnby, John

Capel, Arthur, Baron of Hadham
- Excellent contemplations, divine and moral ... some account of his life ... pious advice to his son ... London: 1683. 1st edn. 12mo. Port, title within black border. A few headlines shaved, a little worming. Old calf, a little worn. Wing C469.
(Robertshaw) **£80 [≈ $144]**

Caradog of Llancarfan
- The historie of Cambria, now called Wales. London: Newberie, 1584. 1st edn. 4to. W'cut title border, 32 w'cut ports in text. Title dusty. Later calf, rebacked & refurbished. NSTC 4606.   *(Marlborough)* **£520 [≈ $936]**

Care, Henry
- English libert[ies] or the free-born subject's inheritance ... with ... additions ... London: B. Harris, n.d. [ca 1706]. 12mo. [viii],244 pp. Upper crnr of title torn with loss of 3 letters, underlining, staining. Contemp sheep,

rubbed, backstrip defective.
(Clark) **£50 [≈ $90]**

Carew, Bampfylde-Moore
- An apology for the life of Bampfylde-Moore Carew, commonly called the King of the Beggars ... London: 1775. 9th edn. 12mo. Fldg frontis. Contemp half calf, crnrs rubbed, jnts cracking.   *(Robertshaw)* **£25 [≈ $45]**
- The life and adventures of Bampfylde-Moore Carew, commonly called King of the Beggars ... origin, government, laws and customs of the gipsies ... London: for J. Buckland ..., 1793. 12mo. 235,[5] pp. Contemp blue bds, spine a bit worn.   *(Burmester)* **£45 [≈ $81]**

Carey, Mathew
- A short account of the malignant fever, lately prevalent in Philadelphia ... to which are added accounts of the plague in London and Marseilles ... Phila: for the author, 1794. 8vo. 4th edn. Wraps.   *(Farahar)* **£225 [≈ $405]**

Caribby Islands ...
- The history of the Caribby Islands ... See De Rochefort, Charles

Carleton, Sir Dudley
- Letters from and to during his embassy in Holland, from January 1615/16 to December 1620. London: 1775. 2nd edn. 4to. lxix,[2], 510,[25] pp. Engvd port frontis. Old calf, crnrs worn, rebacked. *(Young's)* **£50 [≈ $90]**

Caron, Frans & Schouten, Joost
- A true description of the mighty kingdoms of Japan and Siam. London: Robert Boulter ..., 1671. 2nd English edn. 12mo. [viii],152 (numbered 112 in error) pp. Fldg map. Rec panelled calf antique, spine gilt.
(Morrell) **£1,950 [≈ $3,510]**

Carstares, William
- State-papers and letters addressed to William Carstares, confidential secretary to K. William ... To which is prefixed the life of Mr. Carstares. Edinburgh: for W. Strahan, 1774. 1st edn. 4to. Some spotting. Rebound qtr calf.   *(Hughes)* **£65 [≈ $117]**

Carte, Thomas
- A general history of England ... London: for the author, 1747-50-52. 1st edn. 3 vols. Folio. Contemp panelled calf, rebacked, old labels.
(Lloyd-Roberts) **£200 [≈ $360]**
- An history of the life of James, Duke of Ormonde ... account of the most remarkable affairs of his time, and particularly of Ireland,

under his government. London: Knapton, 1736. 3 vols. Folio. Russia, old reback.
(Emerald Isle) **£250 [≈ $450]**

- An history of the life of James, Duke of Ormonde ... account of the most remarkable affairs of his time, and particularly of Ireland, under his government. London: Knapton, 1736-35. 3 vols. Folio. Contemp calf, spines gilt, jnts partly cracked, crnrs rubbed.
(Stewart) **£220 [≈ $396]**

Carter, John
- Specimens of the ancient sculpture and painting now remaining in this kingdom from the earliest period to the reign of Henry VIII. London: 1787. Folio. 2 vols. 80 b/w & 30 cold engvs. Ex lib. Label on endpaper. Contemp calf.
(Camden) **£850 [≈ $1,530]**

Cartwright, Edmund
- Armine and Elvira, a legendary tale. In two parts. Oxford: for J. Murray, London, 1771. 4to. Title vignette, marg tears to 2 leaves reprd, sm strip cut from title marg, lacking half-title & final blank. Mod bds.
(Stewart) **£85 [≈ $153]**
- Armine and Elvira, a legendary tale. In two parts. Oxford: for J. Murray ... 1772. 4th edn. 4to. 37 pp. Half-title, engvd title vignette. Occas browning. New bds.
(Young's) **£48 [≈ $86]**

Cartwright, William
- The royall slave. A tragi-comedy. Presented to the King and Queene by the students of Christ-Church in Oxford. August 30 1636. Oxford: for Thomas Robinson, 1640. 2nd edn. 4to. 1st 3 leaves soiled (from another copy?), lacking A4. Old paper bds. STC 4718.
(Charles Cox) **£65 [≈ $117]**

Carver, Jonathan
- The new universal traveller ... a full and distinct account of all the Empires. London: G. Robinson, 1779. 1st edn. Folio. [ii],iii,668, [6 index] pp. Engvd frontis, 18 maps (1 fldg), 37 plates. A little foxing. Contemp polished calf, scuffed, jnts cracked.
(Morrell) **£380 [≈ $684]**
- Three years travels through the interior parts of North America, for more than five thousand miles. Phila: Key & Simpson, 1796. 8vo. xx,ix,[11]-360, 20 pp. Subscriber list. A few leaves with minor spotting. Contemp sheep, minor wearing & soiling.
(Pirages) **£250 [≈ £138]**
- Travels through the interior parts of North America in 1766, 1767 and 1768. London: for the author, 1778. 1st edn. 8vo. [20],543,[1]

pp. 2 fldg engvd maps, 4 plates. Armorial b'plate. Wormholes at top of 1st few pp. Contemp calf, portion of hinges cracked.
(Argonaut) **$1,200 [≈ £666]**

Casaubon, Meric
- Of credulity and incredulity in things divine and spiritual ... platonick philosophy ... As also the business of witches and witchcraft ... London: for Samuel Lownds, 1670. 8vo. later calf, spine sl worn. Wing C806.
(Charles Cox) **£95 [≈ $171]**
- Of credulity and incredulity in things divine and spiritual ... platonick philosophy as it hath reference to Christianity: ... witches and witchcraft ... London: for Samuel Lownds, 1670. Sm hole on B6 with trivial loss. 19th calf, a little rubbed. Wing C806.
(Waterfield's) **£200 [≈ $360]**
- A treatise of use and custome. London: 1638. 8vo. Red & black title. Minor repr to inner gutter G2. Mod calf. STC 4753.
(Waterfield's) **£450 [≈ $810]**

Casterleagh, Honourable Lord Viscount
- A report of the two speeches ... in the debate on the Regency Bill, on April 11th 1799. Dublin: J. Milliken, 1799. 34 pp. Rebound in bds. *(C.R. Johnson)* **£28 [≈ $50]**

Castiglione, Count Baldassar
- Il Cortegiano, or the courtier; and a new version of the same in English ... prefix'd the life of the author. London: Bowyer, 1727. 1st edn with the life. 4to. [lxii],508 pp. Engvd port frontis. Contemp calf, rebacked, orig spine laid down, recrnrd.
(Frew Mackenzie) **£295 [≈ $531]**

Catherall, Samuel
- [Greek title, then] or, a portraiture of Socrates, extracted out of Plato. Oxford: for A. Peisley, 1717. Sole edn. 8vo. [6],53,[3 blank] pp. Lacking frontis, some waterstaining. Stabbed & stitched as issued.
(Claude Cox) **£20 [≈ $36]**

Catteau
- A general view of Sweden ... a geographical description of the account ... laws, population, natural riches ... Translated from the French. 1790. 410 pp. Prelims sl dampstained. Contemp calf, front bd detchd, worn. *(Old Cinema)* **£35 [≈ $63]**

Cavalry Regulations
- An elucidation of several parts of His Majesty's regulations for the formations and movements of cavalry. 1798. 54 pp. 28 fldg

engvd plates, partly hand-cold. Orig mrbld
bds, rebacked with cloth, worn & soiled.
(Edwards) **£160** [≈ $288]

Cave, William

- Apostolici: or the history of the lives, acts,
death and martyrdoms of those who were
contemporary with ... the Apostles. London:
for R. Chiswell, 1687. 3rd edn, crrctd. Folio.
[xxxii],336 pp. Engvd frontis, 23 engvd
plates. Contemp calf. Wing C1592.
(Lloyd-Roberts) **£100** [≈ $180]

Cavendish, George

- The negotiations of Thomas Woolsey, the
great Cardinall of England. London: for
William Sheeres, 1641. 1st edn. 8vo. 5
prelims, 118 (i.e. 122) pp. Lacking port
frontis. Solitary wormhole in last third, pages
a little yellowed at edges. Mod cloth-backed
bds.   *(Pirages)* **$150** [≈ £83]

Cervantes, Saavedra Miguel de

- The history and adventures of the most
renowned Don Quixote ... now made English
... by J[ohn] P[hillips]. London: Tho.
Hodgkin, 1687. 2nd edn. Sm folio. 8ff, 616
pp. 9 engvd plates. Contemp calf, crudely
rebacked. Wing C1774A.
(Argosy) **$500** [≈ £277]
- The history and adventures of the renowned
Don Quixote. Translated from the Spanish ...
by T. Smollett. London: for A. Millar ...,
1755. 1st edn of this trans. 2 vols. 4to. Errata
leaf at end, 28 copper plates inc frontis.
Minor soiling. 18th c diced russia.
(Pirages) **$450** [≈ £250]
- The history and adventures of the renowned
Don Quixote. Translated ... by T. Smollett.
London: 1782. 5th edn, crrctd. 4 vols. 12mo.
28 plates. Contemp tree-calf, worn, 2 jnts
cracked.   *(Robertshaw)* **£125** [≈ $225]
- The life and exploits of ... Don Quixote de la
Mancha. London: Tonson, 1742. 1st edn of
this trans, 1st iss. 2 vols. 4to. 68 engvd plates.
With a life of Cervantes with sep title (1738)
& port frontis. Some offsetting from plates.
Contemp calf. rebacked.
(Pirages) **$450** [≈ £250]

Chamberlayne, Edward

- Angliae notitiae, or the present state of
England: together with divers reflections
upon the ancient state thereof. In the Savoy:
for John Martyn, 1669. 1st edn. 12mo.
[x],516 pp. 2ff torn, reprd. Contemp calf,
rebacked. Author's pres copy to his nephew.
(Claude Cox) **£75** [≈ $135]

Chambers, Ephraim

- Cyclopaedia: or, an universal dictionary of
arts and sciences ... Fourth edition ...
London: 1741. 2 vols. Lge thick folio. Fldg
frontis, 19 (ex 20?) plates, some fldg. [with] A
supplement. 1753. Folio. 2 vols. 12 plates.
Old calf, rebacked.   *(Weiner)* **£200** [≈ $360]
- Cyclopaedia: or, an universal dictionary of
arts and sciences. London: Rivington,
1786-84-81-83. 5 vols (vol 5 of plates, without
title). Folio. 143 engvd plates, 10 pp printing
types, fldg plate of printing types. Contemp
tree-calf, 1 jnt splitting.
(Frew Mackenzie) **£850** [≈ $1,530]
- Cyclopaedia: or, an universal dictionary of
arts and sciences ... with the supplement and
modern improvements incorporated in one
alphabet by Abraham Rees. 1786-91. 5 vols.
Folio. Frontis, 169 plates. Contemp half calf,
very worn, bds detached.
(Weiner) **£300** [≈ $540]
- Cyclopaedia: or, an universal dictionary of
arts and sciences ... With the Supplement ...
by Abraham Rees. London: Rivington, 1786.
New edn. 4 vols. Folio. 144 engvd plates, 6ff
printing types (2 fldg). Contemp tree-calf,
rebacked, orig spines laid down.
(Gough) **£650** [≈ $1,170]
- Cyclopaedia: or, an universal dictionary of
arts and sciences. London: Rivington,
1786-79-81-83. 5 vols inc plate vol. Lge folio.
141 (ex 145) engvd plates, 8 pp folio type
specimen. Occas spots & stains, 3 short tears.
Contemp reversed calf, hinges cracked.
(Claude Cox) **£250** [≈ $450]

Chambers, William

- A dissertation on oriental gardening. London:
W. Griffin, 1772. 1st edn. 4to. Engvd title,
dedn leaf, x,94 pp, errata leaf. Contemp
mottled calf, rebacked retaining orig gilt spine
& label. Ex lib Kiddington Hall.
(Spelman) **£750** [≈ $1,350]

Chandler, Mary

- The description of Bath. A poem ... added
several poems by the same author. London:
for James Leake ... in Bath, 1736. 3rd (1st
8vo) edn. [xii],77,[xi] pp. Half-title, 5ff pub
advts at end. Some staining, free endpapers
missing. Contemp calf, rubbed & worn.
(Bennett) **£80** [≈ $144]
- A description of Bath: a poem. In a letter to
a friend. London: J. Roberts ..., [1733]. Folio.
Lacking half-title. Sl traces of damp-marking
in crnr not touching the text. A wide copy,
rebound in qtr calf, mrbld bds.
(C.R. Johnson) **£285** [≈ $513]

Chandler, Richard

- Travels in Asia Minor: or an account of a tour made at the expense of the Society of Dilettanti. Oxford: Clarendon Press, 1775. 1st edn. 4to. xiii,[i], 386,[i] pp. Fldg map (browned). Trivial spotting. Contemp tree calf, rebacked, orig spine laid down.
(Frew Mackenzie) **£360 [≈ $648]**
- Travels in Asia Minor: or an account of a tour made at the expense of the Society of Dilettanti. London: J. Dodsley, 1776. 2nd edn. 4to. xiv,[xiv], 283,[i advt],[i errata] pp. Fldg engvd map (laid down, ink stains in margs). Rec half calf, mrbld bds.
(Bow Windows) **£165 [≈ $297]**
- Travels in Greece ... a tour made at the expense of the Society of Dilettanti. Oxford: Clarendon Press, 1776. 1st edn. 4to. 4,xiv,[ii], 304pp. 7 engvd maps & plans (3 fldg). Early inscrptn on title. Contemp tree calf, jnts cracking, crnrs rubbed.
(Morrell) **£280 [≈ $504]**
- Travels in Greece: or an account of a tour made at the expense of the Society of Dilettanti. Oxford: Clarendon Press, 1776. 1st edn. 4to. [iv],304,[ii] pp. 7 engvd maps & plans (2 fldg). Trivial spotting. Contemp tree-calf, rebacked, orig spine laid down.
(Frew Mackenzie) **£360 [≈ $648]**

Chapman, George

- A treatise on education. In two parts. London: for the author, 1790. 4th edn. 242; 37 pp. Half-title. Early 19th c qtr calf.
(C.R. Johnson) **£220 [≈ $396]**

Chapone, Hester

- Letters on the improvement of the mind, addressed to a young lady. London: for J. Walter, 1773. 2nd edn. 2 vols. Sm 8vo. Contemp calf, hinges cracked, crnrs worn, tail of 1 backstrip reprd.
(Claude Cox) **£20 [≈ $36]**
- Letters on the improvement of the mind, addressed to a young lady. A new edition. Edinburgh: for Silvester Doig, 1793. 12mo. vi,210 pp. Contemp sheep, spine sl worn, upper jnt cracked. *(Burmester)* **£28 [≈ $50]**
- Miscellanies in prose and verse. London: for C. Dilly ..., 1787. 12mo. 216 pp. Half-title. Contemp tree-calf, spine gilt, jnts trifle worn.
(Burmester) **£30 [≈ $54]**

Character ...

- The character of a Popish successour ... See Settle, Elkenah

Charles I ...

- Eikon basilike: the pourtraicture of his sacred majestie in his solitudes and sufferings. 1649. Port, fldg plate. leaf bearing royal arms before port. Old calf, rebacked, new endpapers.
(Charles Cox) **£40 [≈ $72]**
- Eikon basilike: the pourtraicture of his sacred majestie in his solitudes and sufferings. Henry Hills, 1649. Red & black title, minor stains & soiling. Contemp panelled mor, spine heavily gilt, jnts cracking, a few minor abrasions. *(Pirages)* **$175 [≈ £97]**
- The papers which passed at Newcastle betwixt his sacred majestie and Mr. Al. Henderson ... London: Royston, 1649. Sm 8vo. Engvd frontis (cut short at foot). Early 19th c calf gilt. New Wing C2535.
(Marlborough) **£60 [≈ $108]**
- Reliquiae sacrae Carolinae. Or the works of the great monarch and glorious martyr King Charles the I. Hague: Samuell Browne, 1651. Some minor stains & marks. Old calf, 1 jnt weak. Wing C2073.
(Charles Cox) **£45 [≈ $81]**

Charles II ...

- Aurea dicta. The King's gracious words for the protestant religion of the Church of England, collected from his majesties letters ... 1681. 4to. 28 pp. Marg of title & last leaf torn. Lacking A1 (blank?). Buckram. STC C2929. *(Allen)* **$30 [≈ £16]**

Charles V ...

- The life of that most illustrious prince Charles V ... See Brune, Jean de la

Charleton, Walter

- Natural history of the passions ... In the Savoy [London]: for James Magnes ..., 1674. 1st edn. 8vo. [xlviii],188 pp. W'cut device on title, anntns on 1 page, sm rust holes & dampstains on 1 or 2 leaves. Contemp mottled calf, rebacked.
(Pickering) **$650 [≈ £361]**

Charlevoix, Father

- The history of Paraguay ... new, curious and interesting particulars ... full and authentic account of the establishments formed there by the Jesuits ... 1769. 2 vols. 8vo. vii,463; viii,415 pp. Contemp speckled calf, gilt spines chipped, jnts cracked.
(Edwards) **£225 [≈ $405]**

Charnock, Robert, et al.

- The tryals of Robert Charnock, Edward King ... for the horrid ... conspiracy to assassinate

... K[ing] William ... London: Samuel
Heyrick ..., 1696. Folio. [iv],76 pp. Some
staining, final leaf dusty. Disbound. Wing
W2255.   *(Clark)* **£38 [≈ $68]**

Charras, Moses
- The Royal Pharmacopoeia, Galenical and
chymical, according to the practice of the
most eminent and learned physicians of
France ... London: John Starkey ..., 1678.
[viii],272, 245,[xv] pp. Sm folio. 4 (ex 6)
plates. Contemp calf, worn at top of spine.
          (Goodrich) **$250 [≈ £138]**

Charters ...
- The Charters of the British Colonies in
America. J. Almon, [1774]. 8vo. ii,132 pp.
Wraps.   *(Farahar)* **£750 [≈ $1,350]**

Chastellux, Marquis de
- Travels in North America, in the years 1780,
1781, and 1782. Translated ... with notes ...
1787. 1st English edn. 2 vols. 8vo. xv,462;
xii,432 pp. 2 fldg engvd maps, 3 fldg plates,
all sl foxed. Contemp tree-calf, spines gilt,
rubbed, 1 spine cracked.
          (Edwards) **£500 [≈ $900]**
- Travels in North America, in the years 1780,
1781, and 1782. Translated ... with notes ...
London: Robinson, 1787. 2nd English edn. 2
vols. 8vo. xv,462; xii,432 pp. 2 fldg maps, 3
fldg plates. Some browning, mostly in margs.
19th c half mor, jnt reprd.
          (Morrell) **£300 [≈ $540]**

Chatterton, Thomas
- Miscellanies in prose and verse. London: for
Fielding & Walker, 1778. 1st edn. 8vo.
xxxii,245 pp, advt leaf. Engvd frontis, plate.
Prelims & final gathering a little crumpled &
waterstained. Contemp calf, hinges cracked.
          (Claude Cox) **£45 [≈ $81]**
- Miscellanies in prose and verse. London:
1778. 1st edn. 8vo. Engvd frontis, half-title.
Contemp calf, spine split.
          (Argosy) **$200 [≈ £111]**
- Poems supposed to have been written at
Bristol, by Thomas Rowley, and others ...
Cambridge: for the editor, 1794. 8vo.
xxix,[iii], 329 pp. Addtnl engvd title, plate.
Later half calf, mrbld bds, extremities
rubbed, upper jnt cracked.
          (Clark) **£120 [≈ $216]**

Chaucer, Geoffrey
- The Canterbury Tales ... To which are
added, an essay upon his languages and
versification ... London: for T. Payne,
1775-78. 5 vols. 8vo. A little light spotting.

Contemp gilt-ruled calf, rebacked.
          (Bennett) **£275 [≈ $495]**
- The Canterbury Tales ... To which are
added, an essay upon his languages and
versification ... London: T. Payne, 1775-78. 5
vols. Engvd port of Thomas Tyrwhitt.
Endpapers spotted, some light spotting
elsewhere. Contemp calf, rebacked,
extremities sl rubbed.
          (Frew Mackenzie) **£350 [≈ $630]**
- The Canterbury Tales ... completed in a
modern version. Oxford: J. Cooke, 1795. 3
vols. 8vo. Some staining to vol 2. Contemp
tree-calf, spines gilt.
          (Frew Mackenzie) **£120 [≈ $216]**
- The works. Compared with the former
editions, and many valuable mss ... London:
for Bernard Lintot, 1721. 1st edn. Folio.
[lii],628,81 glossary, 1 errata pp. 2 ports, 28
engvs in text. Some dust & other marks.
Contemp calf, rebacked, reprd.
          (Bow Windows) **£150 [≈ $270]**
- The works. Compared with the former
editions, and many valuable mss ... London:
for Bernard Lintot, 1721. Folio. [ii],626,82
pp. Port frontis, port, 25 ills in text. Contemp
blindstamped panelled calf, rebacked, sides
restored.   *(Frew Mackenzie)* **£275 [≈ $495]**

Chauncy, Charles
- Ministers cautioned against the occasions of
contempt. A sermon ... Boston: Rogers &
Fowle, 1744. 1st edn. 54 pp.
          (Jenkins) **$50 [≈ £27]**

Cheselden, William
- The anatomy of the human body. London:
Cliff, Jackson & Innys, 1713. 1st edn. 23 fldg
plates, advt leaf at end. Some stains &
discoloration, 1 plate torn, contemp ink
inscrptns on title & another leaf. Half mod
calf, gilt, mrbld bds.
          (John Smith) **£175 [≈ $315]**
- The anatomy of the human body. London:
1792. 13th edn. 8vo. Frontis, engvd title, 40
engvd plates. Qtr calf.
          (Halewood) **£98 [≈ $176]**
- The anatomy of the human body. Boston: J.
White, S. Hall ..., 1795. 1st Amer edn. 8vo.
vi,350 pp. 40 engvd plates (browning &
offsetting). 1 sgntr sl sprung. Contemp tree
calf.   *(Antiq Sc)* **$325 [≈ £180]**
- Osteographia, or the anatomy of the bones.
London: [Bowyer], 1733. 1st edn. Lge paper.
Lge folio. Engvd frontis, engvd vignette on
title, engvd arms, 56 engvd plates each in 2
states. Some marg soiling, inscrptn on title.
Uncut in contemp bds, worn, rebacked.
          (Quaritch) **$3,750 [≈ £2,083]**

Chesterfield, Philip D. Stanhope, Earl of

- The case of the Hanover forces in the pay of Great Britain, impartially and freely examined. London: for T. Cooper .., 1743. 83 pp. Half-title. Disbound.
                    (C.R. Johnson) £50 [≈ $90]
- A farther vindication of the case of the Hanover Troops: in which the uniform influence of the Hanover-Rudder is clearly detected and expos'd ... London: M. Cooper, 1743. 88 pp. Disbound.
                    (C.R. Johnson) £50 [≈ $90]
- The interest of Hanover steadily pursued since the A-----N. being a sequel to ... The Interest of Great Britain Steadily Pursued ... London: M. Cooper, 1743. 51 pp. Disbound.
                    (C.R. Johnson) £55 [≈ $99]
- Letters ... to his son, Philip Stanhope, late Envoy Extraordinary at the Court of Dresden. London: for J. Dodsley, 1774. 1st edn. 2 vols. Folio. Some v sl foxing. Contemp calf, gilt crest on cvrs.   *(Minkoff)* £500 [≈ £277]
- Letters ... to his son. Dublin: Lynch, 1775. 1st Dublin edn. 4 vols. 8vo. Frontis. Contemp calf.   *(Emerald Isle)* £85 [≈ $153]
- A vindication of a late pamphlet, intitled, the Case of the Hanover Troops Considered ... London: T. Cooper, 1743. 56 pp. Half-title. Variant without errata list on p 56. Disbound.
                    (C.R. Johnson) £50 [≈ $90]

Chetwind, Charles

- A narrative of the depositions of Robert Jenison ... plainly proving that William Ireland, lately executed for High Treason, was in London, the nineteenth of August, 1678. London: 1679. 1st edn. Folio. 13 pp. Disbound. Wing C3792.
                    (Robertshaw) £20 [≈ $36]
- A narrative of the depositions of Robert Jenison ... plainly proving that William Ireland ... was in London, the nineteenth of August, 1678. London: 1679. 4to. [18] pp. Disbound.   *(Halewood)* £20 [≈ $36]

Cheyne, George

- The English malady, or, treatise of nervous diseases of all kinds ... in three parts ... London: for G. Strahan ..., 1733. 1st edn. 8vo. [vi],xxxii,370, [vi advt] pp. Divisional titles. Some light browning in some margs. Contemp mottled calf.
                    (Barbary) £230 [≈ $414]
- An essay of health and long life. London: 1724. 1st edn. Contemp calf, jnts cracked.
                    (Goodrich) $295 [≈ £163]
- An essay of health and long life. London: 1724. 1st edn. 8vo. Panelled calf.

                    (Halewood) £85 [≈ $153]
- An essay of health and long life. London: 1725. 4th edn. 232 pp. Title wrinkled & stained, old careless repr of tear. Rec qtr lea.
                    (Fye) $150 [≈ £83]
- An essay of health and long life. London: 1725. 6th edn. Cr 8vo. 232 pp. owner's stamp at hd of title. Contemp calf, jnts tender.
                    (Halewood) £65 [≈ $117]
- An essay of health and long life. London: 1734. 8th edn. 8vo. [iv],xx, [xxiv],232 pp. Contemp calf, worn.   *(Pollak)* £30 [≈ $54]

Chillingworth, William

- The religion of Protestants a safe way to salvation ... The second edition. London: John Clark, 1638. Folio in 6's. [xxx],393 pp. No endpapers, a few margs soiled. Contemp calf, rebacked. STC 5139.
                    (Clark) £75 [≈ $135]
- The religion of Protestants a safe way to salvation; or, an answer to a book entitled 'Mercy and Truth' ... Fifth edition. London: printed by M.C. ..., 1684. Roy 8vo. Contemp calf, rec rebacked, crnrs rubbed. Wing 3892.
                    (Stewart) £75 [≈ $135]

Chomel, J.B.L.

- An historical dissertation on a particular species of gangrenous sore throat ... translated from the French ... London: 1753. 8vo. xvi,128 pp. Welcome Historical Lib stamp on title verso. Linen-backed bds.
                    (Hemlock) $225 [≈ £125]

Chomel, Noel

- Dictionnaire oeconomique: or, the family dictionary ... Done into English ... Dublin: J. Watts ..., 1727. 2 vols. Folio. Many w'cut ills. Occas browning. Contemp calf, rebacked, crnrs reprd, calf a little pitted.
                    (Clark) £380 [≈ $684]

Christian ...

- The Christian's useful companion ... to which is added The companion to the altar, and The whole book of psalms. Birmingham: Martin, 1776. 2 works in 1 vol. Contemp black mor, gilt, a.e.g., worn, hd of spine chipped.
                    (Marlborough) £90 [≈ $162]
- The sincere Christian's devout companion, or, how to live one day to God ... [Nottingham?:] 1798. 8 pp. Uncut & unopened.   *(C.R. Johnson)* £55 [≈ $99]

Christian Piety ...

- The causes of the decay of Christian piety ... See Allestree, Richard

Chrysal ...

- Chrysal; or the adventures of a guinea ... See Johnstone, Charles

Church of England ...

- The claims of the Church of England ... See Fleming, Caleb

Church, Thomas

- An analysis of the philosophical works of the late Lord Viscount Bolingbroke. Dublin: Watson, 1756. Sm 8vo. Sl foxing. Contemp qtr calf, worn. *(Marlborough)* **£300** [≈ $540]

Churchill, Charles

- Poems. London: for the author, 1763. 1st edn. 4to. Contemp calf, inner jnts reprd. *(Argosy)* **$200** [≈ £111]
- Poems. London: for the author, 1763 (vol I); London: for John Churchill ..., 1765 (vol II). 1st edns. 2 vols in 1. 4to. 2 half-titles. Lacking final blank vol I. Rebound in half calf, mrbld bds. *(Hughes)* **£75** [≈ $135]
- Poems. In two volumes. Dublin: Peter Wilson, 1764. Sm 8vo. [6],182, [2],[2],199 pp. Port frontis. Contemp calf. *(Spelman)* **£40** [≈ $72]
- Poems. In two volumes. London: 1766. 8vo. Contemp calf. *(Argosy)* **$125** [≈ £69]
- Poems in two volumes. The third edition. London: for John Churchill, 1766. 2 vols. 8vo. [4],369; [2],330 pp. 2 half-titles. Mod buckram. *(Claude Cox)* **£30** [≈ $54]
- Poems. In three volumes ... To which is added, the life of the author. Adorned with cuts. London: for J. Wilkes, 1767. 6th edn. 3 vols in 1. 12mo. Half-title in vol 1. Contemp patterned calf, new endpapers, scuffed. *(Charles Cox)* **£40** [≈ $72]
- The works. In four volumes. The fifth edition. London: for John Churchill ..., 1774. Engvd frontis & vignette titles in 1st 3 vols. Contemp calf, red labels. From the library of Colquhoun of Luss. *(C.R. Johnson)* **£325** [≈ $585]

Churchman, John

- An account of the Gospel labours and Christian experiences of ... late of Nottingham in Pennsylvania ... Philadelphia printed, London reprinted: 1780. 8vo. Contemp calf, rebacked. *(Waterfield's)* **£60** [≈ $108]

Churchyard, Thomas

- The worthiness of Wales, a poem ... Reprinted from the edition of 1587, for Thomas Evans, 1776. 8vo. xvi,128 pp. Half-title. Occas trivial browning. Uncut in contemp qtr calf, vell tips, mrbld sides, rebacked. *(Frew Mackenzie)* **£95** [≈ $171]
- The worthiness of Wales, a poem ... Reprinted from the edition of 1587, for Thomas Evans, 1776. 8vo. 128 pp. Contemp calf. *(Robertshaw)* **£25** [≈ $45]

Chute, Francis

- The Petticoat: an heroi-comical poem. In two books. By Mr. Gay [pseud. Probably Francis Chute]. London: for R. Burleigh [i.e. Edmund Curll], 1716. 8vo. [iv],39 pp. Half-title. Sl dampstained towards end. Orig blue ptd wraps. *(Burmester)* **£75** [≈ $135]

Cibber, Colley

- An apology for the life of Mr. Colley Cibber, comedian and late patentee of the theatre-royal. With an historical view of the stage during his own time. London: for the author, 1740. 1st edn. [viii],346 pp. Lacking port frontis. Orig bds, untrimmed edges. *(Pirages)* **$750** [≈ £416]
- An apology for the life of Mr. Colley Cibber, comedian and late patentee of the theatre-royal. With an historical view of the stage during his own time. Dublin: for George Faulkner, 1740. 4th edn. Orig calf. *(C.R. Johnson)* **£68** [≈ $122]
- A letter from Mr. Cibber to Mr. Pope, inquiring into the motives that might induce him in his satyrical works, to be so frequently fond of Mr. Cibber's name. London: L. Lewis, 1742. 2nd edn. 66 pp. Half title. rebound in bds. *(C.R. Johnson)* **£75** [≈ $135]

Cicero, Marcus Tullius

- Cato, or an essay on old-age, with remarks [and] Laelius, or an essay on friendship; with remarks ... London: Dodsley, 1773-77. 1st edns. 2 vols. 8vo. Title vignettes, errata leaves. Contemp calf, jnts worn, backs gilt. *(Argosy)* **$50** [≈ £27]
- The first book of Tullies Offices. Translated grammatically ... according to the propriety of our English tongue ... London: for Thomas Mann, 1616. Sm 8vo. [14],320 pp. Lacking A1 blank, crnr of b5 torn away affecting 4 words. Early 20th c half calf. STC 5288. *(Karmiole)* **$200** [≈ £111]
- Three bookes of duties to Marcus his sonne. [London: Richard Tottell], 1583. 10.168ff. Parallel English & Latin text. A few words in old hand on title, some minor darkening. 19th c mottled sheep, gilt, minor scuffing. *(Pirages)* **$600** [≈ £333]

Cipriani

- Cipriani's rudiments of drawing engraved by Bartolozzi. G. Bartolozzi, n.d. [ca 1786]. Obl folio. 10 plates in soft-ground etching, inc dec title. Complete as issued, without the 16 pp text. Plates sl discold. Contemp paper wraps, stitched as issued. *(Spelman)* **£110 [≈ $198]**

Civil Wars ...

- An historical and critical review of the Civil Wars in Ireland ... See Curry, John

Clamours ...

- The clamours of the Dissenters, against the Bill to prevent occasional conformity examined ... By a true Church-of-England-Man. London: 1703. Folio. 16 pp.
  (C.R. Johnson) **£20 [≈ $36]**

Clarendon and Whitlock ...

- Clarendon and Whitlock compar'd ... See Oldmixon, John

Clarendon, Edward, Earl of

- The history of the Rebellion and Civil Wares in Ireland. London: Wilford, 1720. 1st edn. Port. Contemp calf, rebacked.
  (Emerald Isle) **£125 [≈ $225]**
- The life ... written by himself. Oxford: 1759. 1st edn. Folio. Port. Lge paper. Mod half calf.
  (Robertshaw) **£80 [≈ $144]**
- The life ... Oxford: 1760. 2nd, 1st 8vo, edn. 2 vols. [x],512; 525,928 pp. Contemp calf, rebacked. *(Young's)* **£56 [≈ $100]**
- The life ... written by himself. Oxford: Clarendon Printing House, 1760. 3rd 8vo edn. 2 vols. Rather later calf, backstrip rubbed, 1 front jnt cracked.
  (Waterfield's) **£50 [≈ $90]**

Claridge, John

- The shepherd of Banbury's rules to judge the changes of the weather, grounded on forty years experience ... London: W. Bickerton, 1744. 8vo in 4s. viii,43 pp. A bit cropped at ft. Old qtr mor, rubbed. *(Clark)* **£32 [≈ $57]**

Clark, J.

- Observations on the diseases which prevail in long voyages to hot countries, particularly ... the East Indies; ... the same diseases ... in Great Britain. Volume I [all published]. London: 1792. 2nd edn. xxii,252 pp. Orig bds, spine defective, hinges cracked.
  (Whitehart) **£40 [≈ $72]**

Clark, Samuel

- The British gauger: or, trader and officer's

instructor ... rules of vulgar and decimal arithmetic ... London: for J. Nourse, 1765. 2nd edn. Sm 8vo. [iv],v,[i], 432, *433-*448, 433,[1],x pp. 6 fldg engvd plates (1 hand-cold). Sl browning at end. Rec qtr calf.
  (Burmester) **£240 [≈ $432]**

Clarke, Alured

- An essay towards the character of her late Majesty Caroline, Queen Consort of Great Britain. London: J. & P. Knapton, 1738. Half-title, vignette title. 46 pp. Disbound.
  (C.R. Johnson) **£32 [≈ $57]**

Clarke, H.

- A dissertation on the summation of infinite converging series with algebraic divisors. London: for the author, 1779. 4to. xx,222 pp. 2 fldg plates. Contemp bds, roan spine gilt, v sl rubbed & little worn.
  (Whitehart) **£60 [≈ $108]**

Clarke, James

- A survey of the lakes of Cumberland, Westmoreland, and Lancashire ... [Penrith?:] for the author, 1789. 2nd edn. Folio. xlii,194 pp. 11 lge fldg town plans & maps, 2 plates (some wear at flds, 1 shaved at tail marg). Rather browned. Mod calf.
  (Kerr) **£600 [≈ $1,080]**

Clarke, Samuel

- A reply to the objections of Robert Nelson ... London: for James Knapton, 1714. 8vo. Contemp panelled calf, red mor labels, a little rubbed, jnts cracking.
  (Waterfield's) **£45 [≈ $81]**

Clarke, Samuel

- The historian's guide: or Britain's remembrancer ... London: 1688. 3rd imp. Sm 8vo. Lacking leaf before title. [vi],190,[6 advts] pp. Title roughly reprd, occas tiny wormholes. Old worn sheep. Wing C4521.
  (Bow Windows) **£20 [≈ $36]**

Clarke, Sa[muel]

- A geographicall description of all the countries in the known worlds ... London: for Thomas Newberry, 1657. 4to. [ii],225,[viii] pp. Faint staining in fore-marg. Mod half calf. Wing C4516. *(Kerr)* **£175 [≈ $315]**

Clarkson, Thomas

- An essay on the impolicy of the African slave trade. In two parts. London: J. Phillips, 1788. Orig blue bds, paper spine.
  (C.R. Johnson) **£320 [≈ $576]**
- An essay on the impolicy of the African slave

trade. London: Phillips, 1788. 2nd edn. 8vo.
Sl marg foxing. New wraps.
(Marlborough) £110 [≃ $198]
- An essay on the slavery and commerce of the
human species, particularly the African;
translated from a Latin dissertation ...
Dublin: Porter, 1786. 8vo. 256 pp. Irish calf.
(Emerald Isle) £250 [≃ $450]

Clavijero, F.
- The history of Mexico ... London: Robinson,
1787. 1st English edn. 2 vols. xxvii,[4],476;
[4],463 pp. 2 engvd maps, 25 plates. Rebound
in 3/4 calf over bds, orig lea labels.
(Argonaut) $750 [≃ £416]

Clayton, John
- Topicks in the laws of England. London: for
William Leake, 1646. 8vo. Mod panelled calf,
sm snag at hd of backstrip. Wing C4612.
(Waterfield's) £100 [≃ $180]

Clayton, Robert
- The chronology of the Hebrew Bible
vindicated ... London: for J. Brindley, 1748.
4to. 2 engvd maps. Contemp calf, mod paper
labels. *(Waterfield's)* £80 [≃ $144]

Clement XIV
- Interesting letters of the late Pope Clement
XIV translated ... Newcastle: for W.
Charnley, 1777. Engvd frontis, contemp
b'plate. Pub bds, backstrip mildly defective,
front jnt breaking. *(Waterfield's)* £25 [≃ $45]

Clerk ...
- The clerk's magazine: or law-repository ...
Dublin: Oli Nelson, 1759. 12mo. Sl marg
worming. *(Emerald Isle)* £55 [≃ $99]
- The clerk's manual: or ... all the most
improved forms of declarations, pleas, general
issues ... now used in the Court of Kings
Bench. Sawbridge, 1678. 1st edn. 8vo.
[xxiv],464 pp. Sl worming in gutter
throughout. Contemp sheep, hd of spine
reprd. *(Frew Mackenzie)* £115 [≃ $207]
- The young clerk's magazine: or English law-
repository ... London: 1763. 12mo. 4th edn,
revsd & crrctd. Some minor worming, mainly
marginal. Contemp sheep, rubbed.
(Robertshaw) £25 [≃ $45]

Clerke, Richard
- Sermons ... Published for the common good
by Charles White. London: Cotes for
Alchorn, 1637. 1st edn. Folio. 577 pp. Bds,
jnts cracked. STC 5410. *(Argosy)* $75 [≃ £41]

Clery, Jean Baptiste Cant
- A journal of the occurrences at the Temple
during the confinement of Louis XVI, King
of France ... London: 1798. 1st English edn.
8vo. 2 engvd ills, 1 facsimile. Occas light
foxing. Contemp half green mor, gilt, mrbld
paper bds a bit rubbed.
(Deighton Bell) £40 [≃ $72]
- A journal of the occurrences at the Temple
during the confinement of Louis XVI, King
of France ... London: 1798. 1st English edn.
8vo. 2 plates, final leaf of facsimile, half-title,
16 pp list of subscribers. Contemp watered
silk case, rather loose. *(Stewart)* £85 [≃ $153]
- A journal of the occurrences at the Temple
during the confinement of Louis XVI ...
London: Baylis, 1798. 1st English edn. 8vo.
258 pp. 2 engvd ills, 1 facs. Contemp half
mor. *(Lloyd-Roberts)* £35 [≃ $63]

Cleveland, John
- The idol of the clownes, or, insurrection of
Wat the Tyler, with his fellow kings of the
commons. London: 1654. 1st edn, iss with
"Kings". 16mo. xii,148 pp. Old calf, reprd
with tape. *(Argosy)* $300 [≃ £166]
- Poems; with additions never before printed.
London: for John Williams, 1669. 16mo.
[Bound with] Cleveland, J: Poems, orations ...
Fourth edition. London: N. Brooks, 1668.
Old calf. Wing C4698 & C4677
(Argosy) $200 [≃ £111]

Cleveland, Mr.
- The life and entertaining adventures of Mr.
Cleveland, natural son of Oliver Cromwell,
written by himself. London: T. Astley, 1741.
2nd edn. 3 vols. 12mo. Contemp calf.
Fictitious. *(Argosy)* $200 [≃ £111]

Clifton, Francis
- The state of physic ancient and modern,
briefly considered: with a plan for the
improvement of it. London: Bowyer, 1732.
8vo. [20],192 pp. Sgntrs on title. Contemp
panelled calf, rebacked.
(Goodrich) $195 [≃ £108]
- The state of physic ancient and modern,
briefly considered: with a plan for the
improvement of it. London: Nourse, 1732.
1st edn. 8vo. 192 pp. Fldg table. Lacking
front endpaper. Old calf, a little worn.
(Oasis) $125 [≃ £69]

Clinton, Sir Henry
- Memorandums, etc., etc. respecting the
unprecedented treatment which the army has
met with respecting plunder taken after a

siege, and of which plunder the navy ... divided their more than ample share, now 14 years since. London: 1794. 1st edn. 106,8 pp. Sewn. *(Jenkins)* **$110 [≈ £61]**

Clio ...
- Clio: or, a discourse on taste ... See Usher, James

Clube, William
- The Omnium; containing the journal of a late three days tour into France; curious and extraordinary anecdotes ... miscellaneous pieces in prose and verse. Ipswich: George Jermyn, 1798. Orig pink bds, uncut.
(C.R. Johnson) **£110 [≈ $198]**

Coade, Eleanor
- A descriptive catalogue of Coade's artificial stone manufactory ... London: 1784. [with] Etchings of Coade's artificial stone manufacture, London: n.d. [ca 1778-79]. 2 works in 1. 4to & obl folio. [ii],31 pp; 67 etched plates. Occas minor soiling. Lib binding. *(Burmester)* **£3,500 [≈ $6,300]**

Cochrane, Sir Robert
- A detection of the falsehood, abuse, and misrepresentations in a late libel, intitled, the Life of Sir Robert Cochrane. London: T. Cooper, 1735. 60 pp. Disbound.
(C.R. Johnson) **£28 [≈ $50]**
- The life of Sir Robert Cochrane, Prime-Minister to James III of Scotland. London: A. Dodd, 1734. 2nd edn. Rebound in bds.
(C.R. Johnson) **£28 [≈ $50]**

Cockburn, John
- The unfortunate Englishman ... the distresses and adventures ... London: W. Cavell, 1794. 5th edn. Sm 8vo. vi,120 pp. Engvd frontis. Titles, frontis & some leaves dust-soiled. Rec panelled calf. *(Morrell)* **£95 [≈ $171]**

Cocker, E.
- Cocker's decimal arithmetick, wherein is shewed the nature and use of decimal fractions ... London: 1695. [16],436 pp. 2 sm contemp sgntrs on title, sm marg tear reprd, foxed. New lea. *(Whitehart)* **£120 [≈ $216]**

Cockman, Thomas
- Tully's Offices. In English. London: Owen Lloyd ..., 1722. 4th edn, crrctd. 12mo. [2],viii, 265,[25 index] pp. Some soiling. Contemp calf, a little worn.
(Claude Cox) **£18 [≈ $32]**

Cohausen, Johann Heinrich
- Hermippus redivivus, or the sage's triumph over old age and the grave ... prolonging the life and increasing the vigour of man ... London: for J. Nourse, 1749. 8vo. [8],249 pp. Tear in 1 marg with loss of 5 letters. Contemp half calf, top bd nearly loose.
(Claude Cox) **£60 [≈ $108]**

Coke, Arundel
- The tryal and condemnation of Arundel Coke ... and John Woodburne ... for felony, in slitting the nose of Edward Crispe ... London: for John Darby ..., 1723. Folio. 37,[1] pp. Disbound. *(Burmester)* **£45 [≈ $81]**

Coke, Edward
- The first part of the institutes of the laws of England. Or a commentary upon Littleton ... 1639. 4th edn, crrctd. Folio. 395 pp. Title & 2nd port worn, A3 re-mtd, contemp ms anntns in text, waterstained, worn. Contemp calf. STC 1587. *(Edwards)* **£280 [≈ $504]**
- The fourth part of the institutes of the laws of England. Concerning the jurisdiction of the courts. 1681. 6th edn. Folio. 364,ii pp. W'cut port frontis. Calf, rebacked. Wing C4933.
(Edwards) **£150 [≈ $270]**
- The second part of the institutes of the laws of England. London: Flesher & Young, 1642. 1st edn. Folio. [x],745,[xliii] pp. Some light dampstaining & soiling, title & port sl frayed. Contemp calf, sl worn at hd of spine. Wing C4948. *(Frew Mackenzie)* **£180 [≈ $324]**

Coke, Sir Edward
- The compleate copy-holder. Wherein is contained a learned discourse of the antiquity and nature of manors and copy-holds ... London: for W. Cooke, 1641. 4to. Title reprd at crnrs. New calf. Wing C4912.
(Charles Cox) **£135 [≈ $243]**

Coke, Dr. Thomas & Moore, Henry
- The life of the Rev. John Wesley, A.M. ... London: G. Paramore, 1792. Port frontis (stained around edges), 4 pp advts at end. Contemp half calf, mrbld bds, worn, jnts cracked & tender. *(Clark)* **£40 [≈ $72]**

Colbatch, John
- Four treatises of physick and chirurgery ... The second edition corrected and enlarged. London: for J.D. ..., 1698. 1st coll edn. Sm 8vo. xxiii,[i], 122,86 pp, divisional title to each part. Contemp mottled calf, end of upper jnt cracked, a little rubbed.
(Pickering) **$550 [≈ £305]**

- The generous physician, or medicine made easy ... the causes, symptoms, and method proper for cure of several distempers ... London: for J. Roberts, [1733]. 1st edn. 8vo. [ii],iv,90 pp. Some foxing, outer leaves a bit soiled. Disbound. *(Burmester)* £110 [≈ $198]

Collection ...
- A collection of above three hundred receipts ... See Kettilby, Mary
- A collection of all the statutes now in force, relating to the excise on beer, ale, and other liquors ... London: John Baskett, 1722-30. 2 vols. 12mo. Sep pagination. Partly black letter. Contemp calf, jnts cracked.
  (Goodrich) $495 [≈ £275]
- A collection of cases, and other discourses, lately written to recover dissenters to the communion of the Church of England. London: for Thomas Bassett ..., 1694. 2nd edn. Folio. New grey bds. Wing 5116.
  (Stewart) £50 [≈ $90]
- A collection of testimonies concerning several ministers of the Gospel amongst the people called Quakers, deceased. London: Luke Hinde, 1760. 8vo. [xii],372 pp. Inscrptn at ft of title. Lacking front flyleaf, back flyleaf wormed. Contemp calf, spine hd chipped.
  (Bow Windows) £30 [≈ $54]
- A complete collection of all the marine treatises subsisting between Great Britain and France, Spain, Portugal, Austria, Russia ... commencing in the year 1546 ... 1779. 8vo. 400 pp. 1 leaf partly detchd, top edge soiled. Mod buckram, spine gilt.
  (Edwards) £120 [≈ $216]
- A new general collection of voyages and travels ... Europe, Asia, Africa and America ... Thomas Astley, 1745-47. 1st edn. 4 vols. 4 engvd frontis, 288 engvd maps & plates, many fldg, occas sl flaws in margs. Contemp tree-calf, some jnts reprd, sl rubbing.
  (Frew Mackenzie) £1,500 [≈ $2,700]

Colledge, Stephen
- The arraignment, tryal and condemnation of Stephen Colledge for High-Treason ... August 1681. London: Thomas Bassett ..., 1681. 1st edn. Folio. 102 [i.e. 106] pp. Mod wraps. Wing A3761. [Bound with 3 related leaflets]. *(Argosy)* $125 [≈ £69]

Colliber, Samuel
- Columna rostrata: or, a critical history of the English sea-affairs. London: for R. Robinson ..., 1727. 1st edn. 312,[8] pp. Title rehinged. Old calf, rebacked. *(Young's)* £110 [≈ $198]

Collier, George
- Songs, duets, trios, &c. in the dramatic romance of Selima and Azor, as performed at the Theatre-Royal ... London: for J. Wilkie, 1776. 1st edn. 8vo. 22,[2] pp. Half-title, final blank. Disbound.   *(Burmester)* £25 [≈ $45]

Collier, Jane
- An essay on the art of ingeniously tormenting; with proper rules for the exercise of that pleasant art ... London: for A. Millar ..., 1753. 1st edn. 8vo. 234 pp. Engvd frontis. Old calf, front bd detchd.
  (Young's) £45 [≈ $81]

Collier, Jeremy
- An ecclesiastical history of Great Britain ... London: for S. Keble ..., 1708-14. 1st edn. 2 vols. Folio. Engvd frontis. Contemp panelled calf, rebacked. *(Lloyd-Roberts)* £150 [≈ $270]
- Essays upon several moral subjects, in two parts. London: for R. Sare, 1703. 5th edn. [Bound with] Essays, Part III. London: for H. Rhodes ..., 1705. 1st edn. 3 pts in 1 vol. 8vo. Contemp calf, spine v rubbed, hinges tender.
  (Lloyd-Roberts) £50 [≈ $90]
- The great historical, geographical ... dictionary. London: for H. Rhodes ..., 1701. 2nd edn, revsd. [with] A supplement ... For C. Collier, 1727. 2nd edn. [with] An appendix ... Geo. Jane, 1721. 4 vols in 3. Folio. 2 vols contemp polished calf; 1 vol reversed calf.
  (Lloyd-Roberts) £200 [≈ $360]
- A short history of the immorality and profaness of the English stage ... London: for S. Keble ..., 1698. 3rd edn. 8vo. Contemp mottled calf. Wing C5265.
  (Traylen) £120 [≈ $216]
- A short history of the immorality and profaness of the English stage ... London: for S. Keble ..., 1699. 4th edn. Front free endpaper loose. Contemp panelled calf, jnts cracked, trivial loss of lea on front cvr. Wing C5266. *(Waterfield's)* £50 [≈ $90]
- An universal, historical, geographical ... dictionary, exactly describing ... all kingdoms, common-wealths ... in the known world. London: J. Hartley, 1703. 2 vols. 8vo. Unpaginated, ptd double column. Contemp panelled calf, rebacked, orig spines laid down.
  (Frew Mackenzie) £80 [≈ $144]

Collier, John
- The miscellaneous works ... containing his view of the Lancashire dialect ... Also his poem of the Flying Dragon ... Manchester, Haslingden: 1793. Cr 8vo. Port frontis, 9 plates. Lacking final leaf of Flying Dragon,

rather browned. Rec buckram.
(Stewart) **£45 [≈ $81]**
- A view of the Lancashire dialect ... Manchester: for the author, 1775. 8vo. 203 pp. 9 engvd plates inc port frontis. [Bound with, as usual] The battle of the flying dragon ... Manchester: for the author ..., n.d. 8vo. 33 pp. Half-title, plate. 19th c mor.
(Frew Mackenzie) **£130 [≈ $234]**

Collignon, Charles
- The miscellaneous works. Cambridge: Hodson, 1786. 4to. [5],345, errata leaf. Half-title, subscribers' list. Calf, jnts weak.
(Goodrich) **$145 [≈ £80]**

Collins, Anthony
- A discourse on free-thinking occasion'd by the rise and growth of a sect called Freethinkers. London: 1713. 1st edn. vi,3-178 pp. Contemp panelled calf, rebacked.
(Waterfield's) **£185 [≈ $333]**

Collins, Arthur
- Proceedings, precedents, and arguments, on claims and controversies concerning Baronies by writ and other orders ... London: for Thomas Watton, 1734. Folio. [ii],4, 415,[xiii] pp. Sl stain in fore-marg of some leaves. Contemp panelled calf, rebacked.
(Kerr) **£250 [≈ $450]**

Collins, William
- The poetical works ... to which are added, Mr. Hammond's elegies. Glasgow: Foulis, 1775. 12mo. Contemp calf, rather rubbed, lacking label. *(Waterfield's)* **£30 [≈ $54]**
- The poetical works ... to which is prefixed a life of the author by Dr. Johnson. London: T. Bensley, 1798. 8vo. 20 half-page engvs. Later half calf. *(Robertshaw)* **£36 [≈ $64]**

Colloquia Chirurgica ...
- Colloquia chirurgica ... See Handley, James

Collyer, Mary (trans.)
- The death of Abel. In five books. Attempted from the German of Mr. Gessner. London: for W. Oxlade, 1778. 12mo. 150,[5 advt] pp. Engvd frontis. Contemp calf, jnts cracked.
(Burmester) **£15 [≈ $27]**

Colman, Benjamin
- The doctrine and law of the Holy Sabbath ... preached at the lecture in Boston ... Boston: T. Fleet, 1725. 1st edn. 43 pp.
(Jenkins) **$55 [≈ £30]**

Colman, Benjamin & Cooper, William
- Two sermons preached in Boston ... to ask the effusion of the spirit of grace on their children, and on the children of the town. Boston: for J. Edwards, 1723. Sm 4to. [4],iv,38, [2],ii,36 pp. Half-title. Sl browning, lacking final blank. Mod half mor.
(Reese) **$850 [≈ £472]**

Colman, George, Jr.
- The mountaineers. A comic opera. As performed in the theatre at Boston. Boston [Mass]: for William P. Blake, 1796. 2nd Boston edn. 12mo. 44,[3] pp. Contemp mrbld wraps, sheep backstrip, chipped at extremities. *(Karmiole)* **$100 [≈ £55]**

Colonization ...
- History of the colonization of the free states of antiquity ... See Barron, William

Colquhoun, Patrick
- A treatise on the police of the metropolis ... various crimes and misdemeanors by which ... property and security are ... injured and endangered. London: Dilly, 1796. 3rd edn, revsd & enlgd. 8vo. xvii,[vi], 440,xxviii pp. Fldg diag. Contemp half calf, mrbld bds.
(Frew Mackenzie) **£150 [≈ $270]**

Columella ...
- Columella; or, the distressed anchoret ... See Graves, Richard

Combe, William
- The diaboliad, a poem. Dedicated to the worst man in his Majesty's dominions. Second edition. London: for G. Kearsley, 1677 [i.e. 1777]. 4to. Half-title. Disbound.
(C.R. Johnson) **£20 [≈ $36]**
- The Royal interview: a fragment. London: Logographic Press, 1789. 61,1 advts pp. Disbound. *(C.R. Johnson)* **£48 [≈ $86]**

Comber, Thomas
- Friendly and seasonable advice to the Roman Catholicks of England. By "a Charitable Hand". London: for Charles Brome, 1686. 4th edn, enlgd. 12mo. [22],143,[3] pp. Old calf, rubbed, jnts weak. Wing C5470.
(Karmiole) **$75 [≈ £41]**

Combrune, Michael
- An essay on brewing. With a view of establishing the principles of the art. London: R. & J. Dodsley, 1758. 214 pp. Half-title, vignette title. Contemp calf.
(C.R. Johnson) **£350 [≈ $630]**

Comenius, Joh. Amos
- Visible world: or, a nomenclature, and pictures of all the chief things that are in the world and of men's employment therein. Translated ... London: for S. Leacroft, 1777. 12th edn. Cr 8vo. 153 w'cuts in text. Mod crushed mor, rather thumbed.
(Stewart) **£85 [≈ $153]**

Comparison ...
- A comparison of the spirit of the Whigs and Jacobites ... a discourse delivered to an audience of gentlemen in Edinburgh, Dec 24. 1745. Edinburgh: R. Fleming, 1746. 25 pp. Mod wraps.   *(C.R. Johnson)* **£45 [≈ $81]**

Compleat Sheriff ...
- The compleat sheriff. Wherein is set forth, his office and authority ... to which is added, the office and duty of coroners. London: for John Walthoe, 1696. 1st edn. 8vo. 442 pp. Contemp calf, crnrs bumped. Wing C5653.
(Edwards) **£200 [≈ $360]**

Condorcet, M.J.A.N.
- Outlines of an historical view of the progress of the human mind ... Phila: 1796. 1st Amer edn. 12mo. 293 pp. Some foxing & browning, front flyleaf missing. Orig calf, rubbed, edge of front bd blackened. *(Elgen)* **$325 [≈ £180]**

Conduct ...
- The conduct of his Grace the D-ke of Ar--le for the last four years review'd together with his Grace's speech April 15th, 1740. Upon the state of the nation. London: Mr. Wedd, 1740. 57 pp. Disbound.
(C.R. Johnson) **£25 [≈ $45]**
- The conduct of Queen Elizabeth towards the neighbouring nations, and particularly Spain, compared with that of James I, by Palaeophilus Anglicanus. London: J. Robinson, 1629. 8vo. 62 pp. Mod qtr lea.
(Argosy) **$175 [≈ £97]**
- The conduct of the Admiralty in the late expedition of the enemy to the Coast of Ireland, as stated in the House of Commons on the 3rd of March, 1797. London: John Stockdale, 1797. Sm 4to. 27,53 pp. Fldg tables. Mod half calf.
(Emerald Isle) **£225 [≈ $405]**
- The conduct of the allies ... See Swift, Jonathan

Congreve, William
- Amendments of Mr. Collier's false and imperfect citations. London: for J. Tonson, 1698. 1st edn, 1st iss. [iv],109 pp. Half-title,

errata corrected in contemp hand, another brief inked note. Mod mor spine, cloth sides.
(Pirages) **$350 [≈ £194]**
- The dramatic works. London: for S. Crowder ..., 1773. 2 vols. 12mo. Contemp calf, lacking 1 label.   *(Waterfield's)* **£60 [≈ $108]**
- A pindarique ode ... on the victorious progress of her majesty's arms, under the conduct of the Duke of Marlborough ... London: for Jacob Tonson, 1706. 1st edn. Folio. [vi],10 pp. Somewhat browned. Disbound.   *(Bennett)* **£175 [≈ $315]**
- The works ... consisting of his plays and poems. Birmingham: Baskerville, 1761. 3 vols. 8vo. Port frontis, 5 engvd plates. Early 19th c str-grained crimson mor, sides elab gilt, spines gilt, a.e.g.
(Frew Mackenzie) **£350 [≈ $630]**
- The works ... in two volumes. The seventh edition. London: T. Lowndes ..., 1774. 12mo. Port frontis, 5 engvd plates. Contemp calf, spines dec gilt, a little wear at extremities, sm scar on upper bd.
(Clark) **£40 [≈ $72]**
- The works in two volumes ... his plays and poems. London: for Jacob Tonson, 1719-20. 3rd edn, revsd. 2 vols. 12mo. Contemp calf, gilt, old rebacking in mor, gilt.
(Claude Cox) **£75 [≈ $135]**

Consequences ...
- The fatal consequences to be feared ... by our assisting the Queen of Hungary, and the King of Sardinia ... Treaty ... of Worms ... London: 1744. 1st edn. 8vo. 42 pp. Half blue mor.
(Young's) **£70 [≈ $126]**

Consideration ...
- Consideration on the present state of affairs in Europe, and particularly with regard to the number of forces in the pay of Great Britain. London: J. Roberts, 1730. 53 pp. Disbound.
(C.R. Johnson) **£35 [≈ $63]**

Considerations ...
- Considerations concerning the nature and consequences of the Bill now depending in Parliament relating to the Peerage of Great-Britain ... London: J. Roberts, 1719. 28 pp. Disbound.   *(C.R. Johnson)* **£38 [≈ $68]**
- Considerations of the Peerage-Bill; address'd to the Whigs. By a member of the Lower House. London: J. Roberts, 1719. 23 pp. Half-title. Disbound.
(C.R. Johnson) **£38 [≈ $68]**
- Considerations on the conquest of Tanjore, and the restoration of the Rajah ... taken from the records of the East India Company.

London: T. Cadell, 1789. 4to. 74 pp. Disbound. *(C.R. Johnson)* **£55 [≈$99]**
- Considerations on the political and commercial circumstances of Great Britain and Ireland as they are connected with each other ... London: Debrett, 1787. 8vo. 101 pp. Mod wraps. *(Emerald Isle)* **£48 [≈$86]**
- Considerations on the political and commercial circumstances of Great Britain and Ireland, as they are connected with each other, and on the most probably means of effecting a settlement between them ... London: Debrett, 1787. 8vo. 101 pp. Mod wraps. *(Emerald Isle)* **£48 [≈$86]**
- Considerations upon wit and morals ... See Meilhan, Gabriel Senac de

Constable's Guide ...
- The constable's guide and pocket companion; or, plain and easy instructions for high and petty constables ... the method of chusing constables ... London: for J. Worrall ..., 1771. 12mo. [ii],ii, [iv],112 pp. Contemp sheep, lower jnt sl cracked.
(Burmester) **£140 [≈$252]**

Continuation ...
- A continuation of letters written by a Turkish spy at Paris... from the year 1687, to the year 1693. London: W. Taylor, 1718. 12mo. Frontis. Calf, front hinge strengthened.
(Argosy) **$100 [≈£55]**

Cook, Capt. James
- A compendious history of Captain Cook's first and second voyages. The first ... in the 'Endeavour'; the second ... in the 'Resolution' and 'Adventure'. London: G. Kearsley, 1784. Cr 8vo. Orig bds, calf spine.
(Farahar) **£250 [≈$450]**
- See also Hawkesworth, John

Cook, Capt. James & King, James
- A voyage to the Pacific Ocean ... for making discoveries ... London: for Nicol & Cadell, 1784. 1st edn. 3 vols. 4to, atlas vol folio. 5 fldg plates, 19 maps (8 fldg), fldg table. 61 plates & 2 charts in atlas. Contemp 3/4 mor, mrbld bds. *(Argonaut)* **$5,750 [≈£3,194]**
- A voyage to the Pacific Ocean. London: for John Stockdale ..., 1784. 1st 8vo edn. 4 vols. Engvd port vol 1, half-titles vols 2,3 & 4., 49 engvd plates, maps & charts (some fldg)/ Contemp gilt dec tree-calf.
(Gough) **£795 [≈$1,431]**

Cooke, Edward
- Arguments for and against a union between

Great Britain and Ireland considered. Second edition. Dublin printed. London: reprinted December 1798. 58 pp. Rebound in bds.
(C.R. Johnson) **£28 [≈$50]**

Cooke, Edward
- A voyage to the South Sea ... perform'd in ... 1708 [-] 1711 by the ships 'Duke' and 'Dutchess'. London: B. Lintot ..., 1712. 2 vols. 2nd; 1st edns. 8vo. [xxii], 432,[10]; [viii],xxiv, 328,[8] pp. 18 plates, 9 maps, 3 tables. Contemp calf, vol 2 jnts cracking.
(Morrell) **£2,000 [≈$3,600]**
- A voyage to the South Sea, and round the world, performed in the years 1708-11. London: B. Lintot, 1712. 1st edn, 1st iss. [24],456,[12] pp. 15 plates (1 fldg), 5 maps & plans (2 fldg). Contemp panelled calf, rebacked. *(Jenkins)* **$1,250 [≈£694]**

Cooke, William, M.A.
- The medallic history of Imperial Rome ... a general history of Roman medals. 1781. 2 vols. 8vo. xxxix,507; 502 pp. 60 plates, many ills. Some browning & offsetting throughout, paper a little brittle. Ex lib in lib binding, with stamps. *(Edwards)* **£110 [≈$198]**

Cooper, Anthony Ashley
- An essay on painting: being a notion of the historical draught of tablature of the Judgement of Hercules. London: John Darby, 1714. 8vo. 47 pp, advt leaf. Addtnl frontis (not called for) inserted. Ptd price erased from title. Rec qtr blue mor, mrbld bds.
(Spelman) **£80 [≈$144]**
- An essay on painting: being a notion of the historical draught or tablature of the Judgement of Hercules. London: Darby, 1714. 8vo. 1f,47 pp. New qtr mor.
(Marlborough) **£150 [≈$270]**

Cooper, Myles
- Patriots of North America: a sketch with explanatory notes. New York: 1775. Sm narrow 4to. 47,2 advts,1 errata pp. Sm tear to title & advt leaf, crnr of advt leaf clipped & sm marg hole without loss, some minor darkening & fading. later half cloth, mrbld bds. *(Reese)* **$850 [≈£472]**

Cooper, Rev.
- The history of South America. Containing the discoveries of Columbus, the conquest of Mexico and Peru, and other transactions of the Spaniards. E. Newberry, 1789. 1st edn. Sm 8vo. 5 plates. Mod calf.
(Farahar) **£155 [≈$279]**

Corbett, Thomas

- An account of the expedition of the British Fleet to Sicily in the years 1818, 1719 and 1720 under the command of Sir George Byng ... London: 1739. 1st edn. 8vo. A few sm inkstains at beginning, sm hole in fldg table. Contemp half calf, rebacked.
(Robertshaw) **£40 [≈ $72]**

Cordiner, Charles

- Antiquities and scenery of the north of Scotland, in a series of letters to Thomas Pennant. London: 1780. 1st edn. [ii],173,[9] pp. Engvd title, 21 plates (1 fldg). Dampstain throughout in lower marg, 1st 8 leaves reprd. Contemp calf, spine gilt.
(Claude Cox) **£40 [≈ $72]**
- Remarkable ruins, and romantic prospects, of North Britain, with ancient monuments ... London: Peter Mazell, 1788-95. 2 vols in 1. 4to. Engvd title, 97 engvd plates (24 hand-cold). Sl spotting on 3 engvs, 3 sm dampmarks on final plate. Contemp half roan.   *(Lloyd-Roberts)* **£500 [≈ $900]**
- Remarkable ruins, and romantic prospects, of North Britain, with ancient monuments ... London: I. & J. Taylor, 1795. 1st edn. 2 vols. 97 engvd plates, 2 engvd vignette titles. Contemp gilt-panelled mottled calf.
(Gough) **£495 [≈ $891]**

Cornaro, Luigi (Lewis)

- Sure methods of attaining a long and healthy life: with means of correcting a bad constitution. London: for Daniel Midwinter ..., 1727. 4th edn. 12mo. xl,120 pp. Occas spotting. Mod calf. *(Young's)* **£65 [≈ $117]**
- Sure methods of attaining a long and healthy life. Translated ... Edinburgh: A. Donaldson, 1768. 12mo. Contemp calf, jnts cracked.
(Charles Cox) **£40 [≈ $72]**

Coronelli, Vincenzo Maria

- An historical and geographical account of the Morea. London: Gillyflowr, 1687. 1st English edn. 12mo. 42 double-page engvd plates. Contemp calf. New Wing C6342.
(Marlborough) **£750 [≈ $1,350]**

Correspondent ...

- The poetical correspondent ... See Bancroft, Thomas

Corsica ...

- The description of Corsica, with an account of its union to the crown of Great Britain. London: for G.G. & J. Robinson ..., 1795. 1st edn. iii,211 pp. Engvd fldg map. Old calf, jnts

weak.   *(Young's)* **£120 [≈ $216]**

Coryate, Thomas

- Coryats crudities, hastily gobbled up in five months travells in France, Savoy, Italy ... and the Netherlands. London: W.S., 1611. 1st edn. Sm 4to. Engvd title (shaved), ptd title, 4 plates (2 fldg). A few sm tears reprd. 19th c mor, jnts reprd. STC 5808.
(Stewart) **£1,450 [≈ $2,610]**

Cosin, John

- A collection of private devotions. London: Royston, 1672. Engvd title (date 1664). Contemp crimson mor gilt, a.e.g., crnrs & spine rubbed. New Wing C6354A.
(Marlborough) **£110 [≈ $198]**

Cossens, Dr. J.

- The economy of beauty, in a series of fables addressed to the ladies. London: 1777-73. 2 pts in 1 vol. 4to. viii,viii,104; [iv],vi,114 pp. Titles to both pts, 22 plates (lacking the frontis). Owner's stamp on title, some damp & other stains. Rec half mor.
(Bow Windows) **£80 [≈ $144]**

Costigan, Arthur William

- Sketches of society and manners in Portugal, in a series of letters from ... late a Captain of the Irish Brigade in the service of Spain, to his brother in London. N.p., 1787. 2 vols. 8vo. 358; 322 pp. Errata. Contemp lea.
(Emerald Isle) **£100 [≈ $180]**

Cotgrave, Randle

- A dictionarie of the French and English tongues. London: Ada Islip, 1611. 1st edn. Sm folio. Unpaginated. Ptd in double column. Sl affected by damp towards end. 18th c panelled calf, spine gilt, jnts reprd, crnrs bumped.
(Frew Mackenzie) **£260 [≈ $468]**

Cotton, Charles

- Burlesque upon burlesque: or, the scoffer scoft. Being some of Lucian's Dialogues rendered into English fustian ... London: Charles Brome, 1686. 2nd edn crrctd. 8vo. 200,[2] pp. Engvd frontis. 19th c blue calf, hinges rubbed. New Wing C6380A.
(Karmiole) **$200 [≈ £111]**
- The genuine poetical works. Dublin: for Thomas Armitage, 1770. 15th edn, crrctd. 12mo. 7 engvd plates. Contemp calf.
(Robertshaw) **£38 [≈ $68]**
- Poems on several occasions. London: Thos. Bassett ..., 1689. 1st coll edn. 8vo. [viii],729,[i] pp. Contemp speckled calf, spine

elab gilt, lightly rubbed. Wing C6389.
(Frew Mackenzie) £350 [≈ $630]

Cotton, Clement
- A complete concordance to the Bible of the last translation. London: for T. Downs ..., 1631. Folio. Engvd title. Ptd in treble column. Contemp calf, rebacked.
(Traylen) £95 [≈ $171]

Cotton, Nathaniel
- Visions in verse, for the entertainment and instruction of younger minds. London: for J. Dodsley, 1776. 9th edn. 8vo. 141 pp. Engvd frontis. Contemp calf. *(Young's)* £27 [≈ $48]

Cotton, Sir Robert
- An answer to such motives as were offer'd by certain military-men to Prince Henry ... to affect arms more than peace. Henry Mortlock, 1675. 2nd edn. 8vo. [vi],142 pp. Engvd port frontis. Sep titles to each part. 18th c calf, old rebacking. Some worming.
(Blackwell's) £80 [≈ $144]

Countryside ...
- The English countryside, or, rudiments of honour; containing the genealogies of all the nobility of England ... London: 1760. 11th edn. 8vo. 3 vols. 2 frontis, num engvd coats-of-arms. Contemp half calf, worn.
(Stewart) £85 [≈ $153]

Couper, Robert
- Speculations on the mode and appearances of impregnation in the human female ... Edinburgh: C. Elliott; London: Elliott & Kay, 1789. 1st edn. 8vo. 149,[1] pp. Qtr calf over mrbld bds. *(Rootenberg)* $550 [≈ £305]

Courtenay, John
- Philosophical reflections on the late revolution in France, and the conduct of the dissenters in England; in a letter to the Rev. Dr. Priestley. London: T. Becket, 1790. 94 pp. Half-title. Stabbed pamphlet as issued, uncut. *(C.R. Johnson)* £90 [≈ $162]

Coventry, Francis
- The history of Pompey the Little: or, the life and adventures of a lap-dog. London: for M. Cooper, 1751. 1st edn. viii,272 pp. Engvd frontis. Contemp calf, new spine, crnrs worn.
(Pirages) $100 [≈ £55]

Cowell, John
- The interpreter: or book containing the signification of words. Cambridge: John Legate, 1607. 1st edn. 4to. 292ff in double column. Lacking title, 1st section damaged *2-*4. Some light waterstaining elsewhere. 18th c reversed calf, worn. STC 5900.
(Edwards) £180 [≈ $324]

Cowley, Abraham
- Poems: viz. I. Miscellanies. II. The mistress, or, love verses. III. Pindarisque odes. And IV. Davideis ... London: for Humphrey Moseley, 1656. Folio. Old dampstain to some leaves, sl marg worming. Contemp calf, rebacked. Wing 6682. *(Stewart)* £135 [≈ $243]
- The works ... London: for Jacob Tonson, 1707-08. 10th edn. 3 vols. Frontis port. Contemp panelled calf, rebacked.
(Waterfield's) £125 [≈ $225]
- The works ... Now published out of the author's original copies. London: for Henry Herringman, 1668. 1st coll edn. Folio. Port. Inscrptn on title crossed out. Later blindstamped calf, a little rubbed.
(Charles Cox) £85 [≈ $153]
- The works ... published out of the author's original copies. London: for Henry Herringman 1681. [Bound with] The second part of the works ... in his jounger [sic] years ... London: 1682. 4th edn. 2 vols in 1. Cr. 8vo. Port frontis. Contemp calf. Wing 6656 & 6664. *(Stewart)* £125 [≈ $225]

Cowley, John Lodge
- An appendix to the elements of Euclid, in seven books. London: T. Cadell, n.d. [ca 1770]. 2nd edn. 4to. [iv],14 pp. 42 plates of cut-outs. Contemp dark calf, rebacked & recrnrd to match.
(Frew Mackenzie) £1,300 [≈ $2,340]
- The theory of perspective demonstrated; in a method entirely new. London: T. Payne, 1766. 2nd iss (?). [6],xi,[i],117 pp. 11 plates ptd on stiff paper inc 6 cut out for fldg into 3-D models. Some spotting of plates. Contemp str-grained mor, jnts little rubbed.
(Spelman) £480 [≈ $864]

Cowper, William
- Poems ... London: for J. Johnson, 1788. 4th edn. 2 vols. 8vo. Vignette title vol 2. New grey bds. *(Stewart)* £75 [≈ $135]
- Poems ... London: J. Johnson, 1794. 6th edn. 2 vols. 8vo. Contemp diced mottled calf, spines gilt dec. Ex lib Lord Lonsdale.
(Gough) £95 [≈ $171]

Cowper, William (1666 - 1709)
- Myotomia reformata: or an anatomical treatise on the muscles of the human body ... London: for Knaplock ..., 1724. 1st folio edn.

[10],lxxvii, 194,[4] pp. Engvd frontis, 66 plates plus 1 in outline. Anntns in contemp hand throughout. Elab gilt dec calf.
(Rootenberg) **$5,500 [≈ £3,055]**

Cox, Nicolas

- The gentleman's recreation, in four parts: Viz, hunting, hawking, fowling, fishing ... London: 1721. 6th edn. 8vo. Frontis, 4 fldg plates. [Bound with, in contemp calf] An abridgement of Manwood's Forest Laws ...
(Argosy) **$150 [≈ £83]**

Cox, Richard

- Hibernia Anglican: or, the history of Ireland from the conquest thereof by the English ... London: for Joseph Watts, 1689-90. 2 pts in 1 vol. Sm folio. Fldg map, 2 engvd frontis. Contemp speckled calf. Wing 6722.
(Stewart) **£250 [≈ $450]**

Cox, Sir Richard

- A refutation of all the malicious falsehoods and misrepresentations, against Sir Richard Cox, Esq; contained in ... A letter to the Public ... Dublin: Peter Wilson, 1756. 16 pp. Mod wraps, disbound.
(C.R. Johnson) **£32 [≈ $57]**

Coxe, William

- Account of the Russian discoveries between Asia and America, to which are added, the conquest of Siberia ... London: T. Cadell, 1780. 1st edn. 4to. xxii,344, [14],[2] pp. 4 fldg engvd maps. Contemp mottled calf, early rebacking, jnts sl rubbed, mor slipcase.
(Reese) **$1,800 [≈ £1,000]**

- Account of the Russian discoveries between Asia and America ... London: T. Cadell, 1787. 3rd edn. 8vo. [8],v-xxviii, 454,[2] pp. Plate, 4 fldg maps. Mod qtr calf.
(High Latitude) **$375 [≈ £208]**

- Memoirs of the life and administration of Sir Robert Walpole ... London: for T. Cadell ..., 1798. 1st edn. 3 vols. 4to. Engvd port, fldg table, 4 engvd plates. Gilt-panelled calf, spines gilt-dec, hd of 2 jnts reprd.
(Gough) **£235 [≈ $423]**

- Travels in Switzerland, and in the country of the Grisons. 1791. 2nd edn. 3 vols. 8vo. 2 lge fldg maps, plates. Contemp tree-calf, worn.
(Halewood) **£85 [≈ $153]**

- Travels into Poland, Russia, Sweden, and Denmark ... [Jutland, Norway ...] in two [three] volumes. London: for T. Cadell, 1784-90. 1st edn. 3 vols. 4to. 26 maps (mostly fldg), plates, genealogical table, final advt leaf. Occas minor foxing. Contemp calf, gilt.
(Hannas) **£850 [≈ $1,530]**

Crabbe, George

- The library. A poem. London: for J. Dodsley, 1781. 1st edn. 4to. Notes on title, some surface abrasion of imprint. Disbound.
(Waterfield's) **£300 [≈ $540]**

Cradock, Joseph

- Zobeide. A tragedy. London: for T. Cadell, 1771. 1st edn. 8vo. [ii],[vi],80.[iv] pp. Epilogue unsgnd, 2 lines of errata. Title dusty. Disbound.
(Clark) **£24 [≈ $43]**

Cramer, John Andrew

- Elements of the art of essaying metals. In two parts ... For Tho. Woodward ..., 1741. 1st edn in English 8vo. [xii],1-204, half-title, 203-208,[205]-470, viii] pp. 6 fldg engvd plates. Orig calf, upper jnt beginning to crack at hd.
(Bickersteth) **£360 [≈ $648]**

Crashaw, Richard

- Poetry ... With some account of the author, and an introductory address ... by Peregrine Phillips. London: for the editor ..., 1785. 16mo in 8s. xxiv,158 pp. Contemp calf, spine gilt, crnrs sl rubbed.
(Clark) **£65 [≈ $117]**

Craufurd, Quintin

- Sketches chiefly relating to the history, religion, learning and manners of the Hindoos. London: T. Cadell, 1792. 2nd edn, enlgd. 2 vols. Engvd vignette titles, fldg diag. Frontis to vol I sl torn. Contemp mottled calf.
(Waterfield's) **£80 [≈ $144]**

Craven, Lady Elizabeth

- A journey through the Crimea to Constantinople. In a series of letters ... Dublin: H. Chamberlaine, 1789. 8vo. 415 pp. Plates, fldg map. Half lea.
(Zeno) **£85 [≈ $153]**

- A journey through the Crimea to Constantinople ... written in 1786. Dublin: H. Chamberlaine, 1789. 8vo. Contemp Irish tree-calf, spines gilt in compartments.
(Emerald Isle) **£120 [≈ $216]**

- A journey through the Crimea to Constantinople. In a series of letters ... London: for G.G.J. & J. Robinson, 1789. 4to. [vi],327 pp. Fldg engvd map, 6 engvd plates (1 fldg). Contemp tree-calf, spine gilt-dec, lower jnt strengthened.
(Gough) **£185 [≈ $333]**

Crawford, William

- A history of Ireland from the earliest period to the present time, addressed to William Hamilton. Strabane: John Bellew, 1783. 2

vols. 8vo. 350; 387 pp. Mod half calf.
(Emerald Isle) **£220 [≈ $396]**

Creech, Thomas
- The five books of M. Manilius. Containing a system of the ancient astronomy and astrology. London: for Jacob Tonson, 1697. 1st edn. Frontis, 5 plates, half-title, errata leaf. 2 leaves stained. Later half calf gilt, cloth bds. Wing M430. *(Charles Cox)* **£35 [≈ $63]**
- Titus Lucretius Carus his six books of Epicurean philosophy: done into English verse, with notes. London: for T. Braddyl, 1700. 5th edn. Title on poor quality paper (a cancel?). Old calf, rebacked. Wing L3450.
(Charles Cox) **£35 [≈ $63]**

Crevier, Jean Baptiste Louis
- The history of the Roman emperors from Augustus to Constantine. Translated ... London: Knapton ..., 1755-61. 1st edn in English. 10 vols. 8vo. 26 plates, 2 fldg panoramas, 3 fldg maps. Contemp calf, spines gilt dec, minor wear at end of backstrips.
(Clark) **£100 [≈ $180]**

Crisis ...
- The crisis: or a defence against the ... ill-grounded triumph of opposition. London: for the author, 1785. 8vo. New wraps. (On the commercial and political independence of Ireland). *(Marlborough)* **£60 [≈ $108]**

Croft, Herbert
- The legacy of ... Herbert Lord Bishop of Hereford to his Diocese ... all controversies we have with the papists ... London: for Charles Harper, 1679. 4to Imprim leaf. Disbound. Wing C6966.
(Waterfield's) **£40 [≈ $72]**

Croft, John
- Excerpta antiqua; or, a collection of original manuscripts. York: W. Blanchard, 1797. 1st 3 leaves soiled. Uncut in wraps.
(Young's) **£35 [≈ $63]**

Crouch, Nathaniel
- The English acquisitions in Guinea & East India ... London: 1700. 12mo. [iv],179,[ix] pp. W'cut frontis (frayed & mtd), 3 w'cut ills, ctlg at end. Paper browned throughout, some staining, a few crnrs & edges frayed. Contemp calf, rebacked. Wing C7318.
(Clark) **£180 [≈ $324]**

Crowe, William
- Lewesdon Hill. A poem. Oxford: at the

Clarendon Press, 1788. 4to. New bds.
(C.R. Johnson) **£125 [≈ $225]**

Cruden, Alexander
- A complete concordance to the holy scripture of the old and new testament ... London: for A. Cruden ..., 1769. 4to. Port frontis. Contemp calf, rubbed, a few scrapes.
(Hughes) **£45 [≈ $81]**

Cuba ...
- Original papers relating to the expedition to the Island of Cuba. London: 1744. 219 pp. Disbound. *(Reese)* **$450 [≈ £250]**

Cudworth, Ralph
- The true intellectual system of the universe. The first part [all published]. London: for Richard Royston, 1678. 1st edn. Folio. Red & black title, addtnl engvd title. Mod half calf. Wing C7471. *(Waterfield's)* **£300 [≈ $540]**

Cullen, Stephen
- The haunted priory: or, the fortunes of the House of Rayo. A romance. Dublin: for William Jones, 1794. 1st Dublin edn. 12mo. [ii],262 pp. Contemp tree-calf, rebacked, orig label. *(Bennett)* **£165 [≈ $297]**
- The haunted priory: or, the fortunes of the House of Rayo. A romance ... Dublin: for William Jones, 1794. 1st Dublin edn. 12mo. [ii],262 pp. Contemp tree-calf, rebacked.
(Burmester) **£250 [≈ $450]**

Cullen, William
- First lines of the practice of physic. Edinburgh: for Charles Elliot, 1784. 4th edn. 4 vols. 8vo. Titles to vols 2, 3 & 4 a little grubby. New buckram.
(Pollak) **£175 [≈ $315]**

Culpeper, Nicholas
- The English physician enlarged: with three hundred, sixty, and nine medicines made of English herbs ... London: Peter Cole, 1656. 8vo. [22],398,[16] pp. Lacking 1st blank, sl loss to title border, paper flaw in D1, some soiling. Contemp calf, crude respining.
(Spelman) **£160 [≈ $288]**
- The idea of practical physick in twelve books. London: Peter Cole, 1657. Sm folio. [10],345 pp (paginated in sections, with some errors). Foxing. Rec calf. *(Goodrich)* **$1,250 [≈ £694]**

Culverwel, Nathaniel
- An elegant and learned discourse of the light of nature, with several other treatises. London: 1652. 1st edn. 4to. Some light

staining on 1st few leaves. Contemp calf, worn. Wing C7569.

(*Robertshaw*) **£36 [≈ $64]**

Cumberland, Richard

- Anecdotes of eminent painters in Spain. London: J. Walter, 1782. 1st edn. 2 vols. 12mo. 2ff, 225 pp; 1f,224 pp, 1f. Contemp tree-calf gilt.   (*Marlborough*) **£125 [≈ $225]**
- The fashionable lover; a comedy. London: W. Griffin, 1772. 1st edn. 8vo. iii-x,[ii], [64],[iv] pp. Lacking half-title, epilogue leaf misbound before prologue. later inserted mtd plate. Disbound.   (*Clark*) **£20 [≈ $36]**
- The Observer, being a collection of moral, literary and familiar essays. London: for C. Dilly, 1798. 5th edn. 6 vols. Cr 8vo. Contemp tree-calf, gilt spines. (*Traylen*) **£95 [≈ $171]**
- The West Indian, a comedy. As it is performed at the Theatre Royal in Drury Lane. London: 1771. 8vo. 104 pp. New wraps.   (*Argosy*) **$50 [≈ £27]**

Cumberland, Richard (1631-1718)

- An essay towards the recovery of the Jewish measures and weights, comprehending their monies. London: Richard Chiswell, 1686. 1st edn. 8vo. [16],140 pp. Contemp calf, worn, jnts split. Wing C7581.
(*Argosy*) **$300 [≈ £166]**
- A treatise of the laws of nature ... deduced from the nature of things. London: 1727. 1st edn in English. 4to. Red & black gen title. Contemp calf, rebacked.
(*Chaucer Head*) **£300 [≈ $540]**

Cunning Plot ...

- A cunning plot to divide and destroy parliament and the City of London. Made known ... by the Earle of Northumberland ... London: Peter Cole ..., 1643. 1st edn. 4to. 56 pp. Wraps. Wing C7585.
(*Young's*) **£75 [≈ $135]**

Curate, Jacob (pseud.)

- The Scotch Presbyterian eloquence; or, the foolishness of their teachings discovered ... London: for M. Smith, 1719. 4th edn. Title page loosening, lacking A1 (blank?). Later sheep.   (*Waterfield's*) **£60 [≈ $108]**

Curll, Edmund

- An answer to Mr. Mist's journal of the twenty-eight of January, No. 93. In a letter to the author of it. London: for N. Blandford, 1727. 1st edn. 8vo. [ii],30 pp. Disbound.
(*Burmester*) **£150 [≈ $270]**

Currie, James

- Medical reports on the affects of water, cold and warm, as a remedy in fever, and febrile diseases. Liverpool printed: for Cadell & Davies, London, 1797. 1st edn. x,vii, [1 errata], 252,45 pp. Clean tear in 1 leaf. Contemp half calf, mrbld bds, rebacked.
(*Antiq Sc*) **$475 [≈ £263]**

Currie, William

- An historical account of the climates and diseases of the United States of America ... Phila: 1792. 1st edn. 409,v pp. Mod lea, new endpapers.   (*Scientia*) **$475 [≈ £263]**

Curry, John

- An historical and critical review of the Civil Wars in Ireland, from the reign of Queen Elizabeth, to the settlement under King William. Dublin: 1775. 4to. Title spotted. Contemp half calf, rubbed.
(*Robertshaw*) **£45 [≈ $81]**

Curtis, William

- Instructions for collecting and preserving insects ... the nets, and other apparatus necessary for that purpose ... London: for the author, 1771. 1st edn. 8vo. iv,44 pp. Engvd frontis (with old fold mark), some staining on endpapers. Old mrbld bds, calf spine.
(*Burmester*) **£225 [≈ $405]**

Curtius ...

- Curtius rescued from the Gulph; or, the retort courteous ... London: Hookham & Carpenter, 1792. 43 pp. Half-title. Mod wraps.   (*C.R. Johnson*) **£35 [≈ $63]**

Curzon, H.

- The universal library: or, compleat summary of science [and arts], containing about sixty select treatises ... London: for T. Warner, 1722. 2nd edn. 2 vols. 8vo. Fldg pedigree. Contemp panelled calf, gilt panelled spines, ,or labels, gilt.   (*Traylen*) **£250 [≈ $450]**

Cuss, John

- The complete captain, or, an abridgement of Cesars warres ... A particular treatise of modern war ... Englished ... 1640. Sm 8vo. Contemp calf, gilt, sl worn.
(*Edwards*) **£100 [≈ $180]**

Customs and Privileges ...

- Customs and privileges of the Manors of Stepney and Hackney ... prefix'd an Act for perpetual establishment of the said customs ... London: Nutt, 1736. 12mo. [iv],128 pp. Some browning, anntn & underscoring.

Contemp sheep, rebacked, crnrs bumped.
(Frew Mackenzie) £65 [≈$117]

Cygnea Cantio ...
- Cygnea Cantio ... See Featly, Daniel

Da Costa, Emanuel Mendes
- Elements of conchology. London: for Benjamin White, 1776. 1st edn. viii,[iii]-vi, 318,[2 errata] pp, advt leaf. 7 fldg engvd plates, 2 fldg charts. Contemp tree-calf.
(Claude Cox) £110 [≈$198]

da Vinci, Leonardo
- Characturas by Leonardo da Vinci from drawings by Winceslaus Hollar out of the Portland Museum. [London:] J. Clarke, Nov. 1, 1786. 4to. Aquatint port, engvd title, 64 ills on 16 plates. A bit foxed. Contemp mrbld bds, defective. *(Marlborough)* £125 [≈$225]
- A treatise on painting. Translated ... adorn'd with a great number of cuts. London: J. Senex ..., 1721. 1st edn in English. 8vo. xvi,189, [16 index], [3 advts] pp. Frontis, 33 plates (2 fldg), 2 fldg tables. Margs sl browned. Contemp calf, rebacked, new label.
(Claude Cox) £75 [≈$135]

Dale, W.
- Calculations deduced from first principles ... by plain arithmetic, for the use of Societies instituted for the benefit of old age ... London: Ridley, 1772. Sole edn. 8vo. xcvi,[i], 247,[184] pp. Uncut & lgely unopened in orig bds. *(Frew Mackenzie)* £620 [≈$1,116]

Dalrymple, Sir David
- An examination of one of the arguments for the high antiquity of Regiam Majestatem; and an enquiry into the authenticity of Leges Malcolmi. Edinburgh: 1769. 1st edn. 4to. 52 pp. Mod grey bds. *(Robertshaw)* £20 [≈$36]

Dalrymple, John
- An essay towards a general history of feudal property in Great Britain. London: for A. Millar, 1757. 1st edn. 8vo. Mod half calf, new endpapers. *(Chaucer Head)* £120 [≈$216]
- An essay towards a general history of feudal property in Great Britain. London: for A. Millar, 1758. 2nd edn, crrctd & enlgd. x,276 pp. Contemp calf, spine gilt.
(Edwards) £125 [≈$225]

Dalrymple, Sir John
- Memoirs of Great Britain and Ireland from the dissolution of the last parliament of Charles II ... London: 1771-88. 3 vols. 4to.

Contemp speckled calf, gilt spines, vol II rebacked, vol III not quite uniform.
(Bow Windows) £155 [≈$279]
- Memoirs of Great Britain and Ireland from the dissolution of the last parliament of Charles II ... London: 1771-73. 2 vols. 4to. Some spotting & soiling. Contemp calf-backed bds, rubbed, worn, hinges cracking.
(Claude Cox) £35 [≈$63]

Dalrymple, William
- Travels through Spain and Portugal, in 1774; with a short account of the Spanish Expedition against Algiers, in 1775. London: J. Almon, 1777. 1st edn. 4to. iv,187 pp. Engvd frontis, fldg map. Contemp speckled calf, front jnt cracked. Armorial b'plate.
(Frew Mackenzie) £200 [≈$360]

Dalton, John (1766-1844)
- Meteorological observations and essays. London: ... Pennington, 1793. 1st edn, 1st iss. 8vo in 4s. xvi,208 pp. Sev w'cut diags in the text. Uncut in orig lavender bds, a little worn, mor-backed case. Inscrbd by author to William Fothergill.
(Pickering) $3,000 [≈£1,666]

Dalton, Michael
- The country justice. 1655. 6th edn. Folio. 502 pp. Fldg table torn without loss. Contemp calf, worn. Wing D144.
(Edwards) £220 [≈$396]
- The country justice. John Streator ..., 1666. Sm folio. [x],460,[xii] pp. Lacking prelim blank. Old calf, later rebacking, little light wear to crnrs. *(Ash)* £300 [≈$540]
- The country justice. London: E. & R. Nutt, 1727. Folio. [20],679, appendix, tables pp. Half-title. Contemp calf, lower jnt cracked.
(Spelman) £240 [≈$432]
- Officium Vicecomitum. The office and authority of sheriffs ... 1700. 2nd edn. Folio. 564 pp. Mod half calf. Wing D154.
(Edwards) £240 [≈$432]

Dalzel, Archibald
- The history of Dahomy. An inland kingdom of Africa; compiled from authentic memoirs. For the author, 1793. 1st edn. 4to. Fldg frontis map (sl torn), 6 engvd plates. Perf lib stamp on title & map, plates with ink stamp, some browning & staining. Mod cloth.
(Edwards) £150 [≈$270]

Dampier, William
- A new voyage round the world. London: for James Knapton, 1698. 3rd edn, crrctd. 5

maps (4 fldg). No advt leaves at end. Contemp panelled calf, rebacked. Wing D163.
(Charles Cox) £150 [≈ $270]
- The voyages and adventures ... to which is added, a discourse on winds ... Liverpool: Gore, Ansdell ..., 1769. 2 vols. 8vo. iv, [5]-454; 396 pp. A little foxing & browning, 1 leaf torn. Contemp tree-calf, jnts cracking, armorial b'plate.   *(Morrell)* £180 [≈ $324]

Dana, James
- An examination of the late Reverend President Edward's 'Enquiry on Freedom of Will'. Boston [Mass]: Daniel Keeland, 1770. 1st edn. 8vo. xii,140 pp. Without half-title (not called for in pagination). Rec calf-backed mrbld bds, spine gilt.
(Bennett) £185 [≈ $333]

Danebury ...
- Danebury: or the power of friendship, a tale. With two odes. By a young lady. Bristol: W. Pine, n.d. [1755?]. 4to. Half-title. Rebound in qtr calf, mrbld bds.
(C.R. Johnson) £200 [≈ $360]

Danett, Thomas (trans & ed,)
- The historie of Philip de Commines Knight, Lord of Argenton. London: for Iohn Bill, 1614. Folio. 9ff genealogical tables at end. Title dusty, a few sl marg stains. Early calf, gilt, worn. STC 5604.
(Charles Cox) £100 [≈ $180]

Daniel, Gabriel
- The history of France from the time the French monarchy was established in Gaul to the death of Louis XIVth. London: G. Strahan, 1726. 1st English edn. 5 vols. 8vo. W'cut vignettes. Contemp calf.
(Argosy) $200 [≈ £111]

Daniel, Samuel
- The civile wares between the howses of Lancaster and Yorke. London: Simon Watersonne, 1609. 1st complete edn. Sm 4to. [vi],231,[i] pp. Engvd title (cut short at outer marg). Without A4 blank. Str-grained red mor gilt by Hering. Ex lib Richard Heber. STC 6245.   *(Bennett)* £525 [≈ $945]
- The poetical works ... to which is prefix'd, memoirs of his life and writings. London: for S. Gosling, 1718. 1st coll edn. 2 vols. 12mo. Early 19th c polished calf, spines rubbed, numeral labels missing.
(Bennett) £110 [≈ $198]
- The works of Samuel Daniel newly augmented. London: for S. Waterson, 1601. 1st coll edn, 1 iss. Sm folio. W'cut border

round title, outer marg renewed. Blue mor, gilt panelled sides, a.e.g., by Bedford, some fading. STC 6236.
(Traylen) £2,200 [≈ $3,960]

Darell, William
- The history of Dover Castle. London: 1797. 1st edn. 4to. Engvd title, map, 8 plates. Later half roan.   *(Robertshaw)* £80 [≈ $144]

Dart, Rev. J.
- The history and antiquities of the Cathedral Church at Westminster ... 1726. 1st edn. Folio. 2,ix,204,lvi pp. 41 engvd plates (4 fldg), num text ills. Sm repr to title, sl foxing & dampstaining. Half pigskin, mrbld bds, worn.   *(Edwards)* £250 [≈ $450]

Darwin, Erasmus
- The botanic garden. A poem in two parts. London: 1790-91. 4to. Pt 1 1st edn, pt 2 2nd end. 2 frontis, 17 plates (ex 18). Contemp reversed calf.   *(Robertshaw)* £100 [≈ $180]
- Zoonomia or the laws of organic life. London: for J. Dodsley, 1794. 2 vols. 4to. 8 plates. Title of each vol laid down & trimmed. Contemp half calf, rebacked.
(Waterfield's) £300 [≈ $540]

Daulby, Daniel
- A descriptive catalogue of the works of Rembrandt and of his scholars ... Liverpool: M'Creery, 1796. 8vo. Title, xxii pp, 1f, 339 pp, 2ff. Engvd port frontis. Contemp calf.
(Marlborough) £60 [≈ $108]

Davenant, Sir William
- Madagascar; with other poems. London: for Thomas Walkly, 1638. 1st edn. 12mo. Extensively reprd, partic at top edges, two words & a few letters in facsimile, washed, resewn, recased. With 2 of the 4 blanks. Contemp sheep. Ex lib Lord Lowther. STC 6304.   *(Charles Cox)* £1,250 [≈ $2,250]
- The works ... consisting of those which were formerly printed, and those which he design'd for the press. London: for Henry Herringman, 1673, 1st edn. Tear in 1 leaf. Later heavy mor bds. Wing D320.
(Charles Cox) £225 [≈ $405]
- The works consisting of those which were formerly printed, and those which he design'd for the press. London: for Henry Herringman, 1673, 1st coll edn. 4 sectional titles. Contemp calf, rebacked, orig spine laid down. Wing D320. *(Traylen)* £295 [≈ $531]

Davies, Thomas
- Memoirs of the life of David Garrick, Esq., ... characters and anecdotes of his theatrical contemporaries ... a history of the stage ... London: for the author, 1780. 1st edn. 2 vols. Port frontis. Contemp calf, spines gilt, scuffed, a few sm defects. *(Clark)* **£42 [≈ $75]**

Davila, H.C.
- The historie of the Civill Warres of France. London: 1647. 1st English edn. Folio. Engv on title, imprim leaf. Contemp calf, worn, rebacked. Wing D413.
  (Robertshaw) **£70 [≈ $126]**
- The historie of the Civill Warres of France. London: 1647. 1st edn of this trans. Folio. [viii],1478,[ii] pp. Privilege leaf, final errata leaf. Contemp calf, rebacked, crnrs reprd. Wing D413. *(Clark)* **£95 [≈ $171]**

Dawson, Thomas
- Memoirs of St. George the English patron; and of the most noble Order of the Garter. Being an introduction to an intended history of ... Windsor ... London: for Henry Clements ..., 1714. 1st edn. xx,336 pp. Engvd frontis. Some browning. Rec calf.
  (Young's) **£40 [≈ $72]**

Day, Angel
- The English secretoire, or, methode of writing of epistles and letters ... Also the parts and office of a secretorie. Divided into two bookes ... London: William Stansby, [1626]. 8th (?) edn. [xii],441,[9] pp. Some worming. New calf. *(Young's)* **£80 [≈ $144]**

Day, Thomas
- The history of Sandford and Merton, a work intended for the use of children. London: John Stockdale, 1790-88-89. 3 vols. 12mo. 5th, 2nd, 1st edns. Lacking the 3 frontis. Advts at end of each vol. Some early margs vol I stained & torn. Contemp calf, rubbed.
  (Clark) **£105 [≈ $189]**

D'Ancourt, Abbe
- The lady's preceptor. Or, a letter to a young lady of distinction upon politeness ... by a gentleman of Cambridge. London: for J. Watts, 1752. 4th edn. 8vo. [viii],72,[8 advts] pp. Contemp calf-backed mrbld bds, sl wear.
  (Burmester) **£30 [≈ $54]**

d'Andilly, Arnauld
- The works of Josephus. With great diligence revised and ammended, according to the excellent French translation. Also the embassy of Philo Judaeus to the Emperor

Caius Caligula. 1683. 1st edn. 1683. Tall 4to. Port frontis, map, engvs. Calf, rebacked.
  (Edwards) **£100 [≈ $180]**

de Andrada, Jacinto Freire
- The life of Dom John de Castro ... wherein are seen the Portuguese's voyages to the East-Indies ... London: Herringman, 1664. 1st English edn. Sm folio. [vi],xiii,272, [19 index] pp. Sl worming in index margs. Contemp speckled calf, crnrs rubbed, spine reprd.
  (Morrell) **£340 [≈ $612]**

d'Anvers, Arthur
- The daily sacrifice of the Mass ... a sermon ... Dublin: Christopher Dickson, 1736. Sm 4to. 14 pp. Mod wraps.
  (Emerald Isle) **£48 [≈ $86]**
- Salvation scarce possible in the Church of Rome but secure in the Church of Ireland, by law established ... a sermon ... Dublin: Christopher Dickson, 1736. Sm 4to. 20 pp. Mod wraps. *(Emerald Isle)* **£48 [≈ $86]**

D'Anvers, Caleb (pseud.)
- A proper reply to a late scurrilous libel; intitled Sedition and defamation display'd. London: R. Francklin, 1731. 36 pp. (By Richard Pulteney).
  (C.R. Johnson) **£28 [≈ $50]**

de Benyowsky, Count Mauritius Augustus
- Memoirs and travels ... London: Robinson, 1790. 1st edn. 2 vols. 4to. 13 engvd plates (7 fldg), 10 maps & charts (9 fldg), half-titles. Ink inscrptns on titles, some spotting on plates. lacking 2 pp contents vol 1. Contemp calf, spines reprd. *(Morrell)* **£380 [≈ $684]**

De Britaine, W.
- Human prudence; or the art by which a man may raise himself and fortune to grandeur. Dublin: Hoey, 1793. 8th edn. 8vo. Contemp sheep, rubbed. *(Marlborough)* **£60 [≈ $108]**

de Fleury, Andrew-Hercules
- Memoirs of the life and administration of the late ... By an impartial hand. London: for J. Roberts, 1743. 8vo. 101 pp. Title a little dust-soiled. New grey bds.
  (Claude Cox) **£15 [≈ $27]**

D'Israeli, Isaac
- An essay on the manners and genius of the literary character. London: for T. Cadell ..., 1795. Uncut in orig bds, paper spine a little worn. *(C.R. Johnson)* **£180 [≈ $324]**
- Romances. London: for Cadell & Davies,

1799. [iv],xix,[v], 314,[ii] pp. 1st edn. 8vo. Contemp half calf, hd of spine rather worn, front free endpaper missing.
(Bennett) **£95 [≈$171]**

de Lesseps, Jean Baptiste Barthelemy
- Travels in Kamtschatka, during the years 1787 and 1788. London: J. Johnson, 1790. 1st English edn. 2 vols. 8vo. xvi,283; viii,408 pp. Fldg engvd map (sl creased), a little foxing. Contemp polished calf, jnts of vol I cracking, hd & tail of spines chipped.
(Morrell) **£390 [≈$702]**

De Lolme, Jean L.
- The constitution of England, or an account of English government ... London: for G. Robinson ..., 1784. 4th edn, crrctd & enlgd. 8vo. [8],xvi, 540,[20] pp. Engvd port. Contemp calf.
(Fenning) **£35 [≈$63]**
- The constitution of England, or an account of English government ... London: Printed by T. Spilsbury ..., 1775. 1st Edn in English. 8vo. Contemp calf, spine gilt, rubbed, front jnt cracking, crnrs chafed.
(Hughes) **£75 [≈$135]**
- The constitution of England, or an account of English government ... London: for G. Robinson ..., 1784. 4th edn, crrctd & enlgd. 8vo. Title sl dusty & browned & with blind lib stamp at ft. Engvd port. Rebound qtr calf.
(Hughes) **£45 [≈$81]**
- The constitution of England, or an account of English government ... London: for G. Robinson ..., 1781. 3rd edn. 8vo. Contemp calf.
(Stewart) **£60 [≈$108]**

De Moivre, Abraham
- The doctrine of chances: or, a method of calculating the probability of events in play. London: 1718. 1st edn. Lge 4to. [2]ff, xiv,175 pp. Engvd vignettes. Orig calf, rubbed, jnts open.
(Elgen) **$750 [≈£416]**
- The doctrine of chances: or, a method of calculating the probability of events in play. London: for the author, 1718. 1st edn. Lge 4to. [6],175 pp. 2 vignettes (1 on title). Contemp calf, spine & label reprd.
(Rootenberg) **$1,500 [≈£833]**
- The doctrine of chances ... London: 1738. 2nd edn. 4to. Lge paper. [2]ff, xiv,256 pp. Engvd vignette. Title somewhat browned. Lib binding. Ex lib.
(Elgen) **$400 [≈£222]**

de Montesquieu, Baron
- The complete works ... translated from the French. London: for T Evans ..., 1777. 1st comp edn in English. Engvd frontis.

Contemp speckled calf, spines gilt, lacking some labels.
(Waterfield's) **£150 [≈$270]**
- Miscellaneous pieces of M. De Secondat. Translated ... London: D. Wilson ..., 1759. 1st English edn. 8vo. vi,[2],334 pp. Contemp calf-backed mrbld bds.
(Spelman) **£260 [≈$468]**
- The spirit of laws. Translated ... with corrections and additions communicated by the author. London: for J. Nourse ..., 1750. 1st edn in English. 2 vols. 8vo. Contemp tree calf, hds of spines rather chipped, vol 1 rebacked.
(Waterfield's) **£1,000 [≈$1,800]**
- The spirit of laws. London: for J. Nourse ..., 1752. 2nd edn in English. 2 vols. 8vo. Contemp calf, new labels.
(Waterfield's) **£400 [≈$720]**
- The spirit of laws. Translated ... London: for Nourse & Vaillant, 1766. 4th edn. 2 vols. 8vo. Rebound in cloth, sl cut-down.
(Stewart) **£25 [≈$45]**

De Non, M.
- Travels through Sicily and Malta. Translated from the French ... Perth: for R. Morison ... Edinburgh, 1790. Demy 12mo. [4],210 pp. Sl trace of foxing on 6 pp. Uncut in new qtr calf, mrbld bds.
(Orient) **£24 [≈$43]**

de Polnitz, Charles-Lewis, Baron
- The memoirs ... observations made in travels from Prussia thro' Germany, Italy, France ... England, etc. London: for D. Browne, 1737-38. 4 vols. Contemp calf, sl rubbed, lacking 2 spine labels.
(Lloyd-Roberts) **£65 [≈$117]**
- Observations and reflections made in the course of a journey through France, Italy and Germany. London: for A. Strahan, 1789. 1st edn. 2 vols. 3ff advts at end vol 2. Rec half mottled calf, spines gilt.
(Lloyd-Roberts) **£125 [≈$225]**

De Reaumur, Rene Antoinette Ferchault
- The art of hatching and bringing up domestick fowls of all kinds ... by means of the heat of hot-beds or that of common fire. London: for C. davis ..., 1750. 1st English edn. 8vo. 15 fldg engvd plates, 10 engvd vignettes. Contemp calf, gilt, jnts reprd.
(Traylen) **£295 [≈$531]**

De Rochefort, Charles
- The history of the Caribby Islands ... rendered into English by John Davies of Kidwelly. London: 1666. 1st English edn. Sm folio. 351 pp. 9 engvd plates (a little soiled at margs, 1 shaved at hd). Early ink inscrptn on

title. Contemp mottled calf, rebacked.
(Bonham) £750 [≈ $1,350]

D'Urfey, Thomas
- Collin's walk through London and Westminster. A poem in burlesque. Written by T.D. gent. London: for Rich. Parker ..., 1690. 1st edn. Cr 8vo. Half blue mor, gilt. Wing D2719. *(Traylen)* £330 [≈ $594]
- The fool turned critick: a comedy: as it was acted at the Theatre-Royall. London: for James Magnes ..., 1678. 1st edn. 8vo. [4],60 pp. Title browned & with 2 sl tears, reinforced on verso, foxed & darkened throughout. 19th c half calf.
(Pirages) $250 [≈ £138]
- Wit and mirth: or pills to purge melancholy ... the best merry ballads and songs ... fitted to all humours ... London: for J. Tonson ..., 1719-20. 1st coll edn. 6 vols. 12mo. Port frontis vol 1. 1 title cut round & mtd, some page browning. Later mor, gilt.
(Claude Cox) £450 [≈ $810]

Deageant de Saint Martin, Guichard
- The memoirs of Monsieur Deageant ... most secret transactions and affairs of France ... London: 1690. 1st English edn. 12mo. Contemp calf, worn. Wing D490.
(Robertshaw) £38 [≈ $68]

Debate ...
- A friendly debate between Dr. Kingsman, a dissatisfied clergyman, and Gratianus Trimmer ... concerning the late Thanksgiving Day ... London: Jonathan Robinson, 1689. 4to. [viii],78 pp. Disbound, a bit dog-eared, 1 crnr torn affecting a few words. Wing F2218.
(Clark) £18 [≈ $32]

Declaration ...
- The declaration by the Representatives of the United Colonies of North America ... setting forth the causes and necessity of taking up arms. London: 1775. 1st English edn. Title washed, some leaves cut close with loss of catchwords. Mod half calf, mrbld bds.
(Charles Cox) £150 [≈ $270]
- A declaration of the present sufferings of ... Quakers ... See Burrough, Edward
- A declaration of the proceedings of ... Lord General Fairfax in the reducing of the revolted troops ... humble petition of the ... prisoners remaining in the Church of Burford. Oxford, & reprinted London: for John Playford, 1649. 4to. Old wraps. New Wing D745. *(Marlborough)* £65 [≈ $117]

Defence ...
- A defence of the measure of the present administration being an impartial answer to what has been objected against it ... London: J. Peele, 1731. 32 pp. Rebound in bds.
(C.R. Johnson) £28 [≈ $50]
- A serious defence of some late measures ... See Douglas, John

Defoe, Daniel
- The dyet of Poland, a satyr. Printed at Dantzick [i.e. London]: 1705. 1st edn. 8vo. 60 pp. V closely cropped. Old mrbld bds, new lea backstrip, hinges mended.
(Argosy) $300 [≈ £166]
- An essay upon publick credit. London: By the booksellers, 1710. 3rd edn. 8vo. New wraps.
(Marlborough) £350 [≈ $630]
- A general history of the robberies and murders of the most notorious pyrates ... by Captain Charles Johnson. London: for Ch. Rivington ..., 1724. 1st edn. 8vo. 3 plates (1 fldg). Paper sl browned at end. Contemp panelled calf. *(Hannas)* £550 [≈ $990]
- An historical narrative of the Great Plague at London, 1665 ... And some account of other remarkable plagues, ancient and modern. London: W. Nicoll, 1769. 8vo. Some spotting. Mod calf, in calf & cloth slipcase.
(Chaucer Head) £180 [≈ $324]
- History of the plague in London with suitable reflections. Bath: S. Hazard, [1795]. 8vo. W'cut on title. Sewn as issued. An abridgement, Cheap Repository Tract.
(Waterfield's) £30 [≈ $54]
- The history of the Union of Great Britain. Edinburgh: 1709. 1st edn. Thick folio. Contemp panelled calf, rebacked.
(Argosy) $350 [≈ £194]
- A hymn to victory. London: J. Nutt, 1704. 4to. [viii],52 pp. Title soiled, torn at inner margin & mtd with loss of 1 letter, some lesser browning & soiling elsewhere, a few contemp underlinings & marg notes. Mod calf.
(Clark) £85 [≈ $153]
- Jure Divino: a satyr in twelve books. 1706. Cr 8vo. 19th c calf, rubbed.
(Halewood) £75 [≈ $135]
- Jure Divino: a satyr in twelve books. London: 1706. Folio. Engvd frontis. 2 leaves misbound. Early sgntr on title verso. Contemp panelled calf, rebacked.
(Waterfield's) £200 [≈ $360]
- Jure Divino: a satyr. In twelve books. By the author of the True-Born-Englishman. London: 1706. 12mo. Frontis. Polished calf. Spurious edn published by Benjamin Bragg.
(Argosy) $175 [≈ £97]

- The life and strange surprizing adventures of Robinson Crusoe ... Third edition. London: for W. Taylor, 1719. Copperplate port frontis by Clark & Pine, pub w'cut device on title, 4 pp pub terminal advts. Rec half brown calf, red speckled edges. *(Sotheran)* **£385 [≈ $693]**
- The life and strange surprizing adventures of Robinson Crusoe. London: John Stockdale, 1790. 2 vols. 8vo. 2 frontis, 14 plates inc port. Some foxing, crnr torn from vol 1 S6. 19th c half calf, gilt spine. *(Spelman)* **£165 [≈ $297]**
- Memoirs of a cavalier: or a military journal of the wars in Germany ... London: for A. Bell, [1720]. 1st edn. Post 8vo. Contemp panelled calf, sometime rebacked, red speckled edges. *(Sotheran)* **£155 [≈ $279]**
- No Queen: or, no General. An argument, proving the necessity Her Majesty was in ... to displace the D--- of M----borough. 1712. 1st edn. 8vo. 52 pp. Half-title. Last 4 pp mispaginated. Later blue wraps. *(Gough)* **£175 [≈ $315]**
- The re-presentation, or a search for the plunderers of the nation ... London: 1711. 8vo. New wraps. *(Marlborough)* **£280 [≈ $504]**
- A system of magick or a history of the black art ... London: A. Millar, 1728. 2nd edn. 8vo. xii,404 pp. Engvd frontis. Some soiling. New half calf, gilt. *(Lloyd-Roberts)* **£125 [≈ $225]**
- A tour thro' the whole island of Great Britain ... by a gentleman ... the fourth edition. With very great additions ... which bring it down to ... 1748. For S. Birt, 1748. 4 vols. Lge 12mo. Contemp calf, gilt spines. *(Fenning)* **£145 [≈ $261]**
- A tour through ... Great Britain divided into circuits of journies ... continued by the late Mr. Richardson, and brought down to the present time ... London: J. Rivington ..., 1769. 7th edn. 4 vols. Contemp calf. *(C.R. Johnson)* **£450 [≈ $810]**

Delamayne, Thomas Hallie
- The senators: or, a candid examination into the merits of the principal performers of St. Stephen's Chapel. London: for G. Kearsley, 1772. 2nd edn. 8vo. Vignette title. Lacking half-title. Disbound. *(Waterfield's)* **£45 [≈ $81]**

Delany, Patrick
- A sermon preached in Christ-Church, Dublin before His Grace William, Duke of Devonshire ... Martyrdom of King Charles the First ... Dublin: Owen, 1737. Sm 4to. 20 pp. Mod wraps. *(Emerald Isle)* **£45 [≈ $81]**

Delap, John
- The Royal Pavilion, an ode ... Lewes: for W. Lee, 1792. Sole edn. 4to. 11,[i] pp. A little light soiling. 18th c ownership inscrptn on title. Stitched as issued. *(Bennett)* **£350 [≈ $630]**

Dell, William
- Several sermons and discourses ... and now gathered in one volume ... London: reprinted by J. Sowle, 1709. Cr 8vo. 8 pp ctlg. New grey bds. *(Stewart)* **£30 [≈ $54]**

Demonstration ...
- A demonstration of the necessity of a legislative union of Great Britain and Ireland ... by a Philosopher. Dublin: 1799. 8vo. 40 pp. Mod wraps. *(Emerald Isle)* **£25 [≈ $45]**

Demophilus (pseud.)
- The genuine principles of the ancient Saxon, or English constitution ... observations, on their peculiar fitness, for the United Colonies ... Phila: Robert Bell, 1776. [47] pp. Title chipped with loss of 2 letters, 3ff creased, 1 reprd. Later half mor. *(Reese)* **$3,000 [≈ £1,666]**

Demosthenes
- Several orations of Demosthenes, to encourage the Athenians to oppose the exorbitant power of Philip of Macedon. English'd ... by several hands. London: for Jacob Tonson, 1702. [vi],167, 108,[ii], 109-222 pp. Contemp speckled Cambridge calf. *(Pirages)* **$150 [≈ £83]**

Denham, Sir John
- Coopers-Hill. A poem. London: Hills, 1709. 8vo. Disbound. *(Marlborough)* **£45 [≈ $81]**

Deputies ...
- The deputies of the republic of Amsterdam to the States of Holland convicted of High Treason ... London: for Randal Taylor, 1684. Sm 4to. New wraps. Wing 1085. *(Stewart)* **£20 [≈ $36]**

Derham, William
- The artificial clock-maker. A treatise of watch, and clock-work. London: Knapton, 1696. 1st edn. 8vo in 4s. [12],132 pp. W'cut plate, 2 w'cut ills in text. Some waterstaining, dust-soiled throughout. Contemp panelled calf, spine chipped, rubbed. Wing D1099. *(Pickering)* **$3,000 [≈ £1,666]**
- Astro-theology: or a demonstration of the being and attributes of God, from a survey of

the heavens. London: Innys, 1715. 1st edn. 8vo. lviii,[vi], 228,[vii] pp. 3 fldg engvd plates, w'cut vignette on title. Contemp calf, sl rubbed. *(Blackwell's)* **£150 [≈ $270]**

- Astro-theology: or a demonstration of the being and attributes of God, from a survey of the heavens. London: Innys, 1719. 3rd edn, imprvd. 8vo. [xvi],lvi, [viii],246, [x] pp. 3 fldg plates. Contemp calf.
(Lloyd-Roberts) **£90 [≈ $162]**

Derwent Priory ...
- Derwent Priory; or, memoirs of an orphan ... See Kendall, A.

Desaguliers, J.T.
- A course of experimental philosophy. London: 1734-44. 1st edn. 2 vols. 4to. 10ff, 463,12 index & pub ctlg; xv,568,8 index & ctlg pp. 78 fldg plates. 2 pp soiled, few marg stains. Mod half calf. *(Weiner)* **£500 [≈ $900]**

Deulmen, Alf von
- Alf von Deulman; or the history of the Emperor Philip ... See Naubert, Christiane Benedicte Eugenie

Deveil, Sir Thomas
- Memoirs of the life and times of ... London: M. Cooper ..., 1748. 1st edn. 8vo. [11],83 pp. Uncut in wraps. *(Young's)* **£120 [≈ $216]**

Devil in Disguise ...
- The devil in disguise: or, Rome run a roving ... many monsterous cheats and imposters that the popish clergy in France designed to impose upon mankind ... London: for Joseph Marshall, 1710. 8vo. [vii],331,1 pub advts pp. Some browning. Mod calf.
(Kerr) **£175 [≈ $315]**

Dewitt, John
- Fables moral and political, with large explications. Translated from the Dutch. London: 1703. 1st edn in English. 2 vols. 8vo. Engvd frontis. Contemp calf, jnts cracked, labels missing. *(Bennett)* **£85 [≈ $153]**

Diaboliad ...
- The diaboliad, a poem ... See Combe, William

Dialogue ...
- A dialogue between a lady and her pupils ... See Brooke, Charlotte

Diary ...
- A diary kept in an excursion to Little

Hampton ... See Phillips, Peregrine

Dibdin, Charles, the elder
- Hannah Hewit; or, the female Crusoe. being the history of a woman of uncommon mental and personal accomplishments ... supposed to be written by herself. London: [1792]. 3 vols. Contemp qtr calf, rebacked.
(C.R. Johnson) **£750 [≈ $1,350]**
- The younger brother: a novel. in three volumes. London: for the author, [1793]. Half-titles. Contemp qtr calf, mrbld bds.
(C.R. Johnson) **£800 [≈ $1,440]**

Dickenson, Jonathan
- God's protecting providence ... the remarkable deliverance of Robert Barrow ... from the devouring waves of the sea ... the cruel devouring jaws of the inhuman cannibals of Florida. James Phillips, 1790. 7th edn. 8vo. xiv,135 pp. Occas soiling. Wraps. *(Farahar)* **£250 [≈ $450]**

Dickson, Adam
- The husbandry of the ancients. Edinburgh: for J. Dickson ..., 1788. 1st edn. 2 vols. 8vo. Half-titles. Contemp half calf, gilt.
(Traylen) **£220 [≈ $396]**
- The husbandry of the ancients. Edinburgh: J. Dickson ..., and London: G. Robinson ..., 1788. 2 vols. 8vo. Minor marg worming at end vol 2. Contemp calf, spines gilt, lacking numbering-pieces. *(Clark)* **£120 [≈ $216]**
- A treatise of agriculture. Edinburgh: for A. Kincaid ..., 1770. 2nd edn. 2 vols. 8vo. 2 fldg plates. Contemp speckled calf, gilt ribbed spines. *(Traylen)* **£180 [≈ $324]**

Dickson, David
- An essay on the possibility and probability of a child being born alive, and live, in the latter end of the fifth solar ... month. Edinburgh: James Watson, 1712. 1st edn. 12mo. Without half-title. Contemp panelled calf, rebacked.
(Quaritch) **$700 [≈ £388]**

Dictionarium ...
- Dictionarium rusticum ... See Worlidge, John

Dictionary ...
- A classical dictionary of the vulgar tongue ... See Grose, Francis
- A general dictionary of the English language ... By a Society of Gentlemen. London: for J. & R. Fuller, 1768. 1st edn (? Unrecorded?). 4to. [716] pp. Ms family genealogy on endleaves, a little light soiling. Contemp calf,

worn, jnts split.   *(Bennett)* **£550 [≈ $990]**
- The modern dictionary of arts and sciences ... London: for the authors ..., 1774. 1st edn. 4 vols. 8vo. Frontis, 47 engvd plates (a few with outer margs trimmed close with loss of plate numerals). Orig mrbld bds, calf spines with sl wear, 2 jnts cracked.
                        (Bickersteth) **£170 [≈ $306]**
- A new and general biographical dictionary. London: for G.G. & J. Robinson, 1798. New edn. 15 vols. 8vo. Occas foxing. Contemp qtr calf by J.R. Taylor, rather rubbed, ends of some spines a little worn, labels missing.
                        (Burmester) **£300 [≈ $540]**

Difficiles Nugae ...
- Difficiles Nugae ... See Hale, Sir Matthew

Digby, George
- The third speech of the late George Digby to the House of Commons. London: Thomas Walkley, 1640. Sm 4to. 19 pp. Lacking prelim blank. 19th c calf, spine ends worn.
                        (Spelman) **£35 [≈ $63]**

Dillenius, J.J.
- Historia muscorum: A general history of land and water ... mosses and corals, containing all the known species. London: J. Millan, 1768. 4to. 85 engvd plates. Contemp mss notes on plate margs. Half mor bds.
                        (Halewood) **£220 [≈ $396]**

Dimsdale, Thomas
- The present method of inoculating for the smallpox. London: 1767. 3rd edn. 160 pp. No half-title (called for?). Mod qtr lea, cloth bds.
                        (Scientia) **$275 [≈ £152]**

Diodati, John
- Pious and learned annotations upon the Holy Bible ... London: for Nicolas Fussell, 1651. 3rd edn. Folio. Unpaginated. Port frontis, engvd title. Pristine contemp calf, ruled in blind, raised bands
                        (Frew Mackenzie) **£220 [≈ $396]**

Diodorus Siculus
- The historical library of Diodorus the Sicilian. In fifteen books ... the antiquities of Egypt, Asia, Africa ... and other parts of the world. London: for Awnsham ..., 1700. Folio. [xxviii],797, [xxxii] pp. Occas browning. Contemp calf, rebacked, crnrs bumped.
                        (Frew Mackenzie) **£98 [≈ $176]**

Dirom, Alexander
- A narrative of the campaign in India, which

terminated the war with Tippoo Sultan, in 1792. 1794. 2nd edn. 4to. 9 engvd plates & maps. Some foxing, marg stain on a few leaves. Contemp calf, spine lavishly gilt, jnts starting.   *(Allen)* **$225 [≈ £125]**

Discourse ...
- A discourse concerning the laws ecclesiastical and civil, made against hereticks ... Dublin: re-printed by A. Rhames, 1723. Cr 8vo. Contemp panelled calf. *(Stewart)* **£45 [≈ $81]**
- A discourse concerning the nature, power and proper effects of the present conventions in both Kingdoms called by the Prince of Orange ... London: for J.L. ..., 1689. 1st edn. 4to. 18 pp. Disbound. Wing D1588.
                        (Young's) **£30 [≈ $54]**
- A discourse concerning the period of humane life ... See Allestree, Richard
- A discourse on the bookland and folkland of the Saxons ... See Heckford, Reyner

Disney, John
- An essay upon the execution of the laws against immorality and prophaneness. London: Joseph Downing, 1708. 1st edn. 8vo. xxv,200 [i.e. 210] pp. Preceding advts leaf. Contemp calf, rubbed, spine chipped at hd.   *(Frew Mackenzie)* **£115 [≈ $207]**

Dispensary ...
- The dispensary: a poem ... See Garth, Sir Samuel

Dissenting Teachers ...
- The dissenting teachers address to the J--to against the bill for building fifty new churches in and about the cities of London and Westminster ... London: 1711. 20 pp. Rebound.   *(C.R. Johnson)* **£35 [≈ $63]**

Dissertation ...
- A learned dissertation upon old women, male and female, spiritual and temporal, in all ages; whether in church, state, or Exchange-Alley ... London: for J. Roberts, 1720. 2nd edn. 8vo. 31,[1] pp. Disbound.
                        (Burmester) **£150 [≈ $270]**

Dobbs, Francis
- A letter to the Rt. Hon. Lord North on his propositions in favour of Ireland. Dublin: M. Mills, 1780. 8vo. 28 pp. Bds.
                        (Emerald Isle) **£85 [≈ $153]**

Doctor ...
- Doctor dissected: or, Willy Cadogan in the kitchen. Addressed to all invalids, and readers

of a late dissertation on the gout, etc., etc. By a lady. London: T. Davies, 1771. 21 pp. Rebound in qtr mor, mrbld bds.
(C.R. Johnson) **£300** [≈ **$540**]

Dodd, William
- The beauties of history; or pictures of virtue and vice ... selected for the instruction and entertainment of youth. London: Vernor & Hood ..., 1796. 2nd edn. W'cuts by Bewick. Contemp calf. *(C.R. Johnson)* **£70** [≈ **$126**]
- Sermons to young men. London: for J. Knox ..., 1771. 3 vols. Sm 8vo. Panel cut from title in 1 vol removing author's name. Contemp sheep, spines worn.
(Lloyd-Roberts) **£10** [≈ **$18**]

Dodd, William (1729-1777)
- Authentic memoirs of the life of William Dodd ... with particulars of his trial and execution ... Salisbury: Printed & sold by Jos. Hodson ..., [1777]. 2nd edn. 8vo. [iv],48 pp. W'cut port. Outer leaves trifle dusty. Disbound. *(Burmester)* **£200** [≈ **$360**]

Dodington, George Bubb
- The diary of the late ... from March 8, 1748-49, to February 6, 1761 ... Salisbury: E. Easton ..., 1784. 1st edn. 8vo. Advt leaf, halftitle. Orig grey bds, cloth spine, uncut edges.
(Traylen) **£150** [≈ **$270**]
- The diary, with an appendix containing some curious and interesting papers. Dublin: Porter, 1784. Lge 12mo. Contemp calf.
(Marlborough) **£60** [≈ **$108**]

Doddridge, P.
- The rise and progress of religion in the soul ... added a sermon on the care of the soul. London: for J. Buckland ..., 1771. 10th edn. Cr 8vo. Contemp calf, sl damaged.
(Stewart) **£20** [≈ **$36**]
- Some remarkable passages in the life of the honourable Colonel James Gardiner ... slain at the battle of Prestonpans ... 1745. Edinburgh: for Mundell, 1798. 12mo. 268 pp. Contemp calf, rebacked.
(Claude Cox) **£15** [≈ **$27**]

Doddridge, Philip
- A course of lectures on the principal subjects in pneumatology, ethics and divinity ... London: by assignment from the author's widow, 1776. 2nd edn, crrctd. 1 vol bound in 2. 4to. Interleaved throughout. Contemp calf, rec rebacked. *(Stewart)* **£75** [≈ **$135**]
- A course of lectures on the principal subjects in pneumatology, ethics and divinity with

reference to the most considerable authors on each subject ... London: for J. Buckland ..., 1776. 2nd edn, crrctd. 4to. Contemp calf, rather rubbed. *(Waterfield's)* **£120** [≈ **$216**]
- Hymns founded on various texts in the Holy Scriptures. Salop: J. Eddowes ..., 1755. 1st edn. Thick sm 12mo. Mod wraps.
(Argosy) **$60** [≈ **£33**]

Dodsley, Robert
- The oeconomy of human life. In two parts ... Printed at Glasgow, 1765; sold by Robert Bell, Dublin [Reprinted Dublin: ca 1765]. 12mo. [iv],xv, [i],54; iv,[ii],92 pp. Engvd frontis. Contemp mottled calf.
(Burmester) **£45** [≈ **$81**]
- The oeconomy of human life. Translated from an Indian manuscript ... London: for Harding, 1795. One of 25 lge paper. 8vo. 22,119 pp. 49 engvd vignettes. Contemp red mor, gilt, a.e.g., cvrs a little darkened in places. *(Marlborough)* **£550** [≈ **$990**]
- A selection of poems in six volumes. By several hands. London: for J. Dodsley, 1775. 6 vols. 8vo. Half-titles in each vol. Contemp polished calf, spines elab gilt, red & green labels, 1 vol sl chipped at hd of spine.
(Chaucer Head) **£320** [≈ **$576**]

Doe, John
- The whole proceedings on the trial of an ejectment between John Doe ... against Eliza Rankin. London: J. Debrett, 1786. 8vo. [2],259 pp. Advts. Uncut & sl dusty. Orig wraps, respined. *(Spelman)* **£20** [≈ **$36**]

Domestic Happiness ...
- The guide to domestic happiness. In a series of letters. London: for J. Buckland, 1781. 3rd edn. 12mo. [ii],79 pp. Engvd ill on title. Disbound. *(Burmester)* **£45** [≈ **$81**]

Donlevy, Andrew
- The catechism or Christian doctrine by way of question and answer ... An Teagasg Criosduidne ... Paris: James Guerin, 1742. 8vo. 518 pp. English & Irish text. Contemp calf, rebacked. *(Emerald Isle)* **£400** [≈ **$720**]

Donne, John
- Devotions upon emergent occasions, and severall steps in my sicknes. London: for Thomas Jones, 1625. 3rd edn. Sm 8vo. Lacking A1 (blank) & B6 & B7 (text leaves). Rebound in calf. STC 7035.
(Stewart) **£200** [≈ **$360**]
- Letters to severall persons of honour. London: for Richard Marriot, 1651. 1st edn.

4to. [vi],318 pp. Engvd port. Without initial & final blanks. Contemp sprinkled calf, rebacked. Wing D1864.
(Bennett) **£650 [≈ $1,170]**
- Poems, &c. With elegies on the author's death ... added divers copies under his own hand, never before printed. In the Savoy: for Henry Herringman, 1669. 5th edn. 8vo. [viii],414 pp. Initial & final blanks. Contemp mottled calf. Wing D1871. *(Bennett)* **£675 [≈ $1,215]**

Donovan, Edward
- An epitome of the natural history of the insects of China. London: 1798-[1799]. 1st edn. 4to. 50 hand-cold plates. Mod half calf, gilt, a.e.g.
(Wheldon & Wesley) **£3,300 [≈ $5,940]**
- An epitome of the natural history of the insects of China. London: for the author, 1798. 1st edn. 4to. 48ff letterpress, 50 hand-cold plates. Contemp half red mor, mrbld bds.   *(Gough)* **£3,750 [≈ $6,750]**
- Instructions for collecting and preserving various subjects of natural history ... together with a treatise on the management of insects ... London: for the author, 1794. 1st edn. Thick paper. 8vo. [iv],86 pp. 2 engvd plates. Contemp mrbld bds, rebacked.
(Burmester) **£225 [≈ $405]**
- The natural history of British insects. London: Rivington, 1793-1813. 16 vols in 4. 8vo. All vols except 1st in 1st edn. 576 engvd plates, all but 7 hand-cold. Sl spotting of text. Contemp half calf gilt, restored.
(Ash) **£2,000 [≈ $3,600]**
- A natural history of British birds. London: 1794-1819. Roy 8vo. 10 vols in 5. All 1st iss excepting vols 3 & 5, 1815 & 1820 re-issues. 244 hand-cold plates. Some v limited foxing in text. 19th c citron calf, gilt, a.e.g.
(Wheldon & Wesley) **£3,750 [≈ $6,750]**

Dossie, Robert
- The elaboratory laid open, or, the secrets of modern chemistry and pharmacy revealed. London: for J. Nourse, 1758. 1st edn. 8vo. Some marg browning to title & a few other pp. Contemp calf, hinges splitting, crnrs worn.   *(Chaucer Head)* **£200 [≈ $360]**
- Institutes of experimental chemistry ... an essay towards reducing that branch of natural philosophy to a regular system. London: Nourse, 1759. 1st edn. 2 vols. 8vo. xx,[viii], 491,[i]; [iv],437,[xxiii] pp. Occas light foxing. Contemp calf, gilt, rubbed.
(Frew Mackenzie) **£200 [≈ $360]**

Douglas, Gawin
- Select works. Containing memoirs of the author, the Palace of Honour, Prologues to the Aenid, and a Glossary of Obsolete Words ... Perth: R. Morison Jnr ..., 1787. 1st edn thus. 8vo. lxi,156 pp. Engvd port. Uncut in orig wraps, chipped.   *(Young's)* **£40 [≈ $72]**

Douglas, James
- Myographiae comparatae specimen: or, a comparative description of all the muscles in a man and in a quadruped ... muscles peculiar to a woman. London: for George Strahan, 1707. 1st edn. 12mo. Contemp panelled calf, rebacked, mor label, gilt.
(Traylen) **£120 [≈ $216]**
- Myographiae comparatae specimen: or, a comparative description of all the muscles in a man and in a quadruped ... London: for George Strahan, 1707. 1st edn. 12mo. Title & margs a little browned. Contemp panelled calf, spine repaired. *(Quaritch)* **$300 [≈ £166]**
- Myog aphiae comparatae specimen: or, a comparative description of all the muscles in a man and in a quadruped ... a new edition ... London: 1763. 8vo. xxxi,240 pp. Contemp calf, rebacked. Sgntr of "John Hunter, jr" on blank. Soc of Apothecaries b'plate.
(Goodrich) **$195 [≈ £108]**

Douglas, John
- A serious defence of some late measures of the administration ... with regard to the introduction and establishment of foreign troops. London: J. Morgan, 1756. 54 pp.
(C.R. Johnson) **£45 [≈ $81]**

Douglas, William
- The stable trueths of the Kirk require a suitable behaviour ... a sermon ... Aberdeen: J.B. March, 1660. 1st edn. Sm 4to. 47 pp. Title restored at crnr, 2nd leaf defective in crnr, sl browned & frayed at fore-edge. Later qtr calf. New Wing D2044.
(Frew Mackenzie) **£70 [≈ $126]**

Dow, Alexander
- The history of Hindostan. London: for T. Becket ..., 1768. 1st edn. 2 vols. 4to. lxxvi,364; [vi],298,96 pp. 2 engvd frontis, engvd fldg map. Occas spotting. Near-contemp half calf, rebacked.
(Young's) **£140 [≈ $252]**
- The history of Hindostan. London: T. Becket ..., 1768. 2 vols. 4to. 2 engvd frontis, fldg map. Old drab bds, uncut, jnts cracked, backstrips worn.   *(Clark)* **£95 [≈ $171]**

Drage, Theodore
- An account of a voyage for the discovery of a North-West Passage by Hudson's Streights ... performed in the years 1746 and 1747, in the ship 'California'. London: 1748. 2 vols in 1. vii,237; [238]-342,[18] pp. 4 plates, 6 fldg maps. Contemp calf, rebacked.
(Reese) **$4,250 [≈ £2,361]**

Drake, James
- Anthropologia nova; or, a new system of anatomy. London: Walford, 1707. 2 vols. Port, 81 plates (ex 83), of which 30 fldg. Lacking 2 fldg plates vol 2, a few plates with sm tears. Contemp panelled calf, jnts worn, 1 bd nearly detached. *(Pollak)* **£150 [≈ $270]**

Drayton, Michael
- The battaille of Agincourt. London: William Lee, 1627. 1st edn. xii,218 pp. Port frontis in facsimile, trivial discoloration on 3 or 4 leaves. Mod sprinkled calf.
(Pirages) **$325 [≈ £180]**
- England's heroical epistles, with notes and illustrations. London: for J. Johnson, 1788. 8vo. viii,332,[4] pp. Contemp calf, spine rubbed, jnts cracked.
(Burmester) **£120 [≈ $216]**

Drew, Charles
- An authentick account of the life of Mr. Charles Drew ... tried and convicted at Bury Assizes, for the murder of his father ... London: J. Applebee, 1740. 1st edn. 8vo. 48 pp. Outer leaves dusty. Disbound.
(Burmester) **£70 [≈ $126]**

Drexel, Jeremy
- The Christian's Zodiake or twelve signes of predestination unto life everlasting. Samuel Browne, 1647. 24mo. [viii],253 pp. Cut close at upper edge with occas shaving of running title, minor reprs to 2 leaves. Later mottled calf, gilt, a.e.g.
(Frew Mackenzie) **£375 [≈ $675]**

Drinkwater, John
- A history of the late siege of Gibraltar. With a description and account of that garrison. Dublin: for Messrs. Colles ..., 1786. Printing defect on 1 leaf without loss of text. Rebound in qtr calf. *(Hughes)* **£35 [≈ $63]**
- A history of the late siege of Gibraltar. With a description and account of that garrison. Dublin: 1793. 8vo. 339 pp. Port frontis, 2 ports, sm fldg plan. Tear in 3 leaves, sm stains & dustmarks. Rec mrbld bds, mor spine.
(Bow Windows) **£55 [≈ $99]**

Driscoll, Paddy
- A political address to the Catholics of Ireland. Dublin: P. Burne, 1792. 39 pp. Orig stabbed pamphlet, uncut as issued.
(C.R. Johnson) **£28 [≈ $50]**

Drummond, William, of Hawthornden
- The history of Scotland, from the year 1423 until the year 1542. London: for Thomas Fabian, [1680]. 8vo. Engvd port frontis, 5 other ports. Title sl dusty, some minor defects in blank margs. Ex lib with stamps. Mod qtr calf. Wing D2197 *(Hughes)* **£85 [≈ $153]**

Drury, Robert
- Madagascar; or ... journal during fifteen years' captivity on that Island ... London: 1729. 1st edn. 8vo. 464 pp. 5 plates. Contemp calf. *(Argosy)* **$400 [≈ £222]**

Dryden, John
- All for love: or, the world well lost, a tragedy, as it is acted at the Theatre-Royal and written in imitation of Shakespeare's stile. London: for H. Herringman, 1692. 2nd edn. 4to. Title, 80 pp. Unbound. Wing D2230.
(Traylen) **£40 [≈ $72]**
- Amphitryon; or, the two Sofia's. A comedy ... added the musick of the songs, compos'd by Mr. Henry Purcell. London: for J. Tonson ..., 1691. 1st edn, 2nd iss. Title, 66 pp, sep title to music (for J. Tonson, 1690), 13 pp music. Unbound. Wing D2230.
(Traylen) **£120 [≈ $216]**
- The assignation: or, love in a nunnery. As it is acted at the Theatre Royal ... London: for Henry Herringman ..., 1678. 2nd edn. 4to. x,63 pp. Later vellum-backed bds. Wing D2242. *(Young's)* **£65 [≈ $117]**
- Cleomenes, the Spartan Heroe. A tragedy, as it is acted at the Theatre Royal. London: for Jacob Tonson, 1692. 1st edn. 4to. Title, 82 pp. Unbound. Wing D2254.
(Traylen) **£150 [≈ $270]**
- Don Sebastian ... a tragedy acted at the Theatre Royal. London: for Jo. Hindmarsh, 1692. 2nd edn. 4to. Title, 126 pp. 1 leaf torn & reprd, sl affecting ptd surface. Unbound. Wing D2263. *(Traylen)* **£75 [≈ $135]**
- Don Sebastian, King of Portugal: A tragedy acted at the Thetre Royal. London: for Jo. Hindmarsh ..., 1692. 2nd edn. 4to. [xvi],109,[3] pp. Some browning. Wraps. Wing D2263. *(Young's)* **£45 [≈ $81]**
- Eleonora: a panegyrical poem dedicated to the memory of the late Countess of Abingdon. London: for Jacob Tonson, 1692. 1st edn. 8vo. [viii],24 pp. Ample margs. Some leaves sl

& uniformly darkened. Mod mor.
(Pirages) **$250** [≈ **£138**]
- The fables ... ornamented with engravings from the pencil of ... Lady Diana Beuclerc. London: for J. Edwards, 1797. Folio. 241 pp. 9 full-page & num vignette engvs. Some offsetting. Contemp str-grain mor, gilt spine, a.e.g., lightly rubbed.
(Argonaut) **$325** [≈ **£180**]
- The fables ... ornamented with engravings from the pencil of ... Lady Diana Beuclerc. London: T. Bensley, 1797. Lge 4to. xviii,241 pp. 9 stipple-engvd plates by Bartolozzi, Cheesman et al. Rec half mor.
(Spelman) **£150** [≈ **$270**]
- The hind and the panther. London: Jacob Tonson, 1687. 3rd edn. 8vo. [4]ff, 145 pp. Ample margs. Mod paper bds, sl browned & worn.
(Pirages) **$125** [≈ **£69**]
- The kind keeper; or, Mr. Limberham; a comedy as it is acted at the Duke's Theatre ... London: for R. Bentley ..., 1690. 2nd edn. 4to. title, 70 pp. Unbound. Wing D2298.
(Traylen) **£75** [≈ **$135**]
- The kind sleeper; or, Mr. Limberham. London: R. Bentley ..., 1680. 1st edn. 8vo. x,65 pp. Wide margs. 3 gatherings somewhat browned. Thick mrbld paper bds in fldg cloth box.
(Pirages) **$275** [≈ **£152**]
- Oedipus: a tragedy, as it is acted at ... the Dukes Theatre. London: for Richard Bentley, 1692. 4th edn. 4to. Title, 76 pp. Crnr torn from preface affecting last 4 lines. Unbound. Wing D2325.
(Traylen) **£40** [≈ **$72**]
- Of dramatic poesie, an essay. London: for Henry Herringman, 1693. 3rd edn. 4to. Title, 55 pp. Unbound. Wing 2329.
(Traylen) **£40** [≈ **$72**]
- Original poems and translations, now first collected ... in two volumes. London: for J. & R. Tonson, 1743. 1st coll edn. 2 vols. 12mo. [12],336; [12],336 pp. Red & black title. Contemp calf, gilt, upper hinges cracked, a little rubbed.
(Claude Cox) **£60** [≈ **$108**]
- The satires of Decimus Junius Juvenalis. Translated into English verse by Mr. Dryden ... London: Tonson, 1693. 1st edn of Dryden trans. Folio. [lvi],316,[4],87 pp. Old waterstain affecting top marg of approx 80 pp. Contemp calf, rebacked. Wing J1288.
(Karmiole) **$300** [≈ **£166**]
- Secret-love; or, the Maiden-Queen. As it is acted ... London: for Henry Herringman, 1691. 2nd edn. 4to. Title, 60 pp. Unbound. Wing D2357.
(Traylen) **£65** [≈ **$117**]
- The Spanish fryar, or, the double discovery. London: for R. & J. Tonson, 1690. 3rd edn. 8vo. viii,64 pp. Ink anntn on title, 1 inch tear

at bottom of 7 leaves touching text, v sl darkened. Disbound. *(Pirages)* **$100** [≈ **£55**]
- The Spanish fryar, or, the double discovery. London: for E. & J. Tonson, 1695. 4th edn. 8vo. [4]ff, 63 pp. Sl darkened with occas spotting. Mod mor-backed bds, sl rubbed.
(Pirages) **$125** [≈ **£69**]
- The state of innocence, and fall of man. An opera. Written in heroic verse ... London: for Henry Herringman ..., 1678. 3rd edn. 4to. [xx],44 pp. Later vellum-backed bds. Wing D2373.
(Young's) **£60** [≈ **$108**]
- Troilus and Cressida, or, truth found too late, a tragedy as it is acted at the Duke Theatre. London: for Abell Swall ..., 1679. 1st edn. 4to. Title, 95 pp. Unbound. Wing D2388.
(Traylen) **£190** [≈ **$342**]
- The vindication ... London: for Jacob Tonson, 1683. 1st edn. 8vo. [ii],60 pp. Sl darkened at edges, occas spotting. Disbound.
(Pirages) **$150** [≈ **£83**]
- The works of Virgil. Translated by John Dryden, Esq. Glasgow: Foulis, 1769. 3 vols. Port frontis, fldg map, half-title in each vol, advt leaf at back of 2 vols. Contemp calf, minor wear to extremities.
(Pirages) **$225** [≈ **£125**]

Du Bartas, Guillaume de Salluste

- His divine weekes and workes translated ... now thirdly corrected and augm. Humfrey Lownes [colophon: ... 1611]. 4to in 8s. Soiled at beginning & end, extensive reprs to crnrs & margs, num contemp & sl later ms notes. Mod calf. STC 21651. *(Charles Cox)* **£90** [≈ **$162**]
- His divine weekes and workes with a complete collection of all the other most delight-full workes: translated ... London: Lownes, 1621. Folio. [xxviii],1215 pp. Engvd title (trimmed & mtd). Lacking port, sev leaves re-margined. 19th c calf. STC 21653.
(Clark) **£75** [≈ **$135**]
- His divine weekes and workes with a complete collection of all the other most delight-full workes: translated ... London: Young, 1633. Folio. xvi,547 pp. Port, engvd & addtnl title, lge fldg plate. Marg reprs, waterstaining. Contemp calf, rebacked. STC 21654. *(P & P)* **£320** [≈ **$576**]

Du Fresnoy, Charles Alphonse

- The art of painting ... with an original preface ... by Mr. Dryden, also a short account ... by another hand. London: 1695. 1st English edn. lxii,355 pp. 4to. Half calf, mrbld bds.
(Camden) **£600** [≈ **$1,080**]
- The art of painting ... Translated into English. with an original preface, containing

a parallel between painting and poetry: by Mr Dryden. London: 1716. F'cap 8vo. 2nd edn, crrctd & enlgd. [16],lxviii, [4],397,[7] pp. Engvd frontis. Contemp calf, jnts reprd.
(Spelman) £120 [≃ $216]

Du Moulin, Louis
- A short and true account of the several advances the Church of England hath made towards Rome. Printed in the year 1680. Disbound. Wing D2553.
(Waterfield's) £35 [≃ $63]

Du Moulin, Peter
- The elements of logick ... now translated into English by Joshua Ahier. Oxford: Henry Hall, 1647. 2nd English edn. Sm 8vo. [10],155 pp. Title lightly soiled. Sgntr of Richard Cope (1776-1856), Qtr calf over mrbld bds. Wing D2583.
(Rootenberg) $200 [≃ £111]

Du Pin, Louis Ellies
- A new history of ecclesiastical writers ... London: for A.S. & T.C., 1697. 2 vols (later extending to 14 vols) in 1. Folio. Contemp panelled calf, a little worn.
(Charles Cox) £75 [≃ $135]

Du Roveray, J.A.
- An appeal to justice and true liberty; or an accurate statement of the proceedings of the French towards the Republic of Geneva. London: 1793. 1st edn. 8vo. 133 pp. Some foxing. Later bds. *(Robertshaw)* £20 [≃ $36]

Du Vair, Guillaume
- The morall philosophy of the Stoicks ... englished by Charles Cotton, Esq. London: for Henry Mortlock, 1671. Minor staining. Contemp sheep, backstrip rather rubbed, front jnt breaking. Wing D2917.
(Waterfield's) £120 [≃ $216]

Dublin Election ...
- The history of the Dublin Election in the year 1749. With a sketch of the present state of parties in ... Ireland. By a Briton. For John Swan, 1753. 1st edn. 8vo. xv,[1],199 pp. Rec bds. *(Fenning)* £95 [≃ $171]

Dubravius
- A new booke of good husbandry, very pleasant, and of great profite for gentlemen and yomen ... 1599. 1st edn in English. Sm 4to. Black & Roman letter, Headlines of some leaves cropped affecting a few letters. 19th c mor, gilt, a little worn. STC 7268.
(Traylen) £750 [≃ $1,350]

Dubreuil, Jean
- Practical perspective; or an easy method of representing natural objects ... London: Bowles & Carver, [1795]. 4to. xxx,150 pp. Engvd plates. Title soiled. Rebacked.
(Marlborough) £150 [≃ $270]
- The practice of perspective ... London: John Bowles, 1765. 4th edn. 4to. xvi,xvi,150 pp. 2 fldg plates. Some minor foxing to a few margs, front endpaper creased. Contemp calf, rebacked retaining orig label.
(Spelman) £140 [≃ $252]
- The practice of perspective ... representing natural objects according to the rules of art. London: Bowles, 1749. 3rd edn. 4to. xiii,[iv],[300] pp. Red & black title, 2 fldg plates, 150 full-page engvs. Inscrptns at hd of title. Sl staining of 3ff. New calf.
(Frew Mackenzie) £200 [≃ $360]
- The practice of perspective ... representing natural objects according to the rules of art. London: 1749. 3rd English edn. 4to. xiii,[5], 16,150 pp. 2 fldg plates, 150 full page engvs. Red & black title. Contemp calf, jnts cracking, rubbed. *(Edwards)* £150 [≃ $270]
- The practice of perspective ... representing natural objects according to the rules of art. London: Tho. Bowles, 1749. 3rd English edn. 4to. xiii,[5], 16,150 pp. 2 fldg plates. Contemp polished calf.
(Spelman) £225 [≃ $405]

Duck, Stephen
- Poems on several occasions written by Stephen Duck, lately a poor thresher in a barn in ... Wiltshire, at the wages of four shillings per week ... London: J. Roberts, 1730. 5th edn. Crrctd. 32 pp. Rebound in qtr calf, mrbld bds. *(C.R. Johnson)* £125 [≃ $225]

Dufour, Philippe Sylvestre
- Moral instructions of a father to his son, ready to undertake a long voyage ... Edinburgh: for W. Gray ..., 1775. 12mo. 168 pp. Rec bds. *(Burmester)* £70 [≃ $126]

Dugdale, Sir William
- The history of imbanking and drayning of divers fenns ... and of the improvements thereby. London: Alice Warren, 1662. 1st edn. Folio. Engvd port, 11 fldg maps, red & black title, 5 addtnl leaves at end. 18th c polished calf, gilt, edges gilt. Wing D2481.
(Traylen) £720 [≃ $1,296]
- The history of imbanking and drayning of divers fenns ... and of the improvements thereby. London: W. Bowyer ... 1772. 2nd edn. Folio. xii,469 pp. 11 fldg maps. Ex lib

with stamps on title & throughout. Contemp calf, rubbed, rebacked, new endpapers.
(Titles) **£225 [≈ $405]**

- The history of St. Paul's Cathedral in London. London: Tho. Warren, 1658. 1st edn. Folio. [vi],299,[v] pp. Red & black title, port, 14 plates (13 fldg), 30 text engvs (29 full-page). Occas trivial browning. 19th c tan calf, crnrs lightly rubbed.
(Frew Mackenzie) **£480 [≈ $864]**

- A short view of the late troubles in England. Oxford: for Moses Pitt, 1681. 1st edn. Folio. [vi],959,[xiii] pp. Port frontis, vignette title (dusty). Occas browning & foxing. Old calf, rebacked. Ex lib with stamps on each bd & endpapers. Wing D2492.
(Clark) **£100 [≈ $180]**

- A short view of the late troubles in England. Oxford: for Moses Pitt, 1681. 1st edn. vi,960,[6 index],[pub ctlg] pp. Engvd port frontis. New half calf. Wing D2492.
(Lloyd-Roberts) **£200 [≈ $360]**

- A short view of the late troubles in England. Oxford: for Moses Pitt, 1681. 1st edn. Sm folio. Engvd port. Title & port thumbed. Contemp calf, rubbed, later label. New Wing D2492.   *(Marlborough)* **£160 [≈ $288]**

Duhamel du Monceau, Henri Louis
- The elements of agriculture. Translated ... and revised by Philip Miller. London: P. Vaillant, 1764. 1st English edn. 2 vols. 8vo. xx,445; [8],343 pp. 14 engvd plates. Contemp half calf, rebacked & recrnrd. B'plate of Earl Fitzwilliam.   *(Spelman)* **£160 [≈ $288]**
- A practical treatise of husbandry. Wherein are contained many useful and valuable experiments and observations ... London: for C. Hitch ..., 1762. 2nd edn., crrctd & imprvd. 4to. Red & black title, 6 engvd plates (4 fldg). Contemp calf, gilt. *(Traylen)* **£140 [≈ $252]**
- A practical treatise of husbandry. Wherein are contained many useful and valuable experiments and observations ... London: C. Hitch ..., 1762. 2nd edn, crrctd & imprvd. 4to. 6 engvd plates (some fldg), fldg table. Minor browning of early leaves. Calf, scuffed.
(Clark) **£160 [≈ $288]**

Dumourier, General
- Memoirs ... translated by John Fenwick. London: 1794. 1st edn. 2 pts in 1 vol. 8vo. Contemp half calf, rebacked.
(Robertshaw) **£25 [≈ $45]**

Duncan, Andrew
- Annals of medicine for the year 1796 ... for the year 1797. Edinburgh: 1796-97. 1st edn.

2 vols. Lea, backstrips taped with black cloth, inner hinges crudely reprd. Ex lib.
(Fye) **$75 [≈ £41]**

Duncan, William
- The elements of logick. In four books: Of the original of our ideas ... Of the methods of inventions and science ... London: 1770. 12mo. 370,[2 advts] pp. Sm piece torn from 1 leaf with sl loss, free endpapers removed. Contemp calf, a little rubbed.
(Bow Windows) **£36 [≈ $64]**

Dundas, Sir David
- Instructions and regulations for the formations and movements of the cavalry. N.d. [ca 1796]. xv, 342 pp. 16 fldg engvd plates. prelims sl foxed. Contemp calf, rubbed, upper hinge tender.
(Edwards) **£100 [≈ $180]**

Dundonald, Earl of
- A treatise shewing the intimate connection that subsists between agriculture and chemistry ... London: for the author, 1795. Half-title. Rec qtr cloth, mrbld bds.
(Clark) **£160 [≈ $288]**

Dunkin, William
- Select poetical works ... In two volumes. Dublin: W.G. Jones (Vol II S. Powell), 1769-70. 1st coll edn. 2 vols. 4to. [4],392, 395-402, 401 (bis)-463; [6],[34],528 pp (but complete). Margins of 3ff vol I reprd with loss of a few letters. Rec mrbld bds.
(Fenning) **£195 [≈ $351]**

Dunn, Samuel
- A new and general introduction to practical astronomy ... London: for the author, 1744. Roy 8vo. 30 plates & 6 engvd plates. Contemp calf, rebacked, orig spine laid down.
(Traylen) **£110 [≈ $198]**

Dunning, J.
- A defence of the United Company of Merchants of England, trading to the East Indies ... against the complaints of the East India Company. 1742. Folio. 71 pp. Plate. Rebound in calf-backed mrbld bds.
(Old Cinema) **£85 [≈ $153]**

Dunton, John
- Athenian sport: or, two thousand paradoxes merrily argued to amuse and divert the age ... London: B. Bragg, 1707. Sole edn. No half-title, some minor soiling. Contemp calf, gilt, rebacked, crnrs rubbed. *(Clark)* **£75 [≈ $135]**
- Athenian sport: or, two thousand paradoxes

merrily argued, to amuse and divert the age: as a paradox in praise of a paradox. London: for B. Bragg, 1707. 1st edn. 8vo. Half-title (creased & with early ownership inscrptn). Some spotting. Contemp calf, rubbed.
(Hughes) £65 [≈ $117]

Durham, James
- Clavis Cantici: or, an exposition of the Song of Solomon. Glasgow: John Bryce, 1767. Contemp sheep, worn, jnts cracked.
(Waterfield's) £60 [≈ $108]
- The dying man's testament to the Church of Scotland. Edinburgh: Higgins, 1659. 1st edn. Sm 8vo. Contemp calf, hd of spine chipped. New Wing D2810.
(Marlborough) £85 [≈ $153]

Dyche, Thomas & Pardon, William
- A new general English dictionary ... to which is prefixed a compendious English grammar ... London: for Catherine & Richard Ware, 1765. 12th edn. Thick 8vo. Some sl spotting, single wormhole through margs of half the book. 19th c half mor.
(Burmester) £40 [≈ $72]
- A new general English dictionary ... together with a supplement of the proper names of the most noted kingdoms, provinces ... throughout the known world. London: for C. & R. Ware, n.d. [ca 1750]. 12th edn. 8vo. Contemp calf, rebacked, orig spine laid down.
(Stewart) £30 [≈ $54]

Dyer, George
- Memoirs of the life and writings of Robert Robinson. London: for G.G. & J. Robinson, 1796. 8vo. Engvd frontis. Mod qtr calf.
(Waterfield's) £70 [≈ $126]

Dyer, John
- The fleece: a poem in four books. London: 1757. 1st edn. 4to. Half-title, engvd title vignette. Disbound.
(Robertshaw) £45 [≈ $81]
- Poems. Viz. 1. Gronger Hill. II. The Ruine of Rome. III. The fleece, in four books. London: John Hughs ..., 1761. 1st coll edn thus. 188 pp. 3 engvd plates. Old calf, rebacked.
(Young's) £32 [≈ $57]

Dyet ...
- The dyet of Poland ... See Defoe, Daniel

Dykes, Oswald
- The royal marriage. King Lemuel's lesson of 1. Chastity, 2. Temperance ... 6. Industry ... 9. Marriage ... virtues and vices of wedlock.

London: for the author, 1722. 1st edn. 8vo. xxiii,[i],368 pp. Engvd frontis. Contemp calf, rebacked.
(Burmester) £160 [≈ $288]
- The royal marriage. King Lemuel's lesson of Chastity, Temperance, charity, justice ... London: 1722. 8vo. Frontis. Contemp calf, rebacked.
(Argosy) $75 [≈ £41]

Dyvernois, J.L.
- A dissertation upon the sugar of milk ... great efficacy in consumptions, hectic fevers ... translated into English. London: for T. James ..., 1753. 1st edn in English. 8vo. viii,32 pp inc half-title. Outer pages a little soiled. Disbound.
(Pickering) $200 [≈ £111]

Earle of Essex ...
- The Earle of Essex, his desires to the parliament. Also a catalogue of those tradesman volunteers ... [London:] T. Thomson, 1642. 4to. 6 pp. Uncut & unopened as issued. Wing E73.
(C.R. Johnson) £125 [≈ $225]

Eastbourne ...
- East-bourne; being a descriptive account of that village, in the county of Sussex, and its environs. London: Denew & Grant, 1787. 1st edn. 12mo. vii,147 pp. Lacking 1st leaf (blank?). Fldg map (offsetting), 2 engvd plates. Contemp half calf, crnrs sl bumped.
(Frew Mackenzie) £75 [≈ $135]

Echard, Laurence
- A general ecclesiastical history ... London: for Jacob Tonson, 1702. Folio. xiv,472,[xxiv] pp. Engvd frontis, double-page map. Waterstain in inner marg of a few leaves. Rec half calf, gilt.
(Lloyd-Roberts) £90 [≈ $162]
- A most compleat compendium of geography ... Describing all the empires, kingdoms, and dominions in the whole world. Salusbury, 1697. 4th edn. 12mo. Pub advt before title, [xii],136, index, [iii advts] pp. 4 engvd maps. Calf, sl splitting to front hinge.
(P & P) £80 [≈ $144]

Ecton, John
- Thesaurus rerum ecclesiasticarum. Being an account of the valuations of all the ecclesiastical benefices in ... England and Wales ... London: Knapton ..., 1754. 4to. xl,704 pp. 19th c panelled sheep, sl rubbed.
(Frew Mackenzie) £55 [≈ $99]

Eden, Williams
- Principles of penal law [including 'proposal to subject (criminals) during their life to medical experiments']. London: Cadell, 1771. 8vo.

xxvii,[i], 331,[i] pp. Contemp calf, spine ends & edges worn.   *(Pollak)* **£65 [≈ $117]**

Edgar, William
- Vectigalium systema: or, a complete view of that part of the revenue of Great Britain ... called customs ... London: for the author, 1714. 1st edn, 1st iss. [vi],330 pp. Fldg table. Some waterstains, worming in outer margs of 1st 60 pp. Contemp calf, rebacked.
    (Pickering) **$375 [≈ £208]**

Edgeworth, Maria & Richard
- Practical education. London: for J. Johnson, 1798. 1st edn. 2 vols. 4to. 2 half-titles, 3 engvd plates (2 fldg). A little spotting at beginning. Large copy in contemp half calf, rebacked.   *(Bennett)* **£550 [≈ $990]**

Edinburgh ...
- The Edinburgh miscellany: consisting of original poems, translations, etc. By various hands. Volume 1 [all published]. Edinburgh: 1720. 1st edn. Sm 8vo. Half-title. Rebound qtr calf.   *(Hughes)* **£350 [≈ $630]**

Edmonds, Clement
- The commentaries of C. Julius Caesar ... Translated into English. London: 1677. Folio. [xl],332 pp. Engvd port, red & black title, 2 addtnl titles, ctlg leaf, 14 engvd plates & plans (9 fldg). Calf, rubbed, rebacked, rear hinge tender. Wing C200.
    (P & P) **£200 [≈ $360]**

Edmondson, Joseph
- A complete body of heraldry ... historical enquiry ... rise and progress ... historical catalogue ... copious glossary ... London: for the author, 1780. 1st edn. 2 vols. Folio. Lgely unpaginated. Engvd port (offset to title), 24 plates. Contemp calf, rebacked.
    (Frew Mackenzie) **£140 [≈ $252]**

Edmonson, Joseph
- Precedency. London: for the editor, n.d. [ca 1770]. 1st edn. 8vo. 16ff, engvd throughout. Sl cropped at fore-edges. Contemp gilt-panelled & dec red mor, a.e.g.
    (Gough) **£95 [≈ $171]**

Edwards, Bryan
- The history, civil and commercial, of the British colonies in the West Indies. 1794. 2nd edn. 8vo. 9 fldg maps (1 or 2 sm tears reprd), 7 plates. Some occas foxing. Contemp tree-calf, rebacked, orig spines laid down.
    (Farahar) **£450 [≈ $810]**

Edwards, George
- A natural history of uncommon birds ... [with] Gleanings of natural history. London: for the author, 1743-64. & vols. Duplicated French titles, addtnl gen title vol I, text in French & English. 362 hand-cold engvd plates. Contemp mor, gilt, by Benedict.
    (Traylen) **£12,500 [≈ $22,500]**

Edwards, Jonathan
- A careful and strict enquiry into the modern prevailing notions of that freedom of the will which is supposed to be essential to moral agency ... London: Thomas Field, 1762. 1st English edn. 8vo. 414 pp. Contemp calf, cvrs detchd.   *(Argosy)* **$150 [≈ £83]**
- The distinguishing marks of a work of the spirit of God, applied to the uncommon operation that has lately appeared in the minds of many of the people in New-England ... Boston: 1741, London: reprinted by S. Mason, 1742. Half-title. Old calf-backed bds.
    (Waterfield's) **£175 [≈ $315]**
- The life and character of the late reverend, learned, and pious Mr. Jonathan Edwards, President of the College of New Jersey. Glasgow: David Niven, 1785. 2nd edn. 8vo. 396 pp. Some foxing. Contemp calf, spines & crnrs sl rubbed.   *(Morrell)* **£55 [≈ $99]**
- Thoughts concerning the present revival of religion in New-England. Abridg'd by John Wesley. London: W. Strahan, 1745. 1st edn of Wesley's abridgement. 12mo. 24 pp. 1st few leaves somewhat soiled. Contemp calf, rebacked.   *(Bennett)* **£90 [≈ $162]**

Egerton, T.
- General regulations and instructions for the ten troops of Wiltshire Yeomanry. Military Library, Whitehall, 1798. Sm 8vo. 92 pp. Mod calf.   *(Edwards)* **£150 [≈ $270]**
- Instructions for hussars, and light cavalry acting as such, in time of war. A translation. London: T. Egerton, 1799. Slim 8vo. Light waterstaining mainly to lower edge of title & prelims. Contemp half calf, mrbld bds, front hinge cracked. *(Chaucer Head)* **£110 [≈ $198]**

Ekins, Jeffery (trans.)
- Medea and Jason. A poem, in three books: translated from the Greek ... London: for T. Payne, 1772. 2nd edn, crrctd. 8vo. 99 pp. Contemp speckled calf, minor cracking.
    (Burmester) **£50 [≈ $90]**

Elaboratory ...
- The elaboratory laid open ... See Dossie, Robert

Eleanora ...

- Eleanora: from the sorrows of Werter. A tale. London: for G.G.J. & J. Robinson, 1785. 1st edn. 2 vols in 1. 12mo. iv,147; 168 pp. Clean marg tears in 2 leaves. Contemp tree calf.
  (Burmester) **£400 [≈ $720]**

Elements of Trigonometry ...

- The elements of trigonometry ... See Emerson, William

Elliot, Adam

- A modest vindication of Titus Oates the Salamanca Doctor from perjury ... 1682. 1st edn. Folio. [vi],47 pp. Some browning, wormhole in lower crnr. Disbound. New Wing E543.   *(Blackwell's)* **£40 [≈ $72]**

Ellis, George

- History of the late revolution in the Dutch Republic. London: for J. Edwards, 1789. 1st edn. 8vo. [iv],214 pp. Contemp speckled calf.
  (Burmester) **£70 [≈ $126]**

Ellis, George (1758-1815)

- Bath: its beauties and amusements. The second edition. 1777. 4to. Rebound in bds.
  (C.R. Johnson) **£90 [≈ $162]**

Ellis, Henry

- A voyage to Hudson's-Bay ... in the years 1746 and 1747, for discovering a North West Passage ... London: Whitridge, 1748. 1st edn. 8vo. xxviii,336 pp (with the extra 4ff in sgntr G). 9 engvd plates, fldg map. Contemp speckled calf, jnt cracking, crnrs rubbed.
  (Morrell) **£550 [≈ $990]**

Ellis, John

- The natural history of many curious and uncommon zoophytes collected from many parts of the globe ... London: for Benjamin White ..., 1786. 4to. 63 plates. Contemp half calf, lea renewed, uncut.
  (Waterfield's) **£200 [≈ $360]**

Ellis, William

- Ellis's husbandry, abridged and methodized; comprehending the most useful articles of practical agriculture. London: for W. Nicoll, 1772. 2 vols. 8vo. Engvd frontis. Contemp calf, gilt panelled spines, jnts worn.
  (Traylen) **£130 [≈ $234]**

Ellwood, Thomas

- Davideis. The life of David king of Israel: a sacred poem. In five books. London: Assigns of T. Sowle, 1712. 1st edn. 8vo. xiv,310,[viii

pub ctlg] pp. Some browning. Blind-ruled sprinkled sheep by Bernard Middleton.
  (Bennett) **£350 [≈ $630]**
- Davideis. The life of David king of Israel: a sacred poem. In five books. London: T. Sowle, 1749. 3rd edn, crrctd. Cr 8vo. 3 pp ctlg. A few headlines cropped. New grey bds.
  (Stewart) **£45 [≈ $81]**

Elshotz, Johann Sigsmund

- The curious distillatory: or the art of distilling coloured liquors, spirits ... from vegetables ... and metals ... London: for Robert Boulter, 1677. 1st edn in English. 12mo. [xvi],111 pp. Engvd frontis & plate. Minor spotting & offsetting. 19th c half calf.
  (Burmester) **£650 [≈ $1,170]**

Elsum, John

- Epigrams upon the paintings. London: for Dan. Brown ..., 1700. 8vo. 133 pp. Paper browned, a few short tears without loss. Old roan-backed bds, cvrs worn & rubbed. New Wing E63.   *(Marlborough)* **£350 [≈ $630]**

Emerson, William

- The doctrine of fluxions: not only explaining the elements thereof, but also its application and use in several parts of mathematics and natural philosophy. London: Robinson, 1768. 3rd edn. xvi,[iv], 432,[ii errata]. 12 fldg plates. Contemp sheep, spine worn.
  (Pollak) **£80 [≈ $144]**
- The elements of optics. In four books. London: for J. Nourse, 1768. 1st edn. [with, 2nd part] Perspective: or, the art of drawing ... upon a plane. 2 pts in 1. 8vo. [ii],xii,244; vi,[ii],111 pp. 13 & 15 engvd plates. Wanting half-title. Contemp reversed calf.
  (Burmester) **£285 [≈ $513]**
- The elements of trigonometry. Containing the properties, relations, and calculations of sines, tangents ... For W. Innys, 1749. 1st edn. 8vo. viii,186 pp. 6 fldg plates. Contemp calf, rebacked.   *(Bickersteth)* **£110 [≈ $198]**
- The mathematical principles of geography ... [bound with] Dialling or the art of drawing dials, on all sorts of planes whatsoever ... London: Nourse, 1770. viii,ii,172; iv,164 pp. 18 fldg plates. Tree calf, spine rubbed.
  (P & P) **£125 [≈ $225]**
- Navigation; or, the art of sailing upon the sea ... London: for J. Nourse, 1764. 2nd edn. 12mo. xii,216, [112],6 pub advts pp. Worming, with some loss in fore-marg n10-P9. Contemp sheep, rubbed, worn, jnts split.   *(Kerr)* **£75 [≈ $135]**
- The principles of mechanics. Explaining and

demonstrating the general laws of motion ...
projectiles ... construction of machines ... For
J. Richardson, 1758. 2nd edn, crrctd. 4to.
viii,[ii],284 pp. 43 fldg plates. Orig calf,
rebacked.   *(Bickersteth)* **£290 [≈ $522]**
- The projection of the sphere, orthographic,
stereographic and gnomical. For W. Innys,
1749. 1st edn. 8vo. iv,52 pp. 12 fldg plates.
Contemp mrbld bds, new calf spine.
                     (Bickersteth) **£95 [≈ $171]**
- Tracts containing I. Mechanics ... II. The
projection of the sphere. III. The laws of
centripetal ... force. ... Some account of the
life ... of the author. London: Wingrave,
1793. New edn. 8vo. xxii,302 pp. Contemp
roan, rubbed, hd of spine & crnrs chipped.
                 (Frew Mackenzie) **£30 [≈ $54]**

Enchantress ...
- The vocal enchantress presenting an elegant
selection of the most favourite hunting, sea,
love and miscellaneous songs ... with the
music prefixed to each. London: J. Fielding,
1783. 12mo. Frontis, engvd title vignette.
Contemp calf, some wear, lower cvr loose.
                    (Robertshaw) **£25 [≈ $45]**

Encyclopaedia ...
- Encyclopaedia Britannica; or, a dictionary of
all arts and sciences ... 1771. 1st edn. 3 vols.
4to. 160 (ex 161) plates. Stain on lower marg
of last 200 pp vol 3. Calf, all cvrs detchd, all
spines broken.   *(Allen)* **$750 [≈ £416]**

Enderbie, Percy
- Cambria triumphans or Britain in its perfect
lustre shewing the origin and antiquity of that
illustrious nation. London: for Andrew
Crooke, 1661. 1st edn. Folio. [x],356 pp.
Plates. Frontis & pages of arms reprd in
margs. 18th c calf, later reback. Wing E728.
                 (Lloyd-Roberts) **£400 [≈ $720]**

Enfield, William
- An essay towards the history of Liverpool ...
from papers left by the late Mr. George Perry
... London: for J. Johnson, 1774. 2nd edn,
with addtns. Folio. [xii],116 pp. 2 fldg maps,
chart, 9 engvd views. Sl soiling of prelims, 1
map torn at fold. Mod bds.
                  (Deighton Bell) **£135 [≈ $243]**
- Exercises in elocution; selected from various
authors ... A new edition, to which are added,
counsels to young men ... London: for J.
Johnson, 1795. 8vo. viii,448 pp. Frontis, 2
engvd plates. Contemp sheep, a bit worn,
upper jnt weak.   *(Burmester)* **£45 [≈ $81]**

Englefield, Sir H.
- On the determination of the orbits of comets,
according to the methods of father Boscovitch
and Mr. de la Place ... London: 1793.
xi,iv,204, [26],4 pp. 4 fldg plates (2 loose).
Pencil & ink notes on some pp. Later cloth.
                   (Whitehart) **£60 [≈ $108]**

English Topographer ...
- The English topographer ... See Rawlinson,
Richard

Englishmen ...
- The Englishmen: being a sequel of the
Guardian ... See Steel, Sir Richard

Enquiry ...
- An enquiry into the nature of the human soul
... See Baxter, Andrew
- An historical and critical enquiry into the
evidence produced by the Earls of Murray
and Morton, against Mary, Queen of Scots.
Edinburgh: W. Gordon, 1760. Later calf, gilt,
sl scratched & worn.
                   (John Smith) **£50 [≈ $90]**
- An impartial enquiry into ... the Province of
Georgia ... See Martyn, Benjamin
- An impartial enquiry into the properties of
places and pensions, as they affect the
constitution ... London: for H. Goreham,
1740. 1st edn. 8vo. [v],10-52 pp (appears
complete). Disbound.
                   (Burmester) **£35 [≈ $63]**

Epictetus
- All the works ... which are now extant ...
Translated by Elizabeth Carter. Dublin:
1759. 1st Dublin edn. 8vo. 446 pp. Contemp
calf.   *(Argosy)* **$125 [≈ £69]**
- Epictetus: a poem, containing the maxims of
that celebrated philosopher, for the
government of passions in the conduct of life
... London: ... B. Bragge, 1709. 8vo.
[xxiv],147 pp. Contemp sheep, some wear,
rebacked.   *(Burmester)* **£275 [≈ $495]**

Epicurus
- Epicurus's morals collected partly out of his
own Greek text ... faithfully Englished.
London: for Henry Herringman, 1656. 1st
edn in English. Engvd frontis, red & black
title (reprd in gutter). Early panelled calf,
rebacked. Wing E3155.
                  (Waterfield's) **£150 [≈ $270]**
- Epicurus's morals collected partly out of his
own Greek text ... London: for Henry
Herringman, 1656. 1st English trans. Sm 4to.
[xlii],184 pp. Port & title creased in marg,

copious 17th c ms notes on endpapers. Contemp sheep, old repr to fore-edge. Wing E3155. *(Claude Cox)* £150 [≈ $270]

Epigrams ...
- Epigrams upon the paintings ... See Elsum, John

Equiano, Olaudah
- The interesting narrative of the life of Olaudah Equiano ... the African. Written by himself. London: for the author, 1793. 7th edn, enlgd. 12mo. xxxvi,[ii],360 pp. Lists of subscribers, engvd port, fldg engvd plate. Contemp tree-calf, rebacked.
(Burmester) £85 [≈ $153]

Erasmus, Desiderius
- All the familiar colloquies of ... concerning men, manners, and things, translated into English. By N. Bailey. London: for J. Darby ..., 1725. 1st edn thus. Thick 8vo. Contemp panelled calf, rebacked.
(Chaucer Head) £85 [≈ $153]
- Enchiridion militis Christiani ... the hansome weapon of a Christian knight ... London: for Abraham Veale, 1576. 8vo. Black letter. A few sidenotes lightly shaved. Mod calf. STC 10487. *(Waterfield's)* £475 [≈ $855]
- Twenty-two select colloquies ... Pleasantly representing several superstitious levities that were crept into the Church of Rome in his days. London: for S. Sare ..., 1699. 3rd imp, crrctd. Advt leaf at end. Rather browned. Mod calf, a.e.g. Wing E3214.
(Charles Cox) £35 [≈ $63]

Essay ...
- An essay for composing a harmony ... See Harley, Edward
- An essay on brewing ... See Combrune, Michael
- An essay on painting ... See Cooper, Anthony Astley
- An essay on political lying. The second edition. London: S. Hooper, 1757. 28 pp. Disbound. *(C.R. Johnson)* £38 [≈ $68]
- An essay on reason ... See Harte, Walter
- Essay on the natural history of Guiana ... See Bancroft, Edward
- An essay on the possibility and probability of a child being born alive ... See Dickson, David
- An essay on the stage; or, the art of acting. A poem. Edinburgh: John Yair, 1754. 19 pp. Lacking half-title. Disbound.
(C.R. Johnson) £280 [≈ $504]

- An essay on the writings and genius of Shakespear, compared with the Greek and French dramatic poets ... The third edition. London: for Edward & Charles Dilly, 1772. 8vo. [iv],288 pp. Contemp half mor, gilt spine, lacking label. *(Burmester)* £30 [≈ $54]
- An essay towards illustrating the science of insurance ... See Morris, Corbyn
- An essay towards the character of her late Majesty Caroline ... See Clarke, Alured
- An essay upon the execution of the laws against immorality ... See Disney, John

Essays ...
- Essays upon several subjects concerning British antiquities ... See Home, Henry, Lord James
- Essays; read to a literary society ... See Moor, James

Estwick, Nicolas
- A learned and godly sermon preached on the XIX day of December MDCXXXI at the funeral of Mr. Robert Bolton. London: George Miller, 1639. 3rd edn. 4to. Ft of title reprd. Mod wraps. STC 10558.
(Charles Cox) £35 [≈ $63]

Etherege, George
- The man of mode. A comedy ... to which is prefixed the life of the author. Edinburgh: for Martin & Wotherspoon, 1768. 12mo. Disbound. *(Waterfield's)* £15 [≈ $27]
- The man of mode. London: for Henry Herringman, 1676. 1st edn. 8vo. Title & last leaf washed, crnrs reprd, some staining & spotting. later full crushed mor, a little stained & bowed. *(Ash)* £300 [≈ $540]
- The works ... containing his plays and poems. London: for J. Tonson, 1735. 12mo. 3 engvs. Contemp mottled calf, gilt. Robert Gathorne-Hardy's b'plate. *(Charles Cox)* £30 [≈ $54]

Etheridge, Samuel
- Tables for the use of bankers, merchants, tradesmen and others. London: Dilly, 1773. Sm sq 8vo. Contemp tree-calf, gilt.
(Marlborough) £85 [≈ $153]

Euclid
- The English Euclide being the first six elements of geometry. Translated ... by Edmund Scarburgh. Oxford: at the Theater, 1705. Folio. 6ff,282 pp. Half-title, engvd title. Lacking final blank. Sl worming in upper margs & prelims. Contemp calf, rebacked. *(Titles)* £225 [≈ $405]
- Euclides elements of geometry. The first vi

books ... contracted and demonstrated by Captain Thomas Rudd ... whereunto is added. the mathematical preface of Mr. John Dee. London: Tomlins ..., 1651. 1st edn. Sm 4to. [128],254 pp. Num w'cut text ills. Disbound.   *(Argosy)* **$250 [≈ £138]**
- See also Barrow, Isaac

Eusebius, Pamphili
- The history of the Church from Our Lord's incarnation to the ... year of Christ 594. Cambridge: for Nath: Rolis, 1692. Folio. [xlii],700,22 index pp. New half speckled calf. Wing E3424. *(Lloyd-Roberts)* **£150 [≈ $270]**

Evans, John
- The case of kneeling at the Holy Sacrament stated and resolved. London: for T. Basset ..., 1683. 2 pts. 4to. Disbound. Wing E3455 & E3448.   *(Waterfield's)* **£45 [≈ $81]**

Evelyn, John
- Publick employment and an active life prefer'd to solitude ... London: 1667. 1st edn. 8vo. Initial imprim leaf. Sm stain on A1, sm marg repr to title, light dampstaining throughout. Contemp calf, worn, upper cvr missing. Wing E3510.
               (Robertshaw) **£225 [≈ $405]**
- Silva: or, a discourse of forest trees, and the propagation of timber ... London: for J. Walthoe, 1729. 5th edn.Folio. Red & black title, 6 engvs. Contemp mottled calf, gilt, gilt spine.   *(Traylen)* **£295 [≈ $531]**
- Silva: or, a discourse of forest trees, and the propagation of timber ... With notes by A. Hunter. York: 1776. 1st Hunter edn. 4to. Port, 40 engvd plates (1 fldg), fldg table. Contemp calf, rebacked, orig spine laid down, mor label, gilt.   *(Traylen)* **£150 [≈ $270]**
- Sylva: or, a discourse of forest trees, and the propagation of timber ... Pomona ... also Kaledarium Hortense ... London: for Jo. Martyn ..., 1670. Folio. 3 pts in 1. [48],247; 67; 33 pp. 5 text engvs. Contemp calf, rubbed, rebacked. Wing E3517.
                (Karmiole) **$350 [≈ £194]**
- Sylva: or, a discourse of forest-trees, and the propagation of timber ... Pomona ... also Kaledarium Hortense ... London: John Martyn, 1679. 3rd edn. Folio. 3 pts in 1. Engvs, errata with sl tear. Old calf, spine reprd.   *(Halewood)* **£150 [≈ $270]**
- Terra; a philosophical discourse of earth ... York: for A. Ward, 1778. New edn, with notes by A. Hunter. 8vo. Contemp calf, gilt.
                (Traylen) **£65 [≈ $117]**

Examination ...
- An examination of ... 'Enquiry on Freedom of Will' ... See Dana, James
- An examination of the conduct of several comptrollers of the City of London, in relation to the City's estate ... London: 1743. 1st edn. 8vo. 46 pp. Lightly browned, lacking last blank. Disbound.
             (Frew Mackenzie) **£210 [≈ $378]**
- An examination of the scruples of those who refuse to take the oath of allegiance ... See Allix, Peter

Executive of the United States ...
- The proceedings of the Executive of the United States, respecting the insurgents. 1794. Phila: 1795. Edn of 500. 130 pp. Half calf.   *(Reese)* **$550 [≈ £305]**

Expedition ...
- An account of the expedition of the British Fleet to Sicily ... See Corbett, Thomas
- The expedition against Rochefort fully stated and considered in a letter to Thomas Potter ... The second edition, corrected. London: J. Towers, 1758. 68 pp. Disbound.
              (C.R. Johnson) **£28 [≈ $50]**

Experimental Chemistry ...
- Institutes of experimental chemistry ... See Dossie, Robert

Extracts ...
- Extracts from the publications of Mr. Knox, Dr. Anderson, Mr. Pennant and Dr. Johnson, relative to the Northern and North-Western coasts of Great Britain. Macrae: May, 1787. 1st edn. Slim 8vo. Disbound.
              (Marlborough) **£60 [≈ $108]**

Fable ...
- The fable of the bees ... See Mandeville, Bernard

Fables ...
- Fables for the female sex ... See Moore, Edward
- Fables moral and political ... See Dewitt, John

Faction ...
- Faction displayed. A poem ... See Shippen, William

Faden, W.
- Le petit Neptune Francais ... or French coasting pilot for the Coast of Flanders ... and

Mediterranean ... and the island of Corsica. 1793. 1st edn. 4to. 147 pp. Engvd frontis, 42 maps, charts & plans (37 fldg). Sl foxing. Orig calf, rebacked, crnrs worn.

(Edwards) £400 [≈ $720]

Falconer, J.

- Cryptomenysis patefacta: or the art of secret information disclosed without a key. London: for Daniel Brown, 1685. 8vo. [xii],180 pp. Somewhat browned throughout, early sgntr on title. Contemp panelled sheep, a little worn, sometime rebacked. Wing F296.

(Kerr) £200 [≈ $360]

Fanshawe, Sir Richard

- Il pastor fido: the faithful shepheard. With an addition of divers other poems. London: A. Moseley, 1664. 1st 8vo edn. Port (old repr, shaved & a little chipped). 3ff torn without loss, 2ff supplied from another copy. Polished sheep, rebacked. Wing G2176.

(Charles Cox) £35 [≈ $63]

Fanshawe, Sir Richard, et al.

- Original letters and negotiations of ... Sir Richard Fanshawe [et al.] ... matters of importance between England, Spain, and Portugal ... London: 1724. 2 vols. [viii],510; [ii],viii, [iv],415 pp. Fldg port frontis. Contemp calf, rebacked, rubbed. Ex lib.

(Clark) £65 [≈ $117]

Faria, Francisco de

- The narrative of ... wherein is contained the several informations ... touching upon the horrid Popish plot ... For Randal Taylor, 1680. 1st edn. Folio. [iv],35 pp. Some browning. Disbound. New Wing R426.

(Blackwell's) £35 [≈ $63]

Farmer ...

- The framer's lawyer; or every country gentleman his own counsellor. London: W. Strahan ..., 1774. Sole edn (?). Sm 8vo. Contemp law calf, hinges splitting.

(Chaucer Head) £160 [≈ $288]

Fatio de Duillier, Nicolas

- Fruit walls improved by inclining them ... whereby they receive more sun shine and heat ... London: R. Everingham, 1699. 1st edn. 4to. Engvd frontis, vignette on title & dedn leaf, 2 lge fldg engvd plates. Contemp half calf, mrbld bds, reprd. Wing F557.

(Traylen) £390 [≈ $702]

Fawcett, Benjamin

- Observations on the nature, causes and cure

of melancholy. Especially of that which is commonly called religious melancholy. Shrewsbury: 1780. 1st edn. Sm 8vo. A little spotting to title. Contemp half calf, mrbld bds.

(Chaucer Head) £180 [≈ $324]

Fawcett, General Sir W.

- Rules and regulations for the sword exercise of the cavalry. Dublin: R.E. Mercier ..., 1797. 1st edn. xii,92 pp. 29 full-page engvd plates. Orig bds, uncut.

(Young's) £120 [≈ $216]

Featly, Daniel

- Cygnea Cantio: or, learned decisions, and most prudent and pious directions for students in Divinitie ... Robert Mylbourne, 1629. 1st edn. Sm 4to. [viii],41 pp. Title & last 2 leaves with marg reprs, contemp ownership inscrptn on title. Later mor, gilt.

(Frew Mackenzie) £220 [≈ $396]

The Federalist

- The Federalist: a collection of essays written in favour of the new constitution. New York: J. & A. M'Lean, 1788. 1st edn, 1st state. 2 vols. Final 2 leaves vol 2 supplied in facs. Contemp calf, spines restored.

(Jenkins) $3,500 [≈ £1,944]

Fell, John

- The life of the most learned, reverend and pious Dr. H. Hammond. London: for Jo. Martin ..., 1662. 2nd edn. 8vo. [ii], 252 pp. Sl dampstaining 1st 2 leaves, sgntr on title. Old calf, spine gilt, rubbed, hd of backstrip reprd. Wing F618.

(Clark) £55 [≈ $99]

Fenelon, Francis, Archbishop of Cambray

- The adventures of Telemachus ... See also Smollett, Tobias
- The adventures of Telemachus, the son of Ulysses. Translated ... by P. Proctor. London: 1724. 2 vols. 8vo. 2 frontis, 16 plates. Contemp calf, jnts cracked.

(Stewart) £40 [≈ $72]

Fenn, John

- Original letters written during the reigns of Henry VI, Edward IV and Richard III. By various persons of rank ... London: 1787. 2 vols. 4to. [lxxxviii],300; 341,[24] pp. Engvd titles, 3 hand-cold plates, 14 other plates (ex 15), fldg pedigree. Old half roan.

(Bow Windows) £145 [≈ $261]

Ferguson, Adam

- An essay on the history of civil society. London: for T. Cadell ..., 1773. 4th edn, revsd & crrctd. xiii,466 pp. Early 20th c cloth.

Vincent Starratt's sgntr & b'plate, Woodrow Wilson's b'plate.   *(Karmiole)* **$85 [≈ £47]**
- An essay on the history of civil society. London: 1773. 4th edn, revsd & crrctd. 8vo. 466 pp. 2 leaves reprd. Old half calf, worn, jnts cracking. *(Bow Windows)* **£140 [≈ $252]**

Ferguson, James
- The art of drawing in perspective made easy to those who have no previous knowledge of mathematics. London: W. Strahan ..., 1775. 1st edn. 8vo. xii,123 pp. 9 fldg plates, half-title. Contemp sheep, v sl cracks in jnts.
  (Burmester) **£225 [≈ $405]**
- Astronomy explained upon Sir Isaac Newton's principles, and made easy to those who have not studied mathematics. London: for the author, 1757. 2nd edn. 4to. [viii],283, [ix] pp. 13 fldg engvd plates. Occas spotting. Contemp calf, spine restored at hd.
  (Frew Mackenzie) **£300 [≈ $540]**
- An easy introduction to astronomy, for young gentlemen. London: for T. Cadell, 1769. 2nd edn. 8vo. [iv],247,[5] pp. 7 fldg engvd plates. Contemp calf, gilt spine, lacking label, 2 short holes in upper jnt. *(Burmester)* **£100 [≈ $180]**
- Introduction to electricity ... London: 1770. 1st edn. 8vo. 3 fldg plates. Mod wraps.
  (Argosy) **$300 [≈ £166]**
- An introduction to electricity. London: 1778. 3rd edn. 8vo. 140 pp. 3 fldg plates. Old polished calf, worn, rebacked.
  (Weiner) **£100 [≈ $180]**
- Lectures on select subject in mechanics, pneumatics, hydrostatics and optics ... London: for A. Millar, 1764. [with] A supplement ... London: 1767. 2nd & 1st edns. 4to. viii,252,[4]; 23 & 13 fldg engvd plates (some frayed at margs). Contemp calf, rebacked. *(Pickering)* **$425 [≈ £236]**
- Lectures on select subject in mechanics, hydrostatics ... optics ... London: W. Strahan ..., 1770. 2nd 8vo edn. [viii],394, [vi],48 pp. 36 fldg engvd plates. Orig calf, sl worn at ft of spine.   *(Bickersteth)* **£110 [≈ $198]**
- Lectures on select subject in mechanics, hydrostatics ... optics ... with the supplement. London: Strahan ..., 1773. 4to. [viii],252, [iv index],40 pp. 30 fldg engvd plates, some browned. Contemp tree-calf, jnts cracking, cvrs scraped, extremities bumped.
  (Frew Mackenzie) **£250 [≈ $450]**
- Select mechanical exercise: shewing how to construct different clocks orreries and sundials ... London: 1778. 2nd edn. 8vo. Port. 9 plates. Contemp calf, worn, cvrs loose.
  (Robertshaw) **£50 [≈ $90]**
- Select mechanical exercises: shewing how to

construct different clocks, orreries, and sundials ... London: W. Strahan ..., 1778. 2nd edn. 8vo. [xii],xliii,272 pp. Port, 9 fldg engvd plates. Orig calf, rebacked, new label.
  (Bickersteth) **£110 [≈ $198]**
- Tables and tracts, relative to several arts and sciences. London: for Millar & Cadell ..., 1767, 1st edn. 8vo. xvi,328 pp. 3 fldg engvd plates. Rebound in half calf, mrbld bd sides.
  (Pickering) **$400 [≈ £222]**
- Tables and tracts, relative to several arts and sciences. London: Millar & Cadell, 1767. 1st edn. 8vo. xiii,[i errata],328 pp. 3 fldg plates, tables in text. Contemp sheep, jnts cracked, chipped at hd & ft of spine.
  (Frew Mackenzie) **£275 [≈ $495]**

Ferguson, Robert
- An enquiry into, and detection of the barbarous murther of the late Earl of Essex. London: 1689. 4to. Title dusty & sl torn at edge. Mod half roan, sl worn. Wing F739.
  (Charles Cox) **£30 [≈ $54]**
- A just and modest vindication of the Scots design for the having established a Colony at Darien. [Edinburgh]: 1699. 8vo. Contemp calf, later rebacking. New Wing F742.
  (Marlborough) **£420 [≈ $756]**

Fergusson, Robert, Junior, of Craigdarroch
- The proposed reform of the counties of Scotland impartially examined ... Edinburgh: for Elphinston Balfour ..., 1792. 1st edn. 8vo. [iv],iv,31 pp. Half-title, leaf of quotation after title. Old wraps.   *(Burmester)* **£80 [≈ $144]**

Ferne, H.
- Certain considerations of present concernment: touching this reformed Church of England ... London: for R. Royston, 1653. 1st edn. 12mo. Contemp sheep, rubbed. Wing F789. Royston's ctlg bound-in at end.
  (Robertshaw) **£32 [≈ $57]**

Ferne, John
- The blazon of gentrie. London: 1586. 1st edn. 10ff, 341 pp, 1f blank, 130 pp. 71 pp with hand-cold coats of arms, 4 double-page charts. A few contemp & early notes, isolated tears or stains. 17th c mottled calf, 20th c rebacking, sl wear to edges & crnrs.
  (Pirages) **£850 [≈ $472]**
- The blazon of gentrie; Devided into two parts ... London: for Toby Cooke, 1586. [xviii],341,130 pp. Num shields & coats of arms, later hand-cold. Last leaf cropped at hd with loss of title. Mod blindstamped calf, new

endpapers. STC 10824.
(P & P) **£490** [≈ $882]

Festival of Wit ...
- The festival of wit: or, the small talker ... from a voluminous work, in the possession of G***** K****. London: for M. Smith, 1783. New edn. 12mo. [ii],xii, 243,[i] pp. Leaf of 'Advertisement to the Second Edition'. Contemp half calf.
(Bennett) **£325** [≈ $585]

Fiddes, Richard
- A general treatise of morality. form'd upon the principles of natural reason only. London: 1724. 1st edn. Contemp calf, worn.
(Robertshaw) **£40** [≈ $72]
- The life of Cardinal Wolsey. London: for John barber, 1724. Folio. 8 plates 1 fldg). Contemp calf, jnts weak, spine worn.
(Stewart) **£40** [≈ $72]
- The life of Cardinal Wolsey. London: 1726. 2nd edn. Folio. 9 plates, text engv. Contemp calf, rebacked, rubbed.
(Robertshaw) **£38** [≈ $68]

Fielde, John
- A caveat for Parsons Howlet. London: for Thomas Man ..., [1581]. 60ff. Final 2 leaves re-margined, marg repr to another, stab marks at inner marg, pages sl soiled or darkened & sl soft. Rec calf, spine gilt.
(Pirages) **$450** [≈ £250]

Fielding, Henry
- Amelia. London: for A. Millar, 1752. 1st edn. 4 vols. 12mo. Final blank vol 1, advt leaf vol 2. Contemp calf, gilt panelled spines, jnts cracked. *(Traylen)* **£280** [≈ $504]
- Examples of the interposition of providence in the detection and punishment of murder. Containing above thirty cases. Dublin: for James Hoey, 1764. 3rd edn. 12mo. 69,[iii] pp. Pub ctlg at end. Early 20th c buckram-backed bds. *(Bennett)* **£250** [≈ $450]
- The history of the adventures of Joseph Andrews, and his friend Mr. Abraham Adams ... In two volumes. London: for A. Millar ..., 1781. Contemp sheep, hds of spines a little worn. *(C.R. Johnson)* **£65** [≈ $117]
- The history of Tom Jones, a foundling. London: for J. Murray ..., 1792. 3 vols. 8vo. 12 hand-cold plates by Rowlandson. Sev leaves a little offset, foxed, or browned. Contemp tree-calf, rec rebacked. Ex Signet Lib with gilt stamp on all cvrs.
(Pirages) **$550** [≈ £305]
- The history of Tom Jones, a foundling.

London: for A. Millar, 1749. 1st edn, 2nd iss. 6 vols. 12mo. Final blanks in vols 1 & 3. Contemp calf, gilt panelled spines, sl worn at hd of spines. *(Traylen)* **£650** [≈ $1,170]
- The history of Tom Jones, a foundling. London: for H. Millar, 1749. 1st edn. 6 vols. 12mo. Cancels as in Rothschild, with the addtn of B1 in vol IV. Lacking blanks. late 19th c gilt-panelled mor, spines gilt-dec, a.e.g. *(Gough)* **£950** [≈ $1,710]
- The journal of a voyage to Lisbon. London: for A. Millar, 1755. 1st edn, 1st iss. 12mo. [iv],iv,228 pp. Half-title. Polished speckled calf, gilt, by Riviere.
(Burmester) **£200** [≈ $360]
- The journal of a voyage to Lisbon. London: Millar, 1755. 1st edn. 12mo. Without the half-title. Uncut in orig wraps, a little dusty.
(Marlborough) **£260** [≈ $468]
- The modern husband.. A comedy, as it is acted at the Theatre-Royal in Drury-Lane. London: for J. Watts, 1732. 1st edn. 8vo. Unbound. *(Traylen)* **£110** [≈ $198]
- Pasquin. A dramatick satire on the times ... London: for J. Watts, 1736. 1st edn. 8vo. Red & black title, epilogue, advt leaf. Half calf, red mor label, gilt. *(Traylen)* **£120** [≈ $216]
- The works ... With the life of the author. In four volumes. London: A. Millar, 1762. 4to. Port. Sl waterstains to parts of 1st & 4th vols. Contemp polished calf.
(Charles Cox) **£350** [≈ $630]
- The works. Edinburgh: Martin & Wotherspoon, 1767. 4th edn. 12 vols. 6mo. Engvd port. Contemp mor, spines gilt-panelled & dec, lacking tail-band vol 8.
(Gough) **£695** [≈ $1,251]

Fighting Sailor ...
- The fighting sailor turn'd peaceable Christian; manifested in the convincement and conversion of Thomas Lurting ... A true account of George Pattison's being taken by the Turks, 1663. London: J. Sowle, 1710. Cr 8vo. Sl dusty. New wraps.
(Stewart) **£40** [≈ $72]

Filmer, Sir Robert
- Patriarcha: or the natural power of kings. London: printed and are to be sold by Walter Davis, 1680. 1st edn. 8vo. Contemp sheep, blind ownership stamp on front cvr. Wing F992. *(Waterfield's)* **£285** [≈ $513]

Finch, Henry
- Law, or a discourse thereof, in four books. London: Henry Lintot, 1759. 506 pp. Some browning & soiling in 1st section. Mod half

calf.   *(Edwards)* **£200 [≈ $360]**

Finett, Sir John
- Finetti Philoxensis: Some choice observations
  ... touching the reception ... the puntillios and
  contests of forren ambassadors in England.
  London: 1656. 1st edn. 8vo. With 1st & last
  blanks. Contemp calf, worn. Wing F947.
                         (Robertshaw) **£135 [≈ $243]**
- Finetti Philoxensis: Some choice observations
  ... touching the reception, and precedence ...
  of forren ambassadors in England. London:
  for H. Twyford ..., 1656. 1st edn. 8vo.
  Lacking A1 (blank?). Later half calf, lower jnt
  cracked. Wing F947.
                         (Charles Cox) **£110 [≈ $198]**

Fisher, G.
- Arithmetick in the plainest and most concise
  methods hitherto extant. Hitch & Hawes,
  1759. 10th edn. [x],312 pp. Front free
  endpaper almost detchd, ink spillage on 2 pp,
  crnr torn from B1 without loss. Contemp calf.
                         (Hinchliffe) **£40 [≈ $72]**

Fisher, T.
- The Kentish traveller's companion ... The
  fifth edition, revised ... Canterbury: Simmons
  & Kirkby, 1799. 8vo. iv,360,[viii] pp. 3 fldg
  maps, fldg table. Light dust soiling. Uncut &
  partly unopened in orig ptd wraps, backstrip
  defective.   *(Frew Mackenzie)* **£48 [≈ $86]**

Fitz-Harris, Edw.
- The tryal and condemnation of Edw. Fitz-
  Harris, Esq. for high-treason ... as also the
  tryal and condemnation of Dr. Oliver
  Plunket. London: for Francis Tyton ..., 1681.
  1st edn. Folio. [4],56, 61-103,[1] pp inc
  licence lf (with sm hole). Disbound. Wing
  T2140.   *(Hannas)* **£25 [≈ $45]**

Fitzgerald, David
- A narrative of the Irish Popish Plot for
  betraying the kingdom into the hands of the
  French, massacring all English Protestants ...
  London: Cockerill, 1680. Sm folio. License
  leaf. Mod bds.   *(Emerald Isle)* **£85 [≈ $153]**
- A narrative of the Irish Popish Plot for the
  betraying of the kingdom into the hands of the
  French, massacring all English protestants
  there ... Tho. Cockerill, 1680. 1st edn.
  Imprim, [iv],35 pp. Disbound. New Wing
  F1072.   *(Blackwell's)* **£35 [≈ $63]**

FitzGibon, John
- The speech ... delivered in the House of
  Peers, on the second reading of the Bill for the
  relief of his Majesty's Roman Catholic

subjects ... Dublin: J. Milliken, 1798. 69 pp,
appendix.   *(C.R. Johnson)* **£25 [≈ $45]**

Fitzharris, Edward
- The confession ... written with his own hand
  ... the first day of July, 1681 ... the day of his
  execution. S. Carr, 1681. 1st folio edn. 7,[i
  blank] pp, [i advt] f. Browned. Disbound.
  New Wing F1092. *(Blackwell's)* **£35 [≈ $63]**

Fitzherbert, A.
- The new natural brevium of the most
  reverend judge, Mr Anthony Fitz-Herbert;
  corrected and revised. London: W. Rawlins,
  1687. 8vo. [62],600 pp. Sl waterstain to title.
  Contemp panelled calf.
                         (Spelman) **£80 [≈ $144]**

Fitzherbert, Thomas
- The first [second] part of a treatise concerning
  policy and religion. [Douai:] 1606-10. 1st edn.
  2 vols. Titles within ornamental type border.
  Sm marg wormhole latter half vol 1, stain on
  2 pp vol 2. 18th c calf, split in 1 hinge. STC
  11017 & 11019.   *(Stewart)* **£550 [≈ $990]**
- A treatise concerning policy and religion.
  Wherein ... divers principles of Machiavel
  [are] confuted. London: Roper, 1652. 4to.
  Contemp calf, later rebacking, crnrs rubbed.
  New Wing F1102.
                         (Marlborough) **£135 [≈ $243]**
- A treatise concerning policy and religion.
  London: for Abel Roper, 1652. 4to. Title
  reinforced, a few leaves dusty. 17th c calf,
  recased. Wing 1102. *(Stewart)* **£90 [≈ $162]**

Flax-Husbandry ...
- Progress of flax-husbandry in Scotland ... See
  Home, Henry, Lord Kames

Fleet, John
- A discourse relative to the subject of
  animation ... Boston: John & Thomas Fleet,
  1797. 1st edn. 8vo. [3],25,[1] pp. Half-title,
  appendix. Mod cloth.
                         (Rootenberg) **$350 [≈ £194]**

Fleetwood, William
- Chronicum preciosum; or, an account of
  English gold and silver money; the price of
  corn and other commodities ... for six
  hundred years. London: for Charles Harper,
  1707. 1st edn. [xvi],181,[10] pp inc 5 pp
  advts. Panelled calf. *(Young's)* **£175 [≈ $315]**
- Chronicum preciosum; or, an account of
  English gold and silver money; the price of
  corn and other commodities ... for six
  hundred years. London: for T. Osborne,

1745. 2nd edn, revsd. [x],147, [ii index], 30 appendix pp. 12 plates. Contemp calf, rebacked. *(Gough)* £110 [≈ $198]
- Chronicum preciosum; or, an account of English gold and silver money ... London: for T. Osborne ..., 1745. 2nd edn. 8vo. [x],147, [2 index],[1 advt], 30 account, [24 engvd plates], [2 advts] pp. Contemp calf, rebacked, new endpapers. *(Pickering)* $350 [≈ £194]

Fleming, Caleb
- The claims of the Church of England seriously examined: in a letter to the author ... by a Protestant dissenter of Old England. London: for W. Nicholl, 1764. 8vo. Disbound. *(Waterfield's)* £25 [≈ $45]
- Discourse on three essential properties of the Gospel-Revelation ... and a supplemental discourse on the supernatural conception of Jesus Christ. London: for J. Towers, 1772. 8vo. Disbound. *(Waterfield's)* £20 [≈ $36]

Fletcher, Phineas
- Piscatory eclogues, with other poetical miscellanies. Edinburgh: for A. Kincaid & W. Creech, 1771. 2nd edn. 8vo. viii,151,[4] pp. Half-title, engvd title vignette. Mod half calf. *(Young's)* £90 [≈ $162]
- The purple island, or the Isle of Man ... an allegorical poem [on the human body, with anatomical notes] ... London: Frys & Couchman, 1783. 8vo. xvi,189; ix,[2],75 pp. Unobtrusive foxing on 1st pages. Mod buckram. *(Hemlock)* $150 [≈ £83]
- The purple island, or the Isle of Man: together with piscatorie eclogs and other poetical miscellanies. Cambridge: 1633. 1st edn. 4to. Sm area cut from O2 affecting border, without 2 blanks. Early 19th c polished calf, sl scuffed. STC 11082. *(Charles Cox)* £300 [≈ $540]

Flint, George
- Robin's last shift; or, weekly remarks and political reflections upon the most material news foreign and domestick. Part I [all published]. London: for Isaac Dalton, 1717. 12mo. Old calf, sl worn. *(Charles Cox)* £65 [≈ $117]

Florian, Jean Pierre Claris de
- The history of Numa Pompilius, second king of Rome. Translated from the French ... London: for the translator, 1787. 1st edn of this trans. 3 vols. 8vo. 3 engvd frontis. Contemp mrbld bds, sheep spines, rubbed, jnts cracking. *(Burmester)* £180 [≈ $324]

Floyer, Sir John
- Psykhroloysia; or, the history of cold bathing, both ancient and modern. In two parts. London: W. & J. Innys, 1722. 5th edn. [22],491,[31] pp. Orig blindstamped lea, rebacked, orig spine laid down. *(Elgen)* $350 [≈ £194]
- The Sybilline Oracles translated from the best Greek copies, and compar'd with the sacred prophecies ... London: for J. Nicholson, 1713. Cr 8vo. Contemp panelled calf, rec rebacked. *(Stewart)* £45 [≈ $81]

Folly ...
- The folly of appointing men of parts to great offices in a state. London: J. Coote, 1758. 8vo. 24 pp. Half-title. Stitching loose. Disbound. *(Clark)* £12 [≈ $21]

Fonseca, Christopher de
- A discourse of holy love, by which the soul is united unto God. London: for Richard Royston, 1652. 1st edn. 12mo. [x],268 pp. Engvd frontis, engvd & ptd titles (ptd titles red & black). Near contemp gilt panelled mor, a trifle rubbed, a.e.g. Wing F1405. *(Young's)* £170 [≈ $306]
- A discourse of holy love, by which the soul is united unto God. London: for Richard Royston, 1652. 12mo. Engvd frontis & title, red & black ptd title. Old calf, later rebacking. Wing F1405. *(Traylen)* £68 [≈ $122]

Fontenelle, Bernard le Bovyer de
- Conversation with a lady on the plurality of worlds ... translated by Mr. Glanvill. London: for M. Wellington, 1719. 4th edn. 8vo. Frontis, fldg plate. Some minor waterstain affecting a few leaves. Contemp panelled calf, sm tear of back cvr. *(Waterfield's)* £90 [≈ $162]
- Conversation with a lady on the plurality of worlds ... translated by Mr. Glanvill. London: for M. Wellington, 1719. 4th edn. 12mo. Frontis, fldg plate, 4 pp pub ctlg at end. Contemp panelled calf. *(Charles Cox)* £25 [≈ $45]
- Conversations on the plurality of worlds. Translated ... By William Gardiner. London: for A. Bettesworth ..., 1715. 1st edn of this trans. 12mo. [xii],192 pp. Engvd frontis. Contemp panelled calf, rebacked. *(Burmester)* £110 [≈ $198]
- Conversations on the plurality of worlds. Dublin: Peter Wilson, 1761. 12mo. xx,181 pp. 4 engvd fldg plates. Contemp calf, hinges starting. *(Karmiole)* $125 [≈ £69]
- Dialogues of the dead. London: for Jacob

Tonson, 1708. liv,209 pp. Lacking frontis. Contemp unlettered panelled calf, v sl chipped at hd of spine. *(Pirages)* **$50 [≈ £27]**
- The history of oracles, and the cheats of the pagan priests. In two parts. Made English. London: 1688. Sm 8vo. 227 pp. Contemp calf, cvrs detchd.   *(Argosy)* **$250 [≈ £138]**
- A week's conversation on the plurality of worlds ... to which is added Mr. Addison's defence on the Newtonian philosophy. London: 1737. 6th edn. 12mo. Frontis, fldg plate. Contemp calf, lacking label.
    (Robertshaw) **£36 [≈ $64]**

Fool ...
- The fool turned critick ... See · D'Urfey, Thomas

Foot, Jesse
- A complete treatise on the origin, theory, and cure of the lues venerea, and obstructions of the urethra ... London: for the author, 1792. 1st edn. 4to. Lge copy, from the lib of Matthew Boulton. Contemp half calf, jnts reprd.   *(Quaritch)* **$1,550 [≈ £861]**

Forbes, Duncan
- A letter to a Bishop, concerning some important discoveries in philosophy and theology. London: H. Woodfall, 1732. 8vo. Pirated reprint of 4to 1st edn. 64 pp. Title somewhat browned & dusty, couple of marg tears without loss, some foxing. Disbound.
    (Burmester) **£50 [≈ $90]**
- The whole works ... now first collected. Edinburgh: for G. Hamilton ... and T. Durham in London, [1755]. 2 vols in 1. 12mo. Engvd port. Contemp calf, sl snag at hd of backstrip. *(Waterfield's)* **£150 [≈ $270]**
- The whole works ... now first collected. Dublin: Thomas Watson, 1755. 1st Dublin edn. F'cap 8vo. 308 pp, advt leaf. Contemp calf, new label.   *(Spelman)* **£40 [≈ $72]**

Force of Example ...
- The force of example; or, the history of Henry and Caroline: written for the instruction and amusement of young persons. London: for E. Newbery, 1797. 1st edn. 12mo. [iv],159,[4 advts] pp. Engvd frontis, half-title. Contemp calf, jnts partially cracked.   *(Burmester)* **£95 [≈ $171]**

Ford, Simon
- Londons resurrection, poetically represented. London: for Sa: Gellibrand, 1669. 1st edn in English 4to. Advt leaf C4. Loose, stained, disbound, in cloth-backed fldr. Wing F1490.
    (Charles Cox) **£85 [≈ $153]**

Fordyce, James
- The temple of virtue, a dream. London: T. Cadell, 1775. 2nd edn. Contemp calf.
    (C.R. Johnson) **£125 [≈ $225]**

Fordyce, Sir William
- A new enquiry into the causes, symptoms and cure of putrid and inflammatory fevers with an appendix on the hectic fever and on the ulcerated and malignant sore throat. London: 1777. 3rd edn. 8vo. Old calf.
    (Halewood) **£95 [≈ $171]**

Forms for Proceedings ...
- Forms for proceedings on such seizures as by the late Act for preventing frauds ... are to be heard and determined ... London: for Edw. Castle, 1720. 8vo. 37,[3] pp. Disbound.
    (Burmester) **£35 [≈ $63]**

Forrester, James
- The polite philosopher or, an essay on that art which makes a man happy in himself and agreeable to others. Edinburgh: for Robert Freebairn, 1734. 1st edn. Inner gutter of title sl defective without loss of text. Disbound.
    (Waterfield's) **£45 [≈ $81]**

Forsett, Edward
- A comparative discourse of bodies naturall and politique ... the true forme of a Commonweale, with the dutie of subjects ... London: 1606. 1st edn. 4to. 100 pp. Imprint, a few headlines & sidenotes shaved. Later half calf, worn upper cvr detchd. STC 11188.
    (Robertshaw) **£75 [≈ $135]**

Forster, G.
- A voyage round the world in H.M. Sloop 'Resolution', commanded by Capt. James Cook, 1772-75. 1777. 2 vols. Lge 4to. Lge fldg map in pocket. Vol 1 title reprd on edges, ink staining in margs of 4 pp with resultant hole in marg, marg soiling. Half calf.
    (Halewood) **£550 [≈ $990]**

Fortescue, Sir John
- De laudibus legum Anglicae writen by ... Hereto are ioined the two summes of Sir Ralph de Hengham ... London: for the Companie of Stationers, 1616. English & Latin text. prelim & final blank. Full mor, a.e.g., by Riviere. STC 11197.
    (Charles Cox) **£200 [≈ $360]**

Fortis, Alberto
- Travels into Dalmatia; to which are added observations of the Island of Cherso and Osero. London: J. Robson, 1778. 1st English

edn. 4to. x,584 pp. 17 (ex 20) engvd plates (11 fldg), 2 fldg engvd maps. Mod half calf.
(Zeno) **£195 [≈ $351]**

Foster, John
- An accurate report of the speech ... Feb 27th, 1793 ... on the Bill for allowing Roman Catholics to vote at the elections ... London: Debrett, 1793. 8vo. 52 pp. Mod wraps.
(Emerald Isle) **£38 [≈ $68]**

Foster, Samuel
- Miscellanies: or mathematical lucubrations ... Translated ... Leybourn, 1659. 1st edn. Folio. Latin & English titles (inner margs reprd), 7 ptd titles to sections, 10 engvd plates. Some pages & plates strengthened, marg waterstaining. Mod mor. Wing F1634.
(P & P) **£560 [≈ $1,008]**

Fothergill, John
- An account of the sore throat attended with ulcers; a disease which hath of later years appeared in this city ... London: for C. Davis, 1748. 1st edn. 8vo. iv,62 pp. Tear in title reprd, upper margin trimmed close. Orig calf, lower jnt reprd. *(Bickersteth)* **£480 [≈ $864]**

Fougasses, Thomas de
- The generall historie of the magnificent State of Venice ... by Thomas de Fougasses ... Englished by W. Shute. London: Eld & Stansby, 1612, 2 vols in 1. Folio. [vi],579; 500,[xliii] pp. Reprs to some leaves. Contemp calf, armorial gilt, rebacked & restored.
(Frew Mackenzie) **£250 [≈ $450]**

Fourcroy, Antoine Francois de
- Elements of natural history, and of chemistry ... first published in 1782, and now ... translated into English. London: Robinson, 1788. 4 vols. 8vo. 9 fldg engvd tables. Contemp tree-calf, occas sl surface damage to sides. *(Frew Mackenzie)* **£375 [≈ $675]**

Fovargue, Stephen
- A new catalogue of vulgar errors. Cambridge: for the author, 1767. 1st edn. 8vo. [ii],202 pp. Errata slip. Wanting half-title, 1st few leaves sl browned, a few inner margs dampstained. Rec qtr calf. *(Burmester)* **£125 [≈ $225]**

Fox, Charles
- A series of poems containing the plaints, consolations and delights of Achmed Ardebeili a Persian exile. Bristol: for J. Cottle, 1797. Sole edn. 8vo. Title grubby. Contemp tree-calf, newly rebacked.
(Marlborough) **£250 [≈ $450]**

Fox, Charles James
- The speech ... in the House of Commons Dec. 1 1792. On that part of the address to the King which implicated our being involved in a war with France. London: James Ridgway, [1792]. 15 pp. Disbound.
(C.R. Johnson) **£15 [≈ $27]**
- The speech ... in the House of Commons on the Irish Resolutions ... London: J. Debrett, 1785. 100 pp. Rebound in bds.
(C.R. Johnson) **£18 [≈ $32]**
- The speech in the House of Commons on the Irish Resolutions ... London: J. Debrett, 1785. New edn. 104 pp. Disbound.
(Young's) **£25 [≈ $45]**
- Substance of the speech ... upon a motion for the commitment of the bill "for vesting the affairs of the East India Company in the hands of certain commissioners ..." London: for J. Debrett, 1783. 8vo. Disbound.
(Stewart) **£25 [≈ $45]**

Fox, Charles James & Erskine, Thomas
- The speeches ... at a meeting at the Shakespeare Tavern, Covent Garden ... October 10, 1797. London: J.S. Jordon, 1797. 24 pp. Disbound. *(C.R. Johnson)* **£18 [≈ $32]**

Fox, Charles James
- Proceedings in an action for debt between ... Charles James Fox, plaintiff, and John Horne Tooke, defendant. London: for J. Johnson, 1792. 8vo. Some pages detached. Disbound.
(Waterfield's) **£45 [≈ $81]**

Fox, George
- A journal. London: Sowle, 1709. 2nd (1st 8vo) edn. 2 vols. 8vo. New half calf.
(Marlborough) **£120 [≈ $216]**
- The priests fruits made manifest. And the fashions of the world, and the lust of ignorance. 1657. 4to. 8 pp. Half calf, spine worn. Wing F1883. *(Allen)* **$35 [≈ £19]**

Fox, George, et al.
- A battle-door for teachers and professors to learn singular and plural ... London: for Robert Wilson, 1660. 1st edn. Folio. 8 pts. Lge cancel slips at 2nd D6 & at end. Paper browned a little. Mod black mor. Wing 1751.
(Hannas) **£850 [≈ $1,530]**

Foxe, John
- Acts and monuments of matters most special and memorable, happening in the church; with an universal history of the same. London: for the Company of Stationers, 1684. 9th edn. 3 vols. Thick folio. 3 plates (1

reprd), other text engvs. New cloth.
(Stewart) **£200 [≈ $360]**
- The book of martyrs ... Preface by the Rev.
Mr. Madan. 1776. Lge 4to. 815 pp, index.
Copper-plates throughout. Half calf, worn.
(Edwards) **£100 [≈ $180]**

Fragment ...
- A fragment on government ... See Bentham,
Jeremy

Fragmenta Antiquitatis ...
- Fragmenta antiquitatis. Antient tenures of
land ... See Blount, Thomas

Franklin, Benjamin
- The way to wealth, or poor Richard
improved. Paris: for Ant. Aug. Renouard,
1795. Lge paper. 6 prelims, 181,[5],28 pp.
Port frontis (sl freckled), half-title. Contemp
continental calf spine, mrbld bds, extremities
a bit rubbed, sides worn.
(Pirages) **$225 [≈ £125]**
- The way to wealth, or poor Richard
improved. Paris: for Ant. Aug. Renouard,
1795. Lge paper. 12mo. [4],181,[5],31 advts
pp. Port frontis. A few pp sl browned &
foxed. Orig pink bds, extremities worn &
chipped.   *(Heritage)* **$750 [≈ £416]**

Freart, Roland, Sieur de Cambray
- An idea of the perfection of painting ...
London: Henry Herringman, 1668. 1st edn in
English. 8vo. [38],136 pp. Lacking 1st blank.
Contemp blind-tooled calf, hd of spine sl
chipped. Wing C1922.
(Rootenberg) **$950 [≈ £527]**
- An idea of the perfection of painting ...
rendred English by J.E. Savoy [London]:
Herringman, 1668. 8vo. Title, 19ff,136 pp.
Contemp calf, rebacked. Wing F1922.
(Marlborough) **£360 [≈ $648]**

Frederick II, King of Prussia
- The Frederician Code; or, a body of law for
the Dominions of the King of Prussia.
Translated from the French. Edinburgh: A.
Donaldson ..., 1761. 2 vols. 8vo. [i],xlviii,
489; vii,506 pp. Light spotting. Contemp
calf, spines elab tooled, sl worming to jnts.
(Frew Mackenzie) **£200 [≈ $360]**

Free-Citizens ...
- The free-citizens address to Sir Samuel
Cooke, Bart for his unshaken attachment to
the true interest of Ireland ... London: ... at
the Sign of Madam Ragg, beasting Sir Tady
with a Buck's Horn, 1754. [but Dublin?]. 16

pp.   *(C.R. Johnson)* **£55 [≈ $99]**

Free-holder ...
- The free-holder ... See Addison, Joseph

Freeman, John
- The comforter or a comfortable treatise ...
London: for George Purslowe, 1614. 12ff,
title, 16ff, 281 pp, 5ff. Ms notes at beginning
& end. Index leaves with ragged edges, worn.
Parchment cvr, discold, detchd at front.
(Titles) **£60 [≈ $108]**

Freeman, Samuel
- The case of mixt communion, whether it be
lawful to separate from a church upon the
account of promiscuous congregations and
mixt communions? London: for T. Basset,
1684. 2nd edn. Med 4to. [2],41 pp. New
mrbld bds, new blanks. Wing F2139.
(Deighton Bell) **£20 [≈ $36]**

Freind, J.
- The history of physick from the time of Galen
to the beginning of the sixteenth century.
London: Walther, 1726-27. 3rd, 2nd edns.
Orig panelled calf, worn, jnts cracked.
(Goodrich) **$275 [≈ £152]**

French Herauld ...
- The French herauld sent to the Princes of
Christendome. Printed according to the
French copies. London: 1622. 4to. [3]-21,[i]
pp. Lacking A1 (blank?). margs a bit frayed.
Stitching broken, disbound. STC 11375.
(Clark) **£40 [≈ $72]**

French, John
- The York-shire spaw, or a treatise of four
famous medicinal wells ... causes, vertues,
and use thereof ... London: for E. Dod ...,
1652. 1st edn. 8vo. [viii],124,[2 table of
contents] pp. With final blank R4. Rec bds.
(Pickering) **$350 [≈ £194]**

Frend, William
- An account of the proceedings in the
University of Cambridge against ... for
publishing a pamphlet, intituled Peace and
Union, &c ... Cambridge: 1793. 1st edn.
liii,262,[6] pp. Orig bds, uncut, backstrip
renewed.   *(Claude Cox)* **£40 [≈ $72]**

Friend of Virtue ...
- The friend of virtue. A novel from the French
... London: for T. Vernor, 1789. 3 vols.
12mo. Contemp half calf, gilt, mrbld sides.
(Traylen) **£800 [≈ $1,440]**

Fruit walls ...
- Fruit walls improved ... See Fatio de Duillier, Nicolas

Fulke, William
- A most pleasant prospect into the garden of naturall contemplation, to behold the naturall causes of all kinde of meteors ... London: E.G. for William Leake, 1640. Sm 8vo. [3],71ff. Closely trimmed. half mor over mrbld bds. *(Rootenberg)* **$400 [≈ £222]**

Fuller, A. & Holms, T.
- A compendious view of the sufferings of the people called Quakers, both in person and substance, in the Kingdom of Ireland from 1655 to the end of the reign of George I. Dublin: Fuller, 1731. Contemp calf, rebacked. *(Emerald Isle)* **£85 [≈ $153]**

Fuller, Francis
- Medicina gymnastica: or a treatise concerning the power of exercise, with respect to the animal economy; and the great necessity of it ... London: 1728. 6th edn. 8vo. 271 pp. Contemp calf. *(Goodrich)* **$75 [≈ £41]**
- Medicina gymnastica: or a treatise concerning the power of exercise ... London: Knaplock, 1728. 6th edn. 8vo. [36],271,[10 advts] pp. Lower marg waterstained, title verso stamped. Rec half calf. *(Spelman)* **£55 [≈ $99]**

Fuller, Samuel
- A serious reply to ... abusive queries proposed to the consideration of the people called Quakers concluding the works of Joseph Boyse ... Dublin: Sam Fuller, 1728. 8vo. 147 pp. Advt. Contemp calf, cottage tooled. *(Emerald Isle)* **£75 [≈ $135]**

Fuller, Thomas (1608-1661)
- The church-history of Britain. London: for John Williams, 1655. 11 books in 1 vol (some sep paginated). Folio. [With, bound at end, as correct] History of the University of Cambridge. London: 1655. Contemp calf, spine worn, headbands broken, jnts weak. Wing 2416. *(Stewart)* **£200 [≈ $360]**
- Good thoughts in bad times. Together with good thoughts in worse times ... London: for I. Williams, 1659. 12mo. [vi],86; [viii],112 pp. Sgntr leaf before title in both parts. Some minor stains, a few margs cut close with sl loss, Old calf, worn, cvrs detached. *(Bow Windows)* **£40 [≈ $72]**
- The historie of the holy warre. Cambridge: 1640. 2nd edn. Folio. 286 pp. tables, dec title. Text browning & soiled. Contemp panelled calf, worn. *(Edwards)* **£200 [≈ $360]**
- The historie of the holy warre. Cambridge: Thomas Buck, 1651. 4th edn. Sm folio. [xvi],286,[28] pp. Engvd & ptd titles, fldg map. Contemp calf. Wing F2439. *(Lloyd-Roberts)* **£100 [≈ $180]**
- The history of the worthies of England. London: 1662. 1st edn. Folio. Engvd port frontis. Contemp calf, rebacked & recrnrd in red mor, gilt. Wing F2440. *(Traylen)* **£250 [≈ $450]**

Fuller, Thomas (1654-1734)
- Exanthematogia: or ... a rational account of eruptive fevers, especially of the measles and small pox. London: Rivington & Austen, 1730. 1st edn. 4to. 439,[9] pp. Advt leaf. Red & black title. Titles to pts 2 & 3 dated 1729. Contemp lea-backed mrbld bds. *(Antiq Sc)* **$375 [≈ £208]**
- Gnomologia: adages and proverbs; wise sentences and witty sayings, ancient and modern, foreign and British. London: for B. Barker ..., 1732. 1st edn. 12mo. x,297,[5 advts] pp. 19th c half calf, rebacked. *(Burmester)* **£110 [≈ $198]**

Fuller, William
- A plain proof of the true father and mother of the pretended Prince of Wales, by several letters written by the late Queen in France. London: for the author, 1700. 1st edn. 16 pp. Browned & cropped. Rec qtr calf. Wing F2485. *(Young's)* **£33 [≈ $59]**

Fullwood, Francis
- Obedience to the King, not withstanding our oaths to the former. London: for Awnsham Churchill, 1689. 1st edn. Sm 4to. [2],8 pp. With the final blank, ptd on fine paper. Uncut in canvas-backed paper bds. *(Claude Cox)* **£20 [≈ $36]**

Furneaux, Philip
- Letters to the Hon. Mr. Justice Blackstone, concerning his exposition of the Act of Toleration ... in Commentaries on the Laws of England. London: for T. Cadell, 1771. 8vo. Title spotted. Contemp calf, 2 crnrs bumped. *(Stewart)* **£25 [≈ $45]**

G.M.
- Cheape and good husbandry for the well-ordering of all beasts and fowles and for the generall cure of their diseases. 1653. 8th edn. 188 pp. Contemp inscrptn & anntn on 2 leaves. Rebound in calf, gilt, new endpapers. *(Edwards)* **£150 [≈ $270]**

Gadbury, John
- The nativity of the late King Charles astrologically and faithfully performed; with reasons ... of the ... success, and mis-fortune of his whole life ... London: 1659. 1st edn. 8vo. 3 ports, diags & tables. Some soiling. Contemp calf, spine chipped. Wing G89.
(*Robertshaw*) **£110** [≈ $198]

Gage, Thomas
- A new survey of the West Indies. Being a journey of three thousand and three hundred miles within the main land of America ... London: for F. Nicolson, 1699. 4th edn, enlgd. Sm 8vo. [8],477,[18] pp. Lge fldg map. Rebound in green mor.
(*Argonaut*) **$350** [≈ £194]

Gallus, Cornelius
- The impotent lover, accurately described in six elegies upon old age ... made English ... by H. Walker. London: B. Crayle, 1689. 1st edn. Sm 8vo. 78 pp. Some foxing. 19th c cloth, worn. Wing G181B. (*Argosy*) **$250** [≈ £138]

Garat, Dominique Joseph
- Memoirs of the Revolution; or, an apology for my conduct, in the employments which I have held. Edinburgh: G. Mudie, 1797. Contemp calf, red label. From the library of Colquhoun of Luss. (*C.R. Johnson*) **£225** [≈ $405]

Gardiner, John
- An inquiry into the nature, cause, and cure of the gout, and of some of the diseases with which it is connected. Phila: Wiliam Spotswood, 1793. 1st Amer edn. 8vo. xxv,[1], 27-216 pp. Some foxing. Contemp calf, front cvr loose, rear hinge cracked.
(*Hemlock*) **$200** [≈ £111]

Gardiner, Ralph
- England's grievance discovered, in relation to the coal trade; with the map of the River Tyne ... Newcastle: reprinted by D. Akenhead, 1796. 2nd edn. viii,216 pp. Fldg map, 17 engvd oval ports, 3 other plates. 19th c half calf, a little rubbed. (*Young's*) **£90** [≈ $162]

Garnett, John
- A dissertation on the Book of Job. London: for M. Cooper, 1749. 4to. Contemp calf, later rebacked. (*Stewart*) **£30** [≈ $54]

Garrick, David
- Miss in her teens: or, the medley of lovers: a farce in two acts ... London: for J. & R. Tonson, 1748. 4th edn. Half-title. Disbound.
(*Waterfield's*) **£25** [≈ $45]

- Miss in her teens: or, the medley of lovers: a farce in two acts ... London: J. & R. Tonson ..., 1747. 2nd edn. 8vo. [viii],40 pp. Half-title. Disbound. (*Clark*) **£30** [≈ $54]
- Neck or nothing. A farce. In two acts. London: T. Becket, 1766. 1st edn. 8vo. [iv],38 pp. Outer leaves a bit soiled, sm tear at ft of 1st text leaf. Disbound.
(*Clark*) **£35** [≈ $63]

Garth, Sir Samuel
- The dispensary: a poem. In six cantos. London: John Nutt, 1699. 2nd edn, crrctd by the author. 8vo. Engvd frontis. Contemp panelled calf, rec rebacked.
(*Stewart*) **£85** [≈ $153]

Garthwait, Henry
- Monotessapon. The evangelicall harmonie. Cambridge: Thomas Buck ..., 1634. 4to. Lacking engvd title & front & rear endpapers, old stains to final leaves, paper flaws to B1 & E3. Contemp half calf, worn, upper jnt weak. STC 11633. (*Stewart*) **£75** [≈ $135]

Gassendi, Petrus
- The vanity of judiciary astrology, or divination by the stars. London: 1659. 1st English edn. 8vo. Port (sl worming). A little staining at beginning. Contemp sheep, rubbed. Wing G298.
(*Robertshaw*) **£145** [≈ $261]

Gassendi, Pierre
- The mirrour of true nobility and gentility, being the life of the renowned Nicolaus Claudius Fabricius, Lord of Peirisk ... Englished ... London: 1657. 1st English edn. Port. Contemp sheep. Wing G295. Belton House b'plate. (*Robertshaw*) **£95** [≈ $171]

Gauger, Monsieur
- Fires improv'd: being a new method of building chimneys, so as to prevent their smoking ... the manner of making coal-fires ... 1715. 1st edn. 8vo. 161 pp, contents & 2 pp advts. 9 fldg plates (v sl dampstained). Half calf, a little worn. (*Edwards*) **£200** [≈ $360]

Gavin, Antonio
- Observations on a journey to Naples. Wherein the frauds of Romish monks ... are further discover'd ... London: Roycroft, 1691. 1st edn. 8vo. [xxiv],325,3 advts pp. Sm tear in title. Contemp calf, rubbed, spine worn at hd & tail, front jnt cracked. Wing G393.
(*Frew Mackenzie*) **£185** [≈ $333]
- A short history of monastical orders ... primitive institution of monks, their tempers,

habits, rules ... condition they are in at present ... London: for W. Bentley, 1693. 8vo. A1 (advt leaf) frayed & reprd, title discold, some browning. Mod bds. Wing G394. *(Waterfield's)* £30 [≈ $54]

Gay, John

- The beggar's opera ... to which is added the musick engraved on copperplates. London: for John Watts, 1728. 1st edn. 8vo. 56,16 pp. [Bound, in polished calf, with] Gay, John. Polly: an opera. London: for T. Thomson, 1729. 1st edn. 8vo. ix,62,16 pp.
(Argosy) $500 [≈ £277]
- The beggar's opera, to which is prefixed the overture in score: and the musick to each song. London: W. Strahan ..., 1777. 8vo. 96 pp. Engvd frontis. Outer marg a bit cropped. Disbound. *(Clark)* £20 [≈ $36]
- Fables ... with a life of the author. London: John Stockdale, 1793. 1st iss of 1st Stockdale edn. 2 vols. 2 engvd titles, 68 engvd plates. Light foxing. Contemp tree calf, spines gilt, front hinge vol I cracked. Wide-margined lge & thick paper copy. *(Argonaut)* £425 [≈ £236]
- Fables ... with a life of the author, and embellished with a plate to each fable. London: for F. & C. Rivington, 1793. 8vo. xvi,256 pp. Engvd frontis & title, 67 engvd plates on 34 leaves. Some browning, repr to 1 marg. Contemp calf, old reback, crnrs worn *(Bow Windows)* £145 [≈ $261]
- Fables by the late Mr. Gay. In one volume complete. London: 1772. 12mo. 240 pp. 35 plates (all except 2 with 2 ills). Sm inkstains on a few leaves, others dampmarked around margs. Contemp speckled calf, rebacked & reprd. *(Bow Windows)* £70 [≈ $126]
- Fables, in one volume complete. London: Strahan, Rivington, 1772. 12mo. Frontis, 66 plates. Contemp calf. *(Argosy)* £85 [≈ £47]
- Fables. 1757. 2 vols in 1 (running pagination). Frontis, title vignette, copper plates. Contemp speckled calf, rubbed, rebacked. *(Halewood)* £75 [≈ $135]
- The fan. A poem. In three books. London: for J. Tonson, 1714. 1st edn. Folio. 32 pp. Fine paper copy (PH watermark). Disbound.
(Hannas) £580 [≈ $1,044]
- The Petticoat ... See Chute, Francis
- Poems on several occasions. Glasgow: Foulis, 1776. 2 vols. Advt leaf at end of vol 1, fly title in vol 2. Contemp red mor, spines heavily gilt, mrbld endpapers, jnts & extremities sl rubbed. B'plate of Edward, Lord Suffield in each vol. *(Pirages)* £125 [≈ £69]
- The shepherd's week. In six pastorals. London: Ferd. Burleigh, 1714. 1st edn. Sm

8vo. 7ff,60,[4] pp. 7 engvd plates inc frontis. Mod smooth calf, gilt, by Riviere.
(Pirages) $500 [≈ £277]
- The what d'ye call it: a tragi-comi-pastoral farce. London: for Bernard Lintot, [1715]. 8vo. [xii],41 pp. Engvd frontis. '2nd' edn (re-iss of 1st, with cancel title). 19th c half red mor. *(Bennett)* £150 [≈ $270]

Gazetteer ...

- The North-American and the West-Indian gazetteer ... authentic description of the colonies and islands ... London: 1778. 2nd edn. 12mo. 2 fldg maps. Ink sgntr clipped at top of half-title and title. Speckled calf, rebacked, some edge-wear.
(Reese) $850 [≈ £472]

General Assemblie ...

- Reasons for a General Assemblie. [Edinburgh: George Anderson], 1638. 4to. Some sl foxing. New calf with num blanks. NSTC 22054. *(Marlborough)* £85 [≈ $153]

Gentil, Francis & Liger d'Auxerre, Louis

- Le jardinier solitaire; the solitary ... gard'ner ... The compleat florist ... the way of raising all sorts of parterres ... porticoes, columns, and other ornaments ... London: Benj. Tooke, 1706. 1st edn in English. 20 engvd plates (1 fldg). Later calf.
(Gough) £235 [≈ $423]

Gentleman Farrier ...

- The gentleman farrier. Containing instructions for the choice and ... management of horses ... added an appendix, concerning dogs. London: for F. Cogan, 1732. 1st edn. 12mo. [xviii],137, [xiii] pp. Lacking front free endpaper. Contemp panelled calf. *(Bennett)* £110 [≈ $198]

Gentleman's Calling ...

- The gentleman's calling ... See Allestree, Richard

Gentleman's Recreation ...

- The gentleman's recreation ... See Cox, Nicolas

Gerard, Alexander

- Dissertations on subjects relating to the genius and the evidences of Christianity. Edinburgh: for A. Millar ..., 1766, 8vo. Contemp tree-calf.
(Waterfield's) £65 [≈ $117]

Gerard, John

- The herball or general historie of plants.
London: 1597. Folio. [xx],1392,[72] pp.
Engvd title (re-margined), engvd port, 2146
w'cuts in text. last 3 leaves of index reprd with
sl loss of text. Calf, rebacked, worn at jnts &
edges.
(Wheldon & Wesley) **£1,800** [≃ **$3,240**]
- The herball, or generall historie of plantes ...
enlarged and amended by Thomas Johnson.
London: Adam Islip, 1633. 1st Johnson edn.
Folio. Engvd title (sm lib stamp on verso),
num text w'cuts. STC
11751.   *(Traylen)* **£1,200** [≃ **$2,160**]
- The herball, or generall historie of plantes ...
enlarged and amended by Thomas Johnson.
London: Adam Islip, 1636. Thick folio.
Engvd title (sm portion missing from crnr),
num text w'cuts. Contemp calf, rebacked,
mor label. STC 11752.
(Traylen) **£850** [≃ **$1,530**]

Gessner, Salomon

- The death of Abel. In five books. Adapted
from the German. London: for J. Collyer,
1773. 11th edn. Cr. 8vo. Frontis. Sl browned.
Contemp calf.   *(Stewart)* **£20** [≃ **$36**]
- New idylles ... Translated ... with a letter to
M. Fuslin, on landscape painting ... London:
1776. 4to. Engvd title, 8 plates. A few stains.
Contemp diced russia, spine & crnrs rubbed,
upper jnt cracked. *(Robertshaw)* **£50** [≃ **$90**]
- New idylles by Gessner. Translated ... with a
letter to M. Fuslin, on landscape painting ...
London: Hooper, 1776. 1st edn. Sm folio.
[iv],129 pp. Engvd title, 9 engvd plates,
vignettes in text. Contemp tree-calf, some
rubbing & insect damage to front cvr.
(Frew Mackenzie) **£220** [≃ **$396**]

Gibbon, Edward

- The history of the decline and fall of the
Roman Empire. London: for A. Strahan ...,
1789-88. 6 vols. 4to. Mixed edns (vols 1-3
new edns; vols 4-6 1st edns). Half-titles vols
2-6, engvd port, 3 engvd maps (2 fldg).
Contemp speckled calf, gilt.
(Gough) **£895** [≃ **$1,611**]
- The history of the decline and fall of the
Roman Empire. London: W. Strahan & T.
Cadell, 1776-88. 1st edn, vol 1 in crrctd state.
6 vols. 4to. Half-titles in each vol, 3 fldg
maps, port. Contemp mottled calf, rebacked,
orig gilt spines laid down, new labels.
(Dailey) **$3,750** [≃ **£2,083**]
- Miscellaneous works ... with memoirs of his
life and writings ... London: A. Strahan ...,
1796. 1st edn. 2 vols. [with] Miscellaneous

works. Murray, 1815. 1st edn. In all, 3 vols.
4to. Contemp tree-calf, backstrips elab gilt,
front jnt vol III cracked.
(Blackwell's) **£275** [≃ **$495**]
- Miscellaneous works ... with memoirs of his
life and writings ... London: 1796-1815. 3
vols. 4to. xxvi,703; vii,736,[ii]; x,691 pp.
Engvd port frontis vols I & III. 1st 3 ff vol III
sl dampstained. Early 19th c calf, mrbld bds,
hinges reprd, spines worn.
(Frew Mackenzie) **£150** [≃ **$270**]
- A vindication of some passages in the
fifteenth and sixteenth chapters of the History
of the Decline and Fall of the Roman Empire.
London: W. Strahan, 1779. 1st edn. Contemp
qtr calf, mrbld bds, spine rubbed.
(C.R. Johnson) **£160** [≃ **$288**]

Gibson, Edmund

- Codex juris ecclesiastici Anglicani. or, the
statutes, constitutions ... of the Church of
England ... Oxford: Clarendon Press, 1756.
2nd edn. 2 vols. Folio. 1575 pp. Calf, orig
spine, worn, rubbed.
(Edwards) **£200** [≃ **$360**]
- Of visitations parochial and general ... to
which are added some other tracts. London:
1717. 1st edn. 8vo. [xvi],144 pp. Contemp
inscrptn on flyleaf & another more recent.
Contemp Cambridge style calf.
(Bow Windows) **£40** [≃ **$72**]

Gibson, John

- The history of Glasgow ... rise, progress and
present state ... different branches of
commerce and manufactures ... Rob.
Chapman ..., 1777. Fldg frontis. Contemp
calf, red label. Ex lib Colquhoun of Luss.
(C.R. Johnson) **£350** [≃ **$630**]

Gibson, John, Surgeon

- A treatise on bilious disorders and
indigestion, with the effects of quassy and
natron in these disorders. London: for
Murray & Highley ..., 1799. 1st edn. 8vo.
[iv],68 pp. Mod cloth.
(Burmester) **£45** [≃ **$81**]

Gibson, Thomas

- The anatomy of humane bodies epitomized.
London: Flesher, 1682. 1st edn. 8vo.
[viii],510 pp. 13 engvd plates inc imprim leaf
before title. Cancel 2K8 at end. Sm piece torn
from upper marg P1 with sl loss, sm rusthole
in 1 lf. Contemp speckled calf. Wing G672.
(Pickering) **$950** [≃ **£527**]
- The anatomy of humane bodies epitomized.
London: for Awnsham & John Churchill ...,
1697. 5th edn. 8vo. [xvi],vi,626 pp. 20 engvd

plates. Contemp calf, rebacked. Wing G676.
(*Pickering*) **$300 [≈£166]**

Gibson, William
- A new treatise on the diseases of horses ...
London: A. Millar, 1751. 1st edn. 4to.
[10],464,[12] pp. Lge paper. Engvd frontis,
31 plates. Contemp ms recipes on prelim
blanks. B'plates. Contemp calf, rebacked.
(*Rootenberg*) **$650 [≈£361]**

Gifford, John
- A letter to ... Thomas Erskine; containing
some strictures on his view of the causes and
consequences of the present war with France.
London: J. Plymsell, 1797. 171 pp.
Disbound. (*C.R. Johnson*) **£18 [≈$32]**

Gifford, William
- The Baviad, a paraphrastic imitation of the
first satire of Persius. London: R. Fauldner,
1791. 51 pp. Half-title. Disbound.
(*C.R. Johnson*) **£75 [≈$135]**

Gilbert, Benjamin
- A narrative of the captivity and sufferings of
Benjamin Gilbert and his family; who were
surprised by the Indians, and taken from their
farms. In the Spring, 1780. 1785. 1st English
edn. 124 pp. Wraps. (*Farahar*) **£185 [≈$333]**

Gilbert, Samuel
- The florist's vade-mecum ... propagation,
raising ... and preserving the rarest flowers
and plants. London: 1702. 3rd edn, enlgd.
12mo. 149,[19] pp. Sev text diags. Somewhat
browned throughout, light dampstain, a few
other faults. Contemp sheep, jnts cracked.
(*Bow Windows*) **£65 [≈$117]**

Gilbert, Thomas
- A scheme for the better relief and
employment of the poor; humbly submitted
... London: 1764. 1st edn. 8vo. [iv],23 pp.
Blank strip torn from title marg. Disbound.
(*Burmester*) **£125 [≈$225]**

Gilpin, Richard
- Daemonologia Sacra. or, a treatise of Satans
temptations. London: 1677. 1st edn. Sm 4to.
Later half calf, upper jnt cracked. Wing
G777. (*Robertshaw*) **£40 [≈$72]**

Gilpin, William
- The life of Bernard Gilpin. London: for J. &
J. Rivington, 1753. 2nd edn. 311 pp. Engvd
port, engvd vignette title. Contemp gilt-
panelled tree-calf, gilt-dec spine, jnt sl split at
hd. (*Gough*) **£48 [≈$86]**

- The life of Thomas Cranmer. London: for R.
Blamire, 1784. 8vo. Sl foxed. New calf spine,
mrbld bds. (*Stewart*) **£35 [≈$63]**
- The lives of John Wiclif and of the most
eminent of his disciples ... London: for J.
Robson, 1766. 2nd edn, crrctd & imprvd. 5
plates. Contemp calf, rebacked.
(*Waterfield's*) **£70 [≈$126]**
- Observations, relative chiefly to picturesque
beauty, made in the year 1776 ... Blamire,
1792. 2nd edn. 2 vols. vii,xii,221; 195,xvi pp.
40 plates, mainly aquatints (offsetting). Gilt
dec tree-calf, vol 1 rebacked, vol 2 front bd
nearly detached. (*P & P*) **£75 [≈$135]**
- Observations, relative chiefly to picturesque
beauty, made in the year 1776, on several
parts of Great Britain ... London: for R.
Blamire, 1789. 2 vols. 40 plates. Contemp
tree-calf, red & green labels. Ex lib
Colquhoun of Luss.
(*C.R. Johnson*) **£400 [≈$720]**
- Observations, relative chiefly to picturesque
beauty, made in the year 1776, on several
parts of Great Britain; particularly the High-
Lands of Scotland. 1792. 2nd edn. 2 vols.
221; 195 pp. 41 plates. Some foxing on plate
versos. Half calf, gilt, sl worn.
(*Edwards*) **£150 [≈$270]**
- Remarks on forest scenery, and other
woodland views ... illustrated by scenes of
New Forest in Hampshire. 1794. 2nd edn. 2
vols. 340; 342 pp. 32 sepia plates. Offsetting.
Half calf, gilt, sl worn.
(*Edwards*) **£150 [≈$270]**

Giraffi, Lord Alexander
- An exact historie of the late revolution in
Naples. And of their monstrous successes, not
to be parallel'd ... London: 1650. 1st edn in
English. Sm 8vo. Hand-cold engvd frontis,
red & black title, prelims, 206 pp. Rebound in
panelled calf. (*Edwards*) **£110 [≈$198]**

Girardin
- An essay on landscape; or, the means of
improving and embellishing the country
round our habitations. Translated ... London:
J. Dodsley, 1783. 1st English edn. F'cap 8vo.
[2],lv,160 pp. Engvd frontis. B1 & crnr of B4
torn & reprd. Contemp half calf, rebacked.
(*Spelman*) **£240 [≈$432]**

Giraud, Guillaume
- The history of the life of the Duke of
Espernon. Englished by Charles Cotton.
London: 1670. 1st edn. Folio. Red & black
title, 2 ports. Contemp calf, worn. Wing
G788. (*Robertshaw*) **£75 [≈$135]**

Gisborne, John
- The Vale of Wever, a loco-descriptive poem. London: John Stockdale, 1797. 4to. Rebound in qtr calf, mrbld bds.
            (C.R. Johnson) **£125 [≈ $225]**

Gisborne, Thomas
- An enquiry into the duties of men in the higher and middle classes of society in Great Britain, resulting from their respective stations ... London: White, 1794. 1st edn. 4to. vi,[ii],848 pp. Contemp qtr calf, mrbld sides, backstrip rubbed, front cvr scraped.
            (Frew Mackenzie) **£220 [≈ $396]**
- An enquiry into the duties of men in the higher and middle classes of society in Great Britain, resulting from their respective stations ... London: for B. & J. White, 1794. 1st edn. 4to. viii,846 pp. New half calf, mrbld sides.   *(Lloyd-Roberts)* **£125 [≈ $225]**
- An enquiry into the duties of the female sex. London: Cadell & Davies, 1797. 2nd edn. Lge 8vo. Contemp qtr calf, rubbed.
            (Marlborough) **£35 [≈ $63]**
- Walks in a forest: or, poems descriptive of scenery and incidents characteristic of a forest, at different seasons of the year. London: J. Davis, 1796. 2nd edn, crrctd & enlgd. 8vo. [xii],123 pp. Contemp half calf, a little worn.   *(Young's)* **£23 [≈ $41]**

Glanvill, Joseph
- Saducismus triumphatus: or, full and plain evidence concerning witches and apparitions. London: for J. Collins ..., 1681. 1st edn. 3 pts in 1 vol. 2 port frontis, 4 text figs. Paper fault in 1 leaf, a few crnrs defective. Contemp calf, jnts cracked, scuffed. *(Pirages)* **£325 [≈ £180]**
- Saducismus triumphatus: or, full and plain evidence concerning witches and apparitions. London: for S.L., 1689. 3rd edn. Addtnl engvd title. Sm tear in 1 marg. Contemp calf, rebacked. Wing G825.
            (Waterfield's) **£250 [≈ $450]**

Glas, George (trans.)
- The history of the discovery and conquest of the Canary Islands. Dublin: 1767. 2 vols. 12mo. Lge fldg engvd map. Paper flaw on title. Contemp calf, rubbed, lacking 1 label.
            (Marlborough) **£180 [≈ $324]**

Glass, Samuel
- An essay on magnesia alba. Wherein its history is attempted, its virtues pointed out, and the use of it recommended. Oxford: R. Davis, & London: J. Fletcher, 1764. 1st edn. 8vo. 6,38 pp. Title dusty & with sm stain.

Stitched as issued, uncut.
            (Offenbacher) **$275 [≈ £152]**

Glossographia ...
- Glossographia Anglicana nova: or, a dictionary interpreting such hard words of whatever language, as are at present used in the English tongue ... London: for Dan. Brown ..., 1707. 1st edn. 8vo. [viii],[568],[8 advts] pp. Lacking free endpapers. Contemp calf.   *(Claude Cox)* **£100 [≈ $180]**

Glover, R.
- Leonidas. A poem. Glasgow: Foulis, 1769. 8vo. Contemp calf, spine richly gilt.
            (Stewart) **£95 [≈ $171]**

Glover, Richard
- London: or, the progress of commerce. A poem. London: T. Cooper, 1739. 4to. Title & last leaf a little dusty. Rebound in qtr calf.
            (C.R. Johnson) **£245 [≈ $441]**

Godfrey, Thomas
- Juvenile poems of various subjects. With the Prince of Parthia: a tragedy ... Phila: Henry Miller ..., 1765. 1st edn. Sm 4to. Later calf, hinges v sl weakened.
            (Minkoff) **$1,000 [≈ £555]**

Godwin, Francis
- Annales of England containing the reignes of Henry the Eighth, Edward the Sixt, Queene Mary ... London: Islip & Stansby, 1630. 1st edn. Folio. x,342 pp. Engvd title, 2 further titles, 3 engvd ports. Lacking 2 prelims, some minor waterstaining. STC 11947.
            (P & P) **£95 [≈ $171]**

Godwin, Thomas
- Romanae historiae anthologia ... An English exposition of the Roman Antiquities ... for the use of Abingdon School. London: for R. Chiswel, 1680. 4to. Marg of title sl frayed, 1st leaf of text torn without loss, a few stains & marks. New half calf. Wing G995.
            (Charles Cox) **£20 [≈ $36]**

Godwin, William
- The enquirer. Reflections on education, manners and literature in a series of essays. Dublin: for J. Moore, 1798. Sm repr to title gutter. Later half calf, rebacked.
            (Waterfield's) **£225 [≈ $405]**
- Memoirs of the author of a Vindication of the rights of woman. London: for J. Johnson, 1798. 1st edn. Sm 8vo. [iv],199,[v] pp. Engvd port, half-title, errata leaf. Contemp tree calf,

spine gilt, upper jnt reprd.
(Bennett) **£525 [≃ $945]**

Godwyn, Thomas
- Moses and Aaron: civil and ecclesiastical rites, used by the ancient Hebrews ... 1631. 4th edn. 1 leaf torn, final leaf crudely reprd, text stains. Rec cloth.   *(Allen)* **$100 [≃ £55]**
- Moses and Aaron: civil and ecclesiastical rites, used by the ancient Hebrews, and customs borrowed. London: 1678. 11th edn. Sq 8vo. Contemp calf, spine strengthened with tape.   *(Halewood)* **£45 [≃ $81]**

Goethe, Johann Wolfgang von
- The sorrows of Werter: a German story. London: for J. Dodsley, 1784. New edn. 2 vols. 12mo. viii,163; [ii],168 pp. Early 19th c half calf, spine gilt, sides sl rubbed.
  (Burmester) **£110 [≃ $198]**
- The sorrows of Werter: a German story. London: for J. Dodsley, 1789. New edn. 12mo. vii,223 pp. Half-title. Contemp bds, new calf spine.   *(Burmester)* **£45 [≃ $81]**

Goguet, A.Y.
- The origins of laws ... and their progress among the most ancient nations. 1775. 3 vols. 8vo. xxvi,402; vi,424; vi,341 pp. 9 fldg engvd plates, 3 fldg tables. Calf, gilt dec spines, minor wear.   *(P & P)* **£95 [≃ $171]**

Goguet, President de
- The origins of laws, arts, and sciences, and their progress among the most ancient nations. 1761. 1st English edn. 3 vols. xxvi,402; vi,424; vi,341 pp. 7 fldg engvd plates, 3 fldg tables. Contemp calf, spines gilt, rubbed, hinges tender.
  (Edwards) **£130 [≃ $234]**

Golborne, John
- The report of ... Engineer, concerning the drainage of the North Level of the fens, and the outfal of the Wisbeach River. [Chester: ca 1769?]. Sm 4to. 11,[1 blank] pp. Lge fldg map. Old paper wraps.
  (Bow Windows) **£56 [≃ $100]**
- The report of ... Engineer, concerning the drainage of the North Level of the fens, and the outfal of the Wisbeach River. N.d. [ca 1769]. Sole edn. 11 pp. Engvd fldg map, ptd in 2 sections. Contemp (orig?) grey paper wraps.   *(Blackwell's)* **£120 [≃ $216]**

Goldsmith, Oliver
- The deserted village, a poem. The fifth edition. London: W. Griffin ..., 1770. 23 pp.

Half-title. Disbound.
(C.R. Johnson) **£20 [≃ $36]**
- Dr. Goldsmith's Roman history, abridged by himself for the use of schools. London: 1772. 12mo. Contemp calf, spine gilt.
  (Robertshaw) **£75 [≃ $135]**
- Dr. Goldsmith's Roman history, abridged by himself for the use of schools. London: for S. Baker & G. Leich ..., 1782. 12mo in 6's. Foxed. Orig calf, gilt, upper jnt cracked, rubbed.   *(Hughes)* **£10 [≃ $18]**
- Essays ... Collecta revirescunt. Dublin: for James Williams, 1772. 3rd edn, crrctd. 12mo. [ii],ii,248 pp. Pencil sgntrs erased from title, sl soiling, 1st flyleaf removed. Contemp calf, gilt.   *(Burmester)* **£35 [≃ $63]**
- An history of the earth and animated nature. For J. Nourse, 1774. 1st edn. 8 vols. 8vo. 101 engvd plates. Contemp mottled calf, spines rubbed, tops of spines sl worn.
  (Bickersteth) **£260 [≃ $468]**
- The miscellaneous works ... containing all his essays and poems. London: W. Osborne ..., 1780. 2 leaves torn without loss. Contemp sheep.   *(Charles Cox)* **£35 [≃ $63]**
- The poetical works ... Complete in one volume. A new edition. London [i.e. Gainsborough]: for J. Osborne ..., 1785. 12mo. [viii],72 pp. 2 half-titles ('Poems"; "Poems by Dr. Goldsmith'). Contemp sheep, spine a little worn.   *(Burmester)* **£50 [≃ $90]**
- The poetical works ... Complete in one volume. With the life of the author. The vignettes ... by T. Bewick. Hereford: 1794. Sm 8vo. 95 pp. 6 w'cuts. Light occas dampstaining. Contemp calf, gilt.
  (Frew Mackenzie) **£48 [≃ $86]**
- Retaliation. A poem. Including epitaphs on some of the most distinguished wits of the Metropolis. London: for G. Kearsley ..., 1774. 7th edn crrctd. 4to. viii,22 pp. Light dampstaining. Disbound.
  (Young's) **£18 [≃ $32]**
- A survey of experimental philosophy, considered in its present state of improvement. London: for T. Carnan ..., 1766. 1st edn. 2 vols. 8vo. Half-title in vol I. Contemp calf, rebacked, mor labels, gilt.
  (Traylen) **£335 [≃ $603]**
- The Vicar of Wakefield. London: for the booksellers, 1792. 8vo. Lea, hd of spine sl chipped.   *(Emerald Isle)* **£45 [≃ $81]**
- The Vicar of Wakefield. Phila: William Mentz, 1772. 1st Amer edn. 2 vols in 1. 180 pp. Orig sheep.   *(Jenkins)* **$250 [≃ £138]**

Goldsmith, Oliver & Parnell, Thomas
- Poems by Goldsmith and Parnell. W.

Bulmer, 1795. W'engvs by Bewick. Contemp diced calf, rebacked.
(Robertshaw) **£135 [≃ $243]**

Goodwin, George
- Rising Castle, with other poems. Lynn: for the author ..., 1798. 1st edn. 12mo. [iv],151 pp. Contemp black calf.
(Burmester) **£210 [≃ $378]**

Goodwin, Thomas
- Zerubbabels encouragement to finish the Temple. A sermon ... London: for R. Dawlman, 1642. 1st edn (?). 4to. Later half mor, 1 bd loose. Wing G1268.
(Charles Cox) **£20 [≃ $36]**

Gordon, John, of Glencat
- Memoirs of John Gordon of Glencat ... thirteen years in the Scots College at Paris ... wherein the absurdities and delusions of popery are laid open ... London: for John Oswald, 1733. 1st edn. 12mo. Engvd frontis, engvd plate. Rebound in qtr calf.
(Hughes) **£45 [≃ $81]**

Gordon, Patrick
- Geography anatomiz'd: or, the geographical grammar ... London: for J. & P. Knapton, 1737. 15th edn. 8vo. [xxiv],432 pp. 16 fldg engvd maps (1 torn). Some spotting. Contemp calf, jnts & edges a little rubbed.
(Kerr) **£125 [≃ $225]**

Gostling, William
- A walk in and about the City of Canterbury. Canterbury: 1774. 1st edn. 8vo. 138 pp. Lge fldg plan, 3 plates. Later qtr calf.
(Edwards) **£100 [≃ $180]**
- A walk in and about the City of Canterbury. Canterbury: Simmons & Kirkby, 1777. 2nd edn. 8vo. 402,[xvi] pp. Fldg map (reprd), 20 plates. Some offsetting & occas browning. Contemp calf, jnts weak.
(Young's) **£95 [≃ $171]**

Goudemetz, H.
- Judgement and execution of Louis XVI, King of France; with a list of the Members of the National Convention who voted for and against his death. N.p., n.d. [1795]. 1st edn. Title a little stained. Disbound
(Robertshaw) **£18 [≃ $32]**

Gough, John
- A history of the people called Quakers. Dublin: Jackson, 1789. 4 vols. 8vo. Title of one vol trimmed & laid down. Contemp Irish calf.
(Emerald Isle) **£60 [≃ $108]**

Gouland, Thomas
- A treatise on the effects and various preparations of lead ... for different chirurgical disorders. Translated ... Dublin: R. Moncrieffe, 1777. 6th edn. 12mo. [8],231,[1] pp. Contemp calf.
(Elgen) **$95 [≃ £52]**

Goulard, Thomas
- Remarks and practical observations on the venereal complaints and disorders ... with the compositions of ... medicated candles for the cure of those complaints. London: Emsley, 1772. 1st edn in English. Sm 8vo. 261 pp. 1 page torn without loss. Qtr calf.
(Oasis) **$250 [≃ £138]**

Graham, William
- The art of making wines, of fruits, flowers, and herbs ... a succinct account of their medicinal virtues ... many secrets relative to the mystery of vintners ... London: for J. Williams ..., n.d. [ca 1760]. 2nd edn. 8vo. 42 pp. Later qtr calf, uncut.
(Argosy) **$175 [≃ £97]**

Grammar ...
- A short introduction of grammar ... See Lily, William

Grammaticae Questiones ...
- Grammaticae questiones: or a grammatical examination ... for the use of schools ... Bath: S. Hazard, 1794. 4th edn. 12mo. 132 pp. Lacking free endpapers. Orig sheep.
(Claude Cox) **£12 [≃ $21]**

Grammont, Count de
- Memoirs of the life of Count de Grammont ... See Hamilton, Anthony

Grant, William
- An essay on the pestilential fever of Sydenham, common called the gaol, hospital, ship, and camp-fever. London: for T. Cadell, 1775. 1st edn. 8vo. [iv],ix,193 pp. Old lib inscrptn on title. Orig calf, jnts cracked, rubbed.
(Bickersteth) **£45 [≃ $81]**

Grantham, Thomas
- Christianismus Primitivus: or, the ancient Christian religion in its nature, certainty, excellency and beauty ... L: for Francis Smith ..., 1678. 1st edn. Sm folio. Lacking sgntr Q of book II. Old sprinkled calf, rebacked. Wing G1528.
(Bow Windows) **£75 [≃ $135]**

Graves, Richard
- Columella; or, the distressed anchoret. A colloquial tale. London: for J. Dodsley, 1779. 1st edn. 2 vols. 12mo. iv,240; [ii],248 pp. 2 engvd frontis. Contemp tree-calf, spines gilt, sl rubbed, 1 upper jnt reprd, labels missing.
(Burmester) **£425 [≈ $765]**

Gray, Thomas
- Poems by Mr. Gray. London: Dodsley, 1768. 1st London edn. [iv],119,[3] pp. Half-title. Some fore-edge waterstaining throughout. Mod qtr calf, mrbld sides, gilt backstrip.
(Claude Cox) **£75 [≈ $135]**
- The poems ... To which are prefixed memoirs of his life and writings by W. Mason. York: Dodsley ..., 1775. 2nd edn. 4to. [iv],416,110 pp. 2 stamps on half-title, title sl spotted. Contemp half calf, somewhat rubbed, upper hinge cracked, lower partly so.
(Claude Cox) **£35 [≈ $63]**
- Poems. Dublin: William Sleater, 1775. 12mo. 2 pts in 1 vol with 2nd title dated 1776. 185,[6], 180-211; [189]-211 pp. Engvd frontis, vignette titles, engvd & w'cut ills. Blank crnr torn from 1 leaf. Contemp calf, spine sl worn, upper jnt cracked.
(Burmester) **£120 [≈ $216]**
- Poems by Mr. Gray. A new edition. London: for J. Murray, 1776. 12mo. 146 pp. Engvd frontis, title vignette, engvd plate in text. Contemp calf, spine gilt, hinges rubbed. Vincent Starrett's copy with pres inscrptn to his wife.
(Karmiole) **$75 [≈ £41]**

Great Britain ...
- The interest of Great Britain steadily pursued ... See Walpole, Horatio

Greate Abbrydgement ...
- The greate abbrydgement of all ye statutes of Englande, until the xxx. yere of the reygne of ... Lorde Kynge Henry the Eyght ... [L: Robert Redman], before 16 Nov. 1538. 4th edn. Oily stain on many pages. Orig calf-crvrd bds, rec rebacked. STC 9522.
(Allen) **$2,000 [≈ £1,111]**

Greaves, John
- Pyramidographia; or, a description of the pyramids of Egypt. For George Badger, 1646. Sm 8vo. 120 pp. 2 fldg engvd plates (1 reprd), 2 plates, text ills. Lacking prelim blank, occas underlining. Contemp panelled calf.
(Edwards) **£300 [≈ $540]**

Green, Matthew
- The spleen. An epistle inscribed to his particular friend Mr. C.J. ... to which is now added some other pieces ... London: A. Dodd, 1738. 8vo. A4 correctly sgnd. Mod wraps.
(Waterfield's) **£45 [≈ $81]**

Green, Valentine
- The history and antiquities of the City of Worcester. 1796. 2 vols in 1. 4to. xviii,300; iii,114,clv pp. 2 title vignettes, 23 plates (2 double-page), fldg map (partly cold, reprd). Orig mrbld bds, rebacked in mor.
(Edwards) **£125 [≈ $225]**

Greene, Edward Burnaby (trans.)
- The works of Anacreon and Sappho, with pieces from ancient authors; and occasional essays ... London: for J. Ridley, 1768. 1st edn of this trans. 12mo. xxxii,287 pp. Early 19th c green half calf, spine gilt.
(Burmester) **£75 [≈ $135]**

Greenhill, Thomas
- Nekrokedeia: or, the art of embalming ... experiments and inventions of modern physicians ... For the author, [1705]. 1st edn. 4to. [ii],viii,v, [viii],367,[xii] pp. Frontis & fldg map (both with short tears), 13 plates (1 fldg). Contemp calf, rebacked.
(Frew Mackenzie) **£350 [≈ $630]**

Gregory, George
- The life of Thomas Chatterton, with criticisms of his genius and writings, and a concise view of the controversy concerning Rowley's poems. London: for G. Kearsley, 1789. 1st edn. 8vo. [viii],263 pp. Without the facs leaf. Old sheep, worn, early reback.
(Young's) **£60 [≈ $108]**

Gregory, T.
- Discourses upon several subjects. London: R. Sare, 1696. 8vo. [8],251,[3] pp. Text browned, front endpaper missing. Contemp calf, crnrs worn, jnts sl cracked.
(Spelman) **£30 [≈ $54]**

Grelot, William Joseph
- A late voyage to Constantinople ... London: by John Playford ..., 1683. 1st English edn. Sm 8vo. [xiv],243, [8 index],[5 advts] pp. Title within rules, engvd frontis, 8 fldg plates, 6 full-page text ills. A few tears in margs reprd. Contemp tree-calf, gilt.
(Morrell) **£320 [≈ $576]**

Greville, Sir Fulke
- The life of the renowned Sr Philip Sidney. London: for Henry Seile, 1652. 1st edn. Sm

8vo. Rec calf. New Wing B4899.
(Sotheran) **£235 [≈ $423]**

Grew, Nehemiah

- Experiments in consort of the luctation arising from the affusions of several menstruums upon all sorts of bodies ... London: for John Martyn, 1678. 12mo. [xii],118 pp. Browning & marg defects on 6ff without loss. Contemp calf, rubbed.
(Wheldon & Wesley) **£200 [≈ $360]**
- Musaeum Regalis Societatis ... natural and artificial rarities belonging to the Royal Society. London: for the author, 1681. 1st edn. Folio. [xii],386,[2]; title, 43 pp. Port, 43 engvd plates. Some minor stains & dustmarks. Contemp calf, rebacked. Wing G1952.
(Bow Windows) **£495 [≈ $891]**
- Musaeum Regalis Societatis. London: for the author, 1681. 1st edn. 2 vols in 1. Folio. Port frontis, 31 engvd plates. Title smudged at bottom, minor tears, sl foxing & dampstaining. Contemp calf, rebacked, crnrs worn.
(Pirages) **$575 [≈£319]**
- Musaeum Regalis Societatis. London: 1681. Folio. [xii],386, [2],[ii],43 pp. Port, 31 plates. Inscrptn inked out on title. calf, reprd.
(Wheldon & Wesley) **£495 [≈ $891]**
- Musaeum Regalis Societatis. Or ... the natural and artificial rarities belonging to the Royal Society ... London: Newman, 1694. Folio. [xii],386,[ii], [iv],43 pp. 31 engvd plates (1 fldg, torn & reprd). Occas dampstaining & worming. Contemp calf. rebacked.
(Frew Mackenzie) **£265 [≈ $477]**

Grey, Richard (1694-1771)

- A new and easy method of learning Hebrew ... London: Bowyer, 1738. 1st edn. Lge 8vo. Title dusty. New half calf.
(Marlborough) **£110 [≈ $198]**

Grey, Zachary

- A vindication of the government, doctrine, and worship of the Church of England ... against the injurious reflections of Mr. Neale ... London: C. Davis, 1740. 8vo. Re-issue of 1733 edn with cancel title. Sm lib stamp on title verso. 19th c half mor, rebacked.
(Waterfield's) **£40 [≈ $72]**

Griffiths, William

- A practical treatise on farriery; deduced from the experience of above forty years ... Wrexham: R. Marsh, [1784]. 1st edn. 4to. [iv],iii,184,[14] pp. Aquatint frontis. Some outer margs sl stained. Contemp tree-calf, spines elab gilt, jnts reprd.
(Burmester) **£180 [≈ $324]**

- A practical treatise on farriery; deduced from the experience of above forty years ... Wrexham: R. Marsh, [1784]. 1st edn. 4to. Aquatint frontis. Occas spotting. Contemp tree-calf, spines gilt, hinges cracking.
(Chaucer Head) **£180 [≈ $324]**

Grisdale, Browne

- A sermon preached in Whitehall Chapel at the consecration of ... John Douglas, Lord Bishop of Carlisle. London: for T. Cadell, 1788. 8vo. Disbound.
(Waterfield's) **£20 [≈ $36]**

Groans ...

- The groans of Germany: or, the enquiry of a protestant German into the original cause of the present distractions of the Empire ... London: 1741. 6th edn. 32 pp. Some minor worming. Disbound.
(Robertshaw) **£10 [≈ $18]**

Groenveldt, Jan

- A compleat treatise of the stone and gravel ... With an ample discourse on lithontriptick ... London: for Smith & Lintott, 1710. 1st edn. 8vo. 23 engvd plates, 3 fldg (1 with outer marg torn away without loss). Contemp calf, old spine laid down.
(Quaritch) **$1,600 [≈£888]**

Grose, Francis

- The antiquities of England and Wales [and] Scotland [and] Ireland. London: for S. Hooper, 1783-95. 12 vols inc supp vol. 4to. 1097 plates, 56 hand-cold maps. Minor foxing on some plates. Contemp tree-calf, spines heavily gilt, a few jnts & crnrs worn.
(Pirages) **$2,500 [≈£1,388]**
- The antiquities of Ireland. 1791. 1st edn. 2 vols. Lge 4to. 2 engvd frontis & titles, 259 engvd plates. Some occas foxing & offsetting from plates. half mor, mrbld bds, spine gilt, sl rubbed.
(Edwards) **£300 [≈ $540]**
- A classical dictionary of the vulgar tongue. London: S. Hooper, 1785. 1st edn. 8vo. Unpaginated text. Contemp calf, gilt, mrbld endpapers, lightly rubbed, front jnt cracked.
(Frew Mackenzie) **£175 [≈ $315]**
- A classical dictionary of the vulgar tongue. London: S. Hooper, 1785. 1st edn. 8vo. [2],viii,[204] pp. Occas light spotting. Contemp (or sl later) diced calf, rebacked.
(Claude Cox) **£75 [≈ $135]**
- A classical dictionary of the vulgar tongue. London: S. Hooper, 1788. 2nd edn. 8vo. xv,124ff, 2ff advts. Mottled calf gilt, a little rubbed.
(Marlborough) **£130 [≈ $234]**

- A provincial glossary; with a collection of local proverbs, and popular superstitions. London: 1787. 1st edn. 8vo in 4's. xv,[248] pp. Sev inked notes in an early hand, sm damp mark at ft of some leaves. Contemp half calf, worn, jnts cracked.
(Bow Windows) **£48 [≈ $86]**
- A provincial glossary; with a collection of local proverbs, and popular superstitions. London: S. Hooper, 1790. 2nd edn, crrctd & greatly enlgd. 8vo. vii pp, unpaginated text. 19th c half calf, buckram sides, sl rubbed.
(Frew Mackenzie) **£85 [≈ $153]**
- A provincial glossary; with a collection of local proverbs, and popular superstitions. London: S. Hooper, 1787. M6 inlaid. Later half calf, amateurishly recased.
(Waterfield's) **£80 [≈ $144]**
- A treatise on ancient armour and weapons. London: S. Hooper, 1786-9. 1st edn, with the "Supplement to the Treatise". 4to. 118,xviii, [ii]; 10 pp. Engvd frontis, engvd title, 61 engvd plates. Text occas browned. Contemp vellum, extensively gilt, lightly rubbed.
(Blackwell's) **£675 [≈ $1,215]**

Grotius, Hugo

- Of the law of warre and peace with annotations. III parts and memorials of the author's life and death. London: for William Lee, 1655, 2nd English edn. 8vo. 660,69 pp. Port frontis. Contemp anntns on title verso, single spark burn on title. Mod calf.
(Edwards) **£780 [≈ $1,404]**
- The truth of the Christian religion ... London: 1754. 5th edn. Later calf, a little rubbed, spine richly gilt.
(Robertshaw) **£30 [≈ $54]**

Grou, Jean N.

- The characters of real devotion. Translated from the French ... The second edition. Dublin: J. Mehain ..., 1795. Lge 12mo. 158,[2 advts] pp. Contemp unlettered sheep, a little worn. *(Fenning)* **£75 [≈ $135]**

Grove, Robert

- A perswasive to communion with the Church of England. London: for Fincham Gardiner, 1682/83. 4to. With A1 (blank). Mod wraps. Wing 2152. *(Stewart)* **£35 [≈ $63]**

Gualdo Priorato, Galeazzo

- The history of France. London: 1676. 1st English edn. Folio. Contemp calf, rebacked, upper cvr loose. *(Robertshaw)* **£75 [≈ $135]**

Guatimozin

- The letters of Guatimozin ... See Jebb, Fred

Guazzo, Stefano

- The civile conversation ... divided into four bookes ... London: Thomas East, 1586. 1st comp edn in English. Sm 4to. Black letter, colophon leaf at end, title within typo border. Clean tear in R5. 17th c calf, worn upper cvr detchd, spine defective. STC 12423.
(Robertshaw) **£400 [≈ $720]**

Guenee, Antoine

- Letters of certain Jews to Monsieur de Voltaire. Containing an apology for their own people, and for the Old Testament ... Dublin: William Watson, 1777. 1st edn in English. 2 vols. 8vo. 445; [iv],428 pp. Contemp calf, spines gilt, some cracking of jnts.
(Burmester) **£300 [≈ $540]**

Guicciardini, Francesco

- The history of Guicciardin: conteining the warres of Italie ... London: Vautrouiller, 1579. Folio. 1st English edn. [10],1184 pp. Lacking A1 blank, final leaf a little frayed, single wormhole in marg 1st 50 ff, contemp anntns. Early calf, hd of spine reprd.
(Spelman) **£750 [≈ $1,350]**
- The history of Guicciardin: containing the warres of Italie and other parts. London: Richard Field, 1599. 943,[10] pp (errors in pagination). Paper flaws on 2 leaves, isolated minor tears, uniform browning. Contemp or sl later calf, spine gilt, remains of ties.
(Pirages) **$550 [≈ £305]**

Guide ...

- A guide to the knowledge of the rights and privileges of Englishmen. London: for J. Williams ..., 1771. 8vo. viii,12, 32,247 pp. Some pencilled underlining, title sl soiled. Contemp sheep, spine worn, upper jnt cracked. *(Burmester)* **£60 [≈ $108]**

Guidott, Thomas

- A discourse of Bathe, and the hot springs there ... an account of the lives ... of the physicians of Bathe. London: for Henry Brome, 1676. 8vo. [30],200 pp. Explanation leaf before title, engvd title, 4 plates (3 fldg), plan. Contemp calf, a little worn.
(Burmester) **£150 [≈ $270]**

Guillim, John

- A display of heraldry ... sixth edition ... added, a treatise of honour military and civil ... London: R. & J. Bonwicke ..., 1724. Folio. [xxii],460, [iv],275,[i], 58,24,22 pp. 17 ports,

47 plates. 19th c polished calf, trivial rubbing, jnts splitting.
(Frew Mackenzie) **£360** [≈ **$648**]

Gunpowder-treason
- The gunpowder-treason ... See Barlow, Thomas, Bishop of Lincoln

Gunter, Edmund
- The description and use of the sector, cross-staffe ... with a canon of artificiall sines and tangents. 1636. 2 pts in 1. 2nd edn. Sm 4to. Engvd & ptd titles, plate, num w'cut text diags, 2 slips with w'cuts. Some age blemishes. Contemp calf, new spine.
(Halewood) **£250** [≈ **$450**]

Gunton, Symon
- History of the church of Peterburgh. London: for Richard Chiswell, 1686. Folio. 348 pp. 4 full-page engvs (1 fldg), sev text engvs. 1 leaf reprd with sl loss. Later lea, gilt, a.e.g., minor wear to hinges & crnrs.
(Xerxes) **$350** [≈ **£194**]

Guthrie, William
- A new geographical, historical, and commercial grammar; and the present state of the several kingdoms of the world. London: Charles Dilly ..., 1783. 8th edn. 8vo. [2],848 pp. Engvd fldg map frontis (stained), plates, maps (part fldg). Contemp calf, rubbed.
(Heritage) **$150** [≈ **£83**]

Guthrin, James
- A treatise of ruling elders and deacons ... in which ... their office and duty, are clearly and shortly set down ... Edinburgh: George Mosman, 1699. 12mo. Marg worming. Contemp sheep, a little rubbed. Wing G2266.
(Charles Cox) **£35** [≈ **$63**]

Gwinnett, Richard
- Pylades and Corinna: or, memoirs of the lives and writings of ... to which is prefixed the life of Corinna written by her self. London: 1731. 8vo. Some minor waterstaining, sm wormhole in gutter of latter part. Contemp calf, front jnt cracked, crnrs worn.
(Waterfield's) **£65** [≈ **$117**]

Gwynn, John
- London and Westminster improved, illustrated by plans ... prefixed ... observations on the state of art and artists in this kingdom ... London: for the author, 1766. 1st edn. 4to. xvi,132 pp. 4 hand-cold plans. Mod calf, spine gilt.
(Bennett) **£550** [≈ **$990**]

Gyllenborg, Karl, Count de
- Letters which passed between Count Gillenborg, the Barons Gortz ... and others; relating to the design of raising a rebellion ... to be supported by a force from Sweden. S. Buckley, 1717. Folio. [4],39 pp. Mod wraps.
(Deighton Bell) **£50** [≈ **$90**]

Hacke, William
- A collection of original voyages ... London: James Knapton, 1699. 1st edn. 8vo. 3 fldg maps, 3 engvd plates (2 fldg), title within double rules. 18th c half calf, mrbld bds, rebacked, armorial b'plate.
(Morrell) **£1,500** [≈ **$2,700**]

Hacket, John
- Scrinia reserata: a memorial offer'd to the great deservings of John Williams, D.D. ... Keeper of the Great Seal, Ld Bishop of Lincoln ... London: for Samuel Lowndes, 1693. 1st edn. Folio. Port, advt & errata leaves. 19th c calf, rebacked.
(Charles Cox) **£60** [≈ **$108**]

Hakewill, George
- An apologie or declaration of the power and providence of God in the government of the world. For R. Allott, 1635. 3rd edn, much enlgd. Folio. [1],606,378 pp plus index. 1st 2ff of 2nd part imperfect. Contemp calf, well worn. STC 12613.
(Lloyd-Roberts) **£60** [≈ **$108**]

Hakluyt, Richard
- The principal navigations, voyages ... London: George Bishop ..., 1599. 2 vols in 1 (without 3rd vol of 1600). Folio. [xxiv],606; [xvi],312,204 pp. No world map, sporadic staining, insignificant worming in a few margs. 18th c tree-calf, rebacked. STC 126269.
(Clark) **£850** [≈ **$1,530**]

Hale, Sir Matthew
- Difficiles Nugae: or, observations touching the Torricellian experiment ... weight and elasticity of air. London: for W. Shrowsbury, 1674. 1st edn. 8vo. 2 fldg engvd plates (1 with sm rust-hole), initial blank, 2 pp advts. Contemp calf, rebacked. Wing H238.
(Traylen) **£375** [≈ **$675**]

Hale, Thomas
- An account of several new inventions and improvements ... also A treatise of naval philosophy ... by Sir Will. Petty. London: 1691. 1st edn. 2 pts in 1. 12mo. Sep titles, licence lf, 2 fldg charts, 2 fldg leaves. 19th c

calf, gilt, jnts worn. Wing H265.
(Traylen) **£360 [≃ $648]**

Hales, John
- Golden remains, of the ever memorable Mr. John Hales of Eaton Colledge, &c. London: for Robert Pawlet, 1673. 2nd imp. 4to. [viii],291, 190,[ii], 63,7 pp. Engvd title by Hollar (sm hole in upper marg). Contemp calf, rubbed, jnts sl cracked. Wing H271.
(Clark) **£120 [≃ $216]**
- Golden remains, of the ever memorable ... London: for George Pawlet, 1688. 3rd imp. Cr 8vo. Red & black title. Some old staining. Contemp calf. Wing H272.
(Stewart) **£60 [≃ $108]**
- Several tracts, by the ever memorable Mr. John Hales of Eaton Coll. etc. Viz. I. Of the Sacrament of the Lord's Supper. II ... III ... IV ... V. Miscellanies. [L:] 1677. Cr 8vo. New grey bds. *(Stewart)* **£85 [≃ $153]**

Hales, Stephen
- An account of some experiments and observations on tar-water ... London: for R. Manby ..., 1745. 1st edn. 8vo. W'cut. Bds, cloth spine. *(Traylen)* **£110 [≃ $198]**
- An account of some experiments and observations on Mrs. Stephen's medicines for dissolving the stone ... to which is added, a supplement to a pamphlet ... London: [1740]. 1st edn. 66 pp. Plate. Mod bds.
(Scientia) **$175 [≃ £97]**
- Philosophical experiments: containing useful, and necessary instructions for such as undertake long voyages at sea ... London: W. Innys ..., 1739. [4],xxx, [2],163 pp. 6 pp index, 2 pp advts. Plate. Rec half calf, mrbld bds. *(Goodrich)* **$675 [≃ £375]**
- Statical essays: containing vegetable staticks: or, an account of sap in vegetables ... Also ... an attempt to analyse the air ... London: W. Innys, 1731. 8vo. 2nd edn. 8vo. [vi],[viii], 376 pp. 19 engvd plates. Contemp calf, hd of spine worn, jnts cracked.
(Hemlock) **$275 [≃ £152]**

Halfpenny, Joseph
- Gothic ornaments in the cathedral Church of York. York: 1795-[1800]. 1st edn. 4to. Engvd title, 105 plates (2 hand-cold). Some foxing. Rec half lea. *(Spelman)* **£60 [≃ $108]**

Halfpenny, William
- Useful architecture ... for erecting parsonage-houses, farm-houses, and inns ... London: Robert Sayer, 1755. 8vo. 82 pp. 21 plates with architectural plans. Contemp calf.
(Argosy) **$350 [≃ £194]**

Halfpenny, William & John
- The country gentleman's pocket companion, and builder's assistant, for rural decorative architecture. London: Robert Sayer, 1753. 1st edn. 8vo. 25 engvd plates. Some sl foxing. Orig lea, rebacked. *(Minkoff)* **$750 [≃ £416]**

Halhed, Nathaniel B.
- A code of Gentoo laws, or, ordinations of the pundits, from a Persian translation. London: 1776. 1st edn. 4to. lxxiv, blank, 61,321 pp. 8 plates. Uncut in calf-backed orig bds, spine cracked & rubbed. Ex lib John Cator with his b'plate. *(Spelman)* **£380 [≃ $684]**

Hall, Joseph
- The balm of Gilead or, comforts for the distressed ... most fit for these woful times. London: for John Holden, 1650. 2nd edn. 12mo. Port (crnr chipped). A few sidenotes shaved. Old calf. Wing H366.
(Charles Cox) **£40 [≃ $72]**
- Epistles, the first [second] volume: conteining two decads. London: for Eleazor Edgar ..., 1608. 1st edn. 2 vols in 1. A few crnrs worn, some stains and marks, lacking A1 & A8 (blanks?), a few side-notes cropped. Mod qtr calf, mrbld bds. STC 12662.
(Charles Cox) **£120 [≃ $216]**

Hall, Joseph, Bishop of Norwich
- Contemplations upon the remarkable passages in the life of the Holy Jesus. London: for E. Flesher, 1679. 4to. [iv],510, [2 advt & blank] pp. Contemp calf, 19th c rebacking. Wing H376. *(Claude Cox)* **£40 [≃ $72]**

Haller, Albert
- Pathological observations from dissections of morbid bodes. London: Wilson & Durham, 1756. 1st edn in English. 8vo. viii,iii, [1], 197,[3] pp. 3 fldg engvd plates. Title sl foxed. Contemp sheep, front cvr re-hinged.
(Antiq Sc) **$375 [≃ £208]**

Hamill, William
- A memorial by ... agent and trustee for the officers and soldiers of the two late garrisons of London-Derry and Enniskilling in Ireland ... London: 1714. 8vo. Later mrbld bds.
(Emerald Isle) **£85 [≃ $153]**

Hamilton, Alexander
- Observations on certain documents in ... "the History of the United States, for the year 1796" ... in which the charge of speculation ... is fully refuted ... Phila: John Fenno, 1797. 1st edn. 38,[58] pp. Mod half calf.
(Jenkins) **$150 [≃ £83]**

- Report of the Secretary of the Treasury respecting the tonnage of vessels. Phila: Francis Childs ..., January 7, 1794. 1st edn. Folio. 5 pp. Lge fldg chart.
(Jenkins) **$75 [≈ £41]**

Hamilton, Alexander
- A treatise on the management of female complaints and of children in early infancy ... New York: Samuel Campbell, 1795. 8vo. vi,7-304 pp. Contemp calf, dull, cracks in calf.   *(Hemlock)* **$100 [≈ £55]**

Hamilton, Anthony
- Memoirs of the life of Count de Grammont ... the amorous intrigues of the Court of England in the reign of King Charles II. London: for J. Round ..., 1714. 1st edn in English. 2 prelims, 356 pp. Red & black title. Lacking rear flyleaf. Contemp calf, rebacked.
(Pirages) **$200 [≈ £111]**

Hamilton, Charles
- An historical relation of the origin, progress and final dissolution of the Government of Rohilla Afghans, in the Northern Provinces of Hindostan ... 1787. 8vo. xxi,298 pp. Binders' cloth, lea label.
(Farahar) **£185 [≈ $333]**

Hamilton, George
- The Telegraph; a consolatory epistle [in verse, purporting to be] from Thomas Muir, Esq., of Botany Bay, to the Hon. Henry Erskine ... [Edinburgh: 1796]. 4to. 11 pp. Later blue wraps.
(C.R. Johnson) **£250 [≈ $450]**

Hamilton, Hugh
- Philosophical essays on ... I. The ascent of vapours ... II ... Aurora Borealis ... III On ... mechanicks. London: Nourse, 1767. 1st London edn. 12mo. [iv],177,[1] pp. Engvd fldg plate, half-title to each part. Uncut. Orig wraps, vell backstrip cracked.
(Rootenberg) **$225 [≈ £125]**
- Philosophical essays on ... I. ... vapours ... II ... Aurora Borealis ... III ... mechanicks. London: for J. Nourse, 1772. 3rd edn. 8vo. Fldg frontis, 3 part titles, final blank. Stain to upper marg of most leaves. Contemp mrbld bds, sl worn, mod calf spine.
(Stewart) **£225 [≈ $405]**

Hamilton, Robert
- Remarks on hydrophobia or the disease produced by the bite of a mad dog or other rabid animal. London: 1798. 2nd edn. 2 vols. 8vo. 297; 590 pp. List of subscribers. New

paper-cvrd bds.   *(Oasis)* **$200 [≈ £111]**

Hamilton, Sir William
- Observations on Mount Vesuvius, Mount Etna, and other volcanoes. London: T. Cadell, 1772. 1st edn. 8vo. iv,179 pp. 5 fldg plates, fldg map. Contemp calf, gilt.
(Spelman) **£240 [≈ $432]**
- Observations on Mount Vesuvius ... London: T. Cadell, 1772. Fldg map (tear reprd), 5 engvd plates. Contemp tree-calf, a little rubbed & scuffed, upper jnt tender.
(Clark) **£110 [≈ $198]**
- Observations on Mount Vesuvius, Mount Etna, and other volcanos: in a series of letters addressed to the Royal Society. London: 1773. 2nd edn. 8vo. 179 pp. 5 plates. Contemp calf, rebacked, new endpapers.
(Argosy) **$250 [≈ £138]**
- Some particulars of the present state of Mount Vesuvius; with the account of a journey into the Province of Abruzzo ... Read at the Royal Society, May 4, 1786. London: J. Nichols, 1786. 1st edn. 4to. 19 pp. 1 fldg plate (ex 3, lacking 2). Rec qtr calf.
(Deighton Bell) **£55 [≈ $99]**

Hamilton, William
- Letters concerning the Northern Coast of the County of Antrim ... with a plain and impartial view of the volcanic theory ... London: Robinson, 1786. 8vo. Lge fldg map. Mod half calf.   *(Emerald Isle)* **£110 [≈ $198]**
- Letters concerning the Northern Coast of the County of Antrim ... a natural history of its basaltes ... antiquities, manners and customs ... Dublin: Bonham, 1786. 8vo. Fldg map. Contemp calf, spine reprd.
(Emerald Isle) **£95 [≈ $171]**

Hamilton, William, of Bangour
- Poems on several occasions. Edinburgh: for W. Gordon ..., 1760. 8vo. in 4s. Engvd port frontis. Uncut in orig bds, rubbed, new backstrip.   *(Hughes)* **£65 [≈ $117]**

Hammond, Henry
- A paraphrase and annotations upon the Books of the Psalms ... London: R. Norton, 1659. Folio. [xxviii],720,[viii] pp. Contemp inscrptns on endpapers. Contemp calf, crnrs worn, backstrip sl defective at hd. Wing H578A.   *(Clark)* **£40 [≈ $72]**
- A paraphrase and annotations upon the Books of the Old Testament. London: for J. Nicholson ..., 1702. 7th edn, crrctd & enlgd. Folio. iv,viii, 4,841, [19 index] pp. 18th c panelled calf, gilt, hinges & crnrs rubbed &

worn. *(Lloyd-Roberts)* **£45 [≈$81]**

- A view of some exceptions ... made by a Romanist to Viscount Falkland's discourse of the infallibilitie of the Church of Rome ... London: R. Royston ..., 1646. 4to. [viii],204 pp. Minor staining at hd, outer marg sl frayed. Disbound. Wing H271.
(Clark) **£30 [≈$54]**

Hammond, John
- The practical surveyor. London: T. Heath, 1725. 1st edn. 8vo. viii,112 pp. 7 fldg engvd plates, 2 with mtd flaps. Some spotty browning. Contemp blindstamped cloth, rebacked with gilt spine.
(Antiq Sc) **$450 [≈£250]**

Hammond, Nathaniel
- The elements of algebra in a new and easy method ... London: for the author, 1752. 2nd edn, crrctd. 8vo. E4 reprd. Rebound in rexine. *(Stewart)* **£30 [≈$54]**

Hanbury-Williams, Sir Charles
- The foundling hospital for wit, intended for the reception and preservation of such brats of wit and humour, whose parents chuse to drop them. London: for W. Webb, 1749-64. 8vo. 6 pts, all published. Pts 3 & 5 1st edns. Contemp marg anntns. Uncut in half calf.
(Young's) **£100 [≈$180]**

Hancocke, John
- Febrifugum magnum: or, common water the best cure for fevers, and probably for the plague. R. Halsey, 1723. 4th edn. Sm 8vo in 4s. [vi],3-108 pp. New mrbld bds, unlettered.
(Blackwell's) **£75 [≈$135]**

Handley, James
- Colloquia chirurgica: or, the whole art of surgery epitomiz'd and made easie, according to modern practice ... London: Bates & Bettesworth, 1705. 1st edn. 8vo. [16],192,[4] pp. Paste-downs detached. Mottled calf.
(Rootenberg) **£350 [≈£194]**

Handmaid ...
- The new handmaid to arts, sciences, agriculture ... husbandry ... art of painting ... dying silks ... [&c., &c.]. London: for W. Clements & J. Sadler, 1790. 1st edn (?). 8vo. 118 pp. Near-contemp qtr calf, mrbld bds.
(Gough) **£115 [≈$207]**

Hanger, George
- Military reflections on the attack and defence of London; proved ... to have been the most vulnerable part of consequence in the whole

island ... London: J. Debrett, 1795. Rebound in qtr calf, mrbld bds.
(C.R. Johnson) **£75 [≈$135]**

- Military reflections on the attack and defence of London ... the most vulnerable part of consequence in the whole island ... London: J. Debrett, 1795. 1st edn. 8vo. iv,118 pp. Final advt leaf. Uncut in orig blue wraps, frayed, lacks spine, stitched as issued.
(Frew Mackenzie) **£130 [≈$234]**

Hanover ...
- Hanover troops (forces, interest of, &c.) ... See Chesterfield, Philip D. Stanhope, Earl of

Hanway, Jonas
- An historical account of the British trade over the Caspian Sea. London: Dodsley, Nourse ..., 1753. 1st edn. 4 vols. 4to. 9 fldg engvd maps, 19 engvd plates. Sl foxing in places. Contemp polished calf, cvrs scuffed, jnts cracked but firm, crnrs rubbed.
(Morrell) **£550 [≈$990]**
- An historical account of the British trade over the Caspian Sea: with the author's journals of travels ... into Persia. 1762. 3rd edn. 2 vols. 4to. 2 frontis, 17 engvd plates, 9 maps (4 torn). Foxed, marg stains. Calf, worn, jnts broken, 1 cvr detchd. *(Allen)* **$200 [≈£111]**
- Rules and regulations of the Maritime School, on the banks of the Thames ... October, 1781. 1st edn. [viii],xxiv,120 pp. Engvd title, frontis. [with, as usual]. Letter to Mr --- ... a Scholar ... N.p., n.d. [iv],27 pp. Engvd title, frontis. Mod mrbld bds.
(Bennett) **£165 [≈$297]**

Harbin, G.
- The hereditary right of the Crown of England asserted. 1713. 1st edn. Folio. 274,lxiii pp. Panelled calf, new spine laid down.
(Edwards) **£120 [≈$216]**

Hargrave, Francis
- An argument in the case of James Sommerset a Negro, lately determined by the court of King's Bench ... the present unlawfulness of domestic slavery in England. London: for the author, 1772. 1st edn. 8vo. iv,82 pp. Half-title. Rec mor-backed bds, spine gilt.
(Bennett) **£450 [≈$810]**

Harley, Edward
- An essay for composing a harmony between the Psalms and other parts of scripture ... London: J. Downing, 1732. Contemp green calf, gilt border, mrbld endpapers, gilt edges, sm patch of abrasion on front cvr.
(Waterfield's) **£200 [≈$360]**

Harper, Thomas
- The accomptant's companion; or young arithmetician's guide. London: the author, 1765. 2nd edn. 12mo in 6s. [iv],vi, [ii],192 pp. Port frontis. Title cropped at hd. Contemp sheep, worn, backstrip defective.
(Clark) **£60 [≈ $108]**

Harrington, James
- The Oceana and his other works ... with an exact account of his life prefix'd, by John Toland. London: 1700. Folio in 4's, lge paper. Frontis, port. Some sl worming, spotting & offsetting. Contemp calf, rebacked & recrnrd. *(Titles)* **£350 [≈ $630]**
- The prerogative of popular government. A political discourse in two books. London: for Tho. Brewster ..., 1658-57. 1st edns. Sm 4to. [xvi],134,[4]; [iv],84,[4] pp. Vol 1 title v worn & brittle at edges, some browning throughout. Mod calf. Wing H820.
(Pickering) **$650 [≈ £361]**

Harris, J.
- Elements of plane and spherical trigonometry ... and several projections of the sphere in plano ... London: 1723. 207 pp. 6 fldg plates, num text diags. Insignificant worming through inner margs. Contemp calf, rebacked, unsuitable new endpapers.
(Whitehart) **£95 [≈ $171]**

Harris, James
- Hermes or a philosophical enquiry concerning universal grammar ... London: for John Nourse ..., 1771. 3rd edn, revsd & crrctd. Engvd frontis. Contemp calf.
(Waterfield's) **£75 [≈ $135]**
- Hermes or a philosophical enquiry concerning universal grammar. London: for John Nourse ..., 1771. 3rd edn, revsd & crrctd. xix,442,[30] pp. Engvd frontis. Calf, jnts wearring, a.e.g. *(Young's)* **£60 [≈ $108]**
- Philosophical arrangements. London: for F. Wingrave, 1799. New edn. Engvd frontis. Outer margs K2 & K3 cut close. Contemp speckled calf, rebacked.
(Waterfield's) **£50 [≈ $90]**

Harris, John
- The description and uses of the celestial and terrestrial globes; and of Collin's pocket-quadrant. London: 1725. 6th edn. Sm 8vo. 62 pp. Frontis. Contemp calf, upper cvr detached. *(Robertshaw)* **£40 [≈ $72]**
- Lexicon technicum; or, an universal English dictionary of arts and sciences. For Dan Brown ..., 1704. 1st edn. Folio. Red & black

title, engvd port, 7 plates (2 fldg), w'cut ills & text diags. Half calf.
(Halewood) **£325 [≈ $585]**

Harris, Joseph
- The description and use of the globes, and the orrery. London: Wright & Cushee, 1738. 4th edn. 8vo. viii,190 pp. Fldg engvd frontis, 6 fldg engvd plates. Armorial b'plate on title verso (over portion of advt). Contemp panelled calf, jnts cracked.
(Antiq Sc) **$200 [≈ £111]**
- The description and use of the globes, and the orrery. London: 1745. 6th edn. 8vo. viii,190 pp. 6 plates (1 sl cropped). A few sm stains. Contemp lea, rebacked, spine gilt.
(Whitehart) **£60 [≈ $108]**
- An essay upon money and coins. Part 1. The theories of commerce, money and exchanges. Part 2. That the established standard of money should not be violated or altered. London: 1757. 1st edn. Demy 8vo. Half calf, rebacked. *(Halewood)* **£125 [≈ $225]**

Harris, Moses
- The Aurelian: or, natural history of English insects. London: J. Edwards, 1794. 3rd edn. Folio. xv,90,[ii index],[i table] pp. French & English text, hand-cold engvd French title, 44 hand-cold engvd plates. Contemp str-grained red mor, gilt panelled, rebacked.
(Gough) **£4,250 [≈ $7,650]**
- An exposition of English insects, including the several classes of Neuroptera ... described ... with remarks ... White & Robson, 1782. 2nd edn. 4to. [i],viii, 166,[iv] pp. Frontis, 50 cold plates, 1 engv. Some pencil notes, faint browning. Mod mor, gilt.
(Blackwell's) **£550 [≈ $990]**
- An exposition of English insects, including the several classes of Neuroptera ... London: 1786. 2nd edn, 2nd iss. 4to. viii,9-166, [4] pp. Engvd title, cold chart, plain plate, 50 hand-cold plates. V sl foxing. Contemp calf, rebacked.
(Wheldon & Wesley) **£575 [≈ $1,035]**

Harris, W.
- Hibernica, or some antient pieces relating to Ireland ... a project of King James for the Plantation of the Escheated Counties. The report of the Commission to the Establishment of the Plantation ... Dublin: Bate, 1747. 2 vols in 1. Folio. Contemp calf.
(Emerald Isle) **£175 [≈ $315]**

Harris, Walter
- The history of the life and reign of William Henry, Prince of Nassau and Orange ... with

an appendix ... Dublin: Edward Bate, 1749. Folio. maps, charts, plates as called for. Contemp calf, rebacked.
(Emerald Isle) £225 [≈ $405]

Harris, William

- An historical and critical account of the life and writings of Charles I. London: R. Griffiths ..., 1758. 8vo. [viii],428,[ii] pp. Contemp calf, spine gilt, a little rubbed & scuffed. *(Clark)* £50 [≈ $90]
- An historical and critical account of the life of Oliver Cromwell ... Now first published. London: A. Millar, 1762. [viii],543 pp. Contemp calf, spine gilt, rubbed, extremities worn, 1 gathering pulled. *(Clark)* £50 [≈ $90]

Harrison, Joseph

- The accomplish'd practiser in the High Court of Chancery. 1779. 6th edn. 2 vols. 433; 554 pp. Contemp calf. *(Edwards)* £120 [≈ $216]
- Scriptural exposition of the Church catechism. Dublin: Sylvanus Pepyat, 1738. 12mo. Carlow Collage stamp on title. Contemp calf, sl rubbed.
(Emerald Isle) £25 [≈ $45]

Harrison, Sarah

- The house-keeper's pocket book and compleat family cook ... the eighth edition. London: for C. & R. Ware, 1764. Some tables at end shaved at bottom. Contemp sheep, rebacked.
(Waterfield's) £195 [≈ $351]

Harrison, Walter

- A new and universal history, description and survey of the Cities of London and Westminster. London: for J. Cooke, 1776 [1777]. 1st edn in book form. 8vo. [iv],720 pp. Over 190 ills & maps. Text browned in places, some splits & tears. Contemp calf, reprd. *(Ash)* £600 [≈ $1,080]

Harte, Walter

- An essay on reason [in verse]. London: Lawton Gulliver, 1735. Folio. Iss omitting line 504. 30 pp, advt leaf. Disbound.
(C.R. Johnson) £68 [≈ $122]

Hartley, David

- Observations on man, his frame, his duty and his expectations, in two parts ... London: for J. Johnson, 1791. 4to. Engvd frontis (sl foxed). Contemp half calf, rather worn.
(Waterfield's) £215 [≈ $387]

Hartley, David (1705-1757)

- A view of the present evidence for and against

Mrs. Stephen's medicines, as a solvent for the stone ... London: for S. Harding, 1739. 1st edn. 8vo. vi,[2],204 (some mispagination), [4] pp. Rec bds. *(Rootenberg)* $400 [≈ £222]

Hartley, J., et al.

- History of the Westminster election. London: 1785. 2nd edn. 4to. 16 plates by Rowlandson, fldg table. Some dampstaining at beginning. Uncut in orig bds, rubbed, new endpapers.
(Robertshaw) £180 [≈ $324]

Harvard, William

- Regulus. A tragedy. London: for P. Vaillant, 1744. vii,67 pp. 1st edn. 8vo. Title soiled & torn with loss of 2 letters. Disbound.
(Clark) £10 [≈ $18]

Harvey, Gideon

- The art of curing diseases by expectation ... other various discourses in physick ... London: 1689. 1st edn. 12mo. [iv],224 pp. Ink stain on title, some foxing & staining. Contemp mor, gilt, crnrs worn, chipped. Sgntr of Gideon Harvey on endpaper. Wing H1056. *(Pickering)* $1,250 [≈ £694]
- Casus medico-chirurgicus, or a most memorable case of a noble-man deceased, wherein is shewed his Lordship's wound ... how his physicians ... treated him ... London: Rooks, 1678. 1st edn. 12mo. 3ff, 160 pp. Lib b'plate, stamp on title. Old calf, rebacked.
(Hemlock) $350 [≈ £194]
- The City Remembrancer: being historical narratives of the Great Plague at London, 1665; Great Fire, 1666 ... reflections on the plague in general ... London: for W. Nicoll, 1769. 1st edn. 2 vols. 8vo. Contemp tree calf, jnts cracked but sound.
(Quaritch) $350 [≈ £194]
- The vanities of philosophy and physick ... London: for A. Roper ..., 1699. 1st edn. 8vo. [viii],184 pp. Early sgntrs on title, some browning & foxing. Contemp speckled sheep, panelled in blind, crnrs sometime reprd, jnts cracked. Wing H1079.
(Pickering) $650 [≈ £361]
- The third edition of the vanities of philosophy and physick: enlarged ... offering moreover ... different hypotheses ... physick ... and other diseases. London: Roper, 1702. [28],381 pp. Some pencilling. Contemp panelled calf, rebacked.
(Goodrich) $195 [≈ £108]

Harvey, William

- The anatomical exercise concerning the motion of the heart and blood ... to which is added, Dr. James de Back, his discourse on

the heart. London: R. Lowndes, 1673. 2nd edn in English. 8vo. 12ff, 107 pp; 10 ff, 172 pp. Lacking front free endpapers. Old calf.
(Hemlock) **$2,250 [≈ £1,250]**

Haselden, Thomas
- Euclid's elements ... See Barrow, Isaac

Hasted, Edward
- The history and topographical survey of the County of Kent. Canterbury: 1778-99. 1st edn. 4 vols. Folio. 40 fldg engvd maps & plans, 61 copper plates of views, further charts. Sl creasing to some plates. Contemp russia, elab gilt, surface worming.
(Blackwell's) **£1,800 [≈ $3,240]**
- The history and topographical survey of the County of Kent. Canterbury: 1778-99. 1st edn. 4 vols. Folio. 38 engvd maps (36 fldg), 62 engvd plates (4 fldg). Addtnl fldg cold aquatint of Canterbury Cathedral. Occas browning. Contemp calf, rebacked.
(Frew Mackenzie) **£1,650 [≈ $2,970]**

Hastings, Warren
- The defence of Warren Hastings, Esq ... at the Bar of the House of Commons. London: John Stockdale, 1786. New edn. 8vo. Title & last few leaves foxed. Contemp half calf, mrbld bds, spine gilt, crnrs a bit worn.
(Clark) **£38 [≈ $68]**
- Memoirs relative to the state of India. A new edition, with additions. London: J. Murray, 1786. 8vo. Lacking front free endpaper, some staining on a few pages. Orig bds, later rebacked with cloth, uncut, rubbed, a bit marked.
(Clark) **£48 [≈ $86]**
- The present state of the East Indies ... with notes by the editor. London: John Stockdale, 1786. viii,103,[1] pp. Mod blue bds.
(Karmiole) **£60 [≈ £33]**
- The trial of Warren Hastings ... the history of the origin of impeachment, the debate in the House of Commons ... London: J. Owen, 1794. 2 vols. 8vo. Titles a bit soiled, a few lib stamps, some margs re-inforced. Contemp half sheep, mrbld bds, jnts cracked.
(Clark) **£32 [≈ $57]**

Hatsell, John
- Precedents of proceedings in the House of Commons under separate titles with observations. London: for J. Dodsley, 1781, 4to. Contemp calf, somewhat rubbed.
(Waterfield's) **£85 [≈ $153]**

Hatton, Edward
- Comes commercii, or, the trader's

companion. London: C. Hitch, 1759. 10th edn. Narrow 8vo. Some soiling, 1st 4 leaves with reprs. 19th c half mor.
(Spelman) **£30 [≈ $54]**
- A new view of London. London: for John Nicholson ..., 1708. 1st edn. 2 vols. 8vo. Over 800 pp. 2 fldg maps, engvd plates of coats of arms. Plates a little worn at flds, some browning & staining. Old half calf, 1 vol rebacked, new labels.
(Ash) **£350 [≈ $630]**

Haunted Priory ...
- The haunted priory ... See Cullen, Stephen

Havers, G. & Davies, J.
- Collection of philosophical conferences of the French virtuosi upon questions of all sorts ... London: for Thomas Dring ..., 1665. 4to. [8]ff,496 pp. Browned, title with crnr & sm section missing with loss of 4 letters. Contemp calf, worn, jnts open.
(Elgen) **£450 [≈ £250]**

Haward, Lazarus
- The charges issuing forth of the Crown Revenue of England and Wales. London: for M. Wright, 1660. 2nd edn. Sm 4to. [viii],55 pp. Title browned & with hole affecting author's name & imprint. Disbound. Disbound. Wing H1164.
(Young's) **£12 [≈ $21]**

Hawkesworth, John
- An account of the voyages ... for making discoveries ... London: for Strahan & Cadell, 1773. 1st edn, early iss. 3 vols. 4to. 25 maps (22 fldg), 25 plates (16 fldg, lacking 1). Scattered light foxing & minor waterstaining. 3/4 red mor, mrbld bds, by Bayntun.
(Argonaut) **$1,600 [≈ £888]**
- An account of the voyages ... for making discoveries ... London: 1773; [with] Cook, James - A voyage towards the South Pole ... London: 1784; [with] Cook - A voyage to the Pacific Ocean ... London: 1784-85. 2nd, 4th, 2nd edns. 8 vols & atlas vol. Unif calf, mrbld bds.
(Reese) **$7,500 [≈ £4,166]**
- Almoran and Hamet: an oriental tale. London: for Harrison ..., 1780. 2 pts in 1. 8vo. 2 engvd plates. New half mor.
(Stewart) **£25 [≈ $45]**
- Almoran and Hamet: an oriental tale. London: for H. Payne ..., 1761. 2nd edn. 2 vols. Sm 8vo. viii,146; [iv],156 pp. 2 half-titles. Contemp speckled calf, 1 lower hinge cracked.
(Deighton Bell) **£40 [≈ $72]**

Hawkins, Francis

- A narrative, being a true relation of what discourse passed between Dr. Hawkins and Edward Fitz-Harys, Esq; late prisoner in the Tower ... London: Samuel Carr, 1681. Folio. [ii],10 pp. Stained. Disbound, stitching loose. Wing H1173. *(Clark)* £20 [≃ $36]

Hawkins, John

- The life of Samuel Johnson. Dublin: for Messrs. Chamberlain ..., 1787. 8vo. [ii],533,[19] pp. Early 19th c calf, rebacked. *(Burmester)* £140 [≃ $252]

Hawkins, William

- A treatise of the Pleas of the Crown. 1724-26. 2nd edn crrctd. 2 books in 1. Folio. 266; 464 pp. Minor worming to lower margs of 1st few leaves. Contemp calf, jnts splitting. *(Edwards)* £160 [≃ $288]
- A treatise of the Pleas of the Crown ... explanatory preface ... by Thomas Leach. 1795. 7th edn. 4 vols. 28,659; 562; 376; 509 pp. Rec calf. *(Edwards)* £200 [≃ $360]
- A treatise of the Pleas of the Crown ... (Edited and enlarged by Thomas Leach. London: for G.G. & J. Robinson, 1795. 7th edn. 4 vols. Lge 8vo. Vol 1 title dusty. Mod law calf, contrasting labels. *(Chaucer Head)* £160 [≃ $288]

Hay, William

- Religio philosophi: or, the principles of morality and Christianity illustrated from a view of the universe, and of man's situation in it ... London: for R. Dodsley, 1753. Disbound. *(Waterfield's)* £85 [≃ $153]
- Select epigrams of Martial. Translated and imitated. London: for R. & J. Dodsley, 1755. 1st edn. 2ff advts at end. Facing English & Latin text. Contemp calf, a little rubbed. *(Claude Cox)* £30 [≃ $54]

Hayes, Charles

- A treatise of fluxions: or an introduction to mathematical philosophy ... London: for Midwinter & Leigh ..., 1704. 1st edn. Folio. [xvi],xii,315,[1 advt] pp. W'cut diag pasted to ft of p 2, num w'cut text diags. Contemp panelled calf, rebacked, crnrs worn. *(Pickering)* $2,650 [≃ £1,472]

Hayes, Richard

- An estimate of places for life: shewing how many years purchase a place for life is worth ... London: for W. Meadows ..., 1728. 1st edn. 8vo. [viii],263 pp. V light waterstain in outer margs, 18th c sgntr on title. Contemp

calf, rebacked, orig spine preserved. *(Pickering)* $800 [≃ £444]
- Interest at one view, calculated to a farthing ... with a curious table ... also tables for reducing the most common gold coins to pounds. Dublin: 1789. 16th edn. Sq 8vo. 347 pp. Lacking free endpapers. Orig tree sheep. *(Claude Cox)* £25 [≃ $45]

Hayes, Thomas

- A serious address on the dangerous consequences of neglecting common coughs and colds, with ample directions for the prevention and cure on consumptions. Boston: 1796. 1st Amer edn. 12mo. 105 pp. Foxed, stamp on title. New qtr calf. *(Goodrich)* $325 [≃ £180]
- A serious address on the dangerous consequences of neglecting common coughs and colds ... Boston: 1796. 1st Amer edn. Old sgntr on title. Qtr mor, mrbld bds, upper hinge v sl cracked, crnrs sl wear. *(Rittenhouse)* $225 [≃ £125]

Hayley, William

- The triumphs of temper; a poem: in six cantos. London: for T. Cadell, 1788. 6th edn, crrctd. 12mo. xii,162 pp. Half-title, 7 engvd plates. Contemp mottled calf, spine split, labels missing. *(Burmester)* £38 [≃ $68]

Hayter, John

- An essay on a passage of St. Paul, 1 Cor. 11th Ch. 10th verse. London: for G. & T. Wilkie, 1791. 1st edn. 8vo. [ii],31 pp. Prelim advt leaf. Disbound. *(Burmester)* £15 [≃ $27]

Hayward, Sir John

- The life and raigne of King Edward the Sixt. London: Partridge, 1630. 1st edn. S, 4to. 211,179 pp. Engvd title (sm piece torn from upper crnr, cropped on fore-edge with v sl loss). Cropping at lower edge without loss. Later calf & endpapers, rubbed. STC 12998. *(P & P)* £90 [≃ $162]

Haywood, Eliza

- Mary Stuart, Queen of Scots ... secret history of her life and the real causes of all her misfortunes ... Translated from the French by ... London: for D. Browne Junior, 1725. 1st edn. 8vo. iv,240 pp. Red & black title. Contemp panelled calf, rebacked. *(Bennett)* £275 [≃ $495]

Headley, Henry

- Select beauties of English poetry. With remarks ... London: for T. Cadell, 1787. 1st edn. 2 vols in 1. 8vo. xiv,lxvi,113; viii,192 pp,

errata leaf. Without half-titles. front endpapers soiled. Contemp calf, upper hinge cracked & chipped, backstrip worn at ends.
(Claude Cox) **£65 [≈ $117]**

Healde, Thomas
- The new pharmacopoeia of the Royal College of Physicians of London. Translated ... London: for T. Longman, 1788. 2nd edn, crrctd. xvi,350,[i errata],[i blank] pp. Occas marg mark, wanting half-title. New buckram.
(Pollak) **£60 [≈ $108]**
- The pharmacopoeia of the Royal College of Physicians of London ... London: 1793. 6th edn. Lacking front & rear free endpapers. Contemp calf, some wear.
(Robertshaw) **£36 [≈ $64]**

Hearne, Thomas
- The history and antiquities of Glastonbury. Oxford: at the Theater, 1722. 1st edn. 8vo. 5 plates, 3 figs. Old inscrptn on title. Rec qtr calf, new endpapers.
(Bow Windows) **£80 [≈ $144]**

Heckford, Reyner
- A discourse on the bookland and folkland of the Saxons ... and the notion of them advanced by Sir John Dalrymple ... examined and confuted. Cambridge: J. Archdeacon ..., 1775. 1st edn. 8vo. vii,54 pp. Title foxed. Disbound. *(Hughes)* **£18 [≈ $32]**

Helsham, Richard
- A course of lectures in natural philosophy. Dublin: R.Reilly, at the University Press, 1739. 1st edn. 8vo. viii,404 pp. Red & black title, 11 fldg engvd plates. Contemp calf, worn. *(Bennett)* **£250 [≈ $450]**

Helvetius, Claude-Adrien
- De l'esprit: or, essays on the mind and its several faculties. London: for the translator ..., 1759. 1st edn in English. 4to. xvi,331 pp. Red & black title (with 18th c ownership inscrptn). Mod calf-backed mrbld bds.
(Pickering) **$950 [≈ £527]**

Helwich, Christopher
- The historical and chronological theater of Christopher Helvicus, distributed into equal intervals ... London: for George West ..., 1687. 1st English edn. [xxii],213,[43 index] pp. Wing H1411.
(Lloyd-Roberts) **£100 [≈ $180]**

Henderson, Alexander
- A sermon preached at the ... House of Commons ... Wednesday, December 27,

1643. London: for Robert Bostock, 1643. 8vo. Disbound. Wing H1439.
(Waterfield's) **£35 [≈ $63]**

Henderson, William Augustus
- The housekeeper's instructor; or, universal family cook ... to which is added the complete art of carving. London: Stratford, n.d. [1790?]. 5th edn. 448,15 index, 3 subscribers, 1 advt pp. Frontis, 10 engvd plates (1 fldg). Contemp tree-calf, spine gilt-ruled.
(Gough) **£225 [≈ $405]**

Hentzner, Paul
- Travels in England, during the reign of Queen Elizabeth, translated by Horace, late Earl of Orford ... London: Edward Jeffery, 1797. 1st edn thus. 8vo. viii,152 pp. 11 engvd plates, some tinted. Contemp diced calf, a little rubbed. Ex Kimbolton Castle lib.
(Young's) **£90 [≈ $162]**

Hepplewhite, A.
- The cabinet-maker and upholsterer's guide; or, repository of designs for every article of household furniture. London: I. & J. Taylor, 1789. 1st edn. Folio. vi,24 pp, 127 engvd plates (1 double-page), [ii pub advts] pp. Occas light spotting. Later half mor.
(Gough) **£1,350 [≈ $2,430]**

Heraldry ...
- Heraldry in miniature ... the arms, crests, supporters and mottoes of the Peers, Peeresses and Bishops of England ... London: for B. Law ..., 1798. 12mo. 2 vols in 1. 8vo. 36,60,xxxvi index pp. Engvd title, 126 plates. Many ms notes on flyleaves. Contemp calf.
(Claude Cox) **£28 [≈ $50]**

Herbert of Cherbury, Lord Edward
- The life and reign of King Henry the Eighth. London: for Ann Mearn, 1683. Folio. [iv],636 pp. Port frontis, red & black title. Occas minor worming. Later half calf, gilt dec spine faded with sm wormholes, crnrs & edges rubbed, later mrbld endpapers.
(P & P) **£60 [≈ $108]**

Herbert, George
- A priest to the temple: or the country parson's character and rule of holy life. London: 1701. 4th edn. 12mo. Contemp calf, worn.
(Robertshaw) **£38 [≈ $68]**

Hereford, Charles
- The history of Spain from the establishment of the Colony of Gades by the Phoenicians to the death of Ferdinand. London: 1793. 1st

edn. 3 vols. Contemp speckled calf.
(Robertshaw) **£36 [≈ $64]**

Heresbach, Conrad
- Foure bookes of husbandrie ... Newly Englished, and increased by Barnaby Googe. London: John Wright, 1586. Sm 4to. Black letter. W'cut arms on title verso, w'cut in text, final leaf "Olde English Rules", colophon, vignette on verso. Mrbld bds, calf. STC 13198. *(Traylen)* **£685 [≈ $1,233]**

Herle, Charles
- Detur sapienti. In a treatise of the excellency of Christian wisdome ... Two former treatises. Samuel Gellibrand, 1655. 1st edn. 12mo. [iv],242,[v] pp. 1st leaf sl frayed at fore-edge. Contemp sheep, spine defective at hd & tail, rubbed. *(Frew Mackenzie)* **£70 [≈ $126]**

Hermippus Redivivus ...
- Hermippus redivivus ... See Cohausen, Johann Heinrich

Heron, Robert
- General view of the natural circumstances of those Isles ... distinguished by the common name of ... Hebrides. Edinburgh: 1794. 4to. Bds, calf spine. *(Traylen)* **£42 [≈ $75]**

Herschel, Caroline Lucretia
- Catalogue of stars, taken from Mr. Flamsteed's observations ... in ... the Historia Coelestis. With an index ... Sold by Peter Elmsly ..., 1798. 1st edn. Folio. 136 pp. Engvd lf of scales, errata lf. Marg worming throughout, reprd on title. Rec grey bds.
(Pickering) **£600 [≈ £333]**

Hervey, Thomas
- A letter to William Pitt, Esq: concerning the fifteen new regiments lately voted by Parliament. London: W. Webb, 1746. 39 pp & "Bookseller to the Reader". Disbound.
(C.R. Johnson) **£35 [≈ $63]**

Hesperi-neso-graphia ...
- Hesperi-neso-graphia ... See Moffett, William

Hewit, Hannah ...
- Hannah Hewit; or, the female Crusoe ... See Dibdin, Charles, the elder

Hey, Richard
- A dissertation on duelling. Cambridge: J. Archdeacon, 1784. 97 pp. Disbound.
(C.R. Johnson) **£85 [≈ $153]**
- A dissertation on suicide. Published by

appointment. Cambridge: J. Archdeacon, 1785. 90 pp. Disbound.
(C.R. Johnson) **£125 [≈ $225]**
- A dissertation on the pernicious effects of gaming. Cambridge: J. Archdeacon, 1783. 1st edn. 8vo. 100 pp. Contemp half calf.
(Argosy) **$250 [≈ £138]**
- A dissertation on the pernicious effects of gaming. Cambridge: J. Archdeacon, 1784. 2nd edn. 100 pp. Disbound.
(C.R. Johnson) **£95 [≈ $153]**
- A dissertation on the pernicious effects of gaming. Cambridge: J. Archdeacon, 1784. 2nd edn. 8vo. 100 pp. Stitched.
(Argosy) **$75 [≈ £41]**
- Edington: a novel. London: for Vernor & Hood, 1796. 1st edn. 2 vols. 12mo. Errata leaf. Contemp mrbld bds, calf spines.
(Traylen) **£350 [≈ $630]**

Heylyn, P.
- A help to English history, containing a succession of all the Kings of England, the English Saxons, and the Britains ... London: Basset, 1680. 12mo. 634 pp, advt leaf. Many w'cut coats of arms in text. Ex lib with stamp on title & occas elsewhere. Mod calf.
(P & P) **£50 [≈ $90]**

Heylyn, Peter
- Aerius redivivus: or the history of the Presbyterians ... the beginnings, progress, and the successes ... London: for Christopher Wilkinson ... 1672. 2nd edn. Folio. Sm wormhole in outer marg of part. Contemp calf, jnts cracked, crnrs rubbed. Wing 1682.
(Stewart) **£100 [≈ $180]**
- Cyprianus Anglicanus: or, the history of ... William ... Archbishop of Canterbury ... London: for A. Seile, 1668. 1st edn. Folio. 2 crnrs torn without loss. Later half mor, worn & rubbed, cloth bds. Wing H1699.
(Charles Cox) **£40 [≈ $72]**
- Cyprianus Anglicanus: or, the history of ... William ... Archbishop of Canterbury ... London: for A. Seile, 1671. 2nd edn. Folio. [iv],511 pp. Sporadic browning. Contemp panelled calf, rebacked, edges worn. Ex lib with stamps on bds. Wing H1700.
(Clark) **£40 [≈ $72]**
- (Greek title, then) The historical and miscellaneous tracts of ... Peter Heylyn, D.D. Now collected into one volume. London: for Charles Harper, 1681. 1st edn. Folio. Lacking port. Contemp calf, jnts weak, new endpapers. Wing H1680.
(Charles Cox) **£45 [≈ $81]**
- Microcosmos. A little description of the great

world. Oxford: John Lichfield ..., 1625. 2nd edn. 8vo. [xvi],812,[ii] pp. Underlining throughout, stamps on title & a few margs, M2 marg cropped. 19th c half mor, extremities rubbed. STC 13277.
(Clark) **£145 [≈ $261]**

Heynes, Samuel
- A treatise of trigonometry, plane and spherical, theoretical and practical ... To which is added a correct table of logarithms, sines ... London: 1701. 2 works in 1 vol. 12mo. 16 fldg plates, 2 engvd figs with movable flaps, fldg table. Lib buckram.
(Argosy) **$200 [≈ £111]**
- A treatise of trigonometry, plane and spherical, theoretical and practical. London: 1701. [2],135, [52],[92], 8 pp. 16 fldg plates. Old panelled calf, edges & front worn, top of spine sl defective. *(Whitehart)* **£150 [≈ $270]**

Heywood, Samuel
- The right of protestant dissenters to a complete toleration asserted. London: for J. Johnson, 1789. 2nd edn, crrctd. 8vo. [viii],99 pp. Disbound.   *(Young's)* **£32 [≈ $57]**

Heywood, Thomas
- The exemplary lives and memorable acts of nine the most worthy women of the world. London: 1640. 1st edn. Sm 4to. 10 engvd ports. Title & 1st port reprd with sellotape, some dampstaining. Mod half calf. STC 13316.   *(Robertshaw)* **£100 [≈ $180]**
- The hierarchie of the blessed Angells. Their names, orders and offices. The fall of Lucifer ... London: Adam Islip, 1635. Sole edn. Folio. Engvd title, 8 plates. Old stain at top, privilege leaf laid down, lacking terminal blank. Mod calf. STC 13327.
(Charles Cox) **£350 [≈ $630]**
- (Greek title, then) or, Nine bookes of various history concerninge women ... London: Adam Islip, 1624. Sole edn. Folio. Engvd title trimmed, laid down, a couple of marg tears, some staining to prelims. Old polished calf, rebacked. STC 13326.
(Charles Cox) **£425 [≈ $765]**

Hibernica ...
- Hibernica, or some antient pieces relating to Ireland ... See Harris, W.

Hickes, Geo.
- The gentleman instructed, in the conduct of a virtuous and happy life. In three parts ... To which is added, a word to the ladies ... London: for D. Midwinter, 1738. 11th edn. 8vo. Sep title to each part. Contemp calf,

scraped, worn.   *(Hughes)* **£46 [≈ $82]**

Hickes, Dr. George
- Several letters which passed between Dr. George Hickes, and a Popish priest, upon occasion of a young gentlewoman's departing from the Church of England to that of Rome. London: 1705. 1st edn. Contemp panelled calf. John Evelyn's copy.
(Robertshaw) **£46 [≈ $82]**

Hickingill, Edm.
- A speech without-doors: or some modest inquiries humbly proposed to the Right Honourable Convention of Estates ... London: George Larkin, 1689. 1st edn. Sm 4to. [viii],36 pp. Title dust-soiled, edges curled. Disbound. Wing H1287.
(Hughes) **£25 [≈ $45]**

Hierocles
- Hierocles upon the golden verses of the Pythagoreans, translated ... into English by John Norris. London: M. Flesher, 1682. 8vo. Lib stamp on title & 3 other leaves, rather browned. Contemp sheep. Wing H1939.
(Waterfield's) **£100 [≈ $180]**

Higgins, Bryan
- Experiments and observations made with a view of improving ... calcereous cements and of preparing quicklime ... for building, incrustation or stuccoing, and artificial stone. London: T. Cadell, 1780. 1st edn. 8vo. xi,[i],233 pp. Rec half calf, mrbld bds.
(Spelman) **£260 [≈ $468]**

Higgons, Brevill
- A short view of English history. Tho. Edlin, 1723. 1st edn. Lge paper. viii,435 pp. Half-title. Contemp calf, ruled sides, sl rubbed, jnts cracking but firm.
(Blackwell's) **£150 [≈ $270]**

Hill, Aaron
- The dramatick works ... In two volumes. London: T. Lowndes, 1760. Contemp calf, red mor labels. Ex lib Colquhoun of Luss.
(C.R. Johnson) **£360 [≈ $648]**

Hill, James
- The following is an authentic copy of a letter sent by James Hill to his brother in Manchester. [Manchester: 1782]. 4to. 4pp.
(C.R. Johnson) **£75 [≈ $135]**

Hill, John
- Arithmetic both in theory and practice, made plain and easy ... whole numbers and

fractions, vulgar and decimal ... extraction of the square and cube roots ... London: 1764. 12th edn. vi,416 pp. Lacking half-title, 1 or 2 pp stained. Contemp calf, rebacked.
(Whitehart) **£55 [≈ $99]**

Hilton, William
- Caps well fit: or, select epigrams, serious and comic. By Titus, in Sandgate, and Titus, everywhere. Newcastle: for T. Fishburn ..., 1785. 1st edn. 12mo. Title dust-marked. Contemp mrbld bds, rebacked.
(Charles Cox) **£95 [≈ $171]**

Hinde, M., et al.
- A new royal and universal dictionary of arts and sciences ... London: 1772-71. Folio. 2 vols. 1st edn, 2nd ptg & 1st edn. 100 (ex 101) plates. Vol 2 lacking leaf 4P. Contemp calf, v worn. *(Elgen)* **$225 [≈ £125]**

Hints ...
- Hints respecting the culture and use of potatoes. [London?: 1795]. 8vo. 8 pp. Drophead title. *(C.R. Johnson)* **£120 [≈ $216]**

Hippesley, R.
- Bath and its environs, a descriptive poem, in three cantos ... Bath: R. Cruttwell, 1775. 4to. Engvd plate. Orig mrbld bds, rebacked.
(C.R. Johnson) **£165 [≈ $297]**

Hitt, Thomas
- A treatise on fruit trees. London: For Robinson & Roberts, 1768. 8vo. viii,394,[v] pp. 7 fldg engvd plates. Contemp polished calf. *(Bickersteth)* **£125 [≈ $225]**
- A treatise on fruit trees. London: T. Osborne, 1755. 1st edn. 8vo. xv,392 pp. 7 fldg plates (2 reprd, 3 with sl snags in fold). Direction/errata leaf present. Contemp sprinkled calf, upper jnt tender.
(Blackwell's) **£250 [≈ $450]**

Hoadly, Benjamin
- Three lectures on the organs of respiration. Read at the Royal College of Physicians, A.D. 1737 ... London: for W. Wilkins, 1740. 1st edn. 8vo. iv,112,20 pp. 3 engvd plates. Cut close in upper marg & 1st word of title, headlines & plates shaved. Disbound.
(Pickering) **$250 [≈ £138]**

Hoadly, Benjamin, Bishop of Winchester
- The common rights of subjects, defended: and the nature of the Sacramental Test, consider'd. W. Wilkins, 1719. 1st edn. 8vo. viii,[iv], 303,[i] pp. 2 vignettes, decorated initial. Mod wraps. *(Blackwell's)* **£45 [≈ $81]**

Hoare, Michael (pseud.)
- See Halfpenny, William

Hobart, Sir Henry
- The reports of that reverend and learned judge ... purged from the errors of all former impressions. London: for William Lee ..., 1658. Folio. Some foxing, contemp ms notes & underlinings. Mod law cloth. Wing H2207.
(Charles Cox) **£40 [≈ $72]**

Hobbes, Thomas
- Leviathan ... London: for Andrew Crooke, 1651. 1st edn, 1st iss. Folio. Engvd title. Half mottled calf, mottled bd sides. New Wing H2245. *(Traylen)* **£1,650 [≈ $2,970]**
- Leviathan, or the matter, forme, and power of a Common-wealth ecclesiasticall and Civill. London: for Andrew Cooke, 1651. 1st edn, 1st iss. Folio. Pull-out plan. Minor reprs to title border. Mottled calf, gilt.
(Edwards) **£2,000 [≈ $3,600]**
- Leviathan, or the matter, forme, and power of a Common-wealth ecclesiasticall and Civill. London: Crooke, 1651. 1st edn, with head ornament on title. Folio. [vi],396 pp. Addtnl engvd title. Fldg table. Title reinforced on verso, 1 leaf frayed. Mod calf, gilt.
(Frew Mackenzie) **£1,650 [≈ $2,970]**

Hobler, J. Paul
- The words of the favourite pieces, as performed at the Glee Club, held at the Crown and Anchor Tavern, Strand. Compiled from their library. London: for the author, 1794. Contemp tree-calf.
(C.R. Johnson) **£110 [≈ $198]**

Hog, James
- Otia Christiana: or Christian recreations. being a conference betwixt Nicon and Philotheus ... Edinburgh: James Watson, 1708. 1st edn. 12mo. viii,220 pp. 1st few leaves v sl frayed at outer edges, ptd throughout on poor paper. Rec sprinkle panelled calf. *(Bennett)* **£225 [≈ $405]**

Hogarth, William
- The analysis of beauty. London: W. Strahan for Mrs Hogarth, 1772. New (2nd English) edn. 4to. xxi,[3], 153,[2] pp. 2 lge fldg plates taken from later edn. Repairs to back of plates & final advt leaf. Working copy in blue buckram. *(Spelman)* **£120 [≈ $216]**
- Hogarth moralized. Being a complete edition of Hogarth's works. London: sold by S. Hooper & by Mrs. Hogarth, 1768. 1st edn. Sm 4to. Port frontis, engvd & ptd titles, full

& part-page engvs. Contemp calf, rebacked.
(Chaucer Head) **£160 [≈ $288]**

Holdsworth, E.
- Remarks and dissertations on Virgil ... London: for Dodsley, 1768. 1st edn. Lge 4to. [iii],619 pp. 4 fldg, 8 full-page plates & plans, text ills. Some foxing to endpapers. Calf, gilt dec spine, front hinge split.
(P & P) **£78 [≈ $140]**

Holles, Denzil
- The case stated concerning the judicature of the House of Peers in the point of appeals. London: 1675. 1st edn. Prob lacking prelim blank. Mod cloth. Wing H2452.
(Charles Cox) **£30 [≈ $54]**

Holliday, F.
- An introduction to fluxions, designed for the use, and adapted to the capacities of beginners. London: 1777. xx,iv,343 pp. 7 plates. Contemp tree-calf, sl worn, sl damage to label. *(Whitehart)* **£60 [≈ $108]**

Holroyd, John, Lord Sheffield
- Observations on the manufactures, trade and present state of Ireland. London: Debrett, 1785. 3rd edn. Lge 8vo. 3 fldg tables. Near contemp half mor.
(Marlborough) **£400 [≈ $720]**

Holwell, William
- A mythological, etymological, and historical dictionary ... London: for C. Dilly, 1793. 1st edn. 8vo. xix,449,[29] pp. Uncut in contemp bds, a bit worn, 19th c cloth reback.
(Burmester) **£30 [≈ $54]**

Home, Francis
- Experiments on bleaching ... added, I. ... the use of leys and sours ... II. ... the effects of lime upon alkaline salts ... by Joseph Black ... III.... Dublin: Ewing, 1771. 1st Dublin edn. 12mo. [iv],295 pp. W'cut ill. Contemp lea, hd of spine discold. *(Bennett)* **£275 [≈ $495]**
- Medical facts and experiments. London: 1759. 1st edn. 8vo. 288 pp. Mod qtr calf, mrbld bds. *(Goodrich)* **$495 [≈ £275]**
- The principles of agriculture and vegetation. London: for A. Millar ..., 1759. 2nd edn with addtns. 8vo. viii,207 pp. 1st 2ff foxed. Orig calf, gilt, back & crnrs sl worn.
(Titles) **£150 [≈ $270]**

Home, Henry, Lord Kames
- Essays upon several subjects concerning British antiquities ... Introduction of the feudal law into Scotland ... Constitution and parliament ... succession or descent ... Edinburgh: Kincaid, 1747. Contemp calf, red label. Ex lib Colquhoun of Luss.
(C.R. Johnson) **£340 [≈ $612]**
- Progress of flax-husbandry in Scotland. Edinburgh: 1766. 1st edn. 8vo. 31,[1] pp. Disbound. *(Burmester)* **£250 [≈ $450]**

Home, John
- Alonzo. A tragedy. London: T. Becket, 1773. 1st edn. 8vo. [viii],86,[ii] pp. Final leaf a bit soiled. Disbound. *(Clark)* **£20 [≈ $36]**

Hooke, Nathaniel
- An account of the conduct of the Dowager Duches of Marlborough, from her first coming to court, to the year 1710. 1742. Old calf, cvrs detchd. *(Allen)* **$25 [≈ £13]**

Hooke, Robert
- Micrographia restaurata: or, the copper-plates of Dr. Hooke's wonderful discoveries by the microscope ... London: John Bowles, 1745. Folio. 33 plates (2 fldg). Contemp calf, rebacked, orig spine laid down.
(Traylen) **£750 [≈ $1,350]**
- Microscopic observations, or Dr. Hooke's wonderful discoveries by the microscope. London: 1781. Folio. [iv],65,[4] pp. 33 plates. V sl foxed. New mrbld bds, calf back.
(Wheldon & Wesley) **£750 [≈ $1,350]**
- Philosophical experiments and observations of the late eminent Dr. Robert Hooke ... and other eminent virtuoso's in his time. London: W. & J. Innys, 1725. 1st edn. 4 engvd plates (2 fldg), w'cut ills in text, leaf of advts at end. Contemp calf, rebacked.
(Traylen) **£550 [≈ $990]**
- Philosophical experiments and observations of the late eminent Dr. Robert Hooke ... London: Innys, 1726. 1st edn. 8vo. [viii],391, [4] pp. Stamp on title. Old panelled calf, rebacked. *(Goodrich)* **$695 [≈ £386]**
- Philosophical experiments and observations of the late eminent Dr. Robert Hooke... London: Printed by W. & J. Innys..., 1726. 1st edn. 8vo. [viii],391,[7],[2 advts] pp. W'cut headpieces, initials & diags in text. Contemp sprinkled calf, upper jnt cracked.
(Pickering) **$1,500 [≈ £833]**
- The posthumous works ... To these discourses is prefixt the author's life ... London: Sam. Smith & Benj Walford, 1705. 1st edn. Folio. 3ff xxviii,572 pp, 6ff (pp 210-276 omitted in pagination). 15 copperplates. No half-title. Contemp panelled calf, rubbed. *(Offenbacher)* **$1,500 [≈ £833]**

Hooker, Richard
- Of the lawes of ecclesiastical politie. London:, John Windet, [1594]-97. 209.[1] pp, 1f (blank, [xv],270 (i.e. 271) pp, sev errors in pagination. Early 20th c red mor, gilt panels, spine heavily gilt, 3 or 4 shallow scars on cvrs, spine sl darkened.
  (Pirages) **$1,900 [≈ £1,055]**
- Of the lawes of ecclesiastical politie. Eight bookes. William Stansbye ..., [1622]. Folio. [lvi],583,[xv index] pp. Title within engvd border, sep engvd titles to each part. Contemp polished calf, front jnt cracked, rear jnt rubbed, crnrs bumped. STC 13717.
  (Frew Mackenzie) **£180 [≈ $324]**
- Of the lawes of ecclesiastical politie. Eight bookes. London: Stansbye, [1622]. Folio. [liv],583 pp. Tables. Rec endpapers, mod cloth. STC 13717. *(P & P)* **£75 [≈ $135]**
- Of the lawes of ecclesiastical politie. Eight bookes. William Stansbye ..., [1632-31]. Folio. [lviii],583,[xv] pp. Some occas light dampstaining at hd. Contemp calf, spines elab gilt, some reprs to front cvr, spine lightly rubbed. STC 13718.
  (Frew Mackenzie) **£200 [≈ $360]**
- Of the lawes of ecclesiastical politie. Eight bookes. London: William Stansbye ..., [1632]. Folio. Engvd port (not called for) mtd as frontis. A few minor marks. Old calf, rebacked. STC 13719A.
  (Charles Cox) **£60 [≈ $108]**
- The works ... In eight books Of the lawes of ecclesiastical politie. London: for John Walthoe ..., 1723. Folio. Engvd port, engvd title, red & black ptd title. Contemp panelled calf, hinges splitting, crnr of top bd sl damaged. *(Chaucer Head)* **£130 [≈ $234]**

Hoole, John
- Cleonice, Princess of Bithynia: a tragedy. London: T. Evans, 1775. 1st edn. 8vo. [xii],74, [ii] pp. Disbound.
  (Clark) **£20 [≈ $36]**
- Timanthes: a tragedy. As it is performed at the Theatre Royal in Covent Garden. London: For T. Becket, 1770. 1st edn. 8vo. 71 pp. Short tear to title fore-margin. 19th c polished calf. Ex Signet Library.
  (Sotheran) **£68 [≈ $122]**

Hopkins, Charles
- Friendship improved: or, the female warriour. London: for Jacob Tonson, 1700. 1st edn. 8vo. [viii],56 pp. Quite browned, a little ragged. Mod mor-backed cloth bds.
  (Pirages) **$100 [≈ £55]**

Horace
- Odes of Horace. The best of lyrick poets. Containing much in moralitie ... by Sr. T[homas] H[awkins]. London: for William Lee, 1635. 3rd edn. Engvd title laid down & reprd, reprs to marg of ptd title & A2. Old sheep, rebacked. STC 13802.
  (Charles Cox) **£40 [≈ $72]**
- Satires, Epistles and Art of Poetry ... London: W. Mears ..., 1729. 4th edn. 8vo. [2],iv,[6], 477,[6 index] pp. Strip cut from hd of title without loss, light staining at beginning. Contemp panelled calf, rebacked, worn.
  (Claude Cox) **£15 [≈ $27]**
- The works. Translated into English prose ... with the original Latin from the best editions. London: for J. Oswald ..., 1741-43. 1st edn. 2 vols. xxviii,463,[12]; lii,405, [18] pp. Red & black titles, with vignettes. Old calf, worn, jnts weak. *(Young's)* **£40 [≈ $72]**

Horne, William
- A genuine account of the life and trial of William Andrew Horne, Esq; of Butterly-Hall, in the County of Derby ... London: for W. Bristow, 1760. 3rd edn. 8vo. 28 pp. Rec bds. *(Burmester)* **£60 [≈ $108]**

Horneck, Anthony
- The crucified Jesus ... the nature, end, designs, and benefits of the Lord's Supper. London: for Sam. Lowndes, 1686. Cr 8vo. Engvd frontis, red & black title. Contemp calf. Wing 2821. *(Stewart)* **£40 [≈ $72]**
- A sermon preached at Fulham ... on the consecration of ... Gilbert, Lord Bishop of Sarum. London: Richard Chiswell, 1689. 4to. Wing H2850. *(C.R. Johnson)* **£10 [≈ $18]**

Horsley, Samuel
- On the prosodies of the Greek & Latin languages. London: for J. Johnson, 1796. 1st edn. 8vo. [ii],v,171 pp. Half-title. Disbound. *(Burmester)* **£30 [≈ $54]**

Hotoman, Francois
- Franco-Gallia: or, an account of the ancient free state of France, and most other parts of Europe, before the loss of their liberties. London: 1721. 2nd edn. 8vo. Some light browning. Contemp panelled calf.
  (Robertshaw) **£25 [≈ $45]**

Houghton, John
- Husbandry and trade improv'd ... Revised, corrected, and published ... by Richard Bradley. London: Woodman & Lyon, 1727-29. 4 vols. 8vo. Contemp speckled calf,

gilt, mor labels. Vol IV not quite uniform.
(Traylen) **£350 [≈ $630]**

Houghton, Thomas
- Royal institutions: being proposals for articles to establish ... laws, liberties and customs of silver and gold mines ... in Africa and America ... London: Daniel Poplar, [1694]. 1st edn. 126 pp. 2 leaves cut short, a few sl browned. Orig sheep, crnrs worn.
(Pirages) **$1,500 [≈ £833]**

House of Commons ...
- Precedents of proceedings in the House of Commons ... See Hatsell, John

Howard, George Selby
- The New Royal Cyclopaedia and Encyclopaedia; or, complete modern and universal dictionary of arts and sciences ... London: Alex Hogg, [1788]. 1st edn. 3 vols. Folio. 161 engvd plates, 4 pp subscribers' list. Contemp half calf, mrbld sides, rubbed & worn. *(Traylen)* **£330 [≈ $594]**

Howard, Henry, Earl of Surrey
- Poems ... with the poems of Sir Thomas Wiat, and his other famous contemporaries. London: for W. Mears, 1717. 11th edn. 8vo. xvi,263,[vii] pp. Early 19th c diced calf gilt. Lord Leigh's b'plate. *(Bennett)* **£110 [≈ $198]**

Howard, John
- The state of the prisons in England and Wales. Warrington: William Eyres, 1780. 2nd edn (1st 8vo). [viii],449, [xix index] pp. 11 engvd plates, mostly fldg. Contemp qtr calf, rebacked, orig spine laid down.
(Gough) **£225 [≈ $405]**
- The state of the prisons in England and Wales. Warrington: William Eyres, 1777. [with] Appendix ... Warrington: 1784. 1st edn. 2 vols in 1. [8],489,[23]; [8],236,[10] pp. 21 plates. (1 mtd). Some waterstaining in crnrs. Rec half calf. A.l.s. tipped-in.
(Claude Cox) **£450 [≈ $810]**

Howard, Sir Robert
- The history of religion. London: 1694. 1st edn. 8vo. Contemp calf, rebacked. Wing H2998. *(Robertshaw)* **£30 [≈ $54]**
- The life and reign of King Richard the Second. London: for M.L. & H.C., 1681. 8vo. [viii],240 pp. Sl fraying in early mars, minor marg worming at end. Contemp calf, crnrs worn, backstrip defective. Wing H3001.
(Clark) **£40 [≈ $72]**

Howe, John
- A funeral-sermon for that excellent minister of Christ the truly reverend William Bates ... London: for T. Parkhurst ..., 1699. 8vo. xii,115,[5 pub ctlg] pp. Port frontis. Calf. Wing H3028. *(Lloyd-Roberts)* **£40 [≈ $72]**

Howell, James
- Epistolae ho-elianae. Familiar letters, domestick and foreign. Divided into four books. London: 1713. 8th edn. [xiv],510,[21] pp. Contemp panelled calf, rebacked.
(Young's) **£38 [≈ $68]**
- The pre-eminence and pedigree of parliament. London: for Dorman Newman ..., 1677. 4to. 1st word of title shaved, last leaf laid down, a little browned. New qtr calf, mrbld bds. Wing H3108.
(Charles Cox) **£30 [≈ $54]**

Hoyle, Edmond
- Mr. Hoyle's games of whist, quadrille, piquet, chess and back-gammon ... The twelfth edition ... two new cases of whist, never before printed ... London: for Thomas Osborne ..., [1760?]. 12mo. xii,214 pp. Contemp sheep, rubbed, sl splits in jnts. A piracy? *(Burmester)* **£40 [≈ $72]**
- A short treatise of the game of whist ... whereby a beginner may ... attain to the playing it well ... London: for F. Cogan, 1743. 2nd edn. 12mo. Blank segment from top of title missing. Later half calf, rebacked.
(Waterfield's) **£85 [≈ $153]**

Hoyle, John
- Dictionarium musica, being a complete dictionary or, treasury of music. London: for the author, 1770. 1st edn. 8vo. [iv],112 pp. Old plain wraps. *(Burmester)* **£160 [≈ $288]**

Huarte Navarro, Juan de Dios
- Examen de ingenios: or, the tryal of wits. Discovering the great difference of wits among men ... ... made English ... London: for Richard Sare, 1698. 8vo. [40],502 pp, leaf of advts. A few pp with reprd tears. Contemp calf, worn, hinges cracking. Wing H3205.
(Karmiole) **$250 [≈ £138]**

Hubbard, William
- A narrative of the Indian Wars in New-England, from ... 1607, to the year 1677 ... Boston: John Boyle, 1755. 3rd Amer edn, abrdgd. 12mo. viii,[9]-288 pp. Occas light foxing & marg staining. 18th c sgntr on title. Orig sheep, extremities lightly rubbed.
(Heritage) **$250 [≈ £138]**

Hudson, John
- The case and appeal of John Hudson ... tried at the Old Bailey ... upon a charge of committing a robbery in the shop of Robert Davis ... London: for the appellant, 1781. 1st edn. 8vo. [iv],viii,71 pp. Disbound.
(Burmester) **£75 [≈ $135]**

Hughes, Charles
- The compleat horseman; or, the art of riding made easy ... With directions to the ladies to sit gracefully, and ride with safety. London: for F. Newbery, [1772]. Sole edn (?). 8vo. 5 pp of w'cut ills. 19th c polished calf.
(Chaucer Head) **£160 [≈ $288]**

Hughes, G.
- The natural history of Barbados. London: the author, 1750. Folio. [xvi],viii, 314,[20] pp. Fldg map, 30 plates (1 cold). Tear in 1 leaf reprd. Contemp lea-backed bds, rather worn & rubbed.
(Wheldon & Wesley) **£500 [≈ $900]**

Hughes, Robert
- A catalogue of the genuine and most curious collection of Sardonyx's ... and other oriental stones, antique cameo's and intaglia's in rings, pictures ... curious mathematical and optical instruments ... London: Bastin, 1770. 4to. 9 pp. Stitched. *(Marlborough)* **£300 [≈ $540]**

Hulls, Jonathan
- A description and draught of a new-invented machine ... for carrying vessels or ships ... London: for the author, 1737. 1st edn. 12mo. 48 pp. Fldg engvd frontis (dustsoiled, tear reprd, cropped with loss of imprint). Title & last leaf soiled. 19th c calf.
(Pickering) **$4,000 [≈ £2,222]**

Humane Industry ...
- Humane industry ... See Powell, Thomas

Hume, David
- Dialogues concerning natural religion. London: 1779. 2nd edn. 8vo. Half-title. Some spotting of prelims & last few leaves. Contemp calf, rebacked.
(Hughes) **£375 [≈ $675]**
- Dialogues concerning natural religion ... London: 1779. 2nd edn. Uncut in mod qtr calf. *(Waterfield's)* **£400 [≈ $720]**
- An enquiry concerning the principles of morals. London: for A. Millar ..., 1751. 1st edn, 1st iss. 12mo. [viii],253,[3 advts] pp. L3 not a cancel. A little browned. Mod calf.
(Pickering) **$1,650 [≈ £916]**

- Essays and treatises on several subjects in two volumes ... London: for A. Millar ..., 1768. 2 vols. 4to. Lge paper (?).Port frontis. Contemp calf, worn, jnts cracked.
(Waterfield's) **£405 [≈ $729]**
- Essays and treatises on several subjects. London: A. Millar ..., 1767. New edn. 2 vols. 8vo. Half-title in vol 2. Single lib blindstamp. Contemp speckled calf, rebacked.
(Chaucer Head) **£250 [≈ $450]**
- Essays and treatises on several subjects. London: A. Millar ..., 1767. New edn. 2 vols. 4to. 582; [iv],509,[xv] pp. Engvd port frontis (sl browned). Occas foxing. Contemp half calf, mrbld sides, rebacked, crnrs worn, sides lightly rubbed.
(Frew Mackenzie) **£270 [≈ $486]**
- Essays moral and political. London: for A. Millar ..., 1748. 3rd edn, crrctd. 12mo. Contemp calf, rebacked, lacking label.
(Waterfield's) **£200 [≈ $360]**
- Essays, moral and philosophical. The third edition, corrected, with additions. London: for A. Millar ..., 1748. 12mo. iv,312 pp. Contents leaf reprd, some worming in lower blank marg of last 2 sgntrs. Rebound in half calf. *(Hughes)* **£230 [≈ $450]**
- Essays, moral and philosophical. The third edition, corrected, with additions. London: A. Millar ..., 1748. 12mo. [iv],312 pp. Very sl browned, lacking rear free endpaper. Contemp calf, rubbed.
(Blackwell's) **£230 [≈ $414]**
- Four dissertations. I. The natural history of religion ... IV. Of the standard of taste ... London: for A. Millar, 1757. 1st edn, 1st iss. Misspelling "lancing" p 131; 4ff of dedication. 12mo. Half-titles. Contemp calf, gilt. *(Traylen)* **£720 [≈ $1,296]**
- Four dissertations. I. The natural history of religion. II. ... III ... IV. Of the standard of taste ... London: for A. Millar, 1757. 1st edn. 12mo. [iv],240 pp. Contemp mottled calf, upper jnt reprd, spine & crnrs rubbed. Ex Middleton park lib.
(Pickering) **$1,200 [≈ £666]**
- The history of England, from the invasion of Julius Caesar to the Revolution in 1688. London: for T. Cadell, 1773. 8 vols. 8vo. 2 vols with some soiling & foxing. Contemp smooth calf, spines heavily gilt, generally worn, some spine ends ragged.
(Pirages) **$450 [≈ £250]**
- Philosophical essays concerning human understanding. London: for M. Cooper, 1751. 2nd edn. 12mo. Contemp calf, front jnt cracked. *(Waterfield's)* **£200 [≈ $360]**

Hume, Sophia

- An exhortation to the inhabitants of South Carolina ... [with] An epistle to the inhabitants of South Carolina ... London: Luke Hind, 1752-54. 2 works in 1 vols. 1st edn & 1st London edn. 152; 114,[ii] pp. Sl dampstain at end. Orig calf, gilt, jnts sl rubbed.   *(Pirages)* **$300 [≈ £166]**

Humphreys, David

- An essay on the life of the Honorable Major-General Israel Putnam ... Middletown [Ct]: for Hudson & Goodwin, 1794. 2nd edn. 12mo. v,[6]-168 pp. Lacking front free endpaper, occas minor foxing, a few light marg stains, lib stamp on title. Contemp calf.
                    (Heritage) **$125 [≈ £69]**

Hunt, Edward

- An abridgement of all the statutes in Ireland in the Reign of King George I. Dublin: Dobson, 1728. [with] The abridgement of statutes of George II. Dublin: Dobson, 1728. Mod half calf, mrbld bds, somewhat wormed.
                    (Emerald Isle) **£40 [≈ $72]**
- An exact abridgement of all the Irish statutes, from ... Edward II to the end of the eighth year of the reign of ... George II. Dublin: 1736. 4to. [6],770, [98 tables], 28 supplement pp, advt leaf. 2 stamps on title, dampstaining. Contemp calf, worn.
                    (Claude Cox) **£45 [≈ $81]**

Hunt, Henry

- A discoverie of the sect of the Banians ... their history, law ... casts, customs, and ceremonies ... 2 parts in 1 volume ... London: for Fra. Constable, 1630. 1st edn. Addtnl engvd title. Sl worming top crnr last 20ff. New old style calf. NSTC 16825.   *(Stewart)* **£285 [≈ $513]**

Hunt, Thomas

- A defence of the Charter, and municipal rights of the City of London ... London: Richard Baldwin, [1682]. 1st edn. Sm 4to. Lightly browned. Cloth-backed bds. Wing H3570.   *(Frew Mackenzie)* **£70 [≈ $126]**
- A defence of the Charter, and municipal rights of the City of London ... London: Richard Baldwin, n.d. [ca 1682]. 4to. Disbound.   *(Stewart)* **£15 [≈ $27]**

Hunter, John

- The natural history of the human teeth ... structure, use, formation, growth and diseases. London: J. Johnson, 1771. 16 plates. [with] A practical treatise on the diseases of the teeth ... a supplement ... London: 1778. 1st edns. 4to. Half-title to pt 2. Half calf.
                    (Halewood) **£850 [≈ $1,530]**
- A treatise on the venereal disease. London: 1786. 1st edn. 4to. [6],395 pp. 7 engvd plates. Contemp calf, rebacked, preserving orig spine. Author's pres copy.
                    (Goodrich) **$1,295 [≈ £719]**
- A treatise on the venereal disease. London: 1786. 1st edn. 4to. 7 engvd plates. Contemp calf, rebacked, orig spine laid down. Author's pres copy.   *(Traylen)* **£550 [≈ $990]**

Hunter, John (1738-1821)

- An historical journal of the transactions at Port Jackson and Norfolk Island ... John Stockdale, 1793. 1st edn. 4to. xvi,583 pp. Engvd port & title (imprint shaved), 15 engvd maps. charts, plates (2 fldg). Tall copy in contemp tree-calf, backstrip gilt.
                    (Blackwell's) **£4,200 [≈ $7,560]**
- An historical journal of the transactions at Port Jackson and Norfolk Island ... London: John Stockdale, 1793. 1st edn. 4to. xvi,583 pp. Engvd port frontis, 10 engvd plates, 5 maps & charts. Title cropped. Mod sprinkled calf, richly gilt. *(Morrell)* **£2,400 [≈ $4,320]**

Hunter, Thomas

- Observations on Tacitus. In which his character as a writer and an historian, is impartially considered, and compared with that of Livy. London: for Richard Manby, 1752. 1st edn. 8vo. 296 pp. Contemp calf, a trifle worn.   *(Fenning)* **£65 [≈ $117]**

Hurdis, James

- Adriano; or the first of June, a poem. London: for J. Johnson, 1792. 2nd edn. 8vo. [iv],105,[3 advts] pp. Half-title. Disbound.
                    (Burmester) **£45 [≈ $81]**
- Cursory remarks upon the arrangement of the plays of Shakespeare ... London: for J. Johnson, 1792. 1st edn. 8vo. 55 pp. Disbound.   *(Burmester)* **£130 [≈ $234]**
- Poems. London: for J. Johnson, 1790. 1st edn. 8vo. vi,[ii], 154,[2 advts] pp. Fldg engvd plan. Contemp calf, spine rubbed, label chipped.   *(Burmester)* **£120 [≈ $216]**
- Reflections upon the commencement of a new year. London: for James Johnson, 1793. 1st edn. 8vo. 20 pp. Disbound.
                    (Burmester) **£150 [≈ $270]**
- Select critical remarks upon the English version of the first ten chapters of Genesis. London: for J. Johnson, 1793. 1st edn. 8vo. [iv],xii, 34,[2] pp. Half-title, errata leaf, final advt leaf. Disbound.
                    (Burmester) **£90 [≈ $162]**
- Sir Thomas More: a tragedy. London: for J.

Johnson, 1793. 2nd edn. 8vo. 132 pp. Disbound. *(Burmester)* **£35 [≈ $63]**

Hurt, Monsieur, Bishop of Avranches
- The history of the commerce and navigation of the ancients. Made English ... 1717. 1st English edn. [xxx],265 pp. Advts. Foxing throughout. Panelled calf, sl worn, upper jnt cracked, upper bd loose, backstrip chipped.
(Old Cinema) **£65 [≈ $117]**

Hurtley, Thomas of Malham
- A concise account of some natural curiosities in the environs of Malham, in Craven, Yorkshire. London: Logographic Press, 1786. 1st edn. 8vo. 3 fldg plates, subscribers' list, 199 pp appendix. Calf.
(Halewood) **£98 [≈ $176]**

Husbandman ...
- The good husbandman's jewel ... to know the means whereby horses, sheep, &c. come to have ... diseases; the way to cure them perfectly ... Preston: W. Smith, n.d. [ca 1750]. 12mo. W'cuts on title & last page. A bit dog-eared & dust-marked. Mod qtr calf.
(Charles Cox) **£105 [≈ $189]**

Husbandry ...
- Select essays on husbandry, extracted from the Museum Rusticum, and foreign essays on agriculture. Edinburgh: for John Balfour, 1767. 8vo. x,408 pp. Advt leaf, 2 engvd plates, fldg table. Contemp calf, jnts partly cracked, minor wear. *(Pirages)* **$300 [≈ £166]**

Hutcheson, Archibald
- An abstract of all the publick debts remaining due at Michaelmas, 1722 ... some remarks and hints offer'd ... for the improvement of the revenue, by good husbandry ... London: T. Payne, 1723. 1st edn. Folio. 27 pp. Orig mrbld wraps. *(Burmester)* **£45 [≈ $81]**

Hutcheson, Francis
- An inquiry into the original of our ideas of beauty and virtue; in two treatises. London: for J. & J. Knapton, 1729. 3rd edn, crrctd. 8vo. xxii,[2],304 pp. Some occas spotting. Contemp calf, rebacked.
(Spelman) **£280 [≈ $504]**
- An inquiry into the original of our ideas of beauty and virtue; in two treatises. London: for J. & J. Knapton ..., 1729. 3rd edn, crrctd. 8vo. Contemp calf, rebacked.
(Waterfield's) **£165 [≈ $297]**
- A short introduction to moral philosophy, in three books. Glasgow: Robert & Andrew Foulis, 1764. 3rd edn in English. 2 vols.

12mo. ix,[xv],186; [ii],189-373, [3] pp. Occas sl soiling. Contemp speckled calf, a little worn, 1 jnt weak, lacking 1 label.
(Burmester) **£160 [≈ $288]**
- A system of moral philosophy ... prefixed some account of the life, writings, and character of the author ... Glasgow printed: R. & A. Foulis ..., 1775. 1st edn. 2 vols. 4to. Dedn leaf, 6 pp subscribers. Blank margs last 2 leaves reprd. New calf, gilt.
(Traylen) **£900 [≈ $1,620]**

Hutchinson, B.
- Biographia medica; or, historical and critical memoirs of the lives and writings of the most eminent medical characters ... London: 1799. 1st edn. 2 vols. 8vo. Marg repr on 1 leaf. Half niger mor. *(Halewood)* **£150 [≈ $270]**

Hutchinson, Francis
- A defence of the compassionate address to Papists. London: D. Midwinter, 1718. Mrbld bds. *(Emerald Isle)* **£75 [≈ $135]**
- An historical essay concerning witchcraft. London: R. Knaplock, 1718. 8vo. Contemp calf, rebacked, Ex Kimbolton Castle Library.
(Emerald Isle) **£220 [≈ $396]**
- An historical essay concerning witchcraft ... And also two sermons. 1718. Lea, spine rubbed, worn hinges shaken.
(Edwards) **£260 [≈ $468]**

Hutchinson, John
- An abstract from the works ... being a summary of his discoveries in philosophy and divinity. London: for E. Withers, 1755. 2nd edn, crrctd. 8vo. Cancel title. Contemp calf.
(Waterfield's) **£225 [≈ $405]**

Hutchinson, Thomas
- The history of the Colony of Massachuset's Bay, from the first settlement thereof in 1628 until ... 1691. London: M. Richardson, 1765. 2nd edn. 8vo. iv,66 pp. Contemp speckled calf, rebacked, 1 gathering sprung, crnrs lightly bumped.
(Frew Mackenzie) **£180 [≈ $324]**

Hutchinson, W.
- An excursion to the Lakes in Westmoreland and Cumberland; with a tour through part of the Northern Counties, in the years 1773 and 1774. London: J. Wilkie, 1776. 1st edn. 8vo. Many fldg plates, other ills tipped-in. New buckram. *(Argosy)* **$150 [≈ £83]**
- The history of the county of Cumberland ... Carlisle: F. Jollie, 1794. 1st edn. 2 vols. 4to. 2 engvd vignette titles, lge fldg map hand-cold

in outline, 3 fldg plans (worn at folds), 51 plates. Sl browned throughout, occas spotted. Rec qtr calf.   *(Kerr)* £300 [≈ $540]

Hutton, Charles
- The compendious measurer; being a brief, yet comprehensive treatise of mensuration and practical geometry adapted for the use of schools and practice. London: 1790. 2nd edn. xii,323 pp. Num text diags. Contemp lea bds, rebacked.   *(Whitehart)* £40 [≈ $72]
- A mathematical and philosophical dictionary. London: 1795-96. 1st edn. 2 vols. 4to. viii,650; 756 pp. 37 engvd plates, num text ills. Contemp calf, rebacked.
        (Frew Mackenzie) £275 [≈ $495]
- A mathematical and philosophical dictionary containing mathematics, astronomy ... London: J. Johnson, 1796-95. 1st edn. 2 vols. 4to. viii,650; ii,756 pp. 12 & 25 engvd plates. Contemp sgntr of Thos. Maugham on titles. Contemp tree sheep, gilt sides, rebacked.
        (Pickering) $800 [≈ £444]
- A mathematical and philosophical dictionary. London: for J. Johnson ..., 1795-96. 1st edn. 2 vols. 4to. 37 engvd plates. New half antique calf, gilt, mor labels, gilt.
        (Traylen) £190 [≈ $342]
- A mathematical and philosophical dictionary containing an explanation of the terms, and an account of ... mathematics, astronomy ... London: Johnson, 1796-95. 1st edns. 2 vols. 4to. viii,650; ii,756 pp. 17 & 20 engvd plates. Tree-calf, rebacked, crnrs reprd.
        (Pollak) £175 [≈ $315]
- A treatise on mensuration, both in theory and practice. Newcastle-upon-Tyne: for the author, 1770. 1st edn. 4to. Engvd plate, num figs (by Thomas bewick), list of subscribers, errata leaf. Half crimson mor, gilt.
        (Traylen) £330 [≈ $594]

Huxham, John
- An essay on fevers, and their various kinds, as depending on different constitutions of the blood ... London: for S. Austen, 1750. 2nd edn. 8vo. xvi,288 pp. 1st gathering springing. Contemp calf, lightly rubbed.
        (Frew Mackenzie) £140 [≈ $252]
- Medical and chemical observations upon antimony. John Hinton, 1756. 1st edn. 8vo. [iv],78,[ii] pp. Dedn leaf sgnd 'A', half-title, advt leaf at end, interleaved copy. Inscrptn on title. New qtr calf over orig mrbld bds.
        (Blackwell's) £100 [≈ $180]

Hyde, Edward, Earl of Clarendon
- Animadversions upon a book, intituled

Fanaticism fanatically imputed to the Catholic Church ... London: for R. Royston, 1674. 2nd edn. 8vo. [vi],262 pp. Old calf, rebacked. Wing C4415.
        (Young's) £36 [≈ $64]

Hymn ...
- A hymn to victory ... See Defoe, Daniel

Ides, E. Ysbrandszoon
- Three years travels from Moscow over-land to China ... done into English. London: W. Freeman ..., 1706. 4to. [xii],210 pp. Addtnl engvd title, fldg map, 30 plates (8 fldg, 1 panorama, occas tiny wormholes). Light browning. Contemp calf, rebacked, a.e.g.
        (Frew Mackenzie) £700 [≈ $1,260]

The Idler
- The Idler ... See Samuel Johnson

Idol ...
- The idol of the clownes ... See Cleveland, John

Ilavater, John Caspar
- Essays on physiognomy, designed to promote the knowledge and the love of mankind ... Translated from the French ... London: for John Murray ..., 1789-98. 5 vols. 4to. 4to. Num engvd plates, vignettes & ills in text. Contemp diced calf, gilt, v sl worn.
        (Traylen) £595 [≈ $1,071]

Indiana
- The life, misfortunes and adventures of Indiana, the virtuous orphan. Written by herself. London: printed by M. Read, 1755. 3rd edn. Engvd frontis, 2 plates (1 fldg with tear, without loss). Contemp qtr calf, mrbld bds.   *(C.R. Johnson)* £650 [≈ $1,170]

Ingen-Housz, John
- Experiments upon vegetables, discovering their great power of purifying the common air in the sun-shine, and of injuring it in the shade and at night. London: for P. Elmsly & H. Payne, 1779. 1st edn. 8vo. Fldg engvd plate. Contemp calf, rebacked.
        (Traylen) £850 [≈ $1,530]

Inhabitants of Pennsylvania ...
- An address to the inhabitants of Pennsylvania ... See Pemberton, Israel

Innes, Thomas
- A critical essay on the ancient inhabitants of the Northern parts of Britain, or Scotland ...

Glasgow: for William Innys, 1729. 2 vols. 8vo. 2 fldg genealogical tables (1 reprd). Sl foxing. Later mor, gilt extra.
(Cooper Hay) £95 [≈ $171]
- A critical essay on the ancient inhabitants of the Northern parts of Britain, or Scotland ... Glasgow: for William Innys, 1729. 1st edn. Lge paper. 2 vols. 4to. 2 fldg tables. Late 19th c full black crushed mor, gilt borders on sides, gilt panelled spine. *(Traylen)* £240 [≈ $432]

Inquiry ...
- A critical inquiry into the opinions ... of the ancient philosophers ... See Towne, John
- A free and candid inquiry humbly addressed to the representatives of the several counties and boroughs in this kingdom ... Dublin: S. Powell, 1763. 2nd edn. 43 pp. Disbound.
(C.R. Johnson) £38 [≈ $68]
- A free inquiry into the nature and origin of evil. In six letters ... London: 1757. 2nd edn. 12mo. Half-title, vignette title. Contemp calf, spine worn. *(Halewood)* £30 [≈ $54]
- An inquiry into the fitness of attending Parliament in a letter from a member to his friend, who has absented. London: T. Cooper, 1739. 28 pp. Rebound in bds.
(C.R. Johnson) £38 [≈ $68]
- An inquiry into the manner of creating Peers ... See West, Richard
- An inquiry into the share which King Charles I had in the transactions of the Earl of Glamorgan ... See Birch, Thomas

Instructions ...
- Instructions for collecting and preserving insects ... See Curtis, William

Interest ...
- The interest of Great Britain steadily pursued ... See Walpole, Horatio

Interview ...
- The Royal interview ... See Combe, William

Introduction ...
- A concise introduction to the knowledge of the most eminent painters. London: Cadell, 1778. 8vo. Title, 65ff. Qtr calf, rebacked.
(Marlborough) £85 [≈ $153]

Ireland, J.
- Vindicae Regiae; or a defence of the kingly office. In two letters to the Earl of Stanhope. London: for J. Wright, 1797. 2nd edn. 8vo. 79 pp. 4 pp advts at end, half-title. New bds.
(Claude Cox) £15 [≈ $27]

Ireland, Samuel
- Miscellaneous papers and legal instruments under the hand and seal of William Shakespeare. 1796. 1st 8vo edn. Fldg frontis ptd both sides. Half canvas bds, uncut.
(Halewood) £78 [≈ $140]
- A picturesque tour through Holland, Brabant, and part of France ... London: for T. Egerton ..., 1796. 2nd edn. 2 vols. 8vo. xx,217; iv,211 pp. 2 addtnl engvd titles, 48 aquatint plates in sepia. Light marg browning. Contemp mor, hinges & edges rubbed. *(Claude Cox)* £225 [≈ $405]
- A picturesque tour through Holland, Brabant, and part of France; made in the autumn of 1789. London: 1790. 1st edn. 2 vols. 8vo. 47 plates (mainly tinted). Some minor foxing & offsetting. Contemp russia, jnts a little weak, spines sl rubbed.
(Bow Windows) £375 [≈ $675]
- Picturesque views on the River Medway. 1793. 1st edn. xii,206 pp. Half-title, addtnl mezzotint half-title, 28 mezzotint plates, map. Half calf, gilt, upper hinge tender.
(Edwards) £160 [≈ $288]
- Picturesque views on the Upper, or Warwickshire Avon. London: R. Faulder ..., 1795. 1st edn. xviii,284,[i errata] pp. Sepia aquatint frontis, 29 sepia aquatint plates, 2 etched ports, engvd plan. Occas light marg foxing & faint offsetting. Contemp red mor.
(Gough) £295 [≈ $531]

Ives, Edward
- A voyage from England to India in the year MDCCLIV. London: Dilly, 1773. 1st edn. 4to. xii,506 pp. 13 engvd plates (1 fldg), 2 fldg maps (1 with short tear reprd). 1 or 2 leaves sl spotted. Contemp mottled calf, rebacked, orig spine laid down, little rubbed.
(Morrell) £320 [≈ $576]

Ives, John
- Remarks upon the Garianonum ... London: Hooper, 1774. 1st edn. Sm 8vo. [iii],54 pp. Half-title, 6 engvd plates & plans (some fldg). Calf, front hinge split. *(P & P)* £48 [≈ $86]

Jack, Richard
- Elements of conic section in three books. Edinburgh: Tho. Wal & Tho. Ruddimans, 1742. 1st edn. 8vo. [iv],xi,331 pp. 9 fldg engvd plates. Mrbld bds, calf spine.
(Burmester) £85 [≈ $153]

Jackson, Robert (1750-1827)
- A treatise on the fevers of Jamaica, with some observations on the intermitting fever of

America, and an appendix ... on the means of preserving the health of soldiers in hot climates. Phila: 1795. 1st Amer edn. 12mo. Contemp calf, worn. Ex lib.
(Argosy) **$200** [≃ **£111**]

Jackson, Thomas
- The works ... such as were, as such as never before were printed. With the author's life ... London: Andrew Clark, 1673, 3 vols. Folio. Sl marg worming in vol 3. New grey bds, paper labels. Wing J90.
(Stewart) **£100** [≃ **$180**]

Jackson, William
- Thirty letters on various subjects. London: for T. Cadell ..., 1795. 3rd edn. 8vo. viii,236 pp. Without half-title. Contemp tree-calf, gilt backstrip. Capel Cure b'plate.
(Claude Cox) **£30** [≃ **$54**]

Jacob, Giles
- The compleat court-keeper; or, land-steward's assistant ... London: for B. Lintot ..., 1715. 2nd edn. 8vo. viii,480,[21 index],[3 advts] pp. Sm name stamp on title. Contemp calf.
(Fenning) **£85** [≃ **$153**]
- A new law-dictionary. 1750. 6th edn. Folio. Contemp calf, some slitting to hinges.
(Edwards) **£140** [≃ **$252**]
- The new law-dictionary: containing the definition of words and terms ... In the Savoy: 1743. 8vo. [608] pp. Inked initials on title verso, lower crnr torn from leaf with loss of a few letters. Contemp calf, spine ends worn, jnts beginning to crack.
(Bow Windows) **£95** [≃ **$171**]
- A new law-dictionary: containing, the interpretation and definition of words and terms used in the law. London: Henry Lintot, 1744. Folio. Unpaginated. 5th edn. Browned. New panelled speckled calf.
(Frew Mackenzie) **£285** [≃ **$513**]
- A new law-dictionary ... now corrected and greatly enlarged by J. Morgan. London: W. Strahan ..., 1782. 10th edn. Folio. Contemp calf, rebacked. *(Waterfield's)* **£85** [≃ **$153**]

Jacob, J.
- Observations on the structure and draught of wheel-carriages. London: 1773. 1st edn. 4to. Half-title, 14 fldg plates. Contemp half calf, mrbld bds, jnts sl cracking.
(Halewood) **£375** [≃ **$675**]
- Observations on the structure and draught of wheel-carriages. London: E. & C. Dilly, 1773. 1st edn. 4to. 14 fldg plates. Contemp half calf, respined, orig label.
(Spelman) **£550** [≃ **$990**]

Jago, Richard
- Edge-Hill, or, the rural prospect delineated and moralized. A poem. In four books. London: Dodsley, 1767. 1st edn. 4to. xix,[iv],164 pp. Half-title, 4 engvd vignettes. Some light spotting. Contemp half calf, mrbld sides, lightly rubbed.
(Frew Mackenzie) **£200** [≃ **$360**]
- Edge-Hill, or, the rural prospect delineated and moralized. A poem. In four books. London: J. Dodsley, 1767. 4to. Half-title. Contemp calf spine, mrbld bds.
(C.R. Johnson) **£240** [≃ **$432**]

Jamaica ...
- An abridgement of the laws of Jamaica ... St. Jago de la Vega: Alexander Aikman, 1793. Contemp calf, jnts cracked.
(Farahar) **£225** [≃ **$405**]
- The laws of Jamaica ... St. Jago de la Vega: Alexander Aikman, 1792. 2 vols. Thick 4to. Orig calf, rebacked. *(Farahar)* **£500** [≃ **$900**]

James, Robert
- A dissertation on fevers, and inflammatory distempers. The eighth edition ... now first added ... a vindication of the fever powder. London: for Francis Newbery, jnr, 1778. 8vo. Engvd port frontis. Contemp polished calf.
(Quaritch) **$975** [≃ **£541**]
- A medicinal dictionary. London: 1743-45. 1st edn. 3 vols. Thick folio. Unpaginated, ptd in double column. 63 plates. 3 leaves with sm loss of text, replaced in facsimile on old paper. Mod lea. *(Scientia)* **$2,000** [≃ **£1,111**]
- Pharmacopoeia universalis: or, a new universal English dispensatory. London: for J. Hodges, 1747. 8vo. xxxi,[i], 836,[xlviii] pp. Later half calf, 2 lower crnrs with marg tears, half-title & last leaf with some old splashes & some v sm holes. Later half calf.
(Pollak) **£75** [≃ **$135**]
- A treatise on canine madness. London: Newberry, 1760. 8vo. vi,264 pp. Light foxing. Old calf, rebacked, crude endpapers.
(Goodrich) **$495** [≃ **£269**]

James, Thomas
- An account of King's College Chapel, in Cambridge ... Cambridge: for the author ..., 1769. 1st edn. iv,92 pp. Engvd frontis, plate. Disbound. *(Young's)* **£38** [≃ **$68**]

Jameson, Robert
- An outline of the mineralogy of the Shetland Isles, and of the Island of Arran. With an appendix ... observations on peat, kelp, and coal. Edinburgh: for William Creech, 1798.

Roy 8vo. Engvd plate, 2 maps (1 fldg). Contemp half calf, gilt spine.
(Traylen) £150 [≈ $270]
- Outline of the mineralogy of the Shetland Islands and the Islands of Arran, with an appendix on peat, kelp and coal ... Edinburgh: Creech, 1798. Lge 8vo. 2 engvd maps, engvd plate. Final leaf stained. Contemp mrbld bds, uncut, spine renewed.
(Marlborough) £210 [≈ $378]

Jebb, Fred
- Considerations on the expediency of a National Circulation Bank at this time in Ireland. Dublin: R. Marchbank, 1790. 8vo. Bds. *(Emerald Isle)* £110 [≈ $198]
- The letters of Guatimozin on the affairs of Ireland ... to which are added letters of Causidicus [Robert Johnson] that accompanied the essays of Guatimozin. Dublin: R. Marchbank, 1779. 8vo. Bds.
(Emerald Isle) £75 [≈ $135]

Jefferys, Thomas
- An account of the maritime parts of France ... fortified towns, forts, harbours, bays, and rivers ... London: for Faden & Jefferys ..., 1774. 2nd edn. 2 vols. Obl 4to. 87 plates (some misnumbered). Repairs to some leaves of index. Contemp half calf, sl rubbed.
(Hughes) £575 [≈ $1,035]
- An account of the Spanish Islands and settlements ... of the West Indies. London: Faden ..., 1774. 2nd edn. 4to. [iv],xxiv, 106,[2 index] pp. 32 fldg plans & charts, Lightly browned. 19th c half calf, rebacked, orig backstrip preserved, crnrs rubbed.
(Morrell) £2,400 [≈ $4,320]
- The natural and civil history of the French Dominions of North America and South America ... London: 1760. 2 vols in 1. 168; 246 pp (but num errors in pagination). 18 lge fldg engvd maps & plans, some reprd. Mod calf over orig bds. *(Reese)* $7,500 [≈ £4,166]

Jeffries, John
- A narrative of the two aerial voyages of ... with meteorological observations and remarks ... from London into Kent ... from England into France ... London: the author, 1786. 4to. 60 pp. Port frontis, plate. Uncut, orig blue wraps. Author's grandson pres copy.
(Weiner) £500 [≈ $900]

Jenner, Charles
- The placid man: or, memoirs of Sir Charles Beville. In two volumes. London: J. Wilkie, 1770. Contemp calf, red labels.
(C.R. Johnson) £585 [≈ $1,053]

Jenner, Thomas (publisher)
- A description & plat of the sea-coasts of England. London: for Thomas Jenner, 1753. 1st edn. Sm 4to. [vi],41,[46] pp. 2 fldg engvd maps. 1 map shaved to plate-mark at 1 marg, strengthened at folds, 1 or 2 side-notes shaved, a few sl marks. 19th c mor, rubbed.
(Ash) £2,000 [≈ $3,600]

Jenyns, Soames
- The works ... including several pieces never before published. London: Cadell, 1790. 1st edn. 4 vols. 8vo. Engvd port. 2 sm lib stamps on each title. Contemp mottled calf, gilt, 1 jnt strained. *(Marlborough)* £150 [≈ $270]

Jephson, Robert
- The Count of Narbonne, a tragedy. London: for T. Cadell, 1781. 1st edn. 8vo. [viii],80,[iv] pp. Interleaved with blanks. Contemp calf, jnts & edges blank, in fldg cloth box.
(Pirages) $175 [≈ £97]

Johnson, Ben
- The works. 1716. 6 vols. 2700 pp. 3 frontis. Half calf, gilt, sl rubbed, mrbld bds.
(Edwards) £250 [≈ $450]

Johnson, Captain Charles
- A general history of the robberies and murders of the most notorious pyrates ... See Defoe, Daniel

Johnson, Charles
- The victim. A tragedy as it is acted at the Theatre Royal ... London: Ferd Burleigh, 1714. 1st edn. 12mo. [x],64,[4] pp. Engvd frontis. Calf-backed bds.
(Young's) £50 [≈ $90]

Johnson, James
- A sermon preached before the Incorporated Society for the Propagation of the Gospel in Foreign Parts ... February 24, 1758. London: E. Owen ..., 1758. 1st edn. 8vo. 77 pp. Orig wraps. *(Young's)* £28 [≈ $50]

Johnson, John
- The advantages and disadvantages of the marriage state. As enter'd into with religious or irreligious persons. Deliver'd under the similitude of a dream. Leedes: Griffith Wright, 1760. 1st edn (?). Slim 8vo. [32] pp. Title browned, some spotting.
(Chaucer Head) £120 [≈ $216]
- The primitive communicant; in three discourses on the Sacrament of the Church ... Manchester: Mrs Mary Johnson, 1738. 2nd

edn. 151 pp. Orig thick paper wraps, stabbed as issued.   *(C.R. Johnson)* **£45 [≈ $81]**

Johnson, Samuel

- A dictionary of the English language. London: J. & P. Knapton, 1755-56. 2nd edn. Folio. 2 vols. Unpaginated. Ptd in 2 columns. Red & black titles. Lib stamps on title versos, early leaves 1st vol with minor crnr dampstaining. Half calf, rebacked, sides rubbed.   *(Frew Mackenzie)* **£980 [≈ $1,764]**

- A dictionary of the English language .. abstracted from the folio edition ... London: for J. Knapton ..., 1760. 2nd edn, crrctd. 2 vols. Contemp calf, inelegantly rebacked.   *(Waterfield's)* **£125 [≈ $225]**

- A dictionary ... London: Millar ..., 1766. 3rd (abrdgd) edn. 2 vols. 8vo. Contemp calf.   *(Marlborough)* **£250 [≈ $450]**

- A dictionary of the English language. London: for Rivington ..., 1785. 2 vols. Folio. Port frontis (backed). 1st & last leaves in each vol browned, minor discoloration elsewhere. Contemp mrbld bds, later calf spine & crnrs, spine gilt, minor shelfwear.   *(Pirages)* **$750 [≈ £416]**

- Dr. Johnson's table-talk: containing aphorisms on literature, life, and manners. London: for C. Dilly, 1798. 1st edn. 8vo. [vi],446 pp. Old lib stamp on title. Early 19th c half calf, rebacked, bds rubbed.   *(Burmester)* **£85 [≈ $153]**

- The Idler. London: for J. Newbery, 1761. 1st coll edn. 2 vols. 12mo. [viii],294; [vi],285,[3] pp. Contemp speckled calf, spines gilt, spine a little worn, labels missing.   *(Burmester)* **£160 [≈ $288]**

- The Idler ... With additional essays. London: for J. Hodge ..., 1790. 6th edn. 2 vols. Port. Contemp calf, gilt, lacking labels, hinges cracked.   *(Claude Cox)* **£22 [≈ $39]**

- The Idler ... With additional essays. London: for J. Hodge ..., 1790. 6th edn. 2 vols. 12mo. [iv],221,[3]; [iv],247 pp. Contemp half calf, jnts sl rubbed.   *(Burmester)* **£50 [≈ $90]**

- A journey to the Western Islands of Scotlands. Dublin: J. Williams, 1775. 1st Dublin edn. 8vo. Contemp calf.   *(Robertshaw)* **£115 [≈ $207]**

- A journey to the Western Islands. London: Strahan, 1775. 1st edn. D8/U4 cancelled, U4v correctly numbered. Title foxed, some margs thumbed. Later half red mor.   *(Marlborough)* **£260 [≈ $468]**

- A journey to the Western Isles of Scotland. London: for W. Strahan ..., 1775. 8vo. Contemp calf, front jnt cracked. Todd 'B'.   *(Waterfield's)* **£135 [≈ $243]**

- A journey to the Western islands of Scotland. Edinburgh: For Mundell ..., 1798. New edn. 8vo. [iv],288 pp. Some foxing. Contemp tree-calf, by Woodward of Liverpool, sl rubbed.   *(Burmester)* **£60 [≈ $108]**

- The lives of the English poets; and a criticism of their works. Dublin: for Whitestone ..., 1779-81. 3 vols. 8vo. Minor discoloration on a few pages. Contemp smooth calf, rec rebacked.   *(Pirages)* **$325 [≈ £180]**

- The lives of the most eminent English poets. 1781-81-83-83. 4 vols. Vols 1 & 2 1st edn, vols 3 & 4 2nd edn. 480; 471; 432; 485 pp. Port frontis vol I. Prelims spotted in 2 vols. Calf, spines dec gilt, 2 vols rebound.   *(Edwards)* **£100 [≈ $180]**

- The lives of the most eminent English poets ... A new edition, corrected. London: for T. Longman ..., 1794. 4 vols. 8vo. Engvd port frontis. Some sl marg staining in earlier leaves. Mod qtr calf, uncut.   *(Waterfield's)* **£80 [≈ $144]**

- Marmor Norfolcience: or an essay on recent prophetical inscription ... lately discover'd near Lynn in Norfolk. London: for J. Brett, 1739. 1st edn, iss with 'Finis'. 8vo. [3]-55 pp. Lacking half-title. Sl spotting, ink anntns on endpapers. 18th c half calf.   *(Frew Mackenzie)* **£1,500 [≈ $2,700]**

- The poetical works ... now first collected in one volume. London: for the editor, 1785. 1st edn. 8vo 4 pp advts. Contemp calf, hinges strained.   *(Chaucer Head)* **£200 [≈ $360]**

- The poetical works ... now first collected in one volume. London: for the editor, 1785. 1st edn. 8vo. viii,196,4 advts pp. Contemp polished calf, gilt. Ex lib the Lord Clonmore with his engvd b'plate.   *(Frew Mackenzie)* **£400 [≈ $720]**

- The poetical works ... now first collected in one volume. London: for the editor, 1785. 1st edn. viii,196 pp, 2 advts ff. 2 pp yellowed, 1 short tear. Contemp tree-calf, rec rebacked.   *(Pirages)* **$275 [≈ £152]**

- Political tracts. Containing, the False Alarm, Falkland's Islands, The Patriot; and Taxation no Tyranny. London: for W. Strahan ..., 1776. 1st coll edn. 8vo. [iv],264 pp. Fly-title to each part. Contemp calf, spine elab gilt, rubbed, jnts worn. 18th c b'plate.   *(Burmester)* **£300 [≈ $540]**

- The Rambler. London: for A. Miller ..., 1763. 6th edn. 4 vols. 12mo. Contemp calf, spines gilt, minor traces of wear, labels missing.   *(Burmester)* **£90 [≈ $162]**

- The Rambler. Eighth edition. [Edinburgh?:] Printed in the year 1772. 4 vols. 12mo. Contemp speckled calf, spines gilt, 3 labels

defective, some rubbing.
(Burmester) £75 [≈ $135]

Johnson, Samuel, et al.
- Miscellaneous and fugitive pieces. London: for T. Davies (vol III, T. Davies; & Carnan & Newbery), 1774. 2nd edn, crrctd (vol III, 2nd edn). 3 vols. 8vo. [iv],375; [iv],360; viii,311 pp. Some light spotting, tear in 1 leaf. Contemp calf, spines gilt.
(Burmester) £225 [≈ $405]

Johnson, Samuel, Vicar of Torrington
- Scripture-doctrine of Christ's divinity ... necessary supremacy of God considered. London: Samuel Birt, 1729. Lea, hinges & edges worn. *(Xerxes)* $125 [≈ £69]

Johnston, Nathaniel
- The excellency of monarchical government, especially of the English monarchy. London: for Robert Clavel, 1686. Folio. [xii],480, [viii] pp. Initial licence leaf, final errata page, 7 pp ctlg. Tear in 5 leaves reprd. Contemp calf, rebacked. Wing J877. *(Clark)* £135 [≈ $243]

Johnston, Thomas
- General view of the agriculture of the county of Selkirk, with observations. London: W. Bulmer, 1794. 1st edn. 4to. 50 pp, final blank. Half-title. Disbound.
(Claude Cox) £30 [≈ $54]

Johnstone, Charles
- Chrysal; or the adventures of a guinea ... by an adept. London: for T. Becket, 1760. 1st edn. 2 vols. Later half sheep, jnts breaking, rubbed. *(Waterfield's)* £25 [≈ $45]

Johnstone, James
- Antiquitates Celto-Normannicae ... the Chronicle of Man and the Isles ... [and] Antiquitates Celto Scandicae. 2 works in 1 vol. Both Copenhagen: 1786. 1st part Latin & English text. Later calf, rubbed, old reback preserving spine.
(Marlborough) £150 [≈ $270]
- The Norwegian account of Haco's expedition against Scotland; A.D. 1263 ... with a literal English version ... London: for the author, 1782. 1st edn. xv,143,[14] pp. Lacking half-title & dedn leaf. Light staining in crnr throughout. Rec calf-backed mrbld bds.
(Claude Cox) £40 [≈ $72]

Johnstone, John
- An account of the most approved method of draining land; according to the system practised by Mr. Joseph Elkington in the

County of Warwick. Edinburgh: 1797. 1st ed. 4to. 16 plates. Later bds, cloth spine, uncut.
(Robertshaw) £40 [≈ $72]

Jones, David
- A farewel sermon preached to the United parishes of St. Mary Woolnoth, & St. Mary Woolchurch-Haw in Lombard Street. London: 1692. 4th edn. 4to. 41 pp. Disbound. Wing J930. *(Young's)* £40 [≈ $72]

Jones, Griffith
- A short view of the controversie about episcopacy and our church communion. In a letter to a friend of the Presbyterian perswasion in Chester. Chester: W. Cooke, 1720. 2nd edn. 20 pp. Disbound.
(Robertshaw) £10 [≈ $18]

Jones, Henry
- Kew Gardens. A poem. In two cantos. London: J. Browne, 1767. 4to. 45 pp. Qtr calf, mrbld bds.
(C.R. Johnson) £220 [≈ $396]
- Shrewsbury quarry [etc.]. A poem. Shrewsbury: J. Eddowes, 1769. Rebound in bds. *(C.R. Johnson)* £225 [≈ $405]

Jones, Henry, Dr.
- A remonstrance of passages concerning the Church and Kingdome of Ireland. London: G. Emerson, 1642. Sm 4to. Half calf.
(Emerald Isle) £120 [≈ $216]

Jones, Robert
- Artificial fire-works, improved to the modern practice, from the minutest to the higher branches. London: J. Millan, 1766. 2nd edn. 8vo. xxvi, errata, 262 pp. 8 fldg plates. Some faint waterstaining to early lower margs. Rec half calf. *(Spelman)* £420 [≈ $756]

Jones, Stephen
- The history of Poland, from its origin as a nation to ... 1795 ... an accurate account of the geography ... customs and manners of its inhabitants. Dublin: W. Porter, 1795. 1st Irish edn. 8vo. vii,[4],500, [15] pp. Fldg map. Sl later half calf. *(Fenning)* £35 [≈ $63]

Jones, William
- An essay on the first principles of natural philosophy ... in four books. Oxford: 1762. 4to. 3ff, 281 pp. 3 plates (2 fldg). Old polished calf, worn, lacking label, front jnt cracked.
(Weiner) £250 [≈ $450]

Jonson, Ben
- Q. Horatius Flaccus: his art of poetry. Englished by ... With other workes of the author. London: 1640. 1st edn. 12mo. Lacking engvd title (supplied in facs) & 3 of the 4 blanks. 1st few leaves browned, imprim leaf ragged. Early calf, rebacked. STC 13798.
(Charles Cox) **£150 [≈ $270]**

Jordan, John
- Welcombe Hills, near Stratford upon Avon. A poem, historical and descriptive. London: for the author, 1777. 4to. 48 pp. Disbound.
(C.R. Johnson) **£225 [≈ $405]**

Jortin, J.
- The life of Erasmus. London: Whiston & White, 1758. 1st edn. 4to. vi pp, contents leaf, 630 pp, corrigenda leaf. Frontis port (sl cropped on fore-edge), red & black title, mrbld endpapers (v sl dampstaining & sl foxing). Calf, rebacked.
(P & P) **£68 [≈ $122]**

Josephus, Flavius
- See de Andilly, Arnauld
- The works ... London: Fielding & Walker, 1777. 2 vols. 4to in 2s. iv, subscribers' list, 5-719; 644, index pp. 2 frontis, 2 engvd title, ptd title vol 1, num plates & maps. Extensive worming to margs of last 7 leaves vol 2. Calf, rebacked, rec endpapers.
(P & P) **£78 [≈ $140]**
- The works ... To which are added, a dissertation ... and Christopher Noldius's history of ... Herod the Great ... London: R. Penny, 1732. Folio. Frontis, 2 fldg maps, 5 plates. Some marg worming at beginning without loss. New calf spine, grey bds.
(Stewart) **£100 [≈ $180]**
- The works translated into English by Sir Roger L'Estrange, Knight. London: Richard Sare, 1702. 1st edn. Folio. [iv],1130 pp. Engvd frontis, fldg map, fldg plate, engvd plate. Contemp panelled calf, old rebacking, v rubbed. *(Frew Mackenzie)* **£225 [≈ $405]**

Journey ...
- The journey of Dr. Robert Bongout and his lady to Bath ... See Brag, Robert

Joyfull Newes ...
- Joyfull newes from Ireland ... See Loftus, Edward

Junius
- The letters of Junius in two volumes. London: John Wheble, 1775. 2 vols. 8vo.

xxxvi,324; 264 pp. 2 engvd vignette titles. Contemp calf, gilt, rubbed, a little worn, hinges cracked. Trinity College Dublin gilt badges on sides. *(Claude Cox)* **£28 [≈ $50]**
- Letters. London: T. Bensley, 1799. 2 vols. Roy 8vo. Lge paper. Num engvd vignettes by John bewick. Contemp vellum, sl marked.
(Spelman) **£140 [≈ $252]**

Justice, J.
- The British gardener's new director. Dublin: 1765. 4th edn. 8vo. [xvi],443,[12] pp. 4 plates. Upper marg of title cut away with loss of 1st line of title. Contemp calf, trifle worn, jnts cracked.
(Wheldon & Wesley) **£40 [≈ $72]**

Justification ...
- A justification of the whole proceedings of their majesties King William and Queen Mary ... of the convention, army, ministers of state ... in this great revolution. London: for Randal Taylor ..., 1689. 1st edn. 4to. 37 pp. Disbound. Wing J1264.
(Young's) **£40 [≈ $72]**

Kane, Richard
- Campaigns of King William and the Duke of Marlborough; with remarks on the stratagems by which every battle was won or lost, from 1689, to 1712. London: for J. Millar ..., 1747. 2nd edn. 8vo. [vi],140 pp. Fldg map, 16 engvd plans. Contemp calf.
(Young's) **£74 [≈ $133]**

Kearsley, Geo.
- Kearsley's complete peerage of England, Scotland and Ireland. London: for Geo. Kearsley, 1799, 16mo. xxxvi,584 pp. Addtnl 90 pp engvd coats-of-arms inc 37* & 38*. 4pp reprd without loss. Early 19th c half blue mor, spine gilt. *(Gough)* **£50 [≈ $90]**

Keate, George
- An account of the Pelew Islands. Dublin: Luke White, 1788. 1st Dublin edn. 8vo. xxx,378 pp. Fldg chart, port, 14 plates (1 fldg). Contemp half mor, hinges cracking.
(Lewcock) **£120 [≈ $216]**
- An account of the Pelew Islands. London: for Captain Wilson, 1788. 2nd edn. 4to. xxviii,378 pp. Port frontis, fldg map, 15 plates (1 fldg, all sl foxed & some offsetting). Contemp half calf, mrbld sides, jnts patched, bds rubbed & discold.
(Pirages) **$225 [≈ £125]**
- A short account of the ancient history, present government and laws of the Republic of Geneva. London: for R. & J. Dodsley, 1761.

1st edn. 8vo. xv,[v],218 pp. Fldg engv map. Panelled calf antique.
(Burmester) **£175 [≈ $315]**

Keble, J.
- An assistance to justices of the peace, for the easier performance of their duties. 1683. 1st edn. Folio. 719 pp. Black letter, with privilege leaf. Contemp calf, endpapers renewed. Wing 113A.
(Edwards) **£220 [≈ $396]**

Keill, James
- The anatomy of the humane body abridged. London: Keblewhite, 1698. 1st edn. 12mo. xxii,[ii errata lf, recto blank],328,[6 table],[2 advts] pp. Sm waterstain in crnr of 1st few gatherings, sm sgntrs on title & verso. Contemp sheep, jnts splitting. Wing K131.
(Pickering) **$450 [≈ £250]**
- Essays on several parts of the animal oeconomy. Fourth edition, to which is added, a dissertation concerning the force of the heart, by James Jurin ... London: for George Strahan, 1738. 8vo. 16 pp pub advts. Antique calf.
(Traylen) **£38 [≈ $68]**

Keill, John
- An introduction to the true astronomy. London: J. Buckland, 1769. 6th edn, crrctd. 8vo. [6],xiv,[4], 396,[10] pp. Advt leaf. 28 fldg plates (2 not called for). Contemp calf, sm crack to upper jnt.
(Spelman) **£95 [≈ $171]**

Keith, George Skene
- Tracts on weights, measures and coins. London: Murray, 1791. 4to. Sewn as issued, edges frayed.
(Marlborough) **£85 [≈ $153]**

Kelly, George
- The speech ... st the Bar of the House of Lords ... in his defence against the Bill ... for inflicting pains and penalties upon him ... London: A. Moore, 1723. 4th edn. With remarks ... by Britannicus. W. Wilkins, 1723. Folio. 15,[i]; [iv],22 pp. Disbound.
(Clark) **£15 [≈ $27]**

Kelly, Hugh
- Clementina, a tragedy. London: for E. & C. Dilly. 1771, 1st edn. Mod wraps.
(Waterfield's) **£20 [≈ $36]**
- False delicacy: a comedy. London: for R. Baldwin ..., [1768]. New edn. Engvd frontis, vignette title. Mod wraps.
(Waterfield's) **£20 [≈ $36]**
- The romance of an hour: a comedy. London: for G. Kearsley, 1774. 1st edn. Mod wraps.
(Waterfield's) **£20 [≈ $36]**

- The school for wives, a comedy. London: for T. Becket, 1774. 1st edn. Title becoming detchd & sl damaged in gutter. Mod wraps.
(Waterfield's) **£20 [≈ $36]**
- The school for wives. A comedy. London: T. Becket, 1774. 1st edn. 8vo in 4s. [ii],vi, [viii],88 pp. Disbound. *(Clark)* **£20 [≈ $36]**
- A word to the wise, a comedy. London: for the author, 1774. 1st edn. Mod wraps.
(Waterfield's) **£20 [≈ $36]**

Kendall, A.
- Derwent Priory; or, memoirs of an orphan. In a series of letters. Cork: J. Connor ..., 1799. Contemp calf, some wear.
(C.R. Johnson) **£320 [≈ $576]**

Kennedy, John
- A treatise upon planting, gardening, and the management of the hot-house ... Dublin: for W. Wilson, 1784. 1st Dublin edn. 8vo. xvi,462,[ii advts] pp. Contemp calf.
(Gough) **£125 [≈ $225]**
- A treatise upon planting, gardening. London: 1777. 2nd edn. 2 vols. 8vo. Orig bds, spine worn.lf. *(Wheldon & Wesley)* **£35 [≈ $63]**

Kenrick, William
- The Kapelion, or poetical ordinary; consisting of a great variety of dishes in prose and verse ... [L: 1750]. 1st edn. 8vo. 6 pts with continuous pagination & sgntrs. Frontis, 2 plates of music (all sl shaved). A few headlines cut into. 19th c half calf.
(Hannas) **£550 [≈ $990]**

Kent, N.
- General view of the agriculture of the County of Norfolk. 1794. 1st edn. 4to. Half-title, title, advt leaf, [56] pp. 2 hand-cold aquatint plates. Mod bds, lower crnrs bumped.
(Edwards) **£100 [≈ $180]**

Kent, Nathaniel
- Hints to gentlemen of landed property. London: for J. Dodsley ..., 1776. 2nd edn. 8vo. vii,282,2 ctlg pp. 10 fldg engvd plates. Inner marg wormhole occas affecting a letter. Rec half calf. *(Young's)* **£98 [≈ $176]**

Kent, Samuel
- The grammar of heraldry containing 1. Rules ... II. ... III. A large collection of arms by way of example ... London: for J. Pemberton, 1716. Contemp panelled calf, rebacked, retaining orig backstrip.
(Waterfield's) **£100 [≈ $180]**
- The grammar of heraldry containing 1. Rules

... II. ... III. A large collection of arms ... London: Pemberton, 1716. Contemp calf, worn, jnts weak.   *(Stewart)* **£85 [≈ $153]**

- The grammar of heraldry. London: for J. Pemberton, n.d. [1716?]. xliv,179 pp. Sev hundred hand-cold coats of arms, some gold leafed. A few sm anntns, 1 or 2 headlines grazed, 1 blank marg reprd. Rec mor, gilt.
(Pirages) **$300 [≈ £166]**

Ker, John

- The memoirs of John Ker ... his secret transactions and negotiations in Scotland, England, the Courts of Vienna, Hanover ... London: 1726. Curl's name at hd of advts, p 176 misprinted 761. Sl marg fraying, staining throughout. Contemp calf, rubbed, scuffed.
(Clark) **£55 [≈ $99]**
- The memoirs of John Ker, of Kersland in North Britain ... London: 1726. 1st edn. 2 pts in 1. 8vo. xii,iv,180, [4 index]; viii,184, [6 index] pp. 16 pp pub list. Fldg engvd map (torn & reprd) in part II. Contemp panelled calf, rebacked, crnrs restored.
(Morrell) **£180 [≈ $324]**

Kersey, John

- Dictionarium Anglo-Britannicum: or, a general English dictionary. London: for J. Phillips ..., 1715. 2nd edn, crrctd. Unpaginated, ca 700 pp. Title cut round & mtd, tips of 2 crnrs torn away without loss, some staining. Contemp panelled calf, reprd, rebacked.   *(Claude Cox)* **£120 [≈ $216]**
- The elements of that mathematical art commonly called algebra ... R.& W. Mount ..., 1717. Folio. [ii],24,323 pp. Engvd port, sl defective at 1 crnr, occas rubber stamps. Ex lib in contemp panelled calf, rec rebacked.
(Blackwell's) **£160 [≈ $288]**

Kettilby, Mary

- A collection of above three hundred receipts in cookery, physick and surgery ... the second edition, to which is added, a second part ... London: for Mary Kettilby, 1719. 2 pts in 1. Half-title. Light marg staining. Contemp panelled calf.   *(Traylen)* **£390 [≈ $702]**
- A collection of above three hundred receipts in cookery, physick and surgery ... to which is added, a second part ... London: for Mary Kettilby, 1724. 3rd edn. 2 pts in 1. 8vo. Advt leaf. Contemp panelled calf, rebacked.
(Traylen) **£195 [≈ $351]**

Key ...

- A key to the business of the present S----n: Viz. I. His H---'s speech to his Life Guard of Switzers ... II. Certain important hints ...

London: T. Cooper, 1742. Half-title. 63 pp. Disbound.   *(C.R. Johnson)* **£40 [≈ $72]**

Kid, James

- A letter to a Minister of the Gospel; concerning the Parish of Bathgate. [Edinburgh?:] 1720. Sm 8vo. 64 pp. Some soiling. Later cloth-backed bds.
(Spelman) **£30 [≈ $54]**

Kidgell, John

- A genuine and succinct narrative of a scandalous, obscene, and exceedingly profane libel, entitled An Essay on Woman ... London: James Robson ..., [1763]. 4to. 16 pp. Qtr calf, mrbld bds, ex lib. Author's sgntr on title.   *(C.R. Johnson)* **£220 [≈ $396]**

Kimber, Isaac

- The life of Oliver Cromwell. London: for J. Brotherton, 1731. 3rd edn. 8vo. Port. Contemp calf, worn.   *(Stewart)* **£35 [≈ $63]**

Kindersley, Mrs.

- Letters from the Island of Teneriffe, Brazil, the Cape of Good Hope, and the East Indies. 1777. 8vo. Frontis. Mod half calf.
(Farahar) **£365 [≈ $657]**

King, Edward

- Morsels of criticism tending to illustrate some few passages in the Holy Scriptures upon philosophical principles and an enlarged view of things. London: for J. Nichols, 1788. 4to. Contemp half calf.
(Waterfield's) **£85 [≈ $153]**
- Vestiges of Oxford Castle. or a small fragment of a work ... on the progress of architecture. W. Bulmer, 1796. Sole edn. Lge paper. Folio. [iv],iv.30,[2 drctns to binder] pp. 5 aquatint plates. Pencillings at ft of many pages, broken. Contemp mrbld wraps.
(Blackwell's) **£150 [≈ $270]**

King, William

- The art of cookery, in imitation of Horace's art of poetry ... London: for Benjamin Lintott, [1708]. 1st edn. 8vo. Half-title. Contemp panelled calf, rebacked.
(Traylen) **£105 [≈ $189]**
- The art of cookery, in imitation of Horace's art of poetry ... London: for Benjamin Lintott, 1708. 1st edn. 8vo. [viii],160 pp. Half-title (ink-smudge). Initials at ft of title, some moderate water-marking to prelims. Rebound panelled calf.
(Gough) **£125 [≈ $225]**
- Miscellanies in prose and verse. London: for

B. Lintott ..., n.d. [ca 1705]. [32],536,[2] pp.
12 pts, each with sep title. Final leaf Nn, "the
Table'present. Old panelled calf, rebacked,
crnrs & extremities worn.
(Karmiole) **$175 [≃ £97]**

King, William (1650-1729)
- The state of the Protestants of Ireland under
the late King James's Government. London:
Roycroft, 1692. 4th edn. Contemp calf.
(Emerald Isle) **£95 [≃ $171]**

Kippis, Andrew
- The life of Captain James Cook. London:
1788. xvi,527 pp. Port. Calf, rebacked.
(Reese) **$300 [≃ £166]**

Kirby, Joshua
- Dr. Brook Taylor's method of perspective
made easy, both in theory and practice ...
Ipswich: for the author, 1755. 2nd edn. 2 vols
in 1. 4to. 2ff, iv,xvi,78 pp; title, 84 pp, 6ff.
Engvd frontis, 50 plates. Contemp calf,
rebacked. *(Marlborough)* **£360 [≃ $648]**
- An historical account of the twelve prints of
monasteries, castles ... in the County of
Suffolk ... Ipswich: Craighton, 1748. 8vo. 2ff,
36,[4 subscribers' list] pp. 5 engvd plates.
Interleaved. Contemp speckled calf,
rebacked. *(Marlborough)* **£185 [≃ $333]**
- An historical account of the twelve prints of
monasteries, castles ... in the County of
Suffolk ... published March 26, 1748.
Ipswich: Craighton, 1748. [4],36,[4
subscribers' list] pp. 6 plates. Interleaved
throughout. Contemp calf, rejointed.
(Spelman) **£120 [≃ $216]**

Kirby, Thomas
- Essay on criticism in the course of which the
theory of light and the gravity of the earth are
particularly considered. London: W. Owen,
1757. 32 pp. Rebound in wraps.
(Xerxes) **$150 [≃ £83]**

Kirkpatrick, James
- The analysis of inoculation: comprizing the
history, theory, and practice of it ... The
second edition corrected, J. Buckland ...,
1761. xii,xxxii, 429,[i errata],xv pp. Some
dampstaining & foxing throughout. Contemp
sprinkled calf. *(Blackwell's)* **£180 [≃ $324]**

Kirwan, Richard
- An essay on the analysis of mineral waters.
London: for D. Bremner, 1799. 1st edn. 8vo.
viii,279 pp. 7 fldg tables. Contemp calf,
rebacked. Franklin Institute Lib b'plate.
(Offenbacher) **$450 [≃ £250]**

- The manners most advantageously applicable
to the various sorts of soils ... London: for
Vernor & Hood, 1796. 4th edn. 8vo. Title sl
soiled. New wraps. *(Stewart)* **£75 [≃ $135]**

Knight, Samuel
- The Child Jesus the great exemplar of youth.
A sermon ... London: for J. Wyat, 1718.
Engvd frontis of St. Paul's School. Mrbld
wraps, sewn as issued, sl frayed at outer edge.
(Waterfield's) **£30 [≃ $54]**
- The life of Erasmus ... an account of his
learned friends, and the state of religion and
learning at that time in both our universities.
Cambridge: Crownfield, 1726. 1st edn. 8vo.
18 engvd ports. Contemp calf, spine sl
rubbed. *(Marlborough)* **£110 [≃ $198]**

Knowles, Admiral Sir Charles
- An account of the expedition to Carthagena,
with explanatory notes and observations. The
second edition. London: M. Cooper, 1743. 58
pp. Disbound. *(C.R. Johnson)* **£25 [≃ $45]**
- An account of the expedition to Carthagena,
with explanatory notes and observations.
London: for M. Cooper, 1743. 3rd edn. 8vo.
58 pp. Stitched as issued.
(Young's) **£38 [≃ $68]**

Knox, John
- The historie of the Reformation of the
Church of Scotland: containing five bookes:
together with some treatises ... London: for
G.T. ... ; Reprinted Edinburgh: Robert
Bryson, 1644. Sm 4to. 2 leaves sl frayed at ft
without loss. Mod calf. Wing K739.
(Hughes) **£125 [≃ $225]**

Knox, Robert
- An historical relation of the Island of Ceylon
... detaining in captivity of the author ...
miraculous escape ... London: Richard
Chiswell, 1681. Lge 4to. [20],189,[3] pp.
Engvd fldg map, 15 plates (tears reprd).
Lacking port, scattered foxing. Mod 3/4 calf.
(Reese) **$650 [≃ £361]**

Knox, Vicesimus
- Essays moral and literary. A new edition, in
two volumes. London: for Charles Dilly,
1782. 2 vols. 12mo. 2 engvd frontis (spotted).
Contemp calf, sl rubbed.
(Hughes) **£45 [≃ $81]**
- Essays moral and literary. The seventh
edition. In two volumes. London: Charles
Dilly, 1785. 7th edn (hitherto unlocated). 2
engvd frontis. Contemp calf, red labels.
(C.R. Johnson) **£90 [≃ $162]**

- Liberal education: or, a practical treatise of the methods of acquiring useful and polite learning. Dublin: W. Hallhead ..., 1781. 1st Dublin edn. 12mo. xix,267 pp. Sm wormhole running through tail margin. Contemp calf, some sl wear. *(Blackwell's)* **£110 [≈ $198]**

Koehoorn, Minno, Baron of
- The new method of fortification. Translated from the original Dutch ... By Tho. Savery. London: for Daniel Midwinter, 1705. 1st edn in English. Folio. 16 engvd plates. Title & 4 ff a little ragged, light browning & worming, lib stamp on title verso. New mor.
(Young's) **£150 [≈ $270]**

Kolben, Peter
- The present state of the Cape of Good Hope; or, a particular account of the several nations of the Hottentots. London: W. Innys, 1731. 1st edn in English. 8vo. 18 engvd plates. Qtr calf. *(Halewood)* **£165 [≈ $297]**

Koran
- The Koran, commonly called the Alcoran of Mohammed. Translated into English ... 1764. 1st edn. 2 vols. xviii,248,280; vi,523 pp. 4 plates (3 fldg). Speckled calf, sl rubbed, backstrips worn & chipped, upper bd detchd.
(Edwards) **£100 [≈ $180]**

Krantzovius, Irenaeus
- Some thoughts concerning happiness ... See Stillingfleet, Benjamin

Krasheninnikov, Stefan P.
- The history of Kamschatka, and the Kurilski Islands. With the countries adjacent. Translated ... Gloucester: 1764. 4to. Frontis fldg map (crudely reprd), fldg map, 5 plates (2 fldg, 1 v torn). Rebound in gilt edged mor-backed mrbld bds. *(Edwards)* **£350 [≈ $630]**

Kyle, Thomas
- Treatise on the management of peach and nectarine trees; either in forcing houses, or on hot and common walls. Edinburgh: for the author, 1787. 2nd edn, enlgd & imprvd. 128 pp. Fldg plate. lea. *(Xerxes)* **$175 [≈ £97]**

Kyngesmill, Andrew
- A viuevve of mans estate, wherein the greate mercie of God ... is verie comfortably declared. For George Bishop ..., 1580. Sm 8vo. A-L8, M3 (lacks last blank). Black letter. V sm marg dampstain towards end, 2 ff with marg tears. Later sheep. STC 15005.
(Frew Mackenzie) **£350 [≈ $630]**

La Bruyere, Jean de
- The characters, or the manners of the age. F. Leach, 1702. 3rd edn, crrctd. 8vo. [iv],382, [11],xviii, 38 pp. Contemp panelled calf, jnts cracked but holding, backstrip rubbed & chipped at hd & tail.
(Blackwell's) **£80 [≈ $144]**

La Trobe, Benjamin
- Ancient and modern history of the Brethren ... the Protestant Church of the United Brethren. Translated from the German. London: W. & A. Strahan, 1780. 621 pp. Index at end. Front blank loose. Contemp calf, rubbed, worn. *(Xerxes)* **$150 [≈ £83]**

Labelye, C.
- The present state of Westminster Bridge ... a description ... a true account of the time already employed in the building ... London: 1743. 1st edn. 30 pp. Advt leaf at end. Title a little soiled. Mod half calf.
(Robertshaw) **£85 [≈ $153]**

Lacy, Benjamin
- The vanity of the world; or, the folly of those who lead wicked and profane lives ... London: H. Meere, 1720. Cr 8vo. Lacking front & final endpapers. Contemp calf, extremities rubbed. *(Stewart)* **£35 [≈ $63]**

Ladies Calling ...
- The ladies calling ... See Allestree, Richard

Ladies Tales ...
- The ladies tales. Exemplified in the virtues and vices of the quality, with refllections. London: 1714. 1st edn. 12mo. 264 pp. Mod wraps. *(Argosy)* **$85 [≈ £47]**

Lairesse, Gerard de
- The art of painting in all its branches .... Translated by J.F. Fritsch. London: Vandenbergh, Payne ..., 1778. 4to. Red & black title, 10ff, 50 pp. Engvd frontis, 69 plates (some fldg). Contemp half calf, spine gilt. *(Marlborough)* **£350 [≈ $630]**

Lamb, Charles
- A tale of Rosamund Gray and Old Blind Margaret, London: for Lee & Hurst, 1798. 1st edn. Sm 8vo. 134 pp. Contemp calf, worn jnts, half lea box. *(Argosy)* **$85 [≈ £47]**

Lambarde, William
- Eirenarcha, or of the office of the Iustices of Peace, in foure bookes. London: for the Companie of Stationers, 1619. Some marg

staining and worming. Mod calf. STC 15174.
(Charles Cox) £125 [≈ $225]

Lambe, Samuel
- Seasonable observations humbly offered to His Highness the Lord Protector - certain proposalls for establishing a banke at London. London: 1657. 2 pts in 1. Folio. Drop-head title. Lacking A1 blank. Unbound, stitched as issued. Wing L229. *(Robertshaw)* £45 [≈ $81]

Landais, Peter
- Memorial to justify Peter Landai's [sic] conduct during the late war. Boston: Peter Edees, 1784. 115 pp. 15 engvs, engvd errata. Title lacking sm portion, affecting some text, replaced in facs, 1st 12 leaves with marg paper loss in marg. Mod 3/4 calf.
(Reese) $3,750 [≈ £2,083]

Langallerie, Marquis de
- The memoirs ... an account of the most secret intrigues of the French, Spanish and Bavarian Courts ... London: for J. Round ..., 1710. 2nd edn. 8vo. [xvi],416 pp. Contemp panelled calf, early reback. Ex Kimbolton Castle Lib.
(Young's) £45 [≈ $81]

Langbaine, Gerard
- An account of the English dramatick poets. Oxford: for George West ..., 1691. [xvi],556, [xxxvi] pp. Final errata leaf. Old perf lib stamp at ft of title, some minor worming of later leaves. Rec half calf, spine gilt, mrbld bds. Wing L373. *(Clark)* £280 [≈ $504]

Langford, T.
- Plain and full instructions to raise all sorts of fruit-trees that prosper in England. London: 1696. 2nd edn, revsd & enlgd. 8vo. [xxx],220,[6] pp. 2 plates. Contemp calf, trifle worn. *(Wheldon & Wesley)* £140 [≈ $252]

Langham, William
- The garden of health: containing the sundry rare and hidden vertues and properties of all kinds of simples and plants. London: Thomas Harper, 1633. 2nd edn. 4to. Title strengthened, lacking final blank, final leaf of index & fldg table. Contemp calf, rebacked.
(Stewart) £225 [≈ $405]

Langhorne, John
- Frederic and Pharamond, or the consolations of human life. London: T. Becket & P.A. de Hondt, 1769. 1st edn. Sm 8vo. iv,157 pp, leaf of advts. Contemp qtr calf, mor label, mrbld paper bds. *(Deighton Bell)* £25 [≈ $45]
- Solyman and Almena. London: for H. Payne

& W. Cropley, 1762. 1st edn. 12mo. iv,198,[2 advts] pp. B'plate & owner's stamp. Contemp speckled calf, floral gilt border, gilt spine.
(Burmester) £180 [≈ $324]

Langley, Batty
- New principles of gardening; or, the laying out and planting parterres, groves ... labyrinths, avenues ... London: A. Bettesworth ..., 1728. 1st edn. [2],xvi, [8],207, blank, 191, advt pp. 28 plates (22 fldg, 6 double-page). Contemp calf, spine & crnrs reprd. *(Spelman)* £1,400 [≈ $2,520]

Langlois de Francan, F.
- The favourites chronicle. printed according to the French copie. London: 1621. 1st English edn. Slim 4to. Ptd title, 41 pp. Rec bds, parchment backstrip, new endpapers. STC 15203. *(P & P)* £105 [≈ $189]

Langrishe, Sir H.
- Celebrated speech in the Irish House of Commons ... March 4, 1794, on the Motion of Mr. Ponsonby for A Parliamentary Reform. Edinburgh: J. & J. Fairburn, 1794. 15 pp. Rebound in bds.
(C.R. Johnson) £28 [≈ $50]

Laporte, John
- Of the characters of trees, drawn and engraved ... pts I-VI. London: Macklin, 1795-98. Obl folio. 24 plates (4 in each part). Orig wraps, ptd labels on front cvrs.
(Marlborough) £525 [≈ $945]

Lassels, Richard
- The voyage of Italy ... In two parts ... Paris [i.e. London]: John Starkey, 1670. 2nd edn. 12mo. [xliv],251, 447,[iii table] pp. Addtnl engvd title as frontis, sep title to 2nd part. Trivial dampstaining in crnrs of some prelims. Contemp calf, jnts reprd.
(Frew Mackenzie) £250 [≈ $450]

Late Revolution ...
- History of the Late Revolution in the Dutch republic ... See Ellis, George

Late Troubles ...
- A short view of the late troubles in England ... See Dugdale, Sir William

Laud, William
- The history of the troubles and tryal of ... William Laud ... written by him during his imprisonment ... 1695. 1st edn. Folio. 616 pp. W'engvd frontis. Crnr of title missing without loss of text. Contemp calf, worn,

rubbed, upper bd nearly detchd.
(Edwards) **£150 [≈ $270]**

Laurence, John
- The fruit-garden kalendar: or, a summary of the art of managing the fruit-garden ... an appendix on the usefulness of the barometer. London: for Bernard Lintot, 1718. 1st edn. 8vo. Fldg frontis, half-title, 3 pp ctlg. Mod wraps.   *(Stewart)* **£85 [≈ $153]**
- A new system of agriculture, being a complete body of husbandry and gardening ... Tho. Woodward, 1726. 1st edn. Folio. [xxiv],456 pp. Engvd frontis, 2 engvd plates. Occas light soiling. Contemp panelled calf, rubbed, jnts beginning to split.
(Frew Mackenzie) **£250 [≈ $450]**
- A new system of agriculture, being a complete body of husbandry and gardening ... Tho. Woodward, 1726. Folio. [xxiv],456 pp. Frontis, 2 plates. Contemp panelled calf, rubbed, crnrs worn newly rebacked.
(Blackwell's) **£135 [≈ $243]**
- A new system of agriculture, being a complete body of husbandry and gardening ... in five books ... Dublin: 1727. Folio. Engvd frontis, 2 plates. Old calf, new spine.
(Halewood) **£150 [≈ $270]**

Lavater, Johann Caspar
- Aphorisms on man. Translated from the original manuscript. London: T. Bensley, 1789. Vol 1, all published in English. 2nd edn. Engvd frontis by Blake. Contemp calf, rebacked.   *(C.R. Johnson)* **£160 [≈ $288]**
- Essays on physiognomy. London: 1789. 1st English translation. 3 vols. 241; 324; 314 pp. 360 engvs. Lea, rebacked.
(Fye) **£500 [≈ £277]**
- Essays on physiognomy ... Translated ... 1789. 3 vols. 241; 324; 314 pp. 360 engvs in each vol. Vols 1 & 3 lacking half-titles. Rebound in cloth, worn.
(Edwards) **£100 [≈ $180]**
- Essays on physiognomy. Boston: Spotswood & West, [1794]. 1st Amer edn. 12mo. [4],272 pp. Engvd title, 7 engvd plates. Light browning. Contemp calf, front jnt cracked, rear jnt partially so. *(Antiq Sc)* **£140 [≈ £77]**
- Essays on physiognomy. London: H.D. Symonds, 1797. 4 vols. 8vo. Num plates. Some stamps. Contemp calf, rec rebacked.
(Waterfield's) **£250 [≈ $450]**
- Physiognomy: or the corresponding analogy between the conformation of the features and the ruling passions of the mind. London: n.d. [ca 1795]. 8vo. [10],280 pp. Frontis. 4 engvd plates. Calf, worn.   *(Goodrich)* **£55 [≈ £41]**

Lavoisier, Antoine
- Elements of chemistry in a new systematic order ... Edinburgh: Creech, 1799. 4th edn in English. 8vo. 592 pp. 13 fldg engvd plates (moderately foxed). New polished mor. Addtnl 19th c engvd port of Lavoisier, 2 b'plates inc 1 armorial. *(Oasis)* **$600 [≈ £333]**

Law ...
- The practick part of the law. Showing the offices of a complete attorney,in the full prosecution of any action ... London: Thomas Roycroft, 1658. 5th imp. 12mo. 440 pp. Contemp roan, rebacked. Wing 3141.
(Edwards) **£160 [≈ $288]**

Law, William
- A serious call to a devout and holy life. Adapted to the state and condition of all orders of Christians. London: for William Innys, 1729. 1st edn. 8vo. 5 pp book ctlg at end. Contemp panelled calf, rebacked.
(Chaucer Head) **£380 [≈ $684]**
- A serious call to a devout and holy life. London: for W. Innys ..., 1739. 4th edn. Cr 8vo. Some early notes on endpapers & pencil underlining. Contemp calf.
(Stewart) **£30 [≈ $54]**

Lawrence, Herbert
- The passions personify'd, in familiar fables. London: for J. Whiston ..., [1773]. 1st edn. 8vo. [ii],iv,[ii],104 pp. Engvd frontis (with clean tear reprd), 12 engvd plates. Contemp sheep, sl wear.   *(Burmester)* **£110 [≈ $198]**

Lawrence, John
- The clergy-man's recreation: shewing the pleasure and profit of the art of gardening. London: B. Lintott, 1714. 1st edn. 8vo. [12],83,1 pub advts pp. Engvd frontis, w'cut diag in text. Light offsetting on title. Mod calf.   *(Rootenberg)* **$750 [≈ £416]**

Lawrence, Thomas
- Mercurius centralis: or, a discourse of subterranel cockle, muscle, and oyster-shels ... London: for J. Collins ..., 1664. 1st edn. 12mo. [x],94 pp. Some side-notes cropped. 18th c calf, rather rubbed. The Britwell Court copy. Wing L689D.
(Pickering) **$850 [≈ £472]**

Le Brun, Charles
- Heads representing the passions of the soul; as they are expressed in the human countenance ... Laurie & Whittle, 1794. Folio. Engvd title, 2ff preface, 19 engvd plates (i.e. 20 inc title. Stitched as issued in

wraps, crnrs lightly worn, spine defective.
(Frew Mackenzie) **£100 [≈$180]**

Le Clerc, Jean
- The life and character of Mr. John Locke ...
done into English. London: for John Clark ...,
1706. 1st edn in English. 4to. [iv],31, [1 advts]
pp. New qtr calf. *(Pickering)* **$1,000 [≈£555]**

Le Clerc, S.
- Practical geometry: or, a new and easy
method of treating that art. London: T.
Bowles, 1727. 3rd edn. Sm 8vo. [2],195,6
index pp. 82 engvd plates. Front endpaper
stained. Rebound in calf.
(Spelman) **£220 [≈$396]**

L'Estrange, Sir Roger
- Fables of Aesop and other eminent
mythologists: with morals and reflections.
London: 1714. 6th edn, crrctd. Port.
Contemp panelled calf, spines richly gilt.
(Robertshaw) **£55 [≈$99]**

Le Prince de Beaumont, Jeanne Marie
- The young misses magazine, containing
dialogues between a governess and ... her
scholars. London: 1793. 5th edn. 2 vols.
12mo. A few leaves loose in vol 1. Contemp
sheep, rubbed, jnts cracking.
(Robertshaw) **£25 [≈$45]**

Le Sage, Alain Rene
- The bachelor of Salamanca; or, memoirs of
Don Cherubim. London: for Richardson ...,
1767. 2 vols. Top blank marg of 1 leaf torn,
minor discoloration. Contemp sprinkled calf,
minor wear. *(Pirages)* **$135 [≈£75]**
- The history and adventures of Gil Blas de
Santillane ... prefixed some account of the
author's life. London: for J. Massey & W.
Sprout, n.d. [ca 1775]. 4 vols. 8vo. 4 engvd
frontis. Old calf, rebacked.
(Young's) **£40 [≈$72]**

Leadbetter, Charles
- Mechanick dialling: or, the new art of
shadows ... added ... best and most approved
methods of painting sun dials. London:
Edward Wicksteed, 1737. 1st edn. 8vo.
xvi,193,[i] pp. 12 fldg plates. Contemp calf,
rebacked, crnrs reprd.
(Spelman) **£280 [≈$504]**
- The Royal gauger; or gauging made perfectly
easy ... London: 1755. 4th edn. 8vo.
xviii,218; 209-446, 481-510 pp (without
apparent loss). 2 cold plates (1 fldg to 3 ft), 5
other fldg plates, 2 fldg vouchers. Dust
marks. Sm paper fault in 3 ff. Rec half calf.

(Bow Windows) **£110 [≈$198]**

Leake, Stephen Martin
- An historical account of English money ...
London: for R. Faulder ..., 1793. 3rd edn.
8vo. viii,8, 428,[16] pp. 14 plates. Rec cloth.
(Young's) **£57 [≈$102]**

Lediard, John
- The life of John, Duke of Marlborough,
prince of the Roman Empire. London: for J.
Wilcox, 1743. 2 vols. 8vo. Engvd frontis vol
I, engvd plates & maps (some fldg). Vol I title
a bit browned, some spotting. Rebound in qtr
calf. *(Hughes)* **£65 [≈$117]**

Ledwich, Edward
- Antiquitates Sarisburiensis. Containing, I. A
dissertation on the antient coins ... II. The
Salisbury ballad. III. The history of Old
Sarum ... VI ... Salisbury: 1771. 15; 28; 247,5
advts pp. 3 fldg plans. Some foxing &
browning. Half calf, worn, reprd.
(Edwards) **£100 [≈$180]**

Lee, James
- An introduction to botany containing an
explanation of the theory of that science ...
London: 1794. 5th edn, crrctd. 8vo. xxiv,240
pp. 12 copper plates, 2 tables. Contemp calf,
upper front hinge split.
(Hemlock) **$150 [≈£83]**
- An introduction to botany, an explanation of
the theory of that science ... London: J. & R.
Tonson, 1765. 2nd edn. 8vo. xv,iv,479, [12]
pp. 12 engvd plates. Contemp gilt-panelled
calf. Ex lib William Constable with his
b'plate. *(Gough)* **£115 [≈$207]**
- An introduction to botany, an explanation of
the theory of that science ... the second
edition, to which is added, a glossary.
London: J. & R. Tonson, 1765. 8vo. xvi,iv,
1-331; 449-479 pp. Contemp sprinkled calf,
backstrip gilt, jnts beginning to crack.
(Blackwell's) **£55 [≈$99]**

Lee, Nathaniel
- Oedipus: a tragedy ... See Dryden, John &
Lee, Nathaniel
- Lucius Junius Brutus; father of his country. A
tragedy. Acted at the Duke's Theater ...
London: for R. & J. Tonson, 1681. 1st edn.
4to. A little browned, 1st & last leaves sl
creased & dust-marked. Later half calf, mrbld
bds. Wing L852. *(Charles Cox)* **£60 [≈$108]**
- Lucius Junius Brutus; father of his country. A
tragedy. London: for R. & J. Tonson, 1681.
1st edn. 8vo. viii,72,ii pp. Sl darkened, 1 crnr

torn away with catchword lost. Disbound.
(Pirages) **$125 [≃ £69]**
- The rival Queens, or the death of Alexander the Great. Acted at the Theater-Royal ... London: for James Magnes ..., 1677. 1st edn. 4to. Title faintly browned, cut rather close at hd, headlines of a few leaves just touched. Mod qtr cloth. Wing L865.
(Charles Cox) **£60 [≃ $108]**
- Sophonisba, or Hannibal's overthrow. A tragedy acted at the Theatre Royal ... London: for S. Chapman, 1726. 8vo. 70 pp. Engvd frontis. Half blue calf.
(Young's) **£29 [≃ $52]**

Lee, Samuel
- Orbis miraculum, or the Temple of Solomon pourtrayed ... London: Giles Calvert, 1659. Folio. [12],3711,[8 index & errata] pp. Engvd title, 2 plates. Some running heads cut close, a few other minor defects. Old mottled calf, rebacked, crnrs worn. Wing L902.
(Bow Windows) **£250 [≃ $450]**

Lefevre, N.
- A compleat body of chymistry. London: Pulteyn, 1670. 2nd English edn. 4to. 2 pts in 1. [x],286; [vi],320 pp. 2 titles, 6 fldg plates, 2 full-page ills. Contemp calf, 1 rear crnr missing. Wing L926. *(P & P)* **£105 [≃ $189]**

Legh, Gerard
- The accedens of armory. [L: Rychard Tottel, 1586]. 2nd edn. [7],135,[2] ff. W'cut emblems & coats of arms, w'cut title. Title & 2 other leaves tipped-in, some other leaves (perhaps) inserted from another copy. Later vellum, v sl soiled & splayed.   *(Pirages)* **$350 [≃ £194]**

Leibnitz, G.W. von & Clarke, Samuel
- A collection of papers which passed between ... Mr. Leibnitz and Dr. Clarke ... Relating to ... natural philosophy ... London: for James Knapton, 1717. 1st edn. xiii,[iii], 416,46 pp. Advt leaf. Worming in margs of 2 gatherings. Contemp calf, rebacked & reprd.
(Bickersteth) **£385 [≃ $693]**

Leigh, Charles
- The natural history of Lancashire, Cheshire ... Oxford: for the author, 1700. Folio. Errata, postscript & inserted pp at V2. Port (reprd), 2 plates of arms, map, 22 plates. Title dusty, frayed at edges, few tears in marg. Contemp calf, rebacked, reprd.
(Bow Windows) **£240 [≃ $432]**
- The natural history of Lancashire, Cheshire ... Oxford: for the author, 1700. 1st edn. Folio. 26 copper engvd plates inc port frontis

& double-page cold map. Port title & front free endpaper damaged in crnr sl affecting ptd area. Mod qtr calf. Wing L975.
(Blackwell's) **£170 [≃ $306]**
- The natural history of Lancashire, Cheshire and the Peak, in Derbyshire. Oxford: 1700. Folio. Port (crnr defective), cold map, 24 plates. New half calf.
(Wheldon & Wesley) **£225 [≃ $405]**

Leigh, Edward
- Select and choice observations, concerning all the Romane Emperours. London: for John Williams, 1670. 3rd edn. 8vo. 65 medallion ports in text, 2 on addtnl final leaf 2D8. Minor worming to inner margs, crnr torn from title with sl loss. Old calf. Wing 1005.   *(Stewart)* **£85 [≃ $153]**
- Select and choyce observations, concerning all the Romane Emperours ... Certain choyce French proverbs ... London: for John Williams, 1657. 1st edn. 8vo. [xii],277 pp. Early 19.n c calf, spine gilt, gilt edges. Wing L1003.   *(Burmester)* **£75 [≃ $135]**

Leigh, Sir Samuel Egerton
- Munster Abbey. A romance. Interspersed with reflections on virtue and morality. Edinburgh: for W. Creech ..., 1797. 1st edn. 3 vols in 1. 8vo. 34 pp subscribers' list. 19th c mor, mrbld bds.
(Chaucer Head) **£350 [≃ $630]**

Leland, John
- The itinerary published by Mr. Thomas Hearne. Oxford: for James Fletcher ..., 1770. 3rd edn. 9 vols in 5. Lge paper, on fine paper. 3 plates (1 fldg). Rather later half calf, mrbld paper sides. Ex Ipswich Library with b'plates & stamps.   *(Claude Cox)* **£150 [≃ $270]**

Lemery, M.L.
- A treatise of all sorts of foods, both animal and vegetable; also of drinkables ... how to choose the best sort of all kinds. Translated ... London: 1745. 12mo. 396 pp. Red & black title, approbation leaf. Contemp bds, new spine.   *(Halewood)* **£115 [≃ $207]**

Lemery, N.
- A course of chymistry, containing an easie method of preparing those chymical medicins which are used in physick ... London: for Kettilby, 1698. 3rd edn. 8vo. [xxii],815, [xvi] pp. 7 full-page plates. Rebound calf, old calf laid down, new endpapers. Wing L1040.
(P & P) **£340 [≃ $612]**

Lemnius, Levinus
- An herbal for the Bible ... Drawen into English by Thomas Newton. London: E. Bollifant, 1587. 1st edn. Sm 8vo. W'cut initials. Mod mor. STC 15454.
(Traylen) £490 [≈ $882]

Lempriere, J.
- Bibliotheca classica: or, a classical dictionary. London: for T. Cadell ..., 1797. 3rd edn. Lge 8vo. Unpaginated. Contemp calf, gilt, crease in backstrip. *(Claude Cox)* £20 [≈ $36]

Lennox, Charles, Third Duke of Richmond
- A letter ... to Lieutenant Colonel Sharman, Chairman ... appointed by the delegates of forty-five Corps of Volunteers assembled at Lisburn in Ireland. London: J. Johnson, 1792. 16 pp. Disbound.
(C.R. Johnson) £28 [≈ $50]

Leslie, Charles
- An answer to a book intituled The state of the Protestants of Ireland under the late King James's Government [by William King, q.v.]. London: 1692. 8vo. 195,77 pp. Fldg broadside list of ships lost since 1688. Mod half calf. *(Emerald Isle)* £125 [≈ $225]

Leslie, John
- Killarney. A poem. London: for George Robinson, 1773. 4to. Rebound in bds.
(C.R. Johnson) £125 [≈ $225]

Letter ...
- A letter to a Baron of England relating to the late Bill concerning his Royal Highness. London: 1679. Folio. 5 pp. Rebound in qtr calf, mrbld bds. Wing L1631.
(C.R. Johnson) £35 [≈ $63]
- A letter to a Bishop ... See Forbes, Duncan
- A letter to a freeholder, on the latest reduction of the land tax ... By a Member of the House of Commons. London: for J. Peele, 1732. 8vo. Title & final leaf sl dustsoiled. Uncut in new wraps. *(Stewart)* £85 [≈ $153]
- A letter to a Member of Parliament concerning the present state of affairs at home and abroad. By a true lover of the people. London: T. Cooper, 1740. 60 pp. Rebound in bds. *(C.R. Johnson)* £45 [≈ $81]
- A letter to a member of parliament, relating to the Bill for the opening of a trade, to and from Persia through Russia. London: for T. Cooper, 1741. 1st edn. 8vo. [ii],67 pp. Lacking half-title. Disbound.
(Burmester) £58 [≈ $104]
- A letter to his Grace the D--- of N----e on the

duty he owes himself, his king, his country and his God, at this important moment. London: J. Morgan, 1757. 47 pp. Disbound.
(C.R. Johnson) £30 [≈ $54]
- A letter to his Majesty's principal secretaries of State by the Ministers of the several Roman Catholick princes and states ... complaining of a clause relating to Popish priests ... London: E. Owen, 1746. 29 pp. Rebound in bds. *(C.R. Johnson)* £28 [≈ $50]
- A letter to Robert Bertie, relating to his conduct in the Mediterranean, and his defence of Admiral Byng. London: R. Griffiths, 1757. 35 pp. Half-title. Disbound.
(C.R. Johnson) £48 [≈ $86]
- A letter to the jurors of Great Britain ... See Rouse, George
- Letter to the late Rector of Bourton on the Water ... In answer to a letter lately addressed to the Bishop of Chester. London: Brett, 1782. 60 pp. Rebound in bds.
(C.R. Johnson) £18 [≈ $32]
- A letter to the Occasional Writer [q.v.], on receipt of his third. London: for J. Roberts, 1727. 1st edn. 8vo. 36 pp. Disbound.
(Burmester) £45 [≈ $81]
- A letter to the people of Ireland on the subject of tythes ... a second letter ... address to the Dissenters ... Inhabitants of Ulster ... Dublin: 1758. Third letter ... the farmers complaints ... Dublin: Powell, 1758. 3 pts in 1 vol. 8vo. Wraps. *(Emerald Isle)* £75 [≈ $135]
- A letter to the Rev. Doctor O'Leary ... See O'Driscoll, William
- Letter to the Right Honourable Edmund Burke, on the subject of Bengal. London: J. Johnson, 1783. 97 pp. Disbound.
(C.R. Johnson) £45 [≈ $81]
- A letter to William Pitt ... See Hervey, Thomas
- A second letter to the Common Council of the City of London, with some remarks on Lord Chief Justice Pratt's answer to Sir Thomas Harrison the Chamberlain. London: W. Nicoll, 1764. 41 pp. Disbound.
(C.R. Johnson) £32 [≈ $57]

Letters ...
- Letters and essays on the small-pox ... See Quier, John
- Letters concerning the present state of Poland ... See Lind, John
- Letters from a young painter abroad ... See Russell. John
- Letters from Edinburgh; written in the years 1774 and 1775 ... See Topham, Edward
- Letters of certain Jews to Monsieur de

Voltaire ... See Guennee, Antoine

- Letters to married women ... See Smith, Hugh

Lettsom, John Coakley

- The naturalist's and traveller's companion containing instructions for collecting and preserving objects of natural history ... London: 1774. 2nd edn. 8vo. xvi,89,[9] pp. Engvd title & frontis, each with hand-cold ills. Rec half calf by Bernard Middleton. *(Burmester)* **£90 [≈ $162]**

- Some account of the late John Fothergill, M.D. London: Dilly, 1783. 8vo. 193 pp. Qtr calf, rebacked. *(Goodrich)* **$125 [≈ £69]**

Lewesdon Hill ...

- Lewesdon Hill. A poem ... See Crowe, William

Lewin, William

- The birds of Great Britain. London: for J. Johnson, 1795-1801. 8 vols in 2. Thick folio. One of 25 lge paper. 336 hand-cold engvd plates. Full levant mor, spines gilt, gilt edges, by Zaehnsdorf. *(Traylen)* **£6,500 [≈ $11,700]**

Lewis, John

- The history and antiquities ecclesiastical and civil of the Isle of Tenet in Kent. 1723. 1st edn. 4to. viii,140,103 pp. Red & black title with vignette, 4 plates (1 fldg), 3 extra engvd plates inserted. Contemp diced russia, rebacked. Armorial b'plate.
  (Frew Mackenzie) **£95 [≈ $171]**

- The history of the life and sufferings of the reverend and learned John Wicliffe ... London: for Robert Knaplock ..., 1720. 1st edn. 8vo. xxvi,406 pp. Some text browning. Old calf, rebacked. *(Young's)* **£30 [≈ $54]**

Lewis, Matthew Gregory

- Ambrosio, or the Monk: a romance. London: for J. Bell, 1798. 4th edn. 3 vols. 12mo. Some light dampstaining in 1 vol. Early 19th c half calf, spines gilt. *(Burmester)* **£250 [≈ $450]**

Lewis, William

- A course of practical chemistry ... with many new, and several uncommon processes. J. Nourse, 1746. 1st edn. 8vo. [xx],432,ii advts,xx index,ii advts,vii explanation of plates pp. 9 copper engvs. Foxing or browning throughout. Amateur calf, hinge cracked. *(Blackwell's)* **£125 [≈ $225]**

- A course of practical chemistry ... with many new, and several uncommon processes. London: J. Nourse, 1746. 1st edn. 8vo. 10ff,

432 (i.e. 422) pp, 21ff. 9 copperplates. Contemp calf, back gilt, hinges cracked. Franklin Institute Lib b'plate.
  (Offenbacher) **$500 [≈ £277]**

Lewis, William

- The information ... delivered at ... the House of Commons ... November, 1680 ... confirmation of the Popish plot ... justice of the executions ... Randall Taylor, 1680. 1st edn. Imprimatur, [iv],31 pp. Disbound. New Wing L1851. *(Blackwell's)* **£45 [≈ $81]**

Leybourn, William

- The art of dialling performed geometrically ... arithmetically ... instrumentally ... London: 1669. 1st edn, 2nd iss. Sm 4to. 4ff, 175 pp. W'cut port, fldg plate, num w'cut diags. Ink inscrptns at beginning, prelims a little grubby & stained. Old calf, worn.
  (Weiner) **£750 [≈ $1,350]**

- Compleat surveyor: or, the whole art of surveyi..g of land, by a new instrument lately invented. London: 1722. 5th edn. Folio. [12],166, 155 pp. Advt. Engvd port, 14 fldg plates. Old stamps on title, frontis & elsewhere. Some browning. Contemp calf, rebacked. *(Spelman)* **£180 [≈ $324]**

- Dialing ... shewing how to make all such dials, and to adorn them with all useful furniture ... London: Churchill, 1682. 1st edn. Folio. [20],76; 89-187; [12],189-192; 12; 181-226; 273-330 pp. Frontis, 23 engvd plates (10 fldg), Old calf, rebacked. Wing L1912.
  (Rootenberg) **$1,800 [≈ £1,000]**

- The line of proportion of numbers, commonly called Gunter's Line made easie. London: for Hannah Sawbridge, 1684. Sm 8vo. 2 pp bookseller's ctlg. Lacking fldg plate, lib stamp on title verso. Contemp calf, jnts reprd. Wing 1921. *(Stewart)* **£250 [≈ $450]**

Lhuyd, Edward

- Archaeologia Britannica ... languages, histories and customs ... from collections and observations in travel ... Vol I [all published]. Oxford: for the author, 1707. Folio. [xx],438,[iv] pp. Contemp panelled calf, crnrs bumped, front jnt cracking at ft.
  (Frew Mackenzie) **£220 [≈ $396]**

Library ...

- A compendious library of the law: necessary for persons of all degrees and professions. In two parts. In the Savoy, for J. Osborn, 1743. 2nd edn. 8vo. 2 pts in 1, each with sep title. Early law calf. *(Chaucer Head)* **£120 [≈ $216]**

- The library. A poem ... See Crabbe, George

Lightfoot, John (1602-1675)

- Erubhin or miscellanies Christian and Judaicall, and others. London: 1629. 1st edn. Sm 8vo. Some dampstaining. Contemp calf, rebacked. STC 15593.
(Robertshaw) **£55** [≈ $99]
- Works ... revised and corrected by George Bright. London: William Rawlins, 1683-84. 2 vols. Folio. Port frontis, 3 fldg maps, tables. Contemp calf, rec rebacked. Wing 2051.
(Stewart) **£60** [≈ $108]

Lightfoot, John (1735-1788)

- Flora Scotia: or, a systematic arrangement, in the Linnaean method, of the native plants of Scotland and the Hebrides. B. White, 1777. 2 vols. 8vo. Engvd & ptd titles, 35 engvd plates (6 fldg). Light foxing. Contemp mrbld calf, rebacked, crnrs wearing.
(Blackwell's) **£150** [≈ $270]

Ligon, Richard

- A true and exact history of the Island of Barbados ... Together with the Ingenio that makes the sugar ... Humphrey Mosely, 1657. 1st edn. Sm folio. 9 plates (3 fldg, 1 reprd, 1 sl torn), map in facsimile. Sl browned, title rebacked. Lea, gilt. Wing L2075.
(Edwards) **£700** [≈ $1,260]

Lilburne, John

- The engagement vindicated and explained. Or the reasons upon which Lieut. Col. John Lilburne took the engagement. Published by a well-wisher ... London: 1650. 1st edn. Sm 4to. 6 pp. Disbound. A bit dusty. Wing L2101.
(Hughes) **£30** [≈ $54]

Lilly, W. & Colet, J.

- A short introduction to grammar ... of the Latin tongue ... London: 1745-14-39. 3 pts in 1 vol. Sm 8vo. [xx],[76]; [iv],140; 80 pp. Contemp calf, spine ends chipped, jnts cracking.
(Bow Windows) **£45** [≈ $81]

Lilly, William

- Christian astrology. London: Partridge, 1647. Sm 4to. Engvd port frontis (backed). Margs thumbed. Old calf, garish reback. Wing P2215.
(Halewood) **£350** [≈ $630]
- An easie and familiar method whereby to judge the effects depending on eclipses, either of the sun or moon. London: 1652. 1st edn. Slim 4to. Qtr calf, mrbld bds. Lea b'plate of the 'Plesch' Library.
(Halewood) **£145** [≈ $261]

Lily, William

- A short introduction of grammar. London: Will. Norton, 1703. 8vo. [lxxii,ii], 130,[xx] pp. Half-title & final blank, w'cut titles. 18th c panelled calf, spine a little rubbed & worn, a few sl marks.
(Ash) **£150** [≈ $270]

Limitations ...

- Limitations for the next foreign successor, or new Saxon race. Debated in a conference between two gentlemen. 1701. 4to. Disbound.
(Stewart) **£15** [≈ $27]

Lind, James

- An essay on diseases incidental to Europeans in hot climates with the means of preventing their fatal consequences. London: Becket & de Hondt, 1771. 2nd edn, enlgd. 8vo. xv,375 pp, 4ff. Marg staining to 1st few leaves. Contemp calf, dull, hinges rubbed.
(Hemlock) **$250** [≈ £138]
- An essay on diseases incidental to Europeans in hot climates with the means of preventing their fatal consequences. London: Becket, 1776. 3rd edn, enlgd. 387 pp. Inked names on title, tiny piece torn from blank crnr of 13 leaves. Contemp calf, rebacked.
(Oasis) **$350** [≈ £194]
- An essay on the most effectual means of preserving the health of seamen in the Royal Navy. London: Millar, 1757. 1st edn. Sm 8vo. xxiv,119 pp. Lacking half-title, contemp sgntrs on title & another page. Contemp bds, crnrs reprd, rebacked in calf.
(Oasis) **$2,750** [≈ £1,527]
- A treatise on the scurvy ... the nature, causes, and cure of that disease ... London: A. Millar, 1757. 2nd crrctd edn. 8vo. xvi pp, 2ff, 476 pp. Ownership stamp on title, medical ex lib inside front cvr. Contemp half calf.
(Hemlock) **$1,875** [≈ £1,041]

Lind, John

- An answer to the Declaration of the American Congress. 1776. 1st edn, 2nd iss. 8vo. 132 pp. Uncut, stitched as issued in orig wraps.
(Farahar) **£400** [≈ $720]
- Letters concerning the present state of Poland. London: 1773. 1st edn. 8vo. Contemp calf, ruled in gilt.
(Robertshaw) **£60** [≈ $108]

Lindesay, Robert

- The history of Scotland: from Feb. 1436 to Mar. 1565 plus a continuation till 1604. Edinburgh: 1728. Sm folio. Subscribers' list. Sm blemish on title. Contemp half calf, a little worn.
(Halewood) **£85** [≈ $153]

Lindsay, Colin, Earl of Balcarres
- An account of the affairs of Scotland, relating to the Revolution in 1688 ... Never before printed. J. Baker: 1714. 1st edn. 8vo. [i],vi, 5-150,[iv], 16 pp. Contemp panelled calf, crnrs bumped, jnts splitting at hd. Armorial b'plate.   *(Frew Mackenzie)* £75 [≈ $135]

Ling, Nicholas
- Politeuphoria, wits commonwealth. Newly corrected and amended. London: M. Flesher ..., 1647. 12mo. [vi],322,8] pp. Title & last leaf frayed, 1st few leaves stained, some browning & discoloration throughout. Rec mor.   *(Claude Cox)* £75 [≈ $135]

Linnaeus, Carl
- Miscellaneous tracts relating to natural history, husbandry, and physic. Translated from the Latin ... by Benj. Stillingfleet. London: R. & J. Dodsley ..., 1759. 1st edn. 8vo. xxx,[i],230 pp. Contemp qtr calf, mrbld bds, spine worn at hd & ft, jnts cracked.   *(Bickersteth)* £285 [≈ $513]
- Miscellaneous tracts relating to natural history, husbandry and physick. London: 1762. 2nd edn. 8vo. xxxi,391 pp. 11 engvd plates. Lib stamp on title. Contemp calf, rebacked. Author's [Sic. Translator's? - Ed.] pres copy.   *(Goodrich)* $145 [≈ £80]

Lister, Martin
- A journey to Paris in the year 1698. The third edition. London: Jacob Tonson, 1699. 8vo. [v],248 pp. 6 engvd plates (3 fldg). Occas browning. Contemp panelled calf, old rebacking, extremities lightly rubbed. Wing L257.   *(Frew Mackenzie)* £170 [≈ $306]

Lister, Thomas
- Opposition dangerous. London: John Stockdale, 1798. 39 pp. Disbound.   *(C.R. Johnson)* £22 [≈ $39]

Little, Janet
- The poetical works of Janet Little, the Scotch milkmaid. Ayr: John & Peter Wilson, 1793. Half green mor, mrbld bds.   *(C.R. Johnson)* £385 [≈ $693]

Liturgical Discourse ...
- A liturgical discourse of the Mass ... See Mason, Richard Angelus

Livius, Titus
- The Roman history written in Latin ... faithfully done into English. London: Awnsham Churchill, 1686. Folio. [viii],211;

3-940 pp. Engvd frontis, maps, table, fldg battle-plan. Sl spotting to fore-edge. Mod half calf, new endpapers. *(P & P)* £110 [≈ $198]

Lloyd, Charles
- Poems on various subjects. Carlisle: F. Jollie, 1795. 1st edn. 8vo. 104,[ii] pp. Without the author's 'advertisement', sm lib blindstamp at ft of title, lib release stamp on front pastedown. Mod buckram.   *(Bennett)* £125 [≈ $225]

Lloyd, David
- Dying and dead mens living words. Or, fair warnings to a careless world. London: for John Amery, 1682. 12mo. Sl scruffy, with ink blot on title verso & facing page. Contemp calf, worn. Wing L2639.   *(Charles Cox)* £25 [≈ $45]
- The states-men and favourites of England since the Reformation. Their prudence and policies ... London: for Samuel Speed, 1665. 1st edn. 8vo. [xiv],823,[i advt] pp. Red & black title, engvd frontis. Some browning & dustmarks. Contemp calf rebacked. Wing L2648.   *(Bow Windows)* £105 [≈ $189]

Lloyd, Lodowick
- A briefe conference of divers lawes: divided into certaine regiments. London: Thomas Creede, 1602. 1st edn. 4to. [iv],143, [vii] pp. With the final blank.. Rec blind-ruled sprinkled calf. STC 16616.   *(Bennett)* £350 [≈ $630]

Lloyd, William
- Considerations touching the true way to suppress popery in this kingdom. London: for Henry Broome, 1677. 4to. Contemp calf, rebacked, retaining orig backstrip. Wing L2676.   *(Waterfield's)* £45 [≈ $81]
- Considerations touching the true way to suppress popery in this kingdom. London: for Henry Broome, 1677. 4to. Old marg stain to a few leaves. Contemp calf, rebacked. Wing L2676.   *(Stewart)* £65 [≈ $117]

Lobb, Theophilus
- A compendium of the practice of physick, or, the heads of a system of practical physick contained in 24 lectures ... London: 1747. 8vo. 11,9,103,4 advts pp. Contemp calf.   *(Halewood)* £120 [≈ $216]
- Medical practice in curing fevers. John Oswald, 1735. 1st edn. 8vo. xxxii,431,[xxii] pp. Contemp sprinkled calf, sometime rebacked, crnrs reprd.   *(Blackwell's)* £140 [≈ $252]

- Medical practice in curing fevers. Correspondent to rational methods ... which arise from the ... symptoms of the patient. London: 1735. 1st edn. Thick 8vo. Errata/advt leaf. Contemp calf.
(Halewood) **£115 [≈ $207]**
- Medicinal letters. In two parts ... for removing various disorders ... II ... on the most frequent and dangerous diseases ... John Buckland, 1765. 3rd edn. 12mo. [vii],92,viii advts pp. Title stained in margs. Contemp sheep, jnts cracked, lacking f.e.p.
(Blackwell's) **£50 [≈ $90]**
- A practical treatise of painful distempers, with some effectual methods for curing them ... James Buckland, 1739. 1st edn. 8vo. xxxii, 320,[xiv] pp. Some marg foxing throughout. Contemp sprinkled calf, rec rebacked, gilt, crnrs worn.
(Blackwell's) **£100 [≈ $180]**

Lobo, Daniel
- A nomenclature; or, dictionary, in English, French, Spanish ... of the principal articles manufactured in this kingdom ... hardware and cutlery trade ... For the editor, 1776. Sole edn. 4to. vii,172,[iii] pp. 8 pp spotted. Contemp half calf, mrbld sides.
(Frew Mackenzie) **£480 [≈ $864]**

Locke, John
- A collection of several pieces ... Never before printed, or not extant in his works. London: for R. Francklin, 1720. 1st edn, 1st iss. 8vo. Diag at p 187, 3 pp advts at end. Contemp panelled calf, jnts a little worn.
(Traylen) **£350 [≈ $630]**
- An essay concerning humane understanding. In four books. London: Tho. Bassett ..., 1690. 1st edn, 2nd iss. Folio. [xii],362, [xxii] pp. Cancel title. Light occas browning. Mod calf. New Wing 2739 (improperly as "anr. ed.').
(Blackwell's) **£4,000 [≈ $7,200]**
- An essay concerning humane understanding. London: for Awnsham & John Churchill ..., 1694. 2nd edn. Folio. Staining, affecting partic the frontis & title. Contemp mottled calf. Wing L2470.
(Waterfield's) **£375 [≈ $675]**
- An essay concerning humane understanding. In four books. London: for A. Churchill, 1726. 9th edn. 2 vols. 8vo. [xxxii],372; [xvi],340, [xxvii] pp. Port frontis. V sl marg stain towards end vol 2. Contemp panelled calf.
(Frew Mackenzie) **£85 [≈ $153]**
- Some considerations of the consequences of the lowering of interest ... London: 1692. 1st edn, 2nd (?) iss. Sm 8vo. [iv],4,192, [1 errata] pp. Top crnr title torn away, rprd in facs. Some staining & browning. Contemp calf,

rebacked. Wing L2760.
(Pickering) **$2,750 [≈ £1,527]**
- Some thoughts concerning education. London: for A. & J. Millar, 1693. 1st edn (?). vii,262,[2 contents] pp. Contemp panelled calf, sm piece missing from crnr of top cvr. Wing C2762A. *(Pickering)* **$1,850 [≈ £1,027]**
- Some thoughts concerning education. London: A. & J. Churchill, 1705. 5th edn, enlgd. 8vo. [viii],390, [ii contents] pp. 1st & last gatherings browned. Contemp panelled calf, extremities rubbed.
(Blackwell's) **£60 [≈ $108]**
- The works ... in three volumes. The fifth edition. To which is now first added the life of the author ... London: 1751. 3 vols. Folio. Port, plate. Wormhole through lower marg vol II, another through outer marg at end of vol III. Old calf, rebacked & reprd.
(Bow Windows) **£405 [≈ $729]**

Lockhart, George
- Memoirs concerning the affairs of Scotland, from Queen Anne's accession to the throne, to the commencement of the Union ... London: J. Baker ..., 1714. 1st edn. 8vo. Mod qtr calf.
(Hughes) **£48 [≈ $86]**

Lockman, John (trans.)
- Travels of the Jesuits, into various parts of the world: particularly China and the East-Indies ... London: Piety, 1762. 2nd English edn. 2 vols. 8vo. 3 fldg maps, fldg plan, fldg plate. Contemp polished calf, hd & tail of spines & crnrs rubbed, jnts cracking.
(Morrell) **£560 [≈ $1,008]**

Loftus, Edward
- Joyfull newes from Ireland, or a true relation of the great overthrow which the English gave the rebels before Drogheda. London: John Franks, 1642. Sm 4to. 4 pp. Mor-backed cloth bds. Wing L2831. BM duplicate.
(Emerald Isle) **£150 [≈ $270]**

Lomazzo, Giovanni Paolo
- A tracte containing the artes of curious paintinge carvinge & buildinge. Oxford: R[ichard] H[aydock], 1598. 1st edn. 12,119; 218 pp. 18 full-page engvs. 1st & last lf soiled, title mtd, occas faint dampstain. Contemp mor, gilt, hairline cracks on spine.
(Pirages) **$4,000 [≈ £2,222]**

Lommius, Jodocus
- A treatise of continual fevers ... to which are added medicinal observations. London: for J. Brotherton, 1732. 1st edn in English. 8vo. xvi,452,iv pp. Marg dampstain in early

sgntrs. Contemp sprinkled calf, bds & extremities a bit worn & scuffed, in fldg box.
(Pirages) **$250 [≈£138]**

London ...

- London's dreadful visitation ... all the bills of mortality for this present year ... London: sold by E. Cotes, 1665. 1st edn. 4to. 55ff. Fldg table (torn in folds affecting sev letters without loss). Title sl soiled. Contemp panelled calf, worn, jnts cracked.
(Pickering) **$2,400 [≈£1,333]**

- A new view of London ... See Hatton, Edward

Long, Edward

- The history of Jamaica. 1774. 1st edn. 3 vols. 4to. 628; 601; viii,381 pp. 2 fldg map frontis (vols 1 & 2), 11 engvd plates, 4 maps & plans (3 fldg inc 1 not called for). Some offsetting of plates. Half calf, mrbld bds, vol 1 rebacked in mod calf. *(Edwards)* **£350 [≈$630]**

Long, John

- Voyages and travels of an Indian interpreter ... with an account of the posts situated on the River Saint Laurence, Lake Ontario, etc. London: for the author, 1791. 1st edn. 4to. 295 pp. Fldg map (offset & spotted), errata leaf. Contemp tree-calf, rubbed.
(Pirages) **$1,950 [≈£1,083]**

Long, Thomas

- A resolution of certain queries concerning submission to the present government ... What is the constitution ...? ... What obligation lies on the king ...? London: R. Baldwin ..., 1689. 4to. Wing L2980.
(C.R. Johnson) **£25 [≈$45]**

Lord of the Manor ...

- The lord of the manor, a comic opera ... See Burgoyne, John

Loriot, Monsieur

- A practical essay on a cement, and artificial stone ... lately discovered ... for ... all manner of buildings and ... all kinds of ornaments of architecture ... London: Cadell, 1774. 1st English edn. [4],51 pp. Title soiled & marked. Faded contemp wraps.
(Spelman) **£240 [≈$432]**

Louis XIV

- The life and history of Louis XIV. Present king of France and Navarre. In eight parts. For John Morphew, 1709. 1st edn. xvi,602,72 pp. Sm piece snipped from title crnr. Contemp calf, lacking label, some wear to

extremities. *(Claude Cox)* **£30 [≈$54]**

Louis XVI

- The accusation, trial, defence, sentence, execution, and last will of Louis XVI. Edinburgh: J. Elder ..., 1793. [2],108 pp. Frontis, port, plate. Foxed & sl dusty. Later binder's cloth. *(Cooper Hay)* **£14 [≈$25]**

Lounger ...

- The lounger's common-place book ... See Newman, Jeremiah Whitaker

Louvet de Couvray, Jean B.

- An account of the dangers to which I have been exposed, since the 31st of May, 1793. Perth: R. Morison, 1795. 12mo. 240 pp. A little dampstaining at end. Contemp mrbld bds, new calf spine, new endpapers.
(Robertshaw) **£30 [≈$54]**

- Narrative of the dangers to which I have been exposed, since the 31st of May, 1793. Dublin: for P. Byrne, 1795. 1st Irish edn. vi,221 pp. Polished half calf, gilt, a.e.g., jnts weak but holding. *(Fenning)* **£75 [≈$135]**

Love, John

- Geodaesia: or the art of surveying and measuring of land made easy ... also, how to lay out new lands in America, or elsewhere ... London: Betteworth ..., 1731. [20],196,[16], 4,[18],[8] pp. W'cut diags, tables. Rec calf.
(Karmiole) **$150 [≈£83]**

Lovell, Robert

- Sive pammineralogicon. Or an universal history of mineralls containing the summe of all authors ... Oxford: 1661. 1st edn. Sm 8vo. Title, 103 pp. Some dust marks & light stains. Rec half calf. Wing L3245.
(Bow Windows) **£125 [≈$225]**

Lover ...

- The fashionable lover; a comedy ... See Cumberland, Richard

Lovett, Richard

- The electrical philosopher ... new system of physics ... upon the principle of a universal plenum of elementary fire ... Worcester: 1774. 8vo. 2ff,xvi pp,3ff [5]-290 pp, 5ff. 2 fldg plates. Num lib stamps in margs. Contemp bds, spine damaged, uncut.
(Offenbacher) **$450 [≈£250]**

Lowman, Moses

- A dissertation on the civil government of the Hebrews ... to which is added an appendix ...

London: for J. Noon, 1745. 2nd edn. 8vo. Sm hole affecting 1 letter on E2. Contemp calf, rebacked.   *(Waterfield's)* £85 [≈ $153]

Lowth, William
- A commentary upon the prophet Isaiah. London: for W. Taylor, 1714. 4to. Some browning. Contemp calf, rec rebacked.
(Stewart) £35 [≈ $63]

Lozano, Pedro
- A true and particular account of the dreadful earthquake which happen'd at Lima ... a description of Callao and Lima ... and of ... Peru in general. London: Osborne, 1748. 1st English edn. 8vo. 24,342 pp. Advt leaf. Fldg map, plans, 5 fldg plates. Half cloth.
(Halewood) £150 [≈ $270]

Lucas, R.
- Practical Christianity; or, an account of the holiness which the gospel enjoins ... London: for W. Taylor, 1721. 6th edn. 8vo. Lacking front & rear endpapers. Contemp calf.
(Stewart) £25 [≈ $45]

Luckombe, Philip
- The history and art of printing. London: for J. Johnson, 1771. 1st edn, 2nd iss. 8vo. 6ff,502,[4] pp. W'cut frontis. Contemp mottled calf, minor worming at jnts, extremities a bit rubbed, bds & spine a little marked.   *(Pirages)* $450 [≈ £250]

Lucubrations ...
- Lucubrations during a short recess. London: J. Debrett, 1782. 65 pp. Half-title. Inscrbd pres copy from the author. Disbound.
(C.R. Johnson) £28 [≈ $50]

Ludlam, W.
- Mathematical essays. Cambridge: 1787. 2nd edn, with addtns. 97 pp. Sm 8vo. 3 fldg plates of diags. Cropped by binder with some loss of sgntrs. Later 3/4 lea, mrbld bds.
(Whitehart) £50 [≈ $90]

Ludlow, Edmund
- Memoirs of Edmund Ludlow, Lieutenant General of the Horse, Commander in Chief of the forces in Ireland. Vivay: 1698-99. 1st edn. 3 vols. Port in vol 1. Occas browning. Contemp panelled calf, some jnts cracked, most labels missing. Wing L3660 & L3462.
(Robertshaw) £65 [≈ $117]

Ludolphus, Job
- A new history of Ethiopia ... a full and accurate description of the Kingdom of

Abessinia ... London: Samuel Smith, 1682. 1st edn. in English. Sm folio. [viii],398 pp. 9 engvd plates, fldg table. V sl spotting. Contemp mottled calf, jnts cracking. Wing L346.   *(Morrell)* £450 [≈ $810]

Luffman, John
- The Charters of London complete. Luffman, 1793. 1st edn. 8vo. ii,431 (but viii,432) pp. Some anntns. Contemp half calf, spine dec in blind, restored, new label.
(Ash) £125 [≈ $225]

Lupton, Thomas
- A thousand notable things, on various subjects, disclosed from the secrets of nature and art ... London: for T. French, 1795. 12mo. A bit grubby with browning at edges & some fingering. Rec calf.
(Hughes) £25 [≈ $45]

Luther, Martin
- A commentarie of Master Doctor Martin Luther upon the Epistle of S. Paul to the Galathians ... out of Latine faithfully translated ... London: George Miller ..., 1644. 8vo. Some v minor worming in blank margs. Contemp calf, worn, jnts cracking. Wing L3510B.   *(Hughes)* £65 [≈ $117]
- Commentary St. Paul's Epistle to the Galatians ... Wigan: William Bancks, 1791. 4to. xx,339 pp. Title & final leaf sl frayed, intermittent light browning. Old calf, rebacked, crnrs reprd.
(Claude Cox) £18 [≈ $32]

Lynn, Walter
- Niktalopsia: or, the use and abuse of snuffers. London: A. More, 1726. 1st edn. 8vo. [2],28 pp. 2 w'cut ills. Title & last page soiled. mrbld bds.   *(Rootenberg)* $950 [≈ £527]

Lysimachus ...
- Lysimachus, or a dialogue concerning the union of Great Britain and Ireland. Dublin: G. Faulkner, 1770. 8vo. 67 pp. Mod mrbld bds.   *(Emerald Isle)* £75 [≈ $135]

Mably, Gabriel Bonnot, Abbe
- Phocion's conversations: or, the relation between morality and politics. London: for the author, 1769. 8vo. [vi],civ,[ii],303 pp. 1st edn in English. Contemp calf, upper cvr a little marked, upper jnt partially cracked.
(Burmester) £85 [≈ $153]
- Remarks concerning the government and the laws of the United States of America in four letters addressed to Mr. Adams ... with notes by the translator. Dublin: 1785. 1st Dublin

edn. 8vo. Contemp calf, jnts cracked.
(Farahar) **£200 [≈ $360]**

MacAllester, Oliver
- A series of letters, discovering the scheme projected by France ... For an intended invasion upon England with flat-bottom'd boats ... London: for the author, 1767. 2 vols. 4to. vi,263; 268 pp. Contemp qtr calf over bds.   *(Karmiole)* **$150 [≈ £83]**

Macaroni and Theatrical Magazine
- The Macaroni ... or Monthly Register, of the fashions and diversions of the times. London: Oct 1772 - Oct 1773. 13 monthly issues. 8vo. Engvd title, frontis, 26 (ex 27?) engvd plates. Tear in 1 outer margin with loss of 12 lines. Contemp half calf, worn.
(Burmester) **£80 [≈ $144]**

Macaulay, Alexander
- An enquiry into the legality of pensions on the Irish Establishment. London: J. Wilkie and Dublin, reprinted ..., 1763. 16 pp. Disbound.   *(C.R. Johnson)* **£30 [≈ $54]**

Macaulay, Aulay
- Polygraphy, or shorthand made easy to the meanest capacity being an universal character fitted to all languages ... London: for the author, 1747. 1st edn. 12mo. Engvd throughout. Contemp calf, jnts reprd.
(Traylen) **£60 [≈ $108]**

MacCulloch, John
- Malaria: an essay on the production and propagation of this poison ... with ... the means of preventing or diminishing them, both at home and in the naval and military service. London: 1727. 1st edn. 8vo. vi,[2],480 pp. Contemp 3/4 calf, mrbld bds.
(Hemlock) **$225 [≈ £125]**

Machiavelli, Niccolo
- The works ... London: for J[ohn] S[tarkey], 1675. 1st edn in English. 12ff, 529 pp, 11ff (frequently mispaginated). 1 leaf with marg tear, 2 early anntns. Contemp panelled calf, jnts partly cracked, sides pitted.
(Pirages) **$350 [≈ £194]**
- The works ... London: R. Clavel ..., 1695. Folio. [xxiv],528,[xvi] pp. Individual titles to each work. 1st few leaves dampstained, minor marg staining, single wormhole through inner marg. Old panelled calf, jnts cracked, surface of calf scuffed. Wing M131.
(Clark) **£140 [≈ $252]**
- The works ... Newly translated from the originals ... the life ... never before published.

In two volumes. Thomas Davies ..., 1762. 1st edn. 2 vols. 4to. Fldg plans. Contemp calf, spines elab gilt, spines reprd.
(Frew Mackenzie) **£320 [≈ $576]**

MacIntosh, James
- Vindiciae Gallicae. Defence of the French Revolution and its admirers against the accusations of ... Edmund Burke. London: for G.C.J. & J. Robinson. 1791. 3rd edn. Some pencillings. Later red half calf.
(Waterfield's) **£65 [≈ $117]**

Mackenzie, Andrew
- A treatise of maritime surveying, in two parts; with a prefatory essay on draughts and surveys. London: Dilly, 1774. 1st edn. Sm 4to. xxiii,[1], 119,[1 errata] pp. 6 fldg engvd plates. Contemp 3/4 calf.
(Antiq Sc) **$850 [≈ £472]**

Mackenzie, George
- The institutions of the law of Scotland. Edinburgh: 1688. 2nd edn, crrctd & enlgd. 12mo. [12],407 pp. A1 reprd with sl loss of text. Contemp calf, gilt on spine rubbed.
(Spelman) **£65 [≈ $117]**
- The lives and characters of the most eminent writers of the Scots nation ... Edinburgh: James Watson, 1708-11-22. 1st edn. 3 vols. Folio. A little waterstaining & soiling at beginning of vols 2 & 3, 1 title reprd, some biro anntns. Contemp calf, rebacked.
(Hughes) **£150 [≈ $270]**
- Reason. An essay. London: for Joseph Hindmarsh, 1695. 1st edn. 8vo. 158 pp. Title reprd. Contemp calf, old rebacking. Wing M194.   *(Edwards)* **£100 [≈ $180]**

Mackenzie, Henry
- The man of feeling. A new edition. 1794. 12mo. 279 pp. Advt. Contemp calf, rebacked.
(Halewood) **£40 [≈ $72]**

Mackenzie, Lieutenant J.
- A woollen draper's letter on the French treaty, to his friends and tradesmen all over England ... London: for the author, 1786. 1st edn. 8vo. [ii],48 pp. Lacking half-title, a little foxed. Mod paper-cvrvd bds
(Pickering) **$65 [≈ £36]**

Mackenzie, James (1680?-1761)
- The history of health and the art of preserving it. Edinburgh: William Gordon, 1758. 1st edn. 8vo. xii,436 pp. Calf, front jnt tender, hd of spine worn.   *(Elgen)* **$225 [≈ £125]**

Macklin, Charles
- The man of the world, a comedy, in five acts ... Dublin: 1786. 12mo. 72 pp. Contemp anntns on initial blank & on cast list. Disbound.   *(Clark)* **£18 [≃ $32]**

Macky, John
- Memoirs of the secret services of ... during the reigns of King William, Queen Anne, and King George I. Published from his original manuscripts ... London: 1733, 2nd edn. 8vo. New bds.   *(Stewart)* **£150 [≃ $270]**

Maclaurin, Colin
- An account of Sir Isaac Newton's philosophical discoveries, in four books. For the author's children, 1748. 1st edn. 4to. [viii],[xx subscribers], xx,392 pp. 6 fldg plates. Lightly browned throughout. New panelled calf.
                    (Frew Mackenzie) **£275 [≃ $495]**
- An account of Sir Isaac Newton's philosophical discoveries, in four books. London: 1750. 2nd edn. 8vo. Half-title, 6 fldg plates. Qtr calf.   *(Halewood)* **£125 [≃ $225]**
- A treatise of algebra, in three parts ... London: A. Millar ..., 1748. 1st edn. 8vo. xiv,366, [ii],65,i errata pp. 12 fldg engvd plates. Calf, worn.   *(Pollak)* **£85 [≃ $153]**
- A treatise of algebra, in three parts ... London: A. Millar ..., 1748. 1st edn. 8vo. xiv,366; i,65,i pp. 12 fldg engvd plates of diags, num diags in text. Contemp polished sprinkled calf, engvd b'plate.
                    (Blackwell's) **£200 [≃ $360]**

Maclean, Charles
- A view of the science of life ... elements of medicine of John Brown ... epidemics and pestilential diseases ... Phila: 1797. 8vo. 232 pp. Foxing. Antique bds.
                    (Goodrich) **$75 [≃ £41]**

Maclean, John
- Two lectures on combustion. Phila: Dobson, 1797. 1st edn. 8vo. 71 pp. Last leaf with old reprd tear, some staining. Linen-backed blue bds, antique style. *(Antiq Sc)* **$500 [≃ £277]**

Macmillan, Anthony
- Forms of writing used in Scotland ... Edinburgh: Elphingston Balfour, 1786. 2nd edn. [with] Supplement ... Edinburgh: 1786. 2 vols. 12mo in 6's. 1st edn of Supplement. Contemp calf, rubbed & chafed.
                    (Hughes) **£45 [≃ $81]**

McNayr, James
- A guide to Glasgow, to some of the most remarkable scenes in the Highlands of Scotland, and to the Falls of the Clyde. Glasgow: Courier Office, 1797. 1st edn. 8vo. Paper bds.   *(Halewood)* **£52 [≃ $93]**

MacNeill, Hector
- Scotland's Skaith; or the history o' Will and Jean: an owre true tale. Second edition. Edinburgh: P. Hill & A. Guthrie, 1795. 16 pp. Mod wraps. *(C.R. Johnson)* **£45 [≃ $81]**
- Scotland's Skaith; or the history o' Will and Jean: an owre true tale. Ninth edition. Stirling: C. Randall, 1795. 12 pp. Disbound.
                    (C.R. Johnson) **£45 [≃ $81]**

Macpherson, James
- Fingal, an ancient epic poem, in six books. London: for T. Becket ..., 1762. 1st edn. 4to. Red & black title, leaf of advts at end. Some minor worming in blank marg of a few leaves at end. Contemp sprinkled calf, gilt.
                    (Hughes) **£185 [≃ $333]**
- Fingal, an ancient epic poem, in six books. London: for T. Becket ..., 1762. 1st edn. 4to. 8ff, xvi,270 pp. Red & black vignette title. Contemp sprinkled calf, spine a little darkened, jnts rubbed or cracked, crnrs bruised.   *(Pirages)* **$175 [≃ £97]**
- Fingal, a poem in six books, by Ossian: translated from the original Galic ... Oxford: for J. & J. Fletcher ..., 1772. 8vo. viii,180 pp. Some sl staining & signs of use, crnr torn from 1 leaf affecting 2 words. Contemp mottled calf, ends of spine worn.
                    (Burmester) **£75 [≃ $135]**
- An introduction to the history of Great Britain and Ireland. Dublin: Williams, 1771. 12mo. Contemp calf.
                    (Emerald Isle) **£35 [≃ $63]**
- An introduction to the history of Great Britain and Ireland. London: T. Becket ..., 1771. 4to. 3 pp advts at end. Lib stamp at ft of title. Contemp calf, spine gilt, extremities worn, upper hinge cracked.
                    (Clark) **£35 [≃ $63]**
- Temora, an ancient epic poem in eight books, together with several other poems composed by Ossian ... Dublin: A. Leathly, 1763. 8vo. Contemp calf.   *(Emerald Isle)* **£50 [≃ $90]**
- Temora, an ancient epic poem, in eight books. London: for T. Becket ..., 1763. 1st edn. 4to. 2ff, xxxiv,[2],247 pp. Contemp sprinkled calf, spine a little darkened, jnts rubbed or cracked, crnrs bruised.
                    (Pirages) **$175 [≃ £97]**
- The works of Ossian, the son of Fingal. In

two volumes. London: for T. Becket ..., 1765. 3rd edn. 2 vols. 8vo. Contemp calf, rubbed, spines sl chipped, front jnt cracked vol I.
(Hughes) **£45 [≈ $81]**

Madox, Thomas
- Baronia Anglica, an history of land-honors and baronies and of tenures in capite. London: for Francis Gosling ..., 1741. Folio. 292 pp, index at end. W'engvd title. Sl soiled. Contemp calf, rebacked, rubbed.
(Titles) **£150 [≈ $270]**
- Firma burgi. or, an historical essay concerning the cities, towns and boroughs of England. 1726. 1st edn. Folio. 297 pp. Engvd vignettes. Contemp calf bds, rebacked.
(Edwards) **£260 [≈ $468]**
- The history and antiquities of the Exchequer of England. London: John Matthews, 1711. Lge 4to. Blank, 3ff, xvii,752, [xii],[72], [5 contents] pp, subscriber's leaf. Gilt dec panelled calf, hinges v tender.
(Titles) **£285 [≈ $513]**

Maid of the Oaks ...
- The maid of the oaks. A new dramatic entertainment ... See Burgoyne, John

Maimbourg, Louis
- The history of the League ... translated into English ... by Mr. Dryden. London: for Jacob Tonson, 1684. Frontis. Mod qtr calf. Wing M292.
(Waterfield's) **£85 [≈ $153]**
- The history of the League ... translated into English ... by Mr. Dryden. London: for Jacob Tonson, 1684. 1st edn. Engvd frontis. Contemp calf, old reback, a little rubbed, 1 jnt tender. Wing M292.
(Charles Cox) **£50 [≈ $90]**

Maitland, William
- The history of London. Osborne & Shipton ..., 1756. 1st complete edn. 2 vols. Folio. 123 maps & plates, many fldg (2 loosely inserted from smaller copies). A little foxing, a few sl marks. Contemp tree-calf, spines elab gilt, refurbished.
(Ash) **£1,000 [≈ $1,800]**

Malcolm, Alexander
- A new system of arithmetick ... for the purposes of men of science ... for men of business. London: for J. Osborn ..., 1730. 4to. 4,v-xx, 623,[i errata] pp. Contemp calf, rebacked, crnrs reprd, new endpapers.
(Pollak) **£150 [≈ $270]**

Mall, Thomas
- The history of the martyrs epitomised ...

Boston: Rogers & Fowle, 1747. 2 vols in 1. [16],267,[2]; [4],xi,292, [4] pp. Some foxing & staining, 1 sgntr starting. Early calf, worn.
(Reese) **$350 [≈ £194]**

Mallet, David
- Amyntor and Theodora: or, the hermit. A poem. In three cantos. The second edition. London: Paul Vaillant, 1748. 4to. 92 pp. Disbound.   *(C.R. Johnson)* **£65 [≈ $117]**
- Edwin and Emma. Birmingham: John Baskerville, 1760. 1st edn. 4to. [15] pp. Mod polished half calf, mrbld bds.
(Chaucer Head) **£90 [≈ $162]**
- The life of Francis Bacon ... London: for A. Millar..., 1740. 1st edn. 8vo. viii,197 pp. Engvd title vignette. Contemp calf, rebacked.
(Young's) **£50 [≈ $90]**

Mallet, Paul Henry
- Northern antiquities: or, a description of the manners, customs, religion and laws of the ancient Danes ... London: for T. Carnan, 1770. 2 vols. 8vo. Contemp calf, rebacked.
(Waterfield's) **£165 [≈ $297]**
- Northern antiquities: or, a description of the manners, customs, religion and laws of the ancient Danes ... London: for T. Carnan, 1770. 1st edn. 2 vols. 8vo. Rebound in cloth. Ex Royal Marines lib. *(Young's)* **£50 [≈ $90]**

Malone, William
- A reply to Mr. James Ussher his answer. [Douai:] 1627. 4to. Engvd title (mtd). Cut close at hd. Early 19th c calf, spine bumped. NSTC 17213.   *(Marlborough)* **£130 [≈ $234]**

Malton, Thomas
- A compleat treatise on perspective, in theory and practice. London: for the author, 1778. 2nd edn. Folio. [i title],[i blank],iv subscribers,[8 preface],296 pp. Engvd frontis, 48 plates (45 fldg, 5 with overslips). Contemp polished calf, gilt, upper jnt reprd.
(Spelman) **£500 [≈ $900]**

Malvezzi, Virgilio
- Discours upon Cornelius Tacitus ... translated ... by Sir Richard Baker ... London: for R. Whitaker ..., 1642. 1st edn in English. 8vo. [xx],504 [i.e. 492] pp. Some waterstaining, title a little soiled. Contemp calf, jnts cracking, crnrs rubbed. Wing M359.   *(Pickering)* **$850 [≈ £472]**
- The pourtract of the politicke christian-favourite. Originally drawn from from some of the actions of the Lord Duke of St. Lucar ... London: for M. Meighen ..., 1647. 1st edn

in English. 12mo. xlvi,117 pp. Without initial & final blanks, Mod calf. Wing M360.
(Pickering) **$650 [≈ £361]**

- Romulus and Tarquin. First written in Italian ... London: for John Benson, 1637. 1st edn in English. 12mo. Wanting prelim blank (or frontis?). Early 19th c calf, 1 jnt cracked. STC 17219. *(Charles Cox)* **£85 [≈ $153]**

- Romulus and Tarquin. First written in Italian ... London: for John Benson, 1637. 1st English edn. 12mo. Engvd title. Old stain at top of 1st 50 pp, last leaf reprd & reinforced. Mod vell, ruled in gilt, a.e.g. STC 17219.
(Karmiole) **$250 [≈ £138]**

Man of the World ...

- The man of the world, a comedy ... See Macklin, Charles

Mandeville, Bernard

- The fable of the bees ... And a search into the nature of society. London: for Allen & West, 1795. 8vo. 2 pts in 1 vol. Half-title. Contemp calf, old rebacking.
(Chaucer Head) **£85 [≈ $153]**

- The fable of the bees: or, private vices, publick benefits. With an essay on charity and charity-schools. And a search into the nature of society. London: for J. Tonson, 1725. 4th edn. 8vo. Title sl damaged, some marg fingermarks. Contemp calf, rebacked.
(Chaucer Head) **£95 [≈ $171]**

Manilius (fl. ca B.C. 60)

- Astronomicon. London: Woodfall, 1739. 4to. Port frontis, lge fldg engvd plate (remargined). Contemp calf, spine gilt, short split at hd of 1 jnt.
(Marlborough) **£190 [≈ $342]**

Manners and Principles ...

- An estimate of the manners and principles of the times ... See Brown, John

Manningham, Sir Richard

- An exact diary of what was observed upon Mary Toft, the pretending rabbet-breeder of Godalming ... an account of her confession of the fraud. London: for Fletcher Gyles ..., 1726. 1st edn. 8vo. 38 pp. Half-title. Disbound. *(Burmester)* **£75 [≈ $135]**

Manual Defence ...

- The art of manual defence; or, system of boxing: perspicuousley explained in a series of letters. London: for G. Kearsley, 1799. 3rd edn. 12mo. xxxv,133,[9] pp. 9 engvd plates. Frontis laid down, title soiled, some

browning. Lacking leaf of drctns (?).
(Young's) **£250 [≈ $450]**

Manwood, John

- Manwood's treatise of the forest laws. London: for B. Lintott, 1717. 4th edn, crrctd & enlgd by William Nelson. 8vo. 435 pp. Old calf, old rebacking. *(Edwards)* **£150 [≈ $270]**

Manzolli, Pietro Angelo

- The zodiake of life. London: Robert Robinson, 1588. 3rd edn. [viii],242,[xix] pp. Sm hole mended in marg of 1st 2 gatherings. Rec calf. *(Pirages)* **$1,250 [≈ £694]**

Maple, William

- A method of tanning without bark. Dublin: A. Rhames, 1729. 1st edn. 8vo. [6],35,[5] pp. Engvd hand-cold plate. Front paste-down detached & partially lacking. Mottled calf, dec in gilt. *(Rootenberg)* **$950 [≈ £527]**

Marchant, John

- The bloody tribunal: or, an antidote against popery ... cruelties of the inquisition, as practised in Spain ... Italy ... East and West-Indies. London: for Judith Walker, 1756. 1st edn. 8vo. 13 ills on 6 plates (old reprs). Contemp sheep, worn, bds near loose.
(Charles Cox) **£50 [≈ $90]**

Marinet, Johannes Florentina

- The catechism of nature. For the use of children. Boston: David West, 1795. 12mo. 99,[1],[3 advts] pp. Contemp calf over bds, a bit rubbed & soiled. *(Karmiole)* **$75 [≈ £41]**

Markham, Gervase

- Cheap and good husbandry for the well-ordering of all beasts and fowles, and for the generall cure of their diseases. London: for E. Brewster ..., 1657. 4to. W'cut & sev dec head & tail-pieces. Half calf. Wing M613.
(Traylen) **£65 [≈ $117]**

- Markham's farewell to husbandry: or, the enriching of all sorts of barren and sterile grounds in our nation ... London: for E. Brewster ..., 1656. 4to. W'cut ills in text. Calf-backed mrbld bds. Wing M650.
(Traylen) **£75 [≈ $135]**

- The perfect horse-man. Or the experienced secrets of Mr. Markham's fifty years' practice. London: for Humphrey Moseley, 1660. Sm 8vo. Frontis. A few marg tears, sl browning. Contemp rough calf, worn, owner's stamps on endpapers. Wing 672.
(Stewart) **£150 [≈ $270]**

Marlborough, John, Duke of ...
- History of John Duke of Marlborough ... See Banks, John

Marmor Norfolcience ...
- Marmor Norfolcience ... See Johnson, Samuel

Marra, John
- Journal of the 'Resolution''s voyage, in 1772 [-] 1775 ... Also a journal of the 'Adventure''s voyage in the years 1772 [-] 1774. London: Newbery, 1775. 8vo. Lge fldg chart, 5 engvd plates. Old calf, new spine.
  (Halewood) **£495 [≈ $891]**

Marriott, Sir James
- Poems written chiefly at the University of Cambridge ... with a Latin oration upon the history ... of the Roman and Canon laws. [London: Bettenham, 1706]. 1st edn. 8vo. Thick paper. [iv],viii, viii,[ii],156 pp. Frontis, sev vignettes, half-title. Rec qtr calf.
  (Burmester) **£85 [≈ $153]**

Marsden, William
- The history of Sumatra ... account of the government, laws, customs and manners ... ancient political state ... London: for the author, 1784. 2nd edn. 4to. xii,373,[7] pp. Fldg map, plate. Minimal spotting. Mod half calf.
  (Young's) **£180 [≈ $324]**

Marshall, Joseph
- Travels through Holland, Flanders, Germany ... the Ukraine and Poland in 1768, 1769 and 1770. London: for J. Almon, 1772. 1st edn. 3 vols. 8vo. Half-title vol 1, 4 pp ctlg at end vol 3. Contemp panelled calf, spines gilt, upper jnt vol 1 cracked. *(Stewart)* **£185 [≈ $333]**

Marshall, Stephen
- The song of Moses the servant of God, and the song of the Lambe; opened in a sermon preached to the House of Commons. London: 1643. 4to. [iv],48 pp. Minor marg staining. Disbound. Wing M789. *(Clark)* **£35 [≈ $63]**

Marshall, William
- Planting and ornamental gardening; a practical treatise. London: J. Dodsley, 1785. 8vo. 1st edn. xi,[5],638 pp. Half-title. Contemp tree-calf, jnt & hd & tail of spine reprd. *(Spelman)* **£220 [≈ $396]**
- Planting and rural ornament, being a second edition, with large additions, of Planting and Ornamental Gardening, a Practical Treatise. London: for G. Nicol ..., 1796. 2 vols. 8vo.

Contemp half calf, gilt spines, jnts worn.
  (Traylen) **£50 [≈ $90]**
- Planting and rural ornament, being a second edition, with large additions, of Planting and Ornamental Gardening, a Practical Treatise. London: 1796. 2 vols. 8vo. xxxii,408,[8]; xx,454,[4] pp. Contemp half calf, spine gilt.
  (Spelman) **£200 [≈ $360]**
- The rural economy of Norfolk. London: T. Cadell, 1787. 1st edn. 8vo. xix,400; [xvi],392, [iv] pp. Fldg map. Sl worming in gutters vol I & some margs vol II, sgntr Cc vol II misfolded. Orig grey bds, untrimmed.
  (Blackwell's) **£160 [≈ $288]**
- The rural economy of the Midland Counties ... management of livestock in Leicestershire ... Dublin: J. Moore, 1793. 2 vols. 8vo. [8],280; [8],287,[8] pp. Vol 1 endpapers removed & sl wormed in marg. Contemp tree calf. *(Spelman)* **£95 [≈ $171]**
- The rural economy of the West of England: including Devonshire; parts of Somersetshire, Dorsetshire, and Cornwall. London: G. Nicol ..., 1796. 1st edn. 2 vols. 8vo. 34,332; 24,358 pp. Engvd fldg frontis map. Inscrptns cut from endpapers. Mottled calf, gilt.
  (Tara) **£95 [≈ $171]**

Marten, Peter (trans.)
- The common places of the most famous and renowned divine doctor Peter Martyr divided into foure principall parts ... 1583. 4to. 252,165 pp, preface. V sl foxing. Rebound, bds worn. *(Edwards)* **£300 [≈ $540]**

Martial, Marcus Valerius
- The epigrams ... in twelve books. With a comment by James Elphinston. London: Baker & Galabin, 1782. Lge 4to. 1st edn of this trans. xxxviii,574,[2] pp. Engvd port frontis, final advt leaf. Rec calf, orig mrbld endpapers preserved.
  (Karmiole) **$150 [≈ £83]**
- Select epigrams ... Englished. In the Savoy. For Samuel Lowndes, 1689. Engvd frontis. Early 20th c half red mor. Ex lib Viscount Birkenhead with his b'plate. Wing M833.
  (Waterfield's) **£100 [≈ $180]**

Martin, B.
- The philosophical grammar: being a view of the present state of experimental physiology, or natural philosophy. In 4 parts ... London: 1762. 6th edn. 368 pp. 26 fldg plates. Contemp lea, rebacked.
  (Whitehart) **£80 [≈ $144]**

Martin, Benjamin

- The new art of surveying by the goniometer. London: for the author, 1766. 1st edn. 8vo. ii,36 pp. Red & black title. 2 fldg engvd plates. Old lea-backed mrbld bds.
(Antiq Sc) **$475 [≃ £263]**
- A new compleat and universal system or body of decimal arithmetick ... London: for George Keith, 1763. 2nd edn. 8vo. [xiv],403 pp. Prelim advt leaf, num diags & tables. Contemp calf, rebacked, orig spine preserved,
(Burmester) **£90 [≃ $162]**

Martin, Gregory

- A discovery of the manifold corruptions of the holy scriptures ... Reims: Fogny, 1582. 1st edn. Sm 8vo. Old limp vellum. NSTC 17503.
(Marlborough) **£350 [≃ $630]**

Martin, John

- The history and antiquities of Naseby in the County of Northampton. Cambridge: 1792. 8vo. iv, 5-206 pp. Fldg frontis, reprd on verso. Some pencil anntns. Uncut & sl dusty in rec half calf.
(Spelman) **£60 [≃ $108]**

Martin, M.

- A description of the Western Isles of Scotland ... 1703. 1st edn. 8vo. 392 pp. Fldg engvd map (short tear, not affecting text). Sl browning. Contemp calf, upper bd detchd.
(Edwards) **£170 [≃ $306]**

Martyn, Benjamin

- An impartial enquiry into the state and utility of the Province of Georgia. London: 1741. 104 pp. Variant without price ptd on title. Lib stamp on title. 3/4 calf & bds.
(Reese) **$675 [≃ £375]**

Martyn, Thomas

- Aranei, or a natural history of spiders ... As also ... Swedish Spiders ... London: 1793. 2 pts in 1 vol. 4to. Engvd titles, hand-cold frontis, 30 engvd plates (28 of spiders, hand-cold). A little spotting. Old diced calf, reprd, inner jnts cracked.
(Bow Windows) **£975 [≃ $1,755]**
- A chronological series of engravers from the invention of the art. Cambridge: J. Archdeacon, 1770. Sm 8vo. Title, xii,128 pp, 8ff index. 3 engvd fldg tables. New half calf.
(Marlborough) **£110 [≃ $198]**
- The English entomologist exhibiting all the coleopterous insects found in England ... London: 1792. Imp 4to. [vi],33,[iv], 41,[4] pp. Engvd title, 41 hand-cold plates. English & French text. Without the 2 plates of medals.

New qtr mor, uncut.
(Wheldon & Wesley) **£500 [≃ $900]**
- Thirty-eight plates, with explanations; intended to illustrate Linnaeus's system of vegetables ... London: J. White, 1799. 8vo. vi,72 pp. 38 plates. Some minor foxing. 19th c half calf, spine gilt. *(Spelman)* **£70 [≃ $126]**
- Thirty-eight plates, with explanations; intended to illustrate Linnaeus's system of vegetables ... London: J. White, 1799. 8vo. Advt leaf. Some light foxing. Mod bds.
(Stewart) **£90 [≃ $162]**
- A tour through Italy ... travelling in that interesting country ... everything that is curious in architecture, painting, sculpture, &c ... London: for C. & G. Kearsley, 1791. 8vo. xxxix,480,[viii] pp. Fldg cold map. Some foxing. Rec half calf. *(Clark)* **£90 [≃ $162]**
- A tour through Italy ... travelling in that country ... everything that is curious in architecture, painting, sculpture, &c ... London: for C. & G. Kearsley, 1791. 8vo. xxxix, 480,[8] pp. Lge fldg cold map (trifle torn). Uncut in contemp bds, new calf spine.
(Burmester) **£95 [≃ $171]**

Marvell, Andrew

- Miscellaneous poems. London: for Robert Boulter, 1681. 1st edn. Folio. Port & last 2 leaves in facs. Contemp sheep.
(Charles Cox) **£380 [≃ $684]**
- A short historical essay touching General Councils, creeds, and impositions in matters of religion. Very seasonable at this time. London: R. Baldwin, 1687. 2nd edn. Sm 4to. 37 pp. Worming through outer marg effecting text on about 10 leaves. Old wraps.
(Burmester) **£45 [≃ $81]**
- A short historical essay touching General Councils, creeds, and impositions in matters of religion. London: 1680. 1st edn. 4to. Title soiled & defective at crnr, reprd & laid down. With the blank E4. 18th c b'plate. Later calf, rebacked. Wing M888.
(Charles Cox) **£125 [≃ $225]**
- A short historical essay touching General Councils ... London: 1680. 4to. 38,[ii] pp. Final blank. Title dusty, worming in marg affecting some letters. Later wraps. Wing 888. *(Clark)* **£48 [≃ $86]**
- The works ... with a new life of the author by Capt. Edward Thompson. London: Dodsley ..., 1776. 3 vols. 4to. Engvd port frontis. Contemp calf, jnts cracked but holding, some surface damage, spines chipped away at hd & tail. *(Frew Mackenzie)* **£240 [≃ $432]**

Marzin, Cardinal

- Letters to Lewis XIV. The present king of France, on his love to the Cardinal's niece. Together with his secret negotiation with Don Lewis D'Haro. London: for R. Bentley, 1691. 1st edn. 12mo. Contemp panelled calf, rebacked. Wing M1540.
(Traylen) **£70 [≈ $126]**

Mason, John Mitchel

- A sermon preached September 20th, 1793; a day set apart in the City of New York, for public fasting, humiliation and prayer, on account of a mortal and malignant fever prevailing in the City of Philadelphia. New York: Samuel Loudon, 1793. 8vo. 64 pp. Wraps.
(Farahar) **£45 [≈ $81]**

Mason, Richard Angelus

- A liturgical discourse of the Mass. [London:] 1670-69. 2 parts in 1 vol. 8vo. Contemp calf, very worn, jnts cracked. New Wing M936-7.
(Marlborough) **£80 [≈ $144]**

Mason, Richard Oswald

- 'Pro Aris et Focis". Considerations of the reasons that exist for reviving the use of the long bow with the pike. London: for T. Egerton, Military Library, 1798. 1st edn. 8vo. Frontis, engvd title, 2 fldg plates. Orig bds, spine worn.
(Robertshaw) **£30 [≈ $54]**

Mason, William

- Elfrida, a dramatic poem. London: for J. & P. Knapton, 1752. 2nd edn. 8vo. [iv],xx,80 pp. Mod paper wraps. *(Claude Cox)* **£15 [≈ $27]**
- Elfrida, a dramatic poem. London: J. & P. Knapton, 1752. 2nd edn. 8vo. [iv],xix,80 pp. Half-title. Disbound. *(Clark)* **£18 [≈ $32]**
- The English garden: a poem. Book the first. London: 1772. 1st edn. 4to. [iv],30, [ii] pp. Final advt leaf. Outer leaves a bit dusty. Disbound, untrimmed. *(Clark)* **£18 [≈ $32]**
- Musaeus: a monody to the memory of Mr. Pope, in imitation of Milton's Lycidas. London: for R. Dodsley ..., 1747. 1st edn. 4to. 22 pp. Vignette title. Leaves rprd in inner marg. New bds. *(Young's)* **£58 [≈ $104]**
- Poems. London: for Robert Horsfield ..., 1764. 1st coll edn. Vignette title. Contemp calf. Ex lib Colquhoun of Luss.
(C.R. Johnson) **£250 [≈ $450]**

Massinger, Philip

- The bond-man: an ancient storie. As it hath been often acted with good allowance, at the Cock-pit in Drury Lane ... London: for John Harison ..., 1624. 1st edn. Sm 4to. A1-L4.

Title sl stained. Rebound in blind-tooled calf.
(Edwards) **£950 [≈ $1,710]**
- The renegado, a tragaecomedie. As it hath beene often acted by the Queenes Majesties servants, at the private play-house in Drurye-Lane. London: for John Waterson ..., 1630. 1st edn. 4to. A1-m2. Sl tear to marg of A3 not affecting text. Mottled calf.
(Edwards) **£750 [≈ $1,350]**

The Mathematician

- The Mathematician. Numbers 1-4 [of 6 published]. Containing articles on: the rise, progress and improvement of geometry; chief properties of the parabola; conic sections ... London: 1745. viii,259 pp. Diags. 1st title grubby. New 3/4 lea.
(Whitehart) **£150 [≈ $270]**

Mather, Increase

- The mystery of Israel's salvation, explained and applyed. London: 1669. 8vo. 1st edn. With the addtnl title c8. Title sl torn along gutter, tear without loss to c8. Mod calf. Wing 1230A. *(Charles Cox)* **£650 [≈ $1,170]**

Mather, Samuel

- The life of the very reverend and learned Cotton Mather ... Boston: 1729. [24],186 pp. Foxed. Mod 3/4 pebbled calf.
(Reese) **$600 [≈ £333]**

Mather, W.

- The young-man's companion: or, arithmetick made easy ... London: 1734. 14th edn. 8vo. Frontis loose. Contemp calf.
(Robertshaw) **£30 [≈ $54]**
- The young-man's companion: or, the several branches of useful learning made perfectly easy ... London: 1764. 22nd edn. 8vo. Frontis, 4 plates. Contemp sheep.
(Robertshaw) **£30 [≈ $54]**

Mathews, Thomas

- Authentick letters from Admiral Mathews to the Sec--t----s of St---te, the L---ds of the Ad---- -ty, etc. Relating to his expedition to the Mediterranean ... London: W. Webb, n.d. [ca 1744]. 68 pp. Disbound.
(C.R. Johnson) **£25 [≈ $45]**
- A narrative of the proceedings of his Majesty's Fleet in the Mediterranean ... from 1741 to March 1794 ... accurate account of the late fight near Toulon ... London: J. Millan, 1744. 118 pp. Disbound.
(C.R. Johnson) **£25 [≈ $45]**
- A particular account of the late action in the Mediterranean. With the line of battle of both

fleets. London: 1744. 26 pp. Disbound.
(C.R. Johnson) **£25 [≈ $45]**

Mathias, Thomas James
- The shade of Alexander Pope on the banks of the Thames. A satirical poem, with notes. The third edition. London: for T. Becket, 1799. 8vo. [ii],82 pp. Disbound.
(Burmester) **£15 [≈ $27]**

Matho ...
- Matho: or, the cosmotheoria puerilis ... See Baxter, Andrew

Matthews, John
- A voyage to the River Sierra-Leone ... London: B. White, 1788. 1st edn. 8vo. iv,183 pp. Fldg engvd chart & plate. Mod half mor, mrbld bds, spine gilt. *(Morrell)* **£280 [≈ $504]**

Matthieu, Pierre
- The heroyk life and deplorable death of the most Christian King Henry the Fourth ... Translated ...L: printed by George Eld, 1612. 1st edn. 4to. Waterstain to 1st few leaves & elsewhere, last leaf ragged at edges. Old calf, rebacked. STC 17661.
(Charles Cox) **£95 [≈ $171]**

Maude, Thomas
- Viator a poem: or, a journey from London to Scarborough, by way of York. With notes historical and topographical. London: B. White ..., 1782. Half-title, 40,xix pp. Disbound. *(C.R. Johnson)* **£225 [≈ $405]**
- Wensley-Dale; or rural contemplations: a poem. The second edition. London: T. Davies, 1772. 4to. Half-title. Mod wraps.
(C.R. Johnson) **£95 [≈ $171]**

Mauger, Claude
- French grammar with additions, enriched with new words, and a new method ... London: 1698. 18th edn. 8vo. Parallel English & French text. Sm burnhole in C4 touching a few letters. Contemp calf. Wing M1341B. *(Robertshaw)* **£40 [≈ $72]**

Maundrell, Henry
- A journey from Aleppo to Jerusalem. At Easter 1697 ... The fifth edition ... added an account of the author's journey to the banks of the Euphrates ... Mesopotamia. Oxford: 1732. 8vo. 15 plates (9 fldg). Contemp calf, spine trifle worn. Baronial b'plate.
(Halewood) **£85 [≈ $153]**
- A journey from Aleppo to Jerusalem at Easter 1697 ... The fifth edition ... added an account

of the author's journey to the banks of Euphrates ... and Mesopotamia. Oxford: 1732. 8vo. 15 plates (8 fldg). Lacking rear free endpaper. Contemp calf, rubbed.
(Waterfield's) **£85 [≈ $153]**
- A journey from Aleppo to Jerusalem at Easter 1697 ... added an account of the author's journey to the banks of Euphrates ... Mesopotamia. Oxford: 1849. 7th edn. 8vo. xii,171 pp. Vignette title. Sl browned. Contemp speckled calf, inner hinges strengthened.
(Frew Mackenzie) **£130 [≈ $234]**
- A sermon preach'd before the Honourable Company of Merchants trading to the Levant-Seas ... 1695. London: for Daniel Brown, 1696. 1st edn. Sm 4to. [ii],28 pp. Disbound. Wing M1356. *(Hughes)* **£45 [≈ $81]**

Maupas, Charles
- A French grammar and syntaxe ... Translated ... London: for Rich: Mynne, 1634. 1st edn in English. 12mo. xxii,445 pp. Wanting A1 (blank?). Worming, mainly confined to margs, crnr torn from 2 leaves with sl loss to errata. Contemp sheep, rebacked & reprd.
(Burmester) **£160 [≈ $288]**
- A French grammar and syntaxe ... Translated ... London: for Rich: Mynne, 1634. 1st edn. Worming, mostly marginal, 2 crnrs torn with loss of 2 words, last leaf torn & laid down. Old sheep, rebacked. *(Charles Cox)* **£65 [≈ $117]**

Maurice, Henry
- A defence of diocesan episcopacy. London: for James Adamson, 1691. 1st edn. 8vo. viii,456 pp. Contemp calf, worn at hd of spine. Wing M1360.
(Lloyd-Roberts) **£35 [≈ $63]**

Maurice, T.
- Indian antiquities: or, dissertations, relative to the antient geographical divisions ... the whole intended as introductory to the history of Hindostan ... 1794-1800. 1st edn. 7 vols. 7 fldg frontis, 21 plates, 2 fldg maps. Tree-calf, some jnts cracking. *(Edwards)* **£150 [≈ $270]**

Mauriceau, Francois
- The diseases of women with child, and in child-bed: as also the best means of helping them in ... labours ... London: Andrew Bell, 1710. 4th edn. 8vo. xliv,373,[11] pp. 10 plates, most fldg. Browning & spotting, stamps on title & plates. Contemp calf.
(Hemlock) **$275 [≈ £152]**

Maxwell, Robert, of Arkland
- The practical husbandman; being a collection

of miscellaneous papers on husbandry, &c. Edinburgh: for the author, 1757. 1st edn. xii,432,[4] pp. Contemp half calf, upper hinge broken, lower hinge cracked.
(Claude Cox) **£100 [≈ $180]**

May, Thomas
- The history of the parliament of England which began November the third, 1640. London: Thomason, 1647. 1st edn. Sm folio. Old calf, rubbed, rec reback. New Wing M1410.   *(Marlborough)* **£140 [≈ $252]**
- The history of the parliament of England which began November the third, 1640. London: for George Thomason, 1647. 1st edn. Folio. Innocuous repr to ft of title. Old calf, later label, spine worn. Wing M1410.
(Charles Cox) **£50 [≈ $90]**

May, W.
- The Queen's closet opened. Incomparable secrets in physic, chirurgery, preserving ... Part II ... making perfumes ... Part III The compleat cook ... London: Blagrave, 1683. 12mo. [10],190,[8]; 106,[4]; 123,[7]. Pp 95-102 in pt III in facs. Mod calf. Wing M104.   *(Hemlock)* **$550 [≈ £305]**

Mayhew, Jonathan
- A discourse occasioned by the death of the honourable Stephen Sewall ... member of his Majesty's Council for the Province of the Massachusett's-Bay in New England. Boston: Richard Draper, 1760. 8vo. 66 pp. Later half mor. spine & crnrs worn.
(Spelman) **£40 [≈ $72]**
- The snare broken. A thanksgiving discourse, preached at the desire of the West Church in Boston, N.E. May 23, 1766, occasioned by the repeal of the Stamp Act. Boston: 1766. viii,48 pp. Disbound. In fldg cloth case.
(Reese) **$275 [≈ £152]**
- Two discourses delivered October 25th 1759 ... a day of public thanksgiving, for the success of his majesty's arms, more particularly in the reduction of Quebec ... with an appendix ... Boston: 1759. 79 pp. Disbound. In fldg cloth case.
(Reese) **$750 [≈ £416]**

Mayne, Jasper
- Oxlo-maxia. Or the people's war, examined according to the principles of scripture and reason ... Oxford printed: for Mayne, 1647. 4to. Woodcut title border. Sl fraying of title marg. Disbound. Wing 1472.
(Clark) **£40 [≈ $72]**

Maynwaring, Everard
- Tutela sanitatis ... the protection of long life, and detection of its brevity ... London: Peter Lillicrap, 1664. 1st edn (?). 8vo. [24],118,[2] pp. Red & black title. Sm hole B5 affecting 1 letter, possibly lacking last leaf. Contemp calf, rebacked, recrnrd.
(Rootenberg) **$500 [≈ £277]**

Mead, Richard
- A discourse concerning the action of the sun and the moon on animal bodies ... London: 1708. 1st edn. 8vo. 32 pp. Sl foxed. A lge copy in rec mor-backed bds.
(Pickering) **$800 [≈ £444]**
- A discourse on the plague ... the ninth edition corrected and enlarged. London: for A. Millar ..., 1744. Lge paper. 8vo. [viii],xl, 164 pp. Inscribed 'From the author'. Polished calf, gilt, rebacked, orig spine laid down, 2 crnrs reprd.   *(Pickering)* **£450 [≈ £250]**
- A mechanical account of poisons. In several essays. London: 1702. 1st edn. 175 pp. Plate. Stamp on title. Lea, rebacked, new endpapers.   *(Scientia)* **$250 [≈ £138]**
- A mechanical account of poisons in several essays. London: for Ralph Smith, 1702. 1st edn. Sm 8vo. [xvi],183,[i] pp. Contemp sprinkled calf, sl rubbed, rec rebacked.
(Blackwell's) **£160 [≈ $288]**
- A mechanical account of poisons in several essays. London: for Ralph Smith, 1708. 2nd edn, revsd. 8vo. [xvi],189,[2 explanation],[1 blank] pp. Fldg engvd plate. Contemp polished calf, jnts cracked.
(Pickering) **£250 [≈ £138]**
- A mechanical account of poisons in several essays. London: 1708. 2nd edn. Rebound in stiff mrbld wraps.
(Rittenhouse) **$195 [≈ £108]**
- Medical precepts and cautions ... Translated from the Latin by Thomas Stack. London: 1755. 2nd edn. 8vo. xvi,311,[1] pp. Inscrptn on flyleaf. Contemp calf.
(Hemlock) **$240 [≈ £133]**
- Medical precepts and cautions. Translated by Thomas Stack. London: J. Brindley, 1755. 2nd edn. 8vo. xvi,311 pp. Advt leaf. Orig lea bds, rebacked, crnrs bumped, hd of spine chipped.   *(Elgen)* **$250 [≈ £138]**
- The medical works ... with an account of the life and writings of the author ... Edinburgh: Alexander Donaldson, 1765. 1st edn of this coll. 3 vols. 8vo. 18,272; viii,255; 213,[73 index] pp. Contemp polished calf, hd of spine nicked, jnts of 1 vol weak.
(Pickering) **£600 [≈ £333]**
- The medical works. Dublin: Thomas Ewing,

1767. 8vo. 5 plates. Contemp calf, worn, spine broken. *(Robertshaw)* **£25** [≈ **$45**]

- The medical works. London: 1762. 1st edn. 4to. 662 pp. 6 fldg plates. Rec half lea.
(Fye) **$400** [≈ **£222**]

- A short discourse concerning pestilential contagion, and the methods to be used to prevent it ... Dublin: George Grierson, 1720. 4th edn. Portions of lower marg cut away & replaced. Mod mrbld bds.
(Emerald Isle) **£125** [≈ **$225**]

- A short discourse concerning pestilential contagion, and the methods to be used to prevent it ... London: Sam. Buckley ..., 1722. 8th edn, with lge addtns. Lge paper. 8vo. [viii], xxxvi,150 pp. Contemp red mor, spine & sides gilt. *(Pickering)* **$400** [≈ **£222**]

Meager, Leonard

- The English gardener or a sure guide to your planters and gardeners ... For P. Parker ..., 1670. 1st edn. Sm 4to. 24 engvs. Lower portion of 1 plate torn away with some loss, sm piece cut out of the middle of 3 plates. Early calf, rebacked, new endpapers.
(Sotheran) **£585** [≈ **$1,053**]

Means ...

- The legal means of political reformation proposed ... See Sharpe, Granville

Meares, John

- Voyages made in the years 1788 and 1789, from China to the Northwest coast of America ... probable existence of a North West Passage ... London: 1790. xx, xcvi,372, [108] pp. 10 maps & plans, 17 ills inc port frontis. Orig calf, rebacked. *(Reese)* **$3,250** [≈ **£1,805**]

Measures ...

- The measures of the late administration examin'd with an enquiry into the grounds of the present Revolution. London: M. Cooper, 1745. 63 pp. Disbound.
(C.R. Johnson) **£45** [≈ **$81**]

Mede, Joseph

- The works of the pious and profoundly-learned Joseph Mede. London: for R. Royston, 1677, 4th edn, crrctd & enlgd. Folio. [xliv], xlvi, 924, [xxviii] pp. Contemp reversed calf. Wing M1589.
(Lloyd-Roberts) **£80** [≈ **$144**]

Meilham, Gabriel Senac de

- Considerations upon wit and morals. Translated from the French. London: for G.G.J. & J. Robinson, 1788. Sm lib stamp on

title. Contemp qtr calf.
(Waterfield's) **£80** [≈ **$144**]

Memoirs ...

- Memoirs British and foreign of the lives ... of the most illustrious persons who dy'd in the year 1711. London: 1712. 1st edn. Contemp panelled calf, jnts cracked, wear at hd of spine. *(Robertshaw)* **£25** [≈ **$45**]

- Memoirs concerning the affairs of Scotland ... See Lockhart, George

- Memoirs of a cavalier ... See Defoe, Daniel

Memorandums ...

- Memorandums, etc., etc. respecting the unprecedented treatment which the army has met with ... See Clinton, Sir Henry

Memorial ...

- The memorial of the Church of England humbly offer'd to the considerations of all true lovers of our church and constitution. Printed in the year 1705. 4to. Disbound.
(Waterfield's) **£35** [≈ **$63**]

- A memorial of the contractants with Mr. Aislabie. In a letter to Licinius Stolo. London: for J. Roberts, 1721. 1st edn. 8vo. [ii],60 pp. Trife dusty. Uncut, disbound.
(Burmester) **£110** [≈ **$198**]

Memorialls ...

- Memorialls for the government of the Royalburghs in Scotland ... See Skene, Alexander

Memorials ...

- The memorials of the English and French Commissaries concerning the limits of Nova Scotia or Acadia. London: 1755. Lge thick 4to. [4],771 pp. Fldg map, backed at folds, minor stains. Minor reprs to extremities of 1st & last leaves. New half calf, mrbld bds.
(Reese) **$3,500** [≈ **£1,944**]

Mental Amusement ...

- Mental amusement; or, the juvenile moralist ... Calculated for the use of private families and public schools. London: for G. Sael ..., 1798. 2nd edn, revsd. 12mo. viii,136 pp. Engvd frontis. Orig green roan-backed mrbld bds, ptd label sl chipped.
(Burmester) **£160** [≈ **$288**]

Mercier-Dupaty, Charles

- Sentimental letters on Italy; written in French ... in 1785 ... and translated ... at Paris. London: for the translator, 1789. 1st edn of this trans. 2 vols in 1. 12mo. Rec antique-style half mor.   *(Burmester)* £90 [≈ $162]

Meredith, Sir William
- The question stated whether the Freeholders of Middlesex lost their right by voting for Mr. Wilkes at the last election? London: G. Woodfall ..., n.d. [ca 1769]. 72 pp. Half-title. Disbound.   *(C.R. Johnson)* £45 [≈ $81]

Meriton, G.
- An exact abridgement of all the publick printed Irish statutes now in force ... Dublin: A. Crook, 1700. Thick 8vo. Over 700 pp. Some sl marg worming near end. Contemp calf.   *(Emerald Isle)* £110 [≈ $198]

Meriton, George
- Nomenclatura clericalis: or, the young clerk's vocabulary in English and Latin. London: 1685. 1st edn. 8vo. Light dampstaining on a few leaves. Later half calf, worn, upper cvr loose. Wing M1807.
    (Robertshaw) £30 [≈ $54]

Meriton, Thomas
- Love and war. A tragedy. London: Charles Webb, 1658. 4to. [iv],[96] pp. Cropped at hd affecting text of 1st few leaves. Later mor, worn, upper jnt weak. Wing M1822.
    (Clark) £55 [≈ $99]

Merke, Thomas
- The Bishop of Carlisle's speech in parliament concerning deposing of princes. Thought seasonable to be published to this murmuring age. London: 1679. Folio. 5 pp. Rebound in qtr calf, mrbld bds. Wing M1827.
    (C.R. Johnson) £25 [≈ $45]

Method ...
- A method of tanning without bark ... See Maple, William
- A short and easie method with the deists ... See Berrow, Capel

Meyrick, W.
- The new family herbal; or, domestic physician. Birmingham: Pearson, 1790. xxiv,498,[vi advts] pp. Engvd frontis (sl waterstained), 14 plates. Calf, rebacked.
    (P & P) £98 [≈ $176]

Middleton, Charles
- The architect and builder's miscellany, or pocket library ... original picturesque designs in architecture ... London: for the author, 1799. 1st edn. F'cap 8vo. 2 ff, 60 hand-cold etched plates. Contemp speckled calf, gilt

spine, jnts reprd.   *(Spelman)* £450 [≈ $810]

Middleton, Conyers
- A free enquiry into the miraculous powers, which are supposed to have subsisted in the Christian Church, from the earliest ages ... London: for R. Manby, 1749. 1st edn. 4to. Half-title. Contemp calf, rubbed at edges, rec rebacked.   *(Hughes)* £65 [≈ $117]
- The history of the life of Marcus Tullius Cicero. London: for W. Innys ..., 1741. 2nd edn. 3 vols. 8vo. Contemp calf, vol 1 spine worn.   *(Lloyd-Roberts)* £30 [≈ $54]
- A letter from Rome shewing an exact conformity between Popery and Paganism ... London: for William Innys ..., 1733. 3rd edn, with additions. 4to. Title v dusty. Disbound.
    (Waterfield's) £20 [≈ $36]

Miege, Guy
- The present state of Great Britain and Ireland ... Eleventh edition ... completed ... by Mr. Bolton. London: 1757. 8vo. Port. Contemp calf, v worn, jnts cracked.
    (Robertshaw) £20 [≈ $36]
- A short dictionary English and French, with another French and English. London: Tho. Bassett, 1685. Initial advt leaf. Short tear in final leaf. Contemp calf, extremities worn, jnts cracked. Wing 2027.
    (Clark) £100 [≈ $180]

Miles, William
- A letter to Henry Duncombe ... on the subject of an extraordinary pamphlet, lately addressed by Mr. Burke, to a noble Lord. London: J. Debrett, 1796. 4th edn. 100 pp. Mod wraps.   *(C.R. Johnson)* £18 [≈ $32]

Miller, Edmund
- An account of the University of Cambridge, and the Colleges there ... their oaths, statutes and charters. London: J. Baker ..., 1717. 1st edn. 8vo. 200 pp. Without frontis. Contemp gilt panelled vellum, a.e.g.
    (Young's) £100 [≈ $180]

Miller, Philip
- The abridgement of the gardeners dictionary. London: 1771. 6th edn. 4to. Engvd frontis, 12 fldg plates. Plate 5 defective, last few leaves heavily stained, inscrptn cut from title marg. Half calf, worn.
    (Wheldon & Wesley) £65 [≈ $117]
- The abridgement of the gardeners dictionary ... Sixth edition, corrected and much enlarged. For the author, 1771. 4to. [vii,920] pp. Frontis, 10 fldg plates, ptd in double

column. Sl foxing & soiling. New qtr brown mor. *(Blackwell's)* **£85 [≈ $153]**

- The gardeners dictionary ... cultivating and improving the kitchen ... flower-garden ... the physick garden ... London: 1731. 1st edn. Folio. Engvd frontis, 4 fldg plates. Title a bit stained & dusty, some minor staining & worming. Contemp calf, rebacked.
  (Clark) **£250 [≈ $450]**

- The gardeners dictionary ... the kitchen, fruit and flower-garden, as also, the physick garden ... London: for the author, 1731. 1st edn. Folio. Unpaginated. Engvd frontis, 4 engvd plates. Trivial soiling. Contemp panelled calf, rebacked, sides rubbed.
  (Frew Mackenzie) **£290 [≈ $522]**

- The gardeners dictionary ... the kitchen, fruit and flower garden ... London: 1731. 1st edn. Folio. xvi,[841] pp. Frontis, 4 plates. Mod buckram, crnrs trifle bumped.
  (Wheldon & Wesley) **£200 [≈ $360]**

- The gardeners dictionary ... cultivating the kitchen ... flower-garden, as also, the physick garden ... London: for the author, 1733. 2nd edn crrctd. [with] An appendix to ... 1735. Folio. Unpaginated. Engvd frontis, 4 engvd plates. text figs. Contemp calf.
  (Frew Mackenzie) **£265 [≈ $477]**

- The gardeners kalendar; directing what works are to be performed every month in the kitchen, fruit and pleasure gardens ... 1762. 13th edn. Engvd frontis, 4 fldg plates. Contemp calf, rebacked.
  (Halewood) **£58 [≈ $104]**

- The gardeners kalendar. London: 1769. 15th edn. 8vo. lxvi,382,[21] pp. Frontis, 5 plates. New half calf.
  (Wheldon & Wesley) **£45 [≈ $81]**

Milton, John

- A complete collection of the historical, political, and miscellaneous works ... In two volumes. London: A. Millar, 1738. Folio. [iv], xcvii,628; [iv],617,[xxv] pp. A little dampstaining & occas spotting. Contemp calf, spines gilt, heavily worn.
  (Clark) **£110 [≈ $198]**

- A defence of the people of England ... in answer to Salmasius's defence of the King. [Amsterdam:] 1692. 1st edn in English. With blank A8 & final advt leaf. Title a little marked, a few light mostly marg stains, a little underlining. Mod calf. Wing M2104.
  (Charles Cox) **£175 [≈ $315]**

- Paradise lost ...The twelfth edition. To which is prefix'd an account of his life. London: for Jacob Tonson, 1725. Lge 12mo. xxviii,[8], 350,[46] pp. Engvd port, 12 plates. Light

foxing throughout. Rec bds.
  (Fenning) **£85 [≈ $153]**

- Paradise lost. London: S. Simmons, 1678. 3rd edn. Port. Lacking the 2 blanks at end, cut a little close at head, some headlines just touched. Polished calf, gilt, a.e.g, by bedford. Wing M2145. *(Charles Cox)* **£350 [≈ $630]**

- Paradise lost. London: Tonson, 1711. [x],376,[xiii] pp. Frontis, 12 plates. Sl yellowed, 2 sm brown spots on fore-edges throughout. Contemp red mor, spine elab gilt, jnts patched, short crack in spine.
  (Pirages) **$100 [≈ £55]**

- Paradise lost. Glasgow: Foulis, 1770. Folio. B1 cancelled. Reprs to title gutter, occas minor spotting. Mod red qtr mor.
  (Waterfield's) **£150 [≈ $270]**

- Paradise lost. Paradise regained ... London: for J. Beecroft ..., 1775-77. 4to. 3 vols. ci,491; 460,116; 690,2 pp. 3 frontis, 16 plates. Full calf, gilt, spine & crnrs sl worn.
  (Edwards) **£200 [≈ $360]**

- Paradise lost: a poem. In twelve books. J. & H. Richter, 1794. 4to. [iv],493 pp. Port frontis, 11 engvd plates. Trivial marg worming in 1st 3 leaves, v occas browning, 19th c inscrptn on front blank. Contemp mor, gilt, rebacked, crnrs lightly bumped.
  (Frew Mackenzie) **£170 [≈ $306]**

- Paradise regain'd ... [with] Samson Agonistes; and poems upon several occasions, with a tractate of education. The fifth edition. London: for J. & R. Tonson ..., 1713. Lge 12mo. [viii],388 pp. Engvd frontis, 10 plates. Contemp calf, jnts sl rubbed.
  (Pirages) **$125 [≈ £69]**

- Paradise regain'd ... [with] Samson Agonistes; and poems upon several occasions, with a tractate of education. The eighth edition. London: for J. & R. Tonson ..., 1743. Lge 12mo. [8],352 pp. Engvd frontis. Contemp calf, gilt, jnts cracked. *(Fenning)* **£65 [≈ $117]**

- Paradise regain'd ... [with] Samson Agonistes; and poems upon several occasions. Birmingham: J. Baskerville for J. & R. Tonson, 1758. 2 vols. 8vo. Vol 2 with minor marg worming through half. Contemp sprinkled calf, extremities a little worn.
  (Pirages) **$450 [≈ £250]**

- The poetical works. London: for Jacob Tonson, 1695. 2nd coll edn. Follio. Port sans margs & laid down, 1 plate sl torn without loss, leaf of 'Annotations' defective, New half calf, mrbld bds. *(Charles Cox)* **£195 [≈ $351]**

- The poetical works ... Boston (Mass): for E. Larkin, 1796. 3rd Amer edn. xx,[21]-373 pp. Paper uniformly darkened, stain at inner marg in last third of text, lacking rear free

endpaper. Orig sheep.
                              (Pirages) **$225 [≈ £125]**
- A tractate of education ... To which are
added, four papers on the same subject, from
the Spectator. Glasgow: R. Urie, 1746. 8vo.
110 pp. Half-title. Half-title & title browned
& frayed at edges. Contemp tree-sheep,
rebacked.   *(Gough)* **£75 [≈ $135]**
- The works ... London: printed in the year
1697. 1st edn. Folio. Some coll edn. Some minor
stains. New half calf. Wing M2086.
                  (Charles Cox) **£160 [≈ $288]**

Mimosa ...
- Mimosa: or, the sensitive plant ... See Perry,
James

Minsheu, John
- The guide into tongues ... London: John
Haviland, 1627. 2nd edn, 3rd iss. Folio in 6s.
Later half russia. NSTC 17947.
                  (Marlborough) **£450 [≈ $810]**

Minto, Walter
- An inaugural oration, on the progress and
importance of the mathematical sciences.
Trenton [N.J.]: Isaac Collins, 1788. 1st edn.
8vo. 51 pp. Brown staining. Mod blue wraps.
                  (Antiq Sc) **$350 [≈ £194]**
- Researches into some parts of the theory of
the planets ... to determine the circular orbit
of a planet ... London: C. Dilly, 1783. 8vo.
xviii,72 pp. Orig bds, uncut, new paper
backstrip, paper label.
                  (Cooper Hay) **£35 [≈ $63]**

Minucius Felix
- His dialogne [sic] called Octavius. Containing
a defence of Christian religion. Translated ...
Leonard Lichfield, 1636. 1st edn. 12mo.
viii,165,[xi] pp. Sm strip cut from inner blank
hd of title. New calf, gilt.
                  (Frew Mackenzie) **£80 [≈ $144]**
- Minucius Felix's Octavius, and Tertullian's
Apology for the primitive Christians, rendered
into English. London: for B. Barker, 1708.
1st edn thus. [[6],xxii,250 pp. Engvd frontis.
Lib stamp on endpaper & title. Contemp tree-
calf.   *(Lloyd-Roberts)* **£20 [≈ $36]**
- Those two excellent monuments of ancient
learning and piety ... Octavius, and
Tertullian's Apology for the primitive
Christians. London: for B. Barker ..., 1708.
1st edn. Engvd frontis. Contemp panelled
sheep, worn.   *(Charles Cox)* **£20 [≈ $36]**

Minutes ...
- Minutes taken at a court-martial ... into the

conduct of Captain Richard Norris, in the
engagement ... [against] the fleet of French
and Spaniards ... 11th February, 1743. [with]
An appendix ... London: Webb, 1745. 92; 48
pp. Later cloth.   *(Clark)* **£48 [≈ $86]**

Mirabeau, Count de
- On lettres de cachet and state prisons, written
in the dungeon of the Castle of Vincennes.
London: 1787. 1st English edn. Some
dampstaining at beginning. Orig bds, uncut,
lacks spine.   *(Robertshaw)* **£35 [≈ $63]**

The Mirror ...
- The Mirror. A periodical paper, published at
Edinburgh in the years 1779 and 1780. In
three volumes. The fourth edition, corrected.
London: Strahan, 1782. Contemp calf, red
labels.   *(C.R. Johnson)* **£125 [≈ $225]**

Miscellaneous ...
- Miscellaneous and fugitive pieces ... See
Johnson, Samuel, et al.

Miscellany ...
- The moral miscellany: or a collection of select
pieces   ...   for   the   instruction   and
entertainment of youth. Leipzig: 1775. 8vo.
Contemp wraps, sl stained.
                  (Stewart) **£65 [≈ $117]**
- The musical miscellany ... the most approved
Scots, English and Irish songs, set to music.
Perth: J. Brown, 1786. 12mo in 6's. xii,347
pp. Engvd frontis (torn, soiled & mtd) & title.
Browned & foxed throughout. Contemp calf,
rebacked, crnrs worn.   *(Clark)* **£95 [≈ $171]**

Mitchell, Jonathan
- Propositions concerning the subject of
baptism and consocation of churches,
collected ... by a synod of elders and
messengers of the churches in Massachusetts-
Colony in New-England ... [Cambridge:]
1662. [14],18,32 pp. Errata slip pasted-in.
Wing M2292.   *(Jenkins)* **$1,250 [≈ £694]**

Mitchell, Joseph
- The highland fair, or union of the clans. An
opera ... with the musick, which wholly
consists of select Scots tunes ... London: for J.
Watts, 1731. 1st edn. 8vo. [xvi],78 pp. Engvd
frontis by Hogarth, musical notation
throughout, 2 advt leaves. Rec qtr mor.
                  (Burmester) **£200 [≈ $360]**

Mixt Communion ...
- The case of mixt communion ... See Freeman,
Samuel

Mocket, R.
- God and the King: or, a dialogue shewing that our Soveraign ... doth rightly claim whatsoever is required by the Oath of Allegiance. London: 1663. Sm 4to. W'cut port. Mod wraps. Wing M2302.
(Robertshaw) £50 [≈ $90]

Moderation ...
- Moderation displayed. A poem ... See Shippen, William

Modern Conveyancer ...
- The modern conveyancer or conveyancing improv'd. London: for John Walthoe, 1695. 465 pp. Contemp calf. Wing M2336.
(Edwards) £200 [≈ $360]

Moffett, Thomas
- The silkewormes, and their flies ... described in verse, by T.M. ... apprentice in physicke... London: Ling, 1599. 1st edn. 4to. [6],75,[1] pp. W'cut title vignette, errata. Prelim & final blanks sl soiled, inscrptn on title. Contemp calf, rebacked. STC 17994.
(Rootenberg) $3,000 [≈ £1,666]

Moffett, William
- Hesperi-neso-graphia: Or, a description of the Western Isle. In eight cantos. Dublin: Printed by and fot [sic] J. Carson, 1724. 52 pp. Disbound.   *(C.R. Johnson)* £550 [≈ $990]

Molesworth, Robert
- An account of Denmark as it was in the year 1692. London: 1694. 1st edn. 8vo. [lii],271,[i] pp. Outer marg of title a little browned, contemp sgntr on hd of title, notes on blank verso of last leaf. Contemp speckled calf, some wear. Wing M2382A.
(Bow Windows) £135 [≈ $243]

Molyneux, William
- The case of Ireland's being bound by Acts of Parliament made in England stated ... Dublin: Joseph Ray, 1698. 1st edn, 1st iss. 8vo. [xvi],174 pp. Sm tear in M4 marg, somewhat dampstained. Contemp sprinkled calf, spine v rubbed, sides scuffed. Wing M2402.   *(Pickering)* $850 [≈ £472]
- The case of Ireland's being bound by Acts of Parliament made in England stated. To which are added Letters to the Men of Ireland, by Owen Row O'Nial [Joseph Pollock]. Dublin: 1782. 8vo. 93 pp. Bds.
(Emerald Isle) £85 [≈ $153]

Monastical Orders ...
- A short history of monastical orders ... See Gavin, Antonio

Money, John
- The history of the campaign of 1792, between the armies of France ... and the allies ... with an account of what passed in the Thuilleries on the 10th August. For E. Harlow, 1794. 1st edn. 8vo. xv,303 pp. 3 fldg cold maps. Orig bds, spine worn.   *(Fenning)* £55 [≈ $99]

Monk, Mary Molesworth
- Marinda: Poems and translations upon several occasions. London: Tonson, 1716. 1st edn. 8vo. [lii],156,[iv] pp. Endpapers & flyleaves browned. Contemp sprinkled calf, rebacked.   *(Pirages)* $450 [≈ £250]

Monro, Alexander
- A description of all the bursae mucosae of the human body ... Edinburgh: for C. Elliot ..., 1788. 1st edn. Folio. 10 engvd plates (1 fldg), extra-illust with 4 plates (margs of some frayed), some spotting. Lge uncut copy in orig bds, soiled, rebacked.
(Quaritch) $575 [≈ £319]

Monro, Alexander Primus
- The anatomy of the humane bones ... an anatomical treatise of the nerves ... description of the humane lacteal sac and duct ... Edinburgh: for William Munro, 1732. 2nd edn, 1st with treatise on nerves. 8vo. viii,iv, 41,[2 advts] pp. Contemp calf, rebacked.
(Pickering) $750 [≈ £416]
- The anatomy of the humane bones ... an anatomical treatise of the nerves ... Edinburgh: for Wm Munro, 1732. 2nd edn. 8vo. viii,344, iv,41, [i blank],[ii advts] pp. Occas foxing, early names on prelims, lacking rear free endpaper. Contemp calf, sl worn.
(Pollak) £125 [≈ $225]

Monroe, James
- A view of the conduct of the executive ... connected with the mission to the French Republic, during the years 1794, 5 and 6. Phila: 1797. 407 pp. Scattered foxing. Orig paper & bds, spine reprd, uncut.
(Reese) $275 [≈ £152]

Montagu, Walter
- Miscellanea spiritualia, or devout essayes ... [1st & 2nd Series]. London: 1648-54. 1st edns. 2 vols in 1. 4to. Engvd title, ptd title with 2 cms cut away with loss of 2 words, reprd. Contemp calf, 19th c rebacking. Ex

Signet Lib. Wing M2473 & M2474.
(Deighton Bell) **£45** [≈ $81]

Montaigne, Michel de
- Essays written in French by Michael Lord of Montaigne ... Done into English ... by John Florio. London: for Edward Bliunt ..., 1613, 2nd edn in English. Folio. Engvd port. 18th c calf, gilt, rebacked.
(Traylen) **£685** [≈ $1,233]

Montcalm, Marquis de
- Letter from the Marquis de Montcalm, Governor-General of Canada; to Messrs. De Berryer & De la Mole, in the years 1757, 1758, and 1759. J. Almon, 1777. 1st edn. 8vo. English & French text. Some foxing, partic towards end. Wraps.
(Farahar) **£250** [≈ $450]

Montfaucon de Villars, Abbe de
- The diverting history of the Count de Gabalis ... the nature and advantages of studying the occult sciences ... the carnal knowledge of women to be renounc'd ... London: 1714. 2nd edn. 88 pp. Mod half calf.
(Robertshaw) **£130** [≈ $234]

Montreux, Nicolas de
- Honours academie. Or the famous Pastorall, of the fair shepheardesse, Ivlietta. London: Thomas Creede, 1710 [i.e. 1610, altered in ms]. 1st edn. Folio. Light staining, 3 blank crnrs torn, 1 leaf reprd, lacking 2 blanks. Old calf, rebacked. STC 18053.
(Charles Cox) **£300** [≈ $540]

Moor, James
- Essays; read to a literary society ... at Glasgow ... influence of philosophy ... On historical composition. Glasgow: Foulis, 1759. 1st edn. 8vo. [vi],178,[2] pp. Sub-titles & final errata leaf. Contemp polished calf. Ex lib Colquhoun of Luss.
(Burmester) **£160** [≈ $288]

Moore, Edward
- Fables for the female sex. London: 1766. 3rd edn. 8vo. Red & black title with lge vignette, 9 engvd plates. Later half calf, new endpapers. *(Argosy)* **$175** [≈ £97]

Moore, Isabella
- The useful and entertaining family miscellany. Palmer, 1766. 1st edn. 8vo. vii,[i],112 pp. A few sl marks & creases. New half mor. *(Ash)* **£500** [≈ $900]

Moore, John
- Journal during a residence in France from the beginning of August, to the middle of September, 1792. London: for G.G. & J. Robinson, 1793. New edn. 2 vols 8vo. 502; 617 pp. Fldg map cold in outline. Old speckled calf, a little worn, jnts weakening.
(Young's) **£65** [≈ $117]
- A view of society and manners in France, Switzerland, and Germany. London: for A. Strahan, 1786. 6th edn. 2 vols. 8vo. xvi,420; xii,420 pp. Some occas spotting, sm tears in 2 margs. Old calf, jnts worn, lacking labels.
(Young's) **£35** [≈ $63]
- A view of society and manners in France, Switzerland, and Germany. London: 1789. 7th edn. 2 vols. Staining in vol 1. Contemp calf, vol 2 hinges reprd. *(Argosy)* **$75** [≈ £41]
- Zelucco. Various views of human nature, taken from life and manners, foreign and domestic. London: A. Strahan ..., 1789. 2nd edn, crrctd. 2 vols. 8vo. Final advt leaf in vol 1. Contemp tree-calf, gilt spines, jnts worn.
(Traylen) **£20** [≈ $36]

Moore, John Hamilton
- The new practical navigator. London: B. Law ... and the author, 1796. 12th edn. 8vo. viii,309, [1],[222 tables],[6] pp. Engvd frontis, 8 engvd plates, text w'cuts. Scattered spotting, tear to 1 lf. Contemp calf, old rebacking. *(Antiq Sc)* **$175** [≈ £97]

Moore, Sir Jonas
- A mathematical compendium ... arithmetick, geometry, astronomy ... dyalling ... application of pendulums ... London: for J. Philips ..., 1705. 4th edn. 12mo. [24],120, [174] pp. 4 engvd tables (1 fldg), sev tables in text. 19th c calf, rebacked.
(Burmester) **£40** [≈ $72]

Moral Amusement ...
- Moral amusement; or, a selection of tales, histories, and interesting anecdotes; intended to amuse and instruct young minds. Bath: for Vernor & Hood ..., 1798. 1t edn. 12mo. iv,175,[1 adverts] pp. Engvd frontis. Orig green vell spine over mrbld bds, worn.
(Fenning) **£165** [≈ $297]

Moral and Instructive Tales ...
- Moral and instructive tales for the improvement of young ladies; calculated to amuse the mind, and form the heart to virtue. London: John Marshall, [1786]. 1st edn. Sm sq 8vo. [iv],92 pp. Half-title. Contemp sheep-backed mrbld bds, upper jnt cracked.
(Burmester) **£175** [≈ $315]

Moral Essayes ...
- Moral essayes, contain'd in several treatises on many important duties ... See Nicole, Pierre

Moral Philosophy ...
- Outlines of moral philosophy ... See Stewart, Dugald

Mordaunt, Charles
- Remarks on a pamphlet intitled, the thought of a member of the lower house, in relation to a project for restraining and limiting the power of the crown, in the future creation of peers. London: J. Roberts, 1719. 39 pp. Disbound. *(C.R. Johnson)* £38 [≈$68]

More, Hannah
- The inflexible captive: a tragedy. Bristol: S. Farley ..., 1774. 1st edn. 8vo. [viii],83 pp. Outer leaves a bit soiled, 1 gathering pulled. Disbound. *(Clark)* £24 [≈$43]
- Sacred dramas. Chiefly intended for young persons ... to which are added Reflections of King Hezekiah, and Sensibility, a Poem. Phila: Thomas Dobson, 1787. 1st Amer edn. 12mo. 191 pp. Calf, scuffed. *(Argosy)* $150 [≈£83]
- Sacred dramas. Chiefly intended for young persons ... to which is added Sensibility, a Poem. London: for T. Cadell, 1799. 11th edn. Cr. 8vo. Contemp calf, rubbed. Contemp pres inscrptn (not from author) on endpaper. *(Stewart)* £45 [≈$81]
- Strictures on the modern system of female education. Dublin: William Porter, 1799. "Fourth" (1st Dublin) edn. 12mo. [viii],viii, 416 pp. Sl later half purple calf, spine elab blind-tooled. *(Bennett)* £80 [≈$144]

More, Henry
- An antidote against atheisme or an appeal to the natural faculties of the minde of man, whether there be not a God. London: Roger Daniel, 1653. 1st edn. Minimal wormhole in 40 leaves. Mod calf, old calf sides laid down. Wing M2639. *(Waterfield's)* £250 [≈$450]
- An explanation of the grand mystery of Godliness or, a true and faithfull representation of the everlasting gospel ... London: for W. Morden, 1660. Folio. Contemp panelled calf, rebacked. Wing M2658. *(Waterfield's)* £275 [≈$495]
- An illustration of those two abstruse books in Holy Scripture, the Book of Daniel, and the Revelation of St. John ... London: for Walter Kettilby, 1685. 4to. Red & black title. Contemp calf, rec rebacked. Wing 2662.

(Stewart) £30 [≈$54]
- The immortality of the soul so farre forth as it is demonstrable from the knowledge of nature and the light of reason. London: for William Morden, 1659. Red & black title. Lacking A1 blank. Contemp calf. Wing M2663. *(Waterfield's)* £250 [≈$450]

More, Sir Thomas
- Utopia: or the happy republic; a philosophical romance. Glasgow: Foulis, 1753. 8vo. Mezzo frontis port, xxiii,[1], 139,[1 advt] pp. Title grubby, few stains throughout. Contemp calf, rubbed. *(Cooper Hay)* £38 [≈$68]

Morgagni, Giovanni Battista
- The seats and causes of diseases investigated by anatomy: in five books ... from the Latin. London: A. Millar ..., 1769. 1st edn in English. 3 vols. 4to. xxxii,[4], 3-868; vi,[2],3-770; 3-604,[152] pp. Lightly browned. Contemp calf, 19th c rebacking. *(Rootenberg)* $2,000 [≈£1,111]

Morgan, Thomas
- Philosophical principles of medicine, in three parts ... a demonstration of the general laws ... the more particular laws ... chief intentions of medicine ... London: 1725. 8vo. lviii,440 pp. Fldg plate. Contemp panelled calf, spine edges & crnrs sl worn. *(Pollak)* £250 [≈$450]

Morgan, William
- Facts addressed to the serious attention of the people of Great Britain respecting the expense of war ... third edition revised. London: for J. Debrett, 1796 [with] Additional facts ... Debrett, 1796. 2 items. 8vo. Disbound. *(Waterfield's)* £120 [≈$216]

Moritz, Charles P.
- Travels, chiefly on foot, through several parts of England, in 1782. London: for G.G. & J. Robinson, 1797. 2nd edn. 8vo. Lacking front blank. Uncut. Orig calf-backed mrbld bds, little worn, sound. *(Deighton Bell)* £35 [≈$63]

Mornay, Philip de
- Fowre bookes of ... the Holy Sacrament of the Eucharist in the Old Church. London: Windet, 1600. 1st English edn. Sm folio. Contemp calf, rebacked & refurbished. NSTC 18142. *(Marlborough)* £190 [≈$342]

Morris, Corbyn
- An essay towards illustrating the science of insurance ... to fix, by precise calculation,

several important maxims ... to solve various problems ... London: 1747. 1st edn. 8vo. xvi,[i],61 pp. Lacking half-title. Disbound.
(Burmester) **£350 [≈ $630]**

Morritt, John Bacon Sawrey
- A vindication of Homer and of the ancient poets and historians, who have recorded the siege and fall of Troy ... York: 1798. 4to. ii,124 pp. Fldg map, 5 fldg aquatint plates. Orig blue papered bds, new paper spine.
(Farahar) **£185 [≈ $333]**

Morsels ...
- Morsels of criticism ... See King, Edward

Mortimer, Thomas
- Every man his own broker: or, a guide to Exchange-Alley ... And the mystery and iniquity of stock-jobbing laid before the public in a new and impartial light. London: S. Hooper, 1762. 5th edn. 12mo. Tables (1 lge & fldg). Title browned. Contemp calf.
(Chaucer Head) **£140 [≈ $252]**
- Every man his own broker: or, a guide to the stock-exchange ... London: for G.G.J. Robinson, 1791. 11th edn. Sm 8vo. Fldg table. Contemp calf, front bd with sm area of damage. *(Chaucer Head)* **£110 [≈ $198]**

Morton, J.
- The natural history of Northampton-shire; with some account of the antiquities. 1712. 1 vol in 2. 1st edn. Folio. iv,551; 46,z pp. Fldg double-page map, 14 engvd plates. Orig calf, rebacked, orig spines laid down.
(Edwards) **£250 [≈ $450]**

Morton, Nathaniel
- New England's memorial ... [Newport: 1772]. 3rd edn. viii,208,[8] pp. Half calf, bds, spine chipped & worn. Mor slipcase.
(Reese) **$850 [≈ £472]**

Morton, Richard
- Phthisiologia: or, a treatise of consumptions ... three books. I. Of original consumptions ... II. ... III. Of symptomatical consumptions ... London: for Sam. Smith ..., 1694. 1st edn in English. 8vo. Port frontis. Contemp panelled calf, rebacked. Wing M2830.
(Traylen) **£375 [≈ $675]**

Morton, Thomas
- A defence of the innocencie of the three ceremonies of the Church of England. London: for William Barrett, 1619. 2nd imp. 4to. Sm lib stamp on title, cancelled stamp on verso, final endpaper torn, contemp anntns in

margs of 1st 30pp. Contemp vellum. STC 1810. *(Stewart)* **£60 [≈ $108]**

Moseley, Walter Michael
- An essay on archery ... [?London:] 1792. 8vo. Engvd frontis, 4 plates. Later half calf, rubbed. *(Marlborough)* **£110 [≈ $198]**
- An essay on archery: describing the practice of that art, in all ages and nations. London: 1792. 8vo. [2],x,348 pp, errata slip. Frontis, 4 plates. Some occas staining. 19th c half calf, jnts & crnrs rubbed. *(Spelman)* **£140 [≈ $252]**

Mossom, Robert, Bishop of Londonderry
- Englands gratulation for the King and his subjects happy union [a sermon]. 1660. 4to. 40 pp. Lacking A1 (blank?), sev marg tears. Cloth. *(Allen)* **$30 [≈ £16]**

Motte, Andrew
- A treatise of the mechanical powers, wherein the laws of motion ... are explained and demonstrated ... London: Benj. Motte, 1727. 1st edn. 8vo. [6],222,[2] pp. Errata, advt leaf, 3 engvd plates, text w'cuts (1 full-page). Contemp panelled calf, rebacked.
(Rootenberg) **$950 [≈ £527]**

Motte, Benjamin
- The philosophical transactions from the year MDCC (where Mr. Lowthorp ends) to the year MDCCXX. London: for R. Wilkin ..., 1721. 2 vols. 4to. 53 plates or diags (some fldg). Contemp panelled calf, rebacked.
(Waterfield's) **£300 [≈ $540]**

Mount, William & John (publ.)
- Marine architecture: or, the ship-builder's assistant ... from the first laying of the keel, to her actually going to sea. London: for W. & J. Mount ..., 1748. Slim 4to. W'cut diags, full-page w'cut plate, fldg plate. Some browning. Contemp roan, rebacked.
(Chaucer Head) **£240 [≈ $432]**

Moxon, Joseph
- A tutor to astronomy and geography ... London: for Joseph Moxon, 1674. 3rd edn, crrctd & enlgd. 4to. Engvd frontis, text figs. Paper flaw on M4 without loss of text. New grey bds. Wing 3024.
(Stewart) **£175 [≈ $315]**

Mozeen, Thomas
- The lyrick pacquet. Containing most of the favourite songs ... that have been performed for three seasons past at Sadler's Wells. London: J. Dixwell, 1764. 1st edn. 12mo. [iv],118,[2] pp. Engvd frontis (inserted?),

some later insertions. 19th c black half mor.
(Burmester) £275 [≈ $495]

Muir, Thomas
- The Telegraph; a consolatory epistle ... See Hamilton, George

Muirhead, John
- Observations on Dr. Young's Essays on Government, &c. Edinburgh: for the author, [1794]. 1st edn. 8vo. 64 pp. Disbound.
(Burmester) £140 [≈ $252]

Muller, John, Professor of Artillery ...
- Elements of mathematics ... for the use of the Royal Academy of Artillery at Woolwich. London: 1765. 3rd edn, imprvd. 8vo. xxxvi,312 pp. 28 fldg plates. Cloth-backed mrbld bds, worn. *(Weiner)* £45 [≈ $81]

Murphy, Arthur
- The apprentice. A farce, in two acts. London: Paul Vaillant, 1756. 1st edn. 8vo. [x],46 pp. Disbound. *(Clark)* £40 [≈ $72]
- An essay on the life and genius of Samuel Johnson. London: 1792. 1st edn. 8vo. Minimal browning, contemp sgntr on free end leaf. Contemp polished calf, gilt, rebacked. *(Book Block)* £210 [≈ £116]
- An essay on the life and genius of Samuel Johnson. London: for T. Longman, 1792. 1st separate edn. 8vo. Half-title. Contemp calf, rebacked. *(Traylen)* £130 [≈ $234]

Murray, Lindley
- English exercises ... designed for the benefit of private learners ... York: 1798. 3rd edn, crrctd. 12mo. 192 pp. Orig speckled sheep, front jnt cracked & weak.
(Blackwell's) £35 [≈ $63]

Murry, Ann
- A concise history of the Kingdoms of Israel and Judah. London: Frys & Couchman, 1783. 1st edn. 2 vols. 12mo. 2 lge fldg engvd maps. Contemp tree-calf, spines gilt, jnts cracked but firm. *(Bennett)* £75 [≈ $135]

Musaeus
- The loves of Hero and Leander. London: privately printed, 1797. 1st edn. 4to. [2],53 pp. Facing Greek & English text. Contemp half mor, blue bds, rubbed.
(Claude Cox) £35 [≈ $63]

Museum Rusticum ...
- Museum rusticum et commerciale: or, select papers on agriculture, commerce, arts, and

manufactures ... London: 1764-66. 1st edn. 6 vols. 8vo. 14 engvd plates (7 fldg), 9 tables (7 fldg), other ills. Contemp speckled calf, gilt, mor labels (1 lacking).
(Traylen) £280 [≈ $504]

Musgrave, Samuel
- An essay on the nature and cure of the (so-called) worm-fever. London: sold by T. Payne ..., 1776. 8vo. Light staining on title. Mod bds. *(Stewart)* £75 [≈ $135]

Nairn, Katherine & Ogilvie, Patrick
- The trial of Katherine Nairn and Patrick Ogilvie, for the crimes of incest and murder ... Edinburgh: Auld & Smellie, 1765. 12mo. 135 pp. Later plain wraps. Preserved in cloth fldr. *(Karmiole)* $100 [≈ £55]

Naismith, John
- General view of the agriculture of the county of Clydesdale. Brentford: 1794. 1st edn. 4to. 82 pp. Half-title. Disbound, final leaf almost detchd. *(Claude Cox)* £30 [≈ $54]
- General view of the agriculture of the county of Clydesdale. Glasgow: J. Mundell ..., 1798. 8vo. Fldg engvd map. 19th c half calf, mrbld sides, lightly rubbed. *(Hughes)* £75 [≈ $135]

Nalson, John
- The project of peace, or, unity of faith and government, the only expedient to procure peace ... and to preserve these nations from the danger of popery ... London: for Jonathan Edwin, 1678. 8vo. 2 pp ctlg. Final leaves rather stained. New cloth. Wing 113.
(Stewart) £60 [≈ $108]

Nani, Battista
- The history of the affairs of Europe in this present age, but more particularly of the Republic of Venice. 1673. 1st English trans. 4to. [xii],573,[xxiii] pp. (Lacking 1st leaf?). Imprim leaf, 2 ff advts at rear. Bds severely worn & rubbed, hinges cracked.
(Edwards) £120 [≈ $216]

Narrative ...
- An authentic narrative of the late extraordinary proceedings at Cambridge, against the W--------r Club. London: M. Cooper, 1751. 62 pp, errata. Mod bds.
(C.R. Johnson) £45 [≈ $81]
- A narrative of the proceedings of his Majesty's Fleet ... See Mathews, Thomas

National Oeconomy ...
- National oeconomy recommended, as the

only means of retrieving our trade and securing out liberties; occasioned by the perusal of the late report ... relating to the army ... London: for M. Cooper, 1746. 1st edn. 8vo. [ii],51 pp. Lacking half-title. Disbound.   *(Burmester)* **£75 [≃ $135]**

Nature & Place of Hell ...
- An enquiry into the nature and place of hell. London: W. Bowyer. for W. Taylor, 1714. 2 fldg plates, errata. Contemp calf, rebacked. (Situated in the sun, with supporting astronomical arguments).
               (C.R. Johnson) **£75 [≃ $135]**

Naubert, Christiane Benedicte Eugenie
- Alf von Deulman; or the history of the Emperor Philip and his daughters. Translated from the German by Miss A.E. Booth. London: for J. Bell, 1794. 1st edn in English. 2 vols. 8vo. xx,300; [iv],305 pp. Half-title in vol II. Contemp half calf, sl rubbed.   *(Burmester)* **£300 [≃ $540]**

Naylor, Sir George
- A collection of coats of arms borne by the nobility and gentry of the County of Gloucester. London: 1792. 4to. All published. Engvd vignette title, 62 plates. Uncut in orig wraps, frayed.
               (Robertshaw) **£50 [≃ $90]**

Neal, Daniel
- The history of New-England containing an impartial account of the civil and ecclesiastical affairs of the country to ... 1700. London: 1700. 2 vols. [20],320; [4],331-712, [15] pp. Fldg map. Calf, gilt, rebacked, worn at crnrs.   *(Reese)* **$600 [≃ £333]**

Neck ...
- Neck or nothing. A farce ... See Garrick, Davis

Necker, Jacques
- On the French Revolution ... Translated ... London: for T. Cadell Jun ... 1797. 1st edn in English. 2 vols. 8vo. [iv],460; [iv],480 pp. Ptd on blue paper. Sm tear on 1 leaf. Contemp polished tree-calf, gilt. Ex lib Colquhoun of Luss.   *(Pickering)* **$550 [≃ £305]**

Needham, John Turbeville
- An account of some new microscopical discoveries founded on an examination of the calamary ... London: for F. Needham, 1745. 1st edn. 8vo. viii,126,[2 advts] pp. Contemp calf, gilt spine, new label, rubbed, crnrs worn.
               (Pickering) **$450 [≃ £250]**

Negotiations ...
- The negotiations of Thomas Woolsey ... See Cavendish, George

Nelson, Robert
- The practice of true devotion ... to which is added the character of the author. London: for B. Dod, 1749. 12th edn. Cr 8vo. Port frontis. Contemp calf, sl rubbed.
               (Stewart) **£15 [≃ $27]**

Nelson, William
- Lex manoriorum. or the law and customs of England, relating to manors and lords of manors ... 1726. 1st edn. Folio. 198,128 pp. Contemp calf, some wear to spine.
               (Edwards) **£130 [≃ $234]**
- The office and authority of a justice of the peace ... the eleventh edition, corrected, amended ... In the Savoy: 1736. 2 vols. 8vo. xlvii,572; [iv],308,[264] pp. Light damp mark at hd at end vol 2. Contemp calf, jnts cracking.   *(Bow Windows)* **£145 [≃ $261]**

Neri, A.
- The art of glass wherein are shown the wayes to make and colour glass, pastes, enamels ... London: 1662. Sole English trans. 11ff (ex 12), 352 pp (ex 362, lacking 10,[4] at end although final leaf has 'Finis'). 6 plates from another work. Mod half lea.
               (Whitehart) **£200 [≃ $360]**

Neuhoff, Frederic de
- Memoirs of Corsica ... natural and political history ... events, revolutions ... its products, advantageous situation ... London: for S. Hooper ..., 1768. 1st edn. 8vo. Lge fldg map. Some spotting, sm piece torn from title marg. Contemp calf, rebacked.
               (Chaucer Head) **£180 [≃ $324]**

Neumann, Caspar
- The chemical works ... Abridged and methodized. With large additions ... by William Lewis ... London: Johnston ..., 1759. 1st edn in English. 4to. [xvi],586, [xxxviii index] pp. Contemp calf, sl rubbed, spine reprd at hd & ft.
               (Frew Mackenzie) **£575 [≃ $1,035]**
- The chemical works ... Abridged and methodized. With large additions ... by William Lewis ... London: Johnston ..., 1759. 1st edn. 4to. [28],586, [76] pp. Contemp lea, jnts cracked.   *(Antiq Sc)* **$350 [≃ £194]**

Newcastle, William Cavendish, Duke of
- A new method, and extraordinary invention,

to dress horses, and work them according to nature. London: 1667. 1st edn. Lge paper. Folio. [xxii],40, 352,[iv] pp. 1 leaf with minor tear, another ragged at ft, occas light foxing & staining. Contemp calf, rebacked.
(Pirages) **$650 [≈ £361]**

Newman, Henry Charles Christian
- The love of our country, a poem ... R. Faulder, 1783. 1st edn. 4to. viii,34 pp. Stitched in contemp mrbld wraps, wraps curling sl at edges, spine defective.
(Frew Mackenzie) **£120 [≈ $216]**

Newman, Jeremiah Whitaker
- The lounger's common-place book, or miscellaneous anecdotes. A biographic ... and satirical compilation. London: 1796. 2nd edn. 2 vols in 1. 8vo. Contemp calf.
(Argosy) **$75 [≈ £41]**

Newman, Samuel
- A large and compleat concordance to the Bible in English according to the last translation. London: for T. Downes ..., 1658. 3 imp, crrctd & amended. Lge thick folio. Unpaginated. Calf, sl worn. Wing N931.
(Lloyd-Roberts) **£150 [≈ $270]**

News ...
- News from heaven: or dialogue between St. Peter and the five Jesuits last hanged. [London: 1679]. Folio. 4 pp. Rebound in qtr calf, mrbld bds. Wing N964.
(C.R. Johnson) **£25 [≈ $45]**

Newton, Sir Isaac
- The chronology of ancient kingdoms amended ... London: for J. Tonson ..., 1728. 1st edn. xiv,[2],376 pp. 3 fldg plans. 1st half of text v sl mottled, tear in 1 marg. Contemp Cambridge calf, jnts cracked, spine worn & darkened. *(Pirages)* **$200 [≈ £111]**
- Mathematical elements of natural philosophy ... 1720. 1st English edn. xxii,259,[2] pp. 33 fldg plates (2 loose). Marg of title & following page reprd. Contemp lea, spine & edges sl worn, new endpapers.
(Whitehart) **£180 [≈ $324]**
- The mathematical principles of natural philosophy ... laws of the moon's motion ... London: Motte, 1729. 1st edn in English. 2 vols. 8vo. [xxxviii],320; [ii],393,[13 index],viii appendix,71,[1 errata] pp. 2 engvd frontis, 32 fldg engvd plates. Mod calf, gilt.
(Pickering) **$6,000 [≈ £3,333]**
- The mathematical principles of natural philosophy ... Translated into English by Andrew Motte. London: Benjamin Motte,

1729. Vol 1 only. 1st edn in English. 8vo. [xxxviii],320 pp. Title reprd. Contemp calf, jnts cracking. *(Halewood)* **£500 [≈ $900]**
- Observations upon the prophecies of David and the Apocalypse of St. John. In two parts. J. Darby & T. Browne, 1733. 1st edn. 4to. vi,[i],323 pp. Title lightly spotted & sm piece torn from crnr without loss. Contemp half calf, extremities worn, rebacked.
(Frew Mackenzie) **£175 [≈ $315]**
- Opticks: or a treatise on the reflections, refractions, inflections and colours of light. London: Innys, 1721. 3rd edn. 8vo. 382 pp. 12 fldg plates. Advt leaf at end. Contemp name on title. Contemp calf, sl worn, rec rebacked. *(Oasis)* **$750 [≈ £416]**
- The system of the world demonstrated in an easy and popular manner ... London: for J. Robinson, 1740. 2nd edn, crrctd & imprvd. 8vo. 2 plates, cancel title. Contemp calf, front jnt cracked. *(Waterfield's)* **£400 [≈ $720]**
- A treatise of the system of the world. London: for F. Fayram, 1728. 1st edn in English. 8vo. 2 engvd plates, errata leaf. Mod polished calf. *(Chaucer Head)* **£1,100 [≈ $1,980]**

Newton, John
- Trigonometria Britanica: or, the doctrine of triangles in two books ... London: R. & W. Leybourn, 1658. 1st edn. Folio. [4]ff,96 pp, [94]ff, [46]ff, [12 of 14]ff. Title laid down (v worn with some segments missing). Browning, ms notes & scribbles. Lib buckram. *(Elgen)* **$650 [≈ £361]**

Newton, John (1725-1807)
- Twenty six letters on religious subjects. To which are added hymns, &c. by Omnicron. London: J. & W. Oliver, 1808. 8vo. Later roan. Author's pres inscrptn on endpaper. *(Chaucer Head)* **£260 [≈ $468]**

Newton, Thomas
- The works. With some account of his life and anecdotes of several of his friends. Written by himself. London: John Rivington, 1787. 2nd edn. 8vo. Contemp half calf.
(Spelman) **£85 [≈ $153]**

Nichols, William
- A comment on the Book of Common-Prayer, and administration of the Sacrament ... London: for R. Bonwicke ..., 1710. Folio. Port frontis. Contemp panelled calf, rubbed, upper jnt weak, spine gilt. Ex lib, with label.
(Stewart) **£35 [≈ $63]**

Nicholson, P.
- The principles of architecture, containing the fundamental rules of the art, in geometry, arithmetic and measuration ... London: 1795-98. 3 vols. Demy 8vo. Upwards of 200 copper plates. Bds, uncut.
(Halewood) £125 [≃ $225]

Nicholson, William
- The Irish historical library. Dublin: 1724. 8vo. Sm repr to hd of title. Contemp calf.
(Stewart) £160 [≃ $288]

Nicholson, William (1753-1815)
- The first principles of chemistry. London: Robinson, 1790. 1st edn. xxvii,[1],532,[5] pp. Fldg engvd plate. Contemp tree-calf, ends of spine sl chipped, rubbed.
(Antiq Sc) $300 [≃ £166]
- The first principles of chemistry. London: for G.G.J. & J. Robinson, 1790. 1st edn. Fldg plate. Contemp half calf.
(Chaucer Head) £120 [≃ $216]
- The first principles of chemistry ... London: for G.C.J. & J. Robinson ..., 1790. 1st edn. 8vo. xxviii,532,[5 index] pp. Fldg engvd plate. Sm wormhole in marg of 1st few leaves, title a little dust soiled. Early notes on endpaper. Contemp calf, little rubbed.
(Pickering) $1,000 [≃ £555]
- The first principles of chemistry. London: 1790. 1st edn. 8vo. xxvii,532,[5] pp. Fldg engvd plate. Calf, worn. Ex lib.
(Elgen) $300 [≃ £166]
- The first principles of chemistry. London: Robinson, 1796. 3rd edn. xxi,[3],564, [4] pp. Fldg engvd plate. Light unif browning. Contemp tree-calf, lightly worn.
(Antiq Sc) $85 [≃ £47]
- An introduction of natural philosophy. London: Johnson, 1782. 1st edn. 2 vols. 8vo. 25 fldg engvd plates. Contemp calf, rebacked.
(Marlborough) £350 [≃ $630]
- An introduction to natural philosophy. London: for J. Johnson, 1782. 1st edn. 2 vols. 8vo. xx,383, [1 blank],[12 index]; xi,[1 blank], 441, [14 index] pp. 25 fldg engvd plates. Contemp speckled half calf, mrbld bds, hds of spines chipped. The Westport House copy.
(Pickering) $1,000 [≃ £555]

Nicole, Pierre
- Moral essayes, contain'd in several treatises on many important duties ... Done into English by a person of quality. London: for Sam. Manship, 1696. 4 vols in 2. 8vo. 3rd & 2nd edns. Contemp calf, rubbed, rec rebacked. Wing N1137, N1137A/B/C.

(Hughes) £145 [≃ $261]

Nicolson, Joseph & Burn, Richard
- The history and antiquities of ... Westmorland and Cumberland. London: for W. Strahan, 1777. 2 vols. 4to. 2 lge fldg maps (1 shaved). Occas spotting. Contemp sprinkled calf, rec rebacking.
(Kerr) £375 [≃ $675]

Nicolson, William
- The English, Scotch and Irish historical libraries ... short view and character of most of our historians ... account of our records, law-books ... a new edition, corrected. 1776. 4th edn. 4to. xii,241, [iii],114, viii,92 pp. Contemp calf, old rebacking.
(Edwards) £190 [≃ $342]
- The English, Scotch and Irish historical libraries ... short view and character of most of our historians ... account of our records, law-books ... London: for T. Evans ..., 1776. New edn, crrctd. Lge 4to. Contemp red gilt dec mor, a.e.g. (Traylen) £235 [≃ $423]

Nicolson, William, Lord Bishop of Carlisle
- Leges marchiarum, or Border-laws. Tim Goodwin, 1705. 1st edn. 8vo. [viii],388,[iv] pp. V sl browning, sm marg tears to 2 leaves reprd. Contemp calf, rebacked.
(Frew Mackenzie) £115 [≃ $207]

Nihell, James
- New and extraordinary observations concerning prediction by various crises of the pulse ... London: ... sold by James Crokatt, 1741. 1st edn. 8vo. xxviii,[xii], 154,[14 index] pp. Contemp sprinkled calf, spine gilt; Hopetoun b'plate.
(Pickering) $1,000 [≃ £555]

Niktalopsia ...
- Niktalopsia ... See Lynn, Walter

Nisbet, Alexander
- A system of heraldry speculative and practical: with the True art of blazon ... Edinburgh: 1722-42. 1st edn. 2 vols. Folio. 50 engvd plates. Vol 1, contemp panelled calf; vol 2, polished calf. (Spelman) £250 [≃ $450]

Nixon, William
- Prosody made easy. Phila: William Spotswood, 1786. 8vo. xvi (i.e. xiii),36 pp. Contemp anntns on endpapers, lib stamps. Contemp mrbld bds, calf backstrip, worn & rubbed.
(Heritage) $125 [≃ £69]

Noble, Benjamin

- Geodaesia Hibernica, or an essay on practical surveying ... useful improvements ... Dublin: for the author, 1768. Errata slip tipped-in, fldg figs. Some fore-edge reprs. Contemp calf.
(Emerald Isle) **£165 [≈ $297]**

Noble, Mark

- Two dissertations, upon the mint and coins of the Episcopal-Palatines of Durham. Birmingham: for the author, 1780. 4to. 21 engvd text ills. Later half roan, rubbed.
(Marlborough) **£120 [≈ $216]**

Noldius, Christopher

- History of ... Herod the Great ... See Josephus, Flavius

Noorthouck, John

- An historical and classical dictionary ... London: 1776. 1st edn. 2 vols 8vo. Contemp calf, gilt spines dull & worn at ends, jnts cracked, crnrs rubbed.
(Bow Windows) **£20 [≈ $36]**

Norden, Frederick Lewis

- Travels in Egypt and Nubia ... London: Lockyer Davis ..., 1757. 1st edn in English. 2 vols in 1. Lge folio. xii,xxiv,124; iv,155,[1] pp. Engvd frontis to each vol, 161 engvd plates, half-titles, thick paper. Mod half calf antique, mrbld bds.
(Blackwell's) **£1,600 [≈ $2,880]**
- Travels in Egypt and Nubia ... London: Lockyer Davis ..., 1757. 1st edn in English. 2 vols. Folio. [xii],xxiv,124; [iv],viii,155,[1 errata] pp. 2 half-titles, 2 frontis, 161 engvd plates. Contemp calf, rebacked, rubbed, crnrs worn, hinges reinforced.
(Morrell) **£980 [≈ $1,764]**

Norris, John

- A collection of miscellanies: consisting of poems, essays, discourses, and letters. London: for S. Manship, 1699. 3rd edn, crrctd. Mod calf. Wing N1250
(Charles Cox) **£45 [≈ $81]**

North, Roger

- A discourse of fish and fish-ponds. London: E. Curl, 1713. 1st edn. [8],71 pp. Contemp panelled calf.   *(Spelman)* **£280 [≈ $504]**
- Examen: or, an enquiry into the credit and veracity of a pretended complete history [White Kennet: History of England] shewing the perverse and wicked design of it ... London: Fletcher Gyles, 1740. 1st edn. 4to. [xvi],692,[xxiv] pp. Contemp calf, rebacked.
(Frew Mackenzie) **£90 [≈ $162]**

Northcote, William

- A concise history of anatomy, from the earliest ages to antiquity. London: 1772. 1st edn. 8vo. Pencilled notes in text & on rear endpaper. Half calf, rear jnt reprd.
(Argosy) **$150 [≈ £83]**

Noy, William

- Reports and cases, taken in the time of Queen Elizabeth, King James, and King Charles. London: Matthew Walbancke, 1656. 1st edn. Folio. Browned, a few letters of imprint cropped. 18th c calf, rebacked. Sgntrs of Sir Robert Chambers & Lord Eldon. Wing N1449.   *(Charles Cox)* **£350 [≈ $630]**

O'Connor, Roger

- An address to the people of Ireland; shewing them why they ought to submit to an Union. Dublin: the booksellers, 1799. 16 pp. Disbound.   *(C.R. Johnson)* **£28 [≈ $50]**

O'Driscoll, William

- A letter to the Rev. Doctor O'Leary. Found on the Great Road leading from the City of Cork to Cloughnakilty. Dublin: W. Sleater, 1787. 30 pp. Half-title. Some dampstaining in the 1st section.   *(C.R. Johnson)* **£15 [≈ $27]**

O'Halloran, Sylvester

- A general history of Ireland, from the most authentic records. London: Hamilton, 1778. 1st edn. 2 vols. 4to. Irish calf.
(Emerald Isle) **£150 [≈ $270]**

O'Leary, Arthur

- An essay on toleration: or, Mr. O'Leary's plea for the liberty of conscience. Phila: Kline & Reynolds, 1785. 1st Amer edn. 8vo. [viii],70,[ii] pp. Ptd on poor paper, sl marg fraying. Untrimmed, disbound.
(Bennett) **£48 [≈ $86]**
- Miscellaneous tracts. The second edition. Dublin: John Chambers, 1781. Orig calf.
(C.R. Johnson) **£45 [≈ $81]**

Oates, Titus

- A true narrative of the horrid plot and conspiracy of the Popish party against the life of his sacred Majesty. London: Thomas Parkhurst ..., 1679. Folio. [xii],68 pp. Imprim leaf creased & soiled, title & final page dusty, Disbound. Wing O59.   *(Clark)* **£50 [≈ $90]**

Obedience ...

- Obedience to the King ... See Fullwood, Francis

Observations ...

- Observations on a journey to Naples ... See Gavin, Antonio
- Observations on modern gardening ... See Whately, T.
- Observations on the Bedford charity; in a series of letters that were signed Justus. Now first published entire ... London: 1761. 4to. [viii],36 pp. Stitched as issued, uncut & unopened.   *(Clark)* **£30 [≈ $54]**
- The observations on the treaty of Seville examined ... See Walpole, Robert
- Observations upon a treatise intituled Of Humane Reason ... See Stephens, Edward
- Some observations concerning the plague ... occasioned by ... discourse of the learned Dr. Mead ... by a well wisher to the public. Dublin: George Grierson, 1721. Sm triangular piece cut from lower marg & replaced. Mod mrbld bds.
            (Emerald Isle) **£85 [≈ $153]**
- Some observations relative to a late Bill for paying off the residue of the National Debt of Ireland. Dublin: 1754. 39 pp. Disbound.
            (C.R. Johnson) **£45 [≈ $81]**

Occasional Writer ...

- The occasional writer ... See Bolingbroke, Henry St. John

Oeconomy ...

- The oeconomy of human life ... See Dodsley, Robert
- The oeconomy of love ... See Armstrong, John

Ogilby, James

- Homer his Odysses translated, adorn'd with sculpture and illustrated with annotations by James Ogilby. London: for the author, 1669. Folio. Engvd frontis, red & black title, 24 plates (1 with marg tear). Contemp calf, rebacked, new endpapers.
            (Waterfield's) **£275 [≈ $495]**

Ogilby, John

- Africa ... Tho. Johnson, for the author, 1670. 1st edn. Folio. xvi,767,[1] pp, 7ff. Engvd half-title, 58 engvd plates (46 double-page), 40 engvs of scenes in the text, red & black title. Minor waterstaining & sl worming. Contemp panelled calf, rebacked.
            (Blackwell's) **£2,900 [≈ $5,220]**

Ogilvie, John

- The theology of Plato compared with the principles of oriental and Grecian

philosophers. London: for J. Deighton, 1793. Mod half calf.   *(Waterfield's)* **£145 [≈ $261]**

Okell, Bateman

- A short treatise of the virtues of Dr. Bateman's pectoral drops: the nature of the distempers they cure, and the manner of their operation. [1726]. Sm 8vo. vii,48 pp. Mor-backed bds.   *(Rootenberg)* **$350 [≈ £194]**

Oldenbarneveld, Jan van

- Barnevelt displayed; or the golden legend of New St. John ... Translated out of Dutch. London: for Nathanael Butter, 1619. Sm 4to. 45 pp. Title soiled, stained throughout. Mod half mor. STC 18801.
            (Robertshaw) **£40 [≈ $72]**

Oldfield, T.H.B.

- An entire and complete history, political and personal, of the Boroughs of Great Britain. London: for G. Riley, 1792. 3 vols. 8vo. xvi,323; vi,547; 288,148, 52,68 pp. Errata slip vol 1. Mod half calf.
            (Edwards) **£120 [≈ $216]**

Oldham, John

- Poems and translations. London: for Joseph Hindmarsh, 1684. 2nd edn. Cr 8vo. Lacking ai (blank). New bds.   *(Stewart)* **£45 [≈ $81]**
- The works ... Together with his remains. London: for Jo. Hindmarsh, 1684. 1st coll edn. 8vo. Mispaginated. Persistent dampstain throughout most, other stains & spots, some worming, sev inked jottings. Contemp calf, worn, spine ends a little torn. Wing O224 &c.
            (Bow Windows) **£80 [≈ $144]**

Oldmixon, John

- Clarendon and Whitlock compar'd. To which is ... added, a comparison between the History of the Rebellion, and other histories of the Civil War ... London: J. Pemberton, 1727. 8vo. xxxix,344,[xxiv] pp. Initial advt leaf, 7 pp advts at end. Rec half calf.
            (Clark) **£45 [≈ $81]**

Oliver, T. Milwood

- Trial of T. Milwood Oliver in Stafford ... 1797 ... for the murder of Mr. John Wood, an eminent potter, of Brownshill ... Stafford: J. Drewry, [1797]. 76 pp. Disbound.
            (C.R. Johnson) **£65 [≈ $117]**

Oliver, William

- A practical dissertation on Bath-waters ... to which is added a relation of a very extraordinary sleeper near Bath. Printed for Samuel Leake, bookseller in Bath ..., 1764.

Contemp sheep, rebacked.
(Waterfield's) **£65 [≈ $117]**

Onslow, Arthur
- The speech of the Right Honourable A-r O-w, Esq., at the Bar ... upon presenting the Money Bills to his M-----y. April 29, 1740. London: John Clarke, 1740. 4to. Half-title. 14 pp. Disbound. *(C.R. Johnson)* **£35 [≈ $63]**

Opera Mineralia Explicata ...
- Opera mineralia explicata ... See Stringer, Moses

Oracles ...
- The history of oracles ... See Fontenelle, Bernard le Bovyer de
- The lively oracles given to us ... See Allestree, Richard

Order ...
- An Order of the King and Council, concerning the political disputes between the states and the Royal Court, of the Island of Jersey. Issued on the 2nd June 1786. Southampton: 1786. 26 pp. Mod wraps.
(C.R. Johnson) **£45 [≈ $81]**

Origins of Commerce ...
- An historical and chronological deduction of the origins of commerce ... with an appendix ... London: Logographic Press, 1787-89. 2nd edn, crrctd & enlgd. 4 vols. 4to. 3 lge fldg engvd maps. Contemp speckled calf, gilt, rebacked, orig spines laid down.
(Traylen) **£420 [≈ $756]**

Orlandi, Pellegrini Antonio
- Repertorium sculptile-typicum. or a complete collection ... of the several marks and cyphers by which the prints of the best engravers are distinguished. London: Harding, 1730. 12mo. 69 pp, without the fldg table. Tear in 1 lf, title worn. Contemp half calf.
(Marlborough) **£135 [≈ $243]**

Orme, Robert
- A history of the military transactions of the British Nation in Indostan, from the year MDCCXLV. 1775. 2nd edn. 2 vols. 4to. 36 engvd maps & plans, mostly fldg. Contemp mottled calf, rebacked.
(Edwards) **£150 [≈ $270]**

Orosius, Faustus
- The Anglo-Saxon version from the historian Orosius, by Aelfred the Great, together with an English translation from the Anglo-Saxon.

London: Bowyer & Nichols, 1773. Contemp calf. *(Waterfield's)* **£65 [≈ $117]**

Osbeck, Peter
- A voyage to China and the East Indies ... a voyage to Suratte ... an account of Chinese husbandry ... London: White, 1771. 1st English edn. 2 vols. 8vo. xx,396; [ii],367,[31 index] pp. 13 engvd plates. Contemp polished calf, spines cracked, edges rubbed.
(Morrell) **£590 [≈ $1,062]**

Osborne, Francis
- The works. London: 1609. 9th edn. Contemp calf, spine gilt. Wing O507.
(Robertshaw) **£48 [≈ $86]**

Osborne, Thomas, Duke of Leeds
- The thoughts of a private person; about the justice of the gentleman's undertaking at York. Nov 1688. London: 1689. 1st edn. 4to. 1st & last pp dusty, sm repr to edge of title. Mod half calf, cloth bds. Wing L923A.
(Charles Cox) **£35 [≈ $63]**

Osmer, William
- A treatise on the diseases and lameness of horses. London: for T. Waller ..., 1761. 2nd edn. 8vo. [ii][2],300 pp. Half mor.
(Pickering) **$150 [≈ £83]**

Oswald, James
- An appeal to common sense in behalf of religion ... London: 1768. 2nd edn. Contemp calf, a little rubbed.
(Waterfield's) **£85 [≈ $153]**

Other Side ...
- The other side of the question ... See Ralph, James

Otway, T.
- Orphan; or, the unhappy marriage. A tragedy ... London: Bentley & Magnes, 1680. 1st edn. 4to. Title, [vi],71, epilogue pp. Title discold & sl frayed. Some staining throughout, some running headlines cropped. Later half calf.
(P & P) **£30 [≈ $54]**

Over, Charles
- Ornamental architecture in the Gothic, Chinese and modern taste. London: for Robert Sayer, 1758. 1st iss. 8vo. 8 pp. 54 engvd plates. Light soiling to margs. Contemp mottled calf, rebacked, crnrs reprd, mrbld slipcase. *(Spelman)* **£1,000 [≈ $1,800]**

Overall, John

- Bishop Overall's convocation-book, MDCVI. Concerning the government of God's Catholic Church ... London: for Walter Kettilby, 1690. Sole edn. 4to. Imp leaf & final blank. Minor worming to a few inner margs. Contemp calf, worn upper jnt weak. Wing 607.   *(Stewart)* £60 [≈ $108]

Overbury, Sir Thomas

- A true ... account of the ... trial ... and execution of Joan Perry ... for the supposed murder of Will. Harrison ... Also Mr. Harrison's own account how he was conveyed to Turkey, and there made a slave. For J. Atkinson, n.d. [ca 1750]. 8vo. 31pp. Wraps.
                     (Fenning) £35 [≈ $63]

Ovidius Naso, Publius

- Ovid's Art of Love. In three books. Together with his Remedy of Love. Translated into English verse by Dryden (et al.). London [i.e. Edinburgh]: for T. Caslon ..., 1777. 12mo. [ii],261 pp. Some minor soiling. Contemp sheep, rubbed.   *(Burmester)* £55 [≈ $99]
- Ovid's Metamorphosis Englished by G[eorge] S[andys]. London: 1626. 1st edn of this trans. Sm 4to. 10ff, 326 pp, 3ff. Engvd frontis & title. 1st few leaves browned & creased, a few stains & scribbles. Contemp speckled calf, front jnt patched, a little marked.
                     (Pirages) $425 [≈ £236]

Owen, Charles

- An essay towards a natural history of serpents: in two parts ... London: for the author, 1742. 1st edn. 4to. 7 engvd plates. Contemp calf, gilt, rebacked, jnts cracking.
                     (Traylen) £420 [≈ $756]
- An essay towards a natural history of serpents: in two parts ... to which is added a third part ... London: 1742. xxiii,240,[12] pp. Pp 49-56 misbound. Various pp of related ms material bound in. Later half calf.
                     (Whitehart) £285 [≈ $513]

Pack ...

- A pack of Puritans ... See Wentworth, Sir Peter

Pagitt, Ephraim

- Christianographie, or a description of the multitude and sundry sorts of Christians in the world not subject to the Pope. London: for Matthew Costerden, 1635. 1st edn. 4to. 1 lge & 3 sm maps. Contemp calf, rebacked & refurbished. NSTC 19110.
                     (Marlborough) £130 [≈ $234]

Pain, William

- The builder's pocket treasure or Palladio delineated and explained. London: Owen, 1785. 8vo. 55 copper engvs. Calf.
                     (Camden) £385 [≈ $693]

Paine, Thomas

- Letter addressed to the addressers, of the late proclamation. : for H.D. Symonds, 1792. Cr 8vo. Some sl browning throughout. New bds.
                     (Stewart) £125 [≈ $225]
- Letter addressed to the addressers, on the late proclamation. : for H.D. Symonds ..., 1792. 1st edn. 8vo. 50 pp. Some browning throughout, a few leaves spotted. Rec bds.
                     (Bow Windows) £80 [≈ $144]
- Prospects on the War and paper currency of Great Britain. London: 1793. 3rd edn. 8vo. [iii-viii],68 pp. Lacking half-title. Rec bds.
                     (Bow Windows) £70 [≈ $126]
- The rights of man ... Part 1. London: H.D. Symonds, 1792. 78 pp. [with] Rights of man: Part the second ... London: H.D. Symonds, 1792. 90,4] pp. Each part with advt leaf.
                     (C.R. Johnson) £100 [≈ $180]
- The rights of man ... [with] Rights of man: Part the second ... London: for S. Jordan, 1791-92. 1st edn, 2nd iss & 3rd edn. 4ff, [5]-162pp; 7 ff, 178 pp. Lightly foxed throughout, stab holes at inner marg. Early 19th c half calf, mrbld sides, sl worn.
                     (Pirages) $350 [≈ £194]
- Two letters to Lord Onslow ... on the subject of the late excellent proclamation ... London: for James Ridgway ..., 1792. 6th edn. 8vo. 36 pp. Rec bds.   *(Bow Windows)* £30 [≈ $54]

Palafox y Mendoza, Juan de

- The history of the conquest of China by the Tartars together with ... the religion ... and customes of both nations. London: W. Godbid, 1671. 1st edn in English. 588 pp. A few tears & faint dampstaining in margs. Contemp sheep, crnrs worn, spine sl chipped.
                     (Pirages) $600 [≈ £333]

Paley, William

- The principles of moral and political philosophy. Dublin: P. Byrne & L. White, 1788. 4th edn crrctd. Contemp calf.
                     (C.R. Johnson) £38 [≈ $68]
- The principles of moral and political philosophy. Dublin: for P. Byrne ..., 1788. 4th edn, crrctd. Contemp calf, rubbed, hd of backstrip worn. *(Waterfield's)* £75 [≈ $135]
- A view of the evidences of Christianity, In three parts. 1795. 3rd edn. 2 vols. 8vo. Old calf, rebacked.   *(Young's)* £26 [≈ $46]

- The principles of moral and political philosophy. Phila: Thomas Dobson, 1794. New edn (2nd Amer). 8vo. 618,2 pub advts pp. Some browning. Orig calf, front hinge starting. *(Karmiole)* **$150 [≈£83]**

Palmer, Charles
- A collection of select aphorisms and maxims ... extracted from the most eminent authors. London: 1748. 1st edn. 4to. 322 pp. Engvd frontis. Contemp calf, rubbed.
(Argosy) **$175 [≈£97]**
- A collection of select aphorisms and maxims ... extracted from the most eminent authors. London: E. Cave, 1748. Sole edn. 4to. Engvd frontis. Prelims sl foxed. Contemp calf, spine gilt, crnrs rubbed, ft of backstrip worn.
(Clark) **£52 [≈$93]**

Palmer, John
- Malefactor. A full and true account of the horrid murders, robberies and burnings committed at Bradforton and Upton Snodsbury, in the County of Worcester ... Worcester: J. Butler, 1782. 3 engvd plates. Crnr of X2 torn, without loss. Later qtr calf.
(Waterfield's) **£135 [≈$243]**

Palmyra ...
- The ruins of Palmyra ... See Wood, Robert

Panegyric ...
- A panegyric on the town of Paisley. By a North-Country gentleman. Printed in the year 1765. [Paisley?]. Half-title. Later qtr mor, uncut, orig blue wraps bound in.
(C.R. Johnson) **£185 [≈$333]**

Papin, Denis
- A new digester or engine for softening bones. London: H. Bonwicke, 1681. 1st edn. Sm 4to. [4],52,[2 blank] pp. License lf, fldg engvd plate. Early lower margs worn, license lf backed & fore-marg strengthened, a few dampstains. Old calf-backed mrbld bds.
(Antiq Sc) **$1,500 [≈£833]**

Paprrs [sic] ...
- Original paprrs [sic]. Relating to the expedition to Carthagena ... See Vernon, Edward

Paris ...
- The curiosities of Paris ... manner of travelling ... description of Paris ... adapted for the use of chirurgical students and the traveller. London: for W. Owen, 1757. 8vo. xxiv,169,3 pub advts pp. Occas spotting. Contemp calf, rebacked, jnts split, rubbed.

(Kerr) **£85 [≈$153]**
- A view of Paris, and places adjoining. With an account of the Court of France ... by a gentleman lately residing at the English Ambassador's at Paris. London: for Nutt, 1701. 1st edn. 8vo. Half-title. Lacking final advt leaf. Contemp panelled calf, rebacked.
(Hannas) **£75 [≈$135]**

Parker, Henry
- The true portraiture of the Kings of England; drawn from their titles, successions, raigns and ends ... demonstrated that there hath been no ... hereditary right ... London: 1688. 4to. New edn. Wing P430.
(C.R. Johnson) **£35 [≈$63]**

Parker, Samuel
- A discourse of ecclesiastical politie; wherein the authority of the civil magistrate over the conscience of subjects ... is asserted ... London: John Martyn, 1670. 8vo. lvi,326 pp. Errata. Lacking endpapers. 19th c cloth, worn, sm stain at outer edge.
(Spelman) **£60 [≈$108]**

Parker, Wilmot
- An analysis of the practice of the Court of Chancery. London: for J. Butterworth, 1794. 1st edn. 8vo. [iv],172 pp inc prelim blank. Uncut in rec qtr calf.
(Burmester) **£90 [≈$162]**

Parkins, Sir William
- The arraignment, tryal and condemnation of Sir William Parkins Knt for the most horrid ... conspiracy to assassinate ... King William ... London: Samuel Heyrick ..., 1696. Folio. [iv],48 pp. Imprim leaf. Final page a bit soiled. Disbound. Wing A3260.
(Clark) **£24 [≈$43]**

Parkinson, J.
- Thetrum botanicum. The theater of plantes or, an universall and compleate herball. London: 1640. Folio. [xx],1756 (i.e. 1746),[1] pp. Errata leaf at end. W'cut title, letterpress title, 2714 w'cuts. Contemp calf, rebacked.
(Wheldon & Wesley) **£1,500 [≈$2,700]**

Parkyns, Sir Thomas
- (Greek title, then) The inn-play: or Cornish-hugg wrestler ... a method which teacheth to break all holds, and throw most falls mathematically ... For Tho. Weekes ..., 1727. 3rd edn crrctd. 4to. W'cuts in text. Sl browned. Contemp sheep, worn & rubbed.
(Charles Cox) **£225 [≈$405]**

Parliament of Scotland ...

- An account of the proceedings of the Parliament of Scotland ... See Ridpath, George

Parnell, Thomas

- Poems on several occasions ... published by Mr. Pope ... London: for H. Lintot, 1737. 3rd London edn. 8vo. [viii],222,[2 blank], xii,13-64 pp. Dodsley's 8 pp ctlg at end. Red & black title. Contemp calf, rebacked, crnrs reprd.   *(Claude Cox)* **£45 [≈ $81]**
- The poetical works of Dr. Thomas Parnell, late Archdeacon of Clogher. Glasgow: Foulis ..., 1786. Folio. Title & dedn leaf sl spotted, 2 leaves browned, sm hole in 'Contents' leaf & C2. Rebound inn qtr calf.
          (Hughes) **£55 [≈ $99]**
- The works in verse and prose ... Enlarged with variations and poems, not before published. Glasgow: Foulis, 1767. 8vo in 4s. [8],232 pp. Contemp calf, piece missing from top of back, hinge sl cracked, crnrs bumped.
          (Cooper Hay) **£30 [≈ $54]**

Parr, Richard

- The life of James Usher, late Lord Arch-Bishop of Armagh and Primate of all Ireland. London: 1686. 1st edn. Folio. Port. Contemp panelled calf, newly rebacked, rubbed.
          (Robertshaw) **£70 [≈ $126]**

Parr, Samuel

- Discourse on education and on the plans pursued in Charity-Schools. London: for T. Cadell ... & J. & C. Berry, Norwich, [1786]. 1st edn. 4to. [ii],78,[i] pp. Errata leaf at end. Marg closely trimmed, nowhere touching text. Disbound.   *(Bennett)* **£350 [≈ $630]**
- A free translation of the preface to Bellendenus containing animated strictures on the great political characters of the present time. London: Stafford & Davenport, 1788. Half-title. Contemp calf, hinges weakening.
          (C.R. Johnson) **£35 [≈ $63]**

Parsons, J.

- Parsons' select British classics, a well chosen collection of classical essays. London: J. Parsons, 1793-94. 36 vols. Each vol with engvd title & ptd title. Contemp green str-grained mor, gilt, a.e.g., by C. Herring of St. Martin Street, London.
          (C.R. Johnson) **£2,000 [≈ $3,600]**

Parsons, James

- A mechanical and critical enquiry into the nature of hermaphrodites. London: for J.

Walthoe, 1741. 1st edn. 8vo. 2ff, liv,[2],156 pp. Advt leaf before p 1, 3 fldg engvd plates. 2 short tears. Rec polished calf.
          (Pirages) **$450 [≈ £250]**
- Philosophical observations on the analogy between the propagation of animals and that of vegetables. London: C. Davis, 1752. 1st edn. 8vo. xvi,276,[12] pp. Fldg engvd plate. Lightly browned. Contemp calf, jnts lightly cracked.   *(Antiq Sc)* **$275 [≈ £152]**
- Philosophical observations on the analogy between the propagation of animals and that of vegetables. London: 1752. 8vo. xvi,276,[12] pp. Fldg plate. Title & plate somewhat foxed. 1 or 2 pp torn without loss, few lib stamps. Contemp half calf, rebacked.
          (Wheldon & Wesley) **£100 [≈ $180]**

Pascal, Blaise

- Monsieur Pascall's thoughts, meditations, and prayers, touching matters moral and divine. London: for Jacob Tonson, 1688. 1st edn in English. 22ff,263pp, 4ff, 269-375 pp. V sm hole in final leaf. Contemp sprinkled calf, 2 sm wormhole, trivial wear to jnts.
          (Pirages) **$850 [≈ £472]**
- Thoughts on religion and other subjects ... translated from the French. London: for A. & J. Churchil ..., 1704. Contemp calf, rebacked.   *(Waterfield's)* **£125 [≈ $225]**
- Thoughts on religion. And other curious subjects. London: for Jacob Tonson, 1727. 2nd edn. 8vo. xliv,315 pp. Contemp calf, 19th c rebacking, a little worn.
          (Young's) **£60 [≈ $108]**
- Thoughts on religion. And other curious subjects. London: for R. Ware ..., 1741. 8vo. 4th edn in English. 8vo. Contemp polished calf.   *(Chaucer Head)* **£60 [≈ $108]**

Passions Personify'd ...

- The passions personify'd ... See Lawrence, Herbert

Paterson, Daniel

- A new and accurate description of all the direct and principal cross roads in England and Wales ... 1796. 11th edn. Thick 8vo. Engvd map. Lea cloth.
          (Halewood) **£45 [≈ $81]**

Paterson, William

- A narrative of four journeys into the country of the Hottentots, and Caffraria. London: for J. Johnson, 1789. 1st edn. 4to. vi, ix-xii, 171 pp. 2ff. Fldg map, 17 plates (sl offset). Sm tear at inner marg 2 leaves. Contemp tree-calf, spine gilt, jnts sl worn.
          (Pirages) **$1,200 [≈ £666]**

Patin, Charles
- Travels thro' Germany, Swisserland, Bohemia, Holland; and other parts of Europe ... 1697. Sm 8vo. Fldg map, port, 6 plates. Some occas foxing. Contemp panelled calf, recased, reprd.   *(Farahar)* **£95 [≈$171]**

Patrick, Simon
- A commentary upon the historical books of the Old Testament, plus, a commentary upon the three lesser prophets. 1765-66. 4 vols. Lge 4to. Port frontis. Vols 3 & 4 lacking front free endpapers. Mottled calf.
       (Edwards) **£150 [≈$270]**
- A paraphrase upon the books of Ecclesiastes and the Song of Solomon. London: for Rich. Royston, 1685. 2 pts in 1 vol. Cr 8vo. Port frontis. Contemp calf.   *(Stewart)* **£35 [≈$63]**

The Patriot ...
- The patriot or political, moral and philosophical repository consisting of original pieces and selections from writers of merit ... London: for G.G.J. & J. Robinson, 1792-93. 3 vols. Contemp half calf.
       (Waterfield's) **£350 [≈$630]**

Patriots ...
- Patriots of North America ... See Cooper, Myles

Patsall, Mrs.
- An apology for the Catholics of Great Britain and Ireland ... For the author, 1767. 1st edn. 8vo. viii,172 pp. Calf, rebacked.
       (Young's) **£15 [≈$27]**

Paul, John
- Every landlord or tenant his own lawyer. London: W. Strahan 1778. 4th edn. 8vo. [4],178 pp. Orig wraps, uncut, new paper spine, sl dusty.   *(Spelman)* **£25 [≈$45]**
- The laws relating to landlords and tenants. London: 1791. 7th edn. 8vo. [viii],203 pp. Contemp sheep, worn, jnts cracked.
       (Bow Windows) **£55 [≈$99]**
- The laws relating to landlords and tenants; or, every landlord and tenant his own lawyer ... London: for W. Richardson, 1791. 7th edn. 8vo. Early calf-backed bds, hinges splitting.
       (Chaucer Head) **£30 [≈$54]**

Peacham, Henry
- The compleat gentleman ... with other additions. London: for Francis Constable ..., 1627. 2nd edn. 4to. [xii],302 pp. Lacking engvd title, 1st & last few leaves soiled, some headings cropped. Rec half calf.

(Young's) **£95 [≈$171]**
- The compleat gentleman ... to which is added the gentleman's exercise ... London: 1661. 3rd imp. Sm 4to. Engvd frontis (trimmed at top), title, [viii],304; title, [v],455 (continuous pagination from 1st pt). Top edge cropped with sl loss. 19th c calf, rebacked.
       (P & P) **£260 [≈$468]**
- The gentleman's exercise. Or ... for drawing all manner of beasts ... as also the making of all kinds of colours ... London: for I.M., 1634. Sm 4to. [8],163 pp. Num w'cut ills in text. Wide-margined. Outer edges v thin & occas frayed. 19th c cloth-backed bds.
       (Spelman) **£160 [≈$288]**

Peacock, W.
- A compendious geographical dictionary containing a concise description of the most remarkable places ... in Europe. Asia, Africa, and America ... embellished with maps. 1795. 2nd edn. 12mo. 5 maps. Gilt-ruled calf.
       (Tooley) **£50 [≈$90]**
- A compendious geographical dictionary containing a concise description of the most remarkable places ... in Europe. Asia, Africa, and America. London: 1795. 2nd edn. 12mo. 5 maps, double hemisphere map. Later cloth.
       (Robertshaw) **£30 [≈$54]**

Pearce, William
- Windsor Castle; or, the fair maid of Kent, an opera, as performed at the Theatre Royal, Covent Garden ... London: for T.N. Longman, 1795. 1st edn. 8vo. viii,40 pp. Half-title, sl stain on 2 leaves. Disbound.
       (Burmester) **£20 [≈$36]**

Pearson, A.
- The great case of tythes. Dublin: Fuller, 1730. 8vo. Mod bds.
       (Emerald Isle) **£25 [≈$45]**

Peck, Francis
- Academia tertia Anglicana; or, the antiquarian annals of Stamford in Lincoln, Rutland, and Northampton Shires ... in xiv books. London: 1727. Folio. Fldg plate, title, [iii-xvi] pp. 14 books sep paginated. 31 plates. Contemp gilt dec calf, rebacked, orig back.
       (Titles) **£200 [≈$360]**
- Desiderata curiosa: or, a collection of divers scarce and curious pieces. London: for Thomas Evans, 1779. New edn. 2 vols. 4to. 9 engvs. A few upper edges & crnrs damaged without loss of text. Rec half calf, mrbld bds.
       (Titles) **£85 [≈$153]**

Peckham, Harry
- The tour of Holland, Dutch Brabant, the Austrian Netherlands, and part of France ... a description of Paris and its environs. London: for G. Kearsley ..., 1772. 1st edn. 256 pp. Contemp sheep-backed bds, rubbed.
(Young's) £50 [≈ $90]

Peel, Robert
- The substance of the speech ... in the House of Commons ... 14th February, 1799, on the question of receiving the report of the Committee on the Resolutions ... Dublin: John Exshaw, 1799. 22 pp. Stabbed pamphlet as issued, uncut. *(C.R. Johnson)* £22 [≈ $39]

Peerage Bill ...
- The Peerage Bill consider'd as it relates to the Scots. In a letter to a commoner. [Edinburgh: 1719]. 4to. 4 pp. Uncut as issued.
(C.R. Johnson) £28 [≈ $50]

Peerage of Ireland ...
- The peerage of Ireland. London: Almon, 1768. 1st edn. 2 vols. Lge 8vo. 141 engvd coats of arms on 71ff. 1 leaf loose. Contemp calf. *(Marlborough)* £240 [≈ $432]

Pegge, Samuel
- Curalia: or an historical account of the Royal household. London: J. Nichols ..., 1782-1790. 3 pts bound in 1 vol. 78; viii,126; 133 pp. Contemp ms crrctns & drctns to printer in margs, occas light foxing. Rebound in qtr calf, mrbld bds. *(Gough)* £135 [≈ $243]

Peirce, James
- The curse causeless. A sermon preach'd at Exon, Jan 30th, 1716/17. London: for John Clarke, 1717. 8vo. 35,[1] pp. Disbound.
(Burmester) £20 [≈ $36]

Pemberton, Henry
- A view of Sir Isaac Newton's philosophy. London: S. Palmer, 1728. 1st edn. 4to. [1],407 pp. 12 fldg engvd plates, sev engvd decorations. Minor waterstaining. Uncut in 19th c half vell. Stamp of Royal Society of Edinburgh on title.
(Pickering) $1,000 [≈ £555]
- A view of Sir Isaac Newton's philosophy. Dublin: reprinted by & for John Hyde, 1728. 8vo. 12 fldg engvd plates. Contemp calf, spine rubbed, lacks label.
(Marlborough) £190 [≈ $342]

Pemberton, Israel
- An address to the inhabitants of

Pennsylvania, by those Freemen ... who are now confined in the Mason's Lodge, by virtue of a General Warrant signed in Council ... Phila: 1777. 4,52 pp. Half lea, bds.
(Reese) $900 [≈ £500]

Pembroke, Henry, Earl of
- Military equitation: or, a method of breaking horses, and teaching soldiers to ride. Designed for the use of the army. Sarum: E. Easton, 1778. 3rd edn. 4to. [viii],140 pp. 17 engvd plates. Orig bds, uncut, rebacked.
(Young's) £145 [≈ $261]

Penington, Isaac
- The works ... London: Clark, 1761. 2 vols. Sm 4to. Calf, sl wear.
(Emerald Isle) £75 [≈ $135]

Pennant, Thomas
- Arctic zoology. London: 1792. 2nd edn. 3 vols. 4to. Frontis, 2 title vignettes, 2 fldg maps, 25 plates. Sl stain in upper marg vol 2. Contemp mottled calf, worn, rubbed, jnts cracked, front cvr vol 3 detchd.
(Wheldon & Wesley) £380 [≈ $684]
- Genera of birds. London: for B. White, 1781. 2nd edn. 4to. [6],xxvi,68,[2] pp. Engvd title, 16 engvd plates. Lge margs. Lib stamps on title verso & plate rectos & versos. New calf-backed mrbld bds. *(Claude Cox)* £55 [≈ $99]
- The history of the parishes of Whiteford and Holywell. London: for B. & J. White, 1796. 1st edn. [x],328 pp. 22 engvd plates, 3 vignettes. Some spotting to prelims & plate margs. New half calf, mrbld sides.
(Lloyd-Roberts) £120 [≈ $216]
- The journey from Chester to London. London: for B. White, 1782. 1st edn. 4to. iv,452,[vi index] pp. Engvd frontis, 22 engvd plates. Contemp half calf, mrbld sides.
(Lloyd-Roberts) £125 [≈ $225]
- The literary life ... by himself. London: Benjamin & John White ..., 1793. 1st edn. 4to. vi,144 pp. Engvd port frontis, engvd plate. Lib stamp on title & bottom margs of plates. Contemp half calf, rebacked.
(Claude Cox) £65 [≈ $117]
- The literary life, by himself. London: White & Faulder, 1793. 4to. 3ff,144 pp. Engvd port frontis, engvd plate. Later half tan mor, dusty. *(Marlborough)* £175 [≈ $315]
- Some account of London. Dublin: for John Archer, 1771. Roy 8vo. vi,[viii subscribers], 480,[8 index] pp. Fldg map, engvd title, 15 engvd plates. Uncut in orig bds.
(Lloyd-Roberts) £85 [≈ $153]
- Some account of London. The third edition.

London: for Robert Faulder, 1793. 4to. viii,502,8 index pp. 15 engvd plates inc fldg plan. Plan split at flds, frontis reprd & tissue lined. Rebound half calf.
(Lloyd-Roberts) **£105 [≈ $189]**

- A tour in Scotland MDCCLXIX. London: Benj. White, 1790. 5th edn. 4to. Engvd title. 42 engvd plates, lge map. Rebound half calf, mrbld sides, uncut.
(Lloyd-Roberts) **£125 [≈ $225]**

- A tour in Wales. 1778-83. 2 vols. 4to. 2 engvd titles, 26 plates inc 9 fldg with 10 supplementary plates inc 1 fldg. Orig tree calf, rebacked, spine gilt.
(Edwards) **£250 [≈ $450]**

Pennsylvania ...
- A brief state of the Province of Pennsylvania ... See Smith, William

Pepys, Samuel
- Memoires relating to the state of the Royal Navy in England, for ten years, determin'd December 1688. London: for Ben Griffin, 1690. 1st edn, 2nd iss. Marg tear & repr to fldg table, ms crrctns of errata on 8 pp. Contemp sprinkled calf, rebacked. Wing P1449.
(Charles Cox) **£650 [≈ $1,170]**

Perceval, John
- Faction detected, by the evidence of facts. Containing. An impartial view of parties at home, and affairs abroad. London: J. Roberts, 1743. 175 pp. Disbound.
(C.R. Johnson) **£20 [≈ $36]**

Percy, Thomas
- Hau Kiou Choaan or the pleasing history. A translation from the Chinese language. London: R. & J. Dodsley, 1761. 1st edn in English, 4 vols. Sm 8vo. Engvd fldg plate (each with minor repr) & errata leaves in each vol, half-title vol 1. Contemp calf.
(Dailey) **$500 [≈ £277]**
- Reliques of ancient English poetry. 1765. 3 vols. 8vo. 344; 384; 386 pp. Frontis vol 1, 3 vignette titles. Later red grained mor, gilt, a.e.g.
(Edwards) **£160 [≈ $288]**
- Reliques of ancient English poetry. London: for J. Dodsley, 1775. 3rd edn. 3 vols. 8vo. lxxviii pp, 2ff, 376 pp, 1f; iii,402 pp, 2ff; iii,360 pp, 1f. Engvd frontis & titles. 1 leaf reprd. Contemp calf, gilt.
(Titles) **£100 [≈ $180]**

Pernety, Dom Antoine Joseph
- The history of a voyage to the Malouine Islands ... two voyages to the Straits of

Megellan ... T. Jefferys, 1771. 1st English edn. 4to. [iv],xvii, [i blank], 294 pp. Frontis map, 2 fldg plans, fldg chart, 2 maps, 10 plates. Contemp tree-calf, dec gilt.
(Blackwell's) **£2,200 [≈ $3,960]**

Perry, Charles
- A disquisition on the stone and gravel; together with strictures on the gout, when combined with these disorders. By S. [sic] Perry ... London: for T. Becket, 1779. 6th edn. Sm 8vo. Minor marg dampstaining, sm tear to hd of 1 leaf with sl loss. Mod qtr calf.
(Hughes) **£24 [≈ $43]**

Perry, James
- Mimosa: or, the sensitive plant; a poem. Dedicated to Mr. Banks, and addressed to Kitt Frederick, Dutchess of Queensberry, elect. London: 1779. 2nd edn. 4to. 20 pp. Half-title. Calf by Bickers, b'plate of 2nd Marquis of Milford Haven.
(C.R. Johnson) **£550 [≈ $990]**

Perry, John
- An account of the stopping of Daggenham Breach ... And proposals for rendering the Ports of Dover and Dublin ... commodious for entertaining large ships. London: 1721. 1st edn. 8vo. Lge fldg plan (strengthened). Some spotting. Contemp polished calf, rebacked.
(Chaucer Head) **£160 [≈ $288]**

Perry, W.
- The Royal standard English dictionary. Edinburgh: Bell & Bradfute, 1793. 8th edn. 12mo in 6s. Contemp calf, old doeskin spine.
(Marlborough) **£65 [≈ $117]**

Perry, William
- The only sure guide to the English tongue; or, new pronouncing spelling book ... Brookfield, Ma: E. Merriam, n.d. [1790s]. Sm 8vo. x,180 pp. W'engvd frontis, 12 text w'cuts. Contemp calf, rubbed.
(Karmiole) **$100 [≈ £55]**

Perswasive ...
- A perswasive to communion with the Church of England ... See Grove, Robert

Petition ...
- The petition of the Catholics of Ireland, to the King ... at St James's ... Jan 2, 1793. By Messers. Edward Byrne ... Dublin: H. Fitzpatrick, 1793. 27 pp. Disbound.
(C.R. Johnson) **£22 [≈ $39]**
- Petition of the Roman Catholics of Ireland. Intended to have been presented to

Parliament in February 1792. Dublin: P. Byrne, 1792. 16 pp. Disbound.
(C.R. Johnson) **£25 [≈ $45]**

Petrowitz, Alexis
- The tryal of the Czarewitz, Alexis Petrowitz ... 25th of June, 1718, for ... rebellion and treason against the life of the Czar ... London: James Crokatt, 1725. 8vo in 4's. [ii],110 pp. Title cropped at hd, some minor foxing. Later cloth.   *(Clark)* **£40 [≈ $72]**

Pettus, Sir John
- Fodinae Regales ... history, laws ... of the chief mines and mineral works in England, Wales, and ... Ireland. London: Thomas Basset, 1670. 1st edn. Folio. Frontis, 2 fldg plates. Title a little rubbed, sm dampstain on 3ff. Contemp calf, rebacked. Wing P1908.
(Pickering) **$900 [≈ £500]**

Petty, Sir William
- Political survey of Ireland ... added an account of the wealth and expences of England ... London: D. Browne, 1719. 2nd edn. 8vo. [xvi],223, 26,[2 pub advts] pp. Contemp panelled calf, rebacked.
(Pickering) **$675 [≈ £375]**
- Tracts chiefly relating to Ireland. Dublin: Boulter Grierson, 1769. 1st coll edn. Contemp calf, rebacked.
(Emerald Isle) **£550 [≈ $990]**

Petyt, William
- Jus parliamentarium. Or, the ancient power, jurisdiction, rights, and liberties of the most high court of parliament, revived and asserted, In two parts. 1739. 1st edn. Folio. xxiv,400 pp. Red & black title. Contemp calf, little wear to upper hinge.
(Edwards) **£170 [≈ $306]**

Pharmacopoeia ...
- The British dispensatory, containing a faithful translation of the New London Pharmacopoeia ... the whole contents of the Edinburgh Pharmacopoeia. London: Edward Cave, 1747. 8vo. xii,136, 83,[i] pp. Some foxing & old ink marks. New qtr calf.
(Pollak) **£50 [≈ $90]**

Philalethes, Eugenius
- Long livers: a curious history of such persons of both sexes who have liv'd several ages, and grown young again. 1st English edn of Robert Samber's translation. 8vo. [2],lxiv, 199,viii,[3] pp. Index & errata. Little light browning. Full calf.   *(Rootenberg)* **$350 [≈ £194]**

Philidor, Francois Andre
- Analysis of the game of chess. 1777. New edn, greatly enlgd, New half mor.
(Allen) **$200 [≈ £111]**

Philipps, Katherine
- Poems. By the incomparable, Mrs. K.P. London: for Rich. Marriott ..., 1664. 1st edn. [xiv],242,1 errata pp. 2 engvd ports at beginning inc 1 addtnl. Without imprim leaf. Later calf, a.e.g., hd & tail of spine defective.
(Young's) **£210 [≈ $378]**

Philips, Ambrose
- Pastorals, by Mr. Philips. London: H. Hills, 1710. Greyish paper a little browned, a couple of brief tears in lower marg. Mod half calf, cloth bds.   *(Charles Cox)* **£65 [≈ $117]**
- Pastorals, epistles, odes, and other original poems, with translations from Pindar, Anacreon, and Sappho ... London: for J. & R. Tonson ..., 1748. 1st edn. 12mo. Front end paper wanting. Contemp polished calf, gilt, upper jnt weak.   *(Charles Cox)* **£48 [≈ $86]**
- Pastorals, epistles, odes, and other original poems, with translations ... London: for J. & R. Tonson ..., 1748. 1st coll edn. Lge 12mo. [8],147 pp. Contemp calf, rebacked.
(Fenning) **£135 [≈ $243]**

Philips, John
- Cyder. A poem. In two books. London: for Jacob Tonson, 1708. 1st edn. Fly-title (b1) bound before frontis as half-title & bearing 19th c inscrptn, this leaf marked & dusty. New calf.   *(Charles Cox)* **£55 [≈ $99]**
- Cyder. A poem. In two books. London: Jacob Tonson, 1708. 1st edn. Lge & thick paper. Roy 8vo. Engvd frontis. Some spotting to title & elsewhere. Contemp calf, bds dec in blind, rebacked.   *(Chaucer Head)* **£240 [≈ $432]**
- Poems attempted in the style of Milton. With his life by Dr. Sewell. London: for E. Curll, 1744. 10th edn. Lge 12mo. xxx,42; 72 pp. Port, engvd frontis. Wraps.
(Fenning) **£35 [≈ $63]**
- The splendid shilling. An imitation of Milton. London: for Hen. Clements, 1719. Sm 8vo. 28 pp. Occas soiling. Later plain paper bds.   *(Spelman)* **£25 [≈ $45]**

Phillips, Peregrine
- A diary kept in an excursion to Little Hampton ... and Brighthemston ... in 1778; and also ... in 1779. London: for the author, 1780. 2 vols. 2nd & 1st edns. 12mo. viii,100; vii,127 pp. Half-titles. Sl damage to outer crnrs of sev leaves. Rec half calf.

(Burmester) £120 [≈ $216]

Phillips, Robert

- A dissertation concerning the present state of the high roads of England ... wherein is proposed a new method of repairing and maintaining them. London: L. Gilliver, 1737. 1st edn. 8vo. [16],62 pp, advt leaf. 8 plates. Sm repr to title marg. Rec qtr calf.
(Spelman) £280 [≈ $504]

Phillips, Thomas

- The history of the life of Cardinal Pole. Oxford: 1764. 2 parts in 1. Sm 4to. Port frontis, fldg pedigree. Sl foxing. Calf, sl rubbing to jnts. *(Edwards)* £100 [≈ $180]

Philosophical Enquiry ...

- A philosophical enquiry into the origin of our ideas ... See Burke, Edmund

Philosophical Survey ...

- A philosophical survey of the South of Ireland ... See Campbell, Thomas

Philostratus

- The first two books ... By Charles Blount, gent. Nathaniel Thompson, 1680. 1st edn. Folio. [viii],243 pp. Red & black title. Faint marg dampstaining at end, some sections sl browned. Contemp calf, rubbed, upper compartment of spine defective. Wing P1654.
(Frew Mackenzie) £95 [≈ $171]

Phipps, Constantine John

- A voyage towards the North Pole undertaken by his majesty's command 1773. London: W. Boyer & J. Nichols, 1774. 4to. viii,253,[3] pp. Half-title, leaf of drctns to binder, 15 plates & maps, some fldg, fldg tables. Orig bds, rec rebacked in paper, uncut.
(High Latitude) $750 [≈ £416]

Phipps, Joseph

- Cursory observations on a late publication, intitled, an essay on the simplicity of truth signed Catholicus. London: James Phillips, 1779. 1st edn. 39,[1 advt], 30 postscript pp. New canvas-backed paper bds.
(Claude Cox) £15 [≈ $27]
- The original and present state of man briefly considered: wherein is shewn the nature of his fall ... Divine principle of grace and truth held forth to the world by ... Quakers. Trenton: Isaac Collins, 1793. Browned. Contemp sheep, rebacked.
(Waterfield's) £75 [≈ $135]
- The original and present state of man briefly

considered ... London printed: New York: reprinted by William Ross, 1788. Title browned. Old sheep, rebacked, crnrs worn.
(Clark) £15 [≈ $27]

Phocion's Conversations ...

- Phocion's conversations ... See Mably, Gabriel Bonnot, Abbe

Phoenix Britannicus ...

- Phoenix Britannicus: being a miscellaneous collection of scarce and curious tracts ... Vol I [all published]. London: for the compiler ..., 1732. 4to. Complete run of 6 numbers with gen title. [xii],viii,584 pp. Title trifle soiled & frayed. Rec half calf.
(Burmester) £110 [≈ $198]

Phylangus, Theophylus (pseud.)

- The Church of England's new hymn, to the State scaffold at Westminster Hall. London: 1710. Sm 8vo. 16 pp. Lower fore-corner frayed touching one letter of one catchword. A small & somewhat soiled copy in new wraps. *(Bennett)* £225 [≈ $405]

Physik ...

- Primitive physik ... See Wesley, J.

Picture ...

- A complete picture of human life: or, variety of food for the mind ... pleasure and instruction of readers of every class ... York: G. Walker in Coffee Yard, [ca 1793-95]. 8vo. vi,508 pp. Gen title, contents, engvd frontis. Contemp half calf, jnts split.
(Bennett) £325 [≈ $585]

Pike, Nicolas

- A new and complete system of arithmetic, composed for the use of citizens of the United States. Worcester: Isaiah Thomas, 1797. 2nd edn. Thick 8vo. 516 pp. Orig calf, worn.
(Argosy) $100 [≈ £55]

Pike, Samuel

- A plain and full account of the Christian practices observed by the church in St. Martin's-le-Grand, London, and other churches (commonly called Sandemanian) ... Boston: Z. Fowle, 1766. 1st edn. 28 pp.
(Jenkins) $25 [≈ £13]

Piles, Roger de

- The art of painting ... above 300 of the most eminent painters ... a complete treatise of painting, designing ... London: Thomas Payne, n.d. [ca 1750-53]. 3rd edn. 8vo. [xvi],439,[i advt] pp. Some spotting, short

marg tears. Contemp calf, upper jnt cracked.
(Bow Windows) **£75** [≈ **$135**]
- The art of painting ... with reflections on the
works of the most celebrated painters ...
London: J. Nutt, 1706. 8vo. 480 pp. Engvd
frontis. Orig calf sl worn.
(Camden) **£500** [≈ **$900**]

Pilkington, Mrs. Mary
- Edward Barnard; or, merit exalted;
containing the history of the Egerton family.
London: E. Newberry, 1797. Engvd frontis.
Contemp tree-calf.
(C.R. Johnson) **£125** [≈ **$225**]

Pilkington, Mrs.
- A mirror for the female sex. Historical
beauties for young ladies. London: Vernor &
Hood, 1799. 2nd edn. 8vo. xxiv,240 pp. 37
w'engvs. Contemp calf, jnts & crnrs worn.
(Spelman) **£20** [≈ **$36**]

Pinckney, Charles
- Three letters, written, and originally
published, under the signature of a South
Carolina planter. Phila: 1799. 65 pp. Sl
browning, a few leaves closely trimmed. Later
wraps. *(Reese)* **$150** [≈ **£83**]

Pindar, Peter (pseud.)
- See Wolcot, John

Pinkerton, John
- The history of Scotland from the accession of
the House of Stuart to that of Mary. London:
for C. Dilly ..., 1797. 1st edn. 2 vols. 4to.
Engvd port frontis, vol I, half-titles, Extra-
illust with 14 engvd ports. Contemp calf, sl
rubbed. *(Hughes)* **£95** [≈ **$171**]

Pinkney, Miles
- Sweete thoughtes of Jesus and Marie. Paris:
Du Moutier, 1665. 2 parts in 1 vol. 8vo. Old
repr to marg of 1 leaf. Contemp mottled calf,
a.e.g., later reback.
(Marlborough) **£140** [≈ **$252**]

Piozzi, Hester Lynch
- Anecdotes of the late Samuel Johnson, during
the last twenty years of his life. London: for
T. Cadell, 1786. 1st edn. 8vo. viii,306,[2] pp.
Half-title. Without errata slip, sm hole in 1
leaf affecting 2 letters. Old lib stamp on title.
Contemp calf, rebacked.
(Burmester) **£150** [≈ **$270**]
- Letters to and from the late Samuel Johnson,
to which are added some poems, never before
printed. London: for A. Strahan ..., 1788. 1st

edn. 2 vols. 8vo. Errata slip. Contemp tree-
calf, gilt, gilt panelled spines, jnts sl worn.
(Traylen) **£220** [≈ **$396**]
- Observations and reflections made in the
course of a journey through France, Italy and
Germany. London: for A. Strahan, 1789. 1st
edn. 2 vols. 8vo. 3ff advts at end vol 2. Rec
half mottled calf, spines gilt.
(Lloyd-Roberts) **£125** [≈ **$225**]

Piso ...
- Piso's conspiracy. A tragedy - acted at the
Duke's Theatre. London: Popeshead, 1676.
56 pp. Some occas soiling. Later gray wraps.
Wing P2285. *(Karmiole)* **$85** [≈ **£47**]

Pitt, William & Fox, Charles James
- Speeches ... on Mr. Grey's motion for a
reform in Parliament. May 7 1793. London:
J. Debrett, [1793]. Disbound.
(C.R. Johnson) **£18** [≈ **$32**]

Pitt, William, Earl of Chatham
- Anecdotes of the life ... and of the principal
events of his time ... to the year 1778 ...
London: for J.S. Jordan, 1793. 3rd edn,
crrctd. 3 vols. 8vo. Contemp calf, jnts
cracked, lacking labels.
(Waterfield's) **£75** [≈ **$135**]
- Anecdotes of the life ... with his speeches in
Parliament, 1736-1778. Dublin: 1792. 1st
irish edn. 2 vols. 8vo. Lge fldg chart. Upper
crnrs of titles chipped, light staining
throughout. Contemp calf, gilt backs.
(Argosy) **$100** [≈ **£55**]
- Speech in the House of Commons, January
31st, 1799 ... the basis of a union between
Great Britain and Ireland. London: Wright,
1799. 8vo. 95 pp. Advts.
(Emerald Isle) **£35** [≈ **$63**]

Pitts, Joseph
- A true ... account of the religion and manners
of the Mohammetans ... Exon [Exeter]: for
Bishop & Score ..., 1704. 1st edn. 8vo.
[xvi],183 pp. Early crrctns of errata in ink.
Contemp speckled calf, rebacked, orig labels,
new endpapers. *(Morrell)* **£480** [≈ **$864**]

Placid Man ...
- The placid man ... See Jenner, Charles

Plain Reasoner ...
- The plain reasoner wherein the present state
of affairs are set in a new, but very obvious
light ... interests of Great Britain and
Hanover ... whether England be best
defended by an army, or a navy ... London:

M. Cooper, 1745. 2nd edn. 52 pp. Disbound.
(C.R. Johnson) **£35** [≈ $63]

Planting ...
- Planting and rural ornament ... See Marshall, William

Plat, Sir Hugh
- Delights for ladies, to adorne their persons, tables, closets ... with beauties, banquets, perfumes, and waters. London: R.Y., 1632. 12mo. Text within typographical borders. A little light waterstaining. Full blue mor, gilt. STC 19985.   *(Traylen)* **£975** [≈ $1,755]
- The Garden of Eden ... all fruits and flowers now growing in England ... advance their nature and growth ... seeds and hearbes ... London: Leake, 1660. 5th edn. 2 pts in 1. 1st edn of 2nd part. 12mo. Some browning. Contemp calf, rebacked, crnrs reprd. Wing 2387A.   *(Spelman)* **£420** [≈ $756]
- The Garden of Eden. or ... all fruits and flowers now growing in England ... how to advance their nature and growth ... London: for William Leake, 1660. 5th edn. [bound with] The second part ... 1660. 2 vols in 1. Contemp calf, recased, rebacked. Wing 2387A,   *(Stewart)* **£250** [≈ $450]

Plate-Glass Book ...
- The plate-glass book ... authentic tables ... glass-house table ... grinding, polishing, silvering ... London: Wicksteed, 1757. 4to. [with, as issued] The compleat appraiser ... London: 1756. 1st edn. Title & 1st few leaves frayed. Contemp sheep, jnts cracked.
(Marlborough) **£750** [≈ $1,350]

Platt, Sir Hugh [or Plat]
- See Plat, Sir Hugh

Plaw, John
- Ferme ornee; or rural improvements. A series of domestic and ornamental designs ... London: I. & J. Taylor, 1795. 1st edn. 4to. [4],13,[1] pp. 38 aquatint plates with tissue guards. Uncut in later grey bds, orig wraps mtd on cvrs, mod drop-lid cloth box.
(Spelman) **£480** [≈ $864]

Playfair, John
- Elements of geometry ... the first six books of Euclid ... plane and spherical trigonometry. Edinburgh: 1795. 1st Playfair edn. 8vo. xvi,400, 16 advts pp. Sep title to 2nd part. W'cut diags in text. Text sl soiled. Contemp sheep, jnts cracked, crnrs worn.
(Pickering) **$250** [≈ £138]

Playfair, William
- Inevitable consequences of a reform in Parliament ... London: for John Stockdale, 1792. 1st edn. 8vo. 27,[5 advts] pp. Sm ms numbering on title. Uncut in mod paper-cvrd bds.   *(Pickering)* **$200** [≈ £111]

Pliny the Younger
- Pliny's epistles and panegyrick translated by several hands with the life of Pliny ... London: for W. Mears, 1724. 2 vols. 8vo. Contemp calf, rebacked.
(Waterfield's) **£150** [≈ $270]

Plot, Richard
- The natural history of Oxfordshire, being an essay towards the natural history of England. Oxford: for Charles Brome, 1705. 2nd edn. Folio. Lge fldg map, 16 engvd plates. 19th c half mor, gilt, t.e.g. *(Traylen)* **£330** [≈ $594]

Plowden, Charles
- Remarks on a book entitled Memoirs of Gregorio Panzani. Preceded by an address to Rev. Joseph Berington. Liege: sold by J.P. Coghlan, London, 1794. 8vo. Rebound in half mor, rubbed.   *(Stewart)* **£55** [≈ $99]

Plowden, Francis
- Jura Anglorum. The rights of Englishmen. London: for E. & R. Brookes, 1792. 8vo. Contemp calf spine, mrbld bds, uncut.
(Stewart) **£30** [≈ $54]

Plowden, Robert
- A letter to Francis Plowden, Esq. ... On his work entitled Jura Anglorum. By a Roman Catholic Clergyman. London: for J.P. Coghlan, [1794]. 1st edn. 8vo. Title dusty & with early lib stamp, sl frayed in lower marg. Contemp roan, 1 bd chipped, rebacked.
(Chaucer Head) **£60** [≈ $108]

Poems ...
- Poems on various subjects ... See Cameron, William
- Poems supposed to have been written at Bristol ... See Chatterton, Thomas

Pointer, John
- A rational account of the weather, shewing signs of its several changes and alterations, together with the philosophical reasons for them. Oxford: for S. Wilmot ..., 1723. 76 pp. Rebound in panelled calf.
(C.R. Johnson) **£260** [≈ $468]

Poland ...

- The history of Poland ... to 1795 ... See Jones, Stephen

Pole, Thomas

- The anatomical instructor; or, an illustration of the modern and most approved methods of preparing the different parts of the human body and of quadrupeds ... London: 1790. 8vo. lxxx,[6], 304,[7] pp. 10 plates. Calf, jnts split.   *(Goodrich)* **$125 [≈ £69]**

Polite ...

- The polite lady ... See Allen, Charles
- The polite philosopher ... See Forrester, James

Political Dialogues ...

- Second political dialogues between the celebrated statues of Pasqin and Marforio at Rome ... Dedicated to ... the Lord Corruption. London: for T. Boreham, 1737. 8vo. 1st edn. [iv],viii,51 pp. Last leaf a little soiled & creased. Disbound.
                    (Burmester) **£30 [≈ $54]**

Political Tracts ...

- Political tracts ... See Johnson, Samuel

Polwhele, Richard

- The history of Devonshire. 1797. 3 vols in 1. 504 pp. 24 engvd plates (some foxing), map. Vol 3 sl waterstained. Half calf, extremities sl worn.   *(Edwards)* **£370 [≈ $666]**
- The influence of local attachment with respect to home. London: J. Johnson, 1796. 68 pp. Orig bds, uncut, lacking backstrip.
                    (C.R. Johnson) **£225 [≈ $405]**
- The influence of local attachment with respect to home. A poem in seven books. A new edition ... London: Johnson ..., 1798. 2 vols. x,93; 113,[3] pp. Errata & advt. Contemp tree-calf, red label.
                    (C.R. Johnson) **£165 [≈ $297]**
- The old English gentleman, a poem. London: for Cadell & Davies ..., 1797. 1st edn. 8vo. [iv],vii,146,[2 advts] pp. Half-title. Uncut in orig plain wraps, rebacked, ptd label.
                    (Burmester) **£260 [≈ $468]**

Pomet, Pierre

- A compleat history of druggs ... added, what is further observable on the same subject, from Messrs. Lemery, and Tournefort ... London: for R. Bonwicke, 1712. 1st English edn. 2 vols in 1. Red & black title, 86 engvd plates, advt leaf. Contemp calf, rebacked.
                    (Traylen) **£350 [≈ $630]**

Pomey, F.

- Indiculus universalis; or, the universe in epitome wherein the names of almost all the works of nature, or all the arts and sciences ... are in English, Latine and French ... London: 1679. 1st edn. 8vo. Later half calf, rubbed, hd of spine chipped.   *(Robertshaw)* **£40 [≈ $72]**

Pompey the Little ...

- The history of Pompey the Little ... See Coventry, Francis

Pontopiddan, E.

- The natural history of Norway ... different soils ... metals, minerals ... customs and manner of living ... translated ... L. 1755. Folio. xxiv,206; viii,291,[xii] pp. Fldg map, 28 engvd plates. Minor foxing. Contemp calf, rebacked, crnrs restored.
                    (Wheldon & Wesley) **£500 [≈ $900]**

Poole, Joshua

- The English Parnassus: or a help to English poesie ... collection of all the rhyming monosyllables ... London: for Henry Brome ..., 1677. 8vo. Engvd frontis, red & black title (both foxed). Some foxing, 2 letters shaved by binder. 19th c vell, sl dust-marked.
                    (Hughes) **£145 [≈ $261]**

Pope, Alexander

- The Dunciad Variorum. With the Prolegomena of Scriblerus. London: ... for the Booksellers in Dublin, 1729. 12mo. [iv],205 pp. Engvd & ptd titles, former with 'ass' vignette. A little staining. Contemp calf, rebacked.   *(Bennett)* **£85 [≈ $153]**
- The Dunciad. With notes variorum, and the Prolegomena of Scriblerus. London: .for Lawton Gilliver, [1735]. Sl marg waterstain, ink scribbles on 2 margs & last (blank) page. New half calf, mrbld bds.
                    (Charles Cox) **£75 [≈ $135]**
- An essay on man. Address'd to a friend. Part I [and Epistles II, III and IV]. 'London, for J. Wilford,' 1733-34. 4 pts in 1. New calf. All Edinburgh piracies, each. however, 1st 8vo edn.   *(Charles Cox)* **£85 [≈ $153]**
- An essay on man. With notes, critical and explanatory. London: Darton & Harvey, 1796. Sm 8vo. [vi],96 pp. Engvd frontis. Some finger & other marks. Rec half calf.
                    (Bow Windows) **£20 [≈ $36]**
- The first satire of the Second Book of Horace. London: ... A. Dodd ..., 1733. 1st edn, 3rd iss. Folio. 19 pp. Addtnl title from 1st iss tipped-in. Disbound, t.e.g.
                    (Clark) **£90 [≈ $162]**

- The Iliad of Homer. Translated by Mr. Pope
... London: for Bernard Lintot, 1736. 4th
edn. 6 vols. 8vo. Contemp calf, some jnts
cracked, vol I uniformly rebacked.
(Waterfield's) **£60 [≈$108]**
- The Iliad [and Odyssey] of Homer. London:
for T. Osborne ..., 1760. 11 vols. 8vo. 2 ports,
fldg map, fldg plate. Contemp speckled calf,
sl insect damage to calf in 1 crnr, neat repair
to vol 1 spine.
(Frew Mackenzie) **£450 [≈$810]**
- Of false taste. An epistle to the right
honourable Richard Earl of Burlington.
Occasion'd by his publishing Palladio's
Designs ... of Ancient Rome. London: L.
Gilliver, 1731. 3rd edn. Folio. 14,[ii] pp.
Outer marg final advt leaf reprd. Disbound,
t.e.g.   *(Clark)* **£60 [≈$108]**
- Of the knowledge and characters of men. An
epistle to ... the Lord Visct. Cobham.
London: for Lawton Gilliver, 1733. Folio. 13
pp. Half-title. Wanting the advt leaf.
(C.R. Johnson) **£110 [≈$198]**
- Of the use of riches, an epistle to the right
honourable Allen Lord Bathurst. London: for
Lawton Gilliver, 1732. 1st edn. Folio. [ii],20
pp. Single erratum on p 13. Disbound.
(Clark) **£120 [≈$216]**
- Of the use of riches, an epistle to the right
honourable Allen Lord Bathurst. London: for
Lawton Gilliver, 1732. 2nd edn. Folio. 22,[ii]
pp. Last 2 leaves loose, no sgntr on final advt
leaf. Disbound.   *(Clark)* **£75 [≈$135]**
- The poetical works ... in 3 volumes. Glasgow:
Foulis, 1785. Folio. 315; 365; [406] pp.
Contemp half calf. *(Halewood)* **£125 [≈$225]**
- The poetical works. Glasgow: Foulis, 1785. 3
vols. Folio. 1f blank, title, 2ff, v-xxxii, pp, 1f,
41-315 pp; title, 2ff, 365 pp; 1f blank, title,
402 pp, 2ff subscribers. Contemp calf newly
furbished.   *(Marlborough)* **£350 [≈$630]**
- The universal prayer ... London: for R.
Dodsley, 1738. Folio. Some reprs. B'plate of
Lord Esher. Mod half calf.
(Waterfield's) **£150 [≈$270]**
- The works ... Dublin: re-printed for George
Grierson ..., 1718. 8vo. A few stains, sm piece
of top blank marg of title replaced. Contemp
calf, rebacked.   *(Emerald Isle)* **£450 [≈$810]**

Popery ...

- History of popery, with such alterations of
phrase as may ... better accomodate it to the
present state of popery in Great Britain.
London: J. Oswald, 1735-36. 2 vols. 4to. Red
& black titles, 2 engvd frontis. Later half mor,
reprd.   *(Argosy)* **$125 [≈£69]**

Portland Museum ...

- A catalogue of the Portland Museum, lately
the property of the Duchess Dowager of
Portland, deceased ... London: Skinner, 1786.
4to. Engvd frontis. viii,194 pp. Including the
44 pp price-list. Contemp calf, rebacked.
(Marlborough) **£250 [≈$450]**

Potter, Francis

- An interpretation of the number 666 ... how
this number ought to be interpreted ... an
exquisite and perfect character ... Oxford: L.
Litchfield ..., 1647. 2nd edn. 4to. [xvi],214
pp. Engvd title, architectural border. Old
calf, rebacked.   *(Young's)* **£150 [≈$270]**

Powell, Robert

- The life of Alfred or Alured: the first
institutor of subordinate government in this
kingdom ... London: for Thomas Alchorn,
1634. 12mo. Some headlines shaved. 19th c
calf, rather scuffed. STC 20161.
(Waterfield's) **£70 [≈$126]**

Powell, Thomas

- The attourney's academy: or, the manner and
forme of proceeding .. upon any suite, plaint
or action ... London: for Benjamin Fisher ...,
1630. 3rd imp. Sm 4to. 8ff, 230 pp, 28ff, 3ff.
Title reprd, sm tears to 6 pp. Marginalia.
Mod calf.   *(Titles)* **£195 [≈$351]**
- Humane industry: or, a history of most
manual arts, deducing the original progress
and improvement of them ... London:
Herringman, 1661. 1st edn. 8vo. xvi,188 pp.
Prelims lightly browned. Contemp calf,
rebacked. Wing P3072.
(Rootenberg) **$950 [≈£527]**

Power, Henry

- Experimental philosophy in three books;
containing new experiments ... London:
1664. 1st edn. 4to. [xxiv],193,[1 blank] pp.
Errata lea, fldg engvd plate. Title & prelims
dust soiled, sm wormhole in title. Contemp
calf, chipped, worn, jnts weak. Wing P3099.
(Pickering) **$3,500 [≈£1,944]**

Power, Lawrence

- The righteous man's portion. Delivered in a
sermon at the obsequies of ... Henry St. John
... killed by the Tories ... J.M. for Henry
Bonwicke, 1680. Sm 4to. [vi],29,[i] pp. Some
browning, tear in marg. Wraps. Wing P3100.
(Blackwell's) **£30 [≈$54]**

Powers ...

- Powers claim'd by the hierarchy. Occasioned
by a late pamphlet ... In which the author's

vindication of the Codex ... are stated and considered. London: J. Roberts, 1735. 64 pp. Disbound.   *(C.R. Johnson)* **£25 [≈ $45]**

Pownall, Thomas
- The administration of the Colonies. 1764. 1st edn. 8vo. iv,131 pp. 1 gathering a little spotted. Wraps.   *(Farahar)* **£600 [≈ $1,080]**

Poyning's Law ...
- Plain reasons for modelling Poyning's law in such a manner as to assert the ancient rights of the two houses of parliament without entrenching on the king's prerogative. Dublin: W. Hallhead, 1780. Bds.
        (Emerald Isle) **£75 [≈ $135]**

Pozzo, Andrea
- Rules and examples of perspective proper for painters and architects ... in English and Latin ... London: for S. Sturt, 1707. Folio. 1st English edn. Engvd frontis, 2 engvd titles, 1 un-numbered plate, 101 engvd plates with facing text. Contemp calf, rebacked,
        (Spelman) **£850 [≈ $1,530]**

Pratt, Samuel Jackson
- Gleanings through Wales, Holland, and Westphalia. Third edition. To which is added, Humanity; a poem. Fourth edition. T.N. Longman, 1797. 3 vols. 8vo. lxiv,395; xvi,482; xii,413 pp. Sl browned throughout. Contemp tree-calf, some jnts tender, rubbed.
        (Blackwell's) **£100 [≈ $180]**

Prejudices ...
- Popular prejudices against the convention and treaty with Spain, examined and answer'd with remarks on a pamphlet, entitled, Considerations upon the present state of our affairs ... London: T. Cooper, 1739. 30 pp. Disbound.   *(C.R. Johnson)* **£45 [≈ $81]**

Prerogative ...
- The prerogative of man or his soule's immortality and high perfection defended ... Oxford: 1645. Some staining & fraying. Contemp calf, rebacked. Wing P3220.
        (Waterfield's) **£115 [≈ $207]**

Preston, John
- Sermons preached before His Maiestie, fift [sic] impression. London: Norton, 1637. 4to. 19th c half calf. NSTC 20237.
        (Marlborough) **£60 [≈ $108]**

Preston, Robert
- Meditations in the seasons. London: Edward & Charles Dilly, 1773. Sole edn. 8vo.

vi,153,[i] pp. Contemp tree-calf, backstrip gilt, crnrs bumped, jnts beginning to split.
        (Blackwell's) **£25 [≈ $45]**

Price, John
- An account of Leominster. Ludlow: Proctor, 1795. Lge 8vo. Frontis, 6 plates (1 fldg). Orig bds, uncut.   *(Marlborough)* **£75 [≈ $135]**

Price, Richard
- Four dissertations. I. On Providence. II. On prayer. III ... IV. On the importance of Christianity. London: for T. Cadell, 1777. 4th edn. 8vo. Contemp calf, rubbed.
        (Stewart) **£35 [≈ $63]**
- Four dissertations. I. On Providence. II. On prayer. III ... IV. On the importance of Christianity. London: for A. Millar & T. Cadell, 1767. 1st edn. 8vo. vii,439 pp. Contemp speckled calf, upper jnt sl cracked, minor wear at ends of spine.
        (Burmester) **£175 [≈ $315]**

Price, Richard (1723-1791)
- Observations on the nature of civil liberty ... and the justice and policy of the war with America. Dublin: for J. Exshaw ..., 1776. 12mo. [8],180 pp. Fldg table. Early 20th c cloth, gilt.   *(Karmiole)* **$150 [≈ £83]**
- Observations on the nature of civil liberty, the principles of government, and the justice and policy of the war with America. London: for T. Cadell, 1776. 2nd edn. 8vo. 128 pp. Mod qtr calf.   *(Edwards)* **£120 [≈ $216]**

Prideaux, Humphrey
- The origin and right of tithes, for the maintenance of the ministry in a Christian Church, truly stated. London: for R. Knaplock, 1736. 2nd edn. 8vo. rebound in qtr calf.   *(Hughes)* **£35 [≈ $63]**
- The true nature of imposture fully display'd in the life of Mahomet ... London: William Rogers, 1698. 3rd edn, crrctd. 8vo. 2 pts in 1. xxii,[2],166; 182,[2] pp. Contemp calf, minor rubbing. Wing P3418.
        (Karmiole) **$175 [≈ £97]**
- The true nature of imposture fully display'd in the life of Mahomet ... London: for E. Curll ..., 1716-17. 2 pts in 1. 12mo. Continuous pagination. Occas spotting. Rec calf.   *(Hughes)* **£28 [≈ $50]**
- The true nature of imposture fully display'd in the life of Mahomet ... London: 1718. 7th edn. 8vo. [xvi],200 pp. Sgntr on title, some pencilling, title & other leaves browned. Old calf, crnrs worn rec rebacked.
        (Bow Windows) **£45 [≈ $81]**

Prideaux, M.

- An easy and compendious inrtodvction [sic] for reading all sorts of histories ... Oxford: 1682. 6th edn. Sm 4to. [viii],392, [40],57,[3] pp. Longitudinal & 3 sub-titles. A few doodles in margs, stains & dustmarks. Old calf, rebacked. Wing P3445 & P3437.
  (Bow Windows) £50 [≈ $90]

Priestley, Joseph

- A course of lectures on oratory and criticism. London: J. Johnson, 1777. 1st edn. 4to. Half-title, errata leaf, 3 pp advts. Qtr calf.
  (Halewood) £98 [≈ $176]
- A description of a chart of biography. London: for J. Johnson, 1778. 7th edn. 2 fldg tables (frayed, reprd). Mod qtr calf.
  (Waterfield's) £80 [≈ $144]
- Directions for impregnating water with fixed air; in order to communicate to it the peculiar spirit and virtues of Pyrmont Water, and other mineral waters ... London: J. Johnson, 1772. 1st edn. 8vo. [2],iii,22, [3] advts pp. Frontis. Rec qtr calf.
  (Spelman) £280 [≈ $504]
- Disquisitions relating to matter and spirit. London: for J. Jonson, 1777. Frontis. Q2 & Q7 cancelled. Contemp sheep.
  (Waterfield's) £300 [≈ $540]
- Disquisitions relating to matter and spirit, to which is added, The history of the philosophical doctrine ... The second edition ... Birmingham: for J. Johnson, 1782. 2 vols. 8vo. Engvd frontis vol 1. Mod bds.
  (Waterfield's) £165 [≈ $297]
- Experiments and observations on different kinds of air ... the second edition. London: for J. Johnson, 1775-77. 3 vols. 8vo. 5 engvd plates. Contemp calf, backstrips a little rubbed, red mor labels.
  (Waterfield's) £350 [≈ $630]
- Experiments and observations on different kinds of air. London: 1781-84-77. 3rd, 2nd, 1st edns. 3 vols. [With] Experiments ... relating to various forms of natural philosophy. 1779-81-86. 1st edns. 3 vols. Browning & foxing. Vols 1-5, worn calf; vol 6 cloth.
  (Elgen) $1,500 [≈ £833]
- Experiments and observations on different kinds of air, and other branches of natural philosophy connected with the subject. Birmingham: Thomas Pearson, 1790. 3 vols. 8vo. Fldg engv frontis, 8 fldg engvd plates, 6 pp advts vol III. Contemp speckled calf.
  (Traylen) £330 [≈ $594]
- Heads of lectures on a course of experimental philosophy particularly including chemistry delivered at the New College in Hackney,

London: for J. Johnson, 1794. Contemp calf, rebacked.
  (Waterfield's) £300 [≈ $540]
- The history and present state of discoveries relating to vision, light, and colours. London: 1772. 1st edn. 2 vols. 4to. v,[1],xvi, 422; 423-812,[20] pp. Frontis, 25 plates, errata leaf, subscr list, pub advts. Lib stamps on 1st title. Contemp calf, rebacked.
  (Rootenberg) $1,500 [≈ £833]
- The history and present state of electricity, with original experiments. London: for J. Dodsley ..., 1767. 1st edn. 4to. [iv],xxxi, 736,[2 biblio],[5 index],[1 advt] pp. Advt plate, 7 fldg engvd plates. Some foxing & soiling. Contemp sprinkled calf, rebacked.
  (Pickering) $1,800 [≈ £1,000]
- Lectures on history and general policy to which is prefixed an essay on a course of liberal education for civil and active lives. Birmingham: Pearson & Rollason, 1788. 4to. Qq3 cancelled. Lacking pub ctlg at end. Early 19th c diced calf. *(Waterfield's)* £250 [≈ $450]
- Lectures on history and general policy. London: for J. Johnson, 1793. 1st 8vo edn. 2 vols. xvi,408; viii,468,[xx index] pp. 2 fldg engvd plates (foxed) tipped-in. Ownership inscrptns on both titles. Contemp tree-calf, spines cracked, jnts rubbed, edges worn.
  (Pickering) $250 [≈ £138]
- Lectures on history and general policy. London: for J. Johnson, 1793. 2 vols. 8vo. Fldg chart in vol I. Contemp half calf, lea renewed. *(Waterfield's)* £185 [≈ $333]
- A letter to the Right Honourable William Pitt ... on the subjects of toleration and church establishments ... London: for J. Johnson, 1787. 8vo. Disbound.
  (Waterfield's) £65 [≈ $117]
- Miscellaneous observations relating to education. Cork: 1780. Old lea, sl rubbed.
  (Whitehart) £120 [≈ $216]

Prince Lee Boo ..

- Interesting history of Prince Lee Boo, a native of the Pelew Islands ... a short account of those islands ... London: E. Newbery, 1789. 1st edn. 12mo. viii,178,[4 advts] pp. Port. Some reprs to margs inc title & port. Browning. Polished calf by Zaehnsdorf.
  (Bow Windows) £125 [≈ $225]

Prince, Thomas

- A sermon on the death of his late Majesty King George ... Boston: Daniel Henchman, 1727. 1st edn. [2],27 pp. Lacking half-title.
  (Jenkins) $75 [≈ £41]

Principles ...
- Of the principles and duties of natural religion ... See Wilkins, John
- The principles of mechanics ... See Emerson, William
- Principles of penal law ... See Eden, William

Pringle, Sir John
- Observations on the diseases of the army. London: A. Millar ..., 1768. 6th edn, crrctd. 8vo. xxiv,345, appendix, cxx [28 index] pp. Errata leaf. Occas light foxing, stain on title, sm burn hole in front flyleaf. Contemp calf, rubbed, crnrs bumped, jnts tender.
    (Elgen) $275 [≈£152]

Prioleau, Philip G.
- An inaugural dissertation on the use of nitric and oxigenated muriatic acids, in some diseases. Phila: J. Bioren, 1798. 1st edn. 8vo. 72 pp. Title foxed, spotty foxing throughout. Mod linen-backed bds.
    (Antiq Sc) $175 [≈£97]

Prior, Matthew
- Poems on several occasions. 1718. Folio. 506 pp. Engvd title (sl torn), many engvs. Front endpaper loose, occas spotting. Half calf, worn top bd detchd at hd.
    (Edwards) £100 [≈$180]
- Poems on several occasions. London: for Jacob Tonson ..., 1718. 1st edn. Folio. [xl],506,[6] pp. Names on title. Rebound calf, old cvrs laid on.
    (Lloyd-Roberts) £120 [≈$216]
- Poems on several occasions. London: 1718. Folio. Frontis. Contemp calf, worn, upper cvr loose.   *(Robertshaw)* £50 [≈$90]
- The poetical works ... now first collected, with explanatory notes and memoirs of the author. London: for W. Strahan ..., 1779. 2 vols. Frontis, engvd title vignette, half-titles. French 19th c levant, intricately gilt spine, a.e.g.   *(Pirages)* $325 [≈£180]

Prior, Thomas
- An authentick narrative of the success of tar-water ... London: Innys, 1746. 8vo. 192 pp. Mod half calf, mrbld sides.
    (Emerald Isle) £100 [≈$180]
- An authentick narrative of the success of tar-water in curing ... distempers ... See also Berkeley, George

Proceedings ...
- Proceedings at the Catholic Meeting at Dublin ... October 31, 1792 at the Exhibition-Room, Exchequer Street ... Dublin: 1792. 72

pp. Half-title. Disbound.
    (C.R. Johnson) £25 [≈$45]
- The proceedings of the House of Lords concerning the Scottish conspiracy ... London: Charles Bill, 1704. Folio. 67 pp. Disbound.   *(C.R. Johnson)* £25 [≈$45]
- The proceedings of the ... House of Commons of Ireland, in rejecting the altered Money-Bill, on December 17, 1753. The second edition. Dublin: Peter Wilson, 1754. 95 pp. Disbound. *(C.R. Johnson)* £55 [≈$99]

Projection ...
- The projection of the sphere ... See Emerson, William

Proposal for Uniformity ...
- A proposal for uniformity of weights and measures in Scotland ... See Swinton, John

Propositions ...
- Propositions concerning the subject of baptism ... See Mitchell, Jonathan

Prosodies ...
- On the prosodies of the Greek & Latin languages ... See Horsley, Samuel

Protestant ...
- The protestant's plea ... see Woodhead, Abraham

Proud, Robert
- The history of Pennsylvania ... Phila: Zachariah Poulson, 1797-98. 1st edn. 2 vols. 8vo. 508; 373,146 pp. Port frontis in vol 1, map in vol 2. Occas light foxing & dust-soiling. Orig gray bds, cvrs near detchd, spines splitting. Qtr mor fldg case.
    (Heritage) $750 [≈£416]

Pryce, William
- Mineralogia cornubiensis; a treatise on minerals, mines, and mining ... with the methods of ... working of tin, copper, and lead mines. London: for the author, 1778. 1st edn. Folio. Port, 7 plates, 2 fldg tables. Half calf, rebacked, orig spine laid down.
    (Traylen) £485 [≈$873]

Prynne, William
- A breviate of the life of William Laud ... London: for Michael Sparke Senior, 1644. Folio. [vi],255,[ix] pp. Lacking plate, some staining mainly at beginning & end. Old calf, rebacked, spine gilt, short split at hd of 1 jnt. Wing P3904.   *(Clark)* £65 [≈$117]
- A legall vindication of the liberties of England

against illegal taxes ... London: for Robert Hodges, 1649. 1st edn. Sm 4to. [ii],55 pp. Title cut close at ft. Mod bds. Wing P3996.
(Pickering) **$250 [≈ £138]**

- A moderate apology against a pretended calumny. In answer to some passages ... by James Howell ... London: for Michael Sparke, 1644. Mod half mottled calf, by Riviere. Wing P4010.
(Waterfield's) **£200 [≈ $360]**

- A revindication of the anoynting and priviledges of faithfull subjects ... London: 1643. [viii] pp. Cropped at ft. Stitched in old brown wraps. Wing P4053.
(Clark) **£28 [≈ $50]**

- A soveraign antidote to prevent, appease and determine our unnatural and destructive civil warres and dissentions. London: Printed in the year 1642. 4to. 32 pp. Unopened as issued. Not conforming to Wing P4086.
(C.R. Johnson) **£65 [≈ $117]**

- A true and perfect narrative of what was done, spoken by and between Mr. Prynne ... the army officers, and those now sitting ... in the Commons lobby ... London: 1659. 1st edn. 4to. Hd of title reprd, other minor spots. Uncut in later red half mor. Wing P4113.
(Charles Cox) **£110 [≈ $198]**

Psalmanazar, George

- A dialogue between a Japonese and a Formosan, about some points of the religion of the time. London: for Bernard Lintott, 1707. 1st edn. 8vo. [x],41,[iii pub ctlg] pp. Half-title. Browned. Large copy in panelled calf by Bernard Middleton.
(Bennett) **£850 [≈ $1,530]**

- Memoirs of ***. Commonly known by the name of George Psalmanazar ... written by himself ... Dublin: Wilson, 1765. 12mo. 234 pp. Contemp calf.
(Emerald Isle) **£100 [≈ $180]**

Psalms ...

- The Psalms of David for the use of parish churches. The words ... the music ... London: W. Millar, [1774]. 4to. Engvd title, dedn, xlvii,142 engvd pp of music. Title & dedn leaf lightly soiled & dampstained. Uncut in contemp mrbld bds, rubbed, spine defective.
(Frew Mackenzie) **£80 [≈ $144]**

Public Worship ...

- A directory for the public worship of God ... Ordinance of Parliament for the taking away of the Book of Common Prayer. London: for Tyler ..., 1644. 1st edn, 1st iss. Sm 4to. Lic leaf, title, 2ff (black letter), 86pp, 1f contents.

Contemp calf. New Wing D1544.
(Marlborough) **£150 [≈ $270]**

Pufendorf, Samuel

- An introduction to the history of the principal kingdoms and states of Europe ... London: for Thomas Newborough, 1702. 5th edn. 8vo. xiv,528 pp. Contemp panelled calf, a little worn.
(Young's) **£35 [≈ $63]**

- An introduction to the history of the principal kingdoms and states of Europe ... continued down to the year 1743, by M. Martiniere ... London: J. & P. Knapton, 1748. 2 vols. 8vo. xiv,412; [i],382, [liv index] pp. Contemp mottled calf, somewhat rubbed.
(Blackwell's) **£175 [≈ $315]**

Puget de la Serre, Jean

- The mirrour which flatters not. Enriched with faire figures. London: for R. Thrale, 1639. 1st English edn. Imprim & advt leaf. Lacks frontis & explanatory leaf, title laid down, 2 leaves reprd. Mod sprinkled calf. STC 20490.
(Charles Cox) **£30 [≈ $54]**

Puglia, James Philip

- The federal politician. Phila: 1795. Title stained & lacking upper crnr, upper marg sl stained. New buckram.
(Allen) **$50 [≈ £27]**

Pulteney, Richard

- A general view of the writings of Linnaeus. London: for T. Payne ..., 1781. 1st edn. 8vo. iv,425 pp. Contemp calf, spine a bit rubbed, sl wear at ft.
(Burmester) **£200 [≈ $360]**

Pulteney, William, Earl of Bath

- A short view of the state of affairs with relation to Great Britain, for four years past ... London: R. Franklin, 1730. 36 pp. Rebound in bds.
(C.R. Johnson) **£28 [≈ $50]**

Pulton, Ferdinando

- A kalendar, or table, comprehending the effect of all the statutes that have been made and put into print. 1608. 2nd edn. 4to. 445 pp. Lacking A1 blank, penultimate index leaf soiled. Contemp calf, rebacked, old spine laid on. STC 9548.
(Edwards) **£320 [≈ $576]**

Pym, John

- The declaration ... upon the whole matter of the charge of High Treason against Thomas, Earle of Strafford. London: Anno Domini, 1641. 4to. Disbound. Wing P4260.
(Waterfield's) **£45 [≈ $81]**

Quarles, Francis

- Boanarges and Barnabas: judgment and mercy. In two parts. The sixth edition. London: R. Royston, 1664. 12mo. [xviii], 120,[ii]; 121-240,[iv] pp. Port frontis, final advt & imprint leaves. Sporadically dusty & soiled. Old calf, reprd, new endpapers. Wing Q56.   *(Clark)* £52 [≈ $93]
- Emblems divine and moral. Together with hieroglyphics of the life of man. London: Trapp, 1777. 90 Engvs.
                     (Appelfeld) $175 [≈ £97]

Quarles, John

- Regale lectum miseriae; or, a kingly bed of miserie. [London:] 1658. Sm 8vo. Engvd port frontis. Title & frontis grubby & frayed, crnr of 1 leaf missing affecting catchword. Contemp sheep, very worn. Possibly Wing Q138.   *(Marlborough)* £160 [≈ $288]

Queen's Closet ...

- The Queen's closet ... See May, W.

Quesnel, Pasquel

- Moral reflections upon the Gospel of St. Luke. To make the reading of it more profitable ... [London:?] 1707. 1st edn in English. Sm 8vo. Errata leaf at end. Early calf, rebacked. *(Chaucer Head)* £160 [≈ $288]

Question ...

- The question stated whether the Freeholders of Middlesex lost their right ... See Meredith, Sir William

Quevedo y Villegas, Francisco Gomez de

- The comical works ... containing I. The night-adventurer, or the day-hater ... VI. Fortune in her wits, or the hour of all men. London: for J. Woodward, 1709. 2nd edn. 8vo. Port. Title browned. Mod half calf.
                     (Traylen) £35 [≈ $63]
- The visions of ... made English ... London: for H. Herringman, 1678. 6th edn, crrctd. 8vo. Lacking A1 (blank), sm tears to 2 leaves, sm pieces cut from title upper marg, a few scribbles, some light browning. 19th c half calf. Wing 200.   *(Stewart)* £125 [≈ $225]

Quier, John

- Letters and essays on the small-pox and inoculation, the measles, the dry belly-ache and ... the fevers ... of the West Indies ... London: for J. Murray, 1778. 1st edn. 8vo. Half-title. Contemp calf, gilt spine, mor label, gilt, front jnt cracking.
                     (Traylen) £375 [≈ $675]

Quillet, Claudius

- Callipaedia, a poem in four books ... made English by N. Rowe. London: Sanger & Curll, 1712. 1st edn. 8vo. Engvd frontis. Some foxing. Contemp panelled calf, worn, lacking label.   *(Marlborough)* £80 [≈ $144]

Quin, James

- The life of Mr. James Quin, Comedian. With the history of the stage from his commencing actor ... London: 1766. 1st edn. 8vo. 116 pp. Port [Bound with] Quin's jests; the facetious man's pocket companion. 1766. 1st edn. 104 pp. 1 leaf defective. Later calf.
                     (Robertshaw) £115 [≈ $207]

Quincey, Thomas

- A short tour in the Midland Counties of England; performed in the summer of 1772 ... a similar excursion ... September 1774. London: for the author, 1775. 1st edn. 8vo. viii,108 pp. Contemp half calf, rebacked.
                     (Burmester) £90 [≈ $162]

Quincy, John

- Lexicon physico-medicum: or, a new medical dictionary ... London: for T. Longman, 1757. 7th edn. 8vo. Contemp calf, rebacked.
                     (Traylen) £40 [≈ $72]
- Lexicon physico-medicum: or, a new medical dictionary ... London: for J. Osborn & T. Longman, 1730. 4th edn. 8vo. Contemp sgntr on title. Contemp panelled calf, lower jnt cracked.   *(Stewart)* £120 [≈ $216]
- Pharmacopoea officinalis et extemporanea, or a complete English dispensatory. London: 1724. 5th edn. 8vo. xvi,674,[62] pp. Inner blank marg of title restored. Contemp calf, worn, cvrs detchd.
                     (Wheldon & Wesley) £45 [≈ $81]
- Pharmacopoea officinalis et extemporanea, or a complete English dispensatory, in four parts. London: 1736. 10th edn. 8vo. xvi,700,lx pp. Advt leaf. Some foxing. Newly rebound in calf.   *(Spelman)* £120 [≈ $216]

Quintilian

- The declamations ... an exercitation or praxis upon his xii books ... Translated ... For John Taylor, 1686. 1st edn in English. 8vo. [16],272, 259 (bis)-474 pp. Some minor worming. Contemp calf, rebacked. Wing Q224.   *(Fenning)* £85 [≈ $153]
- The declamations ... an exercitation or praxis upon his xii books ... London: for John Taylor, 1686. 1st edn in English. 8vo. 8ff, 474 [i.e. 488] pp. Solitary tiny wormhole through text, rust holes in 2 leaves. Contemp

mor, gilt, sl wear to jnts, faded.
(Pirages) **$175 [≈ £97]**

Rabelais, Francois
- The works ... or, the lives, heroic deeds and sayings of Gargantua and Pantagruel ... [Bound with] The second book of the works ... London: for Richard Baldwin, 1694. Cr 8vo. Port frontis. A few marg flaws & tears. Contemp calf, spine worn, jnts weak. Wing 110.   *(Stewart)* **£100 [≈ $180]**

Raffald, Elizabeth
- The experienced English housekeeper ... London: 1794. 11th edn. Port, 3 plates. Author's sgntr on p 1. Contemp calf, rebacked.   *(Robertshaw)* **£125 [≈ $225]**

Rainolds, John
- The overthrow of stage-plays. Oxford: Lichfield, 1629. 2nd edn. 4to. Contemp calf, rebacked. NSTC 20618.
(Marlborough) **£500 [≈ $900]**

Raleigh, Sir Walter
- The history of the world. In five books. London: G. Conyers ..., 1736. 11th edn. 2 vols. Folio. ccl,[viii], xxxii,[xx], 370; 371-817, [xlvii] pp. Port frontis, 7 fldg maps. Contemp diced russia. *(Frew Mackenzie)* **£400 [≈ $720]**
- The prince, or maxims of state. London: 1642. 1st edn. 4to. [6],46 pp. Engvd port frontis (lightly waterstained), title soiled, browned throughout. 19th c binder's cloth, extremities rubbed & worn.
(Claude Cox) **£95 [≈ $171]**
- Remains of Sir Walter Raleigh; viz. Maxims of State. Advice to his son [&c ...]. London: for Henry Mortlock, 1675. 12mo. Later mottled calf, rebacked. Wing R184.
(Charles Cox) **£85 [≈ $153]**

Ralph, James
- The other side of the question or an attempt to rescue the characters of the two Royal sisters Q. Mary and Q. Anne ... London: for T. Cooper, 1742. 1st edn. 8vo. [iv],468 pp. New qtr speckled calf.
(Lloyd-Roberts) **£60 [≈ $108]**

Ralphson, Joseph
- A mathematical dictionary ... use of the principal mathematical instruments ... London: for J. Nicholson, 1702. [vi],40, [lxxvii], 26,18 pp. 3 fldg plates. Gutter & lower edge of title reprd, lacking final blank. Contemp calf gilt, rebacked, old spine relaid.
(Pollak) **£200 [≈ $360]**

The Rambler
- The Rambler ... See Johnson, Samuel

Ramel, General
- Narrative of the deportation to Cayenne of Barthelemy, Pichegru ... Ramel etc. Important facts relative to that revolution, to the voyage, residence and escape. London: 1799. 2nd edn. 8vo. Half-title. Qtr calf.
(Halewood) **£75 [≈ $135]**

Ramsay, Allan
- The gentle shepherd: a Scots pastoral comedy. Edinburgh: 1776. Contemp sheep, rebacked.   *(Waterfield's)* **£55 [≈ $99]**
- The gentle shepherd. Glasgow: Foulis, 1788. 4to. xii,111 pp, 1 f,17 glossary, 18 engvd music pp. Aquatint port, 12 aquatint plates. Rec half calf. *(Marlborough)* **£360 [≈ $648]**
- The gentle shepherd. Glasgow: Foulis, 1788. 4to. Half-title, aquatint port frontis, 12 aquatint plates. Contemp str-grain mor, gilt, gilt panelled spine, elab endpapers.
(Traylen) **£420 [≈ $756]**
- A poem on the South-Sea. To which is prefix'd, a familiar epistle to Anthony Hammond Esq; by a friend. London: for T. Jauncy, 1720. 1st edn thus. 8vo. 23 pp. A bit foxed. Disbound. *(Burmester)* **£400 [≈ $720]**
- The tea-table miscellany. A collection of choice songs, Scots and English, formerly in four volumes, now wholly comprised in one. Glasgow: 1765. 14th edn. Thick sm 8vo. Contemp calf.   *(Halewood)* **£30 [≈ $54]**
- Wealth, or the woody: a poem on the South-Sea. To which is prefix'd, a familiar epistle to Anthony Hammond Esq.; by Mr. Sewell. The second edition, corrected. London: for T. Jauncy, 1720. 8vo. 18,11-23 pp. Disbound.   *(Burmester)* **£350 [≈ $630]**

Ramsay, Andrew Michael
- An essay upon civil government ... London: Minshull, 1722. 12mo. Contemp sheep, very worn & rubbed. *(Marlborough)* **£90 [≈ $162]**

Ramsay, David
- The history of the American Revolution. Phila: Aitken, 1789. 1st edn. 2 vols. Orig paper bds, 1 bd detchd, spines somewhat chipped.   *(Reese)* **$425 [≈ £236]**

Ramsay, James
- Objections to the abolition of the slave trade with answers ... London: James Phillips, 1788. Half-title. Disbound.
(Waterfield's) **£50 [≈ $90]**

Ranby, John
- A narrative of the last illness of the Right Honourable the Earl of Orford ... 4ff,47 pp. Fldg copperplate. [With] An appendix to the narrative. 43 pp. London: John & Paul Knapton, 1745. 1st edn. 2 pts in 1. Main tract lge margs, appendix cut down. Mod cloth.
(Offenbacher) **$300 [≈ £166]**

Randall, John
- The semi-Virgilian husbandry, deduced from various experiments ... a new discourse of national farming ... with the philosophy of agriculture ... London: for B. Law, 1764. 1st edn. 8vo. 3 engvd plates (2 fldg). Contemp calf, gilt spine, jnts reprd.
(Traylen) **£150 [≈ $270]**

Randolph, Thomas
- Poems with the Muses Looking-glasse; and Amyntas. Oxford: for Francis Bowman, 1638. 1st edn. 4to. Contemp blindstamped cloth, refurbished. STC 20694.
(Charles Cox) **£450 [≈ $810]**

Raspe, Rudolph Eric
- An account of some German volcanos, and their productions ... London: Lockyer Davis, 1776. 1st edn. 8vo. xix,[1],140 pp inc 4 pp pub advts. Half-title, 2 engvd fldg plates. Contemp calf, rebacked.
(Rootenberg) **$525 [≈ £291]**

Rastell, John
- Les termes de la ley. or, certaine difficult and obscure words and termes of the common lawes and statutes of this realm now in use expounded and explained. London: Jo. Beale ..., 1641. Newly imprinted. 272 pp. Some browning. Old calf, old rebacking. Wing R286.
(Edwards) **£180 [≈ $324]**

Rawlet, John
- Poetick miscellanies ... Tidmarsh, 1687. 1st edn. Port, title, iv,143 pp. Prelims & final blank strengthened with tissue, minor staining. Contemp inscrptns on endpapers. Mod qtr calf.
(P & P) **£105 [≈ $189]**

Rawlinson, Richard
- The English topographer. London: Jauncy, 1720. 1st edn. 8vo. [viii], xliv,[288] pp. Old sprinkled calf, spine gilt, restored & refurbished, sev b'plates inc Spencers of Althorp. Author's pres inscrptn.
(Ash) **£250 [≈ $450]**

Ray, Charles
- A sermon preach'd at the Parish Church of St.

Peter's in St. Alban's ... thanksgiving ... for the suppression of the late unnatural rebellion. London: E. Say, 1746. 16 pp. Disbound.
(C.R. Johnson) **£15 [≈ $27]**

Ray, James
- A compleat history of the Rebellion, from its first rise in 1745, to its total suppression at the glorious battle of Culloden. York: 1749. Sm 8vo. 420 pp. Engvd port frontis, 2 battle plans. rebound in calf, bds v lightly scratched.
(Edwards) **£150 [≈ $270]**
- Compleat history of the Rebellion. From its first rise, in 1745, to its total suppression at the glorious battle of Culloden. London: for the author, 1754. 12mo. 451 pp. Engvd frontis, 2 engvd maps. Contemp ownership inscrptn. Some browning. 19th c half calf.
(Claude Cox) **£50 [≈ $90]**

Ray, John
- A collection of English proverbs digested into a convenient method for the speedy finding of any one upon occasion ... Cambridge: John Hayes, 1678. 2nd edn. Cr 8vo. Red & black title. Contemp panelled calf, spine gilt. Wing R387.
(Traylen) **£195 [≈ $351]**
- A collection of English words not generally used ... in two alphabetical catalogues ... with an account of the preparation and refining of such metals as are gotten in England. London: 1691. 11ff,211,[5] pp. Lacking A1 blank. Contemp lea, rebacked, edges worn.
(Whitehart) **£120 [≈ $216]**
- A collection of English words not generally used ... with an account of the preparation and refining of such metals as are gotten in England. London: for Christopher Williams, 1691. 2nd edn. 12mo. 5 pp ctlg at end. Sl browned. Contemp sheep rubbed. Wing R389.
(Charles Cox) **£125 [≈ $225]**
- Observations topographical, moral and physiological; made in a journey through part of the Low-Countries, Germany ... and France. London: for John Martyn, 1673. [xvi],499, [i],[viii], 115,[i] pp. 4 engvd plates, 3 text w'cuts. New half calf, old mrbld bds.
(Pollak) **£250 [≈ $450]**
- Observations topographical, moral and physiological; made in a journey through part of the Low-Countries, Germany ... and France. London: for John Martyn, 1673. 1st edn. 8vo. [xvi],499 pp. Port, 3 plates, text figs. Title sl soiled. Old calf, old rebacking.
(Frew Mackenzie) **£135 [≈ $243]**
- Observations topographical, moral and physiological; made in a journey through part of the Low-Countries, Germany ... and France. London: 1673. [16],499 pp, 4 plates,

[8],115 pp. Lea, spine cracking.
(Scientia) **$600 [≈ £333]**
- Select remains. With his life, by the late William Derham. London: Dodsley, 1760. 1st edn. 8vo. vii,336 pp. Engvd port frontis (sl offsetting to title), text engv. Lacking errata leaf. Contemp mottled calf, spine richly gilt. *(Frew Mackenzie)* **£180 [≈ $324]**
- The wisdom of God manifested in the works of creation. London: 1762. 8vo. [xx],259 pp. Fldg engvd frontis. Half calf, rebacked.
(Wheldon & Wesley) **£120 [≈ $216]**
- The wisdom of God manifested in the works of creation. In two parts ... London: for Sam. Smith ..., 1704. 4th edn. 8vo. Port frontis. Sm lib stamp on title. Rebound in qtr calf.
(Hughes) **£85 [≈ $153]**
- The wisdom of God manifested in the works of creation. London: for W. Innys, 1743. 11th edn, crrctd. 8vo. [xxiv],[17]-405 pp. 3 pp advts. Orig calf, short cracks at hd & ft of jnts, a little spine wear. *(Bickersteth)* **£75 [≈ $135]**

Raymond, John
- An itinerary contayning a voyage, made through Italy, in the yeare 1646, and 1647. London: Moseley, 1648. 1st edn. 12mo. [xliii], 284,[ii errata & imprim] pp. Addtnl w'cut title as frontis, 11 w'cuts in text. Short tear in E2 marg. Mor, spine gilt. Wing R415.
(Frew Mackenzie) **£275 [≈ $495]**

Raynal, Guillaume Thomas Francois
- A philosophical and political history of the settlements ... of the Europeans in the East and West Indies. London: Cadell, 1777. 3rd edn. 5 vols. 8vo. Engvd port frontis, 4 fldg maps (2 with short tears). Occas sl spotting. Contemp tree-calf, jnts rubbed.
(Frew Mackenzie) **£180 [≈ $324]**
- A philosophical and political history of the settlements and trade of the Europeans in the East and West Indies ... Dublin: 1784. 6 vols. 8vo. Port, 7 engvd plates, 4 maps (1 or 2 a trifle torn). Contemp calf, some insect damage to sides & 1 or 2 jnts.
(Bow Windows) **£175 [≈ $315]**
- The Revolution of America. London: Lockyer Davis, 1781. 181,2 advts pp. Rebound in qtr calf, mrbld bds.
(C.R. Johnson) **£125 [≈ $225]**

Ready Reckoner ...
- The ready reckoner; or, trader's sure guide ... by exact tables, ready cast up. Edinburgh: 1778. 8vo. Contemp calf, rubbed.
(Stewart) **£75 [≈ $135]**

Reasonableness ...
- The reasonableness of parliamentary proceedings, by attainders, banishments, pains and penalties, in cases of high treason, shewn by various precedents. London: T. Payne, 1723. 1st edn. 8vo. [iv],48 pp. Half-title. Disbound. *(Burmester)* **£80 [≈ $144]**

Reasons ...
- Reasons for extending the Militia Acts to the disarmed counties of Scotland. Edinburgh: Gavin Hamilton, 1760. 20 pp. Mod wraps.
(C.R. Johnson) **£55 [≈ $99]**
- Reasons for war; from the imminent danger with which Europe is threatened, by the exhorbitant power of the House of Bourbon. London: W. Mears, 1734. 2nd edn. 56 pp. Disbound. *(C.R. Johnson)* **£32 [≈ $57]**
- Reasons why this kingdom ought to adhere to the parliament. [London: 1642]. 15 pp. Uncut & unopened as issued. Wing R592.
(C.R. Johnson) **£65 [≈ $117]**

Rebellion ...
- The history of the rebellion raised against his majesty King George II, from its rise in August, 1745 to ... the glorious victory at Culloden. Dublin: A. Reilly, 1746. 1st edn. 8vo. 46 pp. 2 engvd plans. Some minor worming. Disbound.
(Robertshaw) **£36 [≈ $64]**

Record, Robert
- The castle of knowledge. London: Reginalde Wolfe, 1556. Sm folio. [8] ff, 287 pp. W'cut title, ills & figs. Extensive reprs, marg strengthening & recrnring to title & elsewhere, minor worming, staining, lacking endpapers. Old vell, soiled. New STC 20796.
(Bow Windows) **£3,000 [≈ $5,400]**
- Record's arithmetick: or, the ground of arts ... afterwards augmented by Mr. Dee. And since enlarged ... by John Mellis ... London: E. Flesher, 1673. Sm 8vo. 536 pp. Text figs & tables. Mod 3/4 calf. Wing R648.
(Argosy) **$350 [≈ £194]**

Reeves, J.
- History of the English law. London: for E. Brooke, 1787. 2nd edn. 4 vols. 8vo. 488; 474; 475; 484 pp, plus prelims to each vol & index at end vol 4. Contemp calf.
(Titles) **£350 [≈ $630]**

Reflections ...
- Reflections on a late pamphlet entitled Parliamentum Pacificum .... See Burnet, Gilbert

- Reflections on the National Debt; with reasons for reducing the legal interest; and against a publick loan. [Dublin:] printed in the year, 1731. 1st edn. Sm 8vo. 16 pp. Wanting half-title. Disbound.
(Burmester) **£60 [≈ $108]**

Reform ...
- Reform or ruin ... See Bowdler, John

Reformation ...
- The historie of the Reformation of the Church of Scotland ... See Knox, John

Regimen ...
- Regimen sanitatis Salerni. This booke teachinge all people to governe them in healthe ... translated out of the Latyne tongue in to Englyshire by Thomas Paynell. London: Thomas Berthelot, 1541. 4to. Black letter. Title within w'cut border. Mor gilt. STC 21599.   *(Traylen)* **£1,100 [≈ $1,980]**

Regulations ...
- The regulations lately made concerning the colonies ... See Whately, Thomas

Reid, Thomas
- An inquiry into the human mind, on the principles of common sense. London: for T. Cadell ..., 1769. 3rd edn, crrctd. Mod bds.
(Waterfield's) **£125 [≈ $225]**

Relation ...
- A relation of a journey An Dom. 1610 ... see Sandys, George

Religion ...
- The history of religion ... See Howard, Sir Robert
- The religion of nature delineated ... See Wollaston, William

Remarks ...
- Remarks in the Grand Tour ... See Bromley, William
- Remarks on a false, scandalous and seditious libel ... The conduct of the allies. London: A. Baldwin, 1711. 8vo. Rec blue wraps.
(Stewart) **£250 [≈ $450]**
- Remarks on a late book, intitled, An Essay on the Publick debts of this Kingdom ... being a seasonable warning to the people of Great Britain ... London: for A. Moore ..., 1727. 1st edn. vi,58 pp. Bds.   *(Young's)* **£48 [≈ $86]**

Renaudot, Eusebius
- Ancient accounts of India and China, by two

Mohammedan travellers ... in the 9th century. Translated ... London: 1733. 1st edn in English. 8vo. [xxxviii],99, 260,[12] pp. Damp & other stains throughout, tears & creases. Old calf, worn, roughly rebacked.
(Bow Windows) **£80 [≈ $144]**
- A general collection of discourses of the virtuosi of France, upon ... all sorts of philosophy ... London: T. Dring, 1664. Folio. [xvi],580 pp. Title & license leaf torn, soiled & mtd. Contemp calf, rebacked, crnrs rubbed, wormholes in backstrip. Wing R1034.   *(Clark)* **£115 [≈ $207]**

Renauldot, E. (trans.)
- Ancient accounts of India and China, by two Mohammedan travellers ... 1733. 1st English edn. xxxviii,260 pp. Index. Engvd vignette title. Occas light foxing. Calf, jnts split, lower bd loose, backstrip chipped.
(Old Cinema) **£85 [≈ $153]**

Reply ...
- The reply of a member of parliament to the mayor of his Corporation. London: 1733. 1st edn. 8vo. 39 pp. Title sl soiled & stained. Disbound.   *(Robertshaw)* **£30 [≈ $54]**
- Reply to a short review of the political state of Great Britain, at the commencement of the year 1787. London: for John Bell, January, 1787. 75 pp. Disbound.
(C.R. Johnson) **£25 [≈ $45]**

Report ...
- Report of the Committee of Secrecy of the House of Commons ... respecting the conspiracy of the United Irishmen ... to be presented ... by Mr. Secretary Dundas. Dublin: J. Milliken, 1799. 112 pp. Rebound in bds.   *(C.R. Johnson)* **£45 [≈ $81]**
- Report of the Committee appointed to conduct the application of the inhabitants of Margate for a system of police. N.p.: 1785. 1st edn. 8vo. 27 pp. Possibly wanting half-title. Disbound.   *(Burmester)* **£180 [≈ $324]**
- The report of the general officers, appointed by His Majesty's warrant ... to inquire into the causes of the failure of the late expedition to the coasts of France ... London: A. Millar, 1758. 116 pp. Disbound.
(C.R. Johnson) **£28 [≈ $50]**

Representations ...
- Humble representations and address of the ... Lords spiritual and temporal ... 14th March 1704. London: Charles Bill, 1704. Folio. 20 pp. Disbound.   *(C.R. Johnson)* **£15 [≈ $27]**
- Humble representations or addresses of ... the

Lords spiritual and temporal ... to Her Majesty 31st day of March 1704 ... [victualling the navy, West Indian convoys, &c.]. London: Charles Bill, 1704. Folio. 7 pp. Disbound.   *(C.R. Johnson)* £45 [≈ $81]

Resolution ...

- A resolution of certain queries ... See Long, Thomas

- The resolution of the Earle of Essex ... Wherein is declared his honourable intentions to attaine but what shall tend to advancement of his Majesties honour ... [London:] T. Rider, 1642. 4to. 6 pp. Uncut & unopened as issued. Wing R1147.
       (C.R. Johnson) £65 [≈ $117]

Restitution ...

- A restitution of decayed intelligence ... See Rowlands, Richard

Review ...

- A critical review of the liberties of British subjects ... by a gentleman of the Middle Temple. London: 1750. 2nd edn, crrctd. 119 pp. Disbound.   *(Robertshaw)* £35 [≈ $63]

Revindication ...

- A revindication of the anoynting ... of faithfull subjects ... See Prynne, William

Revolution ...

- The revolution and anti-revolution principles stated and compar'd ... justice and necessity of excluding the Pretender ... By the author of Two Disswasives against Jacobitism. London: Edward Young, 1714. 2nd edn. 8vo. 92 pp. Mod cloth. Ex lib.   *(Hughes)* £46 [≈ $82]

- Revolution politicks. Being a compleat collection of all the reports, lyes, and stories which were the fore-runners of the great revolution in 1688. London: 1733. 1st edn. 8 pts in 1 vol. Contemp calf, rebacked.
       (Robertshaw) £50 [≈ $90]

Reynard the Fox

- The most delectable history of Reynard the Fox ... See Shirley, John

Reynolds, Edward

- Three treatises of The vanity of the creature. The Sinfulness of sinne. The life of Christ. London: for Robert Bostocke, 1634. 3rd edn. [xvi],535 pp. Sep titles. Marg repr to 1 leaf. Disbound. STC 20936.   *(Clark)* £20 [≈ $36]

- Twenty sermons preached upon several occasions. London: for George Thomason, 1660. 1st edn. 4to. Browned. Later half calf,

worn. Wing R1301.
       (Charles Cox) £25 [≈ $45]

Reynolds, John

- Vox Coeli, or newes from heaven ... wherein Spaines ambitions and treacheries ... are unmasked ... Printed in Elisium, 1624. 4to. [xviii],92 pp. Lacking A1 (blank), browned, stitching broken, margs chipped. Disbound. STC 20946.5.   *(Clark)* £50 [≈ $90]

Reynolds, Sir Joshua

- Seven discourses delivered in the Royal Academy by the President. London: for T. Cadell, 1778. 1st edn. 8vo. 4ff,326 pp, 1f advts. Half-title. Contemp calf, crnrs & hd of spine worn, cvrs somewhat marked.
       (Pirages) $325 [≈ £180]

- Seven discourses delivered in the Royal Academy. London: Cadell, 1778. 1st edn. 8vo. 4ff,326 pp. Contemp Etruscan calf, a.e.g., rebacked, crnrs rubbed.
       (Marlborough) £150 [≈ $270]

- The works ... containing his discourses, idlers ... and commentary on Du Fresnoy's Art of Painting. London: 1797. 1st edn. 2 vols. 4to. 362;373 pp. Engvd port. Contemp sheep-backed bds, vell crnrs, jnts cracked, rather worn.   *(Europa)* £140 [≈ $252]

Riccobini, Lewis

- An historical and critical account of the theatres in Europe ... contain'd a review of the manner ... of the actors ... An essay on ... the art of speaking ... London: for T. Waller, 1741. 1st edn in English. 8vo. [xvi],333, [xix] pp. Rec half sprinkled calf.
       (Bennett) £165 [≈ $297]

Rich, Barnaby

- Vox militis: foreshewing what perils are procured when the people of this ... kingdome live without regard of marshall discipline ... London: for Thomas Mansfield, 1625. 4to. [xiv],58 pp. Stitching broken, paper brittle & frayed. Disbound. STC 20980.
       (Clark) £45 [≈ $81]

Richards, William

- An English and Welsh dictionary. Carmarthen: 1798 (1st edn?). 12mo. Some browning & occas soiling. Contemp half calf, worn, upper cvr & spine detached.
       (Robertshaw) £40 [≈ $72]

Richardson, John

- An account of the life of that ancient servant of Jesus Christ, John Richardson ... services in the work of the Ministry in England,

Ireland, America, &c. 1774. 3rd edn.
Contemp speckled bds, jnts cracked.
(Farahar) **£45 [≈ $81]**
- An account of the life of that ancient servant
of Jesus Christ, John Richardson ... services
in the work of the Ministry in England,
Ireland, America, &c. Phila: Crukshank,
1783. 1st Amer edn. 8vo. vi,236,[2 advts] pp.
Contemp calf.   *(Karmiole)* **$100 [≈ £55]**

Richardson, Jonathan
- An essay on theory of painting. London: W.
Bowyer, 1715. 1st edn. 8vo. 240 pp. Orig
panelled calf, jnts reprd.
(Spelman) **£260 [≈ $468]**
- The works ... consisting of the theory of
painting, essay on the art of criticism so far as
it relates to painting ... London: Davies,
1773. 1st coll edn. 8vo. 4ff, xix,346 pp, 1f.
Contemp calf, spine gilt.
(Marlborough) **£90 [≈ $162]**
- The works. Containing 1. The theory of
painting. 2. Essay on the art of criticism. 3.
The science of a connoisseur ... Strawberry
Hill: 1792. 1st edn thus. 4to. 287 pp. 12
tinted port plates. Half calf.
(Young's) **£80 [≈ $144]**

Richardson, Samuel
- Clarissa, or the history of a young lady:
comprehending the most important concerns
of private life. London: for J. Rivington,
1764. 5th edn. 8vols. 1st sgntr of 1 vol
browned. Contemp sprinkled calf, extremities
a bit worn, some hairline cracks in spines.
(Pirages) **$250 [≈ £138]**
- A collection of the moral and instructive
sentiments, maxims, cautions ... contained in
Pamela, Clarissa, and Sir Charles Grandison.
London: for S. Richardson, 1755. 1st edn.
12mo. Contemp calf, rebacked.
(Traylen) **£120 [≈ $216]**
- The history of Sir Charles Grandison. In a
series of letters published from the originals.
London: for S. Richardson, 1754. 1st 8vo
edn. 6 vols. Contemp calf, spines gilt, sl
rubbed, some jnts a little tender.
(Young's) **£180 [≈ $324]**
- The history of Sir Charles Grandison. In a
series of letters published from the originals.
London: for S. Richardson, 1754. 1st 8vo
edn. 6 vols. Contemp calf, spines gilt, 2 jnts
cracked (1 reprd), some wear to extremities,
spines rubbed.
(Frew Mackenzie) **£180 [≈ $324]**

Richardson, William
- Essays on some of Shakespeare's dramatic

characters. To which is added An essay on the
faults of Shakespeare. London: for J. Murray,
1798. 5th edn. 8vo. [viii],401 pp. Contemp
calf, jnts a little cracked.
(Young's) **£45 [≈ $81]**
- A philosophical analysis and illustration of
some of Shakespeare's remarkable characters.
London: J. Murray, 1774. 2nd edn, crrctd.
Contemp calf, red label. Ex lib Colquhoun of
Luss.   *(C.R. Johnson)* **£165 [≈ $297]**

Richer, Adrien
- Great events from little causes. or, a selection
of interesting and entertaining stories.
Dublin: James Hoey, 1768. 1st Dublin edn.
12mo. 226,[ii] pp. Contemp calf.
(Bennett) **£60 [≈ $108]**

Richter, August G.
- Medical and surgical observations.
Translated from the German. Edinburgh:
1794. 1st edn in English. 336 pp. Mod qtr lea,
cloth bds.   *(Scientia)* **$225 [≈ £125]**

Ridley, Humphrey
- The anatomy of the brain. London: for Sam.
Smith & Benj. Walford, 1695. 1st edn. 8vo.
[12],200,[24] pp. Dedn leaf, 5 engvd fldg
plates, errata, lacking imprim leaf. Wellcome
Lib stamp & withdrawal on title verso, sgntr
on 1st free endpaper. Russia. Wing R1449.
(Rootenberg) **$6,000 [≈ £3,333]**

Ridley, Nicholas
- An account of a disputation at Oxford, Anno
Dom. 1554. With a treatise of the Blessed
Sacrament. Oxford: at the Theater, 1688. 1st
edn. 4to. Disbound. Wing R1451.
(Charles Cox) **£20 [≈ $36]**

Ridpath, George
- An account of the proceedings of the
Parliament of Scotland, which met at
Edinburgh, May 6, 1703. [Edinburgh?:]
printed in the year 1704. 1st edn. 8vo. Some
spotting, a few names underlined. Rebound
in qtr calf.   *(Hughes)* **£48 [≈ $86]**
- The border-history of England and Scotland
... to the union of the two crowns. London: T.
Cadell, 1776. Contemp calf, red label. Ex lib
Colquhoun of Luss.
(C.R. Johnson) **£350 [≈ $630]**

Right ...
- The right of British subjects to petition and
apply to their representatives asserted and
vindicated. In a letter to ****. London: for
M. Smith, 1733. 30 pp. Disbound.
(C.R. Johnson) **£38 [≈ $68]**

- The right of the House of Stewart to the Crown of Scotland ... See Tait. A.

Rights ...

- The rights of Great Britain asserted against the claims of America; being an answer to the Declaration of the General Congress. 1776. 2nd edn. 8vo. 96 pp. Fldg chart.
(Farahar) **£180 [≈ $324]**

Rimius, Henry

- A candid narrative of the rise and progress of the Herrnhuters, commonly call'd Moravians ... London: for A. Linde, 1753. 8vo. Title dusty. New grey bds. *(Stewart)* **£40 [≈ $72]**

Ripley, James

- Select original letters on various subjects by James Ripley, now, and for thirty years past, oastler at the Red-Lion, Barnet. London: for the author ..., 1781. Port frontis, 123 pp. Rebound in blue mor.
(C.R. Johnson) **£225 [≈ $405]**

Rivals ...

- The rivals, a comedy ... See Sheridan, Richard Brinsley

Riverius, Lazarus

- The secrets of the famous Lazarus Riverius ... newly translated from the Latin. London: for Daniel Brown ..., 1685. 8vo. 1st English trans. 124 pp. Browning. Old calf, rebacked.
(Goodrich) **$295 [≈ £163]**

Riviere, Lazare

- The practice of physick. London: Sawbridge, 1688. 6th edn. Folio. [xii],645 (pagination errors); [xii],463, [1],[32] pp. Sm worm holes through some margs, paper flaw in M3 with sl loss, title & frontis soiled. Contemp calf, rebacked, crnrs reprd. Wing R1564.
(Pickering) **$550 [≈ £305]**

Roberte ...

- Roberte the Deuyll. A metrical romance, from an ancient illuminated manuscript. London: for I. Herbert, 1798. 14 mezzotint plates. Later calf, gilt, a.e.g, by Murton, spine chipped at hd & ft. *(Charles Cox)* **£45 [≈ $81]**

Robertson, William

- An historical disquisition concerning the knowledge which the Ancients had of India ... London: Strahan & Cadell ...,1791. 1st edn. 4to. Fldg map. Contemp half calf, mrbld bds, some wear at crnrs, jnts cracked.
(Clark) **£75 [≈ $135]**

- An historical disquisition concerning the knowledge which the Ancients had of India ... 1791. 1st edn. 4to. xii,346 pp. 2 fldg maps (with sm crease tears). Rebound in mod green cloth. Sm lib stamps on paste-down & top & bottom edges. *(Edwards)* **£120 [≈ $216]**
- An historical disquisition concerning the knowledge which the Ancients had of India ... 1799. 3rd edn. 8vo. vii,441,19 pp. 2 fldg maps. Sl foxing. Contemp mottled calf, gilt, extremities rubbed.
(Old Cinema) **£35 [≈ $63]**
- The history of Scotland ... London: A. Millar, 1761. 2 vols. 8vo. Contemp calf, rebacked, spine gilt. *(Argosy)* **£150 [≈ $83]**
- The history of Scotland ... The twelfth edition ... London: Cadell, 1791. 2 vols. 4to. Mtd engvd frontis vol I. Rebound in qtr black mor. [With] "Account of the Life of William Robertson ... by Dugald Stewart." London: Strahan, 1801. 4to. iv,202 pp bound in.
(Hughes) **£75 [≈ $135]**
- The history of the reign of the Emperor Charles V. London: Strahan, 1769. 1st edn. 3 vols. 4to. Half-titles. Some spotting on endpapers. Mod qtr mor.
(Hughes) **£75 [≈ $135]**
- An index. Drawn up about the year 1629, of many records of charters, granted by the different sovereigns of Scotland between the years 1309 and 1413 ... Edinburgh: 1798. 1st edn. 4to. liii,195,15 pp. Calf, hinges weak.
(Edwards) **£200 [≈ $360]**
- Proceedings relative to the Peerage of Scotland, from ... 1707 to ... 1788. Edinburgh: Bell & Bradfute, 1790. 4to. viii,479,[16] pp. Fldg tables. Crnr piece missing from title. Contemp polished calf, gilt. Colquhoun of Luss b'plate.
(Cooper Hay) **£145 [≈ $261]**

Robinson, Nicholas

- A treatise on the virtues and efficacy of a crust of bread, eat early in a morning fasting ... by a physician. London: E. Robinson ..., 1756. 1st edn. Half-title, title, v,[7]-76 pp. Orig wraps, backstrip partly off.
(Elgen) **$275 [≈ £152]**

Robinson, Thomas

- The common law of Kent. Or the customs of Gavelkind. With an appendix concerning Boroughs English. London: for F. Cogan, 1741. 1st edn. early law calf.
(Chaucer Head) **£150 [≈ $270]**

Rochefoucald, Francis de la

- Maxims and reflections. Boston: I. Thomas

..., 1794. 72 pp. Calf-backed bds.
(Jenkins) **$45** [≈ £25]

Rochon, Abbe
- A voyage to Madagascar, and the East Indies ... Translated ... London: for G.G.J. & J. Robinson, 1792. 1st edn in English. 8vo. [viii],[lii], 475 pp. Lge fldg engvd map. Damp mark affecting some outer margs. Amateur rebound in qtr calf, some wear at crnrs.
(Barbary) **£140** [≈ $252]
- A voyage to Madagascar, and the East Indies ... added, M. Brunel's memoir on the Chinese trade ... London: Jeffery ..., 1793. 2nd English edn. 8vo. lxiv,[17]-406, [1] errata pp. Fldg engvd map. Without half-title, margs sl browned, occas spots. Rec half calf.
(Morrell) **£175** [≈ $315]

Roesslin, Eucharius
- The birth of man-kinde otherwise named the womans booke ... London: for A.H., 1626. 4to. 204 pp. Black letter. 9 copperplates, initials. Insignificant reprs to outer margs prelims, minimal soiling. Lge paper copy in full mor by Sangorski.
(Rootenberg) **$2,500** [≈ £1,388]

Rogers, Edward
- A catalogue of a capital collection of pictures by much esteemed Masters ... also a collection of prints, drawings and books of prints ... Liverpool: T. Vernon, 1797. 4to. 30 pp. Orig wraps.   *(Marlborough)* **£300** [≈ $540]

Rogers, Robert
- A concise account of North America ... several British colonies on that Continent ... Westerly parts of the Country ... St. Laurence, the Mississippi, and the Great Lakes ... London: 1765. 264 pp. Sl offsetting on to title. Orig calf, rehinged.
(Reese) **$1,250** [≈ £694]

Roland, Madame
- An appeal to impartial posterity ... or, a collection of tracts written ... during her confinement in the prisons ... in Paris. London: J. Johnson, 1796. 8vo. 2 vols. 8vo. viii,192, [2],158, advt leaf; [2],200, 236 pp. Contemp half calf, jnts a little rubbed.
(Spelman) **£65** [≈ $117]

Rolt, Richard
- The lives of the principal reformers, both Englishmen and foreigners ... with an introduction wherein the Reformation is amply vindicated ... London: Bakewell & Parker, 1759. Folio. Title, xii,[2],202 pp. 22

mezzotint ports. Early 19th c half green mor.
(Marlborough) **£210** [≈ $378]

Romaine, W.
- Twelve discourses upon the law and gospel preached at St. Dunstan's Church in the West, London. London: J. Worrall, 1760. 472 pp. Lacking front blanks. Lea, worn.
(Xerxes) **$70** [≈ £38]

Roman History ...
- A new Roman history ... Designed for the use of young ladies and gentlemen. London: E. Newbery ..., 1784. 2nd edn. 12mo in 6's. [ii],vi,136 pp. 6 plates. Orig green vellum-backed mrbld bds, lacking label.
(Clark) **£75** [≈ $135]

Roman Martyrologe ...
- The Roman martyrologe set forth by the command of Pope Gregory xiii ... Translated out of the Latin ... S. Omers: Thomas Geubels, 1667. 2nd edn, revsd & enlgd. Final leaf spotted. 19th c tree-calf. Wing R1892.
(Stewart) **£120** [≈ $216]

Ronayne, Philip
- Treatise of algebra in two books. London: W. & J. Innys, 1727. 461 pp. A few minor spots & stains. Gilt dec lea, a.e.g., a bit worn.
(Xerxes) **$200** [≈ £111]

Roscoe, William
- The life of Lorenzo de Medici. London: for A. Strahan ..., 1797. 3rd edn, crrctd. 2 vols. 4to. xxviii,320,[136 appendix]; [4],312, [111 appendix], [1],[11 index] pp. Frontis, 15 vignettes & plates. Contemp tree-calf, hinges cracked, crnrs little worn.
(Claude Cox) **£45** [≈ $81]
- Mount Pleasant [Liverpool]: a descriptive poem. To which is added an ode. Warrington: W. Eyres, 1787. 4to. New bds.
(C.R. Johnson) **£285** [≈ $513]

Roscommon, Earl of
- An essay on translated verse. London: 1685. 2nd edn, crrctd & enlgd. Sm 4to. 26 pp. Later mrbld wraps, loose in card folder.
(Robertshaw) **£50** [≈ $90]

Roscommon, Wentworth Dillon, 4th Earl of
- Poems ... to which is added, An essay on poetry, by the Earl of Mulgrave ... London: for J. Tonson, 1717. 1st edn. 8vo. [20],536 pp. Title lightly soiled. Rec calf-backed mrbld bds. 18th c sgntr on title.
(Claude Cox) **£85** [≈ $153]

Rose, George
- The proposed system of trade with Ireland explained. London: Nichols, 1785. 8vo. 58 pp. Mod mrbld bds.
(Emerald Isle) £75 [≈$135]

Rosen van Rosenstein, Nicholas
- The diseases of children and their remedies. Translated by Andrew Sparrman. London: 1776. 1st edn in English. 364 pp plus index. Lea, rebacked. *(Scientia)* $1,000 [≈£555]

Ross, Alexander
- (Greek title), or, a view of all religions in the world ... also a discovery of all known heresies in all ages ... London: for Ben. Billingsley ..., 1675. 5th edn. 8vo. Port frontis, 17 engvd ports. N2 torn. Contemp calf, rebacked.
(Traylen) £80 [≈$144]
- Mystagogus poeticus, or the muses interpreter. London: for Thomas Whittaker, 1648. 2nd edn. Cr 8vo. Lacking final leaf (of table). New limp mor. *(Stewart)* £45 [≈$81]

Rouse, George
- A letter to the jurors of Great Britain. Occasioned by an opinion of the Court of King's Bench ... in the case of the King and Woodfall ... London: G. Pearch, 1771. Crnrs torn of last 2 leaves without loss. Disbound.
(C.R. Johnson) £45 [≈$81]

Rousseau, Jean Jacques
- Letters on the elements of botany. Addressed to a lady ... and twenty-four additional letters, fully explaining the system of Linneaus. By Thomas Martyn. London: White, 1787. 2nd edn. xxvi,500,[28] pp. Orig bds, uncut, later paper spine, a little chipped.
(Karmiole) $100 [≈£55]
- Letters on the elements of botany. Addressed to a lady ... and twenty-four additional letters, fully explaining the system of Linneaus. By Thomas Martyn. London: 1787. 2nd edn. xxv,[i],500,[28] pp. Contemp calf, rebacked, gilt spine. *(Whitehart)* £85 [≈$153]
- Letters on the elements of botany. London: for B. & J. White, 1794. 4th edn. 8vo. xxiv, 503,[28 indices] pp. Fldg chart. Occas spotting. 19th c half calf, rebacked with orig worn backstrip. *(Claude Cox)* £20 [≈$36]

Rowe, Mrs. Elizabeth
- Friendship in death: in twenty letters from the dead to the living. London: Henry Lintot, 1740. Contemp calf. Ex lib Colquhoun of Luss. *(C.R. Johnson)* £115 [≈$207]
- Friendship in death: in twenty letters from the dead to the living. To which are added, letters moral and entertaining in prose and verse. London: 1750. 1st coll edn. Contemp calf, worn, jnts cracking.
(Robertshaw) £35 [≈$63]

Rowe, John
- An introduction to the doctrine of fluxions. London: J. & J. March, 1767. 3rd edn. 8vo. xii,218,[ii errata] pp. 13 plates. Contemp sheep, rebacked, crnrs worn.
(Pollak) £100 [≈$180]

Rowe, Nicholas
- The royal convert. London: Jacob Tonson, 1708. 1st edn. 8vo. 6ff, 56 pp. Most leaves somewhat darkened. Mod half calf, cloth sides. *(Pirages)* $75 [≈£41]
- The tragedy of the Lady Jane Gray. As it is acted at the Theatre-Royal in Drury Lane. London: Bernard Lintot, 1717. 2nd edn. 12mo. 91 pp. Frontis, engvd vignette. Mod half calf. *(Argosy)* $85 [≈£47]
- The works in two volumes. Consisting of his plays and poems. London: for J. & R. Tonson, 1756. 2nd edn thus. 2 vols. 12mo. xxiv,417; 360 pp. Fort frontis. Calf, some wear, lacking a label. *(Young's)* £30 [≈$54]

Rowlands, Henry
- Mona antiqua restaurata. An archaelogical discourse on the antiquities ... of Anglesey ... a comparative table of primitive words ... Dublin: 1723. 1st edn. Sq 8vo. [v],viii,383,4 pp. 9 engvd plates. Some marg dampstaining. Calf, lower bd sl damaged.
(Edwards) £160 [≈$288]
- Mona antiqua restaurata. An archaelogical discourse on the antiquities ... of Anglesey ... a comparative table of primitive words ... Dublin: 1723. 4to. Red & black title, 10 engvd plates. Some foxing, sm wormhole. Contemp calf, rubbed, jnts cracked.
(Waterfield's) £90 [≈$162]
- Mona antiqua restaurata. 1766. 2nd edn. 4to. [xiv],357,1 errata,1 pub advt pp. Engvd frontis map, 12 plates. Contemp calf, jnts cracking, rubbed. *(Edwards)* £125 [≈$225]

Rowlands, Richard
- A restitution of decayed intelligence: in antiquities ... London: John Bill, 1628. 2nd edn. 4to. [xxiv],338,[12] pp. Red & black title with vignette. 10 half-page engvs. Later calf. STC 21362. *(Clark)* £168 [≈$302]
- A restitution of decayed intelligence: in antiquities ... By the study and travell of R.V. London: for Joyce Norton, 1634. 3rd edn.

4to. [xxiv],338,[xii] pp. W'cut on title, 10 w'cuts in text. 1st few leaves dusty. Rec half mor. STC 21363.   *(Clark)* £100 [≈ $180]

Rudyerd, Sir Benjamin

- The speech of that worthy knight ... concerning the placing of good and able divines in parishes miserably destitute ... London: W. Ley, 1641. 4to. 8 pp. Sgntrs & catchwords cropped. Disbound. Wing R2198.   *(Clark)* £30 [≈ $54]

Rules ...

- Some rules for the conduct of life: to which are added, a few cautions, for the use of such freemen of London, as take apprentices. [London: ca 1775]. 1st edn. 12mo. 24 pp. Contemp ownership inscrptn on title. Orig blue wraps.   *(Burmester)* £60 [≈ $108]

Rural Improvements ...

- Rural improvements ... See Wimpey, Joseph

Rush, Benjamin

- An account of the bilious remitting yellow fever, as it appeared in the City of Philadelphia, in the year 1793 ... Phila: Thomas Dobson, 1794. 1st edn. 8vo. x,363 pp. Sgntr on flyleaf. Contemp calf. Ex lib Fisher collection.   *(Hemlock)* $625 [≈ £347]
- Medical inquiries and observations. Vol. 2. Phila: 1793. 1st edn. 321,[1] pp. Lea, rec rebacked.   *(Scientia)* $325 [≈ £180]

Rushworth, John

- Historical collections of private passages of state, weighty matters in law ... 1618 ... [to] 1629. London: for George Thomason, 1659. 1st edn (of Vol 1, of 6 vols). Sm folio. 2 ports, fldg plate. Contemp calf, rebacked, spine & crnrs sl worn. Wing 2316.   *(Stewart)* £75 [≈ $135]
- Historical collections of private passages of state, weighty matters in law ... 1618 ... [to] 1649. London: 1659-80-92, 1701. 4 parts in 7 vols. Folio. Occas minor soiling & browning throughout. Contemp calf, rebacked. Wing R2316, R2318, R2319.   *(Clark)* £250 [≈ $450]
- The tryal of Thomas Earl of Strafford ... upon an indictment of high treason ... London: John Wright ..., 1680. Folio. [x],786 pp. Engvd port frontis. Contemp calf, lightly rubbed, lower jnt cracked. Wing R2333.   *(Clark)* £95 [≈ $171]

Russell, John

- Elements of painting with crayons. London:

J. Wilkie, 1774. 2nd edn. 4to. [6],52 pp. Half-title. Near contemp mrbld bds. [bound with] Hogarth's Analysis of Beauty, 1772, lacking the 2 plates issued separately & The Abbey of Kilkhampton, G. Kearsley, 1780.
          (Spelman) £220 [≈ $396]
- Letters from a young painter abroad to his friends in England. London: 1750. 2nd edn. 2 vols. 8vo. Lge paper, some fldg. Contemp calf, v worn, jnts cracked.
          (Robertshaw) £50 [≈ $90]

Russell, P. & Price, Owen

- England displayed. Being a new, complete, and accurate survey and description of the Kingdom of England and Principality of Wales ... London: 1769. 2 vols. Folio. 53 engvd maps, 80 full-page engvs. Contemp calf, worn, crnrs bumped.
          (Halewood) £700 [≈ $1,260]

Russell, Lady Rachel

- Letters ... to which is prefixed, an introduction, vindicating the character of Lord Russell against Sir John Dalrymple ... London: Dilly, 1773. 1st edn. 4to. lxxii,216 pp. Rec half calf.   *(Young's)* £20 [≈ $36]

Russell, Richard

- A dissertation on the use of sea-water in the diseases of the glands. London: for the translator, 1752. 1st English edn. 12mo. Engvd frontis, engvd plate. Contemp polished calf.   *(Quaritch)* $400 [≈ £222]
- A dissertation on the use of sea-water in the diseases of the glands ... Translated from the Latin ... London: W. Owen ..., 1752. 1st edn in English. 12mo. xii,204 pp. Engvd frontis, double-page plate. Orig calf, sl rubbed.
          (Elgen) $275 [≈ £152]
- A dissertation on the use of sea-water in the diseases of the glands ... Also an account of the nature ... of mineral waters in Great Britain. London: for W. Owen, 1760. [with] A treatise ... a proper supplement ... Owen, 1762. 2 plates. Contemp calf, rubbed.
          (Waterfield's) £125 [≈ $225]

Rutty, John

- A history of the rise and progress of the people called Quakers in Ireland from the year 1653 to 1700 ... continued to 1751 ... Dublin: Jackson, 1751. Sm 4to. 484 pp. Index. Contemp calf.
          (Emerald Isle) £75 [≈ $135]
- The liberty of the spirit and the flesh distinguished. Dublin: Jackson, 1756. Sm 8vo. Wraps.   *(Marlborough)* £45 [≈ $81]

- A methodical synopsis of mineral waters, comprehending the most celebrated medicinal waters ... of Great-Britain, Ireland, France, Germany ... London: for William Johnston, 1757. 1st edn. Thick 4to. Tables. Title spotted & frayed. Calf, rebacked.
(Chaucer Head) **£220 [≈ $396]**
- A treatise concerning Christian discipline, compiled with the advice of ... the people called Quakers ... [Dublin:] 1752. 8vo. 142 pp. Contemp sheep.
(Emerald Isle) **£50 [≈ $90]**

Rutty, John, et al.
- The argument of sulphur or no sulphur in waters discussed ... annexed, two tracts. ... analysis of milk ... on the uses of goat's whey. Dublin: Alex M'Culloh, 1762. 1st edn. vii,109; [ii],v,3-19; 21 pp. Fldg table, addtnl leaf between pp 94/5. Disbound.
(Burmester) **£75 [≈ $135]**

Rutty, William
- A treatise of the urinary passages ... their description, powers and uses ... London: for Tho. Worrall, 1726. 4to. [viii],54,[vi] pp. 4 plates. Occas foxing, sm tear in fore-edge of title & half-title, 1st plate trimmed a little close. New paper bds. *(Pollak)* **£150 [≈ $270]**

Rycault, Paul
- The present state of the Ottoman Empire ... Turkish politie ... the Mahometan religion ... military discipline ... in three books. London: J. Starkey ..., 1670. 3rd edn. Sm folio. Frontis, 2 plates, 19 text engvs. Contemp sheep, scuffed, rubbed. Wing R2414.
(Clark) **£230 [≈ $414]**

Ryley, William
- Pleadings in Parliament. With the judgements thereon, in the reigns of Edward I and II ... together with several petitions in Parliament ... 1661. 1st edn. Folio. 719 pp. Addtnl title in Latin. Armorial b'plate. Contemp calf, some wear. Wing 2422.
(Edwards) **£200 [≈ $360]**

Rymer, Thomas
- A short view of tragedy; it's original, excellency, and corruption. With some reflections on Shakespear, and other practitioners for the stage. London: Baldwin, 1693. 1st edn. Sm 8vo. [xvi],182,[ii pub ctlg] pp. Initial blank. Early 20th c sheep. Wing R2429.
(Bennett) **£250 [≈ $450]**

Sackville, Charles
- A treatise concerning the militia, in four

sections ... militia in general ... Roman militia ... proper plan of a militia for this country ... observations upon this plan ... London: J. Millan, 1752. 68 pp. Half-title. Disbound.
(C.R. Johnson) **£55 [≈ $99]**

Sackville, Lord George
- The proceedings of a general court martial ... upon the trial of Lord George Sackville. London: A. Millar, 1760. 224 pp. Rebound in bds. *(C.R. Johnson)* **£25 [≈ $45]**
- A second letter to a late Noble Commander of the British forces in Germany ... London: R. Griffiths, 1759. 51 pp. Rebound in bds.
(C.R. Johnson) **£28 [≈ $50]**

St. Augustine
- Saint Augustines confessions translated and with some marginall notes illustrated. London: for Abel Roper, 1650. 12mo. Title sl chipped at edges, a little worn at crnrs throughout. Old calf, rebacked, new endpapers. Wing A4206.
(Charles Cox) **£30 [≈ $54]**

Saint Germain, Christopher
- The dialogue in English, between a Doctor of Divinitie, and a student in the Laws of England. London: the assignes of John More, 1638. 340 pp. Contemp calf. STC 21582.5.
(C.R. Johnson) **£165 [≈ $297]**
- Doctor and student: or dialogues ... London: S. Richardson ..., 1761. 16th edn. 8vo. Minimal worming, old marg stain to a few leaves. Contemp calf, rec rebacked.
(Stewart) **£40 [≈ $72]**
- An exact abridgement of that excellent treatise called doctor and student. London: Assignes of Iohn More, 1630. Top of title torn with loss of 1st word, lacking A1 (blank?), terminal blanks M7 & M8 retained. Mod calf. STC 21583.
(Charles Cox) **£45 [≈ $81]**

Saint Pierre, Jacques Henri Bernardin de
- Voyages of Amasis. In French and English. Translated by M.M.*****. Boston: printed by I. Thomas ..., 1795. 1st edn in English. 12mo. iii.5-137 pp. Duplicate pagination. Some browning & light staining, sm flaw in 1 leaf. Contemp sheep, jnts rubbed.
(Burmester) **£70 [≈ $126]**

Sallust
- The works, translated into English. Dublin: Reilly, 1744. Foxed. Contemp calf.
(Marlborough) **£55 [≈ $99]**

Salmon, Thomas

- An essay concerning marriage ... added, an historical account of the marriage rites and ceremonies. London: for Charles Rivington, 1724. 2nd edn. [xx],310,[5] pp. Old panelled calf, rebacked.   *(Young's)* **£77** **[≈ $138]**
- A new abridgement and critical review of the State Trials and Impeachments for High Treason. London: for J. & J. Hazard ..., 1738. 1st edn. Folio. [iv],922,[8 index] pp. Contemp calf, rebacked. *(Lloyd-Roberts)* **£130** **[≈ $234]**

Salmon, William

- The country builder's estimator: or the architect's companion. For estimating of new buildings, or repairing of old ... a new method to shew what light is proper for any room ... London: James Hodges, 1746. 3rd edn. 12mo. 2 fldg tables. Contemp roan, rebacked.
         (Chaucer Head) **£140** **[≈ $252]**
- Doron medicum: or, a supplement to the New London Dispensatory, in III books ... completed with the Art of Compounding Medicines. London: 1683. 1st edn. 8vo. xvi,720, [60 index], [4 author's books] pp. Old calf, hinges rubbed, sm repr to hinge. Wing S426.   *(Hemlock)* **$475** **[≈ £263]**
- A new geographical and historical grammar. London: William Johnston, 1757. 5th edn. 8vo. Red & black title, 23 fldg maps. Contemp calf. *(Chaucer Head)* **£180** **[≈ $324]**
- Pharmacopoeia Londinensis: or, the new London dispensatory. In VI books ... As also the praxis of chymistry. London: for R. Chiswell, 1707. 7th edn. Sm 8vo. Most pp browned. Contemp panelled calf, rebacked.
         (Chaucer Head) **£120** **[≈ $216]**
- Polygraphice: or the arts of drawing, engraving, etching ... beautifying and perfuming. London: Passenger & Sawbridge, 1685. 5th edn. 8vo. 64,767 pp. Engvd frontis, engvd title, 20 (ex 25) plates (1 torn without loss, some amateur contemp colouring). Rec calf.   *(Spelman)* **£100** **[≈ $180]**
- Polygraphice: or the arts of drawing, engraving, etching ... beautifying and perfuming. London: Passenger & Sawbridge, 1685. 5th edn. 8vo. 64,767 pp. Orig calf, spine replaced.   *(Camden)* **£250** **[≈ $450]**

Salthouse, John

- Wonderful predictions declared in a message, as from the Lord, to ... Sr. Thomas Fairfax ... London: Robert Ibbeton, 1648. 1st edn. 4to. 8 pp. Mod cloth-backed bds, orig lea spine laid down, new endpapers. Wing 507.
         (Edwards) **£120** **[≈ $216]**

Salusbury, Thomas

- Mathematical collections and translations. In two parts. London: ... George Sawbridge, 1667. 2 pts in 1. Folio. 4 fldg plates. Title & last page soiled, sm reprs at crnrs & inner margs, tear in A2, sm tear in dedn leaf reprd, some staining. Old calf, rebacked.
         (Traylen) **£1,100** **[≈ $1,980]**

Sancho, Ignatius

- Letters of the late Ignatius Sancho, an African. London: Dodsley, 1782. 1st edn. 2 vols. 8vo. Contemp half calf, well worn.
         (Marlborough) **£190** **[≈ $342]**

Sanctorius

- Medicina statica: being the aphorisms of Sanctorius. Translated ... added, Dr. Keil's Medicina Statica Britannica ... As also Medico-Physical Essays ... London: 1723. 3rd edn. 8vo. vii,344, [18],[4], 116 pp. Frontis, fldg plate. Contemp calf, hinges cracked.
         (Hemlock) **$150** **[≈ £83]**

Sandeman, Robert

- The honour of marriage opposed to all impurities: an essay. London: for T. Vernor, 1777. 1st edn. 8vo. Wraps, apparently as issued.   *(Waterfield's)* **£75** **[≈ $135]**

Sanders, Francis William

- An essay on the nature and laws of uses and trusts. Dublin: J. Jones, 1792. Lightly foxed. Mod law cloth.   *(Charles Cox)* **£30** **[≈ $54]**

Sanderson, William

- The excellency of the pen and pencil ... in the arts of drawing and etching. London: Dorman Newman, 1688. Sm 8vo. 123 pp. Engvd frontis, 19 copper plates. Later calf.
         (Camden) **£450** **[≈ $810]**

Sandford and Merton ...

- The history of Sandford and Merton ... See Day, Thomas

Sandford, Francis

- A genealogical history of the Kings and Queens of England ... to the year 1707. Nicholson, 1707. Folio. [xii],878,[xxviii index & errata] pp. Red & black title, engvd frontis, 2 engvd fldg plates, num text engvs. Sl marg dampstain.
         (Frew Mackenzie) **£200** **[≈ $360]**
- A genealogical history of the Kings and Queens of England ... to the year 1677. London: for the author, 1677. 1st edn. Folio. [xii],578,[xi] pp. Red & black title, 5 double-

page plates, num text ills (majority full-page). 19th c diced russia, rebacked, gilt.
(Frew Mackenzie) £295 [≈ $531]

Sandys, George
- A relation of a journey An Dom. 1610 ... Turkish Empire ... the Holy Land ... London: Barrett, 1621. 2nd edn. Sm folio. [iv],309,[1 errata] pp. Engvd title, fldg double-page map. Lacking sm fldg plate. Light waterstain throughout, Contemp calf, early reback.
(Morrell) £110 [≈ $198]
- Travels, containing a history of the original and present state of the Turkish Empire ... London: John William Jr., 1673. 7th edn. Sm folio. 50 lge copperplates in the text. Mod half calf. Wing S680. Engvd title of 1670 6th edn bound in.   *(Argosy)* $400 [≈ £222]

Sargent, John
- The Mine. A dramatic poem. London: for T. Cadell, 1785. 1st edn. 4to. [4],xvi,63 pp. Orig bds, uncut, marked & worn, upper hinge split. "From the author" on endpaper.
(Claude Cox) £80 [≈ $144]

Sarpi, Paulo
- The history of the Council of Trent ... London: for Samuel Mearne ..., 1676. Folio. [xvi],cvi,[2], 889,[47] pp. Red & black title. Some minor dust & dampmarks. Contemp calf, rebacked & reprd, orig spine preserved. Wing S696.   *(Bow Windows)* £165 [≈ $297]
- The history of the inquisition ... for councellors, casuists, and politicians ... Translated ... London: for Mosley, 1639. 1st edn in English. Sm 4to. Red & black title, imprim leaf. Light staining at end, a few catchwords cropped. New qtr calf. NSTC 21765.   *(Stewart)* £135 [≈ $243]

Saugnier & Brisson
- Voyages to the Coast of Africa ... an account of their shipwreck on board different vessels, and subsequent slavery ... London: Robinson, 1792. 1st English edn. 8vo. [iv],viii, 500 pp. Half-title, fldg engvd map. Orig bds, spine a little rubbed & chipped, uncut.
(Morrell) £185 [≈ $333]

Saul, Edward
- An historical and philosophical account of the barometer ... reason and use of that instrument, the theory of the atmosphere ... probable judgement of the weather. London: A. Bettesworth ..., 1730. 100 pp. Contemp panelled calf, rebacked.
(C.R. Johnson) £260 [≈ $468]

Saunders, William
- A treatise on the structure, economy, and diseases of the liver; together with an enquiry into ... the bile, and biliary concretions. Boston: W. Pelham, 1797. 1st Amer edn. 12mo. xx,231 pp. Contemp tree-calf, lea label.   *(Antiq Sc)* $100 [≈ £55]
- A treatise on the structure, economy and diseases of the liver; together with an enquiry into the ... bile and biliary concretions. Boston: 1797. 1st Amer from 2nd London edn. Sm 8vo. 231 pp. Name excised from top of title, mild browning. Calf, v worn.
(Oasis) $85 [≈ £47]

Saunderson, Nicholas
- The elements of algebra, in ten books. Cambridge: University Press, 1740. 1st edn. 4to. [xx],[ii errata],xxvi, [iv],360; [ii],363-748 pp. Port frontis, engvd plate vol I, 8 fldg engvd plates vol II. Without the addtnl title vol I. Rebound in grey bds.
(Pickering) $450 [≈ £250]
- The method of fluxions applied to a select number of useful problems ... London: for A. Millar ..., 1756. 1st edn. xxiv,309,[1 errata] pp. 12 fldg engvd plates. Some browning in margs. Rebound in calf-backed bds.
(Pickering) $850 [≈ £472]

Savigny, J.H.
- Treatise on the use and management of a razor with practical directions relative to its appendages. London: 1786. 12mo. 83 pp. Some browning & cockling, final leaf with sm segment missing not affecting text. Cloth. Ex lib.   *(Elgen)* $125 [≈ £69]

Saxe, Field-Marshall Count
- Reveries, or memoirs upon the art of war ... some original letters, upon various military subjects ... London: for J. Nourse, 1757. 1st English edn. 4to. x,195,[i advt] pp. 40 engvd plates on 34 leaves, mostly fldg. Contemp gilt-panelled calf.   *(Gough)* £325 [≈ $585]

Scale, Bernard
- Tables for the easy valuing of estates, from one shilling to five pounds per acre: also the parts of an acre, from three roods to one perch. London: the author, 1771. 1st edn. 8vo. Engvd title & dedn. Some browning. Contemp tree-calf, upper hinge sl defective.
(Chaucer Head) £120 [≈ $216]

Scamozzi, Vincent
- The mirror of architecture. 5th edn ... added, A compendium of the art of building, by William Leyburn. Sprint, 1708-07. Sm 4to.

[5],111,[i] pp. Frontis, 40 numbered plates, 9 unnumbered (on 8ff). Lacking 2 fldg plates (?). Tears & staining. Contemp calf.
(Spelman) **£95 [≈ $171]**

Scarisbrick, alias Neville, Edward
- The life of the Lady Warner ... in religion called Sister Clare of Jesus. London: Hales, 1692. 2nd edn. Sm 8vo. Engvd frontis. Title & frontis thumbed. 19th c qtr mor, worn. New Wing C575, entered under Carisbrick.
(Marlborough) **£110 [≈ $198]**

Scarron, Paul
- The whole comical works ... a great part of which never before in English. Translated ... London: J. Nicholson, 1712. 3rd edn, revsd & crrctd. 12mo. Engvd frontis. Contemp calf, jnt cracked, front hinge mended.
(Argosy) **$75 [≈ £41]**

Scheffer, John
- The history of Lapland wherein are shewed the original manners, habits ... of that people. Oxford: 1674. 1st English edn. Folio. Fldg map, engvd title, 25 text w'cuts. Edge of 1 lf sl frayed, sl waterstain affecting final 7 pp. Mrbld bds, buckram spine.
(Farahar) **£385 [≈ $693]**

Scheme ...
- A scheme for the better relief ... of the poor ... See Gilbert, Thomas

Scobell, Henry
- A collection of Acts and Ordinances of general use, made in the Parliament ... at Westminster ... November 1640 ... unto ... 1656 ... In two parts ... 1658-7. 1st edn. Folio. 186; 515 pp. Title reprd. Mod half calf. Wing E873.
(Edwards) **£300 [≈ $540]**

Scot, Reginald
- The discoverie of witchcraft. London: William Brome, 1548. 1st edn. 560 pp, 8ff. 12 charts & diags (2 full-page). 2 leaves reprd at inner margs, title & a few leaves stained, soiled or inked, 2 leaves sl trimmed. Rec calf.
(Pirages) **$3,900 [≈ £2,166]**

Scot, Walter
- A true history of several honourable families of the right honourable name of Scot, in ... Roxburgh and Selkirk ... Hawick: George Caw, 1786. 3rd edn. 8vo. 2 pts in 1. Sep pagination for the 2 pts, continuous sgntrs. Contemp calf, rubbed, jnt cracked.
(Hughes) **£75 [≈ $135]**

Scotland's Skaith ...
- Scotland's Skaith; or the history o' Will and Jean ... See MacNeill, Hector

Scott, George
- Select remains of the learned John Ray ... with his life ... London: Ja. Dodsley, 1760. 8vo. vii,[i],336 pp. Port, 3 text engvs. Errata slip pasted to ft of last page. Antique style calf, orig spine label. *(Pollak)* **£80 [≈ $144]**

Scott, J.
- A journal of the life, travels and Gospel labours. 1797. 1st English edn. Sm 8vo. Contemp sheep, jnts cracked.
(Farahar) **£35 [≈ $63]**
- The pocket companion and history of Freemasons ... London: for R. Baldwin ..., 1759. 2nd edn, revsd, crrctd, enlgd. 12mo. viii,380 pp. Engvd frontis. A few contemp anntns in ink. late 19th c gilt-panelled mor, brass clasps. *(Gough)* **£295 [≈ $531]**

Scott, John
- An epistle from Berea, Queen of Otaheite, to Joseph Banks, Esq ... London: for J. Almon, 1774. 2nd edn. Thin 4to. 15 pp. Sev sm creases inc some reprd, sl spotting. Lea-backed mrbld bds. *(Edwards)* **£200 [≈ $360]**

Scott, Thomas
- Vox populi. or newes from Spain ... which may serve to forwarn ... England ... how farre to trust to Spanish pretences. Imprinted in the yeare 1620. 4to. [xxviii] pp. Browned, margs chipped, stitching broken. Disbound. STC 22098.5.

Scribleriad ...
- The Scribleriad: an heroic poem ... See Cambridge, Richard Owen

Scudery, George de
- The female orators. Or, the courage and constancy of divers famous queens, and illustrious women, set forth in their eloquent orations ... London: T. Tebb, 1714. 2nd edn in English. 12mo. Engvd frontis. Later roan.
(Chaucer Head) **£180 [≈ $324]**

Sculptura ...
- Sculptura Historico-technico: or the history and art of engraving. London: J. Marks, 1770. 4th edn. 12mo. [12],264 pp. Fldg table in text, 10 engvd plates. Rebound in half calf, gilt spine & label. *(Spelman)* **£110 [≈ $198]**

Sea-Coasts of France

- The sea-coasts of France from Calais to Bayone. Described in fifteen large charts ... published for the use of His Majesty's Royal Navy. N.d. [ca 1750]. Folio. Half calf, bds frayed, lower bd detchd.
(Edwards) **£400 [≈ $720]**

Seabury, Samuel

- A discourse delivered in St. John's Church, in Portsmouth ... conferring the order of priesthood on the Rev. Robert Fowle. Boston: I. Thomas ..., 1791. 1st edn. 22 pp.
(Jenkins) **$25 [≈ £13]**

Secker, Thomas

- Lectures on the catechism of the Church of England: with a discourse on Confirmation. Dublin: J. Exshaw ..., 1774. 12mo. [viii],387 pp. Sep title to 2nd part. V light browning. Contemp calf, somewhat worn but firm.
(Blackwell's) **£70 [≈ $126]**
- Lectures on the catechism of the Church of England: with a discourse on Confirmation. London: Rivington, 1799. 8th edn. Cr 8vo. Contemp calf, sl worn. *(Stewart)* **£20 [≈ $36]**

Secret Instructions ...

- The secret instructions of the Jesuits. 1746. 2nd edn. 8vo. Parallel English & Latin text. Contemp calf, rubbed, lower jnt cracked.
(Robertshaw) **£36 [≈ $64]**

Secretary ...

- The secretary's guide: in four parts ... choice forms and precedents ... perpetual almanack ... English dictionary ... London: T. Norris, 1721. 12mo. W'cut frontis (sl defective & laid down). 1st & last few leaves browned & chipped. Old sheep, rebacked.
(Charles Cox) **£75 [≈ $135]**

Secrets ...

- Valuable secrets concerning arts and trades; or approved directions ... engraving ... varnishes ... gilding ... making wines ... preparing snuff ... London: Will. Hay, 1775. 1st edn. F'cap 8vo. [8],xxiv,312 pp. Contemp calf, hd & tail of spine chipped.
(Spelman) **£450 [≈ $810]**

Secundus, Johannes

- Kisses, being a poetical translation of the Basia of Johannes Secundus Nicolaius. London: T. Davies, 1778. 2nd edn. 8vo. Frontis (waterstained at bottom), half-title, vignette title. Contemp speckled calf.
(Chaucer Head) **£45 [≈ $81]**

Sedition ...

- Sedition and defamation display'd in a letter to the author of the Craftsman. London: J. Roberts, 1731. Half-title. 48 pp. Rebound.
(C.R. Johnson) **£25 [≈ $45]**

Sedley, Sir Charles

- The miscellaneous works ... collected into one volume. To which is added, the Death of Marc Antony: a tragedy ... London: J. Nutt, 1702. Half-title. Browned. Contemp panelled calf, gilt, sl rubbed.
(Charles Cox) **£80 [≈ $144]**

Seed, Jeremiah

- Discourses on several important subjects to which are added eight sermons ... London: for R. Manby ..., 1747. 5th edn. 2 vols. 8vo. Engvd frontis. Contemp calf.
(Lloyd-Roberts) **£20 [≈ $36]**

Segwick, Obadiah

- The bowels of tender mercy sealed in the everlasting covenant ... London: Edward Mottershed, 1661. Sm folio. Marg reprs to P2 & 2B2, some text browning. New grey bds, paper label. *(Stewart)* **£65 [≈ $117]**

Selden, John

- A brief discourse touching the office of Lord Chancellor of England. 1672. 2nd edn. Folio. 26 pp. Ruled text. Trimmed, just affecting some headings. Mod half calf.
(Edwards) **£225 [≈ $405]**
- The history of tythes. That is the practice of payment of them. The positive laws ... the opinions ... [London:] 1618 (i.e. 1680). 4to. xxii,491 pp. 19th c half calf, later spine. New STC 22173. *(Edwards)* **£160 [≈ $288]**
- Of the Judicature in Parliaments. A posthumous treatise. London: Joseph Lawson, [1681]. 1st edn. With the 2 terminal blanks. Crnr of title marg defective. Mod qtr calf, mrbld bds. Wing S2433.
(Charles Cox) **£145 [≈ $261]**
- Table-talk ... the discourses of ... or his sence of various matters of weight and high consequence relating especially to religion and state. London: for E. Smith, 1689. 1st edn. 4to. Numeral on dedn leaf, rust hole in D1. Mor, gilt, jnts sl worn. Wing S2437.
(Traylen) **£375 [≈ $675]**
- Titles of honour. London: for John Helme, 1614. 1st edn. Sm 4to. xxxviii,391,xliii pp. Some light waterstaining to upper portion of text. Later half calf, rec rebacked. STC22177.
(Edwards) **£180 [≈ $324]**
- Titles of honour. London: William Stansby,

1631. 2nd edn. Folio. [xxxvi],941,[i] pp. Red & black title, w'cuts & dec initials in text. Contemp speckled calf, elab gilt stamps on each cvr, spine restored at hd, 5 v sm wormholes in bottom compartment.
(Frew Mackenzie) **£380 [≈ $684]**

- Tracts. The first: Jani Anglorum facies altera, rendered into English. The second: England's Epinomis. The third ... The fourth ... 1683. 1st edn. Folio. 131,39,24 pp. Lacks port. Sl worming throughout in marg, title reprd in marg. Mod qtr calf. Wing 2441a.
(Edwards) **£125 [≈ $225]**

Sempill, Hugh

- A short address to the public, on the practice of cashiering military officers without a trial and a vindication of the conduct and political opinions of the author ... London: for J. Johnson ..., 1793. 1st edn. 8vo. 47 pp with verso blank. Disbound. *(Hughes)* **£28 [≈ $50]**

Semple, J.G.

- The life of Major J.G. Semple Lisle: containing a faithfull narrative of his alternate vicissitudes of splendour and misfortune written by himself. London: W. Stewart, 1799. Port frontis. Contemp calf. Ex lib Colquhoun of Luss.
(C.R. Johnson) **£280 [≈ $504]**

Senators ...

- The senators ... See Delamayne, Thomas Hallie

Sendivogius, Michael

- A new light of alchymy: taken out of the fountain of nature and manual experience ... a treatise of sulphur ... a chymical dictionary. London: Tho. Williams, 1674. 8vo. Title & final leaf sl soiled, some headlines cropped. New calf, old top cvr. Wing 2507A.
(Stewart) **£600 [≈ $1,080]**

Seneca, Lucius Annaeus

- Morals by way of abstract, to which is added a discourse under the title of An afterthought by Sir Roger L'Estrange. London: for G. Strahan ..., 1739. 14th edn. 8vo. Engvd frontis, plate. 19th c divinity calf.
(Traylen) **£28 [≈ $50]**

- Seneca's morals by way of abstract. London: for S. Manship ..., 1693. 3 pts in 1 vol. 8vo. Engvd frontis. Contemp calf, rubbed, upper jnt cracked. Wing S2518, 2518A, 2519.
(Stewart) **£120 [≈ $216]**

- The works both moral and natural ... Translated by Thomas Lodge. 1614. 1st edn. Folio. 917 pp. Ruled text. W'cut devices &

vignettes throughout (that on title cut out). Contemp calf. STC 22213.
(Edwards) **£275 [≈ $495]**

Sennert, Daniel

- Practical physick: or five distinct treatises of the most predominant diseases of these times [scurvey, dropsie, feavers, agues, French pox, gout]. London: for W. Whitwood, 1676. 1st edn in English. 8vo. [xiv],151, [xii],176, 179 pp. Mod half mor. Wing S2542.
(Bickersteth) **£550 [≈ $990]**

Sense of the Nation ...

- The sense of the nation, concerning the Duke of Marlborough, as it is expressed in several Acts of Parliament ... London: for S. Popping ..., 1702 [but 1712]. 1st edn. 8vo. 28 pp. 19th c skiver mor, rubbed & chafed.
(Hughes) **£30 [≈ $54]**

Sequira, I.

- A new merchant's guide; containing a concise system of information for the Port and City of London ... London: for the author, 1798. 1st edn. 8vo. [xxii],244 pp. 2 engvd plates. Sgnd by author at end of dedn. Contemp half calf, light gen wear. *(Burmester)* **£275 [≈ $495]**

Sergeant, J.

- Schism dispatch't or a rejoinder to the replies of Dr. Hammond and the Ld of Derby. 1657. 1st edn. Some minor marg worming. Contemp calf. Wing S2590.
(Robertshaw) **£30 [≈ $54]**

Sermons ...

- Certaine sermons or homilies appointed to be read in churches. London: John Bill, 1623. Folio. [8],316,[2] pp. W'cut title (marg creased). Lacking DDD3, final leaf of last sermon. Contemp vellum, gilt. STC 13659.
(Spelman) **£160 [≈ $288]**

- Sermons preached by several of the ... Quakers, exactly taken in short-hand as they were delivered ... at their meeting houses ... London: Mary Hinde, 1775. New edn. 8vo. [4],250,[2 blank] pp. Contemp calf, reprd.
(Fenning) **£28.50 [≈ $50]**

Settle, Elkanah

- Carmen Irenicum. The union of the Imperial Crowns of Great Britain. An heroick poem. London: for the author, 1708. 1st edn. Folio. 47 pp. Orig Settle binding of black turkey, richly gilt, arms of Charles Montagu, 1st Duke of Manchester on sides.
(Bennett) **£950 [≈ $1,710]**

- The character of a Popish successour, and

what England may expect from such a one ... London: T. Davies, 1681. Folio. [ii], 22 pp. Outer leaves v dusty, outer marg of title torn. Disbound. Wing S2670. *(Clark)* £20 [≈ $36]
- Ibrahim the illustrious Bassa. A tragedy. London: Tho. Chapman, 1694. 2nd edn. 4to. [vi],62 pp. Cropped at hd, affecting some letters, browned throughout, 1st & last leaves frayed. Later wraps. *(Clark)* £30 [≈ $54]

Sewall, Stephen
- The scripture history relating to the overthrow of Sodom and Gomorrah, and to the origin of the Salt Sea, or Lake of Sodom. Boston: William P. & Lemuel Blake, 1796. 30 pp. Orig blue wraps, somewhat chipped. *(Karmiole)* $50 [≈ £27]

Shade ...
- The shade of Alexander Pope ... See Mathias, Thomas James

Shadwell, Thomas
- Epsom-Wells. A comedy. Acted at the Duke's Theatre. London: for Henry Herringman, 1673. 1st edn. 4to. [vi],96,[ii] pp. Final epilogue/errata lf. Sm repr to title affecting 2 letters, some minor soiling. 19th c half green mor, spine gilt. Wing S2843. *(Clark)* £85 [≈ $153]
- The libertine: a tragedy. London: for Henry Herringman, 1676. 4to. [xii],85,[iii] pp. Cropped at hd affecting a few headlines & page numerals. 19th c half calf, spine gilt, sl rubbed. Wing S2857. *(Clark)* £95 [≈ $171]
- The works. [London:] Printed in the year, 1720. In four volumes. 1st coll edn. Port frontis. Contemp calf, red & green labels. *(C.R. Johnson)* £325 [≈ $585]

Shaftesbury, Anthony, Earl of
- Characteristicks, of men, manners, opinions, times, &c. [London: 1733]. New edn. 3 vols. Thick 12mo. [8],364; 442,[2]; [4],408.[54] pp. Contemp calf, rebacked, extremities quite rubbed. *(Karmiole)* $150 [≈ £83]
- Memoires of the life ... London: Walter Davis, 1682/3. Folio. [ii],10 pp. Creased, title stained. Stitched as issued. Wing M1671. *(Clark)* £30 [≈ $54]
- The proceedings at the Sessions House ... upon the Bill of Indictment for high treason against ... London: Samuel Mearne ..., 1681. Folio. [ii],48 pp. Sm tears on crnrs of title, some staining. Stitched as issued. Wing P3564. *(Clark)* £35 [≈ $63]

Shakespeare, William
- Comedies, histories and tragedies ... with an introduction ... notes critical and explanatory ... London: for J. & R. Tonson, [1767]. 10 vols. Cr 8vo. Contemp calf, rebacked. *(Traylen)* £420 [≈ $756]
- The dramatic works ... Oxford: Clarendon Press and [vols 5-6] J. Cooke ..., 1786-91. 6 vols. 8vo. Half-title in each vol. Owner's name on each title, 1 gathering foxed. Contemp calf, rec rebacked, edges & crnrs worn, a little marked. *(Pirages)* $350 [≈ £194]
- The dramatick writings. With the notes of all the various commentators. London: John Bell, 1786. 10 vols. Sm 8vo. Some foxing to engvd plates. Contemp green mor, a.e.g., gilt spines a little darkened. *(Spelman)* £180 [≈ $324]
- The plays ... in fifteen volumes ... to which are added notes by Samuel Johnson and George Steevens. London: 1793. 4th edn. 15 vols. 8vo. 4 plates (1 fldg). Contemp calf, rebacked. *(Traylen)* £220 [≈ $396]
- The plays ... to which are added notes by Samuel Johnson and George Steevens. London: for C Bathurst ..., 1778-80. 12 vols inc 2 supp vols. 8vo. A few minor tears, stains, or creases. Contemp sprinkled calf, spine ends sl chipped or ragged, 4 jnts cracked. *(Pirages)* $550 [≈ £305]
- The plays. Complete in eight volumes. London: for Bellamy & Roberts, 1791. 8 vols. 8vo. Frontis, engvd title, & 2 stipple plates to each play (2 plays with 1 plate only). Contemp tree-calf, gilt spines with sm reprs. *(Traylen)* £335 [≈ $603]
- The works ... In six [i.e. seven] volumes. Adorn'd with cuts. London: for Jacob Tonson (vol VII, E. Curll), 1709-10. 1st 8vo, & 1st illust, edn. Ports & plates. Some minor foxing, sl marks. Not quite uniform contemp panelled calf, vol VII rebacked. *(Charles Cox)* £750 [≈ $1,350]
- The works ... In eight volumes. Collated with the oldest copies, and corrected ... by Mr. Theobald. London: for H. Woodfall ..., 1767. 8 vols. Port frontis, 36 plates. Minor worming in 3 vols, frequently browned or smudged. Contemp calf, extremities worn. *(Pirages)* $300 [≈ £166]

Sharp, Samuel
- A treatise on the operations of surgery, with a description and representation of the instruments used in performing them ... London: J. & R. Tonson, 1751. 8vo. [8]ff, lii,236 pp. 14 engvd plates. Sl marg browning. Contemp lea bds, rebacked.

(Elgen) **$450 [≈ £250]** - A treatise on the operations of surgery, with a description and representation of the instruments used in performing them ... London: Tonson, 1761. 8vo. 234 pp. 12 (ex 14) plates. Final leaf torn with loss of 3 inch of text at ft. Calf, worn spine defective.   *(Goodrich)* **$65 [≈ £36]**

Sharpe, Granville
- The legal means of political reformation proposed in two small tracts ... The fifth edition. [London: 1780]. 59 pp. Uncut, sewn pamphlet as issued.
          (C.R. Johnson) **£65 [≈ $117]**

Shaw, Thomas
- Travels or observations relating to several parts of Barbary and the Levant. Oxford: 1738. Folio. [vi],xvi, 442,60,[viii] pp. 12 engvd maps & plans, 21 plates. Uncut in qtr calf, mrbld bds, a bit rubbed.
          (Frew Mackenzie) **£450 [≈ $810]**
- Travels or observations relating to several parts of Barbary and the Levant. Oxford: 1738. Folio. xvi,442, 60,[8 index] pp. 9 maps (6 fldg), 3 plans, 20 plates, fldg table. Mod half lea.   *(Zeno)* **£345 [≈ $621]**
- Travels or observations relating to several parts of Barbary and the Levant. Oxford: 1738. Folio. 442,[61 index] pp. Vignette title, 31 fldg maps & plates. Contemp calf, sl cracking.   *(Halewood)* **£325 [≈ $585]**
- Travels or observations relating to several parts of Barbary and the Levant. London: for A. Millar ..., 1757. 2nd edn. Lge cr 4to. xx,513 pp. 37 engvd plates & maps. Contemp calf bds, chipped, reprd, rebacked.
          (Orient) **£170 [≈ $306]**

Shaw, William
- An analysis of the Galic language. Edinburgh: for R. Jamieson, 1778. 2nd edn. 8vo. 171 pp. Occas spotting. Rec qtr calf.
          (Burmester) **£90 [≈ $162]**
- Memoirs of the life and writings of the late Dr. Samuel Johnson. London: Walker, 1785. 1st edn. Sm 8vo. Contemp calf, newly rebacked.   *(Marlborough)* **£420 [≈ $756]**
- Memoirs of the life and writings of the late Dr. Samuel Johnson. London: for J. Walker, 1785. 1st edn. Sm 8vo. [vi],197 pp. half-title. Trace of old lib stamp on title. Rec half calf.
          (Burmester) **£225 [≈ $405]**

Sheffield, John, Duke of Buckingham
- Poems on several occasions. To which are added, the tragedies of Julius Caesar, and Marcus Brutus. Glasgow: Robert & Andrew

Foulis, 1752. 1st edn of this coll. 8vo. viii,280 pp. Contemp speckled calf, spine gilt.
          (Burmester) **£75 [≈ $135]**
- The works ... In two volumes. London: for J.B., 1729. 2nd edn, crrctd. 8vo. xvi,400; iv,272,8 advts pp. Fldg port frontis, fldg plate, text ills. Crnr torn from 2 leaves without loss of text. Contemp panelled calf, spine gilt.   *(Frew Mackenzie)* **£260 [≈ $468]**

Sheffield, John, First Earl
- Observations on the Corn Bill, now depending in Parliament. London: for J. Debrett, 1791. 1st edn. [iv],83 pp. Half-title. Disbound.   *(Burmester)* **£50 [≈ $90]**

Shelvocke, George
- A voyage round the world by way of the great south sea, perform'd in the years 1719, 20, 21, 22. London: 1726. [44],468 pp. Fldg map on 2 sheets, 4 engvs (2 fldg). Contemp blindstamped calf, rebacked, front hinges weak.   *(Reese)* **$1,250 [≈ £694]**

Shenstone, William
- The works in verse and prose. London: for R. & J. Dodsley, 1764. 1st edn. 2 vols. 2 frontis, vignettes, fldg plan (tear in blank panel). Lacking 1 free endpaper. Contemp calf, 1 spine worn at hd. Contemp b'plates of Earl of Haddington.   *(Charles Cox)* **£65 [≈ $117]**
- The works in verse and prose. London: for R. & J. Dodsley, 1764-69. 3 vols. 8vo. Contemp calf, rebacked.   *(Waterfield's)* **£225 [≈ $405]**

Shepherd, A.
- Tables for correcting the apparent distance of the moon and a star from the effects of refraction and parallax. Cambridge: 1772. 1st edn. Lge thick 4to. [2]ff, xii pp, [556] pp. 3 other tables pasted onto last blank leaf. Cloth.
          (Elgen) **$150 [≈ £83]**

Sheppard, William
- The court-keepers guide. or a plain and familiar treatise, needfull and usefull for the help of many imployed in the keeping of Law dayes or Courts Baron. London: 1650. 2nd edn. 12mo. 254 pp. Mod qtr calf.
          (Edwards) **£150 [≈ $270]**
- The touch-stone of common assurances: or, a plain and familiar treatise, opening the learning of the common assurances, or conveyances of the kingdom. Dublin: John Exshaw, 1785. Lge 8vo. Bottom of title rubbed. Contemp (or near) law calf.
          (Chaucer Head) **£75 [≈ $135]**

Sherburne, Sir Edward
- The tragedies of L. Annaeus Seneca ... and the Rape of Helen ... translated ... with annotations ... London: for S. Smith ..., 1702. 1st edn, 2nd iss with cancel title. 8vo. [xvi],39, [ix],377,[xxiii] pp. Engvd port, 5 plates. Contemp calf, spine richly gilt.
(Bennett) £175 [≈ $315]

Sheridan, Richard Brinsley
- A comparative statement of the two bills, for the better government of the British possessions in India, brought into parliament by Mr. Fox and Mr. Pitt. London: J. Debrett, 1788. 3rd edn. 4to. 39 pp. Half-title.
(C.R. Johnson) £85 [≈ $153]
- The critic, or a tragedy rehearsed. A dramatic piece in three acts. London: for T. Becket, 1781. 1st edn. 4th imp. 8vo. Lacking half-title. Later tree-calf, orig backstrip laid down.
(Waterfield's) £90 [≈ $162]
- The critic, or a tragedy rehearsed. London: for T. Becket, 1781 (but actually ca 1795, with paper watermarked thus). [vi],96, [ii] pp. Engvd title (stained), final advt leaf. No half-title. Disbound.   *(Clark)* £28 [≈ $50]
- The critic, or a tragedy rehearsed. A dramatic piece in three acts. London: for T. Becket, 1781. 1st edn. Stain to 1 lower marg, some foxing, no half-title or advt leaf. New qtr calf, cloth bds.   *(Charles Cox)* £55 [≈ $99]
- The rivals, a comedy ... The third edition. London: J. Wilkie, [1776]. 8vo. [viii],123 pp. Engvd title (sl marked). Disbound.
(Clark) £25 [≈ $45]
- A trip to Scarborough. A comedy. As performed at the Theatre Royal in Drury Lane. London: G. Wilkie, 1781. 1st edn. Half-title. A few leaves a little browned. New qtr calf, mrbld bds.
(Charles Cox) £95 [≈ $171]
- A trip to Scarborough. A comedy. As performed at the Theatre Royal in Drury Lane. London: G. Wilkie, 1781. 1st edn, early state. 8vo. [viii],104 pp. Half-title. Blue-green mor by Riviere.
(Bennett) £150 [≈ $270]

Sheridan, Thomas
- British education: or, the source of the disorders of Great Britain. London: for R. & J. Dodsley, 1756. 1st edn. 8vo. Occas spotting. Contemp calf, rebacked.
(Chaucer Head) £260 [≈ $468]
- A course of lectures on elocution ... and some other tracts ... London: for A. Miller ..., 1762. 1st edn. 4to. xxviii,[x],262 pp. Sl marg worming in 1 sgntr. Contemp mottled calf,

gilt.   *(Burmester)* £125 [≈ $225]
- Lectures on the art of reading. In two parts. London: for J. Dodsley, 1787. 3rd edn. 8vo. 409 pp. Mod half calf. *(Young's)* £75 [≈ $135]

Sherlock, Thomas
- Several discourses preached at the Temple Church. London: for J. Whiston ..., 1755. 3rd edn. 4 vols. 8vo. Contemp calf, sl rubbed.
(Stewart) £35 [≈ $63]
- Several discourses preached at the Temple Church. London: for J. Whiston ..., 1754. 2nd edn. 8vo. Title soiled. Contemp calf, sl worn, upper jnt weak. *(Stewart)* £20 [≈ $36]

Sherlock, William
- The case of the resistance of the Supreme Powers stated and resolved according to the doctrine of the Holy Scriptures. London: for Fincham Gardiner, 1684. Contemp sheep, rubbed. Wing S3267.
(Waterfield's) £45 [≈ $81]
- A discourse concerning the knowledge of Jesus Christ, and our union and communion with him ... London: for Walter Kettilby, 1674. Cr 8vo. Early notes on endpapers, sl damage to title. Red mor, spine gilt. Wing 3288.   *(Stewart)* £30 [≈ $54]
- A second letter to a friend, concerning the French invasion. London: 1692. 1st edn. 4to. Imprim, 32 pp. Light stain on upper outer crnrs. B'plate of Earl of Winchilsea. Old cloth-backed bds. *(Claude Cox)* £18 [≈ $32]
- A second letter to a friend, concerning the French invasion ... London: Randall Taylor, 1692. 2nd edn. 4to. 32 pp. Disbound. Wing S3339.   *(Young's)* £27 [≈ $48]
- A vindication of the doctrine of the holy and ever blessed Trinity, and the incarnation of the Son of God ... 1694. 3rd edn. 4to. [8],272 pp. Rec polished bds over mrbld bds. Wing S3378.   *(Fenning)* £35 [≈ $63]

Shippen, William
- Faction displayed. A poem. London: 1704. 1st edn (printing "A"). 8vo. 2ff, 20 pp. Some pages a little foxed. Stitched as issued, later paper wraps.   *(Pirages)* $75 [≈ £41]
- Moderation displayed. A poem. London: 1704. 1st edn. 8vo. 2ff, 20 pp. Leaves sl darkened & faintly foxed. Later paper wraps.
(Pirages) $75 [≈ £41]

Shirley, John
- The honour of chivalry, or the famous and delectable history of Don Bellianis of Greece. London: Passinger, 1683. 2 vols in 1 4to. Predominately black letter. Imprint & some

headlines cropped. 19th c russia, panelled gilt, a.e.g., hinges cracked. Wing S3507.
(Marlborough) **£150 [≈ $270]**
- The most delectable history of Reynard the Fox, newly corrected, and purged from all grossness ... London: for Edward Brewster, 1681. Sm 4to. A-U4, unpaginated. Black letter. Num w'cuts. Title strengthened at gutter. Some browning. Later half mor.
(Frew Mackenzie) **£400 [≈ $720]**

Shirrefs, Andrew
- Poems, chiefly in the Scottish dialect. Edinburgh: for the author, 1790. 1st edn. 8vo. Engvd port, half-title, 14 subscribers list, 41 pp glossary. 2 leaves torn without loss. Orig bds, rebacked, uncut.
(Traylen) **£85 [≈ $153]**

Short, Thomas
- Discourses on tea, sugar, milk, made-wines ... with plain and useful rules for gouty people. London: for T. Longman ..., 1750. 1st edn. 8vo. Advt leaf as frontis, 2 pp advts at end. Contemp calf, 2 line gilt border, gilt panelled spine, mor label, gilt.
(Traylen) **£720 [≈ $1,296]**
- A general chronological history of the air, weather, seasons, meteors, etc ... London: for T. Longman ..., 1749. 1st edn. 2 vols. 8vo. [xxxii],494; [ii],536,[8] pp. Errata leaf. 1st & last few leaves spotted, sm chip in marg of both titles. Rec half calf.
(Pirages) **$450 [≈ £250]**
- The natural, experimental, and medicinal history of the mineral waters of Derbyshire, Lincolnshire, and Yorkshire. London: 1734 [and] ... Cumberland ... Westmoreland, Sheffield: 1740. 1st edns. 2 vols. 4to. 5 engvs (4 fldg). Vol 2 sl browned. Mottled calf.
(Rootenberg) **$475 [≈ £263]**
- The natural, experimental, and medicinal history of the mineral waters of Derbyshire, Lincolnshire, and Yorkshire. London: 1734 [and] ... Cumberland ... Westmoreland, Sheffield: 1740. 1st edns. 2 vols. 4to. 4 fldg plates. Mod mrbld bds.
(Chaucer Head) **£220 [≈ $396]**

Shower, John
- The mourners companion: or, funeral discourses on several texts. London: for J. Dunton ..., 1692. 1st edn. Browned. Contemp sheep, worn. Wing S3673.
(Charles Cox) **£20 [≈ $36]**

Sidney, Algernon
- Discourses   concerning   Government. Booksellers of London & Westminster, 1698.

1st edn. Folio. [ii],462,[v index] pp. Contemp panelled calf, rebacked, gilt-lettered. Wing S3761.
(Blackwell's) **£400 [≈ $720]**
- Discourses   concerning   Government. Booksellers of London & Westminster, 1698. 1st edn. Folio. Some waterstaining in lower part of some leaves. Contemp calf. Wing S3761.
(Waterfield's) **£250 [≈ $450]**
- Discourses concerning Government. London: J. Darby, 1704. 2nd edn. Folio. Engvd port frontis. Contemp panelled calf, label rather chipped.
(Waterfield's) **£165 [≈ $297]**
- Discourses concerning Government. London: 1751. 3rd edn. Folio. lii,495 pp. Port frontis. Later qtr calf, sl soiled.
(Edwards) **£150 [≈ $270]**

Sidney, Sir Philip
- The Countess of Pembrokes Arcadia. Now the sixt time published ... London: for Simon Waterson, 1627. Folio. [vi],624 pp. Title mtd, with loss of our crnrs of border, 1st few leaves frayed, occas marks or stains. Contemp calf, rebacked, crnrs reprd.
(Claude Cox) **£125 [≈ $225]**

Siege of Candia ...
- A relation of the siege of Candia. From the first expedition of the French forces ... to its surrender ... London: T. Williams ..., 1670. Sm 8vo. 119 pp. Contemp calf, extremities rubbed. Wing R868.
(Karmiole) **$200 [≈ £111]**

Sillar, David
- Poems. Kilmarnock: John Wilson, 1789. 247 pp. Rebound in qtr calf, mrbld bds.
(C.R. Johnson) **£285 [≈ $513]**

Simkin the Second ...
- Letters from Simkin the Second ... See Broome, Ralph

Simmons, Samuel
- Elements of anatomy and the animal economy. From the French of M. Person ... London: Wilie, 1775. 1st edn. 8vo. xii,396 pp. Errata leaf. 3 engvd plates. Light pencilling. Old qtr calf, worn.
(Goodrich) **$75 [≈ £41]**

Simpson, Thomas
- The doctrine and application of fluxions ... And the solution of a variety of new ... problems in different branches of the mathematicks. London: for J. Nourse, 1750. 8vo. 2 pts in 1 vol. xi,274; [iv],275-576 pp. Contemp calf, reprd, new back, crnrs worn.

(Pollak) **£100 [≈ $180]**

- Select exercises for young proficients in the mathematics ... new edition ... An account of the life and writings of the author, by Charles Hutton. For F. Wingrave, 1792. 8vo. [4],iv,xxiii, [1 list of books],252 pp. Ink splashes on 4pp. Contemp calf.
(Fenning) **£45 [≈ $81]**

Simson, Robert

- Elements of the conic sections. The first three books translated from the Latin original. Edinburgh: Elliott, 1775. 1st edn. [vi],255 pp. 24 fldg plates. Lacking both free endpapers. Orig qtr calf, a little wear to ft of spine, crnr bent, uncut.
(Hinchliffe) **£70 [≈ $126]**

Sinclair, George

- The hydrostaticks; or, the weight, force, and pressure of fluid bodies ... Edinburgh: 1672. 1st edn. 4to. x,319,[1 blank] pp plus engvd title. Fldg engvd coat of arms, 7 fldg engvd plates. Contemp sgntr on title. Contemp calf, jnts cracking. Wing S3854.
(Pickering) **$2,000 [≈ £1,111]**

Sinclair, Sir John

- General view of the agriculture of the Northern Counties and Islands of Scotland ... London: 1795. 4to. Half-title, 2 fldg cold maps, fldg engvd plate, appendix. Bds, calf spine. *(Traylen)* **£55 [≈ $99]**
- Specimen of the statistical account of Scotland drawn up from the communications of the Ministers of the different parishes. Edinburgh: 1791. 8vo. iv,51 pp. Mod bds. Advertising preprint.
(Pickering) **$250 [≈ £138]**
- The statistical account of Scotland drawn up from the communications of the Ministers of the different parishes. Edinburgh: Creech, 1791. 21 vols. Mod qtr calf, gilt.
(John Smith) **£800 [≈ $1,440]**
- The statistical account of Scotland drawn up from the communications of the Ministers of the different parishes. Edinburgh: Creech, 1791-99. 21 vols. 8vo. Over 13,000 pp. Sev engvd plates & plans, fldg tables. Lacking 1 half-title. Contemp polished calf.
(Pickering) **$2,500 [≈ £1,388]**

Sinking Fund ...

- An annual abstract of the Sinking Fund, from Michaelmas 1718 ... to the 10th of October, 1763. London: for R. Davis ..., 1764. Sole edn. 4to. [2],73 pp. Contemp sprinkled calf, jnts cracked. *(Pickering)* **$125 [≈ £69]**

Skene, Alexander

- Memorialls for the government of the Royalburghs in Scotland ... As also, a survey of the City of Aberdeen ... Aberdeen: John Forbes, 1685. Sole edn. Sm 8vo. 288 pp. Each part with sep title. Contemp calf, sl rubbed, rebacked. Wing S3935.
(Karmiole) **$200 [≈ £111]**

Skene, Sir John

- Regiam Majestatem. The auld lawes and constitutions of Scotland. Edinburgh: Thomas Finlason, 1609. 1st edn. Folio. Dampstains throughout, soiling on p 69. Mod half calf. STC 22624.
(Robertshaw) **£95 [≈ $171]**
- Regiam Majestatem. The auld lawes and constitutions of Scotland faithfullie collected ... whereunto are adjoined twa tratises ... Edinburgh: Thomas Finlayson, 1609. Folio. Orig gilt embossed calf, rebacked. 17th c ownership inscrptn. STC 22626.
(C.R. Johnson) **£380 [≈ $684]**
- Regiam Majestatem. The auld lawes and constitutions of Scotland. 1774. 4to. Foxed. Upper marg of last ten leaves stained. Old calf, rebacked. *(Allen)* **$150 [≈ £83]**

Sketch ...

- A sketch of the debates in both Houses of Parliament of Ireland, on the Roman Catholic Bill passed in the session of 1792 ... Dublin: P. Byrne, 1792. 40 pp. Stabbed pamphlet as issued. *(C.R. Johnson)* **£28 [≈ $50]**
- A sketch of the life and character of Mr. Radcliffe. Containing the part he acted in the Rebellion in 1715. His sentence and escape out of Newgate; His adventures for these 30 years past ... London: T. Gardner, 1746. 28 pp. Half-title. Rebound in qtr calf.
(C.R. Johnson) **£65 [≈ $117]**

Sketches ...

- Sketches chiefly relating to ... the Hindoos ... See Craufurd, Quintin

Skinner, John

- An ecclesiastical history of Scotland ... London: for T. Evans, 1788. 1st edn. 2 vols. 8vo. 471; 698 pp. Some spotting. Contemp half calf. *(Young's)* **£48 [≈ $86]**

Slatyer, William

- The history of Great Britanie from the first peopling of this Island ... London: for Rich: Meighen, [1621]. Sole edn. Folio. Title dusty & v sl chipped, 1 or 2 ink-blots & fingermarks. Old calf, rebacked. STC 22634.

(Charles Cox) **£240 [≈ $432]**

Slavery and Commerce ...
- An essay on the slavery and commerce of the human species ... See Clarkson, Thomas

Smeaton, John
- A narrative of the building and a description of the construction of the Eddystone Lighthouse. 1793. 2nd edn. Folio. xiv,198 pp. Engvd title, 23 maps, plates and charts. Sm lib stamps to title & all plates in margs, browning & foxing. Calf-backed bds.
(Edwards) **£400 [≈ $720]**

Smellie, William
- The philosophy of natural history. Edinburgh: 1790. 4to. Contemp speckled calf, sl rubbing on jnts & wear on lower crnrs.
(Waterfield's) **£80 [≈ $144]**
- The philosophy of natural history. Edinburgh: 1790. 1st edn. 4to. Contemp half calf, gilt, mrbld bds. *(Traylen)* **£85 [≈ $153]**
- The philosophy of natural history. Edinburgh: 1790-99. 2 vols. 4to. Vol 1 calf, vol 2 orig bds, spine sl defective.
(Wheldon & Wesley) **£195 [≈ $351]**
- The philosophy of natural history. Edinburgh: 1790-99. 1st edn. 2 vols (inc the 2nd vol, published posthumously). 4to. xiii,547, errata leaf; xii,515 pp. Old tree-calf, worn. A non-matching set, vol I with larger margins. *(Weiner)* **£175 [≈ $315]**
- The philosophy of natural history. Dublin: for Chamberlaine & Rice ..., 1790. Piracy but 2nd edn. 2 vols. 8vo. Some light dust-soiling, 1 leaf in vol 2 reprd, final leaf of index torn with sl loss. Contemp half calf, sl rubbed & worn, mrbld bds. *(Stewart)* **£250 [≈ $450]**
- A set of anatomical tables ... and an abridgement, of the practice of midwifery. London: [for subscribers], 1754. 1st edn. Lge folio. 39 engvd plates. Light spotting, mainly marg. Ownership inscrptn & ptd stamp on title. Orig mrbld bds, rebacked.
(Quaritch) **$3,750 [≈ £2,083]**
- A set of anatomical tables, with explanations, and an abridgement, of the practice of midwifery. London: 1754. Atlas folio. 39 copperplates. Some marg dustiness & fingerprints. Orig panelled calf, cnrs & headpiece worn.
(Goodrich) **$4,250 [≈ £2,361]**
- A set of anatomical tables, with explanations, and an abridgement of the practice of midwifery. Worcester, Mass: I. Thomas, 1793. 2nd Amer edn. 8vo. 84 pp. 40 engvd plates. Spotty foxing, light browning. Mod

half calf. *(Antiq Sc)* **$500 [≈ £277]**
- A treatise on the theory and practice of midwifery. London: 1762. 4th edn [with] A collection of cases and observations ... London: 1764. 3rd edn [with] A collection of preternatural cases ... London: 1764. 1st edn. 3 vols. 1st complete edn. Some browning. Contemp calf. *(Oasis)* **$450 [≈ £250]**
- A treatise on the theory and practice of midwifery. London: for D. Wilson, 1752. 1st edn. 8vo. Title dust-soiled & rubbed (without loss), some spotting & soiling. Contemp calf, rebacked & recrnrd.
(Quaritch) **$1,600 [≈ £888]**

Smethurst, G.
- Tables of time: whereby the day and the month ... Manchester: 1749. Sm 8vo. viii,132, 48 pp. Embossed stamp on title & a few other pp. Later lib cloth, sl dust-stained.
(Whitehart) **£40 [≈ $72]**

Smith, Adam
- Essays on philosophical subjects ... prefixed an account of the life and writings ... London: for T. Cadell, Jun ..., 1795. 1st edn. 4to. Contemp half calf, gilt spine, mrbld bds.
(Traylen) **£2,950 [≈ $5,310]**
- Essays on philosophical subjects ... prefixed an account of the life and writings of the author by Dugald Stewart. Basil: 1799. 1st Swiss edn. 8vo. Mod half calf.
(Waterfield's) **£365 [≈ $657]**
- An inquiry into the nature and causes of the wealth of nations. Dublin: Whitestone, 1776. 1st Dublin edn. 3 vols. 8vo. Half-title vol 1, 2 advt leaves vol 2. Mod half calf.
(Emerald Isle) **£1,600 [≈ $2,880]**
- An inquiry into the nature and causes of the wealth of nations. London: Strahan & Cadell, 1791. 6th edn. 3 vol. 8vo. Occas spotting. Contemp calf, rebacked.
(Chaucer Head) **£280 [≈ $504]**
- An inquiry into the nature and causes of the wealth of nations. London: Strahan & Cadell, 1796. 8th edn. 3 vol. 3 half-titles. Contemp tree-calf, spines gilt, spines rubbed, crnrs bumped. *(Frew Mackenzie)* **£260 [≈ $468]**
- The theory of moral sentiments. London: for A. Millar ..., 1759. 1st edn. 8vo. [xii],551,[1 errata] pp. Tear in O4 marg with loss of 2 letters, 2 tiny wormholes in last 100 pp margs. Contemp inscrptn on title. Contemp polished calf, spine a little scuffed.
(Pickering) **$8,000 [≈ £4,444]**

Smith, Charlotte
- Ethelinde, or the recluse of the lake. London:

for T. Cadell, 1789. 1st edn. 5 vols. Cr 8vo.
Half-titles. Contemp calf, gilt spines.
(Traylen) **£350 [≈ $630]**
- The old manor house. A novel. London: for
J. Bell, 1793. 1st edn. 4 vols. Cr 8vo. 18th c
sgntr on title. Contemp calf, gilt spine.
(Traylen) **£280 [≈ $504]**
- The romance of real life. London: for T.
Cadell, 1787. 1st edn. 3 vols. 8vo. With the
half-titles. Contemp sheep, reprd, some
extremities of bds wormed.
(Bennett) **£150 [≈ $270]**

Smith, Hugh
- Formulae medicamentorum concinnatae: or,
elegant medical prescriptions for various
disorders. Translated ... To which is prefixed
a sketch of his life. London: J.S. Barr, 1791.
12mo. viii,131 pp. Disbound.
(Burmester) **£45 [≈ $81]**
- Letters to married women. London: G.K.
Kearsley, 1767. 1st edn. 1st edn. Sm 8vo.
viii,246 pp. Browning at extreme margs of
title. Mod bds.   *(Hemlock)* **$950 [≈ £527]**

Smith, John
- The art of painting in oyl ... preparing,
mixing, and working of oyl colours ... art and
mystery of colouring maps ... London:
Samuel Crouch, 1723. 5th imp. 12mo.
[8],108,[4 advts] pp. Contemp calf, rebacked.
(Spelman) **£350 [≈ $630]**

Smith, John (1630-1679)
- The pourtract of old age ... a sacred anatomy
both of soul and body. And a perfect account
of the infirmities of age ... London: for Walter
Kettilby, 1676. 2nd edn, crrctd. 8vo. Fldg
table, imprimatur, title-page in duplicate.
Contemp calf. Wing S4116.
(Traylen) **£295 [≈ $531]**

Smith, John (1747-1807)
- Galic antiquities: consisting of a history of the
Druids, particularly of those of Caledonia ...
and a collection of ancient poems ...
Edinburgh: for T. Cadell ..., 1780. 1st edn.
4to. viii,352 pp. Contemp tree-calf, rebacked,
worn, worming in upper jnt.
(Burmester) **£90 [≈ $162]**

Smith, Thomas
- Poems. Manchester: for the author, 1797. 1st
edn. 12mo. 99,[2 errata] pp. Uncut in orig
cream bds, blue paper spine, v sl wear along
spine.   *(Burmester)* **£200 [≈ $360]**

Smith, William
- A brief state of the Province of Pennsylvania
... and the true cause of the continual
encroachments of the French displayed ...
their late unwarrantable invasion and
settlement upon the River Ohio. London:
1756. 3rd edn. 47 pp. Calf & bds, somewhat
rubbed.   *(Reese)* **$400 [≈ £222]**
- An historical account of the expedition
against the Ohio Indians, in the year 1764.
Phila: William Bradford, 1765. 1st edn.
[2],xiii,71 pp. 2 plates (1 fldg). Lacking the
lge map. Half mor, mrbld bds.
(Reese) **$3,000 [≈ £1,666]**
- An oration in memory of General
Montgomery, and of the officers and men
who fell with him ... before Quebec ... Phila:
John Dunlap, 1776. [4],44 pp. 3/4 mor & bds,
t.e.g., sl wear to front hinge. Ex lib with
b'plate.   *(Reese)* **$425 [≈ £236]**

Smith, William, Dean of Chester (trans.)
- The history of the Peloponnesian War ...
from the Greek of Thucydides. London: John
Watts, 1753. 1st edn of this trans. 2 vols. 4to.
83,308; 484 pp. 2 engvd fldg maps. Contemp
calf, vol 2 cvr sl scraped. *(Tara)* **£95 [≈ $171]**

Smith, William, of Kilmore, Co. Meath
- An authentic account of the life and memoirs
of Mr. William Smith, an unfortunate
convict, executed at Tyburn ... for forgery ...
written by himself. London: for J. Jefferies,
1750. 1st edn. 8vo. 42 pp. Outer leaves a bit
soiled. Disbound. *(Burmester)* **£100 [≈ $180]**

Smollett, Tobias
- The adventures of Ferdinand Count Fathom.
London: for W. Johnston, 1753. 1st edn. 2
vols. Cr 8vo. Full crimson levant mor, gilt
panelled spines, t.e.g., others uncut.
(Traylen) **£520 [≈ $936]**
- The adventures of Peregrine Pickle; in which
are included, Memoirs of a lady of Quality.
London: for the author, 1751. 4 vols. x,288;
x,322; vi,205; viii,315 pp. Later gilt-panelled
mottled calf, spines gilt-dec, a.e.g.
(Gough) **£395 [≈ $711]**
- The adventures of Peregrine Pickle. In which
are included memoirs of a lady of quality.
London: for R. Baldwin ..., 1769. 4th edn.
12mo. Frontis to each vol. Contemp calf, jnts
a little worn.   *(Traylen)* **£50 [≈ $90]**
- The adventures of Sir Launcelot Greaves.
The second edition. Dublin: James Hoey,
1763. 2nd Dublin edn. 12mo. [ii],264,[22
contents & advts] pp. 2 engvd plates.
Contemp sheep.   *(Burmester)* **£90 [≈ $162]**

- The adventures of Telemachus, the son of Ulysses. Translated from the French ... London: for S. Crowder, 1776. 1st edn. 2 vols. 12mo. Half-titles. Contemp calf, rebacked, spines gilt. *(Bennett)* £225 [≈ $405]
- The expedition of Humphrey Clinker. London: W. Johnston, 1771. 1st edn, 1st iss. 3 vols. 12mo. A few ink deletions on 2 pp. Contemp calf, a little worn.
(Traylen) £290 [≈ $522]
- The history and adventures of an atom. London: Cooke, [1795]. 2 vols in 1. 8vo. 98; 80 pp. 2 engvd plates.
(Goodrich) $75 [≈ £41]
- Travels through France and Italy ... particular description of ... Nice. R. Baldwin, 1766. 2nd edn. 8vo. [iv],372; [iv],296 pp. Half-titles (sm piece missing from crnr in Vol II). Some early leaves a little browned at edges. Mod qtr calf, mrbld bds.
(Blackwell's) £160 [≈ $288]

Smollett, Tobias, et al.
- The history of England, from the Revolution to the end of the American War, and peace at Versailles in 1783. Phila: 1796-97. 5 vols. Lacking the 6 ports. Foxed, a few stains. Half calf, worn, spines torn.   *(Allen)* $50 [≈ £27]

Snape, Andrew
- The anatomy of a horse. London: for the authour, 1683, 1st edn. Folio. [xii],237,45 appendix, [iv table] pp. Engvd port, 48 (ex 49) engvd plates (missing plate 1 supplied in facs). Plate 13 restored, without loss. Wide-margined copy in early 20th c half calf.
(Gough) £325 [≈ $585]

Snelling, Thomas
- A view of the silver coin and coinage of England. From the Norman Conquest to the present time. London: the author, 1762. 1st edn. 4to. 55 pp. Engvd plates. Half calf, mrbld bds, a little worn, rebacked, crnrs reprd.   *(Tara)* £50 [≈ $90]

Solyman and Almena ...
- Solyman and Almena ... See Langhorne, John

Somerville, William
- The chase. A poem. London: for G. Hawkins ..., 1735. 1st 8vo. edn. [xx],131 pp. Contemp gilt bordered calf, a trifle worn.
(Young's) £80 [≈ $144]
- The chase. A poem. London: W. Bulmer, 1796. xv,vii,126 pp. 11 w'cut vignettes by the Bewicks. Scattered minor foxing, faintly

browned at edges. Later half mor, mrbld bds, paper sides a bit rubbed.
(Pirages) $200 [≈ £111]
- The chase. A poem. [With] Hobbinol, or the rural games. A burlesque poem ... London: for W. Bowyer ..., 1773. 2 works in 1 vol, as issued. 6th edn of each. 8vo. xvi,122; [4],82 pp. Frontis, 7 plates (faintly waterstained). Contemp calf, rebacked, crnrs reprd.
(Claude Cox) £25 [≈ $45]

Somner, William
- A treatise on the Roman ports and forts in Kent. Oxford: 1693. 1st edn. 8vo. Port. Contemp calf.   *(Robertshaw)* £85 [≈ $153]

Song-writing ...
- Essays on song-writing ... See Aikin, John

Sophocles
- The tragedies ... Translated from the Greek; with a dissertation on ancient tragedy, by the Rev. Thomas Francklin. London: 1766. 2nd edn. 2 vols. 8vo. Frontis, 2 vignette titles. Contemp calf.   *(Argosy)* $150 [≈ £83]

Sorrows of Werter ...
- The sorrows of Werter ... See Goethe, Johann Wolfgang von

Sotheby, William
- A tour through parts of Wales ... With engravings ... London: for R. Blamire, 1794. 1st edn. 4to. 13 sepia aquatint plates. Contemp panelled calf, rebacked, orig spine laid down, gilt.   *(Traylen)* £220 [≈ $396]
- A tour through parts of Wales, sonnets, odes and other poems. With engravings. London: R. Blamire, 1794. 4to. Half-title. Contemp calf, rebacked. *(C.R. Johnson)* £225 [≈ $405]
- A tour through parts of Wales, sonnets, odes and other poems. 1794. 4to. 120 pp. Half-title, 12 sepia plates. Cloth, upper hinge tender.   *(Edwards)* £100 [≈ $180]

South, Robert
- Thirty-six sermons and discourses on several subjects and occasions. Dublin: for P. Dugan ..., 1720. 5th edn. 2 vols. Folio. Contemp calf.   *(Lloyd-Roberts)* £50 [≈ $90]

Southey, Robert
- Letters written during a short residence in Spain and Portugal. Bristol: 1797. 1st edn. 8vo. Half-title, advt leaf at end. Sgntr on title, some leaves stained. Contemp calf, cvrs detchd.   *(Robertshaw)* £45 [≈ $81]

Southworth, John
- The last speech and confession. London: Brome, 1679. Folio. 2ff, binder's blanks. 19th c mor-backed bds, rebacked. Wing S4775.
(Marlborough) £65 [≈ $117]

Soveraign Antidote ...
- A soveraign antidote ... See Prynne, William

Spalding, Lyman
- An inaugural dissertation on the production of animal heat. Walpole, NH: D. Carlisle, 1797. 1st edn. 8vo. 30 pp. Uncut, stitched as issued.   *(Antiq Sc)* $185 [≈ £102]

Spallanzani, Lazzaro
- Tracts on the nature of animals and vegetables. Edinburgh: 1799. 1st edn. 394 pp. 6 plates. Title re-cornered. Mod qtr lea, mrbld bds, new endpapers.
(Scientia) $250 [≈ £138]

Sparke, Edward
- (Greek title, then) vel Scintilla Altaris. Primitive devotion, in the feasts and fasts of the Church of England. London: for J. Flesher, 1666. 4th edn. 8vo. Engvd frontis, red & black title (sl dusty), text ills. Mild waterstaining at end. Rebound qtr calf.
(Hughes) £55 [≈ $99]

Sparke, Michael
- Truth brought to light: or, the history of the first 14 years of King James I. In four parts. London: for Richard Baldwin, 1692. Engvd title, port frontis to 2nd part. Moderately browned throughout. Early 19th c blindstamped calf, nasty reback. Wing S4818C.   *(Charles Cox)* £35 [≈ $63]

Sparrow, Anthony
- A collection of articles, injunctions, canons ... and constitutions ecclesiastical ... London: Pawlet, 1676. 3rd imp. 4to. Engvd frontis, title, [x], title, 402,[iv] pp. Tables at end. Lacking final blank. Calf, sl surface wear, crnrs bumped.   *(P & P)* £60 [≈ $108]
- A collection of articles, injunctions, canons ... and constitutions ecclesiastical ... London: for Blanch Puwlet, 1684. 4th imp. 4to. 406 pp. Sep title to each part, frontis. Contemp calf. Wing S4826.   *(Edwards)* £110 [≈ $198]
- A rationale upon the Book of Common Prayer of the Church of England. London: T. Garthwait, 1657. [x],408,[xii] pp. Engvd frontis, addtnl title, 3 ports. Rec half mor. Wing S4828.   *(Clark)* £50 [≈ $90]

Specimen ...
- A specimen of naked truth ... See Vernon, Admiral Edward

Spectator ...
- The Spectator. London: for J. & R. Tonson ..., [1710-14]. 8 vols. Engvd frontis in each vol. Minor isolated worming. Contemp smooth calf, 2 spines with minor wear, 1 vol sl bowed.   *(Pirages)* $275 [≈ £152]
- The Spectator. London: J. & R. Tonson, 1753. 8 vols. 12mo. Engvd frontis & title in each vol. Sl spotted throughout. 18th c dark calf, spines gilt.
(Frew Mackenzie) £140 [≈ $252]

Speculations ...
- Speculations on the mode and appearances of impregnation ... See Couper, Robert

Speech ...
- The speech of the Right Honourable A-r O-w ... See Onslow, Arthur

Speeches ...
- The dying speeches and behaviour of the several State prisoners that have been executed the last 300 years. London: J. Brotherton ..., 1720. 8vo. [xx],495 pp. Title dusty. Rec half calf, mrbld bds.
(Clark) £32 [≈ $57]

Speed, John
- The history of Great Britain ... London: 1611. 1st edn. Folio. 151-894 pp (correct thus), 25ff. Engvd title. Lacking errata leaf at end. Mod buckram.
(Claude Cox) £150 [≈ $270]

Spelman, Sir Henry
- Villare Anglicum: or a view of all the cities, towns and villages in England ... T.H. for Robert Pawlett, 1678. 2nd edn, crrctd & amended. Engvd armorial frontis. Ink anntns on endpapers & in margs. Contemp calf, lacking label, jnts & backstrip worn.
(Deighton Bell) £30 [≈ $54]
- Villare Anglicum: or a view of all the cities, towns and villages in England ... London: T.H. for Robert Pawlett, 1678. 2nd edn, crrctd & amended. Engvd armorial frontis. Sm piece torn from top of 2 pp without loss. Rec half calf, mrbld bds.
(Cooper Hay) £95 [≈ $171]

Spelman, Sir John
- The life of Aelfred the Great ... With considerable additions and ... remarks, by ...

Thomas Hearne, M.A. Oxford: Atkins, 1709. 1st edn. 8vo. [iv],238 pp. Port, vignette title, addenda & emenda leaf. Contemp blindstamped calf, rebacked.
(P & P) **£98 [≈ $176]**

Spence, Joseph
- A parallel; in the manner of Plutarch: between a most celebrated man of Florence; and one, scarce ever heard of, in England ... Strawberry-Hill: 1758. One of 700. Inner gutter of title reprd. Early 19th c calf.
(Waterfield's) **£200 [≈ $360]**
- A parallel; in the manner of Plutarch: between a most celebrated man of Florence; and one, scarce ever heard of, in England ... Strawberry-Hill: 1758. Sm 8vo. Engvd vignette title, 3-104 pp. Contemp crimson mor gilt, sl rubbed, old reprs to hinges.
(Marlborough) **£450 [≈ $810]**
- Polymetis, or, an enquiry concerning the agreement between the works of the Roman poets and the remains of the ancient artists ... in ten books. London: for R. Dodsley, 1747. Folio. Port frontis, 41 plates. Contemp calf, some wear at crnrs, jnts cracked.
(Waterfield's) **£200 [≈ $360]**

Spencer, Benjamin
- Vox civitatis, or London's complaint against her children in the countrie ... London: for William Hope, 1636. 4to. [iv],31 pp. Lacking A1 (blank?), browned, stitching broken, margs brittle & chipped. Disbound. STC 23075.
(Clark) **£28 [≈ $50]**

Spenser, Edmund
- The Faerie Queene. London: for J. Brindley ..., 1751. 3 vols. 4to. 32 double-page copper plates by William Kent. Contemp mottled calf, rebacked.
(Traylen) **£225 [≈ $405]**
- The Faerie Queene. London: for M. Lownes, 1609-[1613]. Reiss of 1st folio edn. Lacking sep dated title to 2nd half. Title soiled & sl defective, some sl marks, lib label & stamp. Old half vell, some wear.
(Ash) **£200 [≈ $360]**
- Spenser's Faerie Queene. A new edition with ... notes ... by John Upton. London: J. & R. Tonson, 1758. 2 vols. 4to. xlii,[68],673; 673 pp. Contemp calf, rebacked, crnrs reprd.
(Claude Cox) **£150 [≈ $270]**
- The works ... whereunto is added an account of his life ... London: for Jonathan Edwin, 1679. 4to. 5ff, 339,16,[8], 258 [i.e. 254], 369-91 pp. Frontis reprd, 2 leaves re-margined, isolated stains. Contemp calf, rebacked, jnts cracked, crnrs bruised.
(Pirages) **£375 [≈ $208]**

Spilsbury, John
- A collection of fifty prints, from antique gems in the collections of ... Earl Percy ... and T.M. Slade ... London: Boydell, [1785]. 1st edn. 4to. 50 plates. Some light foxing. 3/4 mor, mrbld bds, some wear.
(Argonaut) **$125 [≈ £69]**

Spon, Jacob
- The history of Geneva. London: White, 1687. 1st English edn. Folio. Engvd frontis, 4 engvd plates. Contemp speckled calf, rebacked, new endpapers. Wing S5017.
(Marlborough) **£275 [≈ $495]**

Sportsman ...
- The sportsman's dictionary: or the gentleman's companion ... London: for G.G.J. & J. Robinson, 1785. 3rd edn. 4to. 16 engvd plates. Half polished calf, gilt spine.
(Traylen) **£180 [≈ $324]**

Spotswood, John
- The history of the Church of Scotland ... London: for Royston, 1655. 1st edn. Folio. Port frontis, red & black title, [xiv], port, [iv],546 pp, epitaph leaf, tables, ctlg leaf. 2 lib stamps. Calf, rebacked with new crnrs.
(P & P) **£115 [≈ $207]**

Sprat, Thomas
- The history of the Royal Society of London. London: Scott, 1702. 2nd edn. 4to. [7],438 pp. Plate. Old calf, rebacked.
(Goodrich) **$150 [≈ £83]**
- A true account and declaration of the horrid conspiracy against the late King ... The second edition. London: Thomas Newcomb, 1685. Folio. [vi],167; [ii],141 pp. Imprim leaf. Contemp panelled calf, worn, jnts tender, backstrip defective. Wing S5065.
(Clark) **£35 [≈ $63]**
- A true copy of the last Will and Testament of ... Thomas Lord Bishop of Rochester ... London: 1715. 14 pp. A little foxed, possibly lacking blank at end. Disbound.
(Charles Cox) **£18 [≈ $32]**

Sprengell, Conrad Joachim
- The Aphorisms of Hippocrates, and the Sentences of Celsus ... Aphorisms upon the smallpox, measles ... London: for R. Bonwick ..., 1708. 1st edn of this trans. 8vo. 2 engvd ports. Red & black title. Contemp panelled calf, Constable b'plate.
(Quaritch) **$525 [≈ £291]**

Stackhouse, Thomas
- A new history of the Holy Bible from the beginning of the world to the establishment of Christianity. London: for John Hilton, 1752. 2 vols. Folio. Engvd frontis, 97 plates (some fldg), 7 pp maps, 10 sm engvs. Contemp calf, jnts & spines worn.
(Lloyd-Roberts) **£120 [≈ $216]**

Stafford, William, Viscount
- The tryal of William Viscount Stafford for High Treason. Dublin: Jos. Ray, 1681. Sm 4to. 282 pp. Old calf.
(Emerald Isle) **£125 [≈ $225]**

Standing Armies ...
- A short history of standing armies in England ... See Trenchard, John

Stanley, John Thomas
- An account of the hot springs in Iceland; with an analysis of their waters. [Edinburgh?:] n.d. [ca 1793]. 8vo. Title (loose), 100 pp. Last page soiled, title a little so, marg stains at beginning & end, short tear in last leaf. Sewn (as issued?).
(Weiner) **£300 [≈ $540]**

Stanley, Thomas
- The history of philosophy. London: Thomas Bassett ..., 1687. 2nd edn. Folio. [xxvi],228, 351-[588], 737-1091 pp. Port frontis, 26 ports, 2 text engvs. Outer marg frontis & title frayed, upper marg dampstained. Old reversed calf, worn, shabby. Wing S5239.
(Clark) **£105 [≈ $189]**

Stanyan, Abraham
- An account of Switzerland, written in the year 1714. London: 1714. 1st edn. 8vo. 247 pp. Title within rules with a sm port vignette. Contemp calf, spine elab gilt, a little rubbed.
(Bonham) **£75 [≈ $135]**

Stapleton, Sir Robert
- Juvenal's sixteen satyrs or, a survey of the manners and actions of mankind. London: for Peter Parker ..., 1673. 3rd edn of this trans. Terminal blank. Old calf, rebacked. Wing J1292.
(Charles Cox) **£20 [≈ $36]**

State of the Nation ...
- The state of the nation, with a general balance of the publick accounts. London: M. Cooper, 1748. 2nd edn. 55 pp. Half-title, fldg table. Disbound.
(C.R. Johnson) **£40 [≈ $72]**

State Trials
- A complete collection of State Trials and

proceedings for High Treason ... London: 1742-66. 10 vols. Folio. Red & black titles. Lacking 4 pp vol 10 index, old sgntrs on blank prelims. Contemp mottled calf, uniformly rebacked.
(Bow Windows) **£750 [≈ $1,350]**

Staughton, William
- A discourse, occasioned by the sudden death of three young persons, by drowning. Phila: 1797. 8vo. Disbound. *(Spelman)* **£20 [≈ $36]**

Staunton, Sir George
- An authentic account of an embassy from the King of Great Britain to the Emperor of China. London: G. Nicol, 1797. 3 vols. 8vo. 3 fldg maps (1 reprd). Vol 1 H4 torn without loss. Contemp mottled calf, rebacked, crnrs lightly bumped.
(Frew Mackenzie) **£210 [≈ $378]**

Staveley, Thomas
- The Romish horseleech: or, an impartial account of the intolerable charge of popery to this nation ... London: R. Baldwin ..., 1769. 2nd edn. Sm 8vo. [36],286 pp. Contemp mottled calf, rubbed, outer hinges cracked but holding. *(Karmiole)* **$75 [≈ £41]**

Stebbing, Henry
- An essay concerning civil government. London: Bowyer, 1724. New qtr calf.
(Marlborough) **£75 [≈ $135]**

Stedman, Charles
- The history of the origin, progress, and termination of the American War ... London: 1794. 2 vols in 1. Lge 4to. 446; 502 pp. 15 maps & plans (1 map marginally trimmed). Calf & mrbld bds, some rubbing to spine, front hinge cracking. *(Reese)* **$1,750 [≈ £972]**

Stedman, John Gabriel
- Narrative of a five years' expedition against the revolted negroes of Surinam in Guinea ... the history of that country ... 1796. 1st edn. 2 vols. 4to. xviii,407; iv,4004, index pp. 77 (ex 80) engvd plates inc 2 fldg maps. Lightly browned. Half mor. *(Edwards)* **£550 [≈ $990]**

Steele, Richard
- The crisis: or, a discourse representing ... the just causes of the late happy revolution ... Edinburgh: reprinted ..., 1714. 8vo. 58,[ii advts] pp. Couple of stains on title, some light browning. Later wraps.
(Frew Mackenzie) **£50 [≈ $90]**
- The lover. To which is added, the Reader; by the same author. London: J. Tonson, 1725. 1st coll edn. F'cap 8vo. [12],297,[13] pp.

Some foxing, a few marg reprs. Contemp calf, rebacked.   (*Spelman*) £35 [≈ $63]

Steele, Sir Richard

- The Englishmen: being a sequel of the Guardian. London: Sam. Buckley, 1714. 8vo. [ii],vi, 410,[xiv] pp. Sm nick at hd of title. Contemp calf, rebacked, spine gilt, a little rubbed & scuffed.   (*Clark*) £68 [≈ $122]
- Poetical miscellanies, consisting of original poems and translations. By the best hands. London: J. Tonson, 1727. 2nd edn. 12mo. Engvd frontis. Contemp calf gilt, rebacked.
(*Deighton Bell*) £45 [≈ $81]

Stellatus, Marcellus Palingenious (pseud?)

- See Manzolli, Pietro Angelo

Stephens, Edward

- Observations upon a treatise intituled Of Humane Reason. London: for John Leigh, 1675. Contemp sheep, rather rubbed, text loose in case. Wing S5430.
(*Waterfield's*) £400 [≈ $720]

Stern, Laurence

- The works. In ten volumes complete. London: J. Rivington, 1788. Port frontis & plates, some by Hogarth. Contemp tree-calf, red & green labels, spines gilt.
(*C.R. Johnson*) £550 [≈ $990]

Sterne, Laurence

- Letters ... to his most intimate friends. With a fragment in the manner of Rabelais. London: T. Beckett, 1775. 1st edn. 3 vols in 1. Sm 8vo. Frontis to vol 1. Contemp half calf, gilt spine.   (*Spelman*) £250 [≈ $450]
- Letters to his most intimate friends ... published by his daughter, Mrs. Medalle. London: 1776. New edn. 3 vols. 16mo. Frontis. Contemp calf, gilt.
(*Argosy*) $125 [≈ £69]
- The life and opinions of Tristram Shandy ... London: R. & J. Dodsley ..., 1760-67. 9 vols. Vols 1 & 2 2nd edns, 3-9 1st edns. 2 frontis by Hogarth, 12 hand-cold plates. Lacking some half-titles. Contemp panelled calf, a.e.g., lacking some spine labels.
(*Argosy*) $1,500 [≈ £833]
- The life and opinions of Tristram Shandy ... London: 1760-67. 9 vols in 8. Vols 1 & 2 1st London edns, 3-9 1st edns. Half-titles in vols 4,5,6 & 9, as called for, frontis in vol 3. Contemp calf.   (*Jenkins*) $1,250 [≈ £694]
- The life and opinions of Tristram Shandy. London: J. Dodsley, 1772-73. 6 vols. 12mo. Vols 1 & 2 9th edns, 3-6 new edns. Frontis by

Hogarth vol 1, half-title vol 3. Contemp calf, some rubbing, some cracking to jnts, spines chipped at extremities.
(*Frew Mackenzie*) £80 [≈ $144]
- A sentimental journey through France and Italy. By Mr. Yorick. London: for John Taylor, 1790. 4 vols in 1. 12mo. 224 [i.e. 234] pp. Couple of tears affecting text without serious loss. Contemp sheep, rebacked.
(*Burmester*) £40 [≈ $72]

Stevenson, John Hall

- Crazy tales and fables for grown gentlemen. London: J. Dodsley, 1780. New edn. 8vo. Frontis. Contemp calf, jnts cracked, inner hinges taped.   (*Robertshaw*) £60 [≈ $108]
- The works ... Containing Crazy tales and fables for grown gentlemen, lyric epistles ... monkish epitaphs, &c. ... London: for J. Debrett ..., 1795. 1st coll edn. 3 vols. 8vo. Half-title & engvd frontis in each vol. 19th c polished tan calf, gilt, by Bedford.
(*Traylen*) £150 [≈ $270]

Stewart, Dugald

- Outlines of moral philosophy. For the use of students in the University of Edinburgh. Edinburgh: for William Creech ..., 1793. 1st edn. 8vo. Half-title. Contemp calf, edges a bit worn, rebacked. Sgntr of James Smith Kidston (Edinburgh 1796) on half-title.
(*Hughes*) £165 [≈ $297]

Stiles, Ezra

- A history of three of the judges of Charles I ... who ... fled to America, and were ... concealed, in Massachusetts and Connecticutt, for nearly thirty years ... Hartford: 1794. 358,[1] pp. Port frontis, 2 fldg maps, plates, advt leaf. 19th c mor, gilt.
(*Reese*) $325 [≈ £180]

Stillingfleet, B.J.

- Miscellaneous tracts relating to natural history, husbandry, and physick. To which is added the calendar of flora. London: 1762. 2nd edn. xxxi,391 pp. 11 plates. Contemp sprinkled calf, spine gilt, sl rubbed.
(*Whitehart*) £110 [≈ $198]

Stillingfleet, Benjamin

- Some thoughts concerning happiness. By Irenaeus Krantzovius. Translated from the original German. London: for W. Webb, 1738. 1st edn. 8vo. 31 pp. 1st & last leaves rather soiled. Disbound.
(*Bennett*) £75 [≈ $135]

Stillingfleet, E.

- The grand question, concerning the Bishops right to vote in Parliament in cases capital ... London: M.P. ..., 1680. 1st edn. 8vo. Title, 188 pp. Waterstaining & ink marks in some margs, 1 leaf torn without loss. Front bd detchd. *(P & P)* £25 [≈ $45]

Stillingfleet, Edward

- Fifty sermons preachen upon several occasions. London: 1707. Folio. Port. Contemp panelled calf, crnrs bumped.
  (Robertshaw) £22 [≈ $39]
- Origines Britannicae, or, the antiquities of the British Churches. London: for Henry Mortlock, 1685. 1st edn. Folio. [2],lxxiii, [9],364 pp. Red & black title. Lightly soiled. 18th c half calf, mrbld sides, worn.
  (Claude Cox) £65 [≈ $117]
- A rational account of the grounds of the Protestant religion. London: for H. Mortlock, 1681. 2nd edn. Folio. xxii,608 pp. Sm worming in margs of 1st few leaves. Contemp calf, 2 short splits in jnts. Wing S5625.
  (Lloyd-Roberts) £60 [≈ $108]

Stone, Edward

- A new mathematical dictionary. London: 1743. 2nd edn. 8vo. xii,[278] pp. Num text w'cuts. Old calf, jnts reprd, new labels.
  (Pollak) £85 [≈ $153]

Stone, John Hurford

- Copies of original letters recently written by persons in Paris to Dr. Priestley in America ... London: for J. Wright, 1798. 3rd edn. x,36 pp. Disbound. *(Young's)* £32 [≈ $57]

Store-house ...

- A rich storehouse, or treasury of the diseased ... many approved medicines ... for ... poorer sort of people. By G.W. London: 1650. 274 pp. Calf, rebacked, some scuffing.
  (Rittenhouse) $775 [≈ £430]

Stow, John

- The survey of London. London: 1633. 3rd edn. Folio. W'cut frontis, num w'cuts in text. 2ff reprd without loss of text, crnr of frontis & title reprd. Old calf, rebacked.
  (Robertshaw) £300 [≈ $540]
- The survey of London. London: 1633. Folio. Many hand-cold coats-of-arms in text. 1 leaf supplied in facsimile, lib stamps on title verso, margs of endleaves sl frayed. New mor. STC 23345. *(Stewart)* £165 [≈ $297]

Stringer, Moses

- Opera mineralia explicata: or, the mineral kingdom, within the dominions of Great Britain, display'd. London: n.d. [ca 1713]. Sm 8vo. 4ff,xii, 7-308, 16 ctlg pp. Staining to lower part, sm hole in 1 leaf. Ctlg cropped. Contemp calf, v worn, rebacked.
  (Weiner) £210 [≈ $378]

Strong, Nathan

- Doctrine of eternal misery reconcileable with the infinite benevolence of God. Hartford: Hudson & Goodwin, 1796. 408 pp. Lacking front blank. Lea, rubbed.
  (Xerxes) $200 [≈ £111]

Strother, Edward

- An essay on sickness and health ... for the regulation of diseas'd and healthy persons ... Dr. Cheyne's mistaken opinions ... H.P. for Charles Rivington, 1725. 1st edn. 8vo. lxviii,64, 64 bis-79, 81-463, [1 advts] pp. Contemp panelled calf, reprd.
  (Fenning) £165 [≈ $297]

Strutt, Joseph

- A biographical dictionary ... of all the engravers, from the earliest period ... an essay on the rise and progress of the art of engraving ... J. Davis, 1785-86. 2 vols. 4to. 18 plates. Contemp calf, rebacked. Ex Lincoln's Inn lib with stamp on frontis.
  (Spelman) £140 [≈ $252]
- A supplement to the regal and ecclesiastical antiquities, manners, customs, arms, habits, &c., of the English. London: for the author, 1792. 4to. 12 engvd plates. Some light foxing. Old parchment-backed wraps, a little frayed.
  (Clark) £25 [≈ $45]

Stuart, Andrew

- Letters to ... Lord Mansfield. printed in the month of january, 1773. 1st edn. 8vo. [ii],64,47, [i],47,[i blank] pp. Engvd title with vignette. Lacking half-title. Disbound.
  (Blackwell's) £45 [≈ $81]

Stuart, Gilbert

- A view of society in Europe, in its progress from rudeness to refinement ... Edinburgh: for John Bell ..., 1778. 1st edn. 4to. Half-title, errata leaf. Early 19th c half calf, gilt.
  (Traylen) £775 [≈ $1,395]

Stukeley, William

- Itinerarium curiosum. London: Baker, Leigh, 1776. 2nd edn. 2 vols in 1. Folio. x,[21]; [iv,[290] pp. 210 copperplate engvs, some fldg. Previous owner's ms index. Old calf,

Victorian rebacking.   *(Ash)* £600 [≈ $1,080]

Suckling, Sir John
- The works ... Containing his poems, letters and plays. London: for Jacob Tonson, 1709. 2nd edn. 8vo. Engvd title, sep title to each part. Contemp polished calf.
    (Chaucer Head) £160 [≈ $288]

Sugar and Mutiny ...
- Considerations upon the Sugar and Mutiny Bills, addressed to the people of Ireland in general and the citizens of Dublin in particular. Dublin: Byrne, 1780. 8vo. 31 pp. Advts. Bds.   *(Emerald Isle)* £85 [≈ $153]
- A dispassionate examen of the most popular objections against the Sugar and Mutiny Acts, with some conclusive arguments ... Dublin: J. & W. Porter, 1782. 2nd edn. 8vo. 85 pp. Bds.
    (Emerald Isle) £85 [≈ $153]

Sullivan, James
- Observations upon the Government of the United States of America. Boston: 1791. 55 pp. Mor. The Deering copy, with his b'plate.
    (Reese) £500 [≈ £277]

Sullivan, R.J.
- Philosophical rhapsodies ... containing reflections on the laws, manners, customs ... of certain Asiatic, Afric and European nations. 1784-85. 1st edn. 3 vols. 8vo. vii,286; 463; 315 pp. Sl marg foxing. Half calf, all jnts cracked, extremities sl rubbed.
    (Old Cinema) £65 [≈ $117]

Sully, Duke of
- Memoirs of Maximillian de Bethune, Duke of Sully, Prime Minister to Henry the Great ... London: for A. Millar ..., 1761. 3rd edn. 3 vols. 2 engvd ports, engvd fldg map. Occas v light spotting, sl wear to crnrs. Contemp diced gilt-dec russia. *(Gough)* £195 [≈ $351]

Summers, John
- A short account of the success of warm bathing in paralytic disorders. London: 1751. 2nd edn. 8vo. 38 pp. Rec calf.
    (Goodrich) $125 [≈ £69]

Sutherland, Alexander
- The nature and qualities of Bristol-water; illustrated by experiments and observations ...Bristol: E. Farley, 1758. 1st edn. 8vo. Half mor, gilt.   *(Traylen)* £85 [≈ $153]

Sutton, Samuel
- An historical account ... for extracting the

foul air out of ships ... annexed two relations ... and A discourse on the scurvy by Dr. Mead. London: Brindley, 1749. 1st edn of the Mead. 8vo. viii,120 pp. Fldg engvd plate. Lge copy in contemp calf, sl rubbed.
    (Pickering) $850 [≈ £472]

Swedenborg, Emanuel
- Apocalypse revealed. Manchester: Wheeler, 1791. 2 vols. 639; 629 pp. Some contemp ink notes. 3/4 lea, both top bds detchd.
    (Xerxes) $200 [≈ £111]
- Concerning the earths in our solar system which are called planets. London: Hindmarsh, 1787. 212 pp. Some spotting throughout. New lea spine.
    (Xerxes) $100 [≈ £55]
- The delights of wisdom concerning conjugial love; after which follow the pleasures of insanity concerning scortatory love. London: Hindmarsh, 1794. 1st English edn. 4to. Repr to title & following leaf. Rec qtr calf.
    (Marlborough) £135 [≈ $243]
- Delights of wisdom concerning concerning conjugial love: after which follow the pleasures of insanity concerning scortatory love. Phila: F. & R. Bailey, 1796. xxxii,521,[2] pp. Lea backstrip, lacking bds & blank endpapers.   *(Xerxes)* $200 [≈ £111]
- The wisdom of angels concerning the divine providence. Boston: Isaiah Thomas ..., 1796. 2nd Amer edn (?). 543 pp. Contemp calf.
    (Karmiole) $100 [≈ £55]

Swift, Deane
- An essay upon the life, writings and character of Dr. Jonathan Swift ... London: for Charles Bathurst ..., 1765. 1st edn. [iv],365, [1],53,4 subscription proposal pp. Contemp calf.
    (Young's) £95 [≈ $171]

Swift, Jonathan
- Baucis and Philemon: a poem on the ever-lamented loss of two yew-trees, in the parish of Chilthorne ... London: H. Hide, 1710. 8vo. 16 pp. Later wraps.   *(Argosy)* $75 [≈ £41]
- Cadenus and Vanessa. A poem. To which is added, a true and faithful inventory of the goods belonging to Dr. S--t ... upon lending his house to the Bishop of -- ... London: for N. Blandford, 1726. 4th edn. 8vo. 31,[i] pp. A little soiling. Mod grey wraps.
    (Bennett) £175 [≈ $315]
- A complete collection of genteel and ingenious conversation, according to the most polite mode and method now used at court ... London: for B. Motte ..., 1738. 1st edn, 1st iss. 8vo. Without advt leaf before title.

Untrimmed in orig calf-backed mrbld bds.
(Pirages) **$1,100 [≈ £611]**
- The conduct of the allies, and of the late ministry in beginning and carrying out the present war. London: 1711. 5th edn. 48 pp. Title dustsoiled, Disbound.
(Robertshaw) **£15 [≈ $27]**
- Good Queen Anne vindicated, and the ingratitude, insolence, etc. of her Whig ministry and allies detected and exposed ... The second edition. London: W. Owen, 1748. 72 pp. Half-title.
(C.R. Johnson) **£95 [≈ $171]**
- The history of the four last years of the Queen. London: for A. Millar, 1758. 1st edn. 8vo. xvi,392 pp. Contemp calf, spine heavily gilt, jnts partly cracked, minor wear.
(Pirages) **$175 [≈ £97]**
- The history of the four last years of the Queen. London: for A. Millar, 1758. 1st edn. 8vo. xvi,392 pp. Contemp polished calf.
(Young's) **£60 [≈ $108]**
- A tale of a tub. Written for the universal improvement of mankind. London: for John Nutt, 1704. 3rd edn, crrctd. 8vo. Contemp calf, a little worn, rebacked.
(Traylen) **£95 [≈ $171]**
- A tale of a tub, to which is added an account of a battel between the ancient and modern books in St. James's Library. 1711. [2],310 pp, 1f. Medial blank & blank at end. Contemp Cambridge calf, spine ends & crnrs worn, jnts a little rubbed. *(Pirages)* **$125 [≈ £69]**
- Travels into several remote nations of the world ... by Captain Lemuel Gulliver. London: for P. Turnbull, 1766. 4 pts in 1 vol. 8vo. xviii,86,[2]; 95,[3]; [ii],87,[3]; 109,[5] pp. Sl worming in inner marg. Contemp sheep, rebacked. *(Burmester)* **£150 [≈ $270]**
- Travels into several remote nations of the world; by Lemuel Gulliver. In four parts. London: for C. Bathurst, 1755. 8vo. 10 plates. Lacking half-title. Calf, worn.
(Stewart) **£75 [≈ $135]**
- The works ... in eight volumes. Dublin: George Faulkner, 1751-42-46. 8 vols. 8vo. Engvd ports, maps & plates. Contemp calf, gilt, jnts very worn, most spine labels missing. *(Bennett)* **£150 [≈ $270]**

Swinburne, Henry
- A treatise of testaments and last wills. 1743. 6th edn, crrctd. Folio. 567 pp. Contemp calf.
(Edwards) **£170 [≈ $306]**

Swinton, John
- A proposal for uniformity of weights and measures in Scotland ... With tables of the

English and Scottish standards ... Edinburgh: for Charles Elliot ..., 1779. 1st edn. 8vo. Half-title, Some minor marg staining. Uncut in orig bds, spine defective.
(Hughes) **£65 [≈ $117]**

Switzer, Stephen
- An introduction to a general system of hydrostaticks and hydraulicks, philosophical and practical. London: for T. Astley ..., 1729. 1st edn. 2 vols. 4to. Engvd frontis, 61 plates (60 fldg). 20th c half calf, bds.
(Chaucer Head) **£1,000 [≈ $1,800]**
- The nobleman, gentleman, and gardener's recreation: or, an introduction to gardening, planting, agriculture ... London: 1715. 1st edn. 8vo. Frontis. Contemp calf.
(Robertshaw) **£150 [≈ $270]**
- The nobleman, gentleman, and gardener's recreation: or, an introduction to gardening, planting, agriculture ... London: B. Barker, 1715. 1st edn. 8vo. [8],xxxiv, 266,[16] pp. Engvd frontis. Contemp calf, sm repr on upper jnt. Ex lib Colquhoun of Luss.
(Spelman) **£420 [≈ $756]**

Switzerland ...
- An account of Switzerland ... See Stanyan, Abraham

Sydenham, Thomas
- Dr. Sydenham's compleat method of curing almost all diseases ... To which are now added, five discourses by the same author ... London: for J. Hodges, 1737. 7th edn. 12mo. [viii],202, [6] pp. 18th c cloth.
(Burmester) **£45 [≈ $81]**
- The entire works ... Third edition with all the notes inserted by John Swan, M.D. London: 1753. 8vo. 692 pp. Old calf.
(Halewood) **£85 [≈ $153]**
- The whole works. London: for Richard Wellington ..., 1696. 1st edn in English. [xxiv],592 (i.e. 488) pp. 1st 2 leaves a little chipped, some browning. Mod half calf.
(Ash) **£250 [≈ $450]**
- The whole works. London: for Richard Wellington ..., 1696. 1st edn in English. 8vo. [24],592 pp. Pagination error but complete. Sgntr on title. Mod calf, gilt. Wing 6305.
(Hemlock) **£575 [≈ £319]**

Symmonds, Edward
- A vindication of King Charles I. or a loyal subjects duty. London: 1693. 2nd edn. [xiv],384 pp. Old speckled calf, rebacked.
(Young's) **£42 [≈ $75]**

Symson, Andrew

- Tripatriarchicon; or, the lives of the three Patriarchs Abraham, Isaac & Jacob. Edinburgh: for the author, 1705. 1st edn. 8vo. [ii],8,[xvi], 374 pp. Contemp calf, rebacked. Author's pres copy inscrbd to George Fleming, Archdeacon of Carlisle.
(Bennett) £275 [≈ $495]

Synge, Edward

- A sermon preach'd in Christ's Church, Dublin, before his Excellence The Lord Carteret ... Thanksgiving for the discovery of the Gunpowder Plot ... Dublin: A. Rhames, 1724. Sm 4to. 25 pp. Mod wraps.
(Emerald Isle) £45 [≈ $81]

System of Magick ...

- A system of magick ... See Defoe, Daniel

System of Trade ...

- The proposed system of trade with Ireland ... See Rose, George

Systema Agriculturae ...

- Systema agriculturae ... See Worlidge, John

T.M.

- See Moffett, Thomas

Tables ...

- Tables for correcting the apparent distance of the moon ... See Shepherd, A.

Tait, A.

- The right of the House of Stewart to the Crown of Scotland consider'd. Edinburgh: 1746. 2nd edn. 24 pp. Disbound.
(C.R. Johnson) £35 [≈ $63]

Tanner, John

- The hidden treasures of the art of physick; fully discovered in four books. London: George Sawbridge, 1659. 1st edn. Thick sm 8vo. Errata at end. Old calf, jnts reprd. Wing T138.   *(Traylen)* £675 [≈ $1,215]

Tanner, Thomas

- The entrance of Mazzarini. or; some memorial of the state of France ... Oxford: for Thom. Robinson, 1657. 1st edn. 12mo. Lacking initial blank. Faint waterstains at end. Contemp panelled sheep (damaged by worn & rebacked). Wing T140.
(Hannas) £35 [≈ $63]

Tans'ur, William

- The elements of musick display'd ...

rudimental, practical, philosophical, historical, and technical. London: Stanley Crowder, 1772. 1st edn. 8vo. Engvd frontis (stained). Internally very grubby. New qtr calf.   *(Marlborough)* £250 [≈ $450]

Taplin, William

- The gentleman's stable directory, or modern system of farriery; all the most valuable prescriptions and remedies, etc. Dublin: Wogan, 1793. 2 vols in 1. 8vo. Contemp calf, crack in 1 spine. *(Emerald Isle)* £65 [≈ $117]
- The gentleman's stable directory, or modern system of farriery, prescriptions and approved remedies ... London: 1796. 13th edn. Thick 8vo. 504 pp. Frontis. Bds, uncut.
(Halewood) £65 [≈ $117]

Tarleton, Sir Banastre

- A history of the campaigns of 1780 and 1781, in the Southern Provinces of North America. Dublin: 1787. 2nd edn. vii,533 pp. Paper loss to top outer crnr of title & 1st contents leaf with sl loss. Contemp calf, front hinge & spine rubbed.   *(Reese)* £550 [≈ £305]
- A history of the campaigns of 1780 and 1781, in the Southern Provinces of North America. London: T. Cadell, 1787. 4to. 518,[ii] pp. Fldg frontis map, 4 fldg plans (all partly hand-cold, reprd or rebacked), advt leaf at rear. A bit discold & soiled. Rec calf.
(Pirages) $1,250 [≈ £694]

Tasso, Torquato

- Godfrey of Bullogne: or the recouerie of Jerusalem. Done into English heroicall verse by Edward Fairefax. London: John Bill, 1624. 4to. New half mottled calf, gilt dec spine. STC 23699. *(Traylen)* £240 [≈ $432]
- Jerusalem delivered ... Translated ... by John Hoole. London: for J. Johnson ..., 1797. 2 vols. 12mo. [ii],lviii, 17-286; [iv],264, [48] pp. 2 engvd frontis, 2 half-titles. Contemp calf, spines a bit worn, labels chipped. Pres inscrptn from John Cator.
(Burmester) £45 [≈ $81]
- Jerusalem delivered: an heroic poem translated from the Italian. Printed for the Associated Booksellers, 1797. 2 vols. 8vo. Lge paper. Stipple engvd tinted port, extra illust with steel engvd plates & 20 copper engvs. Str-grained mor, a.e.g., sl rubbed.
(Deighton Bell) £75 [≈ $135]

Tate, Nahum

- Brutus of Alba: or, the enchanted lovers. A tragedy ... London: for Jacob Tonson, 1678. 1st edn. 8vo. 4ff, 56,[2] pp. Title & top of most leaves browned & foxed, a few leaves sl defective in marg. Disbound.

(Pirages) **$125 [≈£69]**

- A congratulatory poem to His Royal Highness Prince George of Denmark ... upon the glorious successes at sea. London: Henry Hills, 1708. A piracy. Disbound.

(Charles Cox) **£45 [≈$81]**

- A duke and no duke. A farce, as it is acted by their Majesties servants. London: for Henry Bonwicke, 1685. 1st edn. 4to. 7 pp typographical music. Disbound. Wing T181.

(Hannas) **£140 [≈$252]**

- Mausolaeum: a funeral poem. London: Aylmer, Rogers ..., 1695. 1st edn. Sm folio. Engvd frontis. 19th c mottled calf, dentelles gilt, cvrs faded. Wing T194.

(Marlborough) **£200 [≈$360]**

- On the sacred memory of our late Sovereign: with congratulations to his present Majesty. London: for Henry Playford, 1685. 1st edn. Folio. [2],6 pp. Title within mourning border. Disbound. Wing T200.

(Hannas) **£110 [≈$198]**

Tauvry, Daniel

- A new rational anatomy ... made English ... London: for D. Midwinter ..., 1701. 1st English edn. [xvi],301 pp. Engvd frontis, 21 plates. 2 leaves of table misbound, dustsoiled & dampstained in places, short tear in 1 leaf. Contemp calf, jnts reprd.

(Pickering) **£650 [≈£361]**

Taylor, Sir James, Lord Mayor of Dublin

- Lucas detected; or a vindication of the Sheriffs and commons of the city of Dublin; from the scandalous aspersions ... Dublin: Peter Wilson, 1749. 2nd edn, crrctd. 16 pp. Rebound in bds. *(C.R. Johnson)* **£25 [≈$45]**

Taylor, Jeremy

- Antiquitates Christianae or ... the life and death of the Holy Jesus ... lives, acts ... of His Apostles. London: for R. Royston, 1684. 7th edn. 2 pts in 1 vol. Folio. vii,lii, x,xxvi,432, [12 index]; 188 pp. Engvd & ptd titles. Contemp calf. Wing T288.

(Lloyd-Roberts) **£150 [≈$270]**

- A dissuasive from popery. The first part ... the second part. London: for R. Royston, 1668-67. 4th, 1st edns. 2 vols in 1. 4to. Early leaves sl browned. Contemp calf, rec rebacked. *(Stewart)* **£60 [≈$108]**

- The golden grove, or manuall of daily prayers and letanies. London: 1655. 1st edn. 12mo. A few headlines shaved, lacking final advt leaf. Later calf, some wear. Wing T336.

(Robertshaw) **£48 [≈$86]**

- The great exemplar of sanctity and holy life. London: 1649. 1st edn. 3 pts in 1 vol. Engvd vignette on 1st title. Sm repr to 1st title. Contemp calf, rebacked, new endpapers.

(Robertshaw) **£75 [≈$135]**

- The great exemplar of sanctity and holy life according to the Christian institution ... In three parts. London: for Francis Ash, 1649. 1st edn. 4to. Red & black title. Contemp calf, rebacked. Wing T342.

(Hannas) **£90 [≈$162]**

- The great exemplar of sanctity and holy life. London: for R. Royston, 1657. 3rd edn. 3 pts. Folio. [lii],600,[x] pp. Engvd frontis, addtnl engvd title, 11 (ex 12) double-page engvs. Contemp calf, spine chipped, stitching weak. Wing T344. *(Lloyd-Roberts)* **£60 [≈$108]**

- The rule and exercises of holy living ... of holy dying. London: T. Horne ..., 1719. 23rd edn. 8vo. 2 vols in 1. 2 frontis, 2 fldg plates. Margs on contents leaves torn, final blank defective. Contemp calf.

(Stewart) **£30 [≈$54]**

- Unum necessarium. Or, the doctrine and practice of repentance. London: for R. Royston, 1655. 1st edn. 8vo. Red & black title, addtnl engvd title, double plate (sm stain in upper crnr). Mod calf. Wing T415.

(Hannas) **£120 [≈$216]**

- The worthy communicant: or, a discourse of the nature, effects, and blessings consequent to the worthy receiving of the Lord's Supper ... London: for John Martyn, 1678. 8vo. Engvd frontis. Tears to 2 leaves, 1 with loss of catchword. Contemp calf, rebacked.

(Charles Cox) **£50 [≈$90]**

- The worthy communicant: or, a discourse of the nature, effects, and blessings consequent to the worthy receiving of the Lord's Supper ... London: for A. Churchil, 1683. Cr 8vo. Engvd frontis. Contemp calf, panelled spine gilt. Armorial b'plate. Wing T421.

(Stewart) **£60 [≈$108]**

Taylor, Michael

- A sexagesimal table, exhibiting at sight, the result of any proportion, where the terms do not exceed sixty minutes ... London: 1780. 1st ed. 8vo. xlv,[i errata],[2],316 pp. Fldg table. Contemp tree-calf, spine gilt, jnts cracked.

(Pickering) **$350 [≈£194]**

- Tables of logarithms ... sines and tangents ... with a preface ... by Neville Maskelyne ... London: 1792. Folio. [xiv], 64 pp. The text only, lacking the tables. A few contemp anntns. Old mrbld bds, mod calf spine.

(Weiner) **£50 [≈$90]**

Taylor, Samuel

- An essay intended to establish a standard for an universal system of stenography or shorthand writing ... London: for the author, 1786. [18],98,x pp. Engvd title, 11 engvd plates (as called for). Old tree-calf, rebacked, crnrs bumped.   *(Karmiole)* **$175** [≈ £97]
- An essay intended to establish a standard for an universal system of stenography or shorthand writing ... London: privately printed, 1786. 1st edn. 8vo. Engvd title, 11 engvd plates. Contemp tree-calf, 19th c rebacking, gilt, 2 sm wormholes, crnrs frayed.
(Chaucer Head) **£200** [≈ $360]

Taylor, Thomas

- The Cratylus, Phaedo, Parmenides, and Timaeus of Plato. London: White, 1793. 8vo. later cloth-backed bds, partly uncut.
(Marlborough) **£350** [≈ $630]

Taylor, Zach.

- The Surrey imposter: being an answer to a pamphlet, entitled The Surrey Demoniack. London: 1697. 8vo. iv,75 pp. W'block ills, errata slip. Sl cropped, sm hole in 1 leaf with loss of 1 word. Rebound in qtr mor, gilt, bds sl worn.   *(Edwards)* **£175** [≈ $315]

Telescope, Tom (pseud.)

- The Newtonian system of philosophy; explained by familiar objects in an entertaining manner for the use of young ladies and gentlemen. London: Ogilvy ..., 1798. 2ff, 137,[ii] pp. Engvd frontis, 4 plates, final advt leaf. Orig sprinkled sheep, jnts cracked.   *(Pirages)* **$150** [≈ £83]

Temple, Sir John

- The Irish rebellion: or, an history of the ... General rebellion ... October, 1641 ... added ... History of the Siege of Drogheda ... Tryal of Connor Lord Maguire ... Dublin: 1724. 3 pts. 4to. Frontis. 1st title red & black. Contemp half calf, rebacked.
(Hannas) **£65** [≈ $117]

Temple, Thomas

- Christ's government in and over his people ... a sermon before the ... house of Commons ... Octob.26, 1642. London: S. Gellibrand, 1642. 4to. [vi],50 pp. Initial license leaf detchd. Disbound. Wing T634.
(Clark) **£20** [≈ $36]

Temple, Sir William

- An introduction to the history of England. W.S. for Richard & Ralph Simpson, 1708. 3rd edn. 8vo. [viii],310 pp. Contemp sprinkled calf, backstrip gilt, front jnt cracked but firm.   *(Blackwell's)* **£50** [≈ $90]
- An introduction to the history of England. London: for Richard Simpson, 1699. 2nd edn. 8vo. Contemp calf. Armorial b'plate. Wing T639.   *(Stewart)* **£75** [≈ $135]
- Letters written by Sir W. Temple ... containing ... the most important transactions that pass'd in Christendom from 1665 to 1672. London: for J. Tonson ..., 1700. 1st edn. 2 vols. 8vo. Port. Some foxing. Contemp polished sheep, vol 1 jnts tender.
(Charles Cox) **£100** [≈ $180]
- Memoirs of what past in Christendom from the War begun 1672 to the peace concluded 1679. London: for Ric. Chiswell, 1692. 1st edn. 8vo. 2 17th c sgntrs on title. Contemp sheep, rubbed. Wing T642.
(Hannas) **£55** [≈ $99]
- Miscellanea. In two parts. London: for Jacob Tonson, 1697. 5th edn. 2 pts in 1 vol. 8vo. [iv],232; [iv],365 pp. Contemp speckled calf, a little rubbed.   *(Claude Cox)* **£75** [≈ $135]
- Observations upon the United Provinces of the Netherlands. London: for Jacob Tonson ..., 1690. 5th edn. 8vo. Initial advt leaf. Contemp calf, gilt spine. Wing T661.
(Hannas) **£35** [≈ $63]
- The works ... to which is prefixed, the life and character of the author. Edinburgh: for G. Hamilton ..., 1754. 4 vols. 8vo. Some sl waterstains. Contemp calf.
(Hannas) **£20** [≈ $36]

Terence

- The comedies ... translated into familiar blank verse by George Golman. London: for T. Becket ..., 1765. 1st edn thus. 4to. lxii,ii, 620 pp. Engvs. Contemp calf.
(Lloyd-Roberts) **£75** [≈ $135]

Terrick, Richard

- A sermon preached before the Incorporated Society for the Propagation of the the Gospel in Foreign Parts ... February 17, 1764. London: E. Owen ..., 1764. 1st edn. 124 pp. Orig wraps.   *(Young's)* **£30** [≈ $54]

Thacher, Peter

- A sermon preached to the Society in Brattle Street, Boston, and occasioned by the death of the Hon. James Bowdoin ... Boston: I. Thomas ..., 1791. 31 pp.
(Jenkins) **$20** [≈ £11]

Thadwell, Thomas

- Epsom-Wells. A comedy. Acted at the Duke's Theatre. London: for Henry Herringman,

1673. 1st edn. 4to. [vi],96,[ii] pp. Final epilogue & errata leaf. Sm repr to title, some minor soiling. 19th c half mor, rubbed.
(Clark) £85 [≈ $153]

Theobald, Lewis
- Shakespeare restored: or, a specimen of the many errors ... by Mr. Pope in his late edition of this poet ... London: for R. Francklin, 1726. 1st edn. 4to. [vi],viii,194 pp. Tear in Q1 reprd. Entirely untrimmed in rec half calf, gilt. *(Bennett)* £650 [≈ $1,170]

Theocritus
- The idylliums. Oxford: Stephens, 1684. 1st edn of Thomas Creech translation. 8vo. Engvd frontis (sl torn), a few sl marks & creases. Contemp calf. *(Ash)* £250 [≈ $450]
- The idylliums ... with Rapin's discourse upon pastorals, made English by Mr. Creech ... the second edition, to which is prefix'd the life of Theocritus by Basil Kennett. London: for E. Curll, 1713. 8vo. Engvd port. Contemp calf, rebacked, bds not matching.
(Waterfield's) £45 [≈ $81]

Thermometrical Navigation ...
- Thermometrical navigation ... See Williams, Jonathan

Thicknesse, Philip
- memoirs and anecdotes of Philip Thicknesse, late Lieutenant Governor of Land Guard Fort, and unfortunate father to George Touchet. For the author, 1788. 1st edn. 2 vols. 8vo. 2 leaves loosening. Contemp qtr calf, mrbld bds, all jnts cracked.
(Hannas) £380 [≈ $684]
- A year's journey through the Pais Bas; or, Austrian Netherlands ... and the routes through Germany, Holland, and Switzerland ... London: for J. Debrett, 1786. 8vo. Fldg plate. Contemp half calf, upper jnt weak.
(Hannas) £140 [≈ $252]

Thomas, Frederick
- The trial of Lieut. Col. Thomas of the First Regiment of Foot-Guards ... [for] neglect of duty before the enemy ... 1780, near Springfield, in the Jerseys ... London: 1781. 118 pp. Lacking initial blank or half-title. Ptd wraps. *(Reese)* $1,250 [≈ £694]

Thomas, John, Bishop of Winchester
- A sermon preached ... in the Abbey Church of Westminster the 17th day of February, 1747 ... London: W. Innys, 1748. 4to. 21 pp. Half-title, advt leaves. Disbound.
(C.R. Johnson) £15 [≈ $27]

Thomas, William
- Good newes from sea, being a true relation of the late sea-fight betweene Captain William Thomas ... against Captaine Polhill ... Lawrence Blaiklock, 1643. 1t edn. Sm 4to. [ii],7 pp. Half calf, mrbld sides, a.e.g., by Riviere. Wing T993.
(Blackwell's) £200 [≈ $360]

Thompson, C.
- Travels through Turkey in Asia, the Holy Land, Arabia, Egypt and other parts of the world, including a curious description of Jerusalem. London: 1767. 2 vols. Cr 8vo. Fldg engvd maps & prints. Calf.
(Halewood) £85 [≈ $153]

Thompson, Isaac
- A collection of poems, occasionally writ on several subjects. Newcastle upon Tyne: for the author, 1731. 1st edn. 8vo. viii,xiv,176 pp. A little insignificant soiling. Contemp panelled calf, spine worn. Lge book-label of James Allan, Darlington, 1738.
(Bennett) £185 [≈ $333]

Thompson, Thomas
- An enquiry into the origin, nature and cure of the small-pox ... added, a prefatory address to Dr. Mead concerning the present discipline in the general administration of physic in this kingdom. London: Millar, 1752. 8vo. 134 pp. Errata leaf. Rec qtr mor.
(Goodrich) $125 [≈ £69]

Thomson, George
- The spirit of general history, in a series of lectures from the 8th to the 18th century ... a view of the progress of society in manners and legislation ... Carlisle: 1791. 1st edn. Demy 8vo. 434 pp. Orig bds, spine worn.
(Halewood) £24 [≈ $43]

Thomson, James
- The Castle of Indolence. An allegorical poem written in imitation of Spenser. London: for A. Millar, 1748. 2nd edn. 8vo. Disbound.
(Waterfield's) £45 [≈ $81]
- Edward and Eleonara. A tragedy. As it was to have been acted at ... Covent Garden. London: for the author, 1739. 1st edn, iss with price on title. 8vo. Disbound.
(Hannas) £30 [≈ $54]
- The seasons. London: for J. Millan ..., 1730. 1st coll 8vo edn. Gen title in red & black. 4 plates. Contemp calf, rebacked. Made up of Spring 2nd edn 1731, lacking half-title, Wing T231; Summer 3rd edn 1730, T223; Autumn

2nd edn 1730, T233; Winter 1730, T217.
(Hannas) **£90 [≈ $162]**
- The seasons. London: A. Millar, 1744. 8vo. 4
engvd plates. Errata slip on verso of dedn leaf
A2. Sm stain in lower marg on 2 or 3 leaves.
B'plate of Earl Gower. Contemp calf,
rebacked.   *(Waterfield's)* **£50 [≈ $90]**
- The seasons. Edinburgh: for A. Kincaid ...,
1768. 12mo. Port, 4 plates. Contemp sheep.
(Hannas) **£15 [≈ $27]**
- The seasons ... with his life, and complete
index and glossary. London: for J. Chapman,
1795. 8vo. Port, engvd title, 4 plates, final
advt leaf. Sm hole in 1 leaf affecting 3 letters.
Contemp tree-calf, gilt. *(Hannas)* **£20 [≈ $36]**
- Spring. A poem. London: A. Millar ..., 1728.
1st edn. 8vo. [xii],57,2 errata &c., 4 ctlg pp.
Red & black title. V light stain to 1st 3 leaves.
Rec mor.   *(Young's)* **£110 [≈ $198]**
- The works ... with his last corrections and
improvements to which is prefixed an account
of his life and drawings. London: for A.
Millar, 1762. 2 vols. 4to. 12 plates, engvd
port, frontis (to vol II), subscribers' list.
Contemp calf, rebacked.
(Waterfield's) **£225 [≈ $405]**
- The works in two volumes. Dublin: for John
Exshaw ..., 1751. 1st Dublin edn thus. 2 vols.
12mo. 360; 390,[2] pp. Engvd port, 4 plates.
Contemp polished calf. *(Young's)* **£38 [≈ $68]**

Thomson, William
- Letters from Scandinavia, on the past and
present state of the Northern nations of
Europe. London: for G.G. & J. Robinson,
1796. 1st edn. 2 vols. 8vo. Half-titles.
Contemp calf, rubbed, lacking labels.
(Hannas) **£120 [≈ $216]**

Thorius, Raphael
- Hymnus tabaci; a poem in honour of tabaco
...Made English by Peter Hausted. London:
for Humphrey Moseley, 1651. 1st edn in
English. 2 pts. 16mo. 18th c half russia. Wing
T1040 (incorporating Wing T1039).
(Hannas) **£320 [≈ $576]**

Thorley, John
- The female monarchy. London: for the
author, 1744. 1st edn. 8vo. Engvd frontis, 4
plates. Contemp calf.
(Marlborough) **£300 [≈ $540]**

Thornton, Bonnell
- City Latin, or, critical ... remarks on the
Latin inscription on laying the first stone of
the intended New Bridge of Black-Fryars.
Proving almost every last word of it to be

erroneous. London: for R. Stevens, 1760. 1st
edn. 8vo. [2],35 pp. Lacking half-title?
(Hannas) **£45 [≈ $81]**

Thorold, Sir John
- A view of Popery. London: for John
Rivington, 1766. 1st edn. 8vo. Thick paper.
Lacking half-title. Contemp mottled calf, gilt.
(Hannas) **£20 [≈ $36]**

Thorowgood, Thomas
- Vindiciae Judaeorum, or, a true account of
the Jews, being more accurately illustrated
than heretofore. London: 1660. [10],30,
[8],28,67 pp. Text cropped, with some loss of
catchwords & sgntr marks. Imprint cropped &
supplied in facsimile. Calf, rubbed.
(Reese) **$7,500 [≈ £4,166]**

Thoughtes ...
- Sweete thoughtes of Jesus and Marie ... See
Pinkney, Miles

Thoughts ...
- Thoughts on civil liberty ... See Brown, John
- Thoughts upon liberty ... See Wesley, John

Thousand notable things ...
- A thousand notable things ... from the secrets
of nature and art ... See Lupton, Thomas

Thunberg, C.P.
- Travels in Europe, Africa and Asia, made
between the years 1770 and 1779. In four
volumes. London: Rivington, 1795. 4 vols.
8vo. Frontis (vol 4), 10 engvd plates. Half
calf.   *(Halewood)* **£495 [≈ $891]**

Thurston, Joseph
- The toilette. London: Motte, 1730. 2nd edn.
8vo. Engvd frontis. Later card wraps, dusty.
(Marlborough) **£55 [≈ $99]**

Tickell, Richard
- Anticipation: containing the substance of his
M---Y's most gracious speech to both H----S of
P---L----T, on the opening of the approaching
Session ... London: for T. Becket, 1778. 1st
edn. 8vo. [8],74 pp inc half-title & a2 advt. Sl
waterstained. Mod qtr calf.
(Hannas) **£55 [≈ $99]**

Tillinghast, John
- Demetrius his opposition to reformation. A
sermon ... London: for Andrew Kembe, 1642.
4to. [viii],48 pp. Title mtd, sm tear in A4,
dampstained. Disbound. Wing T1169.
(Clark) **£25 [≈ $45]**

Tillotson, John
- A discourse against transubstantiation. London: for Brabazon Aylmer ..., 1684. 4to. Disbound. Wing T1190.
(Waterfield's) £30 [≈ $54]
- The rule of faith: or an answer to the treatise of Mr. I.S. entituled Sure-footing ... London: for O. Gellibrand, 1676. 2nd edn. 8vo. Sev ink smudges, 1 or 2 short tears. Rebound in old calf, crnrs reprd, rebacked. Wing T1218.
(Bow Windows) £35 [≈ $63]
- A sermon preach'd before the Queen at White-Hall, March the 8th, 1689. London: Brabazon Aylmer, 1689. 4to. Half-title. Disbound. Wing T1237.
(C.R. Johnson) £10 [≈ $18]
- The works. London: for T. Goodwin ..., 1720. 8th edn. Folio. Engvd frontis laid down, some waterstaining & spotting. 19th c half calf, rather rubbed.
(Waterfield's) £40 [≈ $72]

Tindal, William
- The history and antiquities of the Abbey and Borough of Evesham. Evesham: 1794. 1st edn. 4to. Frontis. 6 plates. Some dampstaining & spotting, mostly marg. Contemp half calf, rubbed, title label chipped.
(Robertshaw) £75 [≈ $135]

Tindall, Matthew
- An essay concerning the laws of nations ... With an account ... upon the question, whether ... [certain seamen] ... might not be looked upon as pirates? London: for Richard Baldwin, 1694. 1st edn. 4to. 34 pp. Mod qtr calf. Wing T1300.
(Edwards) £260 [≈ $468]

Tinney, J.
- A compendious treatise of anatomy. Adapted to the arts of designing, painting, and sculpture ... in which the external muscles of the human body are ... represented. London: for R. Sayer, n.d. [ca 1762]. Folio. 4 ff, 8 plates. Occas foxing. Contemp wraps. Used.
(Pollak) £175 [≈ $315]

Tissot, S.A.D.
- Advice to people in general, with respect to their health ... Translated ... Edinburgh: A. Donaldson, 1766. 2 vols. Contemp calf, red labels. Ex lib Colquhoun of Luss.
(C.R. Johnson) £250 [≈ $450]
- Advice to the people in general with regard to their health ... Translated ... London: 1768. 3rd edn. 8vo. 620 pp. Jnts weak.
(Goodrich) $60 [≈ £33]
- An essay on diseases to literary and sedentary

persons. Notes by J. Kirkpatrick. London: 1769. 2nd edn. 12mo. [Bound with] Tissot: Onanism: or a treatise upon the diseases ... 1766. 12mo. Contemp calf.
(Robertshaw) £136 [≈ $244]
- The life of M. Zimmermann ... Translated ... London: 1797. 8vo. 154,2 pub list pp. Half-title, port frontis. Lea, front cvr detaching, spine gilt.
(Elgen) $75 [≈ £41]
- Onanism: or, a treatise upon the disorders produced by masturbation ... Translated ... London: for the translator, 1766. 1st English edn (?). 12mo. xii,184 pp. Mod qtr calf.
(Hannas) £140 [≈ $252]

Titus, Silius
- Killing no murder: briefly discourse in three questions. London: reprinted ... 1689. 4to. [viii],42 pp. Title & last leaf soiled, other pp a bit dusty. Disbound. Wing T1312.
(Clark) £20 [≈ $36]

Toland, John
- The art of restoring. or, the piety and probity of General Monk in bringing about the last restoration ... London: 1714. 4th edn. 8vo. viii,48 pp. Paper browned. Mod bds.
(Hannas) £35 [≈ $63]

Tomkins, Thomas (ed.)
- Poems on various subjects: selected to enforce the practice of virtue ... London: 1780. 12mo. Half-title. Contemp calf, gilt spine.
(Hannas) £55 [≈ $99]

Tomlins, T.E.
- The law dictionary. Explaining the rise, progress and present state, of the English law, in theory and practice ... originally written by Giles Jacob ... 1797. 2 vols. 4to. Title vol 1 creased. Mod half calf.
(Edwards) £160 [≈ $288]

Tone, Theobold Wolfe
- An argument on behalf of the Catholics of Ireland. Dublin: Re-printed by order of the United Irishmen, 1792. 5th edn. 16 pp. Disbound.
(C.R. Johnson) £22 [≈ $39]

Tooke, John Horne
- Epea Pteroenta. Or, the diversions of Purley. London: for the author, 1798-1805. 1st edn of 2nd part. 2 vols. 4to. 540; 560 pp. Engvd frontis, another plate. Preliminary & final foxing. Contemp calf, spines gilt, spines sl rubbed, upper jnts cracked.
(Deighton Bell) £55 [≈ $99]

Topham, E.
- The life of John Elwes ... Member in three successive parliaments for Berkshire ... London: 1790. 6th edn. 8vo. viii,111 pp. Extndg pedigree, port. Rec half calf, mrbld sides.   *(Bow Windows)* **£55 [≈ $99]**

Topham, Edward
- Letters from Edinburgh; written in the years 1774 and 1775 ... observations on the diversions, customs, manners ... of the Scotch nation, during a six months residency in Edinburgh. London: for J. Dodsley, 1776. 1st edn. 8vo. Title spotted. Mod half calf.
          (Hughes) **£145 [≈ $261]**

The Topographer
- The Topographer. Containing a variety of original articles, illustrative of the local history and antiquities of England. London: for Robson & Clarke, 1789-91. 1st edn. 4 vols. 8vo. 48 engvd plates (6 fldg). Contemp calf, sl wear, some jnts splitting.
          (Young's) **£180 [≈ $324]**

Torbuck, John (ed.)
- A collection of Welsh travels, and memoirs of Wales ... London: for J. Torbuck, [1740?]. 3 pts with sep titles & collation (pts 2 & 3 joint collation). 8vo. 2 frontis. 19th c half roan, gilt spine.   *(Hannas)* **£160 [≈ $288]**

Torriano, Giovanni
- Della lingua Toscano-Romana. Or, an introduction to the Italian tongue. J. Martin ..., 1657. 1st edn. 8vo. [xvi],293,[i blank], [vii index]; [iv],258 (for 260) pp. Contemp sprinkled calf, minor wear to jnts & to hd & tail of backstrip. Wing T1919.
          (Blackwell's) **£250 [≈ $450]**
- The Italian reviv'd: or, an introduction to the Italian tongue. London: for R.C.T.S. ..., 1689. 2nd edn. 3 pts in 1. 12mo. [viii],160; [iv],165-352; [ii],148,[2] pp. Occas rust-marks. Contemp calf, repr to top of spine.
          (Burmester) **£250 [≈ $450]**

Tour ...
- A short tour in the Midland Counties of England ... See Quincey, Thomas

Tower of London ...
- An historical description of the Tower of London, and its curiosities ... London: for J. Newberry, 1754. 2nd edn. Sm 8vo. New half calf, mrbld bds.   *(Stewart)* **£30 [≈ $54]**

Towers, John
- Polygamy unscriptural; or two dialogues between Philalethes and Monogamus ... London: for the author, 1780. 1st edn. 8vo. 61 pp. Title dusty. Old wraps.
          (Burmester) **£30 [≈ $54]**

Towne, John
- A critical inquiry into the opinions and practice of the ancient philosophers concerning the nature of the soul and a future state. London: for C. Davis, 1748. 2nd edn. 8vo. xiv,305,[iii] pp. Red & black title. Contemp gilt-ruled calf, sl rubbed.
          (Bennett) **£55 [≈ $99]**

Townshend, Charles, Viscount
- The Barrier-Treaty vindicated. London: for A. Baldwin, 1712. 1st edn. 8vo. Half-title. Contemp panelled calf, rebacked.
          (Hannas) **£45 [≈ $81]**

Townshend, Heywood
- Historical collections: or, an exact account of the proceedings of the last four Parliaments of Q. Elizabeth. London: for T. Bassett ..., 1680. 1st edn. Folio. Longitudinal title. Contemp calf, rebacked. Wing T1991.
          (Hannas) **£65 [≈ $117]**

Tracts ...
- Miscellaneous tracts relating to natural history ... See Linnaeus, Carl

Trail, Robert
- A vindication of the Protestant doctrine concerning justification ... Edinburgh: for John Trail, 1730. 8vo. 48 pp. Disbound.
          (Hannas) **£15 [≈ $27]**

Transplantation ...
- The great case of transplantation in Ireland discussed ... inconveniences in transplanting the natives of Ireland ... London: 1655. 1st edn. 4to. 32 pp. Last leaf reprd with sm loss. Mod mor-backed bds.
          (Robertshaw) **£145 [≈ $261]**

Trapp, Joseph
- Abra-Mule: or, love and empire. A tragedy. As it is acted at ... Little Lincolns-Inn-Fields. London: for Jacob Tonson, 1704. 1st edn. 4to. Paper sl browned. Half mor.
          (Hannas) **£120 [≈ $216]**

Travell, F.T.
- A sermon upon the present scarcity, preached in the parish church of Upper Slaughter ...

London: J. Smeeton, [1795]. 8vo. New wraps.
(Stewart) £15 [≈ $27]

Travels ...
- Travels through the interior parts of America
... See Anburey, Thomas

Treasure of Poore Men ...
- Here begynneth a good boke of medycynes:
called the Treasure of Poore Men. London: ...
by Thomas Petyt, 1539. 2nd or 3rd edn. Sm
8vo. [iv],44 ff. Title within w'cut border.
Some old anntns on a few leaves. Mor by
Riviere, upper jnt reprd, g.e. STC 24201.
(Pickering) **$3,500** [≈ £1,944]

Treatise ...
- Practical treatise on painting in oil-colours.
London: for E. & J. White, 1795. 1st edn.
8vo. iii-xvi, 246 pp. Without the half-title,
some early ms amplifications in margins, 2 or
3 later notes in ballpoint. Early 19th c half
calf, spine gilt, sl rubbed.
(Bennett) £95 [≈ $171]
- A treatise concerning the militia ... See
Sackville, Charles
- Treatise of algebra in two books. London: J.
Nourse, 1780. 2nd edn. 531 pp. Many fldg
plates. Lacking bds & endpapers.
(Xerxes) **$100** [≈ £55]
- A treatise of use and custome ... See
Casaubon, Meric
- A treatise on the police of the metropolis ...
See Colquhoun, Patrick
- A treatise on the virtues and efficacy of a crust
of bread ... See Robinson, Nicholas

Treaty ...
- The definitive treaty of peace, union,
friendship and mutual defence between the
crowns of Great Britain, Hungary, and
Sardinia, concluded at Worms ... 1743.
London: Edward Owen, 1743. 4to. 28 pp.
Rebound in bds. *(C.R. Johnson)* £20 [≈ $36]

Treble Almanack
- The Treble Almanack for 1797 [Dublin
directory]. Dublin: 1797. 8vo. Map. Contemp
Irish red calf. *(Emerald Isle)* £60 [≈ $108]

Treby, Sir George (ed.)
- A collection of letters and other writings
relating to the horrid Popish plot. London:
for Samuel Heyrick ..., 1681. 1st edn. Folio.
[6],127,[1] pp inc licence leaf (loose, torn).
Disbound. Wing T2102.
(Hannas) £20 [≈ $36]
- A collection of letters and other writings

relating to the horrid Popish plot ... [with]
The second part ... London: for Samuel
Heyrick ..., 1681. Folio. [vi],127; [iv],34 pp.
Imprim leaf to each part. Disbound. Wing
T2102. *(Clark)* £50 [≈ $90]

Trelawney, Jonathan
- A sermon preached before the Queen ... Nov
12 1702 ... for signal success vouchsafed to
her Majesties forces by sea and land ...
London: Tho. Bennet, 1702. 4to. [iv],43 pp.
Rec stiff wraps. *(Clark)* £12 [≈ $21]

Trenchard, John
- An argument, shewing that a standing army is
inconsistent with a free government ...
London: 1697. 1st edn. Sm 4to. iv,30 pp.
Disbound. *(Hughes)* £28 [≈ $50]
- An argument shewing, that a standing army is
inconsistent with a free Government, and
absolutely destructive to the constitution of
the English monarchy. London: 1698. 4to. 31
pp. Rebound in bds. Wing 2111.
(C.R. Johnson) £50 [≈ $90]
- A letter from the author of the argument
against a standing army, to the author of the
Balancing letter. London: 1697. 4to. 15 pp.
Rebound in bds. Wing 2113.
(C.R. Johnson) £45 [≈ $81]
- A short history of standing armies in
England. London: 1698. 4to. 46 pp, errata.
Rebound in bds. Wing 2116.
(C.R. Johnson) £60 [≈ $108]

The Trifler
- The Trifler. A new periodical miscellany. By
Timothy Touchstone of Saint Peter's College,
Westminster. London: the authors, 1788-89.
Pts 1-43 [all published]. Part 1 2nd edn; all
others 1st edn. Sl foxing. Contemp calf,
rebacked, retaining orig spine.
(Spelman) £85 [≈ $153]

Trotter, Thomas
- Medicina nautica: an essay on the diseases of
seamen. Comprehending the history of health
in his Majesty's fleet ... London: 1797. 1st
edn. 8vo. viii,487 pp. Title sl foxed. Contemp
cloth-backed bds, cvrs loose, spine defective
at hd & ft. *(Hemlock)* **$400** [≈ £222]

Trowell, Samuel
- The farmer's instructor; or, the husbandman
and gardener's useful and necessary
companion ... now completed ... by William
Ellis. London: for J. Hodges ..., 1747. 1st
edn. [xiv],276 pp. Engvd frontis. Bottom crnr
shaved without loss. New bds.
(Young's) £98 [≈ $176]

True Portraiture ...

- The true portraiture of the Kings of England ... See Parker, Henry

Trumbull, John

- M'Fingal: a modern epic poem in four cantos. London: for J.S. Jordan, 1792. 5th edn. 1st London edn of the complete poem. 8vo. Half-title (soiled), final advt leaf. Mod half calf.
(Hannas) **£45 [≈ $81]**

Trusler, John

- Proverbs exemplified. London: for the author, 1790. Lge 12mo. Vignette title, 49 w'cut text ills. Paper ageing. Later half mor, gilt, rubbed. *(Marlborough)* **£300 [≈ $540]**

Truth ...

- Truth against craft, or sophistry and falshood detected in answer to a pamphlet intitled The Case Fairly Stated ... Dublin: 1754. 86 pp. Disbound. *(C.R. Johnson)* **£48 [≈ $86]**
- Truth brought to light; or the history of the first 14 years of King James I. In four parts. London: R. Baldwin, 1692. Engvd title, ptd title, [xii],94; 136; 83; 19, table, contents pp. Sep title to each part. Some browning, headlines cropped. Later half calf.
(P & P) **£60 [≈ $108]**
- The truth unvailed, on behalf of the Church of England ... being a vindication of Mr. Standish's sermon preached before the King ... by a person of quality. Printed in the year 1676. 4to. Title soiled. Disbound.
(Waterfield's) **£40 [≈ $72]**

Tryon, Thomas

- A new method of educating children: or, rules and directions for the well-ordering and governing them ... London: for J. Salusbury, 1695. 1st edn. [viii],102,[x] pp. Consistent offsetting & occas browning, sm acid hole on title. Orig calf, extremities worn.
(Pirages) **$2,000 [≈ £1,111]**
- Some memoirs of the life ... written by himself: together with some rules ... in cleanness, temperance, and innocency. London: T. Sowle, 1705. st edn. 12mo. 128 (i.e. 146) pp. Epitaph, 1f, 2 advts pp. Fldg engvd frontis. Calf, sl shelf wear.
(Elgen) **$500 [≈ £277]**
- Wisdom's dictates: or, aphorisms and rules, physical ... divine. For preserving the health of the body ... added, a bill of fare of seventy five noble dishes of excellent food. London: Salusbury, 1696. 12mo. 3ff,144 pp. Browned. Polished calf, gilt, by Bliss.
(Elgen) **$500 [≈ £277]**

Tucker, Josiah

- Letters to the Rev. Dr. Kippis inspired by his ... Vindication of the Protestant Dissenting Ministers ... Glocester: R. Raikes, 1773. 8vo. Mod mrbld bds. *(Waterfield's)* **£65 [≈ $117]**

Tuke, Sir Samuel

- The adventures of five hours. A tragicomedy. London: Henry Herringman, 1663. 1st edn. Folio. Paper browned. Mod gilt-panelled mor. Wing T3299.
(Hannas) **£280 [≈ $504]**

Tull, Jethro

- The horse-hoing husbandry; or, an essay on the principles of tillage and vegetation. London: for the author, 1733. 1st edn. Sm folio. 6 fldg plates, imprimatur lf. Contemp calf, gilt, rebacked. *(Traylen)* **£330 [≈ $594]**
- The horse-hoing husbandry; complete in four parts; or, an essay on the principles of tillage and vegetation ... London: for A. Millar, 1743. 2nd edn [with] A Supplement. 2 pts in 1. Sm folio. 7 fldg engvd plates. Contemp calf, rebacked. *(Traylen)* **£265 [≈ $477]**
- The horse-hoing husbandry; or, an essay on the principles of tillage and vegetation. London: A. Millar, 1762. 8vo. 7 fldg plates. A few crnrs lightly stained. Contemp calf.
(Emerald Isle) **£165 [≈ $297]**

Turbevill, Edward

- The information ... delivered at ... the House of Commons, Tuesday the ninth day of November, in ... 1680. 1st edn. Folio. Imprim leaf (lightly dampstained), 12 pp. Disbound. Wing T3252. *(Blackwell's)* **£30 [≈ $54]**

Turner, Daniel

- De morbis cutaneis. A treatise of diseases incident to the skin. London: 1714. 1st edn. 8vo. Advt leaf. Some foxing & age stains. Old calf. *(Halewood)* **£185 [≈ $333]**
- Syphilis. A practical dissertation on the venereal disease, in two parts. The fifth edition, still farther improved ... London: for R. Wilkin ..., 1737. 8vo. [xxviii],476 pp. Title laid down, lacking A1 (half-title?). Contemp calf, rebacked. *(Pollak)* **£100 [≈ $180]**

Turner, William

- A compleat history of the most remarkable providences ... which have happened in this present age. London: for John Dunton, 1697. 1st edn. Folio. Marg worming at beginning, a few sections browned. Contemp sheep, rubbed, new endpapers. Wing T3345
(Charles Cox) **£75 [≈ $135]**

- The history of all religions in the world ... also a geographical map, shewing in what country each religion is practised. London: John Dunton, 1695. 8vo. [16],684 pp. 3 full-page w'cuts inc map. Red & black title. Contemp calf, rubbed, rebacked. Wing T3347.   *(Karmiole)* **$350 [≃ £194]**

Tusser, Thomas
- Five hundred points of good husbandry, united to as many of good husswiferie ... now lately augmented ... London: ... Richard Tottell, 1574. Sm 4to. Black letter. W'cut title (mtd). Contemp calf, mor label. STC 24378.   *(Traylen)* **£1,600 [≃ $2,880]**
- Five hundred points of good husbandry [in verse] ... London: for the Company of Stationers, 1630. 4to. 164 pp. Old calf, respined. STC 24390.
                     (C.R. Johnson) **£385 [≃ $693]**

Twiss, Richard
- A trip to Paris, in July and August 1792. 1793. 8vo. 131 pp. Engvd frontis, plate. [Bound with] The genuine trial of Marie Antoinette. 1793. 46 pp. Engvd port frontis. Rebound in calf-backed mrbld bds.
                     (Edwards) **£100 [≃ $180]**

Tyers, Thomas
- Political conferences between several great men, in the last and present century. London: T. Cadell, 1781. 2nd edn. 8vo. Half-title, 16 pp book ctlg. Contemp tree calf, spine heavily gilt, crnrs bumped.
                     (Chaucer Head) **£80 [≃ $144]**

Tyrtaeus
- Elegies. Translated into English verse; with notes and the original text. London: for Tho. Payne, 1761. 1st edn of this trans. Sm 8vo. xxiv,36 pp. English & Greek text. Contemp sprinkled calf, spine richly gilt.
                     (Bennett) **£110 [≃ $198]**

Tyson, Edward
- Orang-utang sive homo sylvestris, or the anatomie of a pygmie compared with that of an ape and a man. London: Bennet, 1699. 1st edn. 4to. 2 pts in 1 vol. 108,58 pp. 8 fldg plates (marg tears), advt leaf at end. Imprint leaf in photo facs. Rec half calf.
                     (Oasis) **$2,750 [≃ £1,527]**

Union of Great Britain ...
- The history of the Union of Great Britain ... See Defoe, Daniel

United Company of Merchants ...
- A defence of the United Company of Merchants of England ... See Dunning, J.

Universal Library ...
- The universal library: or, compleat summary of science ... See Curzon, H.

Usher, James
- Clio: or, a discourse on taste. Addressed to a young lady. London: T. Davies, 1772. 3rd edn. Contemp calf, red label, hinges weakening.   *(C.R. Johnson)* **£135 [≃ $243]**

Ussher, James
- The power communicated by God to the prince, and the obedience required of that subject ... printed for Anne Seile, 1661. 1st edn. 4to. [44],76; 105-231 (but complete, with the prelim blank leaf). Engvd port. Contemp unlettered sheep, upper jnt weak.
                     (Fenning) **£165 [≃ $297]**
- Strange and remarkable prophecies ... of James Ussher, late Lord Archbishop of Armagh ... an account of his foretelling the rebellion in Ireland forty years before it came to pass ... London: for R.G., 1678. Sm 4to. 8 pp. Panelled calf, gilt, by Pratt.
                     (Emerald Isle) **£110 [≃ $198]**

Valcaren, John Peter A.
- A relation or diary of the siege of Vienna. London: for William Nott ..., 1684. 1st English edn.. 4to. 2 fldg maps. Lacking initial blank. Contemp calf, rebacked. Wing P1690 & V21 (double entry).
                     (Hannas) **£120 [≃ $216]**

Vallencey, Charles
- A vindication of the ancient history of Ireland ... and several accounts of the ancient Bards ... Dublin: White, 1786. 8vo. 551 pp. Mod half calf, mrbld sides.   *(Emerald Isle)* **£45 [≃ $81]**

Van der Heyden, Hermannus
- Speedy help for rich and poor. or, certain physicall discourses touching the vertue of whey, in the cure of the griping flux of the belly. London: 1653. Lea.
                     (Rittenhouse) **$900 [≃ £500]**

Van Kampen, N. & Son
- The Dutch florist: or, true method of handling all sorts of flowers with bulbous roots ... the particular method of treating the Guernsey Lily. London: 1764. 2nd edn. 8vo. [viii],104 pp. Paper a trifle browned, a few minor stains. Half calf, rebacked.
                     (Wheldon & Wesley) **£85 [≃ $153]**

Van Rymsdyk, John & Andrew

- Museum Britannicum, being an exhibition of a great variety of antiquities ... belonging to the British Museum. London: for the authors, 1778. 1st edn. 2 ff, xvi,84 pp. 30 engvd plates. Contemp calf-backed bds, uncut, dusty, reprd.   *(Marlborough)* £275 [≈ $495]

Van Swieton, Gerard

- The commentaries upon the aphorisms of Dr. Herman Boerhaave ... concerning the knowledge and cure of the several diseases incident to the human body. London: Knapton, 1759-54-65. 14 vols. Foxing. Contemp calf, rebacked.
                          (Goodrich) $995 [≈ £552]

Vanbrugh, Sir John

- A short vindication of the relapse and the provok'd wife, from immorality and prophaneness. London: for H. Walwyn, 1698. 1st edn. 8vo. [4],79 pp inc half-title. Mod half calf. Wing V59.
                          (Hannas) £160 [≈ $288]

Varlo, Charles

- The guide of reason, or floating ideas of nature, suited to the philosopher, farmer, and mechanic ... London: 1798. 2 vols. Orig calf, gilt extra, wear to headbands & hinges.
                          (Reese) $300 [≈ £166]

Vaux, George

- Mathesis juvenilis: or a course of mathematicks for young students ... Made English from the Latin of Jo. Christopher Sturmius ... London: for Dan. Midwinter, 1708-09. 1st edn. 3 vols. 8vo. 111 engvd plates, some fldg. Contemp panelled calf, a little worn.   *(Traylen)* £225 [≈ $405]

Venegas, Miguel

- A natural and civil history of California: containing an accurate description of that country ... the customs of that country ... translated ... London: 1759. 1st English edn. 2 vols. [20],45; [8],387 pp. Fldg map, 4 plates. 3/4 brown crushed levant.
                          (Reese) $1,250 [≈ £694]

Venn, Richard

- King George's title asserted. In a letter to a gentleman at Cambridge. London: W. Bickerton, 1745. 8vo. 101 pp. Final leaf torn along lower marg. Later bds.
                          (Spelman) £20 [≈ $36]

Venner, Tho.

- Via recta ad vitam longam. Or a treatise ... for

attaining to a long and healthy life clearly demonstrated ... famous waters of Bathe ... concerning tobacco ... London: Flesher, 1650. 8vo. [12],417 pp. Sep titles. Light foxing. Mod calf, orig dec panels laid down.
                          (Elgen) $450 [≈ £250]

Ventris, Sir Peyton

- The reports of Sir Peyton Ventris ... In two parts ... Select cases adjudged in the Kings-Bench ... Common-Pleas ... Court of Chancery ... London: 1696. 1st edn. Folio. [xii],368,[xxiv] pp. Port frontis, sep title to each part. Contemp calf, jnts splitting.
                          (Frew Mackenzie) £215 [≈ $387]

Vere, Francis

- The commentaries ...being diverse pieces of service, wherein he had command ... Cambridge: Dillingham, 1657. 1st edn. Lge paper. 4to. [xii],209,[2] pp. 3 engvd ports, 7 fldg maps & plates. Isolated soiling. Contemp calf, rebacked. Author's pres inscrptn.
                          (Pirages) $650 [≈ £361]

Verelst, Harry

- A view of the rise, progress and present state of the English Government in Bengal: including a reply to the misrepresentations of Mr. Bolts ... London: for J. Nourse ..., 1772. 1st edn. 4to. [xii],148, 4,253 pp. Light spotting on title. Near contemp calf.
                          (Young's) £150 [≈ $270]

Vernon, Christopher

- Considerations for regulating the Exchequer ... Tho. Harper ..., 1642. 1st edn. Sm 8vo. [viii],118 pp. Errata leaf at end. Some browning, sm wormholes in lower margs with sl loss. Contemp sheep, rebacked, orig spine preserved, crnrs rubbed. Wing V241.
                          (Pickering) $850 [≈ £472]

Vernon, Admiral Edward

- A specimen of naked truth, from a British sailor, a sincere wellwisher, to the honour and prosperity of the present royal family, and his country. London: for W. Webb, 1746. 1st edn. 8vo. 30 pp. Disbound.
                          (Burmester) £30 [≈ $54]

Vernon, Edward

- Original paprrs [sic]. Relating to the expedition to Carthagena. The second edition. London: M. Cooper, 1744. 154 pp. Rebound in bds. *(C.R. Johnson)* £28 [≈ $50]

Verri, Alessandro, Count

- The Roman nights; or, dialogues at the

Tombs of the Scipios. London: for P. Molini ..., 1798. 1st edn in English. 12mo. [viii],334, [2 errata] pp. Tear in inner margs of a few leaves (with loss of 2 words). Contemp treecalf, spine little worn, jnt tender.
(Burmester) **£180 [≈ $324]**

Vertot, Rene Aubert de
- The history of the Revolutions of Portugal. Translated from the French. Glasgow: Robert Urie, 1760. 12mo. 152 pp. Index. Contemp calf, worn. *(Argosy)* **$75 [≈ £41]**

Vesling, Johann
- The anatomy of the body of man ... Englished by N. Culpepper. London: Peter Cole, 1653. 1st English edn. Sm folio. xii,192 pp. 24 anatomical plates. Lacking engvd frontis. Contemp panelled calf, rubbed.
(Goodrich) **$595 [≈ £330]**

Viator ...
- Viator a poem ... See Maude, Thomas

Viaud, Pierre
- The shipwreck and adventures of Monsieur Pierre Viaud ... translated ... London: for T. Davies, 1771. 1st edn in in English. [12],276 pp. Engvd frontis. Some browning & foxing of last leaves. Contemp calf, rebacked, sl worn at edges. JCB duplicate with stamps.
(Reese) **$750 [≈ £416]**

Victor, Benjamin
- The widow of the wood. London: C. Corbett, 1755. 12mo. [ii],iii,208 pp. Half-title (with 18th c inscrptn). Some browning, front free endpaper removed. Contemp calf, rubbed.
(Frew Mackenzie) **£100 [≈ $180]**

View ...
- A short view of the state of affairs with relation to Great Britain ... See Pulteney, William, Earl of Bath
- A view of some exceptions ... made by a Romanist ... See Hammond, Henry

Villette, John
- A genuine account of the behaviour and dying words of William Dodd ... London: for the author, 1777. 1st edn. 8vo. 24 pp. Outer leaves trifle dusty. Disbound. Villette's sgntr on title. *(Burmester)* **£60 [≈ $108]**

Villiers, George, Second Duke of Buckingham
- The original copy of the conference between George Villars, Duke of Buckingham, and

Father Fitzgerald, an Irish Jesuit ... London: for Sam. Briscoe ..., 1719. (Price four-pence). 8vo. Frontis (ink stains on verso) 6,15-30 pp. Disbound. (A piracy?). *(Hannas)* **£30 [≈ $54]**

Vincent, Thomas
- Gods terrible voice in the city ... London: for George Calvert, 1668. 6th edn. Browned. Early 19th c polished calf, snagged at inside front cvr. *(Waterfield's)* **£60 [≈ $108]**

Vindication ...
- A vindication of natural society ... See Burke, Edmund
- Vindication of the cause of the Catholics of Ireland ... Dublin: H. Fitzpatrick, 1793. Pamphlet. *(C.R. Johnson)* **£22 [≈ $39]**
- A vindication of the government, doctrine, and worship of the Church of England ... See Grey, Zachary
- A vindication of the present m[inistr]y, from the clamours rais'd against them upon occasion of the New Preliminaries. 1711. 1st edn, issue with 'Ruine' in last line of p.43. 8vo. 52 pp. Disbound, wraps.
(Hannas) **£30 [≈ $54]**

Vindiciae Judaeorum
- Vindiciae Judaeorum, or, a true account of the Jews ... See Thorowgood, Thomas

Vines, Richard
- The hearse of the renowned, the right honourable Robert Earl of Sussex ... a Sermon ... London: for Henry Seale, 1646. 1st edn. 4to. Last page stained. Later clothbacked bds, lacking blanks. Wing V554.
(Charles Cox) **£20 [≈ $36]**

Virgil
- The Georgics of Virgil;, with an English translation and notes by John Martyn. London: 1741. 1st edn thus. 4to. xxii,403,[1], 3,[10 index] pp. 13 cold plates. Some finger marks & smudges. Uncut in old mrbld bds, old calf spine, crnrs worn, jnts cracking.
(Bow Windows) **£540 [≈ $972]**
- Virgil's husbandry, or an essay on the Georgics ... With notes ... London: Innys, 1724. 1st edn of this trans (by William Benson). 8vo. [ii],xxviii, 50,[20] pp. Engvd frontis, plate. Lacking half-title, some outer margs trimmed close. Disbound.
(Burmester) **£60 [≈ $108]**
- The works of Publius Virgilius Maro: translated ... with annotations: by John Ogilby ... London: for the author ..., 1675. 3rd edn. 8vo. [viii],320, 296,317 pp. 31 engvd

plates. Title soiled & frayed at gutter, occas soiling & staining. Later half calf.
(Frew Mackenzie) **£75 [≈ $135]**

- The works of Publius Virgilius Maro. Translated by John Ogilby ... London: Tho: Guy, 1684. Engvd title, 32 plates. Mod blindstamped calf. Wing V615.
(Charles Cox) **£95 [≈ $171]**

Vitalba, Giovanni

- A collection of landscapes, containing nine original subjects and a frontispiece, designed, etched, and shadowed in bistre. London: the author, 1792. Obl 4to. Oval title vignette, 2 ff letterpress, 9 oval plates. 19th c cloth.
(Marlborough) **£2,000 [≈ $3,600]**

Vitruvius Pollio, Marcus

- The theory and practice of architecture; or Vitruvius and Vignola abridg'd ... accurately publish'd the fifth time. London: R. Wellington, 1703[-02]. 8vo. [viii],72, [9]-80 pp. Frontis, 30 plates, 32 full-page ills. Browning. Contemp calf, jnts cracked, reprd.
(Frew Mackenzie) **£295 [≈ $531]**

Voltaire, Francois Marie Arouet de

- The age of Louis XIV. London: for R. Dodsley, 1752. 1st English edn. 2 vols. 8vo. 2 frontis. Contemp calf, a bit rubbed.
(Lloyd-Roberts) **£100 [≈ $180]**

- Critical essays on dramatic poetry. London: L. Davis ..., 1761. 12mo. xii,274,[2 pub advts] pp. Half-title. Rec calf.
(Karmiole) **$150 [≈ £83]**

- An epistle ... upon his arrival at his estate near the Lake of Geneva, in March, 1755. London: R. & J. Dodsley, 1755. 4to. 23 pp. Bi-lingual text. 20th c qtr mor.
(Frew Mackenzie) **£275 [≈ $495]**

- Henriade. An epick poem in ten cantos ... The argument to each canto, and large notes ... London: C. Davis, 1732. 1st complete English trans. Engvd frontis. Contemp speckled calf, rebacked, crnrs reprd.
(Clark) **£65 [≈ $117]**

- The history of the misfortunes of John Calas, a victim to fanaticism. Edinburgh: P. Williamson, 1776. 2nd (?) edn. 8vo. vi,48 pp inc 4 pp subscriber's list. Trifle dog-eared, wanting front wrap. Spurious Voltairiana.
(Young's) **£40 [≈ $72]**

- Letters concerning the English nation. London: Davies, 1733. 1st edn. 8vo. Advt leaf. Contemp calf, crnrs a little worn.
(Marlborough) **£350 [≈ $630]**

- Letters concerning the English nation. London: for C. Davies ..., 1733. 1st edn. 8vo.

[16],253,[19] pp. Index. Contemp calf, somewhat rubbed, lacking spine label, outer hinges cracked.
(Karmiole) **$450 [≈ £250]**

- Letters concerning the English nation. London: for C. Davies, 1741. 2nd edn. 12mo. Advts at end. Staining at lower marg of last few sgntrs. Contemp calf, sl rubbed.
(Hughes) **£125 [≈ $225]**

- The philosophical dictionary for the pocket ... Corrected by the author. London: for I. Carnan, & sold by Berry ..., New York, [1767?]. 12mo. v,332 pp. Engvd title with port vignette. Contemp, probably Amer, tree sheep, gilt spine label.
(Bennett) **£175 [≈ $315]**

- The philosophical dictionary for the pocket. Translated from the French ... Catskill: T. & M. Croswell, 1796. 1st Amer edn. Sm 8vo. [8],[2 blank],336 pp. Engvd port on title. Sl browned throughout. Contemp sheep, a little scuffed.
(Dailey) **$450 [≈ £250]**

Volunteer ...

- A volunteer's queries in Spring 1780, humbly offered to the consideration of all descriptions of men in Ireland. Dublin: Pat Byrne, 1780. 8vo. 86 pp. Bds. *(Emerald Isle)* **£85 [≈ $153]**

Vox ...

- Vox coeli, or newes from heaven ... See Reynolds, John

- Vox militis: foreshewing what perils are procured ... See Rich, Barnaby

- Vox populi. or newes from Spain ... See Scott, Thomas

Vox Patriae ...

- Vox patriae: or the resentments and indignation of the free-born subjects of England, against Popery, arbitrary government, the Duke of York, or any Popish successor ... London: for Francis Peters, 1681. 1st edn. Folio. [2],26 pp. Disbound. Wing V725.
(Hannas) **£30 [≈ $54]**

Vyse, William

- A sermon preached before the Honourable House of Commons ... on February 27, 1778 ... a day of solemn feasting and humiliation. London: for T. Cadell, 1778. 4to. Mod binder's cloth. *(Waterfield's)* **£20 [≈ $36]**

Wagstaff, Simon (pseud)

- See Swift, Jonathan

Wagstaffe, William

- Miscellaneous works ... to which is prefix'd his life and an account of his writings ...

London: for Jonah Bowyer, 1726 [i.e. 1725]. 1st coll edn, 1st iss. 9vo. Port, 2 plates, final blank. Contemp panelled calf, rebacked.
(Hannas) **£280 [≈ $504]**

Wake, W.
- The genuine epistles of the apostolical fathers S. Barnabas, S. Clement, S. Ignatius ... trans, and publish'd with a large preliminary discourse ... London: for Ric. Dare, 1693. Cr 8vo. Red & black title. Contemp panelled calf.   *(Stewart)* **£65 [≈ $117]**

Wake, William
- The authority of Christian Princes over their ecclesiastical Synods asserted ... London: for R. Sare, 1697. 1st edn. 8vo. Heavily browned throughout. Contemp panelled calf, rebacked & reprd. Wing W230. *(Hannas)* **£15 [≈ $27]**
- The principles of the Christian religion explained: in a brief commentary upon the Church-Catechism. London: W. Bowyer, 1731. 5th edn, crrctd. 8vo. 4 pp ctlg. Contemp panelled calf, m mark on upper cvr.   *(Stewart)* **£25 [≈ $45]**

Wakeley, Andrew
- The mariner's compass rectified; containing tables, shewing the true hour of the day, the sun being upon any point of the compass ... London: J. Mount, 1765. 12mo. Foxed. Lea, worn.   *(Argosy)* **$125 [≈ £69]**
- The mariner's compass rectified. With the description and use of those instruments most in use in the art of navigation. London: J. Mount, 1767. 8vo. 272 pp. W'cuts in text, 1 with moveable dial. Contemp calf.
(Spelman) **£160 [≈ $288]**

Walker, Adam
- Ideas, suggested on the spot by a late excursion through Flanders, Germany, France and Italy. London: J. Robson, 1790. 1st edn. 8vo. Title, 1f,442 pp, 1f errata. 54 text ills. Some light foxing. Contemp tree-calf, clumsily rebacked, crnrs worn.
(Marlborough) **£135 [≈ $243]**
- A system of familiar philosophy: in twelve lectures. London: for the author ..., 1799. 1st edn. 4to. xviii,571 pp. 48 fldg plates on 47 leaves. Orig half calf, a little rubbed, sl worn at top of spine. *(Bickersteth)* **£185 [≈ $333]**
- A system of familiar philosophy: in twelve lectures. London: 1799. 1st edn. 4to. xviii,571 pp. 47 copper plates. Occas spotting & offsetting. Contemp polished calf, mrbld edges, jnts reprd.
(Frew Mackenzie) **£180 [≈ $324]**

Walker, Sir Edward
- Historical discourses upon several occasions. London: for Sam. Keble, 1705. Folio. [xiv],369 pp. Fldg plate, engvd dedn leaf. Extra-illust with 9 later ports. Sporadic browning & foxing. Contemp half-calf, mrbld bds, worn, jnts cracked. *(Clark)* **£65 [≈ $117]**

Walker, George
- A vindication of the True Account of the Siege of Derry in Ireland. London: Rob. Clavel, 1689. 4to. 33 pp. Licence leaf. Disbound. Wing W354.
(C.R. Johnson) **£110 [≈ $198]**

Walker, George (1734?-1807)
- Sermons on various subjects. London: J. Johnson ..., 1790. 2 vols. 14 pp subscribers' list. Contemp calf, spines gilt, extremities sl worn.   *(Clark)* **£20 [≈ $36]**

Walker, John
- An attempt towards recovering an account of the numbers and sufferings of the clergy of the Church of England. London: for W.S. Nicholson, 1714. Folio. 2 pts in 1 vol. 14 pp subscribers' list, errata leaf. Contemp calf, spine gilt, crnrs rubbed, jnts cracked.
(Clark) **£75 [≈ $135]**
- A critical pronouncing dictionary and expositor of the English language. London: G.G.J. & J. Robinson ..., 1791. 4to. Contemp calf, a little rubbed.
(C.R. Johnson) **£200 [≈ $360]**

Walker, John (1732-1807)
- A dictionary of the English language ... rhyming, spelling, and pronouncing. London: Becket, 1775. 1st edn. Sm 8vo. Contemp calf. *(Marlborough)* **£450 [≈ $810]**

Walker, Thomas
- The true Christian worship explain and recommended. A sermon preached ... In Wakefield, Yorkshire ... Printed for R. Griffiths ..., 1753. 8vo. Disbound.
(Waterfield's) **£25 [≈ $45]**

Walker, W.
- A dictionary of English and Latin idioms. London: Taylor, 1712. 6th edn. 8vo in 4s. Engvd title, title, [xii],488 pp.
(P & P) **£60 [≈ $108]**
- A treatise of English particles ... their significations and uses in English ... London: T. Garthwait, 1668. 2nd edn. 8vo. [xiv],558 pp. Lacking endpapers & engvd title. Contemp calf, inner jnts cracked. Wing

W443.   *(Clark)* **£55 [≈ $99]**
- A treatise of English particles ... shewing much of the variety of their their significations and uses in English ... London: for Robert pawlet, 1683. 8th edn. Advt leaf at end. Mod half calf, mrbld bds. Wing W448.
                    (Charles Cox) **£35 [≈ $63]**

Walkingame, Francis
- The tutor's assistant being a compendium of arithmetic; and a complete question book. London: for the author, 1757. 3rd edn. 12mo. Contemp calf, worn, poorly rebacked.
                (Waterfield's) **£60 [≈ $108]**

Wallace, James
- General and descriptive history of ... Liverpool ... government, police, antiquities ... streets, squares, public buildings ... extensive African trade. Liverpool: [1795]. 1st edn. 8vo. Fldg map. half calf.
                    (Halewood) **£140 [≈ $252]**

Waller, Edmund
- Instructions [in verse] to a painter, for the drawing of the posture and progress of His Ma.ties forces at sea. London: Henry Herringman, 1666. 1st edn (?). Folio. 18 pp. Lacking final blank, some page numerals & catchwords cropped. Mod half calf. Wing 500.   *(Hannas)* **£180 [≈ $324]**
- Poems, &c. Written upon several occasions London: for H. Herringman, 1693. 6th edn [with] The second part ... London: for Tho. Bennet, 1690. 1st edn. 2 vols in 1. The 2nd part sl browned, with advt leaf & blank H7-8 at end. Panelled calf, rebacked. Wing W518 & 521.   *(Charles Cox)* **£80 [≈ $144]**
- Poems, &c. written upon several occasions, and to several persons. London: for Jacob Tonson, 1722. 10th edn. 8vo. Port. 2 advt leaves. Contemp calf, jnts cracked.
                    (Hannas) **£15 [≈ $27]**
- Poems, etc. London: Herringman, 1664. 1st authorised edn. 8vo. Lacking imprim leaf & final blank. Old calf, sl rubbed.
                    (Stewart) **£150 [≈ $270]**
- The second part of Mr. Waller's poems. Containing his alteration of the Maids Tragedy, and whatever of his is yet unprinted. London: 1690. 1st edn. 8vo. Licence leaf, advt leaf at end, lacking final blank. Contemp calf, rebacked. Wing W521.   *(Hannas)* **£160 [≈ $288]**
- The works ... in verse and prose. To which is prefixed, the life of the author by Percival Stockdale. London: for T. Davies, 1772. 1st edn of this 'Life'. Sm 8vo. Contemp calf, gilt.

                    (Hannas) **£35 [≈ $63]**
- The works ... In verse and prose. London: J. Tonson, 1729. Lge 4to. [18],450,xci pp. Engvd port frontis, 3 engvs. Occas stains; waterstain affecting prelims, frontis & title. Mod calf, gilt spine. *(Karmiole)* **$175 [≈ £97]**

Wallis, George
- The art of preventing diseases, and restoring health ... London: Robinson, 1793. 8vo. xx,850,[12] pp. Full tree-calf, front jnt cracked.   *(Goodrich)* **$145 [≈ £80]**

Wallis, John
- Cono-cuneus: or, the shipwright's circular wedge ... a body resembling in part a conus, in part a cuneus, geometrically considered. London: for Richard Davis ..., 1684. 4to. [iv],17,[1] pp. 7 fldg plates. Disbound, stabbed & tied. Fldg cloth box. Wing W565.
                    (Karmiole) **$350 [≈ £194]**

Wallis, Thomas
- The farrier's and horseman's complete dictionary, containing the art or farriery in all its branches ... London: 1759. Cr 8vo. Calf.
                    (Halewood) **£45 [≈ $81]**

Walpole, Horace (Horatio)
- Anecdotes of painting in England ... 4 volumes , and a catalogue of painters. Strawberry Hill: Thomas Farmer, 1762-71, 1763. 1st edn. 4to. Engvd frontis, 112 plates. Contemp calf, gilt, rebacked, 1 new cvr.
                (Marlborough) **£850 [≈ $1,530]**
- An answer to the latter part of Lord Bolingbroke's letters on the study of history ... London: S. Richardson ..., 1762. 1st edn. 4to. 2 pts in 1 vol. Engvd armorial title vignette, sep part-titles, 203 pp, errata leaf. Contemp calf, rebacked. Family pres copy.
                    (Burmester) **£85 [≈ $153]**
- The Castle of Otranto, a gothic story ... London: for R. Dodsley, 1782. 4th edn. 8vo. xxiv,200 pp. Half-title, lge margins. Occas light spotting. Contemp calf, upper hinge cracked.   *(Claude Cox)* **£40 [≈ $72]**
- The Castle of Otranto, a gothic story ... London: for R. Dodsley, 1791. 6th edn. 8vo. xxiv,200 pp. Contemp speckled calf, mor label chipped, hinges & extremities rubbed, upper hinge cracked.
                    (Claude Cox) **£30 [≈ $54]**
- A catalogue of the Royal and noble authors of England, with lists of their works. Strawberry-Hill Press, 1758. 1st edn. 2 vols. Vignette titles, engvd frontis. Contemp panelled calf, rebacked.
                    (Halewood) **£125 [≈ $225]**

- A catalogue of the Royal and noble authors of England, with lists of their works. Strawberry-Hill Press, 1758. 1st edn. 2 vols in 1. 8vo. Frontis, fly-titles & final blank. Title browned, some minor stains. Mor. spine gilt ruled.   *(Bow Windows)* £150 [≈ $270]
- Historic doubts on the life and reign of King Richard the Third. London: Dodsley, 1768. 2nd edn. 4to. Frontis (frayed fore-edge), title, xv,134,[ii] pp. Plate on p 102. Later half calf, mrbld bds, gilt dec spine.
                              (P & P) £55 [≈ $99]
- The interest of Great Britain steadily pursued. In answer to a pamphlet, entitl'd. The case of the Hanover forces impartially examined. Part I. [All published]. London: J. Roberts, 1743. 63pp. Disbound.
                         (C.R. Johnson) £25 [≈ $45]
- The interest of Great Britain steadily pursued ... Part I [all published]. London: for J. Roberts, 1743. 2nd edn. 63 pp. Half calf.
                         (Claude Cox) £20 [≈ $36]
- Miscellaneous antiquities; or, a collection of curious papers ... Number I [II]. To be continued occasionally. Strawberry-Hill: 1772. 1st edn. 2 pts in 1. 4to. 1st title & last page dust-soiled. Later half calf. All published.   *(Hannas)* £220 [≈ $396]
- The sense of an Englishman on the pretended coalition of parties and on the merits of the Whig interest. London: for T. Cooper, n.d. [1735?]. 1st edn. 56 pp. New canvas-backed paper bds.   *(Claude Cox)* £18 [≈ $32]
- The works of Horatio Walpole, Earl of Orford. London: for G.G. & J. Robinson ..., 1798. 1st edn. 5 vols. Lge 4to. Engvd frontis, 165 engvd plates. Light marg waterstaining vol 3. Contemp russia, gilt rose ornaments on sides, gilt panelled sides, mrbld edges.
                          (Traylen) £350 [≈ $630]

Walpole, Robert
- A letter from a Member of Parliament to his friends in the country, concerning the duties on wine and tobacco. London: for T. Cooper, 1733. 1st edn. 8vo. 36 pp. Disbound, uncut.
                           (Hannas) £45 [≈ $81]
- Mr. Walpole's case, in a letter from a Tory member of parliament, to his friend in the country. [London:] 1712. 1st edn. 8vo. [iv],44 pp. Half-title. Disbound.
                         (Burmester) £45 [≈ $81]
- The observations on the treaty of Seville examined. London: R. Francklin, 1730. 34 pp. Mod wraps. *(C.R. Johnson)* 25 [≈ $45]

Walton, Izaak
- The life of Dr. Sanderson, late Bishop of

Lincoln. London: for Richard Marriott, 1678. 1st edn. Port. Some sl marg waterstains. 18th c panelled calf, rebacked. Wing W667.   *(Charles Cox)* £40 [≈ $72]
- The life of Mr. Rich. Hooker. London: J.G. for Rich Marriott, 1665. 1st edn. Sm 8vo. Licence leaf, errata leaf. Lacking final blank (?). Contemp calf, rebacked. Wing W670.
                          (Hannas) £150 [≈ $270]
- The life of Mr. Richard Hooker. London: Tho: Newcombe ..., 1670. 2nd edn. 8vo. 140 pp. Title soiled & relaid. Qtr calf.
                           (Young's) £25 [≈ $45]
- The lives of Dr. Donne; Sir Henry Wotton; Mr. Richard Hooker; Sir George Herbert; and Dr. Robert Sanderson. With notes and the life of the author by Thomas Zouche. York: 1796. 1st edn. 4to. lix,518 pp. 8 engvd plates. Old mrbld bds, rebacked, uncut.
                           (Hannas) £75 [≈ $135]

Walton, Izaak & Cotton, Charles
- The complete angler. London: for F. & C. Rivington ..., 1797. 6th edn. 2 vols in 1. iii-viii, lxxvi, 262,[ii]; xxxii,111,[1] pp, 5ff. 5 plates, 4 text w'cuts. A bit rubbed & soiled, isolated minor stains, a few 19th c pencil anntns. Orig blue paper bds.
                         (Pirages) $375 [≈ £208]

Wanderer ...
- The Wanderer: or surprizing escape. A narrative founded on true facts ... a late very extraordinary adventure ... to ... total defeat ... with some remarks on ... Ascanius ... author thereof very defective ... Glasgow: 1752. 80 pp. Later mor, mrbld bds.
                         (C.R. Johnson) £58 [≈ $104]

Wandesford, Osborne Sidney
- Fatal love: or, the degenerate brother. A tragedy. As acted at ... Hay-Market. London: for T. Worrall, 1730. 1st edn. Disbound.
                           (Hannas) £30 [≈ $54]

Wanley, Nathaniel
- The history of man; or, the wonders of humane nature, in relation to the virtues, vices and defects of both sexes. London: for R. Basset ..., 1704. 1st edn under this title. 8vo. Final advt leaf. Contemp panelled calf, rebacked.   *(Hannas)* £45 [≈ $81]
- The wonders of the little world: or, a general history of man ... collected from the writings of the most approved historians, philosophers, physicians ... and others. London: for T. Basset ..., 1678. 1st edn. Folio. Contemp calf, amateurishly reprd. Wing W709   *(Hannas)* £95 [≈ $171]

Warburton, William

- A sermon occasioned by the present unnatural rebellion ... a manly defence of our happy constitution in church and state ... London: for J. & P. Knapton, 1745. Mod wraps. *(Waterfield's)* £40 [≈ $72]
- Tracts by Warburton and a Warburtonian not admitted into the collections of their respective works. London: for Charles Dilly, 1789. 8vo. Mod qtr calf. *(Waterfield's)* £100 [≈ $180]

Ward, Edward

- Hudibras redivivus: or, a burlesque poem on the times. London: B. Bragge, 1705-07. 2 vols, each with 12 monthly pts. 1st edn of each part. 4to. Bound in 1 vol in contemp panelled calf, rebacked. *(Hannas)* £750 [≈ $1,350]

Ward, Edward

- The wooden world dissected in the character of a ship of war. London: n.d. [ca 1780]. 7th edn. 8vo. [8],72 pp. Title trimmed with loss, generally close cropped throughout. *(Spelman)* £20 [≈ $36]

Ward, John

- The young mathematician's guide: being a plain and easy introduction to the mathematics. London: 1734. 6th edn, crrctd. viii,456 pp. Port frontis. A few pp stained at edges & browned. Orig panelled calf, rebacked. *(Whitehart)* £50 [= $90]

Ward, Richard

- The life of the learned and pious Dr. Henry More ... London: Joseph Downing, 1710. 1st edn. Port frontis. Contemp calf, backstrip sl worn, jnts cracked. *(Waterfield's)* £115 [≈ $207]

Ward, Samuel, of Cambridge

- The wonders of the load-stone or, the load-stone newly reduc't ... E.P. for Peter Cole, 1640. 1st edn in English. 12mo. [xxxix],281 pp (pagination erratic). Engvd frontis. Early leaves thumbed. Contemp sheep, jnts splitting. NSTC 25030. *(Blackwell's)* £475 [≈ $855]

Ward, Thomas

- England's reformation from the time of King Henry the viiith to the end of the Oates Plot. Hambourgh: 1710. 4to. A few dust-stains. 19th c half calf, crnrs rubbed. *(Stewart)* £95 [≈ $171]
- England's reformation [in verse] from ... King

Henry the viiith to ... the Oates Plot. Printed at Hambourgh: 1710. 1st edn. 4to. 4 pts. Errata leaf. Lacking final blank. Crnr of 2ff torn & reprd without loss, faint waterstains at end. 19th c half calf. *(Hannas)* £130 [≈ $234]

Ward, William

- The most excellent, profitable, and pleasant book of the famous doctor, and expert astrologian ... to find the fatal destiny ... of every man and child by his birth ... London: for Thomas Vere, 1670. 1 leaf torn at crnr, 2 reprd. Thumbed, worn. Mod calf. *(Charles Cox)* £145 [≈ $261]

Warder, Joseph

- The true Amazons; or, the monarchy of bees ... London: for John Pemberton ..., 1720. 4th edn, crrctd. 8vo. xvi,120 pp. Without frontis, title soiled, a little worn at crnrs. Late 18th c calf, rebacked. *(Claude Cox)* £75 [≈ $135]
- The true Amazons; or, the monarchy of bees ... also how to make the English wine or mead, equal, if not superior, to the best of other wines. London: 1742. 7th edn. Sm 8vo. Armorial b'plate. Calf. *(Halewood)* £95 [≈ $171]

Ware, Isaac

- The complete body of architecture. London: 1756. Folio. Engvd frontis, 114 engvd plates (some fldg). Calf. *(Camden)* £1,150 [≈ $2,070]

Ware, Sir James

- The antiquities and history of Ireland. Dublin: 1705. 1st English edn. Ca 500 pp. Lengthy inscrptn, some foxing. Calf, worn. *(Edwards)* £130 [≈ $234]

Warmestry, Thomas

- A convocation speech ... against images, crosses ... and the Oath, &c. Printed in the yeare, 1641. Sole edn. Sm 4to. [i],22 pp. Mod grey bds. Wing W882. *(Blackwell's)* £50 [≈ $90]

Warner, Ferdinando

- The history of the rebellion and civil-war in Ireland [1641-60]. Dublin: for James William, 1768. 1st Irish edn. 2 vols. 8vo. xx,288; [2],332 pp. Wanting half-titles. Contemp calf, 1 jnt cracked. *(Fenning)* £125 [≈ $225]
- The history of the rebellion and civil-war in Ireland. London: 1768. 2nd edn. 4to. Map. Contemp calf. *(Robertshaw)* £100 [≈ $180]

Warner, Richard
- Collections for the history of Hampshire, and the Bishopric of Winchester: including the Isles of Wight, Jersey, Guernsey and Sarke. N.d. [ca 1795]. One of 150. 5 vols (ex 6, probably all published) in 3. 57 plates (lacking plan of Jersey). Contemp calf.
(Edwards) £550 [≈ $990]

Warner, Richard (1713 ? - 1775)
- A letter to David Garrick, Esq. concerning a glossary to the plays of Shakespeare ... to which is annexed, a specimen. London: for the author, 1768. 1st edn. 8vo. Title much dust-soiled, lacking final errata leaf. Mod qtr calf. (Hannas) £55 [≈ $99]

Warner, Richard (1763-1857)
- A second walk through Wales ... in August and September 1798. Bath: R. Crudwell, 1799. 8vo. Half-title, aquatint · frontis, aquatint plate. Uncut in orig bds, spine reprd.
(Hughes) £45 [≈ $81]

Warren, John
- Sermons upon several subjects. London: James Bettenham, 1739. 2 vols. 8vo. Contemp calf, lacking 1 label.
(Lloyd-Roberts) £22 [≈ $39]

Warton, Thomas
- Observations of the Fairy Queen of Spenser. London: for R. & J. Dodsley ..., 1762. 2nd ed, crrctd & enlgd. 2 vols. Lge & thick paper. Final blank. Contemp calf, gilt spines.
(Hannas) £120 [≈ $216]

Washington, George
- A letter to the people of the United States of America, from General Washington, on his resignation from the Office of President ... London: for J. Debrett, 1796. 2nd edn. 8vo. 32,[4 advts] pp. Outer leaves sl dust-soiled. Unbound as issued, stitched.
(Heritage) $60 [≈ £33]

Watercolours ...
- The art of drawing and painting in watercolours. Dublin: Potts, 1768. 1st edn. Sm 8vo. 4 copperplates. Contemp calf.
(Camden) £600 [≈ $1,080]

Waterland, Daniel
- A critical history of the Athanasian Creed. Cambridge: University Press, 1724. 4to. Contemp calf, sl rubbed.
(Stewart) £35 [≈ $63]

Watkins, Thomas
- Travels through Switzerland, Italy, Sicily, the Greek Islands, to Constantinople; through part of Greece, Ragusa and the Dalmatian Isles ... in the years 1787, 8, 9. London: T. Cadell, 1792. 1st edn. 2 vols. 8vo. Marg soiling & age-stains. Bds.
(Halewood) £68 [≈ $122]

Watson, R.
- An address to the people of Great Britain [on the new system of finance, &c.]. Dublin: J. Milliken, 1798. 42 pp. Half-title. Rebound in bds. (C.R. Johnson) £28 [≈ $50]
- An apology for the Bible, in a series of letters, addressed to Thomas Paine ... London: for J. Rider ..., 1799. 8th edn. 12mo. Contemp calf, rubbed. (Hughes) £35 [≈ $63]
- An apology for the Bible, in a series of letters, addressed to Thomas Paine ... New York: T. & J. Swords, 1796. 12mo. 178 pp. Endpapers stained, some light foxing, 18th c sgntr on title. Contemp calf, rubbed, front jnt cracked, sm piece missing from front cvr.
(Heritage) $75 [≈ £41]

Watson, R.
- Chemical essays. London: 1784-86. 3rd edn. [12],349; [4],368; [6],376; [23],354,[49] pp. Sl marg worming vol 1. Contemp tree-calf, gilt spines rubbed & worn, lacking some labels.
(Whitehart) £45 [≈ $81]

Watson, Richard
- A sermon preached before the University of Cambridge on October 25, 1776 being the anniversary of His Majesty's accession to the throne. Cambridge: J. Archdeacon, 1776. 4to. Disbound. (Waterfield's) £30 [≈ $54]

Watson, Thomas
- The upright mans character and crown. Preached in a sermon at Pauls ... March 29. 1657. London: for Ralph Smith, 1657. 1st edn. Sm 8vo. [8],54 pp. Possibly lacking a final blank. Some stains. Disbound. Wing W1146. (Hannas) £15 [≈ $27]

Watson, William
- The clergy-man's law. Or the complete incumbent. 1725. 3rd edn. Folio. 652 pp. Contemp half calf, reprd. Ex Christchurch Cathedral Library with b'plate & lib stamp.
(Edwards) £140 [≈ $252]

Watts, Isaac
- A defence against the temptation to self-murther ... together with some reflections on

excess in strong liquors, duelling and other practices akin to this heinous sin. London: for J. Clark ..., 1726. Contemp panelled calf.
(Waterfield's) **£80 [≈ $144]**
- Discourses of the love of God and the use and abuse of the passions in religion ... London: for J. Clark ..., 1729. Some minor staining & marg wormhole in 1st 2 sheets. Contemp panelled calf. *(Waterfield's)* **£80 [≈ $144]**
- An essay against uncharitableness wherein the secret springs of that vice are traced ... London: R. Tookey, 1707. 1st edn. 8vo. Mod mrbld bds. *(Waterfield's)* **£150 [≈ $270]**
- A guide to prayer: or, a free and rational account of the gift, grace and spirit of prayer. London: for D. Farmer, 1735. 6th edn, crrctd. Sm 8vo. Contemp calf.
(Stewart) **£10 [≈ $18]**
- Horae lyricae. Poems, chiefly of the lyric kind. London: S. & D. Bridge, 1706. 1st edn. 8vo. [xx],267,[i] pp. Extra-illust with 14 ports. late 19th c blue mor, richly gilt, by Jenkins & Cecil. *(Bennett)* **£425 [≈ $765]**
- Horae lyricae. Poems, chiefly of the lyric kind. London: for T. Longman ..., 1751. 9th edn. 12mo. Port frontis. Contemp calf, spine rubbed. B'plate of James Colquhoun of Luss.
(Hannas) **£30 [≈ $54]**
- Horae lyricae. Poems, chiefly of the lyric kind. Glasgow: for James Duncan Sen., 1785. 15th edn, crrctd. 12mo. Contemp tree sheep, extremities worn. *(Hannas)* **£25 [≈ $45]**
- The improvement of the mind: or, a supplement to the art of logic ... in religion, in the sciences, and in common life. London: for J. Buckland, 1781. 8vo. Contemp calf, worn. *(Stewart)* **£20 [≈ $36]**
- Logic: or, the right use of reason. Newburyport: W. Garrett for Thomas & Andrews, 1796. 285 pp. Contemp sheep.
(Jenkins) **$35 [≈ £19]**
- Logick: or the right use of reason in the enquiry after truth ... London: for Richard Ford ..., 1736. 6th edn. Marg tear in E3. Contemp panelled calf, rebacked.
(Waterfield's) **£65 [≈ $117]**
- Philosophical essays on various subjects ... with some remarks on Mr. Locke's essay on the human understanding. London: for Richard Ford ..., 1734. 2nd edn, crrctd. 8vo. Sgntr cut from title marg. Contemp panelled calf, jnts cracked, hd of backstrip chipped.
(Waterfield's) **£90 [≈ $162]**
- Philosophical essays on various subjects ... with some remarks on Mr. Locke's Essay on the human understanding ... a brief scheme of ontology, or the science of being in general ... London: for R. Ford ..., 1734. 2nd edn. 8vo.

Contemp calf, worn. *(Stewart)* **£20 [≈ $36]**
- Reliquiae juveniles. Miscellaneous thoughts, in prose and verse, on natural, moral, and divine subjects; written chiefly in younger years. London: for J. Buckland ..., 1789. New edn, crrctd. Sm 8vo. Contemp calf.
(Stewart) **£10 [≈ $18]**
- Sermons on various subjects, divine and moral: with a sacred hymn suited to each other. London: for Longman ..., 1752. 7th edn. 2 vols. 8vo. Contemp calf, rubbed.
(Stewart) **£20 [≈ $36]**

Webb, Daniel
- An inquiry into the beauties of painting; and into the merits of the most celebrated painters, ancient and modern. London: for R. & J. Dodsley, 1760. 1st edn. 8vo. Title dust-soiled. Contemp calf, v worn, amateurishly rebacked. *(Hannas)* **£15 [≈ $27]**
- Remarks on the beauties of poetry. London: for R. & J. Dodsley, 1762. 1st edn, 8vo. Lacking half-title, lib stamp on title & elsewhere. Early tree-calf, gilt.
(Hannas) **£45 [≈ $81]**

Webb, John
- An historical essay endeavouring a probability that the language of ... China is the primitive language. London: Nath. Brook, 1669. vii,212,1 pp. Red & black title. Sm lib stamp, wormhole in final 12 pp affecting a few letters. Contemp speckled calf, rebacked. *(Farahar)* **£300 [≈ $540]**

Webb, John (1611-1672)
- A vindication of Stone-Heng restored: in which the orders and rules of architecture observed by the ancient Romans, are discussed. London: for T. Bassett, 1665. 1st edn. Folio. [viii],232 pp. 11 engvd text ills, red & black title. Qtr old style calf.
(Halewood) **£185 [≈ $333]**

Webster, Alexander
- Heathens professing Judaism, when the fear of the Jews fell upon them. Edinburgh: T. Lumisden ..., 1746. 1st edn. 8vo. 70,[2 blank] pp. Half-title. Disbound.
(Burmester) **£35 [≈ $63]**

Webster, Charles
- Facts tending to show the connection of the stomach with life, disease, and recovery. London: for J. Murray ..., 1793. 1st edn. 8vo. [iv],59 pp. Rec cloth.
(Burmester) **£120 [≈ $216]**

Webster, J.B.
- The domestic instructor. Selected principally from celebrated authors ... with 60 wood cuts, after the manner of Bewick. London: J. Barker, [1798?]. 12mo. 1st edn. iv,13-354, [ii] pp. (Pagination apparently correct). Some w'cuts crudely cold. 19th c cloth.
(Bennett) **£110 [≈ $198]**

Webster, John
- Metallographia; or, an history of metals ... the signs of ores and minerals ... some observations and discoveries of the author himself. London: for Walter Kettilby, 1671. Sole edn. 4to. 388,2 pub advts pp. Wing W1231. *(C.R. Johnson)* **£550 [≈ $990]**

Webster, Noah
- A brief history of epidemic and pestilential diseases; etc. Hartford: 1799. 2 vols. Orig lea, some wear. *(Rittenhouse)* **$375 [≈ £208]**
- The prompter; or, a commentary on common sayings and subjects, which are full of common sense, the best sense in the world. Boston: I. Thomas ..., 1797. 84 pp. Orig calf-backed bds. *(Jenkins)* **$50 [≈ £27]**

Weever, John
- Ancient funerall monuments within the united monarchie of Great Britaine, Ireland, and the ilands adjacent. London: Harper, 1631. Sm folio. Engvd frontis, engvd title, title, 7ff, 871 pp, 7ff. Table, 18 w'cut text ills. 1 marg defective. 19th c diced russia.
(Marlborough) **£800 [≈ $1,440]**

Weld, Isaac
- Travels through the States of North America and ... Canada ... 1795 [to] 1797. London: 1799. 1st edn. 4to. 464 pp. Pub list, err slip, 2 engvd maps (1 fldg & cold in outline), 14 engvd plates & plans. Contemp calf, gilt, jnt a little weak, hd of spine chipped.
(Bonham) **£680 [≈ $1,224]**

Weldon, Sir Anthony
- The court and character of King James. London: 1650. 1st edn. Sm 8vo. Calf.
(Halewood) **£40 [≈ $72]**
- The court and character of King James. London: R.I., sold by John Wright, 1650. 1st edn. Sm 8vo. Port. Final blank with mss index. Paper a little browned. 19th c red mor, gilt, a.e.g. Wing W1273.
(Hannas) **£55 [≈ $99]**

Welles, John
- The soules progresse to the celestiall Canaan,

of heavenly Jerusalem. London: for Henry Shephard, 1639. 1st edn. 4to. Crnr of title reprd. Mod mor. STC 25231.
(Traylen) **£45 [≈ $81]**

Wells, E.
- The young gentleman's astronomy, chronology and dialling. 1718-17-17. 2nd edn. 3 parts in 1 vol. [2],148 pp, 19 plates; [3],86 pp; [3],54 pp, 15 plates. Gen title & sep title to each part. Contemp panelled calf.
(Whitehart) **£180 [≈ $324]**

Welsted, Leonard
- Epistles, odes, &c. Written on several subjects ... prefix'd, a dissertation concerning the perfection of the English language, the state of poetry, &c. London: for J. Walthoe, 1724. 1st edn. 8vo. lxiv,255 pp. Contemp gilt-ruled calf, jnts cracked. *(Bennett)* **£350 [≈ $630]**

Welwood, James
- Memoirs of the most material transactions in England, for the last hundred years, preceeding the Revolution in 1688. Glasgow: Robert Urie, 1744. New edn, crrctd. [300] pp. Old calf, rebacked. *(Young's)* **£35 [≈ $63]**

Wentworth, Sir Peter
- A pack of Puritans, maintayning the unlawfulnesse, or unexpedience or both. Of ... As also a defence of ... princes ... to intermeddle with ... religion ... London: William Sheeres, 1641. 4to. 56 pp. Lacking half-title. Stitched, uncut as issued. Wing W1357. *(C.R. Johnson)* **£45 [≈ $81]**

Wentworth, Thomas
- The office and duty of executors ... Now enlarged with a supplement ... By H. Curzon. London: for John Place ..., 1703. 8vo. Advt leaf before title. Lib stamp on title. Mod half calf. *(Chaucer Head)* **£110 [≈ $198]**
- The office and duty of executors. London: for Henry Twyford ..., 1689. Old calf, sl worn. Wing 1362A. *(Charles Cox)* **£65 [≈ $117]**

Werenfels, Samuel
- Three discourses ... a defence of private judgement ... authority of the magistrate over conscience ... reuniting of protestants ... London: 1718. 1st English edn. 8vo. 103 pp. Disbound. *(Robertshaw)* **£15 [≈ $27]**
- The usefulness of dramatic interludes, in the education of youth. London: R. Dodsley, 1744. 4to. 27 pp. Disbound.
(C.R. Johnson) **£135 [≈ $243]**

Wesley, J.

- Primitive physik: or, an easy and natural method of curing most diseases. Bristol: 1755. 5th edn. 122 pp. Sl staining in top of outer margs. Contemp lea, sl rubbed, spine cracked, inner hinges cracked.
  (Whitehart) **£40 [≈ $72]**
- Primitive physik: or, an easy and natural method of curing most diseases. Bristol: 1755. 5th edn. 12mo. xx,[2],25-122 pp. Apparently correct thus. Upper part of margs lightly soiled. Old calf, worn, jnts cracked.
  (Weiner) **£100 [≈ $180]**

Wesley, John

- A collection of hymns for the nativity of our Lord; and for New-Year's-Day. London: for G. Whitfield, 1797. 8vo. New wraps.
  (Stewart) **£25 [≈ $45]**
- A short account of the life and death of Nathanael Othen, who was shot in Dover-Castle. October 26, 1757. Bristol: for E. Farley, [1758]. 2nd edn. 12mo. 12 pp. Title dusty with some short tears, light waterstains. Rec qtr calf, mrbld bds.
  (Burmester) **£90 [≈ $162]**
- Thoughts upon liberty by an Englishman. London: 1772. Mod qtr calf.
  (Waterfield's) **£165 [≈ $297]**

Wesley, Samuel

- Poems on several occasions. The second edition, with additions. Cambridge: for J. Brotherton ..., 1743. 12mo. [2],iv,ix, [viii],332, [4 advts] pp. Old sgntrs & scribbles on title, 2 sections pulled in binding. Contemp calf, gilt spine, worn.
  (Burmester) **£50 [≈ $90]**

West, Gilbert

- Odes of Pindar ... Translated from the Greek. To which is added a dissertation on the Olympic Games; together with original poems on several occasions. London: J. Dodsley, 1766. 3 vols. 8vo. Frontis in vol 1. Contemp calf, spines worn, lacking labels.
  (Robertshaw) **£38 [≈ $68]**

West, Richard

- An inquiry into the manner of creating Peers. London: J. Roberts, 1719. 74 pp. Disbound.
  (C.R. Johnson) **£38 [≈ $68]**

West, Stephen

- An essay on moral agency containing remarks on a late anonymous publication ... on Freedom of Will ... Salem: Thomas G. Cushing, 1794. Contemp sheep, rebacked.
  (Waterfield's) **£85 [≈ $153]**

West, Thomas

- The antiquities of Furness; or, an account of the Royal Abbey of St. Mary ... For the author, 1774. 1st edn. 4to. 5 subscribers, lvi,288, appendices pp. Fldg map reprd, fldg plan, 2 plates (1 fldg). Some offsetting & foxing. Calf, rebacked, edges rubbed.
  (Edwards) **£250 [≈ $450]**
- A guide to the lakes in Cumberland, Westmorland and Lancashire. B. Law ..., 1784. 3rd edn, revsd & greatly enlgd. 8vo. xii,306 pp, advt leaf. Frontis, fldg engvd map. Some spotting. Contemp half calf, refurbished.
  (Claude Cox) **£45 [≈ $81]**

West, William

- The first part of symboleography ... the art, or description, of instruments and presidents. London: 1632. [with] The second part ... London: Miles Flesher ..., 1641. 2 vols. Excisions from 2 margs & some staining. Half calf, v worn, bds loose. STC 25276.
  (Charles Cox) **£50 [≈ $90]**

Westminster Bridge ...

- The present state of Westminster Bridge ... See Labelye, C.

Weston, R.

- Botanicus universalis et hortulanus. The universal botanist and nurseryman. London: 1770-77. 4 vols. 8vo. 17 engvd plates [with] The English flora. 1775. 8vo. [xiii],259 pp. Together, 5 vols. Contemp calf, sl worming.
  (Wheldon & Wesley) **£195 [≈ $351]**

Wetherald, R.

- The perpetual calendar ... In three parts ... Chronology ... Solar system ... eclipses ... Pneumatics and hydrostatics ... Newcastle upon Tyne: I. Thompson, 1760. 8vo. viii,150,[2] pp. Title & last leaf trifle soiled. Contemp sheep, rebacked.
  (Burmester) **£175 [≈ $315]**

Whaley, John

- A collection of original poems and translations. London: for the author, 1745. 1st edn. 8vo. viii,335 pp. Contemp calf, rebacked.
  (Hannas) **£140 [≈ $252]**

Whalley, T.S.

- The Castle of Montval, a tragedy ... performing with universal applause at the Theatre Royal Drury Lane. London: for R. Phillips ..., 1799. 2nd edn. [xii],81,[3] pp. Half-title. Disbound. *(Young's)* **£22 [≈ $39]**

Whately, Thomas

- Observations on modern gardening, illustrated by descriptions. Dublin: James Williams, 1770. F'cap 8vo. [8],207,[24 advts] pp. Contemp tree-calf, spine gilt, ornate gilt bands.   *(Spelman)* **£160 [≈ $288]**
- Observations on modern gardening, illustrated by descriptions. London: 1771. 3rd edn. 8vo. [viii],257 pp. Contemp calf.
  (Wheldon & Wesley) **£60 [≈ $108]**
- Observations on modern gardening, illustrated by descriptions. London: T. Payne, 1793. 5th edn. 8vo. [8],263 pp. Orig green glazed cloth, some sl wear.
  (Spelman) **£95 [≈ $171]**
- The regulations lately made concerning the colonies, and the taxes imposed upon them, considered. London: 1765. 114 pp. Half calf, mrbld bds.   *(Reese)* **$500 [≈ £277]**

Whichcote, Benjamin

- Moral and religious aphorisms ... Published in MDCCIII by Dr. Jeffery. Now republished ... London: J. Payne, 1753. 8vo. 19th c half red mor, mrbld bds.
  (Chaucer Head) **£85 [≈ $153]**

Whincop, Thomas

- Scanderbeg: or, love and liberty. A tragedy. To which are added a list of all the dramatic authors ... to ... 1747. London: for W. Reeve, 1747. 1st edn. 8vo. Frontis, 5 plates, 18 medallion ports, half-title. Lacking subscribers' list & final bank. Half calf.
  (Hannas) **£90 [≈ $162]**

Whiston, William

- An account of the surprizing meteor, seen in the air, March the 6th, 1715/16, at night. London: Senex, 1716. 1st edn. 8vo. 78 pp. Mod speckled calf. *(Antiq Sc)* **$375 [≈ £208]**
- Astronomical principles of religion, natural and reveal'd. London: for J. Senex ..., 1717. 1st edn. 8vo. [iv],xxxii,304, 14,[2 blank],[4 advts] pp. 7 engvd plates. Sgntr clipped from marg of title, staining at beginning. Contemp calf, extremities sl rubbed.
  (Pickering) **$500 [≈ £277]**
- The calculation of solar eclipses without parallaxes ... some late observations made with dipping needles, in order to discover the longitude and latitude ... London: for J. Senex ..., 1724. 1st edn. 8vo. [iv],94,[2 errata] pp. Half-title, engvd plate. Wraps.
  (Burmester) **£80 [≈ $144]**
- A new theory of the earth, from the original, to the consummation of all things. For Benj. Tooke, 1696. 1st edn. 8vo. [iv],388,[ii

advts],[i errata] pp. Engvd frontis, 7 engvd plates (1 fldg, all foxed), sl marg foxing. Contemp calf, rebacked. Wing W1696.
  (Blackwell's) **£220 [≈ $396]**

Whitaker, John

- The real origin of government. London: for John Stockdale, 1795. 1st edn. 8vo. [iv],71 pp. Title dusty. Stiff wraps.
  (Young's) **£28 [≈ $50]**

Whitby, Daniel

- A discourse concerning the idolatry of the Church of Rome wherein that charge is justified ... London: for Tho. Basset ..., 1674. Contemp calf, crnrs worn, hd of backstrip chipped. Wing W1722.
  (Waterfield's) **£60 [≈ $108]**
- A full answer to the arguments of the Reverend Dr. Jonathan Edwards for the opinion of St. Austin concerning ... the First Sin of Adam ... London: for John Wyat, 1712. 1st edn. 8vo. xxi,196 pp, 2ff advts. Disbound.
  (Hannas) **£15 [≈ $27]**
- An historical account relating to the nature of the English government ... London: for Awnsham Churchill, 1690. 4to. Disbound.
  (Stewart) **£15 [≈ $27]**
- A paraphrase and commentary upon the New Testament. London: for J. Brotherton ..., 1744. 6th edn. 2 vols. Folio. Engvd port frontis. Lacking map vol 2, wormholes in marg vol 1. Contemp calf.
  (Lloyd-Roberts) **£65 [≈ $117]**
- The Protestant reconciler. Humbly pleading for condescention to dissenting brethren ... for the sake of peace ... London: for Awnsham Churchill, 1683. 1st edn. 8vo. 366 pp. Contemp calf, spine rubbed. Wing W1733.
  (Lloyd-Roberts) **£45 [≈ $81]**

White, Charles

- Cases in surgery, with remarks ... to which is added, an essay on the ligature of arteries by J. Aikin. London: for W. Johnston, 1770. 1st edn. 8vo. xv,198,[4] pp. 7 fldg plates. Light browning throughout. Contemp calf, rebacked. Author's pres inscrptn.
  (Rootenberg) **$950 [≈ £527]**
- A treatise on the management of pregnant and lying-in women. Worcester: Isaiah Thomas, 1793. 8vo. Foxed. Orig sheep, worn, jnts cracked.   *(Goodrich)* **$250 [≈ £138]**
- A treatise on the management of pregnant and lying-in women ... the means of curing ... the principal disorders to which they are liable ... Worcester: I. Thomas, 1793. 8vo. [2],vii-xvi, 17-328 pp. 2 plates (1 with marg tear). Title

browned. Rec cloth.

(Hemlock) **$250 [≃ £138]**

White, George
- Reflections on a scandalous paper ... the answer of the East India Company ... character of Francis Davenport ... villanies ... guilty of in several parts of the world. 1689. Sm folio. 16 pp. Title sl foxed. Rebound in half calf, mrbld bds. Wing W1770.

(Edwards) **£140 [≃ $252]**

White, Gilbert
- The natural history and antiquities of Selborne. London: T. Bensley for B. White ..., 1789. 1st edn. 4to. [vi],468,[xii index, list of plates],[i errata] pp. Fldg engvd frontis (old reprs to 2 folds), 2 vignette titles, 6 plates. Contemp tree-calf, rebacked.

(Bow Windows) **£765 [≃ $1,377]**

White, James
- Conway Castle; a poem to which are added verses to the memory of the late Earl of Chatham and the Moon, a simile for the fashionable world. London: J. Dodsley, 1789. Half-title. Rebound in qtr mor, mrbld bds.

(C.R. Johnson) **£250 [≃ $450]**

White, John
- Journal of a voyage to New South Wales. London: Debrett, 1790. 1st edn. 4to. Title vignette, 65 plates (occas light foxing), subscribers' list, 4 pp advts at end. Contemp calf, worn.   *(Halewood)* **£2,000 [≃ $3,600]**

Whitehead, Paul
- Manners: a satire. London: for R. Dodsley [i.e. Edinburgh: Ruddiman], 1739. 8vo. 20 pp. Disbound.   *(Hannas)* **£120 [≃ $216]**
- The poems and miscellaneous compositions ... With explanatory notes on his writings. and his life ... London: for G. Kearsley, 1777. 1st coll edn. 4to. Port frontis & title sl browned. Contemp tree-calf, rebacked.

(Chaucer Head) **£150 [≃ $270]**
- The State dunces. Inscrib'd to Mr. Pope. In two parts. London: for J Dickenson [i.e. Edinburgh: Fleming], 1733. 8vo. [2],29 pp. Title torn across (natural fault) without loss. All name blanks filled in by contemp hand. Disbound.   *(Hannas)* **£130 [≃ $234]**

Whitehead, William
- An hymn to the nymph of Bristol Spring. London: for R. Dodsley ..., 1751. 1st edn. 4to. 27 pp, final advt leaf. Lacking half-title. 3 lge vignettes. Half red roan, sl rubbed.

(Hannas) **£65 [≃ $117]**

- Poems on several occasions, with the Roman Father, a tragedy. London: for R. & J. Dodsley ..., 1754. 1st coll edn. 8vo. Half-title with errata on verso, epilogue leaf, red & black title. Name on half-title, a little dogeared at end.   *(Hannas)* **£130 [≃ $234]**
- Variety. A tale for married people. The fifth edition. London: J. Dodsley, 1777. 40 pp. 4to. Disbound.   *(C.R. Johnson)* **£20 [≃ $36]**

Whitehurst, John
- An attempt towards obtaining ... measures of length, capacity and weight, from the mensuration of time ... London: for the author, 1787. 1st edn. 4to. [iv],xiv,34, pp. 3 fldg engvd plates. Sm piece cut from crnr of title. Mod mor-backed bds. Author's inscrptn.

(Pickering) **$500 [≃ £277]**
- An inquiry into the original state and formation of the earth. For W. Bent, 1786. 2nd edn. 4to. [x],233 pp. 7 fldg plates. [with] Observations on the ventilation of rooms ... 1794. 1st edn. 4to. [vi],52 pp. Fldg plate. Contemp calf, rebacked.

(Bickersteth) **£250 [≃ $450]**
- An inquiry into the original state and formation of the earth; deduced from facts and the laws of nature. London: for W. Bent, 1786. 2nd edn. 4to. Half-title, port frontis (offset to title), 7 plates (6 fldg). Frontis & title waterstained. Mod bds.

(Chaucer Head) **£180 [≃ $324]**

Whitelocke, Sir Bulstrode
- A journal of the Swedish Ambassy, in the years 1653 and 1654 from the Commonwealth of England, Scotland, and Ireland. London: for T. Becket ..., 1772. 1st edn. 2 vols. 4to. Half-titles. Contemp calf, gilt spines v worn.   *(Hannas)* **£85 [≃ $153]**
- Memorials of the English affairs ... from the beginning of the reign of King Charles the First to King Charles the Second ... London: J. Tonson, 1732. New edn. Folio. [x],702,[xiii] pp. Trivial worming in gutter of 1st few leaves. Contemp calf, rebacked.

(Frew Mackenzie) **£110 [≃ $198]**
- Memorials of the English affairs: or an historical account of what passed from the beginning of the reign of King Charles the First to King Charles the Second ... London: 1732. New edn. Folio. Contemp calf, worn, jnts cracked.   *(Robertshaw)* **£35 [≃ $63]**
- Memorials of the English affairs: or an historical account of what passed from the beginning of the reign of King Charles the First to King Charles the Second ... London: for J. Tonson ..., 1732. Folio. [x],702,[xiv]

pp. 19th c calf by Bedford, lightly rubbed.
(Clark) £120 [≈ $216]

Whitworth, Charles, Lord
- An account of Russia as it was in the year 1710. Strawberry-Hill: 1758. Sm 8vo. Engvd vignette title, iii-xxiv,158 pp,1f errata. New qtr calf, old mrbld bds preserved.
(Marlborough) £275 [≈ $495]
- An account of Russia as it was in the year 1710. Strawberry-Hill: 1758. 1st edn. Sm 8vo. Engvd vignette title, xxiv,158 pp. Contemp half calf. *(Argosy)* $250 [≈ £138]

Whytt, Robert
- Observations on the nature, causes, and cure of those disorders ... commonly called nervous hypochondriac, or hysteric. Edinburgh: & London: T. Becket ..., 1765. 1st edn. 8vo. [4],viii,[8], 520,[2] pp. Some light browning. Rec bds, in half mor slipcase.
(Rootenberg) $1,500 [≈ £833]

Wicked ...
- The wicked resolution of the Cavaliers; declaring their malice and hatred to the Parliament, the Commonwealth, and especially the city of London. Lonkon (sic): J. Smith, 1642. 4to. 6 pp. Uncut & unopened as issued. Wing W2080.
(C.R. Johnson) £125 [≈ $225]

Wickliffe, John
- Remarks upon two late presentiments of the Grand Jury of the County of Middlesex. London: A. Moore, 1729. 28 pp. Disbound.
(C.R. Johnson) £28 [≈ $50]

Widow ...
- The widow of the wood ... See Victor, Benjamin

Wild, Robert
- The benefice. A comedy. By R.W. ... Written in his younger days: Now made publick for promoting innocent mirth. London: 1689. 1st edn. 4to. 66 pp. Lacking final epilogue leaf. Disbound. Wing W2123.
(Hannas) £15 [≈ $27]
- Iter Boreale. Attempting something upon the successful and matchless march of the Lord General George Monck ... to London. For George Thomason ... St. Paul's Churchyard, 1660. 1st edn. 4to. Last word & date of imprint cropped. A few wormholes. New mor. *(Charles Cox)* £240 [≈ $432]

Wildman, Thomas
- A treatise on the management of bees ... various methods of cultivating them ... London: for the author, 1768. 1st edn. 4to. xx,170 pp. 3 lge fldg copperplates. Some foxing to title & plates. Contemp faded grey bds, spine russia, gilt. *(Gough)* £435 [≈ $783]
- A treatise on the management of bees ... various methods of cultivating them ... London: for the author, 1768. xx,169 pp, 1f, 5 pp, 3 fldg plates. Some worming, reprd. Calf, rebacked. *(Titles)* £480 [≈ $864]

Wilkes, John
- A complete collection of the genuine papers, letters, &c. in the case of John Wilkes, Esq. ... Berlin: 1769. 1st edn. Sm 8vo. Port. With a 'Supplement'. Title sl finger-marked. Contemp calf, rebacked.
(Hannas) £160 [≈ $288]

Wilkes, Wetenhall
- A letter of genteel and moral advice to a young lady. London: for C. Hitch, 1748. 5th edn, revsd, crrctd & enlgd. 12mo. [vi],198 pp. Title chafed affecting 3 or 4 letters, somewhat spotted & stained. Near-contemp calf, rebacked. *(Bennett)* £55 [≈ $99]

Wilkie, David
- Theory of interest, simple and compound. Derived from first principles ... With an illustration of the Widows Scheme in the Church of Scotland. Edinburgh: for the author, 1794. Sole edn (?). 8vo. Half-title. Early cloth. *(Chaucer Head)* £150 [≈ $270]

Wilkie, William
- The Epigoniad. A poem. In nine books. London: A. Millar, 1759. 2nd edn. Ex lib Colquhoun of Luss.
(C.R. Johnson) £160 [≈ $288]
- Fables [in verse]. : for Edward & Charles Dilly ..., 1768. 1st edn. 8vo. 18 plates. Half-title. Contemp calf, worn.
(Hannas) £45 [≈ $81]
- Fables. London & Edinburgh: 1768. 1st edn. Sm 8vo. Engvd frontis, 17 engvd plates. Contemp calf, rebacked, preserving orig spine. *(Marlborough)* £175 [≈ $315]
- Fables. London: Dilly, & Edinburgh: Kincaid ..., 1768. 1st edn. Engvd frontis, 17 plates. 2 contents leaves misbound at end. Contemp polished calf, 1 jnt cracking.
(Charles Cox) £50 [≈ $90]

Wilkins, John
- An essay towards a real character and a

philosophical language. London: Sa.
Gellibrand, 1668. 1st edn. Folio. [xx],454,[2
blank]; [viii],[149] pp. 3 fldg tables, 2 plates (1
fldg). Imprim leaf & 2nd title. Tables reprd.
Old calf, rebacked & reprd. Wing W2196.
(Bow Windows) **£465 [≈ $837]**
- Mathematicall magick. or the wonders that
may be performed by mechanicall geometry.
In two books. London: Sa. Gellibrand, 1648.
1st edn. F'cap 8vo. [14],295 pp. Text ills, 4
full-page. Wide margs. Lacking prelim blank
A1. Contemp calf, rebacked. Wing W2198.
(Spelman) **£600 [≈ $1,080]**
- Of the principles and duties of natural
religion. Two books ... to which is added a
sermon preached at his funeral ... London: for
T. Basset ..., 1683. 3rd edn. 8vo. Engvd
frontis. Early 19th c red str-grained mor.
Wing W2206 & (the Sermon) L2704.
(Waterfield's) **£80 [≈ $144]**

Wilkinson, Tate
- The wandering patentee; or, a history of the
Yorkshire Theatres. from 1770 ... to which
are added ... the Diversions of the Morning ...
by the late Samuel Foote. York: for the
author, 1795. 1st edn. 4 vols. 12mo. Lacking
half-titles. Contemp half calf.
(Hannas) **£400 [≈ $720]**
- The wandering patentee; or, a history of the
Yorkshire Theatres. from 1770 ... York: for
the author, 1795. 1st edn. 4 vols. 12mo. 4
half-titles. Half brown mor, gilt, t.e.g., others
uncut.   *(Traylen)* **£335 [≈ $603]**

Williams, Sir Charles Hanbury
- The odes of ... London: for D. Lynch, 1768.
1st edn. 12mo. Final 'Addenda' leaf. Contemp
calf, rebacked.   *(Hannas)* **£160 [≈ $288]**

Williams, H.M.
- A tour in Switzerland; or a view of the present
state of the government and manners ... with
comparative sketches of ... Paris. Dublin:
1798. 2 vols in 1. F'cap 8vo. [8],239; [6],240
pp. Contemp qtr calf.
(Spelman) **£90 [≈ $162]**

Williams, Helen Maria
- Letters written in France, in ... 1790, to a
friend in England ... anecdotes relative to the
French Revolution; and memoirs of Mons ...
London: T. Cadell, 1790. 1st edn. 12mo.
Contemp calf, spine gilt, extremities worn,
upper jnt cracked.   *(Clark)* **£50 [≈ $90]**

Williams, John
- An account of some remarkable ancient ruins,
lately discovered in the Highlands, and

northern parts of Scotland ... Edinburgh:
William Creech, 1777. 1st edn. 8vo. [7],[1],
83,[1] pp. Engvd fldg frontis, Half calf over
mrbld bds.   *(Rootenberg)* **£400 [≈ £222]**

Williams, Jonathan
- Thermometrical navigation. Phila: R. Aitken,
1799. 1st edn. 8vo. xii,98,[3] pp. Lge fldg
engvd chart (short tear at fold), mtd errata
slip. Lib perforation on title. Old buckram.
(Antiq Sc) **$800 [≈ £444]**

Williams, Sir Roger
- A briefe discourse of warre. With his opinion
concerning some parts of the martiall
discipline. London: Thomas Orwin, 1590. 1st
edn. 8vo. Later calf. STC 25732.
(Minkoff) **$3,500 [≈ £1,944]**

Williams, William
- The head of the rock, a Welsh landskip. Being
a prospect near Abergwilly palace ... in the
neighbourhood of Carmarthen. London: N.
Conant, 1755. 55 pp. 19th c bds, calf spine
rubbed.   *(C.R. Johnson)* **£240 [≈ $432]**

Willis, Henry Norton
- Biographical sketches of eminent persons,
whose portraits form part of the Duke of
Dorset's collection at Knole. London: for
John Stockdale, 1795. 1st edn. 8vo. 2 plates,
2 advt leaves at end. Orig bds, v worn, new
backstrip.   *(Hannas)* **£25 [≈ $45]**

Willis, Robert Darling
- Philosophical sketches of the principles of
society and government. W. Bulmer ..., 1796.
2nd edn. 8vo. [6],xv,159 pp. Half-title. Rec
calf-backed bds.   *(Fenning)* **£85 [≈ $153]**

Willock, John
- The voyages and adventures of John Willock,
mariner. Interspersed with remarks on
different countries in Europe, Africa, and
America. Phila: 1798. 1st Amer edn.
[2],9-283, [8] pp. Orig calf, hinges rubbed,
front hinge cracking. *(Reese)* **$300 [≈ £166]**

Willughby, F.
- The ornithology of Francis Willughby ...
accurately described ... by John Ray. London:
1678. Folio. [xii],441,[6] pp. 2 tables, 80
engvd plates (4 of which supplied in mod
facs). A few sm stains, a few plates
waterstained, sev margs reprd. Mod half calf.
(Wheldon & Wesley) **£500 [≈ $900]**

Wilmer [or Wilmore], John
- The case of John Wilmore truly and

impartially related; or, a looking glass for all merchants and planters that are concerned in the American plantations. London: 1682. 17 pp. Disbound. In fldg cloth case. Wing W2883.   *(Reese)* **$1,100 [≈ £611]**

Wilmer, B.

- Cases and remarks in surgery to which is subjoined an appendix, containing the method of curing the bronchocele in Coventry. London: 1779. 1st edn. 8vo. 10,260 pp. 2 plates. Half calf.
  (Halewood) **£95 [≈ $171]**

Wilson, Arthur

- The history of Great Britain. Richard Lownds, 1653. 1st edn. Folio. [xii],292,[viii] pp. Engvd port frontis. V faint foxing throughout. 19th c half calf, mrbld sides, front jnt cracked but firm, rubbed. Wing W2888.   *(Blackwell's)* **£125 [≈ $225]**

Wilson, Jasper (pseud. i.e. Currie, James)

- A letter commercial and political addressed to ... William Pitt in which the real interests of Britain ... are considered ... Dublin: for P. Byrne, 1793. 8vo. Disbound.
  (Waterfield's) **£40 [≈ $72]**
- A letter commercial and political addressed to ... William Pitt in which the real interests of Britain ... are considered ... London: G.G.J. & J. Robinson, 1793. 86 pp. Disbound.
  (C.R. Johnson) **£22 [≈ $39]**

Wilson, John, Recorder of Londonderry

- Belphegor, or the marriage of the devil. A tragi-comedy. Lately acted at the Queen's Theatre in Dorset-Garden. London: J. Leake, 1691. 1st edn. 4to. 1st word of title cut into, tears in title marg reprd. Disbound. Wing W2914.   *(Hannas)* **£110 [≈ $198]**

Wilson, Thomas

- A brief journal of the life, travels and labour of love in the work of the Ministry of ... London: James Phillips, 1784. New edn. 8vo. Contemp lea, rebacked.
  (Emerald Isle) **£75 [≈ $135]**

Wilson, William

- A missionary voyage to the Southern Pacific Ocean ... 1796, 1797, 1798 in the ship 'Duff' ...geography and history of the South Sea Islands ... London: for T. Chapman, 1799. 1st edn. 4to. c,395,7 sub list pp. 6 plates, 7 maps (minor reprs). Mod half calf.
  (Young's) **£280 [≈ $504]**

Wilton, W.

- Victory over sin the true triumph of a Christian. A sermon ... Evesham: J. Agg, 1798. 8vo. New wraps. *(Stewart)* **£20 [≈ $36]**

Wimpey, Joseph

- Rural improvements: or, essays on the most rational methods of improving estates; accomodated to the soil, climate, and circumstances of England ... London: for J. Dodsley, 1775. 1st edn. 8vo. Contemp bds, new cloth spine, mor label, gilt, edges uncut.
  (Traylen) **£85 [≈ $153]**

Winchilsea, Anne Finch, Countess of

- Miscellany poems, on several occasions. Written by a lady. London: for J.B., 1713. 1st edn. Contemp panelled calf, rebacked.
  (Hannas) **£260 [≈ $468]**

Windsor Castle ...

- Windsor Castle; or, the fair maid of Kent ... See Pearce, William

Wingate, Edmund

- An exact abridgement of all statutes in force and use ... to ... 1681. London: 1681. 8vo. Title, [ii],688 pp, tables, leaf of statutes. Sm piece torn from title without loss, sl browning to edges. Calf, rebacked, orig spine laid down, later endpapers.   *(P & P)* **£100 [≈ $180]**
- Maximes of reason. or, the reason of the common law of England. 1658. 1st edn. 4to. 772 pp. Fore-marg of 1st 4 leaves re-inforced. Mod blue mor, t.e.g.
  (Edwards) **£220 [≈ $396]**

Winterbotham, William

- An historical ... view of the American United States. London: for the editor, 1795. 1st edn. 4 vols. 8vo. 23 engvd plates or ports, 11 maps, 5 tables. Contemp tree-calf, spines gilt, worn, some jnts strained.
  (Marlborough) **£450 [≈ $810]**

Winthrop, John

- A journal of the transactions and occurrences in the Settlement of Massachusetts and other New-England colonies, from the year 1630 to 1644 ... Hartford: Elisha Babcock, 1790. 3ff, 364 pp, 2 ff. Old calf, rebacked.
  (Reese) **$300 [≈ £166]**

Wintringham, Sir Clifton

- An enquiry into the exility of the vessels of the human body: wherein animal identity is explained ... London: for Thomas Osborne, 1743. 1st edn. 8vo. Wellcome Lib duplicate

with release stamp on title verso. Contemp
calf.   *(Quaritch)* **$325 [≈ £180]**

Wirtzung, Christopher
- The general practice of physick. Containing
all inward and outward parts of the body ...
now translated into English ... London: for
J.L. ..., 1654. Folio. [10],818,[37] pp.
Lacking final 7 index leaves, foxed &
dampstained, early anntns. New half calf.
                         (Goodrich) **$295 [≈ £163]**

Wiseman, Richard
- Severall chirurgicall treatises. London: 1676.
1st edn. Folio. [xvi],498. 79,[15] pp. Contemp
mor, gilt panelled sides, a.e.g.
                            (Fye) **$3,000 [≈ £1,666]**

Wishart, George
- The history of the Kings Majesties affaires in
Scotland, under the conduct of ... James
Marques of Montrose ... in 1644, 1645, &
1646. Printed in the year, 1649. Sm 8vo.
Later half calf. Cut rather short with sl loss of
numerals, 2ff shaved. Wing W3122.
                         (Hannas) **£55 [≈ $99]**

Wither, George
- Abuses stript and whipt: or satirical essayes.
London: T.S. for Francis Burton, 1614. Sm
8vo. Lacking A1 blank. 19th c red roan, richly
gilt, a.e.g. STC 25895.
                         (Hannas) **£480 [≈ $864]**
- Britain's   remembrancer   containing   a
narration of the plague late past [in verse] ...
To be sold by Iohn Grismond 1628. 1st edn.
12mo. Engvd title (lacking the facing
explanatory leaf). Worming at beginning &
end reprd. Early calf, new endpapers. STC
25899   *(Charles Cox)* **£115 [≈ $207]**
- Campo-musae, or, the field-musings of
Captain George Wither, touching his military
ingagement ... London: R. Austin, 1643. 1st
or 2nd edn (Wing & Grolier differ). Sm 8vo.
Engvd frontis. Paper browned, a few
headlines cut into. 19th c panelled calf. Wing
W3145.   *(Hannas)* **£260 [≈ $468]**
- Speculum speculativum: or, a considering-
glass; being an inspection into the present and
late sad condition of these Nations. London:
... MDCLX. 2nd edn with the errata
corrected. Sm 8vo. Margs browned at
beginning & end. 18th c calf, rebacked. Wing
W3192.   *(Hannas)* **£170 [≈ $306]**
- Speculum speculativum: or, a considering-
glass; being an inspection into the present and
late sad condition of these Nations. London:
1660 [i.e. 1661]. 1st edn. Sm 8vo. [12],166
pp. Late 19th c panelled calf, upper jnt split.

Wing W3192.   *(Dailey)* **$550 [≈ £305]**

Withering, William
- An arrangement of British plants; according
to the latest improvement of the Linnean
system. Birmingham: for the author, 1796.
3rd edn. 4 vols. All half-titles & 31 plates as
called for, 1 cold, some fldg. Contemp sheep,
bndgs worn & shabby. *(Pollak)* **£35 [≈ $63]**

Witherspoon, John
- The trial of religious truth by its moral
influence. A sermon ... Glasgow: for James
Wilkem, 1759. 1st edn. 12mo. 45,[1] pp. Title
dust-soiled & with 2 old sgntrs. Disbound.
                       (Burmester) **£28 [≈ $50]**

Withy, Robert
- The laws and customs, rights, liberties, and
privileges, of the City of London. London:
Withy ... & Griffin, 1765. 1st edn. Tall 12mo.
[iv],[xx], xii,[316] pp. Mod qtr calf.
                            (Ash) **£250 [≈ $450]**

Wolcot, John
- Bozzy and Piozzi: or the British biographers,
a town eclogue. London: for G. Kearsley ...,
1786. 4th edn. 4to. Engvd caricature. Sm
lateral tear affecting 1st few leaves. Sewn as
issued.   *(Waterfield's)* **£50 [≈ $90]**
- Ode to Mr. Paine ... on the intended
celebration of the downfall of the French
Empire ... London: for J. Evans, 1791. 4to.
Disbound, the sewing perished, the gutters in
need of guarding. *(Waterfield's)* **£25 [≈ $45]**
- The works of Peter Pindar, Esq. In three
volumes. London: John Walker, 1794. [with]
Volume 4. London: John Waker, 1796. 4
vols. Unif contemp russia. Ex lib Colquhoun
of Luss.   *(C.R. Johnson)* **£225 [≈ $405]**

Wollaston, William
- The religion of nature delineated. London:
Palmer, 1725. 4to. 219 pp. Old calf, rubbed,
rebacked.   *(Goodrich)* **$150 [≈ £83]**
- The religion of nature delineated. London:
sold by B. Lintot ..., 1726. 4to. Sgntr of
Mordaunt Hamilton on title, some marg notes
by him in text. Contemp calf, gilt spine.
                       (Waterfield's) **£90 [≈ $162]**
- The religion of nature delineated. The sixth
edition, to which is added a general account of
the life, character and writings of the author.
London: for John & Paul Knapton, 1738. 4to.
Engvd port. Contemp calf.
                       (Waterfield's) **£80 [≈ $144]**

Wolley, Hannah

- The Queen-like closet. or rich cabinet ... rare receipts for preserving, candying and cookery ... a supplement ... London: for R. Chiswel ..., 1681-84. 4th edn. 12mo. Imprint leaf, w'engvd frontis. Lacks A5 (dedn leaf). A little wear to crnrs & margs. Mod calf.
(Gough) **£545 [≈ $981]**

Wollstonecraft, Mary

- Letters written during a short residence in Sweden, Norway, and Denmark. London: for J. Johnson, 1796. 1st edn. 8vo. Contemp calf, hinges sl worn.   *(Minkoff)* **$650 [≈ £361]**
- A vindication of the rights of women with strictures on political and moral subjects. London: J. Johnson, 1792. 1st edn. [vol 1 only, all published]. 8vo. xix,452 pp. Lacking initial blank. 19th c calf, old rebacking, spine darkened, jnts cracked.
(Frew Mackenzie) **£925 [≈ $1,665]**

Wood, Anthony

- The history and antiquities of the Colleges and Halls in the University of Oxford ... with a continuation to the present time: by the Editor, John Gutch. Oxford: 1786. 4to. [xvi],692 pp. Title creased. Contemp speckled calf, crnrs worn, cvrs just holding.
(Pollak) **£60 [≈ $108]**
- The history and antiquities of the Colleges and Halls in the University of Oxford ... with a continuation to the present time: by the Editor, John Gutch. Oxford: 1786-90. 2 vols. 4to. 692; 330,51 index pp. Half mor, spine gilt, mrbld bds, rubbed.
(Edwards) **£250 [≈ $450]**

Wood, James

- An address to the Members of the Methodist Societies, on several interesting subjects. London: for G. Whitfield, 1799. 8vo. New wraps.   *(Stewart)* **£20 [≈ $36]**

Wood, John (1704-1754)

- The origin of building: or, the plagiarism of the heathens detected. In five books. Bath: S. & F. Farley, 1741. 1st edn. Folio. [6],235 pp, errata leaf. 25 plates (11 double-page). Minor foxing. Late 19th c half calf, mrbld bds.
(Spelman) **£900 [≈ $1,620]**

Wood, Lambert

- Florus Anglicus: or, an exact history of England ... to the death of the late king. London: 1657. 2nd edn. Sm 8vo. Port of King Charles. Contemp calf, worn, loose in binding.   *(Robertshaw)* **£25 [≈ $45]**

Wood, Robert

- The ruins of Palmyra, otherwise Tedmoor, in the desert. 1753. 1st edn. Folio. [vi],50 pp. 57 engvd plates, 1 fldg. Marg dampstain on most plates, sometimes severe. Contemp calf, worn, jnts cracked.
(Frew Mackenzie) **£540 [≈ $972]**

Wood, Thomas

- An institute of the laws of England. In four books. London: Henry Lintot, 1754. 8th edn. Folio x,692,[36 table] pp. Contemp calf, jnts cracked, spine ends worn.
(Spelman) **£140 [≈ $252]**

Woodfall, William

- An impartial sketch of the debate in the House of Commons of Ireland ... to bring in a bill for effectuating the intercourse and commerce between Great Britain and Ireland ... Dublin: Luke White, [1785]. 8vo. ii,200,24 pp. Contemp calf, sl rubbed.
(Emerald Isle) **£110 [≈ $198]**
- A sketch of the debate that took place at the India-House in Leadenhall-Street on ... the 19th October inst ... London: 1794. 1st edn. 4to. Title a little foxed & soiled, ms note in ink at top, Mod bds. *(Pickering)* **$100 [≈ £55]**

Woodhead, Abraham

- The protestant's plea for a Socinian justifying his doctrine from being opposite to scripture or church authority ... London: for Henry Hills, 1686. 4to. Mod cloth-backed bds. Wing W3451.   *(Waterfield's)* **£40 [≈ $72]**
- Two discourses concerning the adoration of our B. Saviour in the H. Eucharist. Oxford printed: 1787. 1st edn. 4to. Sl wormed, some staining. Disbound. Wing W3459.
(Charles Cox) **£20 [≈ $36]**

Woodhouse, James

- Poems on several occasions. London: for the author, 1766. Lge 8vo. Contemp calf, re-jnted. *(Marlborough)* **£105 [≈ $189]**

Woodville, William

- A history of the inoculation of the smallpox, in Great Britain ... review of all publications on the subject ... experimental inquiry into the relative advantages of every measure ... London: 1796. Vol 1 [all published]. 1st edn. 387 pp. Frontis. Mod qtr lea.
(Scientia) **$295 [≈ £163]**

Woodward, Henry

- A letter from Henry Woodward, comedian, the meanest of all characters ... to Dr. John

Hill ... the greatest of all characters.
[London:] for M. Cooper, 1752. 3rd edn. 8vo.
222 pp. Sm hole & heavy stains on title.
Disbound.   *(Burmester)* **£35 [≈ $63]**

Woodward, John
- Fossils of all kinds, digested into a method,
suitable to their mutual relation and affinity
... London: for William Innys, 1728. 1st edn.
8vo. xvi,56,131 pp with 4 unnumbered pp
between pp 92 & 93. 7 plates, some fldg, fldg
printed table. Orig calf, rebacked.
(Bickersteth) **£280 [≈ $504]**
- Fossils of all kinds, digested into a method,
suitable to their mutual relation and affinity
... London: for William Innys, 1728. 1st edn.
8vo. Fldg table, 7 plates. B'plate removed
from title verso. Contemp calf, rebacked, mor
label, gilt.   *(Traylen)* **£175 [≈ $315]**

Woodward, Josiah
- The great duty of love and faithfulness to our
native country ... a sermon ... London: R.
Simpson, 1694. 4to. [vi],26 pp. Marg
dampstaining, final leaf soiled. Later wraps.
Wing W3518,   *(Clark)* **£18 [≈ $32]**
- Some thoughts concerning the stage in a letter
to a lady. London: J. Nutt, 1704. 1st edn. 8vo.
13 pp plus final blank leaf. Mod sheep, gilt
spine.   *(Hannas)* **£240 [≈ $432]**

Woollen Draper ...
- A woollen draper's letter on the French treaty
... See Mackenzie, Lieutenant J.

Woolman, John, of Mount Holly
- Serious considerations on various subjects of
importance. With some dying expressions.
Mary Hinde, 1773. 1st edn. 12mo. Contemp
sheep, headband worn.
(Hannas) **£75 [≈ $135]**

Works ...
- The works of celebrated authors, of whose
writings there are but small remains. London:
for J. & R. Tonson ..., 1750. 1st edn. 2 vols.
12mo. [iv],443; [ii],415 pp. Contemp calf,
rebacked, crnrs reprd. *(Clark)* **£90 [≈ $162]**

Worlidge, John
- Dictionarium rusticum ... or, a dictionary of
husbandry, gardening, trade, commerce ...
London: for J. Nicholson ..., 1717. 2nd edn,
revsd, crrctd & imprvd. 8vo. 2 engvd plates (1
fldg), num ills. Half antique calf, mor label,
gilt.   *(Traylen)* **£85 [≈ $153]**
- Systema agriculturae, the mystery of
husbandry discovered ... an account of several

instruments ... useful in this profession.
London: for T. Johnson ..., 1669. 1st edn.
Folio. Explanation of frontis, engvd frontis,
text w'cuts. New half calf. Wing M3598.
(Traylen) **£375 [≈ $675]**
- Systema agriculturae: or, the art of gardening
... London: Will Freeman, 1700. 4th edn.
8vo. Addtnl engvd title, 3 plates, final advt
leaf. Mod calf. Wing W3606A.
(Hannas) **£150 [≈ $270]**
- Systema horti-culturae; or, the art of
gardening, in three books. London: Tho.
Burrel ..., 1677. 1st edn. 8vo. [xxiv],285,[18
table] pp. Engvd title, gen title, 3 engvd
plates. Later gilt-panelled tree-calf, spine gilt
dec. Wing W3603.   *(Gough)* **£450 [≈ $810]**

Wotton, Sir Henry
- Reliquiae Wottonianae. or, a collection of
lives, letters, poems with characters of sundry
personages ... London: 1651. 12mo. 4 engvd
ports. Title soiled & sl defective. 19th c mor,
rebacked, spine broken. Wing W3648.
(Robertshaw) **£45 [≈ $81]**
- Reliquiae Wottonianae. or, a collection of
lives, letters, poems with characters of sundry
personages ... London: for R. Marriot ...,
1651. 1st edn. 12mo. Contemp calf,
refurbished & rebacked. Wing W3648.
(Charles Cox) **£65 [≈ $117]**

Wotton, William
- The history of Rome, from the death of
Antoninus Pius, to the death of Severus
Alexander. London: for Tim. Goodwin,
1751. 1st edn. Cr 8vo. Contemp panelled calf,
sl worn spine gilt.   *(Stewart)* **£35 [≈ $63]**
- Reflections upon ancient and modern
learning. London: for Peter Buck, 1694. 1st
edn. 8vo. Vellum. Wing W3658.
(Traylen) **£225 [≈ $405]**
- Wotton's short view of George Hickes's
grammatico-critical and archaeological
treasury of the ancient northern languages ...
London: for D. Browne, 1737. 2nd edn. 4to.
2 vignettes. Half calf, gilt.
(Traylen) **£150 [≈ $270]**

Wraxall, N.
- A tour through some of the northern parts of
Europe ... In a series of letters. London: T.
Cadell, 1776. 3rd edn, crrctd. 8vo. iv,411 pp.
Fldg engvd map. V sl worming in marg
throughout. Contemp calf.
(Claude Cox) **£18 [≈ $32]**

Wraxall, Sir Nathaniel
- Memoirs of the courts of Berlin, Dresden,

Warsaw, and Vienna in ... 1777, 1778, 1779. London: for T. Cadell ..., 1799. 1st edn. 2 vols. 8vo. xii,490; xii,414 pp. Contemp calf, jnts wearing. *(Young's)* **£42 [≈ $75]**

Wright, Joseph, of Derby
- A catalogue of pictures, painted by J. Wright of Derby, and exhibited· at Mr. Robins's Rooms ... London: 1785. 4to. 8 pp, 24 items. Unbound. *(Marlborough)* **£300 [≈ $540]**

Wright, Thomas
- Louthiana, or an introduction to the antiquities of Ireland in upwards of ninety views and plans ... ruins ... dwellings ... in Co. Louth. London: Faden, 1748. 1st edn. Lge 4to. Contemp calf, gilt, rebacked. *(Emerald Isle)* **£325 [≈ $585]**

Wyatt, James
- The life and surprizing adventures of James Wyatt ... trumpeter on board the 'Revenge' privateer ... being taken prisoner by the Spaniards ... London: E. Duncomb, 1748. 1st edn. 12mo in 6s. Engvd frontis, 3 plates. Some minor reprs to margs. Mod qtr calf. *(Hughes)* **£65 [≈ $117]**

Wycherley, William
- Love in a wood, or St. James's Park. A comedy. London: for Henry Herringman, 1694. 2nd edn. 4to. Title dust-soiled, a few sl stains in text. Mor-backed paper bds. *(Hannas)* **£110 [≈ $198]**
- Miscellany poems: as satyrs, epistles, love-verses, songs, sonnets, &c. London: for C. Brome ..., 1704. 1st coll edn. Folio. Mezzo port, errata leaf. Contemp panelled calf, worn, rebacked. *(Hannas)* **£320 [≈ $576]**
- The plain-dealer. A comedy. London: for R. Bentley ..., 1686. 4th edn. 4to. Title dust-soiled, sm hole in 1 leaf with loss of 5 letters, reprd, catch-words cropped in 3 leaves. Disbound. Working copy. Wing W3753. *(Hannas)* **£25 [≈ $45]**
- The posthumous works ... in prose and verse ... some memoirs of Mr. Wycherley's life. By Mahor Pack. London: for A. Bettesworth ..., 1728. 1st edn. 2 pts. 8vo. Contemp panelled calf. *(Hannas)* **£300 [≈ $540]**
- The works of the ingenious Mr. William Wycherley, collected into one volume. London: for Richard Wellington, 1713. 1st coll edn of the plays. 8vo. Initial advt leaf. Contemp panelled calf, gilt spine, sl rubbed. *(Hannas)* **£160 [≈ $288]**

Wyndham, Henry Penruddocke
- A tour through Monmouthshire and Wales. Made in ... 1774. And ... 1777. Salisbury: 1781. 2nd edn. xii,214 pp. Half-title, frontis, errata leaf, 16 engvd plates. Rebound in half calf, mrbld bds, spine gilt. *(Edwards)* **£280 [≈ $504]**

Wyndham, Neville, of Ash-Hall (ed.)
- Travels through Europe ... drawn from unerring sources of information ... London: for H.D. Symonds, n.d. [ca 1792]. 1st edn (?). 4 vols. 8vo. Lge fldg map, 22 plates (some fldg). Contemp mottled calf, rebacked. *(Hannas)* **£120 [≈ $216]**

Wyvill, Christopher
- A letter to the Right Honourable William Pitt. York: W. Blanchard, n.d. [ca 1793]. 35 pp. Disbound. *(C.R. Johnson)* **£55 [≈ $99]**

Wyvill, Sir Christopher
- The pretensions of the Triple Crown examined: in thrice three familiar letters ... London: 1672. 8vo. Some worming sl affecting text. Contemp calf, worn. *(Robertshaw)* **£25 [≈ $45]**

Yorke, James
- The Union of Hanover. Containing the armes, matches and issues of the Kings, Dukes, Marquettes and Earles of England from the Conquest ... London: Edward Griffin, 1640. 1st edn. Folio. Hundreds of copper engvs. Calf, lea label. *(Argosy)* **$400 [≈ £222]**

Young, Arthur
- The example of France, a warning to Britain. Dublin: for P. Byrne ..., 1793. 1st Dublin edn. 8vo. [ii],93 pp. Occas sl staining. Disbound. *(Burmester)* **£110 [≈ $198]**
- The example of France. A warning to Britain. Bury St. Edmund's: for W. Richardson, 1793. 8vo. [2],182,[2] pp. Errata leaf & final advt leaf. Disbound. *(Hannas)* **£130 [≈ $234]**
- The farmer's guide in hiring and stocking farms ... also plans of farmyards and sections of the necessary buildings. London: for W. Strahan ..., 1770. 1st edn. 8vo. 10 engvd plates (2 fldg), text ills. Contemp polished calf, gilt, jnts sl worn. *(Traylen)* **£150 [≈ $270]**
- The farmer's kalendar; or, a monthly directory for all sorts of country business ... the oeconomical conduct of the farm. London: for Robinson & Roberts ..., 1771. 1st edn. 8vo. Half-title. Mod calf.

(Chaucer Head) **£130** [≃ **$234**]
- The farmer's tour through the East of England ... to enquire into the state of agriculture. London: for W. Strahan ..., 1771, 1st edn. 4 vols. 8vo. 29 plates (mostly fldg) on 28 sheets. Half-title vol 1, 2 final advt leaves vol 4. Contemp calf, sl worn.
(Hannas) **£280** [≃ **$504**]
- The farmer's tour through the East of England ... to enquire into the state of agriculture. London: 1771, 1st edn. 4 vols. 8vo. 29 engvd plates (mostly fldg), fldg table. Some minor jottings, stains & other marks, Contemp calf, jnts cracked, extremities worn.
(Bow Windows) **£210** [≃ **$378**]
- General view of the agriculture of the County of Suffolk, with observations on the means of its improvement. London: 1794. 4to. Cold map. Bds, calf spine. *(Traylen)* **£50** [≃ **$90**]
- General view of the agriculture of the County of Sussex, with observations on the means of its improvement. London: Nichols, 1793. 1st edn. 4to. Half-title, title, 97 pp. Fldg hand-cold map, 2 hand-cold plates, fldg plan. Mod qtr calf. *(P & P)* **£70** [≃ **$126**]
- General view of the agriculture of the County of Sussex, with observations on the means of its improvement. London: 1794. 4to. Half-title, cold fldg map, fldg engvd plate, 2 hand-cold plates. Bds, calf spine.
(Traylen) **£60** [≃ **$108**]
- Rural oeconomy: or, essays on the practical parts of husbandry ... London: T. Becket, 1770. 1st edn. 8vo. [i],520 pp. Lacking half-title, sl browning, contemp ownership inscrptn on title. Contemp calf, armorial devices on sides, rebacked, armorial b'plate.
(Frew Mackenzie) **£135** [≃ **$243**]
- A six months' tour through the Southern Counties of England and Wales ... London: Nicoll, 1768. 1st edn. 284 pp. Half-title. Mod calf, gilt. *(P & P)* **£165** [≃ **$297**]
- A six months' tour through the North of England ... Dublin: 1770. 1st Irish edn. 3 vols. xvi,297; vi,390; vii,403 pp. 28 plates (15 fldg), 5 fldg tables. 1 leaf torn with loss of sev words. Calf, sl worn, vol 2 split down spine into 3 sections. *(Edwards)* **£125** [≃ **$225**]
- A six months' tour through the North of England ... the present state of agriculture, manufactures and population ... the second edition, corrected and enlarged. London: for W. Strahan ..., 1771. 4 vols. 8vo. 29 plates, 5 fldg tables. Contemp sheep, rebacked.
(Waterfield's) **£275** [≃ **$495**]
- A tour in Ireland: with general observations on the present state of that Kingdom; made in the years 1776-1778. London: for T. Cadell

..., 1780. 2nd, 1st 8vo, edn. 2 vols. 4 engvd plates (3 fldg). Contemp calf, rebacked.
(Traylen) **£130** [≃ **$234**]
- A tour in Ireland: with general observations on the present state of that Kingdom; made in the years 1776, 1777 and 1778. London: for T. Cadell ..., 1780. 1st edn. 2 pts in 1. 4to. Contemp mrbld bds, new calf spine, gilt.
(Traylen) **£220** [≃ **$396**]
- Travels during the year 1787, 1788 and 1789 ... London: for W. Richardson ... Bury St. Edmund's: for W. Richardson, 1794. 2nd edn. 2 vols. 4to. 3 fldg engvd maps (1 hand-cold). Contemp half calf, jnts a little cracked. *(Traylen)* **£225** [≃ **$405**]
- Travels during the year 1787, 1788 and 1789. Bury St. Edmund's: by J. Rackham, 1792. 1st edn. 4to. viii,566,[iv index & errata] pp. 3 fldg engvd maps (1 hand-cold). Later half calf, mrbld bds. *(Gough)* **£295** [≃ **$531**]

Young, Edward
- Busiris, King of Egypt. A tragedy as it is acted at the Theatre-Royal in Drury lane. London: 1719. 1st edn. 8vo. 72 pp. Half-title. Disbound, loose in card folder.
(Robertshaw) **$150** [≃ **$45**]
- The centaur not fabulous. In five letters to a friend, on the life in vogue. London: A. Millar ..., 1755. 1st edn. 8vo. [2],xvi, [2],378 pp. Engvd frontis. Title sl soiled, old sgntrs on title & endpapers. Contemp calf, gilt.
(Dailey) **$150** [≃ **£83**]
- The centaur not fabulous ... London: for A. Millar ..., 1755. 2nd edn. 8vo. Frontis. Contemp calf, sl worn, lacking label.
(Hannas) **£30** [≃ **$54**]
- The centaur not fabulous. London: A. Millar ..., 1755. 2nd edn, crrctd. 8vo. 384 pp. Frontis. Rebound in cloth-backed mrbld bds. *(Dailey)* **$60** [≃ **£33**]
- The centaur not fabulous ... London: for A. Millar ..., 1765. 4th edn, crrctd. Frontis. Stamp on half-title, sgntr on title. Contemp sheep, v worn. *(Hannas)* **£15** [≃ **$27**]
- The complaint: or, night thoughts ... London: for R. Dodsley [part 7-9: for G. Hawkins], 1743-42-65. 9 pts. 4to. 1st edns (part 1 1st 4to edn). Red & black gen title torn across & reprd, other minor tears, lacking 1 half-title. Contemp calf, rebacked.
(Hannas) **£280** [≃ **$504**]
- Love of fame ... London: for J. Tonson, 1730. 3rd edn. 8vo. Contemp calf, rebacked.
(Hannas) **£25** [≃ **$45**]
- Love of fame, the universal passion ... London: for J. Tonson, 1728. 2nd edn crrctd & altrd, 1st coll edn. 8vo. Contemp calf, gilt

& blind-tooled.   *(Hannas)* **£65 [≈ $117]**
- Night thoughts ... with the life of the author and notes critical and explanatory. London: Heptinsall, 1798. Frontis, vignette title, 7 w'engvd plates (with offsetting). Contemp diced calf, gilt.   *(John Smith)* **£150 [≈ $270]**
- Night thoughts. With the life of the author and notes critical and explanatory. London: 1798. 4to. 22,[2],364 pp. Engvd port frontis, engvd title, 8 engvd plates. Browned, some marg staining. Contemp calf, rebacked. Ex lib William Hayley (1745-1820).
        (Dailey) **$250 [≈ £138]**

Young, George
- A treatise on opium, founded upon practical observations. London: for A. Millar, 1753. 1st edn. Thick paper. 8vo. xv,182,[2] pp. Advt leaf. Contemp calf, upper jnt cracked, spine rubbed.   *(Burmester)* **£160 [≈ $288]**

Young, Matthew
- An enquiry into the principal phenomena of sounds and musical strings. Dublin: Joseph Hill, 1784. 1st edn. 8vo. 2 fldg engvd plates. Contemp red str-grained mor, gilt, gilt borders, fully gilt panelled spine, mrbld edges.   *(Traylen)* **£775 [≈ $1,395]**

Yvery, House of
- A genealogical history of the House of Yvery; in its different branches of Yvery, Luvel, Perceval, and Gournay. 1742. 2 vols. xii,455; 533 pp. Engvd ports, table, num ills. Red gilt

dec mor, t.e.g.. B'plates.
        (Edwards) **£200 [≈ $360]**

Zimmermann, John George
- Essay on national pride. To which are added memoirs of the author's life and writings. 1797. xlii,260,[23] pp. Paper-cvrd bds.
        (Whitehart) **£60 [≈ $108]**
- Solitude, considered with respect to its influence over the mind and the heart. Translated ... London: 1801-1799. 2 vols. viii,420; 378,xvii pp. Frontis. Some pp (inc title vol 2) loose, some discold. Old 3/4 lea, mrbld bds, badly rubbed & worn.
        (Whitehart) **£25 [≈ $45]**
- Solitude, considered with respect to its influence over the mind and the heart. Translated ... London: 1791. 2nd edn. 8vo. vii,380 pp. Lacking rear endpaper. Lea, rubbed, jnts tender, spine ends frayed.
        (Elgen) **$55 [≈ £30]**
- Solitude. To which are added, the life of the author, notes historical and explanatory ... London: Vernor & Hood, 1799. 2 vols. 12mo. xlviii,310, [20],[6 advts]; [4],338, [26],[4 advts] pp. Contemp polished calf.
        (Spelman) **£60 [≈ $108]**

Zobeide ...
- Zobeide. A tragedy ... See Cradock, Joseph

Zouch, Thomas
- The crucifixion: A poetical essay. Cambridge: 1765. 1st edn. 4to. Limp mrbld bds.
        (Halewood) **£25 [≈ $45]**

Catalogue Booksellers Contributing to IRBP

The booksellers who have provided catalogues during 1987 specifically for the purpose of compiling the various titles in the *IRBP* series, and from whose catalogues books have been selected, are listed below in alphabetical order of the abbreviation employed for each. This listing is therefore a complete key to the booksellers contributing to the series as a whole; only a proportion of the listed names is represented in this particular subject volume.

The majority of these booksellers issue periodic catalogues free, on request, to potential customers. Sufficient indication of the type of book handled by each bookseller can be gleaned from the individual book entries set out in the main body of this work and in the companion titles in the series.

Allen	=	William H. Allen, 2031 Walnut Street, Philadelphia, PA19103, U.S.A. (215 563 3398)
Allix	=	Charles Allix, Bradbourne Farmhouse, Sevenoaks, Kent TN13 3DH, England (0732 451311)
Allsop	=	Duncan M. Allsop, 26 Smith Street, Warwick CV34 4HS, England (0926 493266)
Ampersand	=	Ampersand Books, P.O. Box 674, Cooper Station, New York City 10276, U.S.A. (212 674 6795)
Antic Hay	=	Antic Hay Rare Books, P.O. Box 2185, Asbury Park, NJ 07712, U.S.A. (201 774 4590)
Antiq Sc	=	The Antiquarian Scientist, P.O. Box 367, Dracut, Mass. 01826, U.S.A. (617 957 5267)
Any Amount	=	Any Amount of Books, 62 Charing Cross Road, London WC2H 0BB, England (01 240 8140)
Appelfeld	=	Appelfeld Gallery, 1372 York Avenue, New York, NY 10021, U.S.A. (212 988 7835)
Argonaut	=	Argonaut Book Shop 786-792 Sutter Street, San Francisco, California 94109, U.S.A. (415 474 9067)
Argosy	=	Argosy Book Store, Inc., 116 East 59th Street, New York, NY 10022, U.S.A. (212 753 4455)
Ash	=	Ash Rare Books, 25 Royal Exchange, London EC3, England (01 626 2665)
Barbary	=	Barbary Books, C.P. Counihan, Fortnight, Wick Down. Broad Hinton, Swindon, Wiltshire SN4 9NR, England (079373 693)
Beasley	=	Beasley Books, Paul & Beth Garon, 1533 W. Oakdale, Chicago, IL 60657, U.S.A. (312 472 4528)
Bennett	=	Stuart Bennett, Rare Books & Manuscripts, 3 Camden Terrace, Camden Road, Bath BA1 5HZ, England (0225 333930)
Between the Covers	=	Between the Covers, Tom & Heidi Congalton, 575 Collings Avenue, Collingswood, NJ 08107, U.S.A.
Bickersteth	=	David Bickersteth, 38 Fulbrooke Road, Cambridge CB3 9EE, England (0223 352291)
Blackwell's	=	Blackwell's Rare Books, B.H. Blackwell Ltd., Fyfield Manor, Fyfield, Abingdon, Oxon OX13 5LR, England (0865 390692)
Black Cat	=	Black Cat Books, Ann Mackenzie, 1 Granby Road, Edinburgh EH16 5NH, Scotland (031 667 6341)

Bonham	=	J. & S.L. Bonham, Flat 14, 84 Westbourne Terrace, London W2 6QE, England (01 402 7064)
Book Block	=	The Book Block, 8 Loughlin Avenue, Cos Cob, Connecticut 06807, U.S.A. (203 629 2990)
Boston Book	=	Boston Book Annex, 906 Beacon Street, Boston, MA 02215, U.S.A. (617 266 1090)
Bow Windows	=	Bow Windows Book Shop, 128 High Street, Lewes, East Sussex BN7 1XL, England (0273 480780)
Braiterman	=	Marilyn Braiterman, Antiquarian Bookseller, 20 Whitfield Road, Baltimore, Maryland 21210, U.S.A. (301 235 4848)
Burmester	=	James Burmester, Manor House Farmhouse, North Stoke, Bath BA1 9AT, England (0272 327265)
Camden	=	Camden Books, 146 Walcot Street, Bath, Avon BA1 5BL, England (0225 61606)
Chaucer Head	=	The Chaucer Head, Daniel McDowell, 41 Low Petergate, York YO1 2HT, England (0904 22000)
Clark	=	Robert Clark, 24 Sidney Street, Oxford OX4 3AG, England (0865 243406)
Clearwater	=	Clearwater Books, 19 Matlock Road, Ferndown, Wimborne, Dorset BH22 8QT, England (0202 893263)
Cooper Hay	=	Cooper Hay Rare Books, 203 Bath Street, Glasgow G2 4HZ, Scotland (041 226 3074)
Cortie	=	R.H. Cortie, 3 Hillway, Highgate, London N6 6QB, England (01 340 3738)
Charles Cox	=	Charles Cox, 20 Old Tiverton Road, Exeter, Devon EX4 6LG, England (0392 55776)
Claude Cox	=	Claude Cox, The White House, Kelsale, Saxmundham, Suffolk IP17 2PQ, England (0728 2786)
Dailey	=	William & Victoria Dailey, 8216 Melrose Avenue, P.O. Box 69160, Los Angeles, California 90069, U.S.A. (213 658 8515)
Dalian	=	Dalian Books, David P. Williams, 81 Albion Drive, London Fields, London E8 4LT, England (01 249 1587)
Darees	=	Darees Books, 22 Wanley Road, London SE5 8AT, England (01 737 4557)
Davis & Schorr	=	Davis & Schorr Art Books, 14755 Ventura Boulevard, Suite 1-747, Sherman Oaks, CA 91403, U.S.A. (818 787 1322)
Deighton Bell	=	Deighton, Bell & Co., 13 Trinity Street, Cambridge CB2 1TD, England (0223 353939)
Edrich	=	I.D. Edrich, 17 Selsdon Road, London E11 2QF, England (01 989 9541)
Edwards	=	Francis Edwards, The Old Cinema, Castle Street, Hay-on-Wye, via Hereford HR3 5DF, England (0497 820071)
Elgen	=	Elgen Books, 336 DeMott Avenue, Rockville Centre, New York 11570, U.S.A. (516 53 6276)
Emerald Isle	=	Emerald Isle Books, 539 Antrim Road, Belfast BT15 3BU, Northern Ireland (0232 771798)
Europa	=	Europa Books, 15 Luttrell Avenue, Putney, London SW15 6PD, England (01 788 0312)
Farahar	=	Clive Farahar, XIV The Green, Calne, Wiltshire SN11 8DG, England (0249 816793)
Fenning	=	James Fenning, 12 Glenview, Rochestown Avenue, Dun Laoghaire, County Dublin, Eire (01 857855)
Fine Art	=	Fine Art Catalogues, The Hollies, Port Carlisle, Near Carlisle, Cumbria CA5 5BU, England (096 55 1398)

Frew Mackenzie	=	Frew Mackenzie plc, 106 Great Russell Street, London WC1B 3NA, England (01 580 2311)
Fye	=	W. Bruce Fye, Antiquarian Medical Books, 1607 North Wood Avenue, Marshfield, Wisconsin 54449, U.S.A. (715 384 8128)
Gant	=	Elizabeth Gant, 52 High Street, Thames Ditton, Surrey KT7 0SA, England (01 398 0962)
Gekoski	=	R.A. Gekoski, 33B Chalcot Square, London NW1 8YA, England (01 722 9037)
Goodrich	=	James Tait Goodrich, Antiquarian Books & Manuscripts, 214 Everett Place, Englewood, New Jersey 07631, U.S.A. (201 567 0199)
Gough	=	Simon Gough Books, 5 Fish Hill, Holt, Norfolk, England (026371 2650)
Green Street	=	Green Street Book Shop, 5 Green Street, Cambridge CB2 3JU, England (0223 68088)
Greyne	=	Greyne House, Marshfield, Chippenham, Wiltshire SN14 8LU, England (0225 891279)
Halewood	=	Halewood & Sons, 37 Friargate, Preston, Lancashire PR1 2AT, England (0772 52603)
Hannas	=	Torgrim Hannas, 29a Canon Street, Winchester, Hampshire SO23 9JJ, England (0962 62730)
Hawthorn	=	Hawthorn Books, 7 College Park Drive, Westbury-on-Trym, Bristol BS10 7AN, England (0272 509175)
Hazeldene	=	Hazeldene Bookshop, A.H. & L.G. Elliot, 61 Renshaw Street, Liverpool L1 2SJ, England (051 708 8780)
Hemlock	=	Hemlock Books, 170 Beach 145th Street, Neponsit, New York 11694, U.S.A. (718 318 0737)
Heraldry Today	=	Heraldry Today, 10 Beauchamp Place, London SW3, England (01 584 1656)
Heritage	=	Heritage Book Store, Inc., 8540 Melrose Avenue, Los Angeles, California 90069, U.S.A. (213 659 3674)
High Latitude	=	High Latitude, P.O. Box 11254, Bainbridge Island, WA 98110, U.S.A. (206 842 0202)
Hinchliffe	=	Hinchliffe Books, 15 Castle Street, Thornbury, Bristol BS12 1HA, England (0454 415177)
Howes	=	Howes Bookshop, Trinity Hall, Braybrooke Terrace, Hastings, East Sussex TN34 1HQ, England (0424 423437)
Hughes	=	Spike Hughes Rare Books, Leithen Bank, Leithen Road, Innerleithen, Peeblesshire EH44 6HY, Scotland (0896 830019)
Ivelet	=	Ivelet Books Ltd., 18 Fairlawn Drive, Redhill, Surrey RH1 6JP, England (0737 64520)
James	=	Marjorie James, Flat 1, 53 Onslow Gardens, London SW7, England (01 373 0614)
Jenkins	=	The Jenkins Company, Box 2085, Austin, Texas 78768, U.S.A. (512 280 2940)
C.R. Johnson	=	C.R. Johnson, 21 Charlton Place, London N1 8AQ, England (01 354 1077)
Johnson Arch	=	Johnson Architectural Books, Tynings House, Sherston, Malmesbury, Wiltshire SN16 0LS, England (0666 840404)
Jolliffe	=	Peter Jolliffe, 2 Acre End Street, Eynsham, Oxon OX8 1PA, England (0865 881095)
Karmiole	=	Kenneth Karmiole, Bookseller, 1225 Santa Monica Mall, Santa Monica, California 90401, U.S.A. (213 451 4342)
Kerr	=	Ewen Kerr, (Brian Peate), 1 New Road, Kendal, Cumbria LA9 4AY, England (0539 20659)

Lewcock	=	John Lewcock, 4 Cobble Yard, Napier Street, Cambridge CB1 1HP, England (0223 312133)
Lewton	=	L.J. Lewton, Old Station House, Freshford, Bath BA3 6EQ, England (022 122 3351)
Lloyd-Roberts	=	Tom Lloyd-Roberts, Old Court House, Caerwys, Mold, Clwyd CH7 5BB, Wales (0352 720276)
Lopez	=	Ken Lopez, Bookseller, 51 Huntington Road, Hadley, MA 01035, U.S.A. (413 584 4827)
Lydian	=	Lydian Bookstore, Bockmer House, Medmenham, near Marlow, Buckinghamshire SL7 2HL, England (0491 571218)
Lyon	=	Richard Lyon, 17 Old High Street, Hurstpierpoint, West Sussex BN6 9TT, England (0273 832255)
McKay	=	Barry McKay Rare Books, 29 Nethercote Road, Tackley, Oxfordshire OX5 3AW, England (086 983 228)
Mansfield	=	Judith Mansfield, Books, 60A Dornton Road, London SW12 9NE, England (01 673 6635)
Marlborough	=	Marlborough Rare Books Ltd., 144-146 New Bond Street, London W1Y 9FD, England (01 493 6993)
Marlborough B'Shop	=	Marlborough Bookshop, 6 Kingsbury Street, Marlborough, Wiltshire, England (0672 54074)
Minkoff	=	George Robert Minkoff Inc., Rare Books, Box 147, Great Barrington, Mass 01230, U.S.A. (413 528 4575)
Monk Bretton	=	Monk Bretton Books, Somerford Keynes House, Cirencester, Gloucestershire GL7 6DN, England (0285 860554)
Moore	=	Peter Moore, P.O. Box 66, 200a Perne Road, Cambridge CB1 3PD, England (02223 411177)
Morrell	=	Nicholas Morrell (Rare Books) Ltd., 77 Falkland Road, London NW5 2XB, England (01 485 5205)
Muns	=	J.B. Muns, Fine Arts Books, 1162 Shattuck Avenue, Berkeley, California 94707, U.S.A. (415 525 2420)
Norton	=	The Norton Bookshop, Christopher Casson, 66 Bishopton Lane, Stockton, Cleveland TS18 2AJ, England (0642 601676)
Nouveau	=	Nouveau Rare Books, Steve Silberman, P.O. Box 12471, 5005 Meadow Oaks Park Drive, Jackson, Mississippi 39211, U.S.A. (601 956 9950)
O'Reilly	=	John O'Reilly, Mountain Books, 85/87 King Street, Derby DE1 3EE, England (0332 365650)
Oasis	=	Oasis Books, P.O. Box 171067, San Diego, CA 92117, U.S.A. (619 272 0384)
Offenbacher	=	Emile Offenbacher, 84-50 Austin Street, P.O. Box 96, Kew Gardens, New York 11415, U.S.A. (718 849 11415)
Old Cinema	=	The Old Cinema, Castle Street, Hay-on-Wye, via Hereford HR3 5DF, England (0497 820071)
Orient	=	Orient Books, Little Blakes, Halse, Taunton, Somerset, England (0823 432466)
Ottenberg	=	Simon Ottenberg, P.O. Box 15509, Wedgwood Station, Seattle, WA 98115, U.S.A.
Pacific	=	Pacific Book House, 1016G Kapahulu Avenue, Honolulu, Hawaii 96816, U.S.A. (808 737 3475)
Palladour	=	Palladour Books, Greenlands, Foot's Hill, Cann, near Shaftesbury, Dorset SP7 0BW, England (0747 3942)
Pharos	=	Pharos Books, P.O. Box 17, Fair Haven Station, New Haven, Connecticut 06513, U.S.A.
Pickering	=	Pickering & Chatto Ltd., 17 Pall Mall, London SW1Y 5NB, England (01 930 2515)

Pirages	=	Phillip J. Pirages, Post Office Box 504, 965 West 11th Street, McMinnville, Oregon 97128, U.S.A. (503 472 5555)
Pollak	=	P.M. Pollak, Ph.D., F.L.S., 'Moorview', Plymouth Road, South Brent, Devon TQ10 9HT, England (036 47 3457)
Polyanthos	=	Polyanthos Books Inc., P.O. Box 343, 8 Green Street, Huntington, NY 11743, U.S.A. (516 673 9232)
Post Mortem	=	Post Mortem Books, Ralph Spurrier, 58 Stanford Avenue, Hassocks, Sussex BN6 8JH, England (07918 3066)
Pye	=	Mr. Pye (Books), M.S. & E.J. Kemp, 47 Hailgate, Howden, Goole DN14 7ST, England (0482 25236)
P & P	=	P & P Books, J.S. Pizey, 27 Love Lane, Oldswinford, Stourbridge, West Midlands DY8, England (0384 393845)
Quaritch	=	Bernard Quaritch Ltd., 5-8 Lower John Street, Golden Square, London W1R 4AU, England (01 734 2983)
Rayfield	=	Tom Rayfield, The Blacksmiths, Radnage Common, Buckinghamshire HP14 4DH, England (024 026 3986)
Reese	=	William Reese Company, 409 Temple Street, New Haven, Connecticut 06511, U.S.A. (203 789 8081)
Rittenhouse	=	Rittenhouse Book Store, 1706 Rittenhouse Square, Philadelphia, Pennsylvania 19103, U.S.A. (215 545 6072)
Robertshaw	=	John Robertshaw, 5 Fellowes Drive, Ramsey, Huntingdon, Cambridgeshire PE17 1BE, England (0487 813330)
Rootenberg	=	B. & L. Rootenberg, P.O. Box 5049, Sherman Oaks, California 91403-5049, U.S.A. (818 788 7765)
Sanders	=	Sanders of Oxford Ltd., 104 High Street, Oxford OX1 4BW, England (0865 242590)
Scientia	=	Scientia, Box 433, Arlington, Mass. 02174, U.S.A. (617 643 5725)
Sherick	=	Michael J. Sherick, Bookseller, P.O. Box 91915, Santa Barbara, CA 93190, U.S.A. (805 966 5819)
Sherington	=	Nick Sherington, 11 Clifton Hill, Exeter, Devon EX1 2DL, England (0392 216532)
Sinclair	=	Iain Sinclair Books, 28 Albion Drive, London E8 4ET, England (01 254 8571)
Sklaroff	=	L.J. Sklaroff, Craiglea, The Broadway, Totland, Isle of Wight PO39 0BW, England (0983 753968)
Alan Smith	=	Alan Smith, 15 Oakland Avenue, Dialstone Lane, Stockport, Cheshire SK2 6AX, England (061 483 2547)
John Smith	=	John Smith & Son (Glasgow) Ltd., 57-61 St. Vincent Street, Glasgow G2 5TB, Scotland (041 221 7472)
Snowden Smith	=	Snowden Smith Books, 41 Godfrey Street, London SW3 3SX, England (01 352 6756)
Sotheran	=	Henry Sotheran Ltd., 2, 3, 4 & 5 Sackville Street, Piccadilly, London W1X 2DP, England (01 734 1150)
Spelman	=	Ken Spelman, 70 Micklegate, York YO1 1LF, England (0904 24414)
Spire	=	Spire Books, 38 Rosebery Avenue, New Malden, Surrey KT3 4JS, England (01 942 2111)
Stewart	=	Andrew Stewart, 11 High Street, Helpringham, Sleaford, Lincolnshire NG34 9RA, England (052 921 617)
Tara	=	Tara Associates Ltd., South End House, Church Lane, Lymington, Hampshire SO41 9RA, England (0590 96848)
Thompson	=	Keith Thompson, 4 Sunset Close, Beachlands, Pevensey Bay, East Sussex BN24 6SA, England (0323 766959)
Titles	=	Titles, 15 Turl Street, Oxford OX1 3DQ, England (0865 727928)

Tooley	=	Tooley, Adams & Co. Ltd., 83 Marylebone High Street, London W1M 4AL, England (01 486 9052)
Traylen	=	Charles W. Traylen, Castle House, 49-50 Quarry Street, Guildford, Surrey GU1 3UA, England (0483 572424)
Typographeum	=	Typographeum Bookshop, The Stone Cottage, Bennington Road, Francestown, New Hampshire 03043, U.S.A.
Upcroft	=	Upcroft Books Ltd., 66 St. Cross Road, Winchester, Hampshire SO23 9PS, England (0962 52679)
Virgo	=	Virgo Books, Mrs. Q.V. Mason, Little Court, South Wraxall, Bradford-on-Avon, Wiltshire BA15 2SE, England (02216 2040)
Waddington	=	Geraldine Waddington, Home Farm Cottage, Knowle, Nr. Braunton, North Devon EX33 2LY, England (0271 815011)
Warnes	=	Felicity J. Warnes, 82 Merryhills Drive, Enfield, Middlesex EN2 7PD, England
Washton	=	Andrew D. Washton, 411 East 83rd Street, New York, New York 10028, U.S.A. (212 751 7027)
Waterfield's	=	Waterfield's, 36 Park End Street, Oxford OX1 1HJ, England (0865 721809)
Weiner	=	Graham Weiner 78 Rosebery Road, London N10 2LA, England (01 883 8424)
Weinreb	=	Weinreb Architectural Books, at Henry Sotheran Ltd., 2 Sackville Street, Piccadilly, London W1V 0AA, England (01 434 2019)
Wheldon & Wesley	=	Wheldon & Wesley Ltd., Lytton Lodge, Codicote, Hitchin, Hertfordshire SG4 8TE, England (0438 820370)
Whitehart	=	F.E. Whitehart, Rare Books, 40 Priestfield Road, Forest Hill, London SE23 2RS, England (01 699 3225)
Whiteson	=	Edna Whiteson, 66 Belmont Avenue, Cockfosters, Hertfordshire EN4 9LA, England (01 449 8860)
Willow	=	Willow House Books, The Cottage Bookshop, 5 Hill Street, Chorley, Lancashire PR7 1AX, England (025 72 69280)
Wolff	=	Camille Wolff, Grey House Books, 12A Lawrence Street, Chelsea, London SW3, England (01 352 7725)
Wood	=	Peter Wood, 20 Stonehill Road, Great Shelford, Cambridge CB2 5JL, England (0223 842419)
Words Etcetera	=	Words Etcetera, Julian Nangle, Hod House, Child Okeford, Dorset DT11 8EH, England (0258 860539)
Xerxes	=	Xerxes, Fine & Rare Books & Documents, Box 428, Glen Head, New York 11545, U.S.A. (516 671 6235)
Young's	=	Young's Antiquarian Books, Tillingham, Essex CM0 7ST, England (062187 8187)
Zeno	=	Zeno, 6 Denmark Street, London WC2H 8LP, England (01 836 2522)

Antiquarian Booktrade
Reference Books from Picaflow

Picaflow's range of annual reference works relating to the antiquarian and collector's book world is made up of *Cole's Register of British Antiquarian & Secondhand Bookdealers* (normally referred to merely as *Cole's Register*), together with five separate titles in the *International Rare Book Prices* series (*IRBP*).

Cole's Register

This volume was recognised, on its first appearance in 1985, as setting a new standard for accuracy of information in its field. The title, completely revised and re-issued each April, provides details of some 1,900 antiquarian and secondhand bookdealers and bookshops in Britain. These details are arranged both alphabetically and geographically. The value of the information is further enhanced by extensive cross-indexing of the specialist fields of individual bookdealers and of bookdealers from whom catalogues are available.

Covering the whole spectrum of book collector, *Cole's Register* enables the librarian or collector to contact specialist bookdealers in practically any subject area at any price level.

International Rare Books Prices

The *IRBP* series, published to the same high standard of accuracy, concentrates on books themselves, rather than bookdealers. The series was established to provide modestly-priced, yet extensive, annual records of the current pricing levels of old, rare, and out-of-print books which come onto the market in Britain and the United States; to draw attention to unusual and infrequently found books which have become temporarily available; and to introduce collectors to dealers.

The subject areas covered by individual volumes of *IRBP* are:

The Arts & Architecture
Books on the fine and applied arts from the 17th century to the 1960s with particular emphasis on the 19th and early 20th century.

Early Printed Books
Concentrating entirely on books, in all subject areas, published prior to 1800. Early books in nearly all disciplines are included. Opportunities to obtain such books are diminishing each year.

Modern First Editions
The most authoritative and extensive annual record available of the demand for literary first editions of this century. Some 8,500 entries appear each year in this particular volume.

Science & Medicine
Books published during the development periods of all major branches of science and medicine form the basis of many developing collections across the world. Such books are found here.

Voyages, Travel & Exploration
Hardly a country or area in the world is not represented in this wide-ranging compilation of long out-of-print and increasingly sought-after titles.

New editions are published in April each year